CRIMINAL COURT PROCESS

CRIMINAL
COURT PROCESS

Ellen Hochstedler Steury
University of Wisconsin—Milwaukee

Nancy Frank
University of Wisconsin—Milwaukee

WEST PUBLISHING COMPANY

Minneapolis/St. Paul New York Los Angeles San Francisco

Copyeditor: Polly Kummel
Text Design: John Edeen
Composition: Carlisle Communications, Ltd.
Indexer: Schroeder Indexing Services

WEST'S COMMITMENT TO THE ENVIRONMENT

In 1906, West Publishing Company began recycling materials left over from the production of books. This began a tradition of efficient and responsible use of resources. Today, 100% of our legal bound volumes are printed on acid-free, recycled paper consisting of 50% new paper pulp and 50% paper that has undergone a de-inking process. We also use vegetable-based inks to print all of our books. West recycles nearly 22,650,000 pounds of scrap paper annually—the equivalent of 187,500 trees. Since the 1960s, West has devised ways to capture and recycle waste inks, solvents, oils, and vapors created in the printing process. We also recycle plastics of all kinds, wood, glass, corrugated cardboard, and batteries, and have eliminated the use of polystyrene book packaging. We at West are proud of the longevity and the scope of our commitment to the environment.

West pocket parts and advance sheets are printed on recyclable paper and can be collected and recycled with newspapers. Staples do not have to be removed. Bound volumes can be recycled after removing the cover.

Production, Prepress, Printing and Binding by West Publishing Company.

British Library Cataloguing-in-Publication Data. A catalogue record for this book is available from the British Library.

 TEXT IS PRINTED ON 10% POST CONSUMER RECYCLED PAPER

Printed with Printwise
Environmentally Advanced Water Washable Ink

COPYRIGHT ©1996   By WEST PUBLISHING COMPANY
610 Opperman Drive
P.O. Box 64526
St. Paul, MN 55164-0526

Printed in the United States of America

03 02 01 99 98 97 96   8 7 6 5 4 3 2 1 0

Library of Congress Cataloging-in-Publication Data

Steury, Ellen Hochstedler.
    Criminal court process / Ellen Hochstedler Steury, Nancy Frank.
        p.   cm.
    Includes index.
        ISBN 0-314-06320-X (Hard : alk. paper)
        1. Criminal procedure—United States.   2. Criminal courts—United
States.   I. Frank, Nancy.   II. Title.
KF9619.S73   1996
345.73'05—dc20
[347.3055]
                                                                                    95-30489
                                                                                    CIP

To Richard and Winona,
in appreciation of your sense of justice

To Bill

PREFATORY LETTER TO STUDENTS: STUDYING THE CRIMINAL COURT PROCESS

Our primary reason for writing a textbook on criminal court process was to help students of the criminal justice system to better understand a process that is often only vaguely understood. Many criminal justice courses focus on policing and corrections. Often less attention is given to the intervening processes that turn an arrestee into a convicted criminal. In writing this book four primary goals shaped our treatment of the material.

First, we place a heavy emphasis on describing criminal court processes. It seemed to us that students too often come away from studying the criminal courts with bits of knowledge about particular issues, such as plea bargaining, pretrial detention, and sentencing practices, but have only a vague understanding of the court procedures within which these issues arise. We have tried to describe what happens and who does what to whom with what results. An important aspect of describing the criminal court process is to acknowledge and describe *variation*. For example, initial appearances may "look" and proceed quite differently, depending on the jurisdiction and the court within that jurisdiction. Although it is impossible to describe all variations, we have tried to suggest those areas in which variation is quite broad and to summarize the more common variations among the states. Inevitably, the jurisdiction with which you are most familiar may conduct its work in ways that differ from the process we describe. When you notice such differences, you need to think about how those differences might influence the outcome of the criminal process. When we identify variations, we try to report the results of research that explores the consequences of variation. For example, what consequences are there for the defendant detained before trial compared to one who is released on bail? What are the consequences of being processed in the lower courts rather than in a court of general jurisdiction?

We trust that our descriptions answer the questions of who, what, when, where, and how. Our second goal in writing this book was to begin to suggest why the courts work the way they do. We examine the history of criminal court processes to explain the evolution of the courts. And we describe foreign systems of criminal court process in order to explore alternatives to the Anglo-American process found in the United States. The historical chapter suggests that differing cultural emphases influence the shape of criminal processes.

We also explore why contemporary court processes vary from place to place. For example, why do some states use the grand jury process and others use the preliminary hearing? Why have some states abolished bail bonding? The way individual defendants are treated also varies. Some defendants are charged, and others are not. Why? What factors explain prosecutors' charging decisions? Some defendants are released on recognizance, and others are not. Why? The answers to these questions attempt to explain how criminal court actors use their discretion.

We also wanted to evaluate how well the criminal courts achieve the goals society expects them to fulfill. Clearly, any answer requires an exploration of what those goals might be. As it turns out, criminal courts are expected to meet more than one goal, some goals are contradictory, and different interest groups support some goals more than others. In large part this book leaves evaluation up to you, the reader. Our goal is to give you some basic information you need to begin to assess how well the courts achieve their goals.

Where the courts are not achieving certain goals, reform is often the next step. In this book we have tried to explain the reforms of the past and to describe current reform efforts. Nearly every chapter describes some reform or proposal. Reform is impossible without vision and a sense of possibility. The historical and comparative chapters (Chapters 4 and 5) are offered in part to give you an opportunity to see the court process in the United States as just one in a range of techniques for resolving disputes between individuals and the larger society. Many procedures described in this book have evolved from fundamental societal values that remain as alive today as ever. Others, however, may have made sense in an earlier time but make little sense in relation to current social conditions and cultural values. Our hope is that this book stimulates your sense of possibilities and gives you the analytical tools you need to evaluate the advantages and disadvantages of proposed reforms.

We begin our task by placing the criminal courts in a broader context—examining the criminal courts as just one of several means used to resolve disputes. Criminal courts are a specialized process for resolving disputes framed in a special way. Disputes are the raw material of the courts. To become subject to the criminal courts disputes are packaged in particular ways and routed through the system. How well the courts fulfill their goals, and the outcomes that result, depends at least in part on the kinds of cases the courts are asked to resolve. Ultimately, a full understanding of how well the courts do their job means exploring whether other methods might fulfill those goals better or in a less costly way. In short, although much of this book describes what courts do and why courts do those things in the ways they do, your task is to continually ask whether the way courts work is the only or best way to accomplish their goals.

◻ ACKNOWLEDGMENTS

Several people were especially helpful to us as we worked on this manuscript. We owe special thanks to Bruce Harvey, justice system review coordinator for the Milwaukee County circuit courts, especially for his insights concerning court administration, and to Nick Bokas for his thoughtful comments on comparative systems of criminal court process. We also wish to thank the following reviewers: Thomas Allen, University of South Dakota; William A. Bailey, Gloucester County College; Robert H. Chaires, University of Nevada-Reno; Daniel S. Compagna, Fayetteville State University; John A. Conley, Buffalo State College; Daniel P. Doyle, University of Montana; Chris W. Eskridge, University of Nebraska-Omaha; Catherine Gallo, University of Hartford; Marc G. Gertz, Florida State University;

A. J. Goubler, Delgado Community College; Ron Graham, Fresno City College; Peter Haynes, Arizona State University; Michael H. Hazlett, Western Illinois University; Barbara J. Keith, Rio Hondo College; Gary N. Keveles, University of Wisconsin-Superior; Roger Klaphake, St. Cloud State University; Mary Lee Luskin, Indiana University; James L. Maddex, Georgia State University; Dale Nute, Florida State University; Rudy Prine, Valdosta State University; Peter Renstrom, Western Michigan University; Ellen D. Riggle, University of Kentucky; George Schrader, Auburn University; and Nancy T. Wolfe, University of South Carolina. Their comments were particularly valuable in shaping the manuscript.

Finally, we thank Thomas Schneider, Joseph Caton, Herman John, Dean Strang, and Peter Goldberg, who have shared with us many insights gleaned from their experiences as practicing attorneys. Many of their insights are reflected in this book.

CONTENTS

CHAPTER 4   HISTORY OF COURTS AND CRIMINAL PROCESS   65

PART III   PROCESSING CASES

CHAPTER 9   THE PROSECUTOR'S INITIAL CHARGING DECISION   192

CHAPTER 10   PROCESSING LESSER OFFENSES IN LOWER COURTS   214

CHAPTER 11

INITIAL APPEARANCE: SETTING BAIL AND OTHER CONDITIONS OF RELEASE   233

CHAPTER 14   ARRAIGNMENT: PLEADING TO THE CHARGE   313

CHAPTER 18   APPEALS AND OTHER POST-CONVICTION REMEDIES   417

INTRODUCTION TO THE CRIMINAL COURT PROCESS

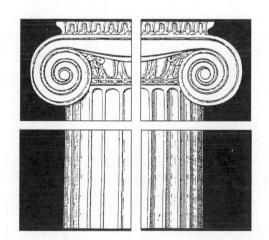

CHAPTER 1

THE ROLE
OF CRIMINAL
COURTS

Few institutions of government are as dramatic as the criminal courts. Our imagination seems drawn to the uncertain fate of the criminal defendant, to the clever maneuvering of the prosecutor and defense counsel, and to the awesome authority of the judge. Here is an institution that literally holds the power of life and death. The state musters all its power against the accused. Against these mighty forces stands the defense lawyer, the only person the defendant can count as an ally against the sordid and humiliating accusations of the state. In the end the defendant's fate is decided by a jury of twelve ordinary citizens, people not unlike ourselves, who for the space of a few hours or days are asked to determine the fate of the defendant. Such is our fascination with criminal courts.

These are idealized images of the criminal courts, which contrast sharply with both the reality of modern criminal court processes and changing public perceptions of the courts. The reassuring themes of *Perry Mason,* in which justice is always served in the end, have been eroded as the public has become increasingly aware of the routines of modern criminal courts. The drama of the jury verdict has been replaced—in reality and in the public mind—by the plea bargain. The deal struck by prosecutor and defense attorney has replaced the judgment of twelve good citizens. To many, justice seems to have been left on the front steps of the courthouse, and chaos seems to have taken over inside.

The true picture of the criminal courts stands somewhere between the two images. The courts have never been as pristine as our romanticized images. Nor are courts today as corrupt and chaotic as many fear. In many ways the quality of justice delivered by the criminal courts today is better than at any time in history. And yet in other ways powerful societal pressures to control crime threaten the justice and fairness of procedures. Through it all, judges, prosecutors, and defense lawyers continually struggle to define what justice truly requires.

Some of our most basic values are played out in the criminal courts. Justice, fairness, and the rights of the individual are balanced against our fears and uncertainties, our need to feel safe from those who might harm us or who threaten to throw our lives into chaos. We demand to see the guilty punished. We fervently hope that the innocent are vindicated. Criminal courts are entrusted with the task of meeting these conflicting needs.

This book is about criminal courts and the processes used to deal with cases brought to them. This introductory chapter describes the role of the criminal courts as one form of dispute resolution. Criminal courts have developed specialized procedures for fulfilling this role. However, as this chapter points out, criminal court processes are not the only—or necessarily the best—way to deal with the various kinds of disputes that find their way to the criminal courts.

DISPUTE RESOLUTION

Conflict is a natural part of human interaction. Conflicts can be minor—such as arguing over who will take out the garbage. Or conflicts can be monumental, resulting in death, destruction, and even war. All social groups, from families to large societies, require mechanisms for resolving disputes between their members. The mechanisms may rely entirely on voluntary action by individuals, or they may require the use of force or the intervention of an authority to compel individuals to resolve their dispute.

Matters that used to be handled privately are now often settled in court. "Throughout the twentieth century, the courts have assumed a burgeoning share of interpersonal domestic, friend and neighbor disputes" (Merry 1982a, 172). Taking a case to criminal court is often a sign that other, less drastic, means of resolving the dispute have failed. Because the courts are often a last resort, we should not be surprised that the courts often fail where other social institutions have already given up.

> Courts cannot solve the problem of crime or even make a significant dent in it. Thus, in a very real sense the courts—charged with handling society's failures—will always fail. What the family, the church, the workplace, and the school cannot do, neither can the courts. (Feeley 1983, 19)

However, failure is a serious challenge to the legitimacy of the criminal courts. If the criminal courts lose their legitimacy, disputing parties may resort to force to obtain the justice they seek. Consequently, the loss of legitimacy could threaten the peace and order of the community.

Because criminal courts are only one means of resolving disputes, an understanding of other dispute resolution mechanisms helps to clarify the special role of the courts and the special procedures used to resolve disputes in criminal courts. Alternatives include negotiation, mediation, force, arbitrary authority, and noncriminal adjudication.

Negotiation and Mediation

negotiation

Sometimes parties to a dispute voluntarily agree to resolve the dispute through negotiation. In **negotiation** the parties discuss their differences in an attempt to find some mutually acceptable solution (Sander 1982). Negotiation often involves an exchange in which one party agrees to give something up in exchange for the right to keep whatever was under dispute.

Negotiation occurs in a wide variety of personal, organizational, and national contexts. Nations negotiate disputed territorial boundaries. One nation may agree to give up the disputed territory in exchange for payments or trade concessions. Employee unions negotiate with employers about wages and conditions. The union may be willing to agree to lower wages in exchange for better health insurance coverage. Even small children negotiate. If Sarah offers Billy another toy in exchange for the ball, Billy may willingly give up the ball that moments earlier he had claimed was his. Spouses might work out a satisfactory division of household tasks through negotiation, with each agreeing to take on part of a particularly messy task in exchange for assistance with other tasks. Negotiation is such a constant part of social interaction that we often begin to negotiate even before we fully realize there is a dispute.

mediation

A variation of negotiation is mediation. In **mediation,** a neutral third party handles the negotiation between the disputing parties (Sander 1982). The mediator does not impose a decision. Rather the mediator works to bring the disputants to a resolution that satisfies both by bringing to light points on which the parties agree. With the solution identified, the disputants voluntarily give up the fight. Both come away with something, and neither loses completely. The parent who manages to get both children to agree that first Billy will play with the ball and then Sarah will get a turn has mediated the dispute.

Because negotiation and mediation are entirely voluntary, they often fail when one or both parties are unwilling to agree to an exchange (Merry 1982b). When the parties place great value on the thing in dispute, neither party may be willing to give in. Billy may feel that no toy is as wonderful as the disputed ball. Adults are often just as stubborn, particularly when they believe that their rights are at stake. "It's mine," "It's my right," "You have no right"—all these phrases spell failure for negotiations. When negotiation fails, the disputants may search for alternative mechanisms for resolving the dispute.

Might Makes Right

Perhaps the most primitive means of resolving disputes is through the use of force. From feuding tribes during the Middle Ages to fighting children on the playground to nations warring over territory, force is used to vanquish opponents and thereby win the dispute. When negotiation fails, one party simply takes by force whatever was under dispute, whether family honor, the use of the baseball diamond, or land.

Using force obviously entails risks. The aggressor, who was initially confident of victory, may find that the foe is stronger or more clever in battle than originally assumed. In addition, the use of force often leads to the use of more force. Unless the victor thoroughly destroys the loser, the loser may rise up with renewed force at some future time. The resolution of the dispute is never final. Where might makes right, right is continually in dispute.

Legitimate Authority

social contract

Seventeenth- and eighteenth-century **social contract** philosophers, such as Thomas Hobbes and John Locke, suggested that governments were originally established in order to end the instability and uncertainty that comes from living in a world in which might makes right. To resolve disputes with any finality, people had to establish some legitimate authority or procedure that would declare the final winner and prevent the loser from retaliating. For the declaration to have the power to end a dispute, both disputants had to voluntarily agree that the decision of the authority was valid and that both were obligated to follow it. In early cultures the mantle of authority fell to groups of individuals, such as a council of elders, or to authoritative individuals, such as the king, queen, chieftain, or empress. These authorities might engage the disputants in mediation, or they might simply resolve the dispute by fiat. In rule by fiat the decision is held to be legitimate so long as the ruler is considered the legitimate ruler. That legitimacy may rest on heredity, moral character, or other qualifications. Legitimacy later was vested in the law rather than in people, which is called the **rule of law**. In rule of law the decision is recognized as legitimate so long as lawful procedures are properly followed.

rule of law

Rule by Fiat

Some societies recognize certain groups or individuals as having the power to resolve disputes according to their personal judgment. This judgment could rest on the arbitrary whim of the authority. If one party had an annoying voice or "looked" untrustworthy, or had a bad reputation, that party might lose, regardless of the facts of the case or any rights that the party might claim. Such rule by arbitrary authority is called rule by fiat.

Although we usually associate rule by fiat with more primitive societies, even today dispute resolution based on arbitrary authority exists in many contexts. Within the family the authoritative declaration of the parent often resolves disputes between siblings—for example, "Johnny, give Billy the ball" or "Mary, stop pulling your sister's hair." No negotiation, no attempt to understand the facts of the situation, no inquiry into fault precedes the decision. The parent merely decides and issues a command. Mary's plea that her sister started it, and Johnny's claim that it is his ball are to no avail. The parent simply responds, "I don't care, you heard what I said."

At work the employer has broad authority to resolve disputes between employees. If two employees are arguing about whose job it is to perform a particular task, the boss may simply order the job done by a particular employee. The employees' dispute may have stemmed from their mutual concern about each getting only their fair share of the work. The employer may use grounds entirely different than fairness to assign the task to one employee rather than another. Perhaps one employee is more hard working and can be relied on to do more work. Perhaps the employer is annoyed that one employee is always complaining. An arbitrary authority does not have to consider notions of right and fairness when making a decision.

The earliest courts probably relied exclusively on the legitimate authority of a ruler, backed by military might, to resolve disputes that arose within the ruler's sovereign territory. Rather than engaging in fact-finding and adjudication according to formal rules, as occurs in modern courts, the early courts relied to a greater extent on the judgment and declaration of the ruler.

Dispute resolution based upon the arbitrary rule of a legitimate authority also has its limitations. Often, the legitimacy of an authority's decision rests upon that individual's personal character. Charismatic leaders who are perceived as possessing good judgment may succeed in having their orders followed, whereas less skillful and commanding personalities find their decisions and their authority being challenged. The king's subjects revolt, the children become rebellious and uncontrollable, or the employees go out on strike. When this happens, the authority may need to fall back on force or negotiation. Another problem with rule by fiat is that it can lead to despotism, that is, absolute rule that exploits or oppresses.

Rule of Law

The opposite of rule by fiat is the rule of law. In the U.S. legal system the principle of the rule of law derives from early English legal principles. Specifically, in England the rule of law referred to the limits on the sovereign's (king's or queen's) power. The rule of law means that no one is above the law, not even the sovereign ruler of the country. In a monarchy such as England's during its early history this meant that even the king was required to follow the laws of the land in order to maintain legitimacy. In the United States the rule of law means that no one in the government—not Congress, not the president, not the police, not judges, no one—is above the law. The law may be found in a number of different places or sources.

constitutional law

Constitutional Law.   The structure of government and the powers of the various parts of government, as well as the limits on government power, are defined in **constitutional law**. For example, the U.S. Constitution describes a government composed of three branches (executive branch, legislative branch, and judicial branch) and defines the powers of each. The Constitution also defines certain rights of individuals in relation to the government, such as those found in the first ten amendments to the Constitution, known as the **Bill of Rights**. Several of these amendments define the rights of individuals accused of crimes and outline the procedures courts must follow in adjudicating criminal cases.

Bill of Rights

statutory law

Statutory Law.   Laws created by authorized legislative bodies, such as Congress and state legislatures, are called **statutory law**. For example, most state legislatures have codified their criminal laws in statutes published in statute books. Statutory laws also specify the procedures the courts must follow in deciding criminal cases. For example, many states have statutes defining the procedures for selecting jurors in a criminal trial.

case law

Case Law.   Another important source of law is found in the decisions of courts. Many of the laws of England were originally created through the pronouncements of courts in deciding specific disputes. The law that evolved in this way is called English common law. The definitions of crimes in the United States and many court procedures trace their ancestry directly to common law, although most states have adopted statutes that codify and revise the original common law provisions. The decisions of courts in the United States also have the force of law. The legally enforceable provisions that arise out of court cases are called **case law**. By applying constitutional law and statutory law to the particular facts presented by a dispute at hand, and reviewing past cases and tradition, the courts announce principles that have the force of law. The courts then use these principles to decide future disputes in which the facts are similar.

administrative law

Administrative Law.   Finally, the legislature empowers some administrative agencies to draft rules that have the force of law. **Administrative law** defines illegal conduct in relation to a wide variety of activities, including environmental crimes, racial and gender discrimination, and fraudulent business practices. For example, the Environmental Protection Agency (EPA) writes regulations prohibiting the release of toxic chemicals into the environment. If a manufacturing plant violates one of these regulations by releasing one of the prohibited chemicals, the EPA can impose penalties or, in some cases, initiate a criminal prosecution.

Adjudication

Dispute resolution that recognizes the rule of law differs from dispute resolution by fiat in that the authority must follow certain legal procedures and standards in arriving at a decision. The rule of law obligates the courts to follow all relevant constitutional and statutory laws, case law, and administrative laws in deciding the cases brought before them. The dispute is not resolved by the whims of the authority (or judge) but by the authoritative application of legal rules in weighing the proof of an allegation. This kind of dispute resolution is called adjudication.

adjudication

Adjudication is "a method of peaceful conflict resolution in which parties present arguments and evidence to a neutral third party for a decision in their favor according to established procedures and rules of law" (Howard 1986, 58). Adjudication usually involves one party to the dispute compelling another party to answer before a board, commission, court, or other such forum. For example, a student who disputes the grade a teacher awarded might take the dispute to an established grievance committee that will decide whether the grade was awarded according to fair criteria. The student would present evidence and arguments supporting the contention that the grade was given in an arbitrary or unfair manner. The grievance committee would follow certain procedures and apply certain rules to decide whether the grade was fair and come to a decision.

Unlike the other forms of dispute resolution, adjudication depends upon the rule of law. The adjudicatory body is required to apply established rules in deciding the dispute at hand. Such rules typically define the nature of evidence that will be accepted and the standards the fact-finders must follow in deciding whether the allegation has been proved. The rule of law also concerns lawful procedures. Under the rule of law all actors involved (disputants and adjudicators) must follow certain prescribed procedures in resolving the dispute.

Although adjudication is most often associated with the courts and other government agencies that engage in fact-finding, adjudication also occurs in private organizations. For example, a corporation may establish a grievance board for resolving disputes among employees. A corporation might also set up a commission for resolving disputes with consumers regarding the quality and performance of the corporation's product. Many private adjudicatory bodies are expected to engage in both mediation and adjudication. In many contexts the adjudicator may encourage the parties to arrive at a negotiated solution; the parties proceed to adjudication if negotiation or mediation fail.

Adjudication is carried out by a variety of agencies and tribunals within government. Hundreds of administrative and regulatory bodies at the local, state, and federal levels of government have adjudicatory responsibilities. For example, the National Labor Relations Board adjudicates disputes between employers and employees relating to labor-management relations. Similarly, an industrial corporation accused of violating pollution rules may be entitled to an adjudicatory hearing before an administrative board that decides whether the corporation broke the law. These administrative boards and commissions engage in the same kind of adjudicatory process as courts but usually operate under less stringent procedural rules.

Adjudication in private and governmental organizations exists alongside other goals and objectives of these organizations. Adjudication is a last resort for dealing with problems that arise in the normal course of the organization's operation. The adjudicatory board may have other responsibilities as well, such as mediation, rule making, and administration. Courts, in contrast, exist for the sole purpose of adjudicating disputes. Adjudication is a service that courts provide to other individuals and organizations.

■ CIVIL AND CRIMINAL ADJUDICATION: SIMILARITIES AND DIFFERENCES

One evolving characteristic of Anglo-American law is the distinction between civil disputes and criminal disputes. Once a distinction between civil and criminal law was recognized, specialized courts and procedures evolved for criminal matters; they differed in important ways from civil courts and civil procedures. (Chapter 4 describes in greater detail the evolution of criminal courts and criminal procedure in England and North America.)

Distinguishing Crimes from Noncriminal Violations

Despite centuries of evolution in the law the criminal and civil law continue to overlap in many ways. The boundary between criminal and civil matters is imprecise. In general, criminal matters involve some combination of the following: violation of a criminal law, a public accusation made and prosecuted by the government rather than the victim, stigma of public condemnation, potential loss of liberty following conviction, and special court procedures. Decisions by victims, police, prosecutors, legal counsel, and others influence whether a dispute is handled as a criminal or civil matter and whether it is resolved in criminal court using criminal procedures.

conduct,
crime

For a dispute to be criminally prosecuted one disputant must have engaged in **conduct** (behavior) prohibited by a criminal law. Strictly speaking, **crime** is any conduct—act or omission—that violates the criminal law. If there is no law defining the conduct as a crime, the dispute cannot be prosecuted as a crime. This require-

nullem crimen
sine lege,
actus reus

ment was recognized in the ancient legal maxim: ***nullem crimen sine lege***. Roughly translated, this phrase means that without law there can be no crime. In addition, there must be an ***actus reus***, that is, conduct that allegedly violates the law. Criminal courts consider only allegations of conduct that the law has declared criminal.

Even if conduct has been declared a crime, such conduct will not necessarily be adjudicated in a criminal court. Many disputes that could be resolved in the criminal courts are not, because the parties to the dispute choose not to frame the conduct as a crime and choose not to bring a complaint to criminal court. For example, in minor assaults between friends neither party may wish the government to interfere in their own private resolution of the conflict. Sometimes a party to a dispute is more interested in recovering monetary damages than in punishing the person responsible. In this case a person may bring a civil suit even though criminal charges are legally possible. In other cases, even if one party seeks resolution of the matter in criminal court, the government may decline to prosecute the conduct as a crime. Perhaps the government views the conduct as

THE EXXON *VALDEZ* CASES

An example of the overlap of various kinds of law is the legal reaction to the Exxon *Valdez* oil spill off the coast of Alaska in 1989. The captain of the oil tanker was charged with a crime and tried in a criminal court (Frank and Lynch 1992, 32–33). The Exxon Corporation was also charged with crimes, two felonies and three misdemeanors (Galen 1990, 39). The incident also violated a number of administrative regulations concerned with oil pollution. Finally, hundreds of civil suits were brought against the Exxon Corporation by the state of Alaska, environmental and Native American groups, and fishermen whose livelihood was harmed by the contamination of fish in Prince William Sound. All these actions stemmed from one incident but involved different legal forums applying different procedures and standards of conduct. Only when the conduct was framed as a violation of the criminal law could it be brought before a criminal court and adjudicated through criminal procedures.

too trivial to expend resources by taking the matter to court, or perhaps there is insufficient evidence that the alleged conduct took place, or there is a question about whether the alleged conduct violates a criminal law.

In many cases a particular dispute might involve more than one set of laws. A decision to pursue a matter in the criminal courts does not foreclose other alternatives. A claim might be taken to an administrative agency for resolution, to a civil court, to a criminal court, or to all three simultaneously.

Unlike other forms of dispute resolution and other court actions, a criminal prosecution is a public accusation made by the government. In the United States a private individual may not bring a criminal complaint without the cooperation and formal action of the government. In this respect all criminal prosecutions are disputes between the government and the defendant rather than between the defendant and another private individual. Even if the initial dispute that brought the case into the criminal system was a private dispute, such as a quarrel between neighbors that escalated into a physical fight, once the dispute is framed as a criminal dispute, the complaining victim becomes a mere witness. The government takes the role of the complainant in the criminal court process.

stigma

The willingness of the government to prosecute and to label an act as a crime against all the people creates the stigma of criminal prosecution. **Stigma** refers to the social disrepute attaching to the defendant in a criminal prosecution. To be declared a criminal is a form of degradation. Through public accusation, trial, and conviction the defendant is transformed into a stigmatized criminal. Although criminal law and other kinds of law overlap in many ways, criminal prosecution is thought to carry a greater social stigma than other kinds of court action relating to the same conduct. The real difference between criminal and civil breaches is "the degree to which people condemn those who violate the law" (Reid 1992, 3).

Because of this condemnation, combined with the threat of incarceration that accompanies a conviction for most crimes, criminal courts are required to follow more rigorous procedures than civil courts. Therefore an additional difference between criminal courts and other forms of dispute resolution concerns the procedures that are followed in deciding the result.

Although many similarities remain in the ways that criminal and civil courts operate, the differences are significant. This book focuses on the operation of the criminal courts.

◼ TYPES OF DISPUTES ADJUDICATED IN CRIMINAL COURTS

Criminal courts, like other courts, resolve two distinct types of disputes: disputes of fact and disputes of law. Disputes of fact arise when the disputing parties disagree about what really happened or what the true facts of the situation are. Disputes of law arise when the disputing parties disagree about the requirements of the law.

Disputes of Fact

At least initially, almost all criminal cases present disputes of fact. In general, the criminal courts are asked to resolve disputes about whether the defendant actually did what the government has accused the person of doing. The prosecutor accuses; the defendant denies it. The disputed fact is whether the defendant did what the government alleges. For example, a prosecutor accuses someone of being in a Michigan bank on a particular day and threatening the teller with violence unless he hands over some money. The accused disputes these allegations, claiming to have been in New Jersey at the time the prosecutor says she was in the bank. In deciding questions of fact criminal courts base their decisions on evidence. Both parties have an opportunity to present evidence supporting their version of the facts. A fact-finder, either a jury or a judge, decides which set of evidence is most credible or believable, subject to the special rules of criminal adjudication.

Disputes of Law

substantive law, procedural law

Many criminal cases also involve disputes about the law. These disputes may concern substantive law or procedural law. **Substantive law** refers to the body of law that defines certain conduct as a crime and specifies punishments. **Procedural law** refers to the body of law that prescribes the procedures to be followed in prosecuting a case, including a description of the rights of defendants.

In legal disputes about substantive law the issue is whether a given set of facts constitutes a crime as defined in substantive law. Such disputes occupy a sort of middle ground between pure disputes of fact and pure disputes of law, because they require the court to apply the law to particular facts. For example, a computer hacker breaks into the financial data files of a bank and credits his account for several thousand dollars. The defendant does not dispute that he did precisely that. The dispute concerns whether this conduct fits the legal definition of burglary and therefore whether the government can convict the defendant of burglary.

More common are disputes concerning procedural law. For example, a defendant in a criminal case may argue that when an undercover officer asked the defendant questions regarding her criminal behavior, it was an interrogation, and the defendant was entitled to have a lawyer present. The government may dispute the legal claim, arguing that because the defendant was not in custody during the interrogation, she was not entitled to the presence of her lawyer. This is a dispute about what the law requires. Both sides agree about what the police did and what the defendant said. That is, there is no dispute about the facts. They dispute only the requirements of the law. One side claims that the right to counsel extends to this situation, whereas the other side maintains that the right to counsel is not so broad as to include this situation.

Although disputes about the facts may be submitted to a judge or a jury, juries may not decide issues of law. Judges have sole responsibility for deciding disputes about the law. In resolving such disputes the judge makes a legal finding. In making a finding the judge must attend to the texts of constitutional, statutory, and administrative laws relevant to the case, as well as binding **precedents**— earlier decisions related to the issue. The reliance on precedent also distinguishes questions of fact from questions of law. In disputes about the facts the only concern is the evidence in the current case. In disputes about the law the facts and findings in similar cases that have been resolved in the past become relevant to the judge's finding of law in relation to the current case.

precedents

◼ SUBSTANTIVE CRIMINAL LAW

Substantive criminal law defines the types of conduct that are punishable as crimes. Substantive criminal law is typically divided into felonies and misdemeanors. In addition, the criminal law and criminal court jurisdiction sometimes overlap with certain noncriminal offenses that generally are considered less serious than misdemeanors.

Felonies and Misdemeanors

felony, misdemeanor

In general, a **felony** is defined as a criminal offense that carries a potential punishment of more than one year's imprisonment. A **misdemeanor** is any crime that is not designated as a felony. States vary somewhat in where they draw the line between felonies and misdemeanors (for example, two years rather than a year), but all states make a distinction between felonies and misdemeanors. For a variety of different types of conduct, states designate less serious forms of the conduct as misdemeanors and the more serious or aggravated forms of the same conduct as felonies. Furthermore, the court to which a case is assigned, the procedures followed by the court, the defendants' rights, and the care with which cases are treated often differ according to whether the charge is a felony or a misdemeanor.

elements

Each offense is made up of one or more **elements**, which are the facts that the state must prove in order to obtain a ruling that the defendant committed the crime as charged. For example, for the crime of simple battery the elements would be (1) that the defendant inflicted bodily harm on another person, (2) that the infliction of harm was intentional, and (3) that the person harmed did not consent to the battery. Aggravated battery includes additional elements related to the particularly heinous nature of the battery.

Noncriminal Offenses

civil forfeitures, ordinance

Noncriminal offenses, including ordinance violations, traffic offenses, and regulatory violations, often overlap with criminal offenses and may be adjudicated in the same courts that hear criminal cases. Beginning about the end of the nineteenth century the number and variety of "offenses" punishable by fines, or **civil forfeitures** (another term for fine) exploded. Municipalities were given the authority to create local laws, called **ordinances,** and to specify penalties for violations. Ordinances might relate to conduct also controlled through the criminal law, such as disorderly conduct, theft, and fighting. In addition, during the late nineteenth and early twentieth centuries, state and local governments

FELONIES AND MISDEMEANORS

Wisconsin statutes 940.19 defines battery and aggravated battery. Wisconsin's definitions are quite similar to definitions of these crimes in other states. Note the differences between the offenses. Like many states Wisconsin divides its offenses into different classes, which are distinguished by the severity of the penalty attached. In Wisconsin a Class A misdemeanor carries a maximum sentence of nine months in jail, whereas a Class E felony carries a maximum penalty of two years in prison, and a Class C felony entails a maximum penalty of ten years in prison. A Class C felony therefore involves a much more severe potential penalty than a Class A misdemeanor. What differences in conduct or state of mind distinguish the seriousness of these offenses?

940.19 Battery; aggravated Battery. (1) Whoever causes bodily harm to another by an act done with intent to cause bodily harm to that person or another without the consent of the person so harmed is guilty of a Class A misdemeanor.

(1m) Whoever causes great bodily harm to another by an act done with intent to cause bodily harm to that person or another without the consent of the person so harmed is guilty of a Class E felony.

(2) Whoever causes great bodily harm to another by an act done with intent to cause great bodily harm to that person or another with or without the consent of the person so harmed is guilty of a Class C felony.

(3) Whoever intentionally causes bodily harm to another by conduct which creates a high probability of great bodily harm is guilty of a Class E felony. A rebuttable presumption of conduct creating a substantial risk of great bodily harm arises:

(a) If the person harmed is 62 years of age or older; or

(b) If the person harmed has a physical disability, whether congenital or acquired by accident, injury or disease, which is discernible by an ordinary person viewing the physically disabled person.

created "public order offenses" that concerned the regulation of commerce (such as peddling regulations), the protection of health and safety, and the regulation of traffic.

Late twentieth-century developments have resulted in still further increases in noncriminal offenses. In the 1970s the expansion of health, safety, and environmental regulation resulted in a growing number of noncriminal offenses relating to potentially dangerous activities by individuals and corporations. Violating these regulations can cause devastating harm to individuals and the environment. Just because the offenses are designated noncriminal does not necessarily mean that they relate to trivial kinds of harm. In addition, although these noncriminal offenses are called civil, they are prosecuted by the government rather than by the victim.

decriminalization

Also during the 1970s legislatures sometimes alleviated overcrowding in the criminal courts by decriminalizing minor criminal behavior, such as disorderly conduct or public drunkenness. **Decriminalization** takes two forms. In one form of decriminalization the legislature repeals the criminal statute prohibiting the act. In place of the criminal statute the state or local government enact laws that describe noncriminal offenses proscribing the same conduct that once was a crime. In the mid–1970s some jurisdictions decriminalized possession of marijuana because of its widespread use, removing the offense of possession of small amounts of marijuana from the criminal code. After decriminalization, individuals caught in possession of marijuana are given a citation, similar to a traffic ticket, and are penalized by only a small fine.

The second form of decriminalization simply provides an alternative to criminal processing. In this situation the proscribed act remains a crime, but the legislature also provides for a noncriminal prohibition by relying on existing municipal ordinances or creating a state infraction or violation. This results in simultaneous criminal and civil jurisdiction over the matter. In this case a single act might be treated as either criminal or noncriminal, or both. How the act is treated depends on the discretion of actors in the criminal justice system. If police and prosecutors consistently apply the noncriminal process rather than the criminal, the result is decriminalization in practice, even if the criminal law is still on the books.

Decriminalization is one way to control the criminal caseload of the courts and the associated costs of processing offenses. Even though decriminalized offenses are frequently adjudicated in the same courts that hear criminal cases, prosecution of noncriminal offenses does not require the elaborate procedures that the law requires for criminal defendants. Defendants charged with noncriminal offenses have fewer rights in the courts. Consequently, the state can avoid the cost of observing these rights (Lindquist 1988, 27). Increasing caseloads in the criminal courts produce continuing pressure to relieve the system by treating the least serious offenses as noncriminal.

■ CRIMINAL PROCEDURE

Criminal courts have evolved specialized procedures in relation to the roles of the state and the defendant in a criminal prosecution. These procedures prevent the government from interfering in the lives of its citizens unless the state has some specific justification for doing so. Without the rule of law, government officials might search our homes, listen in on our telephone conversations, or bring us in for questioning with no justification at all. The rule of law means that the government is accountable to the law in carrying out its legitimate functions.

The rule of law is an abstract concept or ideal. One measure of the fairness of any government or judicial system is the degree to which it achieves this ideal on a daily basis. The mark of a dictatorship is the absence of the rule of law. Although the legislature, courts, and other machinery of government may exist in a dictatorship, and may appear to carry out their tasks, the unpredictability of the government's actions terrorizes the citizens. Security forces may sweep through a neighborhood and arrest suspected dissidents. The government may throw opponents in jail for indefinite periods of time and subject them to torture. Powerful allies of the government may use the machinery of the security forces and the courts to eliminate business and political competitors. All these activities may be formally illegal but are carried out because the government refuses to be limited by the laws of the nation. The government deems itself a power unto itself and above the law.

Even within the United States the rule of law is a goal toward which we strive but that is achieved with varying degrees of success. When courts are perceived as failing to uphold the rule of law and failing to provide justice, court decisions quickly lose legitimacy and risk extrajudicial and extralegal solutions.

Criminal procedure is defined by the U.S. Consitution, particularly the Bill of Rights, and state consitutions and state and federal statutes relating to the criminal process. In addition, as courts decide questions of law relating to procedural issues, their decisions become part of the body of procedural law that other courts must follow. Procedural law defines the circumstances under which a person may be arrested and charged with a crime, the specific steps in the criminal prosecution, and the rights of the defendant, such as the right to a jury trial or the right to counsel. In addition, criminal procedure includes rules of evidence that define the types of evidence that may be presented in court.

RODNEY KING AND THE 1992 LOS ANGELES RIOTS:
A Lesson About Legitimacy

In the spring of 1991 the nation was stunned by a videotape in which police officers appeared to beat an African-American man who had been stopped in a routine traffic stop. Critics of police brutality claimed that the beating of Rodney King was unusual only because a bystander had filmed the entire incident. These critics observed that beatings of suspects, particularly of African-Americans and Hispanics, are all too common in Los Angeles and other cities.

Four police officers were indicted on felony charges. Many wondered what the courts would do. The case was closely monitored by local and national news media, and many people found themselves intently watching the trial on television.

Because of extensive pretrial publicity the defense requested that the trial be moved to another county. The judge ordered the trial moved to Ventura County, a largely white suburban county with a disproportionate number of current and retired police officers residing in it.

The jury, composed of ten white jurors, one Hispanic, and one Filipino acquitted three officers of all felony charges and was unable to reach a verdict in relation to the fourth officer who in the videotape appeared to be most actively involved in using force against Rodney King.

Members of the African-American community and others immediately criticized the verdicts. Once again it appeared to many that African-Americans cannot find justice in American criminal courtrooms. The verdict touched off two days of rioting, perhaps the most violent and destructive in the nation's history.

Legal experts will no doubt debate for decades whether the trial of the four Los Angeles police officers adhered to the rule of law. Some have suggested that moving the trial to Ventura County was unnecessary and interfered with both proper fact-finding in the case and the perceived legitimacy of the verdicts. Whether the jurors' verdicts were influenced by racism or not, the composition of the jury suggested to many that racism rather than the facts best explained their decision.

Clearly, many believed that the jury did not follow the rule of law. The verdicts of acquittal were viewed as illegitimate, the trial as a farce. Under such circumstances it was tragic but hardly surprising that many who felt victimized by police brutality and racist justice sought retribution in the streets of Los Angeles.

The acquittals in state court prompted federal prosecutors to seek justice for Rodney King through the federal courts. The four officers were indicted on federal charges for violating Rodney King's civil rights. Two officers were convicted in federal court and sentenced to prison. Rodney King also won a large damage award in his civil suit against the four officers and the City of Los Angeles.

Formal Versus Informal Procedures:
Negotiating Disputes in Criminal Court

Criminal courts are designed to be an adjudicatory forum for deciding particular kinds of disputes. The formal procedures of criminal courts specify how to adjudicate cases. In the United States this means that evidence is submitted to a fact-finder (judge or jury) who decides whether there is sufficient evidence that the defendant committed the crime. Also, court actors negotiate in order to avoid formal adjudication. Most cases in the criminal courts are resolved through negotiation. Although negotiation is a departure from formal procedure, negotiation in criminal cases is inevitably influenced by the rule of law and the formal adjudication processes of the courts. Because negotiation is voluntary, either party can refuse to negotiate whenever the formal process appears to offer a more satisfactory result.

A continuing controversy concerns the degree to which a defendant accused of a crime can negotiate voluntarily. Is the threat of criminal punishment so inherently coercive that negotiation in the criminal courts is a farce? If so, negotiation may be viewed as a breakdown in the rule of law. On the other hand, if defendants retain the ability to reject negotiated offers and demand formal adjudication (trial), negotiation may complement rather than subvert the adjudicatory process of the criminal courts.

☐ VALUES AND POLICY IN THE CRIMINAL COURTS

The discussion thus far has focused on the role of the criminal courts. How well do the courts fulfill their role? Answering this question involves more than simply gathering facts about the operation of the courts, how many cases are processed, how quickly they are processed, and with what results. Information of this sort is important, but it is not enough. Evaluating the quality of the work done by the criminal courts requires some sense of what constitutes a good job versus a poor job.

Criminal courts are expected to conduct their work in ways that maintain their legitimacy and the legitimacy of the criminal law. The criminal courts also are expected to be reliable in separating the guilty from the innocent. The American system of justice also holds high the values of fairness and equity. At the same time the reality of limited resources necessitates a concern for efficiency. Finally, people value visibility and accountability because they allow the public to determine whether the courts are meeting the expectations of legitimacy, reliability, fairness, and efficiency.

All these values are important. But it is difficult to prioritize these values. Which are the most important? Trade-offs are inevitable. For example, at what point is reliability in the fact-finding process undermined by efforts to make the process more efficient?

Due Process Versus Crime Control: Competing Values, Different Policies

due process model

Herbert Packer (1968), an eminent legal scholar, describes the trade-off as an ideological tug-of-war between the due process model and the crime control model. According to Packer, the **due process model** is principally concerned with preventing the conviction of innocent people. Advocates of the due process model argue that it is better to let ten guilty criminals go free than to convict one innocent person. Packer compares the due process model to an obstacle course; the criminal justice system puts various procedural obstacles in the path to conviction, and each case must be able to clear each hurdle. At each procedural hurdle the court decides whether there is enough evidence and whether the evidence is strong enough for the case to proceed to the next stage, the next hurdle in the process. The due process model places individual rights ahead of the goal of efficiency. According to the due process model, the greatest threat to the legitimacy of the courts occurs when the courts trample individual rights and risk conviction of innocent people. Formal rules of procedure are valued as a means of assuring the visibility of court processes and accountability to the public.

crime control model

In contrast, the **crime control model** "is based on the proposition that the repression of criminal conduct is by far the most important function to be performed by the criminal process" (Packer 1968, 158). If criminals run rampant in society, law-abiding citizens become frightened prisoners in their own homes. The more efficiently the justice system can process criminals, the more effective it will be in repressing crime. The crime control model trusts criminal justice officials to screen out the innocent at an early stage in the process. Those who are not screened out are probably guilty and can be processed quickly through the remaining stages. Reaching a final decision without unnecessary delaying procedures is one means of improving efficency. This model views the conviction of a few innocent persons as the price society must pay to protect its citizens from predatory crime. So long as such errors do not interfere with the system's ability to repress crime, citizens will tolerate errors. The crime control model has been dubbed "assembly-line justice" because of its emphasis on the efficient processing of cases, as if the cases were products on an assembly line. According to the crime control model, the greatest threat to the legitimacy of the criminal courts occurs when the courts are perceived as coddling criminals and ineffectively repressing crime.

These models describe two competing sets of values that permeate almost every issue within the criminal justice system. Proponents of the due process model are called liberals and are often characterized by their opponents as caring more about criminals than about victims. Advocates of the crime control model are called conservatives and are often characterized by their opponents as being more interested in punishing *someone* than in punishing the *right* someone. The struggle between the due process model and the crime control model plays out time and again in the political process. Policy debates about criminal court processes inevitably revolve around these ideological positions.

◼ POLICY REFORM AND THE CRIMINAL COURTS

Reformers seek to remedy defects in the law and court practice in order to protect the legitimacy of the courts as an institution of government and to improve the reliability of the fact-finding process. Some reforms are instituted out of a desire to improve the fairness of the court process. Other reforms emphasize crime control objectives, seeking increased efficiency. Because the goals of promoting fairness and promoting efficiency often conflict, the reforms proposed by some will often be viewed as problems by others. These conflicts impede any reform effort.

Moreover, because the courts are extremely resistant to change, the problems of yesterday remain the problems of tomorrow. Reforms fail because they often do not affect the factors that are most influential in shaping court participants' behavior. Specifically, criminal court reform is often impeded by informal practices, attitudes and norms, and incentives that support the status quo (Church and Heumann 1992, 4).

Like most people, court actors (that is, judges, prosecutors, and defense counsel, among others) behave in the ways to which they are accustomed and that offer the greatest incentives. Reforms that significantly interfere with established norms or important incentives will meet great resistance. Policymakers need to consider these factors in designing new policies intended to improve the criminal court process.

Almost every chapter of this book describes both reform efforts and evolving practices in the criminal courts. Rather than judge criminal court practice against an arbitrary and idealized standard of perfect justice, we must look at the criminal courts in relation to how they have performed their role in the past and how they might *realistically* perform their role in the future. Given the difficult task assigned to the courts, the disagreement about the most important values to be achieved through the criminal court process, and limited resources, what can be done to improve the quality of justice for defendants, victims, and society as a whole? How might we continue to improve the criminal courts' legitimacy, reliability, fairness, efficiency, and accountability?

■ SUMMARY

Throughout history people have used a variety of measures to resolve disputes between individuals and groups. The criminal courts possess some unique features as forums for resolving disputes. First, for the dispute to be brought before a criminal court one party must have engaged in specific behavior and the other party must frame that behavior as a violation of the criminal law. If the prosecuting party is unable to make a minimally convincing argument that the conduct of the other party is a crime, the parties must rely on some other dispute resolution mechanism rather than criminal adjudication. Once in a criminal court, all parties must follow procedures that conform to the rule of law so that the judgment of the court retains legitimacy.

Courts decide two kinds of disputes: disputes about facts and disputes about law. In disputes about facts the issue before the court usually relates to whether the defending party engaged in behavior that violates criminal law. Unless the defendant admits to committing a crime, the factual dispute continues until a judgment is entered. Disputes about the law concern conflicting or differing interpretations of the legal requirements. Legal disputes may relate to either substantive or procedural law. These formal aspects of criminal law provide structure for the informal negotiations and exchanges that occur in most criminal court cases in the United States. Although these informal processes push formal aspects of law and procedure into the background, the formal aspects remain highly relevant to how cases are processed and the types of exchanges that can be made between the parties.

Throughout this book you will learn of the ways in which the criminal courts have evolved. The debate between the due process model and the crime control model serves as a continuous spur to reform of the criminal courts. At the same time, although courts have certainly changed and evolved over the years, any reform effort or policy change confronts tremendous inertia: informal practices, attitudes, norms, and the various incentives that influence practitioners to ignore policies and continue to behave as they have in the past.

The reforms of the past offer important lessons for the future. Rising concern about crime and shrinking budgets requires a clear understanding of what the criminal courts do well, what they do poorly, and how they might do better in the future. Although this book cannot answer those questions for you, we hope it will give you the tools you need to search for the answers.

■ FOR FURTHER DISCUSSION

1. Consider each dispute resolution mechanism described in the chapter. Can you think of examples in which any of these mechanisms are used today— instead of or in addition to using the criminal courts—to respond to conduct that is defined as criminal?

2. One issue that arises repeatedly in relation to the criminal process relates to the efficiency of the criminal justice system. Efficiency relates to both direct

costs (such as the costs of paying judges, prosecutors, and defense counsel) and indirect costs (such as creation of inequality in society, the generation of civil unrest, the encouragement of new crimes, and so on.) Efficiency is concerned with the costs incurred in reaching a result. Compare each dispute resolution mechanism described in this chapter in relation to the costs incurred in reaching a result. What kinds of potential costs are entailed by each of these mechanisms?

3. In 1994, when O. J. Simpson was charged in the homicides of Nicole Brown Simpson and Ronald Goldman, a CNN/USA Today/Gallup poll found that 50 percent of white Americans believed O. J. Simpson would get a fair trial, but only 29 percent of African-Americans thought that ("Opinion Poll" 1994). What do these poll results suggest about the legitimacy of the criminal court process to African-Americans?

4. Identify a criminal justice reform relating to the criminal process (as opposed to substantive reforms, such as creating new offenses, increasing sentence lengths, and so on) being debated in your community or state, or nationally. Would you characterize the proponents of the reform as primarily advocates of the crime control model or the due process model? How would the reform advance the goals of that model?

   With respect to the same reform proposal in what ways might the reform be impeded by informal practices, attitudes, norms, and incentives that support the status quo?

■ REFERENCES

Church, Thomas W., and Milton Heumann. 1992. *Speedy Disposition: Monetary Incentives and Policy Reform in Criminal Courts.* Albany: State University of New York Press.

Feeley, Malcolm M. 1983. *Court Reform on Trial: Why Simple Solutions Fail.* New York: Basic.

Frank, Nancy, and Michael J. Lynch. 1992. *Corporate Crime; Corporate Violence.* Albany: Harrow and Heston.

Galen, Michele, and Vicky Cahan. 1990. "The Legal Reef Ahead for Exxon." *Business Week* (March 12): 39.

Howard, J. Woodford, Jr. 1986. "Adjudication Considered as a Process of Conflict Resolution." In Walter F. Murphy and C. Herman Prithchett, eds., *Courts, Judges, and Politics,* 4th ed. New York: Random House.

Lindquist, John H. 1988. *Misdemeanor Crime: Trivial Criminal Pursuit.* Newbury Park, CA: Sage.

Merry, Sally Engle. 1982a. "Defining 'Success' in the Neighborhood Justice Movement." In Roman Tomasic and Malcolm M. Feeley, eds., *Neighborhood Justice: Assessment of an Emerging Idea.* New York: Longman.

———1982b. "The Social Organization of Mediation in Nonindustrial Societies: Implications for Informal Community Justice in America." In Richard Abel, ed., *The Politics of Informal Justice.* New York: Academic.

"Opinion Poll Says Race Plays Role in O. J. Simpson Case." 1994. *Jet* (July 25): 16–18.

Packer, Herbert L. 1968. *The Limits of the Criminal Sanction.* Palo Alto, Calif.: Stanford University Press.

Reid, Sue Titus. 1992. *Criminal Law,* 2d ed. New York: Macmillan.

Sander, Frank E. A. 1982. "Varieties of Dispute Processing." In Roman Tomasic and Malcolm M. Feeley, eds., *Neighborhood Justice: Assessment of an Emerging Idea.* New York: Longman.

OVERVIEW OF THE CRIMINAL COURTS: STRUCTURE AND PROCESS

Chapter 1 describes the purpose and philosophy of criminal courts and adjudication as a method for resolving disputes. This chapter takes a closer look at the structure of the criminal court and the major decision points in processing cases through the courts. Many concepts and terms introduced in this chapter are important for understanding the remainder of this book. The goal of this chapter is to provide a working vocabulary for studying criminal court process.

■ COURTS AND THEIR JURISDICTION

jurisdiction

Any understanding of the structure and function of the criminal courts requires an understanding of the concept of jurisdiction. **Jurisdiction** refers to the range of boundaries of judicial authority and can be conceptualized in three distinct ways. Jurisdiction is first of all geographic. The criminal courts of the state of California, for example, have jurisdiction (or authority) over conduct that violates the criminal law of California and that occurs within the geography of the state.

Jurisdiction also relates to the subject matter over which a court has authority. Some courts have authority to hear only certain kinds of cases. For example, a state may structure its court system so that some courts have jurisdiction over civil cases and other courts have jurisdiction over criminal cases. In other states the same court may have jurisdiction over both civil and criminal cases. States may create specialized courts that have exclusive jurisdiction in cases of divorce or in cases involving crimes committed by juveniles. The federal system has specialized courts to deal with offenses committed in the military and other specialized courts to decide disputes related to the tax code.

Finally, jurisdiction also has a hierarchical dimension. Every court system in the country has divided its courts into levels. The upper levels of the court system possess appellate jurisdiction. That is, they review the procedures followed in the courts below and determine whether these procedures conform to the law of that jurisdiction. In addition, the upper courts within any jurisdiction may prescribe the procedures to be followed in the lower courts. In this respect the higher courts have greater authority than the lower courts. They have hierarchical jurisdiction over the lower courts.

dual court system

In simplest terms courts in the United States are divided into two main groups, state courts and federal courts. Instead of one national system of criminal courts, the courts are divided into state systems and the federal system. The separation between the state courts and federal courts is sometimes referred to as the **dual court system.** Federal courts have jurisdiction over cases involving federal law. Each state court system has jurisdiction over cases involving the laws of that state. The dual nature of the American court system results in two consequences: concurrent jurisdiction of federal and state courts for some crimes and hierarchical jurisdiction of the U.S. Supreme Court over state courts in issues relating to the U.S. Constitution.

concurrent jurisdiction

If a single act violates both federal law and the law of the state in which the act is committed, the courts have **concurrent jurisdiction** because of the dual court system. An accused may be charged in both the federal system and the state system simultaneously. For example, if someone assaults the president of the United States while he is visiting Wichita, Kansas, the perpetrator can be prosecuted in federal court for assault on the president, a federal crime, as well as by the state of Kansas under the state law prohibiting assault on any person. In the Rodney King case, in which four Los Angeles police officers were charged in the beating of King, a black motorist, the officers were first tried under California state law. After the California jury acquitted the officers, federal prosecutors

FIGURE 2-1   Basic Structure of United States Court System

Source: Extracted from *Want's Federal-State Court Directory, 1995.* Copyright © 1994 WANT Publishing Co. (Washington, D.C.). Reprinted by permission.

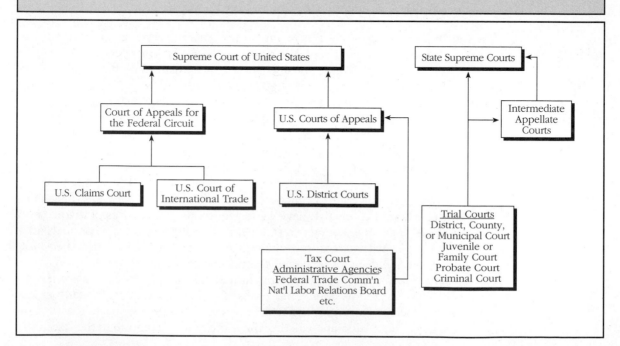

initiated criminal charges for the federal crime of violating a person's civil rights. Two defendants were subsequently convicted on the federal charges. Such double prosecution in the state and federal courts is not recognized as a violation of the protection against double jeopardy.

hierarchical jurisdiction

Another consequence of the dual court system is that the U.S. Supreme Court has **hierarchical jurisdiction** over state courts in matters relating to the federal constitution; that is, the state courts must uphold any rights that are protected by the U.S. Constitution. A defendant who claims a violation of a federal right may appeal to the U.S. Supreme Court (see Figure 2-1). The U.S. Supreme Court in turn may mandate certain procedures that all states must follow if the procedures are required by the U.S. Constitution (see Chapter 3 for a discussion of the concept of incorporation and the historical and legal basis for this authority).

Each court system has its own structure or division of jurisdiction among a number of levels and specialized courts. The structure of the federal court system is relatively simple and uncluttered. In contrast, many states have complicated and often arbitrary divisions between courts that have varying and often overlapping jurisdictions.

■ THE STRUCTURE OF STATE COURTS

trial courts, questions of fact, questions of law

appellate courts

Within any state court system the jurisdiction of particular courts may be divided into smaller geographic units, such as counties or multicounty circuits or districts. In addition, every state has courts with trial jurisdiction and courts with appellate jurisdiction. **Trial courts** hear evidence in order to decide **questions of fact,** specifically whether the accused committed the crime as charged. Trial courts also must decide **questions of law** that arise in the course of trying cases. Questions of law concern the interpretation of substantive and procedural law as it applies to the case at hand. **Appellate courts** do not take direct testimony. Instead they review the record of the trial court to determine whether errors were made during the trial process that require some remedy, including reversing a conviction or ordering a new trial for the accused. Appellate courts focus primarily on deciding questions of law and establishing precedents to direct the procedures in the lower courts.

Many states divide trial court jurisdiction into two levels of original proceedings. Courts of limited jurisdiction have authority to hear minor disputes. "All other cases are heard in the trial court of general jurisdiction or in a specialized court" (American Bar Association [ABA] Commission 1973, 7).

Courts of Limited Jurisdiction

courts of limited jurisdiction

Most criminal cases are disposed of in **courts of limited jurisdiction**, also referred to as *lower courts*. All but six states and the District of Columbia have courts of limited jurisdiction. Of the forty-four states with courts of limited jurisdiction, a few limit their jurisdiction to civil matters only. The vast majority (thirty-nine) have courts with jurisdiction over minor criminal matters. Typically, these courts conduct all stages of processing for misdemeanors. In addition, the typical lower court processes noncriminal offenses, some of which are identical to criminal matters (see Chapter 1). In many places the same lower court has the authority to handle the matter, whether it is designated as a crime or as an ordinance violation. Finally, the lower courts frequently have limited jurisdiction in felony cases, typically limited to setting bail, conducting preliminary hearings, and issuing search and arrest warrants. Beyond this description of what is typical lie many variations.

The jurisdiction of all these courts is established through state law and may vary even within a single state. States often establish several different kinds of limited jurisdiction courts. As a result the 44 states that have lower courts have 122 different categories of lower-court jurisdiction (National Center for State Courts 1988). These different courts may be established in different kinds of political units (county courts, municipal courts, and rural justice of the peace courts), each with a different jurisdictional range. For example, the largely rural justice of the peace courts in Arizona have criminal jurisdiction that is limited to misdemeanors in which the maximum sentence is a fine less than $300 or less than six months in jail. In contrast, municipalities in Arizona are authorized to establish courts that have limited jurisdiction to hear municipal ordinance violations and misdemeanor cases in which the maximum sentence is a fine of less than $2,500 or less than six months (see Figure 2-2).

Kansas, Missouri, and Wisconsin have courts of limited jurisdiction with authority over traffic and ordinance violations but no jurisdiction at all over criminal matters (misdemeanor and felony), which are heard exclusively in the court of general jurisdiction. Nonetheless, ordinance violations often involve the same kind of conduct that might be handled as a misdemeanor (for example, disturbing the peace, disorderly conduct, prostitution, petty theft, and minor assaults). For example, a person who is making a lot of noise in the middle of the night in a residential area might be criminally prosecuted for the crime of disorderly conduct or noncriminally prosecuted for violating the municipal ordinance that prohibits breaches of the peace. In Kansas, Missouri, and Wisconsin the decision to process the case as an ordinance violation means that the case goes to a court different than if the police decide to press criminal charges. In most places, however, the matter will be processed in the same court, no matter what it is called.

Lower court jurisdiction over felonies also varies widely. Some states authorize the courts of limited jurisdiction to conduct preliminary proceedings in felony cases, whereas other states lodge this authority exclusively in the courts of general jurisdiction. Where the lower courts have authority over preliminary matters for felonies, a felony case begins in the lower court and is later transferred to the court of general jurisdiction. Some states even authorize the lower courts to accept guilty pleas and impose sentences in felony cases (National Center for State Courts 1988). Lower courts generally may not hold trials for felonies, however. Because of these variations the term *court of limited jurisdiction* must be used carefully. Although the jurisdiction of each of these courts is clearly limited, what those limits are varies considerably from one court to another.

In many states the courts of limited jurisdiction are not courts of record. This means that the court maintains no record of the proceedings. Consequently, there is no record for an appellate court to review. To provide defendants in limited jurisdiction courts with an opportunity for review of their convictions, many states allow decisions of the courts of limited jurisdiction to be reviewed by a

de novo review

court of record in a proceeding called a de novo review. In a **de novo review** the court of general jurisdiction holds a new trial. The court hears the evidence as though there had been no trial in the court of limited jurisdiction and reaches a verdict on the merits of the case. Following conviction in the de novo trial, some states may allow a defendant to appeal through the usual appellate processes on the basis of the record established in the de novo trial. Other states make the verdict of the de novo trial final and allow no further appeals.

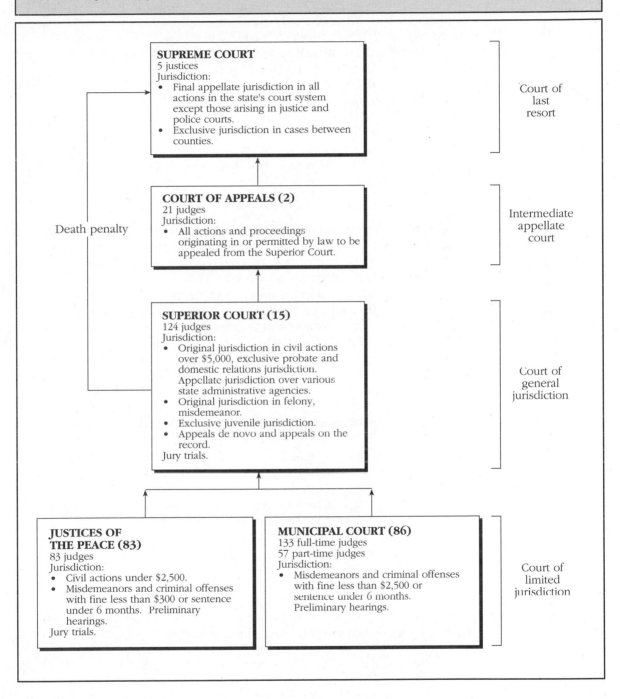

FIGURE 2-2 Arizona Court System

SOURCE: Extracted from *Want's Federal-State Court Directory, 1995.* Copyright © 1994 WANT Publishing Co. (Washington, D.C.). Reprinted by permission.

Courts of General Jurisdiction

courts of general jurisdiction

Courts of general jurisdiction typically have exclusive jurisdiction over all felonies but retain jurisdiction over misdemeanors under a variety of circumstances, including trials de novo. Again, states vary in where they draw the jurisdictional lines between the lower courts and courts of general jurisdiction. Some states draw the line between felonies and misdemeanors. Other states draw the line by using the maximum sentence, so that the courts of general jurisdiction hear all felonies as well as the more serious misdemeanors.

Some states also establish more than one category of courts of general jurisdiction. Michigan, for example, has circuit courts in most parts of the state but has also established the special Recorder's Court of Detroit to hear all felony cases within the city of Detroit (*Want's* 1994; see Figure 2-3). Indiana extends felony trial jurisdiction to superior courts and circuit courts (*Want's* 1994; see Figure 2-4). The names of these courts are not important (for example, superior court versus circuit court). Different states adhere to different conventions in naming their courts. What is important is the role these courts play as courts of general jurisdiction.

Regardless of the structure of a state's court system, states typically divide their courts of general jurisdiction into geographic districts or circuits. Only crimes committed within the district may be processed by the court for that district. Districts may be drawn along county lines, for example, and a crime committed in a given county will be tried in the district court for that county. Each district may have a large number of judges assigned to it. For example, Florida's courts of general jurisdiction are divided into 20 circuit courts to which 434 judges are assigned (*Want's* 1994, 128; see Figure 2-5). However, all the district court judges have jurisdiction over the same types of subject matter and are equal in terms of their hierarchical jurisdiction. In states that have simplified court structures, such as Florida's, judges can be temporarily reassigned from one circuit to another as caseloads demand. Even though the selection of judges may be geographically bound by counties or other judicial subdivisions, the court's structure is consolidated to allow greater flexibility as needed. In some cases court administration is organized according to geography, whereas in other states court administration may be carried out centrally at the state level. Finally, even within a district or circuit the courts may be subdivided into branches or departments, with one judge assigned to each branch or department. A large county district court, for example, may have more than one hundred branches, with one judge assigned to each branch. Each district will have a procedure for assigning cases to a particular branch or department.

Appellate Courts

Every state has established appellate courts for the purpose of reviewing the actions of the courts below. Appellate jurisdiction involves a procedural review of the trial court's record to determine whether the trial court appropriately followed and applied the law. The appellate court rarely disturbs the findings of fact made at the trial level. The principal activity of appellate courts is to clarify the law and decide what law to apply under specific circumstances. The published decisions of appellate courts establish rules that the lower courts in the same jurisdiction must follow, according to the doctrine of *stare decisis*.

stare decisis

The general principle of **stare decisis** says that courts must follow the decisions they have made in previous cases, yet this does not require a mechanical

FIGURE 2-3   Michigan Court System

Source: Extracted from *Want's Federal-State Court Directory, 1995.* Copyright © 1994 WANT Publishing Co. (Washington D.C.). Reprinted by permission.

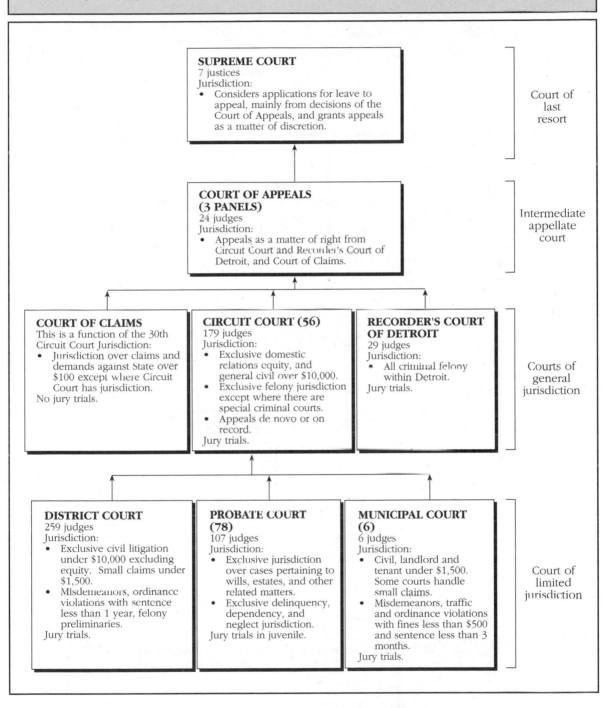

SUPREME COURT
7 justices
Jurisdiction:
• Considers applications for leave to appeal, mainly from decisions of the Court of Appeals, and grants appeals as a matter of discretion.

Court of last resort

COURT OF APPEALS (3 PANELS)
24 judges
Jurisdiction:
• Appeals as a matter of right from Circuit Court and Recorder's Court of Detroit, and Court of Claims.

Intermediate appellate court

COURT OF CLAIMS
This is a function of the 30th Circuit Court Jurisdiction:
• Jurisdiction over claims and demands against State over $100 except where Circuit Court has jurisdiction.
No jury trials.

CIRCUIT COURT (56)
179 judges
Jurisdiction:
• Exclusive domestic relations equity, and general civil over $10,000.
• Exclusive felony jurisdiction except where there are special criminal courts.
• Appeals de novo or on record.
Jury trials.

RECORDER'S COURT OF DETROIT
29 judges
Jurisdiction:
• All criminal felony within Detroit.
Jury trials.

Courts of general jurisdiction

DISTRICT COURT
259 judges
Jurisdiction:
• Exclusive civil litigation under $10,000 excluding equity. Small claims under $1,500.
• Misdemeanors, ordinance violations with sentence less than 1 year, felony preliminaries.
Jury trials.

PROBATE COURT (78)
107 judges
Jurisdiction:
• Exclusive jurisdiction over cases pertaining to wills, estates, and other related matters.
• Exclusive delinquency, dependency, and neglect jurisdiction.
Jury trials in juvenile.

MUNICIPAL COURT (6)
6 judges
Jurisdiction:
• Civil, landlord and tenant under $1,500. Some courts handle small claims.
• Misdemeanors, traffic and ordinance violations with fines less than $500 and sentence less than 3 months.
Jury trials.

Court of limited jurisdiction

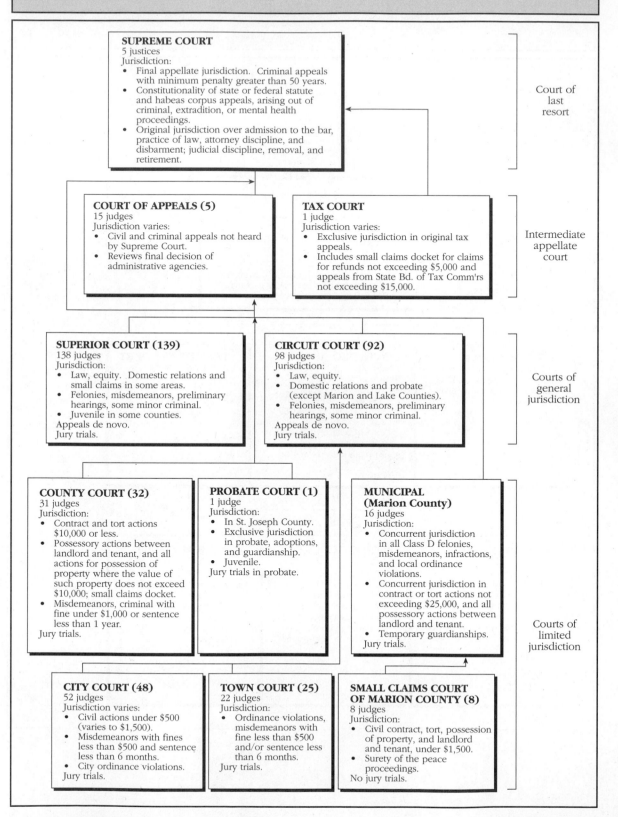

FIGURE 2-4 Indiana Court System

SOURCE: Extracted from *Want's Federal-State Court Directory, 1995*. Copyright © 1994 WANT Publishing Co. (Washington D.C.). Reprinted by permission.

SUPREME COURT
5 justices
Jurisdiction:
- Final appellate jurisdiction. Criminal appeals with minimum penalty greater than 50 years.
- Constitutionality of state or federal statute and habeas corpus appeals, arising out of criminal, extradition, or mental health proceedings.
- Original jurisdiction over admission to the bar, practice of law, attorney discipline, and disbarment; judicial discipline, removal, and retirement.

Court of last resort

COURT OF APPEALS (5)
15 judges
Jurisdiction varies:
- Civil and criminal appeals not heard by Supreme Court.
- Reviews final decision of administrative agencies.

TAX COURT
1 judge
Jurisdiction varies:
- Exclusive jurisdiction in original tax appeals.
- Includes small claims docket for claims for refunds not exceeding $5,000 and appeals from State Bd. of Tax Comm'rs not exceeding $15,000.

Intermediate appellate court

SUPERIOR COURT (139)
138 judges
Jurisdiction:
- Law, equity. Domestic relations and small claims in some areas.
- Felonies, misdemeanors, preliminary hearings, some minor criminal.
- Juvenile in some counties.
Appeals de novo.
Jury trials.

CIRCUIT COURT (92)
98 judges
Jurisdiction:
- Law, equity.
- Domestic relations and probate (except Marion and Lake Counties).
- Felonies, misdemeanors, preliminary hearings, some minor criminal.
Appeals de novo.
Jury trials.

Courts of general jurisdiction

COUNTY COURT (32)
31 judges
Jurisdiction:
- Contract and tort actions $10,000 or less.
- Possessory actions between landlord and tenant, and all actions for possession of property where the value of such property does not exceed $10,000; small claims docket.
- Misdemeanors, criminal with fine under $1,000 or sentence less than 1 year.
Jury trials.

PROBATE COURT (1)
1 judge
Jurisdiction:
- In St. Joseph County.
- Exclusive jurisdiction in probate, adoptions, and guardianship.
- Juvenile.
Jury trials in probate.

MUNICIPAL (Marion County)
16 judges
Jurisdiction:
- Concurrent jurisdiction in all Class D felonies, misdemeanors, infractions, and local ordinance violations.
- Concurrent jurisdiction in contract or tort actions not exceeding $25,000, and all possessory actions between landlord and tenant.
- Temporary guardianships.
Jury trials.

CITY COURT (48)
52 judges
Jurisdiction varies:
- Civil actions under $500 (varies to $1,500).
- Misdemeanors with fines less than $500 and sentence less than 6 months.
- City ordinance violations.
Jury trials.

TOWN COURT (25)
22 judges
Jurisdiction:
- Ordinance violations, misdemeanors with fine less than $500 and/or sentence less than 6 months.
Jury trials.

SMALL CLAIMS COURT OF MARION COUNTY (8)
8 judges
Jurisdiction:
- Civil contract, tort, possession of property, and landlord and tenant, under $1,500.
- Surety of the peace proceedings.
No jury trials.

Courts of limited jurisdiction

FIGURE 2-5   Florida Court System

SOURCE: Extracted from *Want's Federal-State Court Directory, 1995.* Copyright © 1994 WANT Publishing Co. (Washington D.C.). Reprinted by permission.

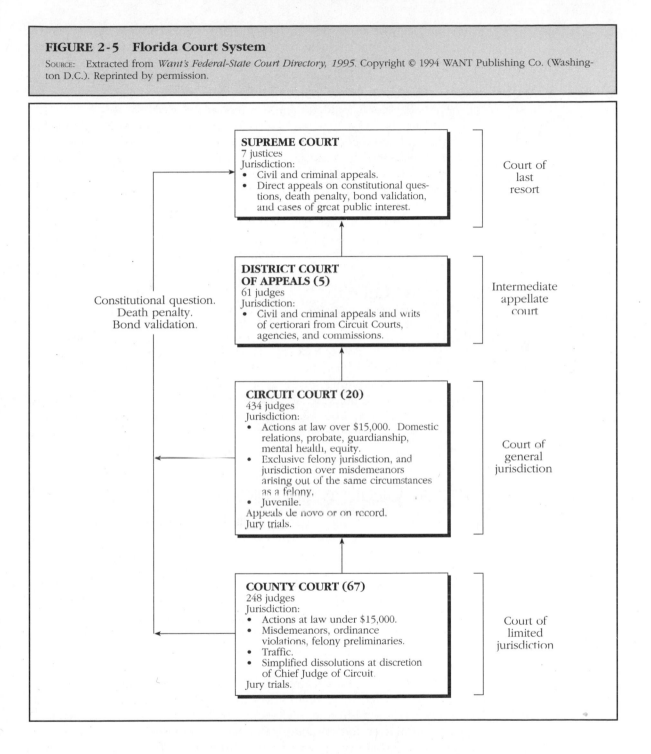

application of prior rulings. First, the principle of stare decisis extends only to those courts in the same jurisdictional hierarchy. If a higher court within the same judicial system decided a similar case in the past, the lower courts in that system are expected to follow that decision as precedent. Second, the court considers whether the facts of the present case are sufficiently similar to the earlier case to justify applying the same rulings. Different facts may require a different outcome.

Courts frequently find reasons for distinguishing between earlier cases and the cases they are deciding. Finally, on rare occasions a court may simply reject the precedent as wrongly decided. Therefore for a variety of reasons, courts may decide not to follow a particular decision as binding precedent. Nonetheless, the principle of stare decisis requires the court to justify the departure, explaining why a prior decision should not apply in the present case.

Most states have created two levels of appellate courts: an intermediate appellate court and a court of last resort. The decision to create an intermediate level of appellate courts is usually based on the volume of appellate cases, both criminal and civil. If the volume is too high for a single appellate court to handle, the legislature may create an intermediate level of appellate courts to ease the burden on the highest court. In most states the highest court is called the Supreme Court, but in New York and Maryland the highest court is called the Court of Appeals. Two states, Texas and Oklahoma, have created a specialized court of last resort for criminal cases, called the Court of Criminal Appeals.

Specialized Courts

specialized courts

In some jurisdictions **specialized courts** have exclusive jurisdiction over certain kinds of subject matter, such as divorce cases, offenses committed by juveniles, and tax or bankruptcy cases. The judges serving in these courts have an opportunity to gain experience dealing with sensitive and often emotional matters or matters requiring special expertise (ABA Commission 1973, 7). These courts generally have no criminal jurisdiction. Although the juvenile courts deal with conduct that would be criminal if committed by an adult, the judgments of juvenile courts are not criminal convictions, and the procedures followed in the juvenile courts are not identical to those in the criminal courts.

▣ FEDERAL COURT STRUCTURE

The structure of the federal courts is relatively simple. The federal courts are frequently referred to as a three-tiered system (U.S. District Court, U.S. Courts of Appeals, and U.S. Supreme Court; see Figure 2-1). The federal system also has a variety of specialized courts, such as the U.S. Claims Court, U.S. Tax Court, and U.S. Court of International Trade. None of the federal special courts has jurisdiction over crimes committed by civilians.

All federal crimes committed by civilians are tried in one of the ninety-four federal district courts. Attached to each district court are federal magistrates who have responsibilities similar to judges' in courts of limited jurisdiction. Each district court has jurisdiction over a specific geographic area of the United States. Large districts may be further divided into divisions. For example, Arkansas is divided into two federal court districts (the Western District and the Eastern District). Each district is further divided into five or six multicounty divisions.

There are thirteen federal courts of appeals, comprised of eleven numbered circuits plus the Court of Appeals for the District of Columbia and the Court of Appeals for the Federal Circuit. The Federal Circuit is a specialized appellate court with jurisdiction over the specialized federal courts. The appellate court for the District of Columbia hears appeals arising from the district court in the District of Columbia. The District of Columbia has a separate appellate court because of the large number of civil lawsuits filed there as the seat of the federal government. Each of the eleven numbered circuits serves a geographic area comprising one or

FIGURE 2-6 The Thirteen Federal Judicial Circuits

SOURCE: Reprinted from *West's Law Finder.* 1987. St. Paul, Minn.: West Publishing, p. 4.

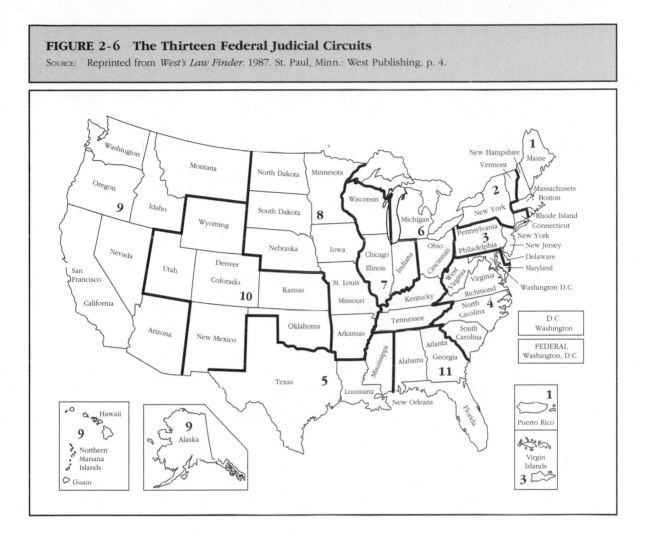

en banc

more district courts (see Figure 2-6). The Courts of Appeals hear appeals in panels of three judges, except when they consider a case ***en banc***, which means that the entire court hears the case. The Courts of Appeals sit en banc in order to resolve conflicts in decisions made by different panels or when the case presents issues of unusual importance.

The U.S. Supreme Court is the court of last resort in the federal jurisdiction. The U.S. Supreme Court accepts appeals from the federal circuit courts, including the specialized Federal Circuit, and from state courts in which the parties raise a federal question. In criminal cases state defendants may appeal their convictions to the U.S. Supreme Court by claiming that state authorities denied them a right guaranteed by the U.S. Constitution.

SIMPLIFYING THE STRUCTURE OF STATE COURTS

This review of court structures gives only a slight indication of the enormous variability in court organization. Many states retain complex structures with overlapping jurisdictions that arose as demands required, with little concern for any overarching structure. As early as 1906 Roscoe Pound, a renowned legal scholar, called for the reform of court structures. He advocated a simple structure with one court to hear trials and one to hear appeals (National Institute of Justice [NIJ] 1984, 3). All cases would originate in the trial court, and the appellate court would supervise the proceedings of the trial court. This two-tiered court system would eliminate the confusing overlap of jurisdictions frequently found in state court systems. In addition, a simplified court structure would make procedures more uniform across the court system.

court unification

The continued variation and complexity in court structures is the result of uneven progress toward the goal of **court unification.** After Pound's initial recommendation for a simplification in court structure, little progress was made for forty years. New Jersey became the first state to take Pound's advice and simplified its court structure in 1947 (NIJ 1984, 4). Since then progress has been slow but steady. During the 1960s and 1970s, most states implemented at least some recommendations of the court unification movement. This movement sought to simplify court structure and consolidate many administrative aspects involved in managing the courts. Reformers hoped that unified court systems would offer better and more consistent processing of cases. Opponents of court unification feared that centralization would result in a large overbearing bureaucracy that would be insensitive to local concerns (NIJ 1984, 5). Because of this resistance and the inertia of tradition court unification has progressed unevenly across the states.

Many states have created more unified court structures with simpler lines of jurisdiction and unified court administration. Other states have succeeded only in eliminating some of the worst confusion and duplication within their court structures. Local tradition and circumstances often prevent the complete unification of a state court system. Attempts to simplify court structure by eliminating the lower courts have sometimes been followed by renewed specialization and the creation of new court officers with limited authority. These judicial officers are not the same as judges and are not selected through the same process as judges. Wisconsin, for example, uses court commissioners in its courts of general jurisdiction. Idaho, Alaska, Kansas, and South Dakota have magistrates, and Iowa uses associate judges as well as judicial magistrates. These judicial officers execute tasks that lower court judges conducted before court reform. For example, they may issue warrants, preside over initial appearances, set and review bail, conduct preliminary hearings in felonies, and determine indigency. Thus even where court reorganization has abolished the lower courts, the functional equivalent of the lower-court magistrate can often be found.

It is important to keep in mind the broad variation in court organization and authority in relation to the various court proceedings described in this book. Even within a single state the practices found in the justice of the peace courts may be different from those in the municipal courts. Similarly, where several different courts of general jurisdiction exist, such as superior courts and circuit courts, procedures and practices may differ substantially in relation to such matters as setting bail, the rigor of preliminary hearings, plea-bargaining practices, the time spent on trials, and so forth.

■ THE ADVERSARIAL PROCESS

Regardless of how they are organized, American courts share a basic approach to the resolution of cases: the adversarial process. All courts in the United States share this common heritage and overarching philosophy of justice. Understanding criminal court processing in the United States requires an understanding of the adversarial process. Chapters 3 and 4 describe in greater detail the theory of the adversarial process and the historical evolution of adversarial procedures. Chapter 5 describes the inquisitorial process, which is the major alternative to the adversarial process, used in other parts of the world.

The main idea of the adversarial process is that the courts rely on the parties to a dispute to bring forward the evidence needed to decide the matter. In a criminal case the parties to the case are the state, represented by the **prosecutor,** and the **defendant**, who is also usually represented by an attorney called the **defense counsel.** Court cases are named by referring to the names of the parties to the dispute. For example, a criminal case might be referred to as *State v. John Smith*. Cases are processed according to formal legal rules enforced by the judge.

prosecutor, defendant, defense counsel

Because adversarial theory is the model underlying the criminal courts, the formal processes of the criminal courts and the legal rules that are applied by the courts are critical to an understanding of the outcomes of the criminal court process. Alongside the formal process, participants redefine and negotiate their tasks in ways that sometimes seem to conflict with the underlying philosophy of the adversarial system. Both formal and informal aspects take place within the broad boundaries set by the adversarial system and the U.S. Constitution.

■ PROCESSING CASES IN CRIMINAL COURT

Only about one-third of all criminal case filings are processed in courts of general jurisdiction (Ostrom et al. 1994, 6, 8). Case processing in the courts of general jurisdiction receives much greater attention (from court participants, court researchers, and the public) than cases in the lower courts. In addition, felony processing is more procedurally complex than misdemeanor processing. These differences must be kept in mind throughout this overview of the movement of cases through the criminal court process.

Most criminal cases in the courts of general jurisdiction are initiated when the police arrest a suspect and refer the case to the prosecutor for charges. After arrest, the processing of serious criminal cases has four major stages: pretrial procedures, adjudication, sentencing, and appeals.

Moving through these stages can take just a few weeks to more than a year, and courts in different jurisdictions vary widely in their processing time for a felony case (see Figure 2-7). For example, a study of the pace of criminal litigation found that in 1987 fewer than 1 percent of cases in Dayton, Ohio, took longer than a year from arrest to final disposition, and more than 90 percent of the cases were decided within 180 days of arrest. In contrast, the courts in Newark, New Jersey, moved more slowly, with most cases taking more than 180 days to process from arrest to final disposition. More than 40 percent of felony cases in Newark were still pending a year after arrest (Hewitt, Gallas, and Mahoney 1990, xi).

A major feature of criminal court processing is the screening function of various steps in the process (see Figure 2-8). Many cases enter the criminal justice process when the police make an arrest. Cases then move through a series of formal and informal screening stages. At each stage some cases are rejected, whereas others are sent on to the next stage. The screening is analogous to the sorting of rocky material from a gravel pit. Rocky materials of all sorts, from large rocks to fine sand, are loaded into the sorting mechanism together. Within the sorting mechanism are screens. Initially, the screens have relatively large holes, so only the biggest rocks are screened out. As the material moves through the

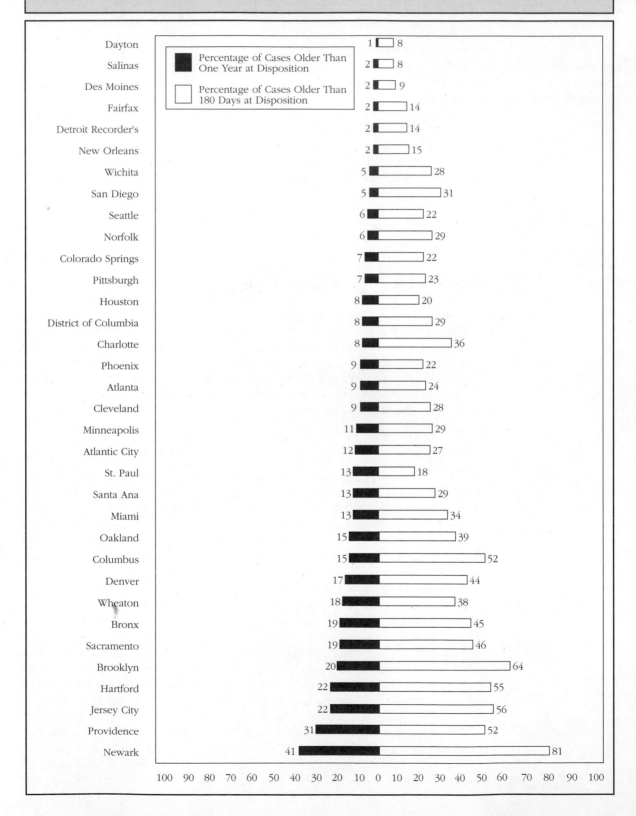

FIGURE 2-7   Felony Case Processing in Selected Courts
Percent of cases older than one year and older than 180 days at disposition

SOURCE: Reprinted from Willam E. Hewitt, Geoff Gallas, and Barry Mahoney, 1990. *Courts That Succeed: Six Profiles of Successful Courts*. Williamsburg, Va.: National Center for State Courts, 1990, p. xi.

FIGURE 2-8   Typical Outcome of 100 Felony Arrests Brought by the Police for Prosecution

Source: Reprinted from Barbara Boland, Paul Mahanna, and Ronald Sones. 1992. *The Prosecution of Felony Arrests, 1988*. Washington D.C.: U.S. Department of Justice, Bureau of Justice Statistics, front cover.

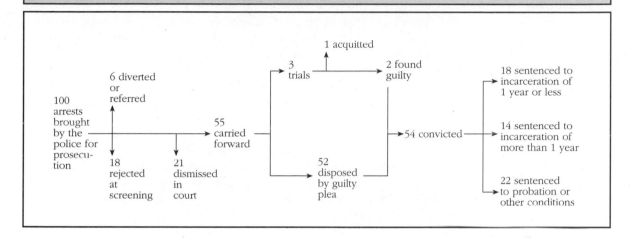

mechanism, the screens are made of finer and finer mesh, so eventually only the finest sand remains.

This is roughly the same process that occurs in the processing of criminal cases. Cases of all types enter the system at the point of arrest. Police and prosecutors engage in a sorting process. As a case moves through the system, the evidentiary screens become progressively tighter. Some screening processes are formal stages in the court process. At other points the prosecutor engages in informal screening to determine whether a case should be sent on or screened out. As Figure 2-8 shows, almost half of all arrests are screened out during the pretrial stages of the court process.

Pretrial Procedures

The three most important stages of the pretrial process are the filing of charges, the setting of bail, and the formal screening of the charges. These three stages may happen in almost any order, depending on law and tradition within the court system and the particular circumstances of the case. In particular, bail setting may occur either before or after charges are filed, whereas in other cases bail is set after the formal screening of the charges.

Filing Charges

filing charges

The process of screening and charging cases differs considerably from one jurisdiction to another. The most common arrangement is for police arrests to be referred to the prosecutor within hours of the arrest and for the prosecutor to be responsible for formally **filing charges** in court (Boland, Mahanna, and Sones 1992, 14). The prosecutor typically screens the case to determine what charges, if any, are appropriate under the circumstances. This informal screening may occur either before or after formal charges are filed, depending on local tradition and variations in the legal time limits for filing charges.

Regardless of when prosecutors review the evidence, they screen out many felony arrests. A recent national study of felony case processing found that 39 percent of all felony arrests were rejected by the prosecutor or dismissed by the court (Boland, Mahanna, and Sones 1992, 6). Some unknown proportion of these cases was subsequently prosecuted as misdemeanors. This loss of cases is referred to as **case attrition,** most commonly the result of lack of evidence or credible witnesses (Boland, Mahanna, and Sones 1992, 35–39). In other words, although police have arrested a suspect and sent the case to the prosecutor for charges, the prosecutor may decide not to charge because evidence is insufficient. Although the amount and quality of evidence appears to be the most important factor in making these decisions, other circumstances, including organizational, pragmatic, and humanitarian considerations, influence the charging decision.

case attrition

In addition, case attrition may reflect a practice of **overcharging** by the police, in which the police arrest and forward the case for prosecution on scant evidence. On the other hand, case attrition may reflect the differences in the ways in which prosecutors and police look at cases. Prosecutors are mindful of the evidence that will be required to convict, as opposed to the more minimal amount of evidence the police need to arrest a suspect (Jacoby 1977).

overcharging

Initial Appearance and Bail

Shortly after the arrest, either before or after the filing of formal charges, the defendant must be brought before a judge (or an authorized judicial officer, such as a magistrate or court commissioner) for an initial appearance. In most jurisdictions the initial appearance is held in a court of limited jurisdiction. In many jurisdictions, this stage is referred to colloquially as the arraignment. In felony cases, the arraignment is a separate proceeding, usually in the court of general jurisdiction, some weeks after the initial appearance. A large proportion of misdemeanor defendants plead guilty at the initial appearance. In felony cases, the main purpose of the **initial appearance** is to inform the defendant of the charges, either arrest charges or filed charges, and to determine under what conditions the defendant may be released before trial. In addition, the judge may be required to make a probable cause determination, assuring that at least a minimal amount of evidence exists suggesting that the defendant is guilty of a crime.

initial appearance

A majority of defendants are released on recognizance. If **released on recognizance**, the defendant agrees to return to court voluntarily for the further processing of the case. The court allows defendants to be released on their promise to return and requires no additional assurance of appearance.

release on recognizance

If the judge believes that the defendant may not return for trial if released on recognizance, the judge may order the defendant to post a bond or cash bail in order to gain release pending trial. A **bond** is a monetary guarantee in the form of collateral from the defendant or the guarantee of a professional bondsman. **Cash bail** refers to money that must be deposited with the court before the defendant is released. In both cases the defendant forfeits property or money upon failure to return for subsequent proceedings in the case.

bond, cash bail

In some cases the initial appearance is also the final appearance. Courts of limited jurisdiction may enter final judgments only in cases over which they have jurisdiction to do so. In most states this includes misdemeanors and some felonies. Consequently, when such cases come to the initial appearance, the magistrate may accept a guilty plea and immediately impose sentence. In this event the defendant immediately pleads guilty to the charges and is sentenced then and there. This is particularly common in those cases in which the only likely penalty is a fine.

Formal Screening

formal screening

In felony cases the charges are formally screened before being sent forward for trial in a court of general jurisdiction. **Formal screening** is a procedure in which either a judge or jury reviews the evidence in the case and decides whether the evidence is sufficient to continue the prosecution. Two different systems are used in the United States to formally screen felony charges: the preliminary hearing and the grand jury.

preliminary hearing

probable cause

In those states in which the **preliminary hearing** is used to formally screen felony charges, a hearing is held before a judge (typically in a court of limited jurisdiction) to determine whether there is probable cause to believe that the defendant committed the crime(s) as charged by the prosecutor. **Probable cause** means there is enough evidence to reasonably believe that the defendant committed the crimes as charged. If the court finds evidence sufficient to support probable cause, the defendant is bound over for felony trial in the court of general jurisdiction. The prosecutor files a formal charging document, called an **information,** with the felony court. The information lists the charges against the defendant. More than half the states follow some variation of this procedure.

information

grand jury

In a somewhat smaller number of states and in the federal jurisdiction the **grand jury** is the mechanism established for formally screening and referring felony cases to the court of general jurisdiction. In some grand jury jurisdictions the prosecutor may choose whether to take a felony case to a preliminary hearing or a grand jury, or may do both (see Figure 2-9). Six to twenty-three citizens (depending on the jurisdiction) are called to serve as grand jurors and hear evidence in cases that the prosecutor wishes to prosecute as felonies. As in the preliminary hearing the task of the grand jurors is to consider the evidence and decide whether evidence is sufficient to show probable cause that the defendant committed a felony. Unlike the preliminary hearing, where a judge makes this determination, no judge is present at the grand jury. The decision to issue felony charges is left to the judgment of the jury of laypeople. If the grand jury decides the evidence supports probable cause, it issues an **indictment,** or **true bill,** which is the formal charging document listing the charges against the defendant. When evidence is insufficient to charge, the grand jury decision is called a **no-bill.**

indictment, true bill

no-bill

bindover

About 90 percent of felony cases presented for formal screening result in either a **bindover** decision at the preliminary hearing or an indictment by the grand jury (Boland et al. 1990, 5). If the defendant is not bound over on felony charges at the preliminary hearing or if the grand jury returns a no-bill (again, depending on the jurisdiction), the case may still be processed in the court of limited jurisdiction on any remaining misdemeanor charges against the defendant.

The time between initial court filing and the preliminary hearing or grand jury decision ranges from about two weeks to a month. During this time the prosecutor may reduce felony charges to misdemeanors or lesser felonies. When this occurs, it may be the result of continued screening, during which the prosecutor eliminates charges because of lack of evidence or decides the charges are too severe under the circumstances. For instance, a prosecutor may choose to drop felony charges, even if they are provable, as a way of showing leniency to a first offender.

FIGURE 2-9   Criminal Case Processing in Fairfax County, Va.

SOURCE: Reprinted from Willam E. Hewitt, Geoff Gallas, and Barry Mahoney. 1990. *Courts that Succeed: Six Profiles of Successful Courts*. Williamsburg, Va.: National Center for State Courts, 1990, p. 62.

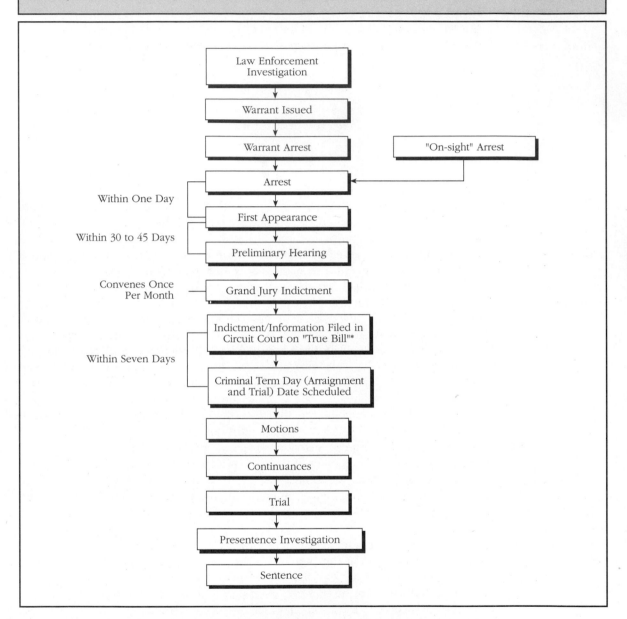

Plea Negotiations

plea bargaining

In other cases the prosecutor's decision to drop felony charges or reduce charges to a misdemeanor may be the result of active negotiations involving the defendant, defense counsel, and the prosecutor, a process commonly referred to as **plea bargaining.** Prosecutors' offices differ widely in the extent to which they engage in plea negotiations, the types of plea agreements they offer, and whether plea agreements result in felony charges being reduced to misdemeanors (Boland et al. 1990, 6).

Both prosecutorial screening and plea negotiations are informal processes. The law does not require prosecutors to screen cases or to negotiate with defendants. Informal screening and negotiations take place outside of court. Prosecutors are not required to articulate reasons or specific standards for the decisions they make. Nonetheless, the outcome of most cases is determined on the basis of these informal processes rather than what happens in the formal proceedings in criminal court.

In recent years prosecutors' offices have tried to develop criteria to guide individual prosecutors in making charging and plea-bargaining decisions. Although the decisions remain informal, the articulation of such policies makes the charging and negotiation processes more visible and subject to supervision. In addition, although prosecutorial screening and plea negotiations are informal, they are influenced by the formal aspects of the court process. For example, the key determinant of a prosecutor's charging decisions appears to be the amount and quality of evidence available. Although only about 10 percent of all defendants charged go to trial, the standards of proof at trial set the yardstick by which most prosecutors measure the evidence while they are screening cases.

Research on a sample of urban jurisdictions found that for every one hundred felony arrests, only three defendants go to trial. The other cases are rejected by the prosecutor, are dismissed, or are resolved by the defendant's pleading guilty (Boland, Mahanna, and Sones 1992; see Figure 2-8). Going to trial is the exception in the criminal court process. Nevertheless, trials are important. The cases that go to trial play an important role in setting legal standards. The right of defendants to demand a trial deters prosecutors from charging for offenses that cannot be proved. In addition, in most instances only those cases that go to trial can be appealed. Because appellate decisions play an important role in interpreting the law, the few cases that go to trial greatly influence the issues that are presented to the appellate courts and therefore influence the interpretation of procedural laws. Ultimately, these interpretations influence the informal processing of cases as prosecutors and defense counsel assess the strength of a case in light of existing rules.

Arraignment and Trial

arraignment

The **arraignment** is a proceeding at which the defendant formally pleads to the charges. In felony cases the arraignment takes place a few weeks after the arrest. If the defendant pleads not guilty, a trial date is set. In most cases the defendant pleads guilty, waiving the right to trial. Even defendants who plead not guilty when first arraigned frequently change their plea to guilty before trial.

waiver

Because a guilty plea **waives,** or gives up, the defendant's right to a trial, the judge must ascertain that the defendant understands the charges and the consequences of pleading guilty and that the plea is being made voluntarily and is not the result of coercion. The judge may ask whether any promises other than the plea agreement were made or whether any threats or pressures caused the defendant to plead guilty. Judges reject only 2 percent of the guilty pleas they consider (U.S. Bureau of Justice Statistics [BJS] 1988, 83).

Of all criminal cases, serious felonies are the most likely to go to trial. For example, in Manhattan criminal courts 30 percent of the defendants arrested on homicide charges go to trial, but fewer than 10 percent of the larceny and auto theft cases go to trial (Boland et al. 1990, 22). Defendants facing long sentences are more apt to decide to go to trial than to plead guilty.

bench trial, trier of fact

reasonable doubt, standard of evidence, burden of proof

Although criminal defendants have a right to a jury trial in all but petty cases, many trials are **bench trials** in which the judge serves as the **trier of fact.** In jury trials the jury serves as trier of fact. The role of the trier of fact, whether judge or jury, is to decide whether the evidence proves the guilt of the defendant beyond a **reasonable doubt.** Because of the serious consequences of a criminal conviction, the law requires this rigorous **standard of evidence.** It is the prosecutor's job to convince the trier of fact that the only reasonable interpretation of the facts is that the defendant is guilty.

If the prosecution fails to meet its **burden of proof,** the defendant is acquitted. An acquitted defendant is freed but typically is not entitled to compensation for the loss of freedom or investment of time and money in defending against the charges. If the judge or jury finds the defendant guilty, the judge is authorized to sentence the defendant.

Sentencing

Whether defendants are convicted by guilty plea or by guilty verdict at trial, sentencing is the stage at which the court decides on the appropriate consequences for their violation of the law. Usually, the judge is responsible for imposing the sentence. Sometimes, especially in death penalty cases, the authority to impose the sentence is shared with the jury instead. The statute defining the offense for which the defendant was convicted sets the limits within which the sentence must fall. These limits may be broad, giving wide discretion, or they may be quite narrow, allowing little or no discretion in sentencing. Usually, statutory law will specify at least a maximum fine and a maximum period of incarceration. Recent legislative changes have made statutory minimum sentences more common as well. Some statutes even impose mandatory fines or prison terms.

probation

Many defendants are sentenced to probation. A sentence of **probation** means that the judge suspends any sentence of incarceration and places the defendant under the supervision of a probation officer. In addition, judges have a good deal of authority to order specialized treatment and close supervision. For example, the judge may require that a drug-dependent defendant participate in a drug treatment program. Similarly, many states are now authorizing judges to order that convicts be electronically monitored in their homes rather than sent to jail or prison.

Appeals

The final stage in the criminal court process is the appellate process. After a verdict of guilty, a defendant has an opportunity to appeal the conviction. The first appeal is generally offered as a right. The defendant must file an appeal within certain time limits set by law, but once an appeal is filed, the appellate court must consider the appeal. If the appeal is unsuccessful, the defendant may file to have the appeal heard in the court of last resort. This appeal is not usually offered as a right. Instead, the court of last resort has the discretion to decide which cases it will hear and which it will reject without a hearing. In states with no intermediate appellate court the court of last resort usually hears criminal appeals as a matter of right. Following appeal in the state court of last resort a defendant may petition the U.S. Supreme Court if state procedures violated the U.S. Constitution.

An appeal must point to errors made by the trial court. In general, the appellate court makes no attempt to determine whether the outcome of the trial was correct. Instead, the appellate court is concerned with procedural errors and violations of the defendant's rights during the court process. The decisions of appellate courts generally relate to issues of law, not issues of fact. If the appellate court finds that the trial court made a procedural error, the appellate court decides whether that error probably affected the outcome of the case. If it finds that the error was **harmless error,** that it probably did not affect the outcome of the case, it will not overturn the conviction. Only if the court finds that a fundamental right was violated or that the error probably affected the outcome of the case will an appellate court reverse the conviction.

harmless error

Appeals are uncommon and are rarely successful in getting a conviction overturned. Despite the small numbers of appeals, however, the appellate process helps to assure that trial judges understand and correctly apply the law. Judges try to avoid having their cases overturned on appeal. The appellate process is also an important means of preventing a miscarriage of justice. The emphasis on procedure rather than the defendant's guilt in the appellate process underscores the central assumption of the adversarial process. Following fair procedures is thought to be the best way to assure the correct verdict. If procedural errors are made, the appellate court may overturn the conviction, necessitating a new trial to assure that the guilty verdict was not a product of the irregular procedures followed in the first trial. Finally, appellate court decisions create new law that guides lower courts in applying substantive law and establishes procedures that police, prosecutors, and trial courts must follow.

◻ DIFFERING APPROACHES TO CASE PROCESSING

Although the major steps in criminal court processing are similar from one jurisdiction to another, the ways in which cases move through these processes vary widely. Researchers have identified a number of factors that influence the way in which cases are processed. Some studies of case processing have concluded that the norms of the courtroom work group (judge, prosecutor, defense counsel, and other courtroom personnel) and the local legal culture influence case processing. Other research suggests that the nature of the work assigned to the court (types of cases) is the critical factor in shaping court processing.

Courtroom Work Group

courtoom work group

Like any group of people who work together day after day, the **courtroom work group** develops norms that influence its handling of cases. Work group norms define the characteristics of typical cases or normal cases (Sudnow 1965). These normal cases can be handled rapidly, without much discussion or controversy, so long as all members of the work group recognize the case as normal. Normal cases receive normal dispositions. However, at any point, one participant can signal that the current case is not normal and force the other participants to adopt a more adversarial approach (Eisenstein and Jacob 1977; Heumann, 1977; Nardulli 1978).

Local Legal Culture

local legal culture

In addition to the norms of the courtroom work group, the **local legal culture** influences the ways in which cases are handled. The legal professionals involved in the criminal courts—judges, prosecutors, and defense counsel—often share basic understandings of the ways in which criminal courts should operate. In some communities the local legal culture may tolerate many delays in the processing of cases, allowing all participants as much time as they need or want in preparing for court appearances. In other communities such delays might be viewed with great disdain. Such local norms influence the pace of case processing and other characteristics of the ways in which cases are treated in the courts (Church 1985).

Nature of the Work

The nature of the work assigned also influences the attention the cases receive. Cases in courts of limited jurisdiction, for example, are more likely to involve minor crimes, simple fact situations, and defendants who are not represented by counsel. The defendants, facing only a small fine, are often eager to get out of court as quickly as possible. These case characteristics result in lower courts' adopting simplified procedures in order to dispose of cases as quickly as possible (Henderson et al. 1984).

Variations in work group norms, local legal culture, and the nature of the work facing the courtroom actors are valuable for understanding the enormous variation in court practices from place to place and even within the same geographic jurisdiction. These factors may affect the speed at which cases are processed, the individualized attention that cases receive from court participants, and the likelihood that the outcome of the case will be just.

SUMMARY

This overview merely touches on some primary features of the criminal court process. This chapter introduced the structure of the court system (the dual court system, courts of limited jurisdiction, courts of general jurisdiction, specialized courts, and appellate courts) and the major decision points in the processing of cases (filing charges, bail, formal screening of charges, plea negotiations, arraignment, trial, sentence, and appeal). Two important conclusions emerge from this overview. First, jurisdictions vary widely, both in relation to court structure and the processing of cases. Some courts have a highly decentralized structure, whereas others are tightly unified. Some courts take a highly formal and adversarial approach to adjudication, whereas others are more concerned with resolving cases quickly and without a lot formality. Similarly, the formal rules of procedure and the order in which certain procedures occur can vary from jurisdiction to jurisdiction. Work group norms and local legal culture further influence the ways in which cases are processed. Subsequent chapters further explore these variations, their causes and consequences.

Informal out-of-court decisions play an enormous role in shaping the outcome of cases in virtually every jurisdiction. The prosecutor's initial charging decision and later plea negotiations have an enormous influence on most case outcomes. To understand the criminal court process requires as much understanding of what goes on outside the courtroom as what goes on within it.

■ FOR FURTHER DISCUSSION

1. What are two consequences of the existence of a dual court system in the United States?

2. Draw a diagram similar to those in figures 2-1 through 2-5 showing the structure of the court system in the state in which you live.

3. To what does the principle of stare decisis refer? How is this principle related to the appellate courts?

4. This chapter introduced key terms and concepts needed to understand the chapters that follow. For most students much of the material may review material covered in other courses. What terms or concepts were unfamiliar to you before reading this chapter?

■ REFERENCES

American Bar Association. 1973. *Standards Relating to Court Organization.* [n.p.]: Commission on Standards of Judicial Administration.

Boland, Barbara, Catherine H. Conly, Paul Mahanna, Lynn Warner, and Ronald Sones. 1990. *The Prosecution of Felony Arrests, 1987.* Washington, D.C.: U.S. Department of Justice, Bureau of Justice Statistics.

Boland, Barbara, Paul Mahanna, and Ronald Sones. 1992. *The Prosecution of Felony Arrests, 1988.* Washington, D.C.: U.S. Department of Justice, Bureau of Justice Statistics.

Church, Thomas W., Jr. 1985. "Examining Local Legal Culture." *American Bar Foundation Research Journal* 1985:449–518.

Eisenstein, James, and Herbert Jacob. 1977. *Felony Justice: An Organizational Analysis of Criminal Courts.* Boston: Little, Brown.

Henderson, Thomas A., Cornelius M. Kerwin, Randall Guynes, Carl Baar, Neal Miller, Hildy Saizow, and Robert Grieser. 1984. *The Significance of Judicial Structure: The Effect of Court Unification on Trial Court Operations.* Washington, D.C.: National Institute of Justice.

Heumann, Milton. 1977. *Plea Bargaining.* Chicago: University of Chicago Press.

Hewitt, William E., Geoff Gallas, and Barry Mahoney. 1990. *Courts That Succeed: Six Profiles of Successful Courts.* Williamsburg, Va.: National Center for State Courts.

Jacoby, Joan. 1977. *The Prosecutor's Charging Decision: A Policy Perspective.* Washington, D.C.: U.S. Department of Justice.

Nardulli, Peter F. 1978. *The Courtroom Elite: An Organizational Perspective.* Cambridge, Mass.: Ballinger.

National Center for State Courts. 1988. *State Court Organization 1987.* Williamsburg, Va: National Center for State Courts.

National Institute of Justice. 1984. *The Significance of Judicial Structure: The Effect of Unification on Trial Court Operations.* Washington, D.C.: U.S. Department of Justice, National Institute of Justice.

Ostrom, Brian J., Karen Gillions Way, Natalie B. Davis, Steven E. Hairston, and Carol R. Flango. 1994. *State Court Caseload Statistics: Annual Report 1992.* Williamsburg, Va: National Center for State Courts.

Sudnow, David N. 1965. "Normal Crime: Sociological Features of the Penal Law in a Public Defender's Office." *Social Problems* 12:209–15.

U.S Bureau of Justice Statistics. 1988. *Report to the Nation on Crime and Justice,* 2d ed. Washington, D.C.: U.S. Department of Justice.

Want's Federal-State Court Directory, 1995 Edition. 1994. Washington, D.C.: WANT Publishing.

CHAPTER **3**

RIGHTS OF THE ACCUSED IN AN ADVERSARIAL SYSTEM

Most Americans are familiar with the images of the adversary system. In movies and television we have all seen the prosecutor and defense counsel going head to head in a battle of wits to win the case. The judge sits high above the fray, acting only in response to a specific request or objection from one of the attorneys. The jury sits mutely to one side. This scene is so familiar that it is sometimes difficult to appreciate the underlying theory of judicial process. And although people in the United States would find the scene familiar, people in other countries might find the adversarial process a peculiar way to arrive at a verdict. Both the prosecutor and the defense counsel seem to be more concerned with winning the case and outwitting their opponent than learning the whole truth. How can this display of clever maneuvering lead to justice?

The value of the adversarial system has been much disputed in recent decades. Legal scholars as eminent as Chief Justice William Rehnquist of the U.S. Supreme Court have argued that basic adversarial practices ought to be modified to make justice more certain and efficient. Some commentators have suggested that we borrow from European judicial models and practices.

Understanding the debate about the adversarial process requires a clear understanding of the theory of the adversarial process, how the process works in practice in the United States, and what the alternatives to the adversarial process might be like. This chapter explains the theory of the adversarial process. Chapter Four sketches the historical evolution of criminal courts and procedure within the Anglo-American adversarial process, and Chapter Five explores alternatives to the adversarial process by describing several foreign systems of criminal adjudication. The rest of this book describes and analyzes the adversarial process as it is practiced in criminal courts today.

◼ TWO KINDS OF JUSTICE

The goal of the adversarial process is justice. Philosophers have identified a variety of different kinds of justice or aspects of justice, two of which are particularly relevant to understanding the theory behind the adversarial process: substantive justice and procedural justice.

substantive justice

Substantive justice concerns the accuracy or correctness of the outcome of the case. If the defendant is actually guilty, a verdict of guilty is just. If the defendant is really innocent, a verdict of not guilty is just. In this sense substantive justice is primarily concerned with the truthfulness of the allegation, the accuracy of the verdict, and the appropriateness of the sentence. The value we place on reliability in the court process stems from our concern with substantive justice.

procedural justice

Procedural justice is not concerned with the outcome of the case. Instead, **procedural justice** concerns the fairness of the procedures used to arrive at a result. If fair procedures are followed, justice is achieved. If fair procedures are not carried out, the action is not just. This is the case regardless of the substantive justice of the result. In other words, a truly guilty person could be convicted (substantive justice), but if the trial involved unfair procedures, that person's conviction is unjust in terms of procedural justice.

It is tempting to excuse lapses in procedural justice when we are sure of the substantive justice of the result. We are less inclined to object to questionable procedures if we are confident that a guilty person was convicted nonetheless. Unfortunately, this is also the logic of the mob. Lynchings and kangaroo trials have frequently taken place in situations in which people were convinced that the accused deserved punishment. The substantive justice of their actions seemed to excuse the lack of a fair trial. In terms of procedural justice, of course, the action of the mob is wrong, no matter how self-evident the guilt of the accused may be.

Although substantive justice and procedural justice are separate concepts, they are clearly related. The theory of the adversarial system values fair procedures as the best way to ensure substantive justice in the greatest number of cases. By giving each and every accused—no matter how guilty they appear—a fair trial, the adversarial process seeks to achieve substantive justice.

But what is "a fair trial"? What should the rules be? The delineation of fair procedures and defendants' rights is a continuing process. The very nature of the common law tradition is to allow for the continual evolution of law and individual rights. Much of American legal history has seen a struggle between those who would expand defendants' rights (due process model) and those who wish to promote the efficiency of the criminal justice system by constraining the expansion of rights (crime control model).

The Nature of an Adversarial System

The logic of the adversarial process permeates the entire legal system of the United States. All courts, whether handling civil or criminal matters, adhere formally to the requirements of adversarial justice. Even when attempts have been made to adopt a different style of decision making, such as juvenile court adjudication and administrative rule making, the adversarial process reasserts itself. In part the pervasiveness of adversarial procedures may be the result of the training lawyers receive in law school. Because lawyers are trained to serve as advocates, they tend to adopt this role in relation to every type of dispute. Our culture of individualism and personal rights also calls forth adversarial procedures. Each person demands her "day in court" to present her side of the story.

adversarial
system

An **adversarial system** of justice may be defined by three main characteristics. First, the disputing parties control the presentation of evidence, and each party seeks victory. This characteristic derives from the historic practice of private prosecution in the English judicial system. Under this system both the plaintiff and the defendant were trying to win their cases. The rules of procedure that developed in England presupposed a system in which interested parties sought victory rather than justice. This tradition has evolved into the adversarial system.

In the adversarial criminal process the prosecutor and defense counsel represent the two adversaries, the state and the defendant. Because the prosecutor represents the state, and because the state has an interest in justice (as opposed to merely winning the case), the modern prosecutor is required to seek justice, not simply to get as many convictions as possible. The prosecutor's control of the charging decision requires that the prosecutor issue charges only if there is evidence to support the charges. The prosecutor should not seek to convict someone if he believes the person is innocent.

Once the charges are initiated, however, the prosecutor is expected to behave like an adversary out to win the case. The prosecutor is not expected to search for evidence that would exonerate the defendant, although the prosecutor is required to turn over to the defense any exculpatory evidence that turns up during the investigation of the case. Each side seeks to present to the court only that evidence that fits its version of the facts. Each adversary hopes to make its witnesses and evidence appear to be the more reliable and truthful. Each adversary tries to use the law, particularly the rules of evidence, to keep inconvenient or damaging information from coming to light.

A second characteristic of the adversarial process is that the decision in the case is made by a neutral and passive fact-finder who takes no part in the investigation of the case or the presentation of evidence at trial. The fact-finder, whether judge or jury, does not take a leading role in presenting evidence or questioning witnesses.

Third, a detailed set of procedures controls the adversaries. These are the rules that set limits on the conduct of the contestants, drawing the boundary between fair play and cheating. The judge serves as referee. If one party violates an established procedure, the other party may object to that violation, and the judge decides whether the specific rule was violated or not.

The terms *contestant, referee,* and *victory* conjure up images of a game. Indeed, the adversarial process has frequently been compared to a sporting meet. This analogy also helps to underscore the necessity of rules in the adversarial process. Imagine a football game with no rules against holding, going offside, or beating opponents with a stick. The game would quickly dissolve into chaos. Rules are just as necessary in the adversarial process. Because both parties are seeking to win, they might resort to unfair and underhanded tactics if they were not forced to follow established rules. The rules of procedure create a level playing field and keep both sides honest.

■ DEFENDANTS' RIGHTS IN THE ADVERSARIAL SYSTEM

Without rules the parties in the adversarial process would be free to engage in conduct that would undermine the ability of the system to attain substantive justice, that is, to find the truth. These procedural rules and limits on the conduct of the adversaries have many sources. Some rules are dictated by the lawyers' code of ethics. Others are derived from statutory laws that define the rules of criminal procedure. The final authority on the minimum rights to which defendants are entitled is the U.S. Constitution.

The Constitution and the Rights of Criminal Defendants

The Bill of Rights, which consists of the first ten amendments to the U.S. Constitution, is a testament to the importance that the founders of this nation placed on fair procedures in an adversarial system of justice. Of the first ten amendments four are directly related to criminal procedures (see Figure 3-1). As ratified in 1791, the Bill of Rights articulated specific freedoms that the national (federal) government was required to recognize. The U.S. Bill of Rights did not initially limit the action of state governments or guarantee any rights to defendants in state criminal prosecutions.

This changed with the passage of the Fourteenth Amendment in 1868. The ***due process*** **due process clause** of the Fourteenth Amendment proclaimed:
clause

> No State shall make or enforce any law which shall . . . deprive any person of life, liberty, or property, without due process of law.

incorporation The meaning of the due process clause has evolved since, resulting in the **incorporation** of much of the Bill of Rights in the interpretation of "due process of law" in the Fourteenth Amendment.

total Some legal scholars have argued that the Bill of Rights is a concise statement of ***incorporation*** the minimum requirements of due process. According to this view, called **total incorporation**, the Fourteenth Amendment's due process clause should be interpreted as guaranteeing all those rights that the U.S. Supreme Court has found within the first ten amendments to the Constitution. Under this view, if the Supreme Court holds that certain procedures are required by the Constitution in federal prosecutions, the states should be held to identical standards.

The doctrine of total incorporation has never been accepted by a majority of Supreme Court justices. Consequently, the content of the Fourteenth Amendment's due process clause has been determined through a process of **selective** ***selective*** **incorporation**. The Court has examined each right on a case-by-case basis, ***incorporation*** sometimes finding that the right or procedure is so fundamental to due process that states are obliged to recognize the right in order to comply with the Fourteenth Amendment. Each decision has involved a balancing of the competing goals of the due process and crime control models. For example, the Court has concluded that representation by counsel is so fundamental to a fair trial in our adversary system of justice that the Sixth Amendment right to counsel has been incorporated as part of the meaning of the Fourteenth Amendment's due process

---

FIGURE 3-1   Criminal Procedure in the Bill of Rights

Article IV

The right of the people to be secure in their persons, houses, papers, and effects, against unreasonable searches and seizures, shall not be violated, and no Warrants shall issue, but upon probable cause, supported by Oath and affirmation, and particularly describing the place to be searched, and the person or things to be seized.

Article V

No person shall be held to answer for a capital, or otherwise infamous crime, unless on a presentment or indictment of a Grand Jury, except in cases arising in the land or naval forces, or in the Militia, when in actual service in time of War or public danger; nor shall any person be subject for the same offence to be twice put in jeopardy of life or limb; nor shall be compelled in any criminal case to be a witness against himself, nor be deprived of life, liberty, or property, without due process of law; nor shall private property be taken for public use without just compensation.

Article VI

In all criminal prosecutions, the accused shall enjoy the right to a speedy and public trial, by an impartial jury of the State and district wherein the crime shall have been committed; which district shall have been previously ascertained by law, and to be informed of the nature and cause of the accusation; to be confronted with the witnesses against him; to have compulsory process for obtaining witnesses in his favor, and to have the assistance of counsel for his defence.

Article VIII

Excessive bail shall not be required, nor excessive fines imposed, nor cruel and unusual punishments inflicted.

Article XIV

No State shall make or enforce any law which shall abridge the privileges or immunities of citizens of the United States; nor shall any State deprive any person of life, liberty, or property, without due process of law; nor deny to any person within its jurisdiction the equal protection of the laws.

---

clause. The Court required this despite the added expense entailed for states required to provide free counsel to indigent defendants.

At other times the Court has allowed states a measure of autonomy in fashioning fair procedures in criminal cases, holding that due process does not require the exact protections outlined in the Bill of Rights. For example, the Supreme Court has ruled that the Fifth Amendment right to indictment by grand jury does not apply to the states. In other words, the use of a preliminary hearing or other charging mechanism meets the minimum requirements of due process, even though the Fifth Amendment requires the grand jury for the federal system. These decisions provide states with flexibility that allows for greater efficiency.

The Bill of Rights and the incorporation of those rights through the Fourteenth Amendment set the minimum standards of justice and fairness that state courts must follow. States may do more, that is, afford greater protections for accused defendants than is required by the U.S. Constitution. Indeed, since the 1970s, with more conservative (crime control–oriented) justices in the majority on the Supreme Court, state courts have frequently held that their own state constitutions impose more stringent protection of defendants' rights than the U.S. Constitution had imposed on the state (Howard 1986, 317).

Defendants' Rights Protect the Law-Abiding

The impulse to protect the rights of defendants is really a self-protective impulse. The ransacking of a home by police is a frightening invasion of privacy. The courts' willingness to enforce the Fourth Amendment right against unreasonable searches and seizures helps to ensure that the police have good reasons for searching before they interfere in people's lives. To be falsely accused and punished for a crime is a nightmare no one wishes to experience. Consequently, defendants are afforded certain rights to reasonably minimize the chances of error or corruption in the operation of the criminal process.

When the Bill of Rights was drafted, the founders of this nation recalled how the criminal courts had been used as a weapon against dissidents and political opponents. Many citizens demanded that the new state and federal constitutions affirm certain rights of defendants in criminal trials. The type of trial contemplated by these procedures was adversarial in form. The rights of defendants were viewed as an essential protection against the mighty power of the state. Because the state possesses vast resources of investigation and prosecution, and because the state controls a police force that is capable of directly intervening in the lives of citizens and disrupting their lives and livelihood through accusation, arrest, and imprisonment, the citizen must be afforded certain rights to prevent the government from using its powers arbitrarily or oppressively.

The rights of defendants serve to equalize the power between the lone citizen suspected or accused of a crime and the enormous powers of the state. In a variety of ways the defendant is given certain advantages over the state to compensate for the citizen's relative lack of power when being accused by the government. One such compensating right is the defendant's right to be presumed innocent until proved guilty, placing the burden of proof on the government to show good reasons for accusing the defendant and ultimately proving guilt. Related to the presumption of innocence and burden of proof is the defendant's right against self-incrimination, which protects people from being forced to admit guilt. Without the right against self-incrimination the presumption of innocence would be a hollow promise. Defendants are also assured of certain rights at trial that are designed to safeguard the adversarial process itself. These rights include the right to trial by jury (ensuring the impartiality of the fact-finder), the right to confront and cross-examine witnesses, and, most important, the right to counsel. Among these rights the right to counsel is the cornerstone of the adversarial process. Having a professional advocate to present the defendant's case is fundamental to the adversarial process and the means by which all other rights of the defendant are protected. For this reason in 1932 the Supreme Court of the United States declared that the defendant's right to counsel is a "fundamental" right in our adversarial system of justice (*Powell v. Alabama*).

The Right to Counsel

The Sixth Amendment to the U.S. Constitution, as well as provisions in state constitutions, guarantees the right to counsel. The Sixth Amendment states: "In all criminal prosecutions, the accused shall enjoy the right . . . to have the assistance of counsel for his defence." Many constitutional experts view this as the most important right of defendants because it is through counsel that a defendant is assured protection of all other rights. Because the adversary system relies heavily on the parties in a case to ensure that lawful procedures are followed and to bring forward any and all evidence supporting their side of the case, having a trained representative as an advocate is essential. A trained lawyer can provide the defendant with information about all the rights that apply and how they apply in the defendant's specific circumstances. Counsel also has the legal expertise to file motions or take other actions to uphold the defendant's rights. By protecting the defendant's rights, counsel ensures that the rules of the process are enforced. Thus, counsel is essential to the proper functioning of the adversarial process itself.

Scope of the Right to Counsel

Although the right to counsel is clearly stated in the Sixth Amendment and in most state constitutions, these documents do not clearly state what the "right to counsel" means. One of the most important questions about the interpretation of the "right to counsel" concerns the right to counsel for indigents. Specifically, does the right to counsel, guaranteed by the Sixth Amendment and applied to the states through the Fourteenth Amendment, mean that defendants merely have a right to hire an attorney if they can afford to do so? Or, does it mean that defendants have a right to be represented by counsel even if they cannot afford to hire an attorney? And if poor defendants have a right to be represented by counsel even if they cannot afford it, is this a right of all criminal defendants? Or does it apply only to defendants in some kinds of cases? The current law, as expressed in Supreme Court decisions, is relatively clear on these points.

Right to Counsel for the Poor

For many years, lawyers understood the Sixth Amendment right to counsel to mean simply that defendants in criminal cases could hire an attorney to represent their interests in court. However, defendants began to challenge this interpretation early in the twentieth century. The right to counsel for indigent defendants was first recognized in death penalty cases, where ensuring a fair trial is of utmost importance because of the irreversible consequences of conviction and punishment. During the nineteenth century and early twentieth century, many states were unwilling to recognize a right to counsel for indigents except in capital cases.

In 1938 the U.S. Supreme Court held that the Sixth Amendment includes a right to counsel for indigents in federal criminal trials (*Johnson v. Zerbst*). Indigent defendants in state prosecutions who had been denied counsel at trial then turned to the U.S. Supreme Court to seek a ruling requiring all states to provide counsel to indigents in noncapital trials. Defendants appealed to the Supreme Court to incorporate the Sixth Amendment right to counsel as part of the meaning of the due process clause of the Fourteenth Amendment. For several decades the Supreme Court refused to interpret the Fourteenth Amendment as requiring states to provide counsel for poor defendants. In 1942 the Supreme Court reaffirmed a longstanding interpretation of the right to counsel in state cases, holding that the right to counsel should be determined on a case-by-case basis (*Betts v. Brady*). According to the Court, due process would demand the appointment of counsel for the indigent only in cases with special circumstances, such as a capital offense, a mentally disabled defendant, or unusually complex legal issues. But the Court recognized no such right for the ordinary defendant facing incarceration as a penalty.

Felony Cases

In 1963, however, the Court overturned its longstanding decision that allowed the states to decide when counsel must be provided. In *Gideon v. Wainwright* the Court held that the right to counsel is fundamental and essential to a fair trial:

> The right of one charged with crime to counsel may not be deemed fundamental and essential to fair trials in some countries, but it is in ours. From the very beginning, our state and national constitutions and laws have laid great emphasis on procedural and substantive safeguards designed to assure fair trials before impartial tribunals in which every defendant stands equal before the law. This noble ideal cannot be realized if the poor man charged with crime has to face his accusers without a lawyer to assist him. (p. 344)

As the Supreme Court typically does, it limited its holding to the facts of the case. Gideon had been charged with a felony. Thus it was clear after this decision that the Court's interpretation of the Sixth Amendment right to counsel for the poor applied to felony cases in state courts. It was still unclear whether misdemeanor defendants were also entitled to state-appointed counsel if they were too poor to afford to hire their own.

Nonfelony Cases

Many states simply instituted appointed-counsel and public defender systems that applied to all poor defendants, whether they were charged with a felony or a misdemeanor. Other states limited the appointment of counsel to felony cases or felonies and serious misdemeanors. Because the wording of the Sixth Amendment specifically refers to "all criminal prosecutions," defendants argued that the right to counsel for indigents announced by the Supreme Court in *Gideon* applied to "all criminal prosecutions," not just to serious crimes.

The Court first addressed this issue in *Argersinger v. Hamlin* (1972). In this case the Supreme Court held that "no person may be imprisoned for any offense, whether classified as petty, misdemeanor, or felony unless he was represented by counsel" (p. 37). The Court emphasized the actual deprivation of liberty suffered by a defendant. This interpretation was later reaffirmed in *Scott v. Illinois* (1979), in which the Court made it clear that it was not the threat of incarceration but actual incarceration that triggers the right to counsel. If a defendant is charged with a misdemeanor for which the maximum penalty is nine months in jail, that person is not entitled to counsel under the U.S. Constitution unless a sentence of incarceration is actually imposed. This gives judges the discretion to deny appointed counsel in misdemeanor cases in which the judge is willing to forego a jail sentence if the defendant is convicted. Despite these limits on the Sixth Amendment right to counsel, many states have more extensive right-to-counsel provisions that may entitle a poor defendant to appointed counsel for petty offenses even if the defendant is not incarcerated.

Representing Yourself: The Right to Proceed *Pro Se*

Although the Supreme Court has held that being represented by legally trained counsel is fundamental to a fair trial, the Sixth Amendment "does not force a lawyer upon a defendant" (*Adams v. United States* ex rel. *McCann* 1942, 279). Under most circumstances defendants retain the right to defend themselves. This is called proceeding ***pro se***, that is, for yourself.

pro se

In *Faretta v. California* (1974) the Supreme Court found within the Sixth Amendment an implied right to act as your own lawyer: "The right to defend is given directly to the accused; for it is he who suffers the consequences if the defense fails" (pp. 818–19).

Proceeding pro se constitutes a waiver of the right to assistance of counsel. A judge can accept a defendant's waiver of any constitutional right only if it is made voluntarily, knowingly, and intelligently. For the waiver of counsel to be valid a defendant must be mentally competent to understand the gravity of this decision and must be under no coercion. The important factor is not whether the defendant can defend as successfully as an attorney could but whether the defendant fully understands the risks of proceeding alone and is doing so voluntarily.

Right Against Self-Incrimination

Another right that is implied by the adversarial process is the right against self-incrimination. This right is specifically guaranteed by the Fifth Amendment, which states: "No person . . . shall be compelled in any criminal case to be a witness against himself."

This right has often been cited as the key distinction between an adversarial and an inquisitorial system of justice. As Chapter 5 describes in greater detail, the early development of the inquisitorial procedure sought confession as the key element in proving a crime. Torture and coercion were used to force the defendant to admit to the crime and confess in court.

The adversarial system proceeds from the presumption that the accuser (the government) must prove its case without compelling the defendant to provide the proof. After all, the defendant is cast in the role of the adversary of the prosecution. The defendant has no duty to cooperate with the accusers and has a clear right to refuse to testify. The key issue is how far this right extends to interrogations that occur before the defendant gets to trial.

The Fifth Amendment protects defendants during custodial police interrogations, in the course of which defendants might make admissions that later would be introduced in court. The Supreme Court has held that anyone in police custody has the right to remain silent and the right to refuse to be questioned by the police. A person also has the right to have counsel present during any interrogation, as a means of safeguarding this important right against self-incrimination. The Court has held that if the police or other officials violate these rights, the information obtained through such illegal questioning may not be used at trial. To use such statements of the defendant would be equivalent to compelling the defendant to testify (*Miranda v. Arizona* 1966). To further protect these rights the Court requires that all suspects be informed of these rights before any questioning—the famous *Miranda* warnings.

The Right to Due Process

The due process clause of the Fourteenth Amendment was patterned after a similar clause in the Fifth Amendment. The Fifth Amendment to the Constitution states that no person may be deprived of life, liberty, or property without "due process of law."

due process of law

The meaning of **due process of law** is far from clear and has been disputed in many of the most famous decisions of the Supreme Court. In general, the phrase means that the government must use fair procedures and standards whenever its actions, such as a criminal prosecution, threaten the person's life, may result in imprisonment or other significant loss of liberty, or may result in the person's having to forfeit money or property. Due process is the minimal standard of fairness to which all individuals are entitled. But what are the minimal standards of fairness? How shall courts determine what is fair and consistent with the ideal of due process?

The Supreme Court has the ultimate authority to dictate the minimal standards of fairness to which both federal and state procedures must conform. In reaching its decisions the Supreme Court considers the history of judicial practice in this country, the traditions of common law, and current practice among the states. The Court also considers which procedures are necessary to preserve the adversarial system of justice. Finally, due process is understood to be an evolving ideal. What is needed to ensure due process today may be quite different from what was required yesterday or will be tomorrow.

In *Mathews v. Eldridge* (1976) the Court outlined how courts should analyze due process requirements. Courts must consider and weigh:

1. The nature and importance of the private interest that will be affected by the government's action;
2. The risk of erroneous deprivation of such interest by using current procedures and the probable value, if any, of additional or substitute procedural safeguards;
3. The government's interest, including the function involved, and the fiscal and administrative burdens that the additional or substitute requirements would entail.

This formula is a double-edged sword. Prior to *Mathews,* courts were apt to recognize procedural rights only if the individual was in jeopardy of suffering a "grievous loss." The *Mathews* test expands the range of situations in which courts might find the need for procedural rights. Even if the potential loss to the individual is slight (for example, a small monetary loss), *Mathews* requires procedural protections if the chances of error are high or if the government's interest (such as the cost of providing protection) are minimal. On the other hand the *Mathews* test has been criticized because it appears to allow even the most significant private interests, such as life and liberty, to be subjected to a sort of cost-benefit analysis. *Mathews* appears to say that individuals, even those facing death or loss of liberty, can be denied procedural protections if offering such protections would interfere with an important government interest.

Both before and after the *Mathews* decision the Court recognized certain fundamental rights as part of the notion of due process. These include protections relating to the burden of proof and the standard of evidence.

Burden of Proof

burden of proof

The key element of the adversarial process is the notion that the government has the duty to prove the defendant guilty without compelling that person to assist in providing the evidence. This idea is referred to as the **burden of proof.** In accusing the defendant, the government takes the responsibility of proving every crime with which the defendant is charged. Defendants are not required to prove their innocence. "Due process commands that no man shall lose his liberty unless the Government has borne the burden of producing the evidence and convincing the fact-finder of guilt" (*Speiser v. Randall* 1958, 526).

Standard of Evidence

probable cause, preponderance of the evidence, clear and convincing evidence, proof beyond a reasonable doubt

Due process requires that the government show good reasons for taking actions that deprive citizens of life, liberty, or property. The greater the invasion of rights by the government, the greater the amount of evidence required to show good reason for denying those rights. The purpose is to minimize the possibility of error, especially as the stakes for the individual increase. Arresting someone, which involves a temporary loss of liberty, requires only enough evidence to show **probable cause**. In civil disputes courts decide the outcome by the standard of **preponderance of the evidence**. Under this standard whichever side presents the more credible evidence wins. A somewhat more stringent standard, **clear and convincing evidence,** is required to involuntarily commit an individual to a mental institution, for example. Finally, to convict someone of a crime the standard of evidence is more stringent still: **proof beyond a reasonable doubt**. Evidence beyond a reasonable doubt has no precise meaning. Some legal scholars suggest that it means that each juror must be 95% or 99% certain of the defendant's guilt. Another way to look at this standard is that the prosecution has met its burden of proving the defendant's guilt if no other interpretation of the evidence is reasonable.

> The requirement of proof beyond a reasonable doubt has this vital role in our criminal procedure for cogent reasons. The accused during a criminal prosecution has at stake interest of immense importance, both because of the possibility that he may lose his liberty upon conviction and because of the certainty that he would be stigmatized by the conviction. Accordingly, a society that values the good name and freedom of every individual should not condemn a man for commission of a crime when there is reasonable doubt about his guilt. (In re *Winship* 1969, 363–364)

Trial Rights and the Sixth Amendment

The Sixth Amendment states clearly and succinctly the trial rights of criminal defendants.

> In all criminal prosecutions, the accused shall enjoy the right to a speedy and public trial, by an impartial jury of the State and district wherein the crime shall have been committed; which district shall have been previously ascertained by law, and to be informed of the nature and cause of the accusation; to be confronted with witnesses against him; to have compulsory process for obtaining witnesses in his favor, and to have the assistance of counsel for his defence.

The right to counsel is widely recognized as an important means of protecting all the other rights of defendants, including the trial rights spelled out in the Sixth Amendment. These rights include a speedy and public trial, the right to be informed of the nature and cause of accusation prior to the trial, and the right of confrontation.

While the language of the Sixth Amendment names these rights, the Supreme Court interprets the full scope and meaning of each and whether they are incorporated through the Fourteenth Amendment.

Right to a Speedy and Public Trial

The right to a speedy trial protects criminal defendants from long-term incarceration without trial. Even a defendant who is free on bail is entitled to a speedy trial, however. The speedy trial requirement prevents prosecutors from bringing charges and then delaying prosecutions so that defendants are indefinitely under suspicion but never, or only belatedly, get their day in court. Although the Sixth Amendment guarantees the right to a speedy trial, no clear-cut rule states *how speedily* a criminal case must be processed to fulfill this requirement. The Supreme Court has noted that the amount of delay that would amount to a violation of this right varies with the type of charge and the circumstances of the case (*Barker v. Wingo* 1972). For example, a complex case takes longer to prepare, necessitating greater delay between charging and trial. Typically, states have statutory provisions that offer more specific guidelines, but the time limits set by these statutes are relatively easily waived. The Supreme Court has also held that speedy trial is a right of the public (*Barker v. Wingo*). In some instances the public's interest in a speedy trial may outweigh the defendant's desire to delay the trial.

The right to a public trial was originally designed to prevent government authorities from holding secret trials. Both the public and the defendant have this right. In some instances the defendant might prefer a closed trial to avoid the publicity that a public trial might bring. Despite the defendant's wishes, the public is entitled to attend the trial and observe the evidence presented (*Richmond Newspapers, Inc. v. Virginia* 1980). This right of the public preserves the public's confidence in the fairness of the court system by preventing secret proceedings. Consider, for example, the loss of legitimacy that would occur if government officials charged with wrongdoing were acquitted in a secret (non-public) trial.

Right to a Jury

The right to a jury is widely acknowledged as a cornerstone of the Anglo-American system of justice. This is the right of defendants to have their guilt or innocence determined by the people rather than by representatives of the government. Historically, the jury has served to protect unpopular figures from government harassment and to prevent the enforcement of unpopular laws.

The right to a jury trial has several facets, including the scope of the right in state trials, the composition of the jury, and the question of impartiality of jurors. These questions are examined in detail in Chapter 16.

Right to Be Informed of Nature and Cause of Accusation

Within an adversarial process a defendant cannot raise a proper defense unless she is informed of the charges being brought against her and the specific circumstances giving rise to the charges. In other words, the defendant must be told in plain English what she is accused of doing and when she is alleged to have done it.

The Right of Confrontation

Given the adversarial nature of the criminal process, it is axiomatic that the defendant has a right to face his accusers in court. It is not acceptable under this right for the government to summarize the accusations made by others. Although the right of confrontation appears straightforward and noncontroversial, here too the rights of defendants can conflict with the public's interest in substantive justice. For example, prosecutors have sought to protect child abuse victims from the trauma of facing the accused while testifying. Recently, the Supreme Court was called on to decide whether closed circuit testimony by the child violates a defendant's right to confront the witnesses against him (*Maryland v. Craig,* 1990).

The right of confrontation also means that the defendant has a right to be present at trial. Unlike other countries, where a defendant may be tried in absentia, in the United States, the defendant has a right to be present at trial, except in unusual circumstances.

The Right of Compulsory Process

compulsory process, subpoena

The right to counsel and the opportunity to raise a defense are implied by the adversarial process. However, these rights would be meaningless without the right to compulsory process. **Compulsory process** means that the defense may ask the court to subpoena witnesses. A **subpoena** is an order issued by the court requiring a person to appear in court at a specified time. Witnesses are often reluctant to testify in ways that might help a criminal defendant. Compulsory process gives the defense a tool for ensuring that all witnesses who have knowledge related to the crime are brought to court and required to testify under oath. Although the defense cannot guarantee that witnesses will tell the truth, compulsory process at least assures that witnesses must appear and respond to questions from both the prosecution and the defense.

Double Jeopardy

The protection against double jeopardy arises from the Fifth Amendment clause stating that no person shall be "twice put in jeopardy of life or limb" for the same offense. This does not mean that a defendant may never be tried twice for the same offense. In general, this Fifth Amendment protection means that once a defendant has been acquitted of an offense, that person may not be reprosecuted for the same conduct by the same sovereign (the federal government or a state). If the defendant appeals a conviction and the conviction is overturned by the appellate court, double jeopardy does not bar the government from retrying the defendant. If the trial results in a hung jury or a mistrial caused by procedural error, a new trial may be held. If the defendant is acquitted on state charges, double jeopardy does not bar a new prosecution in federal court (different sovereign) on federal charges related to the same conduct. Consequently, the real thrust of the protection against double jeopardy is to ensure that an acquittal is final within any single sovereign jurisdiction.

Additional Rights

The Eighth Amendment protects defendants from the imposition of excessive bail (see Chapter 11) and protects those convicted of crimes from being forced to suffer cruel and unusual punishment (see Chapter 17). The Fourth Amendment protects people in the United States from unreasonable searches of their property and from arrests that are not based on probable cause. Although the Fourth Amendment serves primarily as a restraint on the police in conducting investigations, the courts enforce the Fourth Amendment through the exclusionary rule (*Mapp v. Ohio* 1961). In addition, defendants may claim other rights through the due process clause that are not specifically declared in the Constitution. Defendants in state prosecutions may be entitled to rights beyond those demanded by the U.S. Constitution for state trials. These rights may be found in state constitutions, statutes, and court decisions.

Regardless of the specific rights to which a specific defendant is entitled in any particular state, all states recognize that defendants have certain rights and that these rights are intrinsic to the adversarial process of adjudicating cases.

Enforcing the Rights of Defendants

Whatever the rules are, they must be enforced if the adversarial process is to be successful in achieving both substantive and procedural justice. Counsel for the defendant can work to ensure that these rights are protected. Counsel may take several actions to protect defendants' rights and remedy violations of those rights. These include motions and appeals.

Motions

motion

A **motion** is a request to the judge to order some particular action in relation to the case. Motions frequently relate to the rights of the defendant. Motions ask the judge to enter an order upholding a particular right and ordering a remedy for any violation of the right that has already occurred. A motion may request that the trial be scheduled immediately to protect a defendant's right to a speedy trial, or it may request that trial be postponed to protect the defendant's right to prepare a defense. A motion may request an order from the judge to move the trial to another locale to protect the defendant's right to an impartial jury. A motion may request that the charges be dismissed because the indictment does not adequately inform the defendant of the nature and cause of the accusation. In cases of gross violations of the defendant's rights that seriously jeopardize the defendant's right to a fair trial, a motion may even request a mistrial to stop the trial that is in progress. In each case the motion would refer to a rule of procedure or a right of the defendant and would describe why the order requested is necessary to enforce the rule (see Figure 3-2).

The Exclusionary Rule.   Among the motions that are used to enforce the rights of defendants, one of the most controversial is the motion to suppress evidence. The purpose of the motion to suppress is to obtain an order from the judge prohibiting the prosecution from introducing evidence that was obtained in violation of the rules of procedure. The Supreme Court has identified a number of situations in which evidence ought to be suppressed by the trial court judge. Current Fourth Amendment law relating to search and seizure and the applicability of the exclusionary rule is vast and complex. Defense counsel's job requires a good working knowledge of this law in order to identify violations of the defendant's rights and to seek exclusion of evidence obtained as a result. If the defendant was the subject of an illegal search that produced evidence that the prosecutor wishes to introduce against the defendant, the defense may move to suppress the evidence (*Mapp v. Ohio* 1961). If the defendant was interrogated in custody without being advised of the right to remain silent and the right to an attorney, any statements made by the defendant during the interrogation are excluded from trial if the judge grants a motion to suppress (*Miranda v. Arizona* 1966). In addition, according to the doctrine known as "fruit of the poisonous tree," any evidence uncovered as a result of an illegal search, arrest, or interrogation must also be excluded. For example, if a defendant is arrested without probable cause and confesses to a crime while being interrogated in police custody, the illegality of the arrest makes the confession subject to suppression, even if the police followed correct procedure in carrying out the actual interrogation. The confession is the "fruit" of the "poisonous tree"—illegal arrest.

Those who oppose the exclusionary rule argue that it distorts the adversarial process by preventing the prosecution from using evidence that is relevant and reliable. The exclusionary rule, these critics contend, decreases the likelihood that the adversarial process will achieve substantive justice. Instead, guilty

---

FIGURE 3-2   Frequently Requested Motions

Change of Venue	To change the location of the trial in order to lessen the influence of pretrial publicity. See Chapter 15.
Request for Recusal	To request the removal of the judge or prosecutor because of some prior relationship to the case. See Chapter 16.
Severance or Joinder	To sever or join defendants or charges to be tried together at a single trial.
Continuance	To request a postponement of court proceedings.
Suppression of Evidence	To request that the judge order that specific pieces of evidence are inadmissible at trial.
Discovery	To request access to investigate information, evidence, forensic test results, and so on in advance of trial. See Chapter 12.
Mental Examination	To request a mental examination of the defendant for the purpose of obtaining information related to the defendant's competence or sanity. See Chapter 14.

---

defendants may go free because of technical violations of the rules of procedure, even though the violations do not threaten to undermine the substantive justice of the verdict.

The arguments in favor of suppressing illegally seized evidence rest on deterrence and procedural justice. Controlling police and prosecutorial misconduct, preventing police and prosecutors from engaging in illegal searches and illegal interrogations, is difficult. When law enforcement officials are eager to make an arrest or are convinced that a suspect is guilty, they are often tempted to bend and even break the rules. One way the courts can try to prevent illegal searches and interrogations is to remove the rewards. If police know that any evidence obtained through an improper search cannot later be used in court, they have less incentive to conduct the search illegally. If evidence cannot be used because of the way it was obtained, perhaps police and prosecutors will be motivated to use proper procedures.

In addition, proponents of the exclusionary rule argue that excluding illegally obtained evidence is the price a civilized society pays for upholding the ideal of procedural justice. The justice system itself should not be tainted by allowing illegally obtained evidence to be introduced—it makes the judge an accessory after the fact to the illegal actions of the police or other law enforcement officials.

Given the enormous controversy around the exclusionary rule, researchers have tried to determine whether the rule in fact reduces police effectiveness in fighting crime and allows the guilty to go free. The research suggests that law enforcement officers' fears are largely unfounded. Research shows that suppression of confessions obtained in violation of *Miranda* requirements do not pose a serious impediment to police investigation or successful prosecution (Guy and Huckabee 1988).

Continuing dissatisfaction with the exclusionary rule has resulted in much litigation. In particular, prosecutors have sought various exceptions to the rule in order to get evidence admitted that would otherwise be excluded. The Supreme Court has identified exceptions to the exclusionary rule when police officers acted in "good faith." For example, the exclusionary rule was held not to apply to a situation in which the police conducted a search in compliance with a search warrant, but the warrant was later ruled invalid (*Massachusetts v. Sheppard* 1984; *United States v. Leon* 1984).

Appeals

Another means of protecting defendants' rights is through an appeal. If the defense makes a timely objection to some action that is arguably in violation of the rules of procedure, and the judge rules against the defense, the defense may later bring an appeal claiming that the judge erred. If the appellate judges find that the rules of procedure were violated and that the trial court's error either contributed to the guilty verdict or was a violation of one of the defendant's fundamental rights, the appellate court may reverse the conviction, erasing it as a matter of law. The prosecution is then free to reissue criminal charges against the defendant and start the process again from the beginning.

■ BENEFITS OF THE ADVERSARIAL MODEL

Proponents of the adversarial system claim several benefits of conducting court business through an adversarial process. First, the adversarial model provides a clear division of labor—the attorneys, the judge, and the jury have a clear understanding of their respective roles in the proceedings. The attorney's role is to present evidence in a way that is most likely to result in winning the case. The judge's role is to oversee the legality of procedures and the fairness of the trial process. The fact-finder's role, whether judge or jury, is to keep an open mind until all evidence has been presented (Fuller 1961; Landsman 1984, 45).

Another benefit attributed to the adversarial process is that it results in a more far-reaching search for evidence and airing of the facts than would occur under an alternative arrangement. Because the adversaries are trying to win their case, they want to dig out the facts that will be most beneficial to their case. At least two versions of the truth are presented at each trial. The prosecution, for example, may wish to gloss over inconsistencies in its version of the facts or details that do not fit into its construction of the crime. Because such inconsistencies undermine the prosecution's case, the defense will highlight them or present other evidence that undermines the prosecution's version (Fuller 1961, 39).

A third benefit identified with the adversarial system is that it promotes the legitimacy of the system. "Adversary theory holds that if a party is intimately involved in the adjudicatory process and feels that he has been given a fair opportunity to present his case, he is likely to accept the results whether favorable or not" (Landsman 1984, 44). The judge's detachment and neutrality are also seen as contributing to the appearance of fairness in the adversarial process. "It is not his place to take sides. He must withhold judgment until all the evidence has been examined and all the arguments have been heard" (Fuller 1961, 31). As Professor Lon L. Fuller points out, "In the absence of an adversary presentation, there is a strong tendency . . . to reach a conclusion at an early stage and to adhere to that conclusion" (1961, 39) even in the face of conflicting evidence that may later come to light.

■ CRITICISMS OF THE ADVERSARIAL SYSTEM

The adversarial system also imposes some costs on a system of justice. Two principal criticisms of the system are that it is cumbersome and time consuming and that it puts too little emphasis on discovering the truth, or substantive justice.

Using Time in the Adversarial Process

Compared to other systems of adjudication, the adversarial process does have the potential to be extraordinarily slow. In addition, the adversaries are able to use the rules of procedure to purposely delay the process.

Some critics have noted that adversarial trials are more time consuming than inquisitorial trials (Landsman 1984). Because the jury is composed of laypeople who will deliberate without the guiding hand of a trained judge to assist them, all trial participants take pains to make sure that each juror follows the evidence being presented and the logic of the arguments. Lawyers and judges are familiar with legal concepts such as intent and causation, and have experience in drawing inferences from facts that may be less than clear. Jurors are unfamiliar with these concepts and must be educated with each step. This takes time.

In addition, because the evidence is being presented by the parties to the case, rather than by the fact-finders, the parties can never be sure when they have presented enough evidence to persuade the fact-finders. As a result they are likely to engage in evidentiary overkill. Neither side wants to be caught in an oversight. Every conceivable hole must be plugged to make sure that the opponent cannot point it out as a weakness in the case. Any weakness will make the entire case look less convincing to the fact-finder. So each side takes time to painstakingly avoid looking foolish during the trial.

The rules of procedure also slow down the process. First, both parties must be given an opportunity to prepare their cases and to present their evidence in court. Because the adversarial process depends upon oral presentation of evidence, all evidence must be presented through a question and answer format. The parties cannot simply summarize their versions of the facts. Each fact must be elicited through questioning at trial.

Finally, the rules of procedure offer the adversaries opportunities to object to the procedures and actions of the opponent. These objections take additional time as the parties debate the law and the judge makes legal rulings.

Moreover, some objections are made only for the purpose of slowing the process. Although it is more typical for defense counsel to use delaying tactics, prosecutors may also have reason to delay. Defense counsel frequently seek to delay the case to avoid the inevitable and to weaken the prosecution's case. A defendant who is free on bail but anticipates a prison sentence if convicted has every reason to postpone the trial. The defense may also hope that if the case can be delayed long enough, the prosecution's case will deteriorate. Witnesses move away. Memories fade. Similarly, a prosecutor may wish to stall for time to locate a witness or to encourage a defendant to plead guilty.

The rules of procedure can be a refuge to the attorney who wishes to orchestrate delay. Because the process depends on the parties to bring evidence forward, attorneys can request postponements on the ground that they need extra time to prepare the case. And they can file motions that will require extra time to hear and decide.

Discovering the Truth Takes a Backseat

In the adversarial process learning the truth is viewed as a hoped-for by-product of adversarial procedures. Neither party is necessarily seeking truth. Although the modern prosecutor has an ethical and legal obligation to reveal exculpatory evidence, the prosecutor may not know the real truth concerning the defendant's guilt. The prosecutor only knows what she believes to be the truth. Even defense counsel may not know the true facts of what happened. Moreover, if the defendant is guilty, the defense may not want the truth to be found. Nonetheless, the two parties control whatever evidence is going to be presented in court. Neither side is expected to present all relevant facts. The prosecutor need not volunteer, for example, that a prosecution witness has a bad reputation. The prosecutor may even try to prevent the defense from bringing in evidence that casts doubt on the witness's credibility.

This situation is exacerbated by the single-minded pursuit of victory. The attorneys are partisans whose self-esteem and reputations are wrapped up in their ability to win cases. They have undergone a socialization process that encourages them to use all legally available means to win. The rules of evidence may be maneuvered to keep relevant and reliable evidence from trial if it undermines the attorney's case. Although there are legal and ethical limits, especially on prosecutors, in relation to the extent to which lawyers may keep reliable evidence from coming to light, these limits are relatively narrow and not easily enforced.

Finally, the rules of evidence limit the relevant information that can be admitted at trial. "No matter how useful or important certain items may be, if they fall afoul of the evidence rules, they cannot be considered" (Landsman 1984, 39). For example, a confession given in violation of the *Miranda* requirements may be reliable evidence of guilt but will nonetheless be excluded.

Americans tend to assume that our system has the most restrictive rules of evidence in the world. Chapter 5 explores variations in the rules of evidence from one country to the next. Although the rules of evidence in U.S. courts are more stringent in some ways than those found in some countries (for example, France), they are more permissive than others (Saudi Arabia, for example).

◼ LIMITS OF THE ADVERSARIAL MODEL

Discussion of the pros and cons of the adversarial model often misses an important point: adversarial procedures are often abandoned or subverted in day-to-day practice in the courts. Pressures toward efficiency and certainty undermine both parties' desire to rely on adversarial procedures. As a result negotiation and exchange frequently short-circuit the formal adversarial procedures.

Administrative Pressures and Efficiency

assembly-line justice

Critics observe that our criminal courts resemble an assembly line much more than a sporting competition. Unlike adversarial justice **assembly-line justice** relies on cooperation between the parties, which undermines the goal of procedural justice in favor of efficiency. Chapter 2 notes that some courts are especially susceptible to pressures toward assembly-line justice. Courts that handle many minor crimes with relatively simple fact situations are particularly prone to adopt an assembly-line approach to cases. This situation is commonly observed in the lower criminal courts. Caseload pressures and local legal culture have also been cited as causes of assembly-line justice.

According to critics, assembly-line justice results when judges, prosecutors, and defense counsel are too overworked, too pressured by overburdened caseloads, or too cynical to use the adversarial procedures available to them. When defense attorneys begin to assume, along with prosecutors and judges, that all defendants are guilty of something, the protections of the adversarial process may appear to

THE DEFENDANT'S PERSPECTIVE

He seemed like he didn't care one way or the other. He just cop out, you know. Like, you see a police walking on the street writing a ticket out, you know. He puts a ticket on the car. He don't care whose car it is. [The public defender] say, just, you know, You cop out to this, and you say no, and he says, I see if I can get a better deal. Then he brings another offer: You cop out to this. Just like that, you know. Just checking on the cop-outs.

He just playing a middle game. You know, you're the public defender; now, you don't care what happens to me, really. You don't know me, and I don't know you; this is your job, that's all; so you're gonna go up there and say a little bit, make it look like you're tryin to help me, but actually you don't give a damn.

SOURCE: Excerpted from Jonathan D. Casper, © 1972. *American Criminal Justice: The Defendant's Perspective.* Englewood Cliffs, N.J.: Prentice-Hall, pp. 107–108. Reprinted by permission of Prentice Hall/A Division of Simon & Schuster.

lose their value. Getting to sentencing as quickly as possible becomes the goal of all members of the courtroom work group. Critics view the court system, and defense counsel in particular, as selling out defendants' interests for the sake of administrative efficiency. The pressures of the assembly line simply limit the extent to which defense counsel feels free to exercise the rights of defendants. Novice defense counsel quickly learn that the system discourages the filing of motions to protect the defendant's rights (Heumann 1978). As a result defendants may become passive victims of a criminal justice machine that works to convict as many defendants as possible in as short a time as possible.

Other observers take a less critical view of the symptoms of assembly-line justice. Defendants too have reasons to prefer the quick justice of the assembly line over the ideal of adversarial justice. Defendants charged with minor crimes are especially likely to seek quick resolution so they can get on with their lives. In addition, defendants and prosecutors may wish to avoid the risks inherent in the adversarial process.

Achieving Certainty Through Negotiation

Experienced lawyers can look at the available evidence and fairly well predict which cases are winners and which are losers and adjust their strategy accordingly. Even so, uncertainty remains. Opposing counsel may be especially skilled or present information that alters the way the fact-finder views the evidence. So long as the decision is left in the hands of a neutral fact-finder, the outcome remains uncertain. In most cases uncertainty revolves around such matters as whether the defendant will be convicted of the highest degree charged or for a lesser offense and whether the judge will impose a short or a long sentence. Any trial attorney can tell stories of cases that were supposed to be "dead bang" cases, a cinch to win that were lost; similarly, attorneys know that sometimes the "total loser" cases unexpectedly become winners.

This uncertainty is stressful, and both adversaries seek ways to reduce uncertainty through negotiation. The most obvious form of negotiation in the criminal process is plea negotiation, or plea bargaining. Rather than risk a conviction for a serious crime, defendants frequently prefer the certainty of pleading guilty to a less serious charge. Rather than risk the acquittal of a

THE RISKS OF TRIAL

Beginning in the mid-1980s the federal government launched a four-year investigation of the Chicago futures markets that led to the August 1989 indictments of forty-five traders and trader's clerks. The difficulties of taking complex financial cases to trial are clearly illustrated in the results of the trials:

The trials had looked like easy winners as the government meticulously laid out its cases. But after the opening arguments, the trials had quickly bogged down with trade-by-trade explorations of each charge. . . . The yen trial often seemed to bog down, with the prosecutors themselves appearing to be confused by some of the nuances of trading. After the singularly lackluster closing arguments, the yen verdict would not be much of a shock [not a single guilty verdict out of 240 counts]. . . .

Despite the yen result, the feds remained convinced that a jury could understand the charges and would even accept weeks of mind-numbing testimony about the trades from the FBI agent and traders cooperating with the government. . . .

Defense lawyers, however, saw [the] promise to press forward as little more than opening bluster in what were expected to become long and tedious settlement negotiations. They speculated that the government would settle most charges against the yen traders and [try] only those counts it considered certain winners against some of the most notable defendants, focusing particular attention on the racketeering charges against four yen brokers.

SOURCE: Excerpted from David Greising and Laurie Morse, © 1991. *Brokers, Bagmen, and Moles: Fraud and Corruption in the Chicago Futures Markets.* New York: John Wiley and Sons, pp. 284, 287. Reprinted by permission of John Wiley and Sons, Inc.

dangerous offender, the prosecutor may prefer the certainty of a conviction on a reduced charge.

Consequences of Negotiated Justice

Because of the pressures of efficiency and uncertainty, negotiation is likely to remain an adjunct to the adversarial process. At times the pressures of assembly-line justice may become so overwhelming that any vestige of adversarial procedures disappears. The rules of procedure are ignored, judges take an active role in searching for a quick resolution, and the interests of the defendant, the victim, and the public are compromised for the interests of the courtroom work group.

More often, however, negotiation occurs within the context of the adversarial process, without totally corrupting that process. The terms of negotiation are set by the rules of the adversarial process. The merits of the "deal" are judged in light of the strength of the evidence and the likelihood of conviction at trial. The defense counsel, while negotiating with the prosecutor, can maintain the role of advocate, seeking the best outcome possible for the defendant. Thus formal processes both encourage and shape the nature and extent of informal processes.

■ WEIGHING THE ALTERNATIVES

Because the adversarial process—both in theory and in practice—offers benefits and costs, the real question is how these costs and benefits compare to alternative systems of adjudication. Rather than have evidence presented by opposing parties, why not have a system in which unbiased investigators look into an accusation, search for the truth, and reach a conclusion?

Other systems might be more efficient, better at convicting the guilty, quicker in reaching a final disposition. In Chapter 5, we examine some alternative systems for resolving cases that put less emphasis on the rights of defendants. In comparing these alternatives to the adversarial system, keep two issues in mind. First, how do these systems compare in their ability to attain substantive justice? And second, how do these systems compare in their ability to attain procedural justice and the legitimacy of the system of justice as a whole?

It may well be, as some have argued, that the adversarial system is a marvelous invention in theory but that our system is simply not adversarial in practice. Consequently, we must attend to both the way things are meant to be (law in theory) and the way things are (law in action) in evaluating the merits of the adversarial system. The adversarial system may be a quaint relic that worked in a simpler age. Perhaps the pervasiveness of negotiated and assembly-line justice is an indication that the adversarial process can no longer cope with the demands of modern society. A historical look at the criminal courts may help answer this question (see Chapter 4).

Maybe an alternative system would better fit the environment of modern criminal courts. A number of critics have suggested that the adversarial system could benefit by adopting some elements of the inquisitorial system or alternative dispute resolution. Conversely, perhaps the adversarial process remains our best hope for achieving a fair system of justice for all. As we shall see, even modern inquisitorial procedures have injected a fair amount of adversariness in the trial process to counteract the potential for erroneously jumping to conclusions. Do we really want to abandon centuries of tradition and experience, or will tinkering with reforms solve some persistent problems facing the criminal courts?

■ SUMMARY

The U.S. legal system is an adversarial system of justice. Its central principles hold that (1) achieving procedural justice is the best way to ensure substantive justice in the greatest number of cases; (2) the disputing parties control the presentation of evidence; (3) a neutral fact-finder (judge or jury), who takes no part in the investigation and preparation of the case, is responsible for the verdict; and (4) a detailed set of procedural rules, refereed by a judge, controls the adversaries. For the adversarial process to achieve substantive justice the parties must compete on a level playing field. Defendants are granted a variety of rights and procedural protections to equalize the power of the state and the defendant in the adversarial competition.

In the United States the core of defendants' rights is found in the Bill of Rights as incorporated through the due process clause of the Fourteenth Amendment, thereby applying those requirements to the states. States may grant rights and procedures beyond the minimum set by the U.S. Constitution. The right to counsel has been recognized as a fundamental right that enables defendants to know and effectively exercise their other rights.

The extent to which all parties can meaningfully exercise their rights may be undermined by pressure for efficiency. Assembly-line justice is an analogy for the reality in many criminal courts, which abandon adversarial procedures and defendants' rights in favor of quick guilty pleas. Even where the adversarial system has not been thoroughly corrupted by the pressures of the assembly line, negotiation and cooperation often characterize the resolution of cases. Although negotiation and guilty pleas are often the norm, the adversarial procedures of trial remain an option and shape the negotiations between the parties. Attorneys can maintain an adversarial posture while seeking a negotiated solution.

The adversarial model imposes specific roles on the attorneys, judge, and jury. Because of the parties' interest in winning, the adversarial model is thought to result in more thorough airing of the facts than other systems of adjudication. In addition, the adversarial process promotes the legitimacy of the court process by allowing the defendant to present the evidence to best advantage.

Despite these advantages the adversarial process has been criticized as too slow and too focused on procedural rather than substantive justice. Negotiated justice may be one way in which the adversarial process has accommodated the pressure to process cases more quickly. Alternatively, some reformers argue that certain elements of inquisitorial procedures or alternative dispute resolution mechanisms might improve both the efficiency and quality of justice.

FOR FURTHER DISCUSSION

1. Create an example of a situation in which substantive justice is done but procedural justice is not attained. Create an example of a situation in which procedural justice is maintained but substantive justice is not achieved. Which situation most offends your sense of justice?

2. Why is the Fourteenth Amendment so important in understanding the rights of defendants in the criminal process? What is the relationship between the Fourteenth Amendment and the Bill of Rights? How are the Fourteenth Amendment and "incorporation" of the Bill of Rights related to the dual court system described in Chapter 2?

3. Why is the right to counsel considered so important in the United States?

4. What is due process?

5. What is the difference between burden of proof and standard of evidence?

6. Is negotiated justice in conflict with the goals of adversarial justice?

REFERENCES

Adams v. United States ex rel. *McCann*, 317 U.S. 269, 63 S. Ct. 236 (1942), mandate stayed 63 S. Ct. 442 (1943).
Argersinger v. Hamlin, 407 U.S. 25, 92 S. Ct. 2006 (1972).
Barker v. Wingo, 407 U.S. 514, 92 S. Ct. 2182 (1972).
Betts v. Brady, 316 U.S. 455, 62 S. Ct. 1252 (1942).
Faretta v. California, 422 U.S. 806, 95 S. Ct. 2525 (1975).
Fuller, Lon L. 1961. "The Adversary System." In Harold Berman, ed., *Talks on American Law*. New York: Random House.
Gideon v. Wainwright, 372 U.S. 335, 83 S. Ct. 792 (1963).
Guy, Karen L., and Robert G. Huckabee. 1988. "Going Free on a Technicality: Another Look at the Effect of the Miranda Decisions on the Criminal Justice Process." *Criminal Justice Research Bulletin* 4(1):1–3. Huntsville, Tex.: Criminal Justice Center, Sam Houston State University.
Heumann, Milton. 1978. *Plea Bargaining*. Chicago: University of Chicago Press.
Howard, A. E. Dick. 1986. "State Courts and Constitutional Rights in the Day of the Burger Court." In Walter F. Murphy and C. Herman Pritchet, eds., *Courts, Judges, and Politics*, 4th ed. New York: Random House.
In re *Winship*, 397 U.S. 358, 90 S. Ct. 1068 (1970).
Johnson v. Zerbst, 304 U.S. 458, 58 S. Ct. 1019 (1938).

Landsman, Stephan. 1983. *The Adversary System: A Description and Defense.* Washington, D.C.: American Enterprise Institute.

Mapp v. Ohio, 367 U.S. 643, 81 S. Ct. 1684 (1961).

Massachusetts v. Sheppard, 468 U.S. 981 (1984).

Mathews v. Eldridge, 424 U.S. 319, 96 S. Ct. 893 (1976).

Miranda v. Arizona, 384 U.S. 436, 86 S. Ct. 1602 (1966).

Powell v. Alabama, 287 U.S. 45, 53 S. Ct. 55 (1932).

Richmond Newspapers, Inc. v. Virginia, 448 U.S. 555, 100 S. Ct. 2814 (1980).

Scott v. Illinois, 440 U.S. 367, 99 S. Ct. 1158 (1979).

Speiser v. Randall, 357 U.S. 513, 78 S. Ct 1332 (1958).

United States v. Leon, 486 U.S. 897, 104 S. Ct. 3405 (1984).

CHAPTER **4**

# HISTORY OF COURTS AND CRIMINAL PROCESS

Chapter 1 describes a variety of dispute resolution mechanisms and briefly shows how the criminal courts evolved as a special forum for resolving certain kinds of disputes. Understanding why criminal courts exist and why they take the shape they do requires an appreciation of the evolution of the courts as a means of resolving disputes. This chapter offers an overview of the development of the criminal court process, focusing particularly on the evolution of such important components as bail, preliminary hearings and grand jury proceedings, the jury trial, and the rights of the accused.

Frequently, the origins of criminal procedures bear little relation to the functions those procedures serve today. The grand jury was originally conceived as a means of increasing the number of criminals being processed through the courts; only later did the grand jury become a mechanism for protecting people from unwarranted prosecution. Trial by jury was once so mistrusted that defendants had to be tortured until they agreed to have a jury determine their guilt or innocence. Commonly accepted rights of today, such as the right to counsel and the right to call defense witnesses, are of relatively recent origin.

The history of criminal courts describes the evolution of modern criminal court structure and procedures. This evolution was not inevitable, nor is it complete. Prior generations should not be viewed as quaint figures groping ever closer to some ideal of justice that is our ideal of justice. Modern court procedures and practices are merely the latest stage in a continuing evolution. Our ideals of justice are products of this evolution, themselves subject to evolution and change. Just as criminal courts have been transformed many times over the last thousand years, we can be assured that the courts will continue to adapt to changing ideas and social conditions.

The court systems of the federal government and most states are direct descendants of British institutions and practices. Because Louisiana was colonized by France, Louisiana's courts show significant influence from the French.

This chapter focuses on the major developments in English court structure and procedure, because of the importance of English legal institutions to the development of law and courts in the United States.

Little is known about legal institutions before written records were maintained. The earliest records describe a system of private justice that probably dominated tribal society for many centuries before it was recorded.

▨ JUSTICE WITHOUT COURTS

Although the Romans had invaded and occupied England from about 1 to 450 A.D., Roman law never gained a strong foothold. During the waning years of Roman administration in England from 200 to 450 A.D., Roman legal traditions disintegrated and appear to have left little trace on the customs of the indigenous residents (Lyon 1980; Baker 1990, 2). About this same time Germanic tribes that inhabited the western coastal areas of northern Europe began to migrate across the channel to England; these were the Anglo-Saxons.

Justice in the new settlements followed the primitive legal customs of Germanic tribes in Europe. During this period extended family members, referred to as the kindred, protected individuals from the predation of others. Justice followed the tradition of the feud, also called blood vengeance (Harding 1966, 14). Feuding was a form of private justice, based on the concept of reciprocity. If a member of the kindred was killed or severely injured, this wrong could be compensated by killing the wrongdoer or a member of the wrongdoer's kindred. Alternatively, the kindred could demand that the wrong be compensated by paying *wergeld* (literally, man-price) to the victim's kindred. The amount of wergeld was determined by the rank of the person injured or killed (Lyon 1980).

Although feuding and payment of wergeld continued for five centuries, blood vengeance declined in response to pressure from Anglo-Saxon kings who discouraged the practice. The Christian church had long deplored the shedding of blood to avenge wrongs, claiming that vengeance was God's right alone. The feud also created the potential for disorder. Feuds between great noble families could lead to periods of warfare within the kingdom. Over time Anglo-Saxon kings developed incentives to persuade the kindred to forego vengeance and settle for the payment of the wergeld (Simpson 1981, 14). These payments were supervised by bringing the dispute to court, whether the court of the king or the ruling noble of the area. The court frequently ordered the losing party to pay compensation (called *bot*) to the victim or victim's family, as well as a fee (known as *wite*) to the king or noble that might be payment for the service of resolving the dispute or compensation for breaking the king's peace (Simpson 1981, 7).

In time the payment of wite evolved into court fees and fines as punishment. Successive kings found that these payments offered a source of revenue that few subjects opposed, and changes in the law were brought about to increase the king's revenues from these sources. As a result the government (in the person of the king or other ruling noble) became a party to the proceeding (Sanborn 1986, 115). Although feuding was legally recognized up to the Norman Conquest of 1066 A.D., kings continuously struggled to bring the feud under their control. For example, they required that certain procedures had to be followed for the feud to retain legitimacy. If these procedures were not followed, the feud itself could be found illegal and the kindred subjected to severe fines, which also went into the king's coffers (Lyon 1980, 84).

■ MEDIEVAL COURTS AS FORUMS FOR DISPUTE RESOLUTION

The Norman Conquest of 1066 brought feudalism to England. Feudalism was a system of social organization based on reciprocity and military power. The word *feudal* derives from the Latin word *feodum,* referring to the fee of land paid as a retainer to a knight on the promise to serve his lord in time of war. An elaborate hierarchy based on landholding and blood arose along with the division of property according to the promise of service to the lord.

In the feudal society of medieval England *court* referred to much more than a judicial forum. When the king called court, or when a lord called his manorial court, a combination of activities transpired. First, to hold court was to put on a celebration, usually to commemorate a religious festival or some important occasion, such as a royal birth, wedding, or coronation. When the king held court, all the lords would gather at the appointed place. Consequently, court was also an opportunity for the lords to meet and discuss issues of common concern. For the king, holding court was a means of conferring with the great lords concerning matters of war and government. They would discuss and enact new laws. Finally, court also offered an opportunity to resolve disputes that had arisen since the last court was held. These disputes might involve landownership, debts, or accusations of theft or violence. There was no distinction at that time between civil and criminal accusations.

Pretrial Procedures: Ensuring Appearance at Trial

The law encouraged people to bring disputes to court, but there were no police to make an arrest, and courts were held only twice or four times a year. Instead the victim was required to raise the "hue and cry," calling neighbors of the surrounding village and countryside to search for the person believed to be the culprit (Harding 1966, 172). The victim could then take a felony complaint (called an appeal) to court (Baker 1990, 574). Notorious offenders or people accused of serious offenses would be locked up, usually in the dungeon of the noble's castle. In less serious cases laws required that another person guarantee the appearance of both the accuser and the accused. Initially, the guarantor was a member of the accuser's kindred, but later revisions and restatements of these laws required that the lord of the manor be responsible for the appearance of each of his subjects in court. This system, called the *bohr*, was an efficient means for assuring appearance at court. But the nobility opposed the system because it required nobles to be responsible for the fines incurred by their tenants (Lyon 1980, 80). Consequently, the nobles began to force their subjects to secure their appearance and the payment of fines from among their own kin. This system came to be called the tithing. Each freeman (citizen) was placed in a group of ten men. If any one of the ten was accused of a crime or other offense, the other nine had to produce him in court or pay the fine themselves (Harding 1966, 22). If the suspect ran off, the tithing group might first try to track him down. Failing that, the tithing group would be liable for the crime with which he was charged and would have to pay the wergeld plus an additional fine for their failure to produce the suspect. In this way the social group (the tithing) was collectively responsible for the conduct of each member. The function of the tithing was the rough equivalent of the modern functions of police and bail. They were responsible for the preliminary procedures leading up to the actual appearance of the accused in court.

By the eleventh century, England had developed procedures for bringing wrongdoers to justice; these changed little during the next five centuries. The victim of a crime was required to raise the hue and cry immediately, calling his kindred and the surrounding community to help find the culprit. Everyone in the community was required to assist. If the victim could name a suspect, special responsibility fell upon the tithing of the accused to produce that person.

Trial Procedure from 1066 to 1215 A.D.

Court procedure during the Middle Ages was a combination of informal collection of evidence and highly formalized rituals for determining the verdict. The two means for arriving at a verdict were compurgation and ordeal. The first step in either proceeding was for the accuser, or plaintiff, to swear an oath that the accusation was made in good faith (Lyon 1980, 100). Next the plaintiff had to pledge property or the property of his bohr or tithing that he would prosecute the case. Then the plaintiff would have the opportunity to present evidence of the defendant's guilt. When evidence of guilt was strong (for example, the criminal was caught in the act or the defendant was a known outlaw), the case might be resolved immediately without further judicial proceedings. When the evidence was less clear, compurgation was the more common means of finding guilt. Ordeal was reserved for the difficult cases in which compurgation was unsatisfactory for one reason or another.

Trial by Compurgation: Origins of the Adversarial Process

Compurgation was a complex and highly legalistic form of adjudication based upon the practice of oath taking. Oath taking resembled a contest in which both sides competed to produce a sufficient number of oaths to prove their case. The competitive aspect of compurgation probably influenced the evolution of adversarial procedure.

When the evidence of guilt was unclear or questionable, the plaintiff in a suit at court was required to support the allegation with oaths claiming the suspect was guilty. The oath of the plaintiff alone was often not enough, however. Typically, the plaintiff needed to have "oath helpers" who would swear to the guilt of the defendant. Two factors determined the number of oaths required in any particular case: the seriousness of the crime charged and the rank of the plaintiff as determined by the plaintiff's wergeld. For example, if the crime was theft, and theft required oaths equivalent to 1,200 shillings, a nobleman whose wergeld was 1,200 shillings could swear the oath and thereby fulfill the oath obligation with no need for oath helpers. If an ordinary freeman—whose wergeld was worth only 200 shillings—was accusing someone of the same crime of theft, however, the plaintiff would have to take the oath and find five other freemen to act as oath helpers to make up the remaining 1,000 shillings worth of wergeld. No money was paid. The wergeld of a man was taken as a measure of his worth and therefore of the worth of his oath (Lyon 1980).

The higher the accuser's rank, the easier it was to gain the conviction of the accused. Where an ordinary freeman would need to find several kinsmen or friends to risk potential fines for false accusation if the defendant should mount a successful defense, a nobleman could bring accusations and prove them through his own oath. Conversely, a nobleman could also more easily defend himself against accusations brought by a person of inferior rank. Women, slaves, and others who possessed no wergeld needed to rely on the oaths of others to uphold or defend against an accusation. The notion that all people are equal before the law was unknown in this period.

Once the plaintiff and any oath helpers made the necessary oaths, the burden shifted to the defendant to counter those oaths with oaths attesting to his innocence. According to Anglo-Saxon law, the strength of the defendant's oaths was greater than those of the accuser, so that an equal amount of oaths, in terms of the wergeld, was sufficient to show innocence. Thus in the example of the theft worth 1200 shillings, oaths from the accused and oath helpers whose combined wergeld was 1200 shillings would be sufficient to clear the accused of the crime (Lyon 1980, 100). Today we might say that the burden of proof was on the accuser.

The success of a prosecution or defense also depended on the ability to complete the oaths without mistake. Mistakes included removing a hand from the Bible while taking the oath, using the wrong hand, neglecting to kiss the book afterward, and not saying the precise words of the oath. Such mistakes were understood to be the product of divine intervention, revealing the truth of the matter to all who observed the court process (Beckerman 1992, 203–204).

The oath helpers were not witnesses in the modern sense of the word; they did not offer factual evidence in defense of the defendant. Instead they were merely swearing that if the defendant swore he was innocent, he was telling the truth. Essentially, the compurgators were swearing to the court that they were confident that the defendant would not swear falsely. False swearing was considered a terrible sin that would endanger a person's immortal soul. Compurgators did not take the threat of eternal damnation lightly (Beckerman 1992, 203; Hyams 1981, 92–93). Known thieves or scoundrels in the community would be unlikely to find oath helpers to risk immortal punishment and earthly fines for making false oaths. Consequently, some accused persons were unable to find oath helpers. Such a defendant might choose not to contest the charges (plead guilty), or the defendant could try to prove his innocence through trial by ordeal.

The persistence of compurgation as a method of adjudication is a matter of some historical dispute. The Assize of Clarendon in 1166 included a provision that has been interpreted as an "implied prohibition" of compurgation. There is substantial evidence, however, that the practice persisted in local and ecclesiastical courts and that some criminal cases, including murder, were decided by compurgation as late as 1440 (Beckerman 1992; Thayer 1891, 59).

Trial by Ordeal

Ordeal was used in cases in which a defendant was unable to secure the necessary number of oath takers and in certain cases in which compurgation was not allowed as a means of proof (Hyams 1981, 93). For example, "suspicious characters with a record of numerous accusations and with conviction of perjury were not considered oath-worthy," even if friends and relatives were willing to swear to the defendant's innocence (Lyon 1980, 101). In other cases the evidence of guilt was so strong that the defendant would first be required to provide the required number of oaths and undergo the ordeal to be acquitted. Thus when evidence of guilt was uncertain, and the defendant was able to secure the necessary oath takers, the burden of proof rested with the accuser. But when belief in the suspect's guilt was strong, the burden of proof weighed heavily on the accused.

Like compurgation, ordeal was based on the belief that God would intervene to prove the guilt or innocence of an accused person. The ordeal was highly formalized, with exacting procedures to be carried out by a priest. The defendant was required to confess to a priest before participating in the religious ceremony of the mass. If the defendant was guilty, hiding the crime during confession and then accepting the sacrament at mass would be a mortal sin. Consequently, a guilty offender was under enormous pressure to confess (Hyams 1981, 98). After the mass the priest would say prayers, bless the instruments of the ordeal, and the ordeal would begin.

The court could choose from three different kinds of ordeals: trial by cold water, trial by hot water, and trial by hot iron, sometimes referred to as trial by fire (Johnson 1988, 48; Lyon 1980, 102). In trial by cold water the defendant was given a drink of water that had been blessed. Then the defendant would be thrown into a stream or pond or other body of water that had also been blessed. The priest prayed that the water would reject a guilty man. If the accused sank to the bottom, the water was judged to have accepted him, and he would be cleared of all guilt. If the accused floated in the water, the water was judged to have rejected or thrown out the guilty. The accused was then liable to whatever punishment was prescribed by law.

A second form of the ordeal was trial by hot water. In this case a stone was placed at the bottom of a cauldron of boiling water and blessed by the priest. The accused was required to reach into the water and pull out the stone. If the accused could not pull out the stone, she was immediately declared guilty. If she was successful in pulling the stone from the boiling water, her wounded hand was bound in bandages. Three days later the judge would examine the wounds. If the scalded flesh was healing normally, and there was no sign of infection, the accused was declared innocent. If the wounds were festering and showing signs of pus and infection, the defendant was found guilty and the judge would declare sentence.

In the ordeal of the hot iron the accused was required to carry a glowing hot rod of iron for a distance of nine feet. For serious crimes the ordeal was made more rigorous by increasing the weight of the rod. Again the defendant's burned hand would be bound, and the person would be judged innocent if the wound was healing properly after three days and declared guilty if it showed signs of infection. In the case of capital offenses such as murder, the defendant might be required to undergo the threefold ordeal, subjected to trial by cold water, then trial by hot water, and finally trial by fire.

Court records indicate that the ordeal convicted the accused in about half the cases and acquitted the other half (Bartlett 1988, 161). Although some twelfth-century commentators were skeptical about the results of ordeals and described instances in which ordeals were falsified, the ordeal offered a means of resolving disputes in a way that was recognized as legitimate by the people subject to it (Hyams 1981, 98). For this reason it served justice well in arriving at an undisputed resolution of cases.

The role of the judge in both compurgation and ordeal was relatively limited but could be pivotal to the outcome of the case. The principal role of the judge was to declare the law. This required making sure that proper procedures were followed and the proper form of trial was used for the particular circumstances. In trial by ordeal the judge was responsible for declaring whether the defendant passed the ordeal. Finally, the judge declared the sentence but had no discretion in deciding what the sentence should be. The judge imposed whatever sentence the law demanded.

Trial by Battle

Trial by battle, sometimes called judicial combat, offered yet another means of resolving disputes. Trial by battle was not universally available as an option, and its use seems to have varied according to the status of the parties and the nature of the accusation. Trial by battle appears to have been imported from France by the Normans and was viewed as a means of resolving disputes between knights, although peasants were from time to time subjected to trial by battle (Baker 1990; Beckerman 1992).

Trial by battle could occur between the litigants, but both parties had the option of selecting a champion to fight for them. Because trial by battle was not surrounded by the religious mysticism of the ordeal, the roles of priests and religious ritual were less important than in trial by ordeal. For this reason, when the Roman church condemned trial by ordeal in 1215, it allowed trial by battle to continue. Judges erected so many restrictions around the use of trial by battle, however, that by 1250 this form of trial was being displaced by trial by jury.

Justice and the Royal Treasury

After the Anglo-Saxons first appeared on British shores, dispute resolution gradually changed from blood feuding to trials in courts and the use of fines or judicially supervised executions. Fines and forfeitures of a condemned person's property meant the king and other nobles made money by dispensing justice.

All fees collected through the royal courts went into the king's treasury or were paid to a noble for serving as a knight in the king's army. The king's interest in increasing royal revenues led to a continual growth in the variety of offenses considered offenses against the king. English kings also sought to make the justice in royal courts sufficiently attractive to their subjects to persuade complainants to use royal courts rather than the local courts maintained by the lords of the manor. A variety of innovations arose to increase the king's revenue from the judicial system and to expand the king's authority (Baker 1990, 17).

◼ DEVELOPMENT OF THE JURY

One innovation, the inquest, laid the foundations for the grand jury and eventually trial by jury. After a period of war the king needed to ascertain which lands were owned by the Crown. He directed royal officers to conduct an inquest, asking questions of men called to court. The men called to court were required to swear to tell all they knew about the ownership of the lands in the vicinity. In the years to come this tool would be used to settle private disputes between the king's subjects over the ownership of land and ultimately to become the principal means of bringing a case to trial (the grand jury) and determining the guilt of the accused (trial by jury).

The Grand Jury

The development of the grand jury as a means of charging persons with crimes can be traced to an 1166 law called the Assize of Clarendon, passed because cracks were appearing in the justice system. The judicial system was fraught with delays and technical difficulties that caused accusers to drop their cases. And it relied upon private prosecution, in which the individual victim was responsible for bringing a case to trial and assuming all risks and expenses of prosecution. Technicalities made it difficult for accusers to win and even placed the accuser at risk of being fined for false prosecution. If individual victims dropped their cases because of legal technicalities, the guilty person would go free. The community would not be vindicated or protected, and the king would not be able to collect a fine.

King Henry II (1154–1189) searched for a more efficient system for obtaining law and order. The Assize of Clarendon "clearly formulated the institution of the grand jury" (Lyon 1980, 295). The law required that in each county twelve men from each hundred (a political subdivision between the county and the township) and four men from each township be summoned to court. At court these men were required under oath to name everyone in the county reputed to be guilty of murder, larceny, or harboring criminals (Baker 1990, 576). The sheriff arrested the individuals identified and placed them in custody to await trial (Harding 1966, 40).

Such orders went out about every six months. This coincided with the circuits of the itinerant justices, who were appointed by the king to travel throughout the kingdom hearing royal pleas, which included many actions related to conduct that we now call crimes. Initially, the purpose of the grand jury was merely to name those individuals suspected of crime so that they might be brought to justice. Mere suspicion was sufficient to cause an arrest. As the practice evolved between 1166 and 1215, grand jurors were allowed to determine whether they believed the basis of the suspicion was credible (Shapiro 1991, 47). By 1360 a justice of the peace could refer private accusations to the grand jury (Harding 1966, 76). If there was no good evidence pointing to the accused person's guilt, the suspect would go free. Only those truly suspected of committing felonies were held for trial. Thus the function of the grand jury as a charging body was established. The grand jury ultimately evolved into an institution that protects citizens from prosecution when evidence that the accused has committed a crime is inadequate.

Evolution of the Jury Trial

The use of a jury to resolve factual disputes also arose initially in relation to land and property disputes. Early medieval records indicate that groups of men were sometimes asked to witness the buying and selling of property. In the event of a dispute over ownership these men might be asked to resolve the dispute based on their personal knowledge of the sales transaction (Harding 1966, 27).

Criminal accusations were still subject to trial by compurgation or ordeal. One exception to the usual practice had emerged by 1180 and involved the use of a jury to resolve some kinds of criminal accusations. In those cases in which an accuser brought an accusation to court (that is, where the accusation was not originally made by the grand jury), the accused might challenge the accusation by pleading that it had been made out of hate and spite. The accused could purchase a royal writ asking a jury to decide whether the accusation had some basis other than simple maliciousness. The jury would not decide the ultimate question of the accused's guilt. Thus, the use of juries to decide certain kinds of issues was an established practice almost a century before the jury was used to determine guilt or innocence at a criminal trial (Groot 1988, 8).

The jury was also specified in another set of circumstances spelled out in an enactment known as the Grand Assize. In 1179 King Henry II issued the Grand Assize, permitting a knight to decline trial by combat in land disputes and instead submit the matter to a jury by purchasing a royal writ. Again money paid for the writ went into the royal treasury. "If he took this course and purchased the writ, then four knights of his community were chosen to elect a jury of twelve knights who were required under oath to say which litigant had the better right to the land in question" (Lyon 1980, 293). The jurors were expected to resolve such disputes according to their own knowledge of the situation. Such jury trials must have been popular, because trial by battle declined sharply after this assize. By the middle of the thirteenth century jury trial was a common means of settling land ownership disputes of ordinary freemen as well. These were disputes that in today's terms would be considered civil suits.

Despite the use of juries to settle disputes, trial by ordeal in criminal cases continued until the church took action to end the practice. The church had long objected to the ordeal because it required the miraculous intervention of God, and asking for such a miracle was tempting God (Bartlett 1988). In 1215 the Fourth Lateran Council of the Roman Catholic Church forbade priests from participating in the ordeal. Without the participation of a priest to conduct the Mass and bless the instruments of the ordeal, the results of the ordeal could not be trusted. Consequently the ban on trial by ordeal created a vacuum. The ordeal could not be trusted to determine guilt, but what method of finding guilt could be relied upon instead?

In England the church's ban on trial by ordeal quickly led to a decline in its use, except in remote parts of the country where the custom appears to have persisted for several centuries. Nonetheless, the ban on the ordeal created a temporary crisis for the justice system. The first nationwide court session after 1215 started in 1219. Instructions were sent to the justices, "noting that the ordeal had been abolished and that an appropriate judicial response had not been determined" (Groot 1988, 10). The instructions ordered that those accused of serious crimes for which there was strong suspicion be held in prison for the time being. Those held for less serious offenses were to be allowed to abjure the realm, that is, leave the country. Others accused of minor crimes under slight suspicion were to be released under good conduct pledges (Groot 1988, 10). From the cultural perspective of the thirteenth century it seemed almost a sacrilege to condemn a person to die on the basis of human judgment alone (Lyon 1980, 450). Although a jury might release an accused person from charges (as in the newly evolved grand jury or the jury in "hate and spite" actions), conviction by a trial jury was quite another matter. Although records show royal justices condemned prisoners to death on the basis of the verdict of an extremely strong and reliable jury as early as 1221, most justices were reluctant to force the defendant to accept the jury's verdict, especially when the sentence was death. Because trial by jury was so new, judges felt that a person accused by grand jury should be required to choose trial by jury rather than have it imposed upon them (Johnson 1988, 63).

Because the justices had been instructed to hold suspects of serious crimes in prison, the justices were faced with a growing number of prisoners being held in dungeons who had been sent to prison without a trial and who had no prospect for a trial in the future. They solved the problem by giving the prisoner an option: continued indefinite imprisonment without trial or consenting to trial by jury (Groot 1988, 19–20). Given the substantial pains of imprisonment in medieval dungeons, some defendants agreed to put themselves, in the vernacular of the day, "for good or ill on the verdict of the countryside" (Groot 1988, 18). By the end of the century trial by jury was no longer presented as an option, and indefinite painful imprisonment had been institutionalized as a way to force defendants to accept trial by jury. By a royal statute of 1275 accused persons who refused to submit to jury trial were subjected to *la peine forte et dure,* (strong and hard punishment), a form of extremely painful imprisonment. Defendants who refused trial by jury were "loaded with heavy chains and placed on the ground in the worst part of the prison; they were fed a little water one day and a little bread the next" (Lyon 1980, 451). The objective of this painful imprisonment was to persuade the defendant to submit to a jury trial.

This coercive technique might have been successful except for another quirk in the law. Convicted felons forfeited all their lands and property to the king. However, if the defendant died in prison under this "strong and hard imprisonment" while awaiting trial, there was no conviction and the property passed to the defendant's heirs rather than to the king. Consequently, many men endured la peine forte et dure rather than leave their family impoverished after their execution for a felony conviction (Baker 1990, 581). Nonetheless, the dread created by this practice was so great that many defendants submitted to trial by jury rather than endure la peine forte et dure.

The records show an increase in the use of jury trials during the thirteenth century. However, jury trial in this period bore little resemblance to the jury trials of today. No evidence was formally presented to either the grand jury or the trial jury. The jurors were expected to know the facts and give their opinion about whether the defendant had committed a crime (Lyon 1980, 452). The reputation of the accused and common knowledge about the events of the neighborhood were critical in the jury's determination of guilt. Frequently, the same jurors would serve on the charging grand jury as on the trial jury. Some questioned the fairness of having guilt determined by the same group of jurors that had accused the defendant in the first instance (Baker 1990, 579). Surely, the grand jurors would be prejudiced against the defendant (Lyon 1980, 451). Jurors were unlikely to admit that they had been in error in accusing the defendant, especially because false accusation could result in serious fines.

Several changes were initiated to deal with this problem. In some cases defendants paid special fees to obtain additional jurors who had not served on the jury that charged the defendant (Baker 1990, 579). Eventually, the practice evolved so that the grand jury was augmented with additional men from neighboring communities in forming the trial jury. This change in membership allowed a trial jury to come to a conclusion that was different from that of the grand jury. By the end of the thirteenth century a special trial jury of twelve members was formed from a combination of members of the grand jury and one or more jurors selected from the grand juries of other jurisdictions. In 1352 a statute was passed that allowed a defendant to remove prospective jurors who had been members of the grand jury that had indicted the defendant (Green 1985, 22). This may be viewed as an early forerunner of the principle that jurors should be impartial and that defendants may excuse from the jury any jurors who are not impartial.

The practice of including on the trial jury people from outside the jurisdiction in which the crime occurred created new dilemmas for the operation of the jury trial. Ordinarily, jurors were expected to know all they needed to know to determine whether the defendant was guilty. The jurors lived in the vicinity and were expected to inform themselves about the crime and the personalities involved. Jurors from outside the vicinity could not be expected to share this knowledge, however. Thus it became necessary to take the testimony of witnesses in court to bring the facts to light for the jury. Initially, it seems, jurors would conduct informal investigations by going about the neighborhood asking people who might have information related to the case (Harding 1966, 127). By the end of the fifteenth century, 250 years after the introduction of the trial jury, the jury had ceased being "primarily a body of men who knew the criminal facts and became a body examining criminal evidence presented to it" (Lyon 1980, 637).

Once the trial jury was established, it quickly became a powerful institution. "The jury's power to determine the defendant's fate was virtually absolute" (Green 1985, 19). In a variety of circumstances the jury could use this absolute power to bring verdicts that were contrary to the evidence. "Whether such verdicts resulted from mercy, fear, or outright corruption, they evidenced the trial jury's domination of the system of justice" (Green 1985, 26). Judges frequently attempted to limit the power of the jury, refusing to accept not guilty verdicts and threatening to imprison jurors who voted to acquit obviously guilty defendants (Sanborn 1986, 120). Nonetheless, juries continued to act independently and even unpredictably in many cases, despite pressures from judges. This independence became the source of the jury's power and the key to its cherished position as the bulwark of English liberty.

MAGNA CARTA AND THE CONCEPT OF DUE PROCESS

Although the processes of accusation and adjudication were beginning to resemble modern forms, defendants did not possess the rights that are today considered fundamental to the trial process. The origins of the concepts of due process and limited government are found in an ancient document called the Magna Carta, which dates from the same period in which the grand jury and trial jury originated. The Magna Carta (1215) traditionally has been cited as the origin of the fundamental rights of English subjects. It established the principle of the rule of law in England. Although many English monarchs were tempted to assert that they were above the law, the Magna Carta limited the legitimacy of attempts to establish absolute power.

During the reign of King John (1199–1216), a despotic and power-hungry ruler, the feudal nobility had revolted. The Magna Carta was a reactionary document forced upon King John in 1215 by feudal nobles who felt that their traditional rights were being taken away by a selfish and arbitrary king. The barons forced King John to make concessions by reaffirming centuries-old legal and political customs. The king was forced to agree that if he violated the provisions of the Magna Carta, he would forfeit his land and possessions (Harding 1966, 55–56).

The Magna Carta was an acknowledgment by King John that the king is subject to the law. In other words, the Magna Carta created the fundamental principle that England is a nation ruled by law, not by kings. Most provisions in the Magna Carta relating to justice merely reaffirmed judicial practices that had already developed and, in some cases, had fallen into disuse. The Magna Carta was no document of liberty for the average person in 1215. Although it did reaffirm the rights and liberties of the barons, burgesses, and clergy, even the rights that it spelled out were largely feudal rights, making the Magna Carta a conservative rather than a revolutionary document of liberal ideals.

The immediate effect of the Magna Carta was fairly limited (Lyon 1980, 312–13, 321). Nonetheless, certain principles of government were recorded in the Magna Carta establishing a precedent that royal powers were limited. Eventually, the provisions of the Magna Carta and the protections that evolved from them came to be reconfirmed by kings at every opening of Parliament (Lyon 1980, 323). The notion that rulers are limited in their power and must follow lawful procedures was revolutionary in its influence on English legal and political thought. The notion of the rule of law would become particularly important during the conflicts of the sixteenth, seventeenth, and eighteenth centuries in both England and the English colonies in America.

◼ CIVIL WARS AND CHALLENGES TO TRIAL BY JURY

From the sixteenth to the eighteenth centuries English government suffered 150 years of unrest and revolt because of religious conflict and uncertain succession to the throne. During the mid-sixteenth century King Henry VIII (1509–1547) broke with the Church of Rome in order to take a new wife who he hoped would produce a male heir to the throne. Although a male heir was finally born, conflict over the legality of Henry's marriages created political strife, especially after Henry's son died shortly after succeeding to the throne. The struggle between those loyal to the church in Rome and those who upheld Henry's new Church of England led to more than a century of conflict and religious intolerance. During this time the courts were used as tools of political and religious persecution.

During the fifteenth, sixteenth, and seventeenth centuries, the common law judicial procedures of accusation, grand jury, and trial by jury changed little. Nonetheless, the power of the jury was challenged as judges sought to set aside verdicts that were contrary to the court's wishes. In addition, a separate court had emerged in the fifteenth century to deal particularly with political crimes, including religious dissent. This court, known as the Star Chamber, is significant for the development of Anglo-American judicial procedures—not because its innovations survive but because it became so despised that it reaffirmed the necessity of many protections traditionally provided under the common law. The rights of defendants recognized in the eighteenth century were largely a reaction against the arbitrary and harsh practices of the Court of Star Chamber.

Court of Star Chamber

Although trial by jury was firmly established in common law courts by the middle of the fifteenth century, these courts seemed unequal to the task of controlling political crimes and treason. The criminal jurisdiction of the Court of Star Chamber was limited to misdemeanors, but the offenses included riot, unlawful assembly, conspiracy, criminal libel, and perjury. In addition, a judge could seek to have jurors tried by Star Chamber on perjury charges if the judge thought they had violated their oath to convict the guilty (Baker 1990, 591). Lay jurors sometimes did not recognize the legitimacy of the laws and sought to lessen their effect on actual defendants (Green 1985). On the other hand jurors might be intimidated by defendants of high position who could retaliate against them (Harding 1966, 153). "In such cases jury trial was a mockery and an injustice because no juror dared hand down a verdict of guilty" (Lyon 1980, 615).

Jurisdiction in these troublesome cases went to the judicial branch of the king's inner council, the Court of Star Chamber. The Star Chamber adopted methods more commonly used on the continent of Europe, where interrogation of the suspect, sometimes in secret and accompanied by torture, was a common fact-finding tool. The procedures of the Star Chamber were swift and informal (Lyon 1980, 616). The king's attorney would initiate the case by information; there was no grand jury indictment (Baker 1990, 578). There was no right to trial by jury. The accused was forced to accuse himself, and torture was used extensively to extract confessions (Walker 1985, 14). Accusations could be brought without evidence, and the accused was not informed of the identity of the person making the accusation. Such procedures were unknown in the common law system. The Star Chamber came to be used with increasing frequency during decades of civil unrest and war in England during the sixteenth and early seventeenth centuries to deal with treason and religious heresy.

Ironically, because the difficult cases were sent to the Court of Star Chamber, where defendants were denied the rights that had developed as part of the common law, the Star Chamber preserved the common law system for the vast majority of ordinary offenders. Rather than transform the entire judicial structure to suppress revolt and dissent, England created a separate court to deal with those particular problems, with procedures falling outside the common law. Moreover, the abuses of the Star Chamber highlighted to many legal scholars of the day the importance of the judicial procedures of the common law courts in preserving liberty. The abuses of the Star Chamber led to its abolition in 1641 (Johnson 1988, 83; Lyon 1980, 616).

Decline of the Star Chamber: Powers of the Jury Increase

The abolition of the Star Chamber had an additional effect. After 1641 more political cases were tried by common law courts, and defendants had the right to a jury trial. During the 1660s a series of trials against Quakers, a dissident religious sect that was being persecuted by the English government, resulted in a number of trials in which jurors refused to convict defendants who were probably guilty of the crimes with which they were charged. The jurors' refusal was based on their disagreement with the law rather than on the sufficiency of the evidence against the defendants. Judges struggled with juries for power. Some judges responded to jury acquittals by fining and even imprisoning the jurors until the jurors agreed to bring a verdict of guilty (Green 1985, 200). Ultimately, however, the power of the jury in determining questions of fact was upheld.

One result of this episode was to emphasize the distinction between questions of law and questions of fact. Judges would have the authority to decide questions of law, but jurors would maintain control over the decision to convict or acquit once the judge had instructed them in the law (Green 1985, 254).

◼ CRIMINAL PROCEDURE INTO THE EIGHTEENTH CENTURY

Increases in the amount of crime in England, particularly property crime in the larger towns, created new strains on the judicial system. The number of capital offenses was greatly increased. Almost two hundred new capital offenses were created between 1660 and the end of the eighteenth century (Harding 1966, 272). These strains, combined with changing ideological concerns, brought about additional changes in judicial practice in England.

By the early part of the eighteenth century, common law courts charged suspects by grand jury and guaranteed the right of trial by jury for most felony offenses, which were capital crimes. The role of the jury had been transformed since the sixteenth century. Unlike the juries of the thirteenth, fourteenth, and fifteenth centuries, trial juries in the seventeenth and eighteenth centuries heard evidence from witnesses and based their decisions on the evidence. However, the law remained unsettled in regard to the type of evidence that could prove a crime and the amount of evidence needed to convict (Shapiro 1991).

Judges struggled for three centuries to find an appropriate way to instruct juries about the amount of evidence needed to convict a defendant of a crime (Shapiro 1991, 1). Although a body of law defining a standard of proof had developed in ecclesiastical courts and had been adopted in France and other European countries since 1215, the English were reluctant to adopt these rules in the common law courts. Too often English subjects had seen extraordinary non-common law courts, such as the Court of Star Chamber, adopt just such rules of proof. Because of their association with absolute monarchy, these practices were highly suspect (Shapiro 1991, 121–123).

private prosecution

Despite legislators' evident concern about crime in England, the traditional system of private prosecution continued into the eighteenth century. **Private prosecution** is a system of justice in which private individuals initiate a prosecution and take on all the attendent responsibilities, including presenting witnesses and proving the guilt of the defendant. During the eighteenth century 80 percent of indictable offenses were privately prosecuted (Hay 1983, 167). Private prosecution was a costly endeavor. The victim had to pay fees for the subpoena of witnesses and for a warrant for the accused. Additional fees were required if the case was bound over for trial. The government required monetary guarantees that the victim would prosecute the case and that the witnesses would appear to testify. Once in court, a variety of other fees were assessed: a fee to obtain an indictment, a fee to the officer to swear witnesses, to the doorkeeper of the courtroom, to the crier, and to the bailiff who took the prosecutor from the court to the grand jury room. When victims and witnesses lived in the countryside or small towns far from where court was held, the victims also had to pay for food and lodging for themselves and their witnesses (Beattie 1986).

During the early part of the eighteenth century victims usually prosecuted cases without legal assistance. By the latter part of the century, however, some victims were hiring professionals to handle various aspects of the procedure. Victims would offer rewards for assistance in the apprehension of a criminal. Occasionally, the victim would hire a solicitor (lawyer) to prepare the case for court and counsel to present the case in court. In addition, merchants and other propertied men began to form prosecution associations to "share the costs of catching and prosecuting thieves" (Beattie 1986, 48; see also Hay 1983, 171).

The increased use of attorneys by citizens pressing charges appears to have been a central factor leading to the right to counsel for defendants, which was not guaranteed in England until 1836 (Baker 1990, 583). The appearance of counsel for the defense is noted in court records after 1730, but defendants could not be assured that a lawyer would be allowed to participate at trial. Judges had complete discretion to prohibit the participation of defense counsel, and many judges did just that. A lawyer in 1741 noted that the judges act as they see fit on these occasions, and few of them (as far as I have observed) walk by one and the same rule in this particular: some have gone so far, as to give leave for counsel to examine and cross-examine witnesses; others have bid the counsel propose their questions to the Court; and others again have directed that the prisoner should put his own questions: the method of practice at this point is very variable and uncertain. (Beattie 1986, 359)

Counsel for the defense became quite common by the end of the eighteenth century, however.

Magistrates' Courts

The first step in prosecuting a case in England during the eighteenth century was to take a complaint to the justice of the peace. Since the thirteenth century English kings had appointed royal justices of the peace to dispense justice in the local community. The Crown created the office of justice of the peace to undermine the power of the sheriff, who was appointed by local nobles (Conley 1985, 258–59).

The justices of the peace, also called magistrates, served several functions. One was to mediate minor crimes arising from such disputes as trespass and assaults (Beattie 1986, 268). If mediation was inappropriate or failed in the particular case, the second function of the justice of the peace was to summarily dispose of misdemeanors. This practice allowed the magistrate to convict without a jury trial (Baker 1990, 584). After 1670, defendants convicted in a summary trial by a magistrate were typically given the opportunity to appeal the conviction in the county court, which could correct any mistakes (Baker 1990, 584).

Origins of the Preliminary Hearing

The justices of the peace were not permitted to try felonies, which included most property crimes, but fulfilled a preliminary fact-finding role (Beattie 1986, 270). The origins of the preliminary hearing, like those of the grand and petty juries, are found in practices in earlier centuries that crystallized into their more familiar modern forms only after years of experimentation and evolution.

Before the advent of the grand jury individuals could bring accusations against suspected offenders. Direct accusation did not disappear with the development of the grand jury, although the risk of being counter-charged with an accusation of hate and spite probably minimized the practice of direct accusation. During the fifteenth century the law encouraged accusation by means of a document called an information. During the sixteenth and seventeenth centuries the Court of Star Chamber adopted charging by information, in which the officers of the king brought the charges to the attention of the Court. Obtaining an indictment from a grand jury was unnecessary. The association of the practice of accusation by information with the practices of the grand jury may have caused this form of accusation to be tainted as unfair and contrary to the common law of England (Baker 1990, 578). Nonetheless, this form of accusation later crept back into practice, although as an additional step in the criminal process rather than as a substitute for the grand jury.

During the sixteenth and seventeenth centuries, procedures for magistrates in felony cases were still governed by statutes first passed in the middle of the sixteenth century. They required the magistrate to take depositions from the victims and witnesses and to examine the accused and put the accused's statement in writing. This examination was designed to search out evidence that would prove the defendant's guilt. It then fell to the defendant to deny the accusations and evidence in court. The magistrate was not supposed to make a judgment regarding the likely guilt or innocence of the accused. Indeed, "a magistrate could not dismiss a charge that had been sworn to on oath by a respectable prosecutor [accuser]" (Beattie 1986, 275). By the end of the eighteenth century, however, this preliminary examination had been transformed, so that magistrates would dismiss cases if they believed the accusation to be groundless (Shapiro 1991, 178). Magistrates also were responsible for setting bail for the accused or ordering the accused held in jail before trial. The magistrate also had to assure the appearance of the prosecutor and witnesses at trial by ordering monetary guarantees. The discretion of the magistrate to dismiss charges supported by insufficient evidence appears to be a forerunner of the late-nineteenth-century innovation in the United States, the preliminary hearing.

Grand Jury and Trial Procedure in the Eighteenth Century

Felony courts met only twice or four times a year in the eighteenth century. When the court was in session, the town was bustling with activity and even celebration as complainants, witnesses, and jurors came to town to attend court. Court was a highly ritualized and ceremonial affair. The first major piece of business was to empanel and conduct the grand jury. Members of both the grand and trial juries were drawn from the gentry and propertied classes. Statutes enacted as early as 1414 required jurors to possess a minimum amount of property, generally land, in order to be eligible for jury service (Hay 1988, 310). Service on the grand jury tended to enhance a person's social standing, although the wealthiest members of the community frequently sought to avoid jury service, even paying fines for failure to answer the summons for jury duty (Beattie 1986, 320). As a result of laws limiting eligibility for jury service the economic status of jurors tended to be higher than that of the parties before the court. Only 21 percent of private prosecutors owned sufficient property to qualify as jurors, and only 2 percent of the defendants owned that much property (Hay 1988, 350–51).

After the grand jury had heard all cases bound over for court by the magistrates, the judges proceeded to the arraignment and pleas. A guilty plea was rare in the eighteenth century and actively discouraged in capital cases, because it denied the judge an opportunity to collect information that might be used to grant leniency in sentencing (Beattie 1986, 336). If the defendant refused to enter any plea to the charges, and a jury determined that the refusal was deliberate, the prisoner would be subjected to la peine forte et dure. This practice was not officially abolished until 1772.

In eighteenth-century England, most defendants pled not guilty. Trial by jury followed immediately. The burden of proof was on the prosecution (Shapiro 1991, 178), but juries placed at least as much weight on the defendant's reaction to the charges as they placed on the evidence presented by the prosecutor's witnesses (Baker 1990, 581; Beattie 1991, 223). Because the trial was often the first time a defendant heard the charges, the jury could observe the defendant's spontaneous reactions to the charges. Because defendants often had no opportunity to call witnesses, the ability to convey their innocence through their reactions to the prosecutor's witnesses was critical.

In addition, until the end of the eighteenth century, the participation of defense counsel was often limited. Legal commentators of the day viewed counsel for the defense as an impediment to learning the truth, because lawyers would get in the way of observing defendants' honest efforts to explain their conduct and answer the charges. Judges were active participants, taking it upon themselves to see to it that defendants had every opportunity to clear themselves. Judges asked questions and clarified points related to the elements of the offense charged (Beattie 1986, 343).

A single jury would ordinarily hear all cases scheduled for that session of court. Although defendants were allowed to excuse jurors who might be prejudiced, in practice few did so; thus calling more than a dozen or so men to serve for trial juries was unnecessary (Beattie 1986, 340, 395; King 1988, 277). In the seventeenth century juries commonly heard all the trials before deliberating on any of the verdicts. The jury might hear dozens of cases before adjourning to deliberate. By the early decades of the eighteenth century, however, the jury reached its verdict at the conclusion of each case. In most cases the jury would not even leave the courtroom for its deliberation but would simply huddle in the courtroom to come to a verdict (King 1988, 294). Verdicts had to be unanimous, and the jury would be denied food and water until it reached its verdict. When the jury deadlocked, the pressure to reach a decision increased as night fell and everyone became hungry and thirsty. Sometimes, the jury would resort to other means for reaching a verdict, such as tossing a coin or taking a majority vote (King 1988, 293). Although these tactics were illegal and a violation of the jurors' oaths, authorities could do little to control such juries.

If the jury decided to acquit the defendant, it was not uncommon for the judge to try to persuade the jurors that they had made a mistake and ask them to reconsider. If the jurors stood by their decision to acquit, the judge had no choice but to abide by their decision, although judges occasionally would find some other pretext on which to imprison the defendant (Beattie 1986, 408–409). The judge was equally bound by a jury's decision to convict, even if he disagreed, but the judge retained the authority to pardon defendants sentenced to death (Beattie 1986, 409).

Many essential elements of modern criminal procedure can be found in eighteenth-century criminal cases: the preliminary examination of the defendant after which the defendant was dismissed or bound over to the grand jury, the grand jury as a forum for determining whether evidence was sufficient to bind the defendant over for trial, the opportunity to excuse jurors who might be prejudiced, and the finality of the jury's verdict of acquittal.

Many of these familiar procedures existed only in embryonic form. The preliminary examination was less a hearing than an interrogation. The right of the defendant against self-incrimination was not consistently recognized or protected. The concepts of probable cause and presumption of innocence had not yet crystallized. Although late eighteenth-century courts were inclined to allow defendants to be represented by counsel, the assistance of counsel was not recognized as a right, and counsel was actually prohibited in some kinds of cases. The jury had become a symbol of English freedom, yet how jurors were selected reflected deep class inequalities.

Although the political prosecutions of the English Civil War and the abuses of the Star Chamber had created impulses toward protecting the rights of defendants, eighteenth-century England had only begun to recognize these rights. The unique environment of colonial and Revolutionary America made the New World the incubator for these rights.

JUDICIAL PRACTICES IN COLONIAL AMERICA

Practices followed in England strongly influenced court procedures and practices in the colonies of North America. Nonetheless, the experiences of colonists from other countries, such as France and Holland, and the unique conditions of colonial life created an environment in which innovations in criminal procedure were tolerated and even welcomed (Friedman 1973, 39). The colonists adapted familiar systems of law and procedure to their circumstances. For example, the New England colonists, who were religious refugees, sought to reform the law to accommodate their religious beliefs (Rankin 1965). As one judge noted in 1813,

> Every country has its Common Law. Ours is composed partly of the Common Law of England and partly of our own usages. When our ancestors emigrated from England, they took with them such of the English principles as were convenient for the situation in which they were about to place themselves. . . . By degrees, as circumstances demanded, we adopted the English usages, or substituted others better suited to our wants, till at length before the time of the Revolution we had formed a system of our own. (Steinberg 1989, 6)

Beginning with the first permanent settlement in Virginia in 1607, the English established colonies in New England, Maryland, Virginia, and the Carolinas. In most cases, colonies were established by a grant to an individual or company. The Crown granted ownership of land and complete authority over the colony in exchange for a cut of the profits from the exploitation of resources in the New World.

The colonies were composed of remote outposts in a vast wilderness. Sharp status differences among the colonists created complex social relations. The northern colonies (Massachusetts, New York after its acquisition from the Dutch in 1664, and Pennsylvania) were founded largely by religious dissenters, though many settlers in these areas came for the more mundane purpose of making a better life for themselves than possible in the Old World. The southern colonies (Virginia, Maryland, and the Carolinas) were founded by the English gentry who attempted to maintain dictatorial control over the colonial settlers. Many settlers were indentured servants who had obtained ship's passage to the colonies by promising to work for a master for a specified number of years. Other settlers were prisoners who had been offered transportation to the New World as a means of escaping a death sentence. Finally, almost as soon as the colonies were established, Africans were forcibly brought to the colonies to work the large tobacco and rice plantations in the Southern colonies and to serve as domestic servants in the Northern colonies.

To cope with the unique circumstances of the colonies, early colonial rulers appear to have actually increased the severity of the law. Unlike their counterparts in England, colonial judges did not mitigate the harshness of seventeenth century laws. Nor did they appear to be overly concerned with protecting the rights of defendants (Billings 1981, 579). American colonial experience contains numerous examples of brutal and even reactionary movements in criminal practice (Surrency 1967, 254).

During the earliest period of settlement, the governor of the colony acted as judge in both civil and criminal cases (Surrency 1967, 258). As the population grew and cases became more numerous, regular courts were organized and regular procedures were followed to a degree. Cruel punishments were not uncommon during the early colonial period, including mutilation, whipping, and the stocks or pillory. In addition, colonial judges were less likely than their English counterparts to pardon criminals sentenced to death (Chapin 1983, 50–61). The harshness of colonial justice may have stemmed from the increased need for order in a community lacking the "steadying effect of the family, the institutional church, or a well-defined social order" (Billings 1981, 579–80). Law and punishment may have seemed the only protection against disorder, anarchy, and barbarity.

As colonial settlements became more stable, court practice in the colonies more closely followed contemporary practices in England, although without many of the formalities commonly associated with British justice (Friedman 1973, 42). For the most part the colonial courts adopted English judicial practices, although they eliminated some of the complexities of English law.

Colonial Court Process Prior to 1750

Criminal cases could be initiated by citizen complaint, on the action of the justices themselves, or occasionally by grand jury indictment. Justice of the peace courts, or magistrates' courts, were established in the counties to try misdemeanors and petty offenses. These courts were close to the people, offered ready access, and adopted informal summary procedures like those of the magistrates' courts in England (Steinberg 1989, 6–7). These courts also conducted preliminary examinations of felony defendants but were not authorized to hear cases involving capital offenses. Serious crimes were adjudicated before a central colonial court that held sessions only once or twice each year. Felony defendants would be held in jail while they awaited the next session of the court.

Although the custom of private prosecution was initially transplanted from England to the colonies in North America, by the time of the Revolution public prosecution had largely supplanted the earlier custom, especially for felonies (Shapiro 1991, 180). Prosecuting cases privately was expensive and difficult, especially given the lack of familiarity with judicial procedure and the shortage of lawyers to assist in prosecution. Attorneys general for the colonies began to serve as public prosecutors early in the eighteenth century (Goldstein 1983, 1286). Public prosecution may also have been introduced by colonists from Scotland, Holland, and France (Jacoby 1980).

English common law practices of indictment by grand jury and the right to trial by jury were adopted by colonial America with few changes. As in England at the time, colonial defendants were not informed of the nature of the evidence against them until trial. Until the mid-eighteenth century defendants were not entitled to counsel for their defense (Billings 1981).

"Justice" in the Southern Colonies:
Slavery and the Courts

The first slaves were brought to Virginia in 1619. Initially, landowners and merchants relied primarily on indentured servants from England, Scotland, Ireland, and Europe for most of the labor needs in the colonies. In the South the cultivation of labor intensive crops, such as tobacco and rice in the South, the poor working conditions in the swampy low country of the plantation areas, and rising wages in Britain and Europe combined to increase the Southern colonies' reliance on slave labor. Although the Northern colonies also used slave labor, the institution of slavery became an integral part of Southern society by the end of the seventeenth century.

The institution of slavery in the colonies presented a challenge to colonial governors. Although indentured servitude was common in England, slavery had not been practiced for many centuries. The English common law had evolved to resolve disputes between free men. Colonial governors saw little need to extend the protections of the common law to slaves.

Each colony evolved its own set of laws for regulating the slave trade and controlling the slave population. "The objective was simple—to keep the slave population, small though it was, under absolute control" (Spindel 1989, 20). Most punishment of slave offenses occurred on the plantation at the discretion of the slave owner. This punishment could be as autocratic and severe as the slave owner saw fit. Masters were authorized to beat, whip, and even castrate slaves under certain circumstances (Conley 1985, 275). Only serious offenses or offenses involving people or property from off the plantation were taken to the courts for resolution. Local magistrates' courts, which were normally used only for misdemeanors, were adapted during the seventeenth century for felony trials of slaves (Billings 1981, 577; Hindus 1976; Spindel 1989; Flanigan 1974). The burden of proof in these courts was lower than in common law courts, and usually there was no opportunity for a jury or appeal of the court's verdict. Even in cases in which there was a jury, "the hysterical atmosphere that pervaded the communities in the wake of a particularly serious crime could make it almost impossible for a slave to secure an unbiased jury" (Flanigan 1974, 551). Punishment was swift and public; the punished slave was to serve as an example to other slaves who might contemplate rebellion or violence. The master of an executed slave was compensated by the court for the loss of his property.

The consensus of most scholars who have studied these courts is that they offered little justice for black slaves. These courts merely put a gloss of legitimacy on whatever punishment the white community wanted. The institution of slavery in the Southern colonies necessitated adaptations of the common law that violated the standards of justice and equality that colonists demanded for themselves. Even as the colonists demanded greater rights for themselves, they denied the same rights to the slaves. These practices continued through the Civil War with few changes. Whether emancipation brought equal justice for African-Americans is a topic addressed throughout this book.

Building on the Common Law: Rights of Individuals

The colonies in America were settled during a period of rapid social change and political turmoil in England. The Star Chamber was still fresh in colonists' memories. Many people who came to the New World were escaping political and religious repression. Many had risked criminal prosecution for following nonconformist religious beliefs. Their experiences in England had left the colonists with a particularly strong respect for trial by jury and procedural rights to protect their other liberties, such as freedom of religion.

Given these experiences, the philosophy of the Enlightment, promoting liberty, limits on government power, and equality, found fertile ground. Political philosophers, including Immanuel Kant and John Locke, were arguing that all

SLAVE LAW IN THE AMERICAN COLONIES

Indentured servants were a vital part of the labor system in the North, Southern towns, and in frontier regions. But in the tobacco, rice, and sugar colonies, black slavery more and more replaced white servitude. The first blacks were servants, not slaves; their status was hardly different from that of white servants or Indian captives. But the Negro was pagan, and a different race. A special sentiment gradually crystallized about the status of the growing number of blacks. The American style of black-white relations, a peculiar mixture of bigotry, dread, sexual envy, and economic oppression, can be traced far back into the colonial past. The exact origins of the *legal* meaning of slavery are obscure, though, clearly, developing custom guided the lawmaker's hand. Before the end of the 17th century, slavery had become a definite legal status in both North and South; it was peculiarly associated with the Negro; it had become a terrible, timeless condition, inherited by children from their mothers. The legal status of the slave, as it took shape in the statute books, reflected and ratified social discrimination and sense of race. In Virginia, insofar as these developments can be dated, evidence points to the period between 1660 and 1680 as the period in which the status was formalized. In 1662, it became law in Virginia that children of slave mothers would themselves be slaves, regardless of the status of the father. Originally, only pagans could be lawfully enslaved; but as early as a Maryland law of 1671, baptism no longer brought escape from slavery. . . .

Slaves themselves had few legal rights. Slaves could not testify in court against white men. They could not vote, own property, or marry. The master was bound by law to treat the slave with minimal fairness, to feed him and clothe him, and to punish him no more severely than the situation demanded. These rights were occasionally enforced in court. But no one believes that these legal restraints had much effect on the way that masters behaved. . . .

Slaveholders . . . had many fantasies about black men—about their intelligence, strength, and sensibilities. They were capable of believing, and saying, that the slave was best off as a slave. Yet white men never quite convinced themselves that slaves were happy with their lot. On the contrary, the white man had an almost paranoid fear of slave revolt. . . . The slave codes grew steadily more repressive. In North Carolina, for example, the Fundamental Constitutions codified the custom that slaveowners had "absolute power and authority over negro slaves." A statutory revision of 1715 restricted trading with slaves, and outlawed intermarriage of blacks and whites. . . . The master himself was law, judge, and jury over most aspects of slave life: this was inherent in the system. But in North Carolina, at least as early as 1715, there were special courts for slaves who disobeyed the law. Whipping was the common mode of punishment. Serious crimes called for the death penalty; but a dead slave injured his owner's pocketbook; hence owners were repaid out of public funds. Castration was an alternative punishment for serious crimes. Happily, this punishment was eliminated in 1764. But in 1773 a Negro was burned alive for murdering a white man. . . .

There were many free Negroes in the colonies in the 18th century. Some were emancipated slaves, some the descendants of the early class of free blacks. As the racist element in the slave codes increased, the legal position of free slaves deteriorated. The great fear that blacks as a group might conspire against whites cost the free Negroes dearly. Free Negroes were discriminated against by law, and hounded from colony to colony.

Source: Copyright © 1973, 1985 by Lawrence M. Friedman. *A History of American Law.* New York: Simon & Schuster, pp. 73–76. Reprinted by permission of Simon and Schuster, Inc.

men were endowed with certain natural rights and that the consent of the governed is the only true basis of the right to rule (McDonald 1985). Although most Enlightenment philosophers aimed their criticisms of criminal procedures at the harsh practices in France, colonists who had fled persecution in England were acutely aware of the abuses of arbitrary government power. The colonists reinvigorated traditional common law practices, like trial by jury, as protections against tyranny. The procedures they adopted as part of the U.S. Constitution were in part a reaffirmation of both traditional common law protections and later innovations influenced by Enlightenment philosophy.

Recognizing the importance of protections against unreasonable search and seizure and tortured confessions, many colonies had drafted documents that reaffirmed these and other rights for the colonists in the New World. For example, beginning in 1648 the Massachusetts Bay colony drafted a comprehensive piece of legislation called the Body of Liberties, which spelled out precise definitions of criminal acts and stated the rights and privileges to which accused persons were entitled. Other colonies passed similar legislation (Johnson 1988, 104). The New England colonies adopted these declarations of the rights of individuals as legal codes. In the South, where the colonies were typically royal charters to private entrepreneurs, the charter provisions usually included some statement that colonists were entitled to the same rights as other English subjects (Rutland 1955, 22–23).

These declarations of rights covered religious freedom, freedom of speech, and a variety of rights for accused persons, including the right to trial by jury, protection against cruel and unusual punishment, and a limited right to counsel for the accused. It is important to remember, however, that how the colonists interpreted these rights often differed dramatically from how these rights have come to be interpreted since. For example, the Massachusetts Body of Liberties in 1672 prohibited the use of torture to coerce a confession from the accused. Nonetheless, a person might be tortured after conviction in order to obtain information about conspirators or confederates, so long as the torture was not "barbarous and inhumane" (Friedman 1973, 61).

Building on Experience

The colonists' common law heritage and historical experience with repression were further reinforced by their experiences in the colonies. By the middle of the eighteenth century the colonists had experienced a variety of repressive measures that violated their understandings of the rights of English subjects. To control smuggling and tax evasion the British colonial governors had instituted measures that were both effective in apprehending suspects and repugnant to the ideal of due process of law. The British ransacked houses under general warrants, looking for untaxed items that had been smuggled into the colonies. Courts of vice admiralty were used to prosecute cases of smuggling and tax evasion, and the common law protections of indictment by grand jury, trial by jury, and right to counsel were denied the colonists in these military tribunals. Experience with the harsh judicial practices of the British in suppressing revolt renewed colonists' fears of unrestrained government power and the potential of judicial procedures to crush dissent. These fears further strengthened the colonists' notions of the rights of the individual (Johnson 1988).

Blending their (often erroneous) interpretations of the protections of Magna Carta with Enlightenment philosophy, the colonists came to view some rights as natural rights—those to which all persons were entitled and which no government was authorized to violate under any circumstances. As the movement toward independence gained momentum and it became clear that a declaration of independence was inevitable, the colonies began to organize new state governments. The Enlightenment concept of the social contract led the colonists to write constitutions that would define the structure and processes of the new governments. In addition, many state constitutional conventions concluded that some statement of the rights of the individual against government power was a necessary prerequisite to establishing any government.

Forging the Bill of Rights

On June 12, 1776, even before the Declaration of Independence was signed, Virginia passed its Declaration of Rights. It included rights against self-incrimination, the right to be informed of the criminal charges, the right to a speedy trial and trial by jury, and the right against excessive bail and cruel and unusual punishments, in addition to freedom of the press, freedom of religion, and the assertion of equality and majority rule (Rutland 1955, 43–77).

After the Declaration of Independence on July 4, 1776, other states followed Virginia's example, and many used the Virginia Declaration of Rights as a rough model for their own statements of the rights of citizens. None offered what might in retrospect be considered a complete bill of rights. For example, Virginia's Declaration of Rights

> omitted the freedoms of speech, assembly, and petition; the right to the writ of habeas corpus; the right to grand jury proceedings; the right to counsel; separation of church and state; and freedom from double jeopardy and from ex post facto laws. The rights omitted were as numerous and important as those included. Twelve states, including Vermont, had framed constitutions, and the only right secured by all was trial by jury in criminal cases. . . . Four neglected to ban excessive fines, excessive bail, compulsory self-incrimination, and general search warrants. . . . Nine failed to provide for grand jury proceedings, . . . while eleven were silent on double jeopardy. (Levy 1988, 305)

It is unclear whether these omissions were a matter of oversight or whether there were serious disagreements about which rights ought to be preserved in a bill of rights. Although the common law rights to which English settlers were accustomed were an important influence, the common law was being supplemented by a theory of natural rights. The specific content of these natural rights was not entirely clear.

After the Revolution, the Articles of Confederation, which had held the states together in a loose confederation during the war, needed to be revised. A new constitution for a federal government was written and sent to the states for ratification. One issue that emerged in the debate over the new constitution was whether a bill of rights should be included in the national constitution. Some argued that a bill of rights was unnecessary because state constitutions had already secured these rights. Others argued that a bill of rights was necessary to restrain the federal government from encroaching on the rights of citizens. A number of other arguments were offered as well. The debate over a bill of rights also became a rallying point in the struggle between the Antifederalists, who sought to preserve states' rights and powers, and the Federalists, who sought a strong central government. The Constitution was passed by the Constitutional

Convention of 1787 and sent to the states for ratification without a bill of rights. However, most states refused to ratify the new constitution without assurances that amendments would be added that would guarantee the rights of individuals.

When the First Congress of the new national government was convened in 1789, James Madison brought forward a proposal for amendments that would create a federal bill of rights. Madison based his list on state bills of rights and proposals that had been made by state ratifying conventions (Levy 1988, 315). His proposal met with little enthusiasm in the new Congress. Nonetheless, after some delay Congress passed twelve amendments that it sent to the states for ratification. Ten of the amendments were ratified and became what is known as the Bill of Rights. Four of these amendments concerned the rights of those accused of crimes (see Chapter 3). These rights extended only to defendants in federal prosecutions, however.

Madison unsuccessfully sought an amendment that would have extended to the states the protections of freedom of conscience, freedom of the press, and the right to jury trial in criminal cases. Madison believed that the bills of rights in the states were "very defective" and viewed his proposed amendment as "the most valuable in the whole list" (Levy 1988, 316). It received the necessary two-thirds majority in the House, but failed to pass the Senate. As a result the Bill of Rights referred only to the rights of citizens in relation to the federal government. Limitations on state power required state bills of rights.

Role of the Courts in Preserving Rights

The drafters of the various bills of rights at both the federal and state level were very much aware that putting rights on paper was no guarantee they would be preserved in action. Even before the passage of the federal Bill of Rights state provisions had been violated and ignored. "Constitutional protections of rights meant little during times of popular hysteria; any member of the Constitutional Convention could have cited examples of gross abridgements of civil liberties in states that had bills of rights" (Levy 1988, 304).

Despite the obvious limitations of "parchment provisions" to realistically protect the rights of citizens, the framers of the Constitution also recognized that the courts would be the ultimate protector of those rights. In March 1789 Thomas Jefferson wrote to James Madison: "In the arguments in favor of a declaration of rights you omit one which has great weight with me: the legal check which it puts into the hands of the judiciary." Jefferson expected courts to strike down or invalidate actions of the government that violated the fundamental rights of the citizens, but he believed that courts would be better able to do this if there was a written declaration of these rights. In 1803 this role of the courts was recognized in the Supreme Court decision of *Marbury v. Madison*.

The framers also appear to have recognized the advantages of creating broad general principles that would require interpretation by courts in relation to the facts of specific cases. Stare decisis, deciding cases based on precedent, had long been the tradition in common law, a tradition with which the framers were both familiar and comfortable. Thus rather than specify the particular punishments that were cruel and unusual, the framers left it to the courts to interpret the meaning of the phrase. This lack of specificity has given both the federal and state bills of rights the flexibility to adapt to changing circumstances that the framers could not anticipate. The appellate courts continue to reinterpret the rights of citizens of the United States in their decisions. As Chapter 3 discussed, since the passage of the Fourteenth Amendment in the mid-nineteenth century the role of the federal courts has been expanded to include interpreting the rights of citizens in relation to state governments. This role of the courts, to continually review the law and the applicability of constitutional protections, is fundamental to courts and the law in the United States.

■ SUMMARY

The history of the development of courts and judicial procedures in England and early America demonstrates several important points. First, people have relied on a variety of dispute resolution mechanisms at different periods of time. The feud once was viewed as the only legitimate means of resolving disputes over property or personal security. Later, as kings outlawed the feud, emerging court practices relied on the swearing of oaths and the submission to ordeal. These means of resolving disputes were recognized as legitimate and reliable. The abolition of the ordeal created a temporary crisis of legitimacy; the substitution of trial by jury did not gain automatic acceptance as a legitimate means of determining guilt or innocence.

Second, judicial structures and procedures that were initially adopted as an administrative expedient, whether to make justice quicker and more efficient or to increase the king's revenue from the courts, only later came to be viewed as essential to justice. This is particularly true with respect to the grand jury and the trial jury. Indeed, at one time people so distrusted the jury trial that they preferred to suffer la peine forte et dure. Only a few hundred years later the trial by jury would be recognized on both sides of the Atlantic as a fundamental right.

Third, English law created the principle that the rule of law must be obeyed by the rulers as well as by the ruled. This idea evolved into the right to due process and the tenet that some rights are fundamental and may not be abridged under any circumstances, including several related to the apprehension and trial of persons accused of crime.

The rights and procedures that evolved were neither inevitable nor perfect. The history of Anglo-American criminal procedure demonstrates the influence of economic and political considerations in the development of law and practice. Although the founders of the new American Republic declared the rights they recognized as "natural rights," the rights included in the Bill of Rights possess no special magic or finality. Indeed, as the remainder of this book makes clear, our understandings of the rights of the criminally accused continue to evolve, and that evolution, as in the past, has been and will be influenced by economic and political considerations.

■ FOR FURTHER DISCUSSION

1. Trial procedure before 1215 differed dramatically from modern trial procedure. Nonetheless, some similarities emerge. What similarities do you see in compurgation, ordeal, and trial by battle and modern trial procedures?

2. Why was trial by jury so distrusted in the thirteenth century? What historical factors led the English and later the North Americans to put so much value on trial by jury?

3. Assess the quality of justice in each period described in this chapter in relation to the following criteria: accessibility, reliability, and legitimacy.

4. Describe two changes in court procedure that were at least partly motivated by the desire to raise revenue. How do revenue concerns influence reforms in criminal processes today?

5. At the time of the Revolution and ratification of the Constitution and Bill of Rights many criminal procedures and rights of defendants now considered essential to fair adjudication were nonexistent. The only right granted in all state bills of rights was the right to a jury trial. The evolution of rights since has occurred largely, although not exclusively, through court decisions. Would this have surprised the framers of the Constitution? Explain.

◼ REFERENCES

Baker, J. H. 1990. *An Introduction to English Legal History,* 3d ed. Boston: Butterworths.

Bartlett, Robert. 1988. *Trial by Fire and Water: The Medieval Judicial Ordeal.* Oxford, England: Clarendon.

Beattie, J. M. 1991. "Scales of Justice: Defense Counsel in the English Criminal Trial in the Eighteenth and Nineteenth Centuries." *Law and History Review* 9 (Fall): 221–67.

———— 1986 *Crime and the Courts in England, 1660–1800.* Oxford, England: Clarendon.

Beckerman, John S. 1992. "Procedural Innovation and Institutional Change in Medieval English Manorial Courts." *Law and History Review* 10 (Fall): 197–252.

Billings, Warren M. 1981. "Pleading, Procedure, and Practice: The Meaning of Due Process of Law in Seventeenth Century Virginia." *Journal of Southern History* 40 (November): 573–84.

Chapin, Bradley. 1983. *Criminal Justice in Colonial America, 1606–1660.* Athens: University of Georgia Press.

Conley, John A. 1985. "Doing It by the Book: Justice of the Peace Manuals in English Law in Eighteenth-Century America." *Journal of Legal History* 6 (December): 257–98.

Flanigan, Daniel. 1974. "Criminal Procedure in Slave Trials in the Antebellum South." *Journal of Southern History* 40 (4): 537–64.

Friedman, Lawrence M. 1973. *A History of American Law.* New York: Simon & Schuster.

Goldstein, Herman. 1983. "History of Public Prosecution." In Sanford Kadish, ed. *Encyclopedia of Criminal Justice.* Vol. 3. New York: Free Press.

Green, Thomas Andrew. 1985. *Verdict According to Conscience: Perspectives on the English Criminal Jury Trial, 1200–1800.* Chicago: University of Chicago Press.

Groot, Roger D. 1988. "The Early-Thirteenth-Century Criminal Jury." In J. S. Cockburn and Thomas A. Green, eds. *Twelve Men Good and True: The Criminal Jury in England, 1200–1800.* Princeton, N.J.: Princeton University Press.

Harding, Alan. 1966. *A Social History of English Law.* London: Penguin.

Hay, Douglas. 1988. "The Class Composition of the Palladium of Liberty: Trial Jurors in the Eighteenth Century." In J. S. Cockburn and Thomas A. Green, eds. *Twelve Men Good and True: The Criminal Jury in England, 1200–1800.* Princeton, N.J.: Princeton University Press.

———— 1983. "Controlling the English Prosecutor." *Osgoode Hall Law Journal* 21 (2): 165–86.

Hindus, Michael. 1976. "Black Justice Under White Law: Criminal Prosecutions of Blacks in Antebellum South Carolina." *Journal of American History* 48 (December): 575–99.

Hyams, Paul R. 1981. "Trial by Ordeal: The Key to Proof in the Early Common Law." In Morris S. Arnold, Thomas A. Green, Sally A. Scully, and Stephen D. White, eds. *On the Law and Customs of England.* Chapel Hill: University of North Carolina Press.

Jacoby, Joan E. 1980. *The American Public Prosecutor: A Search for Identity.* Lexington, Mass: Lexington Books.

Johnson, Herbert A. 1988. *History of Criminal Justice*. Cincinnati: Anderson Publishing.

King, P. J. R. 1988. "Illiterate Plebians, Easily Misled: Jury Composition, Experience, and Behavior in Essex, 1735–1815." In J. S., Cockburn and Thomas A. Green, eds. *Twelve Men Good and True: The Criminal Jury in England, 1200–1800*. Princeton, N.J.: Princeton University Press.

Levy, Leonard. 1988. *Constitutional Opinions: Aspects of the Bill of Rights*. New York: Oxford University Press.

Lyon, Bryce. 1980. *A Constitutional and Legal History of Medieval England*, 2d ed. New York: W. W. Norton.

Marbury v. Madison, 5 U.S. (1 Cranch) 137 (1803).

McDonald, Forrest. 1985. *Novus Ordo Seclorum: The Intellectual Origins of the Constitution*. Lawrence: University Press of Kansas.

Rankin, Hugh F. 1965. *Criminal Trial Proceedings in the General Court of Colonial Virginia*. Charlottesville: University Press of Virginia.

Rutland, Robert Allen. 1955. *The Birth of the Bill of Rights, 1776–1791*. Chapel Hill: University of North Carolina Press.

Sanborn, Joseph B. 1986. "A Historical Sketch of Plea Bargaining." *Justice Quarterly* 3 (June): 111–37.

Shapiro, Barbara J. 1991. *"Beyond Reasonable Doubt" and "Probable Cause": Historical Perspectives on the Anglo-American Laws of Evidence*. Berkeley: University of California Press.

Simpson, A. W. B. 1981. "The Laws of Ethelbert." In Morris S. Arnold, Thomas A. Green, Sally A. Scully, and Stephen D. White, eds. *On the Law and Customs of England*. Chapel Hill: University of North Carolina Press.

Spindel, Donna J. 1989. *Crime and Society in North Carolina, 1663–1776*. Baton Rouge: Louisiana State University.

Steinberg, Allen. 1989. *The Transformation of Criminal Justice: Philadelphia, 1800–1880*. Chapel Hill: University of North Carolina.

Surrency, Edwin C. 1967. "The Courts in the American Colonies." *American Journal of Legal History* 11 (July): 253–276.

Thayer, J. B. 1891. "The Older Modes of Trial." *Harvard Law Review* 5:45–70.

Walker, R. J. 1985. *The English Legal System*, 6th ed. London: Butterworths.

CHAPTER **5**

COMPARATIVE SYSTEMS OF CRIMINAL COURT PROCESS

$\mathbf{M}$any Americans have found themselves accused of crimes in foreign countries because of the illegal drug trade and international drug trafficking laws. In most cases American defendants are shocked and frustrated to learn that the U.S. government cannot get them out of the country and that other countries do not follow the procedures of U.S. courts. Their experiences include detention for years without trial, torture to coerce confessions, conviction without benefit of counsel or even the opportunity to put on a defense, and harsh and inhumane conditions of confinement.

Although many Americans are highly critical of their own justice system because it is "too soft" on criminals, they are frequently dismayed by the harshness and lack of procedural rights common in some other systems of justice.

This chapter examines three nonadversarial systems of justice: the civil law system as practiced in France, the Islamic system as practiced in Saudi Arabia, and the mediation and adjudication system used in China. These three systems represent distinct philosophical approaches to justice and adjudication.

Any system of criminal justice must address some basic issues: ensuring that the accused and witnesses appear for trial, the role of the victim in the criminal court process; the kind of evidence that may be used in court; the standard of proof to be used to establish the guilt of the accused, and protections to prevent the accusation and conviction of innocent persons. Although these issues are common to all systems of criminal court process, the means used to address them vary in important ways from one country to another. Examining how other systems of justice have addressed these issues may increase our understanding of our own.

A caveat before proceeding. Whereas American scholars have intensively studied the "real practices" of the criminal justice system, especially in the last thirty years, such studies are much less common—or are nonexistent—for most other systems of justice. Consequently, this examination of court procedures in other countries of necessity focuses primarily on the formal processes and the procedural law on the books, which may be quite different from the law in practice.

■ CLASSIFYING SYSTEMS OF JUSTICE

families of law

In the comparative study of law legal scholars have classified systems of law and justice into different groups, or **families of law.** Rene David and John Brierly have classified contemporary world legal systems into three major families: the Romano-Germanic family, the common law family, and the socialist family (1985, 22). Many scholars of modern comparative law accept their classifications.

Romano-Germanic family, civil law

The **Romano-Germanic family** of law includes those legal systems that have evolved from Roman **civil law**, which is sometimes referred to as the *civil law system*. Most countries in continental Europe have legal systems that fall within the Romano-Germanic family. In contrast to the common law tradition in England the civil law places greater importance on the text of written statutory law. Countries in the Romano-Germanic tradition place great emphasis on codification of the law. Courts are not recognized as having the authority to "make" law.

common law family

The main identifying feature of the **common law family** is its tradition of "creating" law through the decisions of judges resolving specific disputes (David and Brierly 1985, 24). Whereas the judge in a court in a Romano-Germanic system would search the written statutory law to find and apply the abstract rule to a particular dispute, the common law judge would be more likely to look for a practical solution and formulate a decision based on the facts of the case and general principles of justice and fairness. Characteristic of England, the United States, and Canada, the common law family organizes law and the courts in relation to disputes between private individuals. Historically, the common law developed on a case-by-case basis as a framework within which private disputes could be worked out to the advantage of society. In contrast the Romano-Germanic family of law focused more on the application of written legal codes.

socialist family

The **socialist family** of law originated in the Soviet Union after the 1917 Bolshevik Revolution. The socialist family of law represents a variation of the civil law system and is characterized by its emphasis on the revolutionary power of the legislature to express the popular will (David and Brierly 1985, 26). One central tenet of Marxist philosophy is that there will no longer be a need for a state or for law after the attainment of pure communism, and that the state will wither away. The law is viewed as a temporary expedient for moving society toward the communist ideal. The rules of criminal procedure are subordinated to the goals of progressing toward the communist ideal. Historically, the criminal justice systems in communist countries used this reasoning to justify purges of political dissidents.

Because the former Soviet Union and Eastern bloc countries were originally part of the Romano-Germanic family of law, their criminal courts are typically organized in much the same fashion as in the Romano-Germanic countries. China's court system also bears the marks of Soviet influence and has some characteristics associated with the socialist family of law, especially in the way it elevates revolutionary goals over formal procedure. With the changes in government that have been sweeping the socialist world since 1989 it is unclear whether a distinction between the Romano-Germanic and socialist families will exist at all in the future.

These three families of law have received the most attention from scholars of comparative law. Because of colonial expansion and the imposition of European and English legal systems in Africa, Asia, and the Americas, the influence of the Romano-Germanic and common law families reaches far beyond the borders of continental Europe and England. Through European colonial occupation of many parts of the world, the civil law tradition became the most widely distributed legal system. It influences modern Europe, Central and South America, and many parts of Asia and Africa, as well as Quebec, Canada, and (to a much more limited extent) the state of Louisiana, a former French colony. The common law tradition has been transplanted from England to Ireland, the United States, Canada, Australia, New Zealand, and many countries of Asia and Africa.

Non-Western Legal Traditions

Among the major legal traditions competing, and often coexisting, with the Western families of law are those based on Islamic law, Hindu law, Jewish law, Chinese, Japanese, and Korean law, and the customary law of numerous regions of Africa (Merryman and Clark 1978, 6). Many of these legal traditions are closely related to religious beliefs and customs and often do not draw the sharp distinction between religious and secular law that has developed in the civil and common law countries. In many countries such traditions have been modified by the importation of Western legal values. In other cases countries have made specific efforts to purge Western ideas from the law and to conform to either precolonial traditions or to forge a new set of legal principles.

ADVERSARIAL AND INQUISITORIAL SYSTEMS OF JUSTICE

Classifying legal systems by families of law is useful for examining their history but is less useful for analyzing differences in criminal court processes. An alternative approach is to classify criminal process as either adversarial or inquisitorial. These two distinct processes arose from the divergent historical evolutions of the Anglo-American and European judicial systems. Romano-Germanic legal systems typically use what is referred to as an inquisitorial procedure, whereas those systems evolving out of the common law tradition use an adversarial process for criminal adjudication.

History of the Inquisitorial Process

Before 1215 criminal processes in continental Europe were not much different from those in England. In both England and on the Continent accusation was made by a private individual, usually the victim of the crime. This characteristic made the criminal process essentially adversarial in nature (Johnson 1988, 59). In both England and continental Europe trials by compurgation and ordeal were common means of resolving doubts about the guilt or innocence of someone accused of a crime.

When in 1215 the Fourth Lateran Council in Rome effectively abolished trial by ordeal by forbidding the participation of priests, courts in both England and on the Continent cast about to develop a system for authoritatively resolving disputes in cases in which the evidence was unclear. As Chapter 4 noted, this crisis led to the eventual adoption of trial by jury in England. Trial by jury, combined with the tradition of private prosecution, established what has come to be known as the adversarial process. In continental Europe, however, trial by jury never gained a strong foothold and was abandoned in many parts of Europe by the fifteenth century (Terrill 1987, 134).

Even before 1215, however, the seeds of the inquisitorial process were taking root on the European continent. The Roman Catholic Church was worried about the spread of heresy (unorthodox beliefs) and immoral conduct among priests and monks, particularly in southern France (Johnson 1988, 59). When lesser measures failed, Pope Gregory IX (1227–1241) created a special papal court to *Inquisition* root out and destroy heretics. So began the **Inquisition.** Dominican and Franciscan friars, acting as ecclesiastical judges, were sent out to communities, preached sermons, and offered forgiveness and leniency to any heretic who would confess within a specified grace period. After the grace period the judges would begin an investigation by interrogating witnesses about any known heretics in the vicinity. Sometimes the witness would admit to practicing heresy; other times, the witness would accuse someone else of heresy. If a person was accused of heresy, the person came under strong suspicion and would be harshly interrogated. "Under this procedure it was almost impossible for the accused to prove himself innocent. He was not allowed to see the testimony against him or to learn the names of his accusers. This secrecy was necessary to protect witnesses from recrimination, but it also encouraged false accusations. The accused was not allowed counsel nor was he allowed witnesses in his own behalf" (Hoyt 1957, 362).

The crisis created by the abolition of the ordeal, the desire to root out heresy, and the lingering Roman tradition of using torture to extract confessions transformed criminal procedures in the civil law countries. The idea evolved that only an individual's confession was sufficient to prove a serious offense like heresy. The role of the interrogator was to secure the confession. Confession established the accused's acceptance of the charges and reassured the court and the public that the truth had been found (Johnson 1988, 60).

Torture and trickery were simply means of obtaining that proof in the inquisitional system. One common technique for extracting a confession was to stretch the accused naked over a wooden horse and pour water down his throat (Johnson 1988, 61). Another was to tie the accused's hands behind her back with a rope attaching her wrists to the ceiling. The accused was then dropped from some height, causing excruciating pain as her arms were wrenched up behind her. Because of the church's declared abhorrence of violence the pope forbade inquisitors to torture for more than one-half hour at a time (Hoyt 1957, 363). Canon law also forbade a conviction to be based on a coerced confession. Consequently, after the accused was revived from the half-hour of torture, the inquisitors would seek to have him repeat his confession. If the accused repeated the confession, it could be used as evidence at the trial. If he did not ratify the confession given under torture, it was invalidated. Nothing, of course, prevented the inquisitors from putting the accused through the entire process again and again until the confession was finally ratified.

Originally, the use of torture was limited to extraordinary cases in which proof through testimony was impossible, especially in cases of heresy. However, the use of torture in the inquisitorial process gradually became more and more common in the trials of ordinary criminal offenses. During the sixteenth century the king of France ordered that the inquisitorial process be used in all French courts. A royal official was made the prosecutor, eliminating the traditional system of private prosecution. Criminal procedure was divided into two stages—the inquisition and the trial. During the inquisition one judge served as an examiner, who would interrogate and, if necessary, torture the accused to learn the truth of the matter. All evidence was put in writing. All evidence, including the confession of the accused, would be placed in evidence before another judge at a public trial, and the guilt of the accused would be formally declared (Mueller and Le Poole-Griffiths 1969, 7).

Innocent people frequently would be condemned because they had broken down under torture and were unable to prove their innocence at trial. Such practices fueled the revolutionary spirit reflected in Enlightenment philosophy. French judicial practices were a prime target of the French revolution. The success of revolutions and the exchange of ideas with the British and Americans resulted in a number of changes in the **inquisitorial process.** What remained was the organization of the process around the centralized search for evidence and the presentation of the investigatory record as the main evidence at trial. What changed was the role of the defendant. Defendants' rights were recognized, the defendant was given an opportunity to present a defense in court, and the brutal features of the early inquisitorial process were abolished.

inquisitorial process

Contemporary Inquisitorial Process

Modern European criminal process is still described as inquisitorial because of the central role the judge plays in examining the accused and the witnesses and developing evidence during the pretrial investigation which plays an important role in European criminal adjudication. Over time, however, this process has been tempered by concern for the rights of the accused and basic standards of humanity. Torture and coerced confessions have been abolished. The defendant now has the right to legal counsel and may raise a defense against the charges. Consequently, the distinction between adversarial and inquisitorial adjudication is less marked than in earlier periods.

Defendants are not presumed innocent as this concept is understood in an adversarial system nor are they presumed guilty. Rather the examining magistrate has a legal duty to search out all evidence, whether it points to the accused's guilt or innocence. Both the prosecutor (or examining judge) and the trial judges are given the task of discovering all the facts surrounding a charge. There is strong emphasis on conducting a complete investigation of any criminal matter, including a search for evidence that might absolve the defendant.

The inquisitorial process also puts great emphasis on the written record of the investigation before the trial. In many instances the written record of the investigation serves as the basis for the conviction. Unless a defendant requests an opportunity to examine a witness, the trial may proceed on the written record of the judicial investigation.

■ MODERN FRENCH CRIMINAL PROCESS

The French system of criminal investigation and trial is a classic example of the modern inquisitorial process. In contrast to their counterparts in Britain and the United States, judges in France play a central role in investigating the case, questioning the various witnesses as well as the accused, and conducting the trial.

The process is dominated by law-trained civil servants who have gone through a special three-year training program and passed a qualifying exam. Those who pass the exam are assigned to serve either as a procurator or a judge. Both are magistrates and members of the same judicial organization but fulfill different roles (Vouin 1970, 483). The **procurator,** roughly equivalent to an American prosecutor, directs the police investigation, determines the likelihood that a crime

procurator

has been committed, and decides whether a judicial examination should be ordered. Judges conduct judicial investigations (involving the more serious offenses) and hear trials.

Defense counsel must have a university law degree and pass several qualifying exams. Defense lawyers work in private practice rather than for the government. Defendants who cannot afford to hire an attorney may apply for legal aid. If granted, the president of the local bar association appoints an attorney to represent the defendant. Attorneys receiving legal aid, however, are paid only for their direct expenses, such as secretarial or investigative assistance. They are not compensated for the time they spend on the case. This situation has made the system quite unpopular with the private attorneys, who may provide less than zealous representation of the indigent as a result (Terrill 1987).

Criminal offenses in France are classified in three categories of varying seriousness. The more serious the offense, the more elaborate the judicial procedures used in prosecuting the offense. Minor criminal offenses, called *contraventions,* are prosecuted by the police before a single judge. These offenses are similar to petty misdemeanors in the United States (Terrill 1987, 129; Goldstein and Marcus 1977, 250). *Delits* are crimes punishable by imprisonment for two months to five years. The most serious crimes, called *crimes,* are punishable by imprisonment for five years or more (Goldstein and Marcus 1977, 250). *Delits* and *crimes* are tried in different courts and, although in theory the procedures for prosecuting *delits* and *crimes* are similar, in practice the prosecution of *delits* is much more streamlined.

In addition to these three categories of offenses, French law distinguishes between flagrant and nonflagrant offenses. An offense may be defined as flagrant in a number of circumstances, most commonly because the offender is caught in the act or the police are in hot pursuit of the offender. Flagrant offenses are expected to trigger immediate action to apprehend the accused and to secure any evidence or witnesses that may be available. If an offense is flagrant, the police have much broader powers to investigate than they have in other cases. Some studies suggest that most offenses are treated as flagrant offenses. As a result the police do most of the investigative work on their own rather than follow the more formal process of investigation under the supervision of the procurator or examining magistrate (Goldstein and Marcus 1977, 253).

Initiation of Cases

When a crime is reported to the police, the police initiate the investigation. If the offense is deemed flagrant, the police may secure the crime scene, search for evidence and weapons, and detain and interview witnesses (Terrill 1987, 142). The police are also required to report the crime to the procurator, but in many cases, particularly for *delits,* the police complete the investigation before the procurator receives notice of the offense. In these cases the police report becomes the main evidence at trial (Goldstein and Marcus 1977, 255).

The procurator has ultimate responsibility for the investigation of the offense and the pretrial procedures that are followed. Although in most cases the police carry out the actual investigation, the procurator retains a supervisory role and may influence the amount of effort and the direction of the investigation by the police. If the procurator does not intend to issue charges, the police need not invest time and effort in investigating the crime and developing evidence.

In some cases the investigation of a crime may be carried out by a magistrate. This procedure is called a judicial investigation. For *delits* the procurator has discretion whether to order a judicial examination, but less than 10 percent of *delits* are investigated in this way (Frase 1990, 575). A judicial examination is required for all *crimes*. If a judicial examination is required, an examining magistrate is assigned to conduct a complete and impartial investigation. Assisted by the police, the examining magistrate interviews witnesses, issues search warrants, and authorizes the arrest of a suspect (Frase 1990, 575). Clearly, the examining magistrate has enormous investigative powers and responsibilities.

Whether a case is investigated by the police under the distant supervision of the procurator, by the procurator directly conducting the investigation, or through the judicial examination, the role of investigating officials is viewed not simply as "making a case" against the accused but as finding the truth of the matter. In this nonadversarial context French law does not require that a neutral third party authorize search and arrest warrants. Under French law the investigating procurator or magistrate is deemed neutral. The procurator is not trying to win a case, but simply to find the truth.

The procurator may also decide whether to prosecute an offense as a *crime* or as a *delit*. It is common for the procurator to process as *delits* cases that could have been treated as *crimes* (Goldstein and Marcus 1977). Treating the offense as a *delit* eliminates the necessity of holding a judicial examination. The defendant may challenge this decision and demand that the case be treated as a *crime* so that the case undergoes a judicial examination. In most cases, however, defendants are grateful to have the charges reduced to a lesser category and do not object to this procedure. The procurator's discretion may also be checked by the victim or by the court; a procurator's decision to lower the seriousness of the charges is not unilateral (Goldstein and Marcus 1977, 252).

Interrogations

The French trial process depends heavily on the written record of interrogations conducted during the investigation by the police, procurator, and examining magistrate. The statements of witnesses and the accused are obtained through formal interviews. Witnesses are interrogated under oath. All statements are then included in the *dossier,* the complete investigative file that becomes part of the central evidence at trial.

During an interrogation of the accused the examining magistrate is required to inform the person of the charge, the right to remain silent, and the right to an attorney (Terrill 1987, 145). In some cases the interrogation of the accused and the victim are carried out simultaneously in a proceeding called a confrontation. The confrontation allows both parties to hear the accusations and responses of the other. Counsel for the accused and for the victim may also ask questions that are approved by the examining magistrate. All this occurs in the magistrate's chambers rather than in open court.

In this sense the judicial investigation is analogous to the taking of depositions in an American civil case, with one important difference. The French judicial investigation is not adversarial. The examining magistrate is the person responsible for deciding which witnesses will be interrogated and what questions will be asked. The accused may request that additional witnesses be questioned, and ordinarily these requests are granted, but the examining magistrate is still fully in control of the process.

A full judicial examination is conducted in only a small proportion of cases. Most cases are relatively routine and straightforward, the evidence is clear, the accused has confessed to the crime, and the procurator concludes that it is not necessary to refer the case to an examining magistrate for a judicial examination. Just as jury trials are relatively rare in the United States, full judicial examinations are relatively rare in France, except for the most serious offenses.

Trial Procedure

Unlike the United States, where trials are held for only a small proportion of all defendants, trials are held in all cases in France. However, the fact that a trial is held does not necessarily mean that the defendant contests the charges. In most cases the defendant has confessed to the crime before the trial and repeats the confession in court. The judges have before them the record of the investigation. As a result in most cases the trial in a French court resembles the taking of a guilty plea and sentencing in an American court. Although defendants are undoubtedly encouraged to confess in order to obtain a more lenient sentence, plea bargaining does not exist in the French system because there is no guilty plea. A confession, which is essentially a description of what happened in the defendant's own words, is not the same as pleading guilty to the charges brought by the prosecution. A confession relates one version of the facts to which the law still must be applied. A guilty plea in the American system, in contrast, is a decision not to contest the legal charges as they have been applied to the defendant.

Three judges preside over trials for *crimes*. Nine lay jurors are then selected to hear and decide the case with the three judges. Selection of the jurors includes an opportunity for both the procurator and defense counsel to challenge jurors and have them dismissed from the panel (Terrill 1987, 149). Note that the panel of judges and jurors in the French criminal trial is twelve persons, exactly the same number on the jury in the traditional Anglo-American system.

Although the judicial examination is conducted in private, the trial is generally open to the public (Terrill 1987, 149). The central piece of evidence at trial is the *dossier,* the official report of the preliminary investigation, but additional witnesses and evidence may be requested at trial by the head judge or by the defense counsel. The defendant and defense counsel have an opportunity to review the *dossier* before trial and prepare a defense. In most cases the defense has little to do once the case reaches trial. Usually, the defense strategy is to emphasize the character of the defendant and mitigating circumstances that explain the defendant's behavior (Merryman and Clark 1978, 703).

The *president*, or head judge of the panel, has the primary responsibility of assuring that all potential evidence relating to the offense has been uncovered so that the truth can be ascertained. The other judges and the jurors may ask questions with the permission of the *president*. The procurator may pose questions directly to witnesses, but the accused or counsel for the defense may ask questions only through the *president* (Terrill 1987, 150). All types of evidence may be admitted at trial, including hearsay and evidence illegally obtained by the police. In deliberating, the judges are expected to take the nature of the evidence into account in deciding whether to convict. As a result French trials are not punctutated by the objections of counsel the way Anglo-American trials frequently are (Merryman and Clark 1978, 703).

In about 20 percent of criminal cases the victim brings a civil action simultaneously with the criminal action, seeking compensation for injuries suffered because of the crime (Frase 1990, 613). The victim, referred to as the civil party, may be represented by counsel. During the criminal trial the civil party may also ask questions through the *president*.

After the introduction of the evidence the procurator, the civil party, and the accused have an opportunity to make final statements to the court, and the judges and jurors retire to deliberate. The vote on the verdict is taken by secret ballot. Unanimity is not required. Eight of the twelve judges and jurors must vote to convict. Following a vote to convict, the judges and jurors vote again on the sanction. A majority must agree to the punishment imposed. The civil claims brought by the civil party are decided by the judges alone, without the help of the lay jurors.

The trial process for *delits* is similar, but the case is heard by a panel of three judges, and no lay jurors are involved. Because of the heavy reliance on the *dossier* in proving the charges, trials of *delits* are usually quite brief.

Summary: French Criminal Court Process

Distinguishing between *crimes* and *delits* is an important determination that influences the type of criminal procedures that will be followed in the case. The procurator has broad discretion to handle a case as a *crime* or as a *delit*. Most criminal cases are resolved with little formal action, with the police report and confession of the accused serving as the principal pieces of evidence at trial. The trial is likely to be brief and in most cases focuses primarily on issues relating to the sentence to be imposed rather than contesting the charges.

The defendant retains the opportunity to put on a complete defense to the crime. Normally, the defense would seek to shape the *dossier* by suggesting avenues for investigation that the procurator or examining magistrate may have overlooked. As a last resort the defense may seek to present witnesses in court to rebut the charges of the procurator. In most cases, however, the chief goal of defense counsel is to obtain leniency in sentencing.

▢ CRIMINAL PROCESS IN SAUDI ARABIA

Despite European colonial expansion in the Middle East during the nineteenth century, a number of Middle Eastern nations have retained or reinstated systems of criminal law and criminal procedure based on Islamic teachings. Although the true content of an Islamic legal system remains a matter of debate, the ideal of government under Islamic law, or *Shari'a,* is strong among many people in the Middle East. Having an understanding of the nature of criminal law and criminal procedure in Islamic culture is increasingly important for Americans today. Islam is the dominant religion in an area stretching from northwestern Africa to the islands of Malaysia and the Philippines in the South Pacific. Twenty-three countries have declared Islam their official religion.

Islam was founded in Medina (in present-day Saudi Arabia) by the prophet Muhammad in 622 A.D. (Coulson 1964, 10). The most holy writings of the faith are in the *Qur'an* (Koran), which is understood to be the direct word of Allah (God). The *Qur'an* is a poetic book containing a blueprint for an orderly society. Part of this blueprint consists of detailed rules for relationships between people.

Muhammad established and ruled a community of the faithful in Medina. The laws of the community were borrowed from local customs but subject to the changes demanded by the new faith. Muhammad served as judge in disputes that arose in the community. The *Sunna* of the prophet, which means the practice of Muhammad, is the second most important source of Islamic law, second only to the *Qur'an* (Coulson 1964, 39). The judicial decisions of Muhammad offer an example of divinely inspired practice for other judges to follow in deciding cases in which the *Qur'an* does not make clear which rules apply.

Following Muhammad's death, there was no clear successor to the role of religious leader for the community. The caliphs, or temporal successors of Muhammad, assumed the judicial responsibilities (Coulson 1964, 23; Pipes 1983, 43). Frequently, neither the *Qur'an* nor the *Sunna* offered a clear answer to some questions of law. Over time different schools of legal thought arose, each specifying a different procedure for interpreting the *Shari'a* and finding correct Islamic rules. By the end of the ninth century four schools had evolved that agreed on the core principles for finding the law. Nonetheless, the followers of Islam continued to be divided by differing understandings of the requirements of the *Qur'an* as applied to their lives and the governing of a nation.

Substantive Law of the *Shari'a*

The separation between church and state enshrined in the U.S. Constitution is a distinctly foreign concept under Islamic law. Islamic society does not separate the religious and the secular (Cottrell 1980, 283). Both are part of the continuous fabric of society. Islam requires that within the *umma* (community of faith) all law and policy should conform to divine will (Cottrell 1980, 283). "While Western law has few regulations governing everyday life, preferring to limit only those things that need to be controlled, Islamic law prescribes clear-cut rules for daily living" (Knudten 1992, 15).

The distinction in Western law between criminal and civil offenses is not a concept that Islamic law recognizes (Knudten 1992, 18). Instead, Muslim scholars classify crimes in three categories.

The *hudud* are offenses defined and punished according to specific directives in the *Qu'ran* and *Sunna*. The *Qu'ran* specifies penalties for only a handful of offenses. Muslim scholars agree that the *hudud* includes adultery (sexual inter course outside of marriage), theft, banditry (theft by means of force), and defamation (false accusation of unchastity). Some scholars include three additional offenses within the *hudud*: transgression (rebellion against a legitimate Islamic ruler), drinking alcohol, and apostasy (departure from religious principles) (Sanad 1991, 50).

Qisas involve offenses against bodily integrity, punishment for which is a right of the victim or the victim's family. *Qisas* include murder, voluntary and involuntary killing, and intentional and unintentional physical injury to another. For intentional *qisas* offenses the victim or victim's male blood relatives may claim the right of *talion* (retaliation); the retaliation is equivalent to the injury committed. According to the Prophet Muhammad,

> And we prescribed for them therein: The life for the life, and the eye for the eye, and the nose for the nose, and the ear for the ear, and the tooth for the tooth, and for wounds retaliation. (Sanad 1991, 61)

Rules circumscribe the execution of the *talion* to ensure that it does not exceed the severity of the original offense. In contrast to the severe penalties of *talion* for intentional injuries, only monetary penalties are imposed for unintentional killing and injury in relation to the status of the person who is injured (Sanad 1991, 61–62).

Ta'zir are the least serious offenses in Islamic law. They are based on the Muslim state's right to criminalize and punish inappropriate behaviors, although the ruler must make *ta'zir* laws consistent with the *Shari'a* (Sanad 1991). These crimes are defined by legislation and may be tried in administrative tribunals rather than in *Shari'a* courts (Newman 1982, 568, note 21; "The Legal System of Saudi Arabia" 1990, 5.240.13).

Ta'zir are punished through a range of penalties, including death, flagellation, imprisonment, and fines (Sanad 1991, 65). During much of the nineteenth and twentieth centuries governments in Islamic countries have used *ta'zir*, fashioned after European laws, to both fill in the gaps in *Shari'a* law and to bypass the severe punishments demanded by *hudud* and *qisas*. Because the laws pronounced in the *Qur'an* are stated in relatively general terms, it is possible to borrow more specific variations of offenses from European codes and attach less draconian penalties to these "new offenses" (Newman 1982).

For example, for the *hudud* crime of theft the hands of the thief are cut off. By creating *ta'zir* that define more precise crimes of theft (theft of food, theft of machinery, and so on) and by attaching less severe penalties governments can avoid the harsh penalties of the *hudud*.

Procedural Law of the *Shari'a*

Shari'a requires that the ruler establish a judicial system and that the judges be selected from among the legal scholars of the community. Except when Muslim rule is threatened, the ruler is required to adhere to the *Shari'a*, establishing the principle of the rule of law in the Islamic legal system.

Little concern is given in *Shari'a* to procedural requirements, because the judges are expected to be just in their rulings (Newman 1982). In this respect the emphasis is more on the justice of the final decision than on the procedural rules that are followed to obtain any particular result. Perhaps because of the severity of the law revealed in the penalties prescribed, Islamic law includes a strong presumption of innocence. The Prophet Muhammad said, "Avoid condemning the Muslim to *hudud* whenever you can and when you can find a way out for the Muslim then release him for it. If the Imam errs it is better that he errs in favor of innocence than in favor of guilt" (Sanad 1991, 72).

Consequently, the rules of evidence and standards of proof are quite rigorous under Islamic law. A defendant cannot be convicted of an offense on the basis of circumstantial evidence, but the defendant may raise circumstantial evidence to prove innocence. Authorities disagree about whether this rule applies only to *hudud* and *qisas*, or whether it applies to *ta'zir* as well (Sanad 1991, 73). Because of the rule against circumstantial evidence witnesses must have direct knowledge of the crime, which usually means that they witnessed the crime. For most crimes the *Shari'a* requires that at least two male Muslims testify orally to their direct knowledge of the truth (Coulson 1964, 125). Some crimes require more witnesses. For example, for the crime of fornication four witnesses must personally observe the act of intercourse for the testimony to qualify under the rules of evidence. "As a result of requiring four witnesses in adultery, it is reported that during the whole Islamic history not one adultery crime has been proven by testimony. Only the confession of the accused has been the grounds of conviction" (Sanad 1991, 100).

In lieu of the testimony of witnesses, confession of the accused may serve to convict (Mayer 1987, 174). Islamic law includes injunctions against coerced confessions. The right to retract a confession, making it inadmissible for proof of the crime, offers protection against the temptation to coerce confessions (Sanad 1991).

A defendant under *Shari'a* law has an explicit right to make a defense (Sanad 1991). Defendant rights include

- The right to be informed of the charges and evidence being brought to establish the case.
- The right to retain counsel. This right is extended equally to the accused and the accuser.
- The right to have a reasonable opportunity to present evidence and raise a defense.

Despite the formal right to counsel, retaining defense counsel is discouraged, and the defendants are expected to defend themselves (Moore 1987; Fairchild 1993). False accusations are discouraged by severe punishment. For example, if a person accuses another person of unchastity but is unable to produce the necessary eyewitnesses, the person making the accusation is liable for punishment, in this case eighty lashes, according to the *Qur'an*.

Differing Interpretations of the *Shari'a*

For many reasons predominantly Islamic countries vary widely with respect to their interpretation and application of the *Shari'a* (Mayer 1987, 132). Some differences date from the centuries just after the founding of Islam and the death of Muhammad. Different Islamic sects and different legal schools hold differing interpretations of the requirements of *Shari'a*. Additional differences have arisen in response to foreign influences and the pressures toward modernization.

Originally, Islamic law was tolerant of the diversity of interpretations of the law (Mayer 1987, 154; Newman 1982, 565). More recently, however, particularly since the 1967 Arab-Israeli War, the Middle East has experienced an upsurge in political movements calling for a return to the "true meaning" of Islamic law. Some countries, notably Iran, Pakistan, Libya, and the Sudan, have engaged in a political process of establishing an Islamic state that is intended to be an expression of the true meaning of Islam. Although each of these countries has established a legal system that it purports to be the sole authoritative statement of *Shari'a* requirements, their versions of Islamic law are quite different from each other and from the classical *Shari'a* law practiced in Saudi Arabia (Mayer 1987, 153–154).

Consequently, it is neither possible nor proper to speak of a single Islamic law. Even after studying the legal systems of predominantly Islamic countries and recognizing the cultural and political significance of the Islamic religion in these countries, it is impossible to make blanket assumptions about what the criminal justice system of each country is like. Similarly, despite the principles of *Shari'a* law described above, a particular Islamic country may differ from these generalities in a variety of ways without necessarily considering itself any less an Islamic state than another.

Criminal Justice in Saudi Arabia

The Saudi Arabian legal system has been described as the most traditional within the Islamic world; it follows one of the early legal schools for resolving those questions of law that could not be answered by direct reference to the *Qur'an* or the *Sunna* of the prophet (Cottrell 1980, 304; Mayer 1987, 134). Saudi Arabia has been described as the leader in the use of orthodox *Shari'a* law today (Sanad 1991). Saudi Arabia is the seat of Islam, the home of Islam's holiest places, and the destination of the pilgrimage (the *haj*) that all faithful are enjoined to make at least once in their lives.

Although most Muslim countries adopted European criminal codes during the last 150 years and abolished the *Shari'a* criminal law, this did not occur in large areas of the Arabian Peninsula (Coulson 1964, 154). Unlike other Middle Eastern nations, parts of Saudi Arabia escaped the foreign domination of European imperialism. As a result whole areas of law in Saudi Arabia have been relatively untouched by Western secularizing influences (Mayer 1987, 134). These characteristics of Saudi Arabia are perhaps all the more important because of the country's wealth and political power, both in the region and around the world.

Criminal Courts in Saudi Arabia

Saudi Arabia has a four-tiered system of *Shari'a* courts to deal separately with petty cases, serious cases, and appeals. In addition to the *Shari'a* courts, Saudi Arabia has established a variety of commissions and tribunals to adjudicate cases arising under administrative regulations, most of which pertain to commercial activity. However, some matters considered by these non-*Shari'a* tribunals, involve conduct that would be considered criminal in other countries, for example, bribery and forgery ("The Legal System of Saudi Arabia" 1990, 5.240.19).

The *Shari'a* courts deal with two kinds of cases: public right cases, involving offenses against the prerogatives of God, and private right cases, involving personal injury offenses. The same court and the same judges hear both types of cases, and a private right case may be joined with a public right case at a single court hearing. The same court procedures are used for both private right and public right cases. In other words, there is no distinction between civil and criminal procedure as there is in the United States (Brand 1986, 10).

Courts of limited jurisdiction hear petty cases only. Decisions in these courts are made by a single judge. Punishments are at the discretion of the judge, because no penalty is prescribed by the *Shari'a* for these offenses. The general court has jurisdiction over crimes, torts, and personal and family law. Decisions in the general court are made by one judge unless the case involves a death sentence, mutilation, or other specific characteristics, in which case a panel of three judges decides the case ("The Legal System of Saudi Arabia" 1990, 5.240.15).

A court of appeals handles most appeals from both the limited courts and general courts. Exceptional cases may be appealed to the Supreme Judicial Council, which is primarily a supervisory body of the *Shari'a* courts.

Criminal Procedure

Initiation of prosecution varies by the type of offense. Because *hudud* are crimes against God, any Muslim can bring charges against a defendant. *Qisas* and *ta'zir* that involve personal injury can be brought by the injured party (Sanad 1991, 66). The police have responsibility for commencing a public right of action. The police officer who investigates the case is also responsible for representing the government as the prosecutor at trial (Brand 1986, 12).

Once a charge has been made, the defendant must be notified of the charges and allowed a reasonable time to prepare a defense. Procedure in *Shari'a* court is informal. There is no uniform code of procedure that all courts must follow. The *qadi* (judge) is responsible for questioning the parties. Although a defendant may be represented by counsel, because of the simplicity and lack of technical expertise required in *Shari'a* courts there is little concern with having attorneys represent the parties. Indeed Saudi Arabia has few lawyers.

Trials are formally public ("The Legal System of Saudi Arabia" 1990, 5.240.18), but spectators and the press generally are not present. Trials are usually held in a small office and may be held in secret if the "interests of morality" require it. The defendant has a right to be present at trial, but this right is effectively waived if the defendant fails to appear after two notices. In such a case the defendant may be tried in absentia (Moore 1987, 66).

The court is required to make a record of its finding of facts and legal reasoning. The burden is on the government to prove that the accused committed the offense charged. Thus the *Shari'a* presumes that the defendant is innocent until proved guilty (Brand 1986, 12; Hagel 1983, 136).

As noted earlier, *Shari'a* law requires proof by the testimony of a set number of witnesses (two or four, depending on the offense) or the confession of the accused. A non-Muslim may not give evidence against a Muslim defendant. Generally, only men are allowed to testify, but some jurists allow the testimony of two women to substitute for the testimony of one male witness. All witnesses must be of good character and integrity, and their righteousness must be beyond doubt. A witness may not testify against a member of his immediate family or if he would benefit from the outcome of the case in any way (Lippman, McConville, and Yerushalmi 1988, 69). If the government produces the required witnesses, the defendant may not present contradictory evidence.

No crime may be proved by circumstantial evidence alone. "A homicide, for instance, cannot be proved by the fact that the witness overheard a violent struggle, saw the accused emerge from his house with a blood-stained knife, and then discovered the victim's body in the house" (Lippman, McConville, and Yurashalmi 1988, 70). Such evidence can convict only if accompanied by fifty oaths of relatives of the victim.

When the government is unable to produce the necessary witnesses the defendant may be required to take an oath denying the crime. The law assumes that a person would not take a false oath, because to swear falsely would be a terrible sin. Moreover, perjury, if discovered, is punishable by imprisonment or lashing. If the defendant refuses to take the oath, the defendant is found guilty despite the lack of proof. The judge decides the verdict and pronounces sentence. If the defendant takes the oath, the defendant is found not guilty (Brand 1986, 12).

Appeals are automatic in cases involving death or mutilation. In less serious cases the losing party may file for appeal within fifteen days of the judgment (Fairchild 1993, 182). Petty crimes, carrying penalties of no more than forty lashes or ten days' imprisonment, may not be appealed (Moore 1987, 64). Following a successful appeal, the case is returned to the original court for reconsideration (Fairchild 1993, 182).

Summary: Saudi Arabian Criminal Process

The Saudi Arabian legal system is based on the religious teachings of the Prophet Muhammad. Compared to other countries, Saudi Arabia's criminal process has changed little since the ninth century. Unlike other Islamic countries that have experienced reform of their court and legal systems, the Saudi Arabian system continues to carry out the traditions of the *Shari'a*. Laypersons do not take part in deciding cases; all decisions are made by professional judges. Although the trial is formally public, it is typically held in a small office and observers are usually not present. The burden is on the government to prove the guilt of the accused. Because of strict rules of evidence that prevent the use of circumstantial evidence, conviction requires the testimony of a certain number of witnesses or, as is more often the case, the confession of the accused. Unlike our own courts, which assume that witnesses on either side of a court case may have reason to lie in court, the Saudi Arabian procedure assumes that people will speak the truth under oath or not speak at all. To lie would be a terrible violation of the teachings of the *Qur'an*. As a result court procedure is simple and straightforward.

◼ CRIMINAL PROCESS IN CHINA

Criminal process in China offers yet another contrast. China is a land of traditions quite different from our own. Chinese rulers throughout history have sought to insulate the Chinese people from foreign influences. As a result Chinese criminal courts retain a purely Chinese element that has not been contaminated by colonial domination (Cheng 1988, 191). Nonetheless, the Chinese criminal court system has absorbed elements of the socialist system and civil law system through its emulation of the Soviet legal system during the 1960s. In addition, the legal ideals held by the leaders of the short-lived Chinese Republic early in the twentieth century continue to exert an influence on Chinese legal philosophy. Thus, the Chinese court process offers another interesting contrast to the adversarial system of common law.

Early Chinese philosophy de-emphasized law in favor of informal norms and persuasion. Confucius, the great Chinese philosopher of the fifth century B.C., observed harmony in nature and advocated harmony in all things human. Because of this traditional stress on harmony Chinese legal traditions have emphasized the value of compromise and viewed formal legal systems as inferior to persuasion and mediation in resolving disputes. During most of China's history the Confucian philosophy of harmony and mediation has been dominant. Since the communist revolution of 1949 these traditional philosophies have been revised and adapted in ways that would be consistent with "Marxist-Leninist-Mao Zedong" thought.

When China was under the influence of the Soviet Union in the 1950s, the Chinese drafted legal codes patterned after Soviet models. Nonetheless, Mao Zedong believed that "the persuasive force of right ideological thinking" was the key to social harmony. Mao advocated the use of persuasion, mediation, and self-criticism to resolve disputes between people. Punishment was reserved for enemies of the revolution (Folsom and Minan 1989, 9–10). During the Cultural Revolution (1966–1976), the Chinese repudiated written law in favor of the rule of the masses. "Trial by the masses," in which the crowd observing the public condemnation of the accused decided both guilt and sentence, was a common event (Cheng 1988, 195).

Since the end of the Cultural Revolution in 1976 many former "enemies of the revolution" have again obtained positions of power in China. These leaders still value informal mediation of private disputes over formal prosecution, because mediation emphasizes the communal obligations of the individual. Nonetheless, through hard personal experience these leaders have learned the importance of law as a limit on power (Cheng 1988, 192). Consequently, a number of laws passed since the end of the Cultural Revolution, including the Code of Criminal Procedure of 1980 and the 1982 Constitution, emphasize the rule of law and explicitly state that the law is the supreme authority (Folsom and Minan 1989, 52).

Two Methods of Resolving Disputes

The Chinese distinguish between minor criminal offenses and more serious offenses. In minor cases the situation may be handled through mediation rather than through formal adjudication in the courts. However, the law does not make clear which offenses are suitable for mediation and which for formal prosecution. Consequently, the police and local mediation officials have much discretion in that decision (Folsom and Minan 1989, 330).

In China, an administrative sanction of "rehabilitation through labor" also may be imposed on individuals without following the procedures of criminal courts. Under rehabilitation through labor a person may be confined to a labor camp for as long as four years (Cohen 1982, 136).

Mediation

Mediation practices have evolved from the Confucian tradition emphasizing harmony and compromise. Mao also favored mediation as consistent with his theory of social justice and social control (Felkenes 1986, 345). The intention is to maintain public order by ending disputes without creating bad feelings between the parties. Mediation also serves the interests of the government by stressing the importance of communal values over individual rights (Folsom and Minan 1989, 97).

Much mediation occurs outside the formal mediation procedures established by the state. Grandparents, neighborhood leaders, and friends mediate disputes within the family or social group (Folsom and Minan 1989, 87). State-sponsored mediation committees organized in neighborhoods and work groups conduct state mediation to resolve disputes among residents and employees. "The role of the mediation committees is to hear the parties [sic] concerns, investigate facts, be polite and patient and employ 'the method of persuasion' " (Folsom and Minan 1989, 88).

China has more than eight hundred thousand mediation committees, each composed of three to eleven members (Folsom and Minan 1989, 88; Leng and Chiu 1985, 68). Mediators are elected by popular vote for a two-year term (Leng and Chiu 1985, 68), although party activists are more likely to be nominated for these positions (Lubman 1969, 98). In the mid-1980s the Ministry of Justice reported that 6.25 million cases were mediated each year (Felkenes 1986, 346). These cases included minor criminal matters, including theft and minor assaults, and about 90 percent of all civil cases. In 1981 mediation committees handled almost thirteen times as many civil and minor criminal cases as the local courts. Although mediation does not foreclose the option of bringing a legal suit, most cases end at this stage. However, in some cases, one party may choose to pursue the matter in court, or the mediation committee may refer relatively serious cases to court or to local prosecutors (Folsom and Minan 1989, 88).

Individual disputes are frequently translated by the mediators into expressions of national policy issues. For example, "a husband who mistreats his wife is characterized by a judge as feudal; a mother-in-law who squabbles with her son's wife is told that the disagreements are caused by old ideology; a young married couple unable to adjust their married life to their employment schedules is told that they must 'serve national construction' " (Lubman 1969, 99–100).

Mediation does not mean that the process is necessarily less invasive or disruptive of a person's autonomy and privacy than a criminal prosecution would be. Mediators do not merely respond to disputes that may be brought to them. They also intervene in situations that threaten social harmony and societal values.

Mediation committees institutionalize informal social control, perhaps reducing the number of cases that need to be brought into the criminal justice system. At the same time mediation committees sometimes extend the agents of government into what Westerners would consider strictly private affairs, refusing to relent until the matter is resolved to the satisfaction of the mediation committee.

Adjudication

Adjudication of criminal cases is carried out through the joint efforts of the public security organ (police), the people's procuratorates (prosecutors), and the people's courts. "The public security organs are responsible for investigation, detention and preliminary interrogation in criminal cases. The people's procuratorates are responsible for approving arrests, performing procuratorial work (including investigation) and instituting public prosecution. The people's courts are responsible for trying cases. No other organ, group or individual has the authority to exercise these powers" (Kim Chin 1985, Article 3, p. 33). Citizens have the duty to report suspected violations of the law to public security organs, procuratorates, or courts. When any of these receives evidence that a crime has likely been committed by a particular person, the case is filed. Once the case is filed, the formal investigation of the case may commence (Folsom and Minan 1989, 306; Kim Chin 1985). In other cases a public security officer or, in limited circumstances, a citizen may seize and detain a suspect and turn the person over to the public security organ, procuratorate, or people's court (Folsom and Minan 1989, 306), which may hold the person for a maximum of seven days. The procurator then may authorize a longer period of detention during the investigation of the case.

Once the case is filed or a suspect apprehended, members of the public security organ and the procuratorate investigate the evidence supporting the complaint. The investigation may include interrogation of the accused, questioning of witnesses, examination of physical evidence, and expert evaluations, if necessary. Searches for evidence may be conducted with a warrant, but the procedures and standards for obtaining a warrant are not spelled out (Chin Kim 1985, Articles 79–83). If the procurator finds the complaint is supported by evidence that is "reliable and complete," a prosecution in people's court is initiated (Folsom and Minan 1989, 307). Several different government organs may review the decision to prosecute or not prosecute (Folsom and Minan 1989, 308). Nonetheless, the procuratorate is able to screen out cases that do not warrant criminal prosecution, and the law specifies a variety of reasons for not prosecuting, including circumstances that do not warrant treating the conduct as a crime (Cheng 1988, 202).

Throughout the investigation and interrogation of the accused, the accused is not informed of the charges. Only when the procurator serves a bill of prosecution outlining the charges, which may occur any time up to seven days before trial, is the accused notified of the charges. Further, a suspect has no right to defense counsel until after being informed of the charges (Folsom and Minan 1989, 309). Once notified of the charges, defense counsel may examine the materials relevant to the case, including taking notes on the case file, interviewing the defendant, and corresponding with a defendant in custody.

Defense Counsel

The role of defense counsel in China is more limited than in the United States or even in civil law countries. In 1986 China had only about seven thousand lawyers;

its population was about one billion (Felkenes 1986, 346). Most of these lawyers do criminal defense work. They view themselves as working for and on behalf of the government, rather than on behalf of the defendant. Criminal defense lawyers in China see their role as working to assure that the truth is found, not to question the evidence in order to make it difficult to convict the defendant. A lawyer who deliberately shields a guilty defendant from prosecution is liable for criminal punishment (Epp 1989, 319). The sole role of counsel is to present any facts that tend to exculpate the defendant and that the prosecution may have overlooked.

If the defendant admits guilt to the attorney, the attorney is required to plead the defendant guilty at trial. There is no attorney-client privilege between the Chinese attorney and client. Any information given or statements made to defense counsel that implicate the defendant in the crime are to be turned over to the prosecution.

The Chinese justice system places a premium on confession. A defendant must confess in order to be considered worthy of lenience in punishment. The defense attorney's role frequently involves persuading the defendant to confess. The criminal defendant in China has no right to remain silent, and if the defendant chooses to remain silent, the court may infer guilt from the defendant's failure to speak (Epp 1989, 317–320). After the confession the attorney's other principal task is to argue for a mitigation of the penalty. For example, defense counsel may point out that the crime was not premeditated, that the defendant was not the ring leader, or that this was the defendant's first serious transgression (Lehman and Niemeyer 1989, 4).

Trial and Standard of Evidence

Trials in the people's courts are open and public, carried out either by a judge acting alone (minor cases only) or by a judge sitting with lay assessors elected by the people to serve two-year terms. The assessors serve for about two weeks each year. The professional judges and lay assessors have equal powers and equal roles at trial. Both may ask questions, and both may decide what evidence may be admitted (Epp 1989, 317).

As in many European countries a civil action may be combined with the criminal prosecution to determine whether the civil party is to be compensated for losses arising from the crime. The civil action is tried simultaneously with the criminal action (Chin Kim 1985, Articles 53–54).

The trial begins with the questioning of the accused, first by members of the court, then—with the permission of the presiding judge—by the procurator, the victim, the plaintiff in a civil action, and the defense counsel. Then they may examine other witnesses and physical or documentary evidence. All parties may ask questions through the presiding judge unless the judge allows questions to be put directly to witnesses. All parties may request additional witnesses to appear in court and to introduce evidence not uncovered by the procurator. Finally, the procurator, the victim, and then the accused make closing statements.

Because the accused often confesses before the trial, and because other written evidence is often submitted to the court before trial, the Chinese trial deemphasizes the taking of testimony. Rather, the trial is an opportunity for the court to express its condemnation of the conduct of the defendant and for the defendant to express remorse. In addition, the court does not narrowly focus on the actions and motives of the accused but may also turn on others whom the court may partially blame for the offense. During a visit to a Chinese criminal trial an American trial lawyer observed the court chastising a witness for lax security procedures in a factory that enabled the defendant to steal from the plant (Strachan 1986, 68).

The Chinese legal standard of evidence requires the courts to "take facts as their basis and law as their criterion" (Chin Kim 1985). Article 36 of the Chinese Criminal Procedure Code requires that testimony of witnesses not be used as the basis for deciding the case until all parties have had an opportunity to confront witnesses in open court. In addition, although the Chinese have no right to remain silent, a defendant may not be convicted solely on the basis of a confession, and coerced confessions are at least formally illegal. "The extortion of confessions by means of torture and the collection of evidence by threat, enticement, deceit or other illegal means are strictly forbidden" (Chin Kim 1985, Article 32). However, given the explicit promise of leniency to defendants who admit their guilt and the practice of defense attorneys to counsel defendants to confess their guilt, the pressures to confess are quite strong. Not surprisingly, 97 percent of people arrested are found guilty (Epp 1989, 315).

The defendant, the procurator, or parties to the supplementary civil action or their legal representatives may appeal the decision of the first-level people's court. If the defendant appeals, the appellate court may not impose a sentence more severe than the original sentence. However, if the procurator appeals, the appellate court may increase the sentence or remand the case to the trial court for retrial, exposing the defendant to double jeopardy (being tried twice for the same crime). The Chinese view this as appropriate, because the goal of the system is to identify and convict guilty persons. The purpose of appellate review is to "seek truth from facts and correct mistakes whenever discovered" (Leng and Chin 1985, 308).

Summary: Chinese Criminal Court Process

The Chinese court process is significantly different from the American adversarial process. Some Chinese legal scholars describe the American system as "two very bright people hired for the purpose of obscuring the truth" (Baker 1989, 340). Many Americans would agree with this characterization. In contrast, the Chinese court system aims first at mediation and self-criticism. If this fails, the task of the courts, and all participants in the court process, is to uncover the truth. In routine cases the processing of cases may not seem very different in China and in the United States. After all, in both systems defendants often admit guilt, and defense counsel focus on minimizing the sentence. The differences between the two systems become most obvious in the difficult cases—when the facts are contested, the defendant does not confess the crime, and especially when the political character of the defendant may be more at issue than the defendant's conduct.

◼ SUMMARY

The French, Saudi Arabian, and Chinese criminal court processes offer a number of important comparisons and contrasts to the American way of "doing justice." As in the U.S. each of these systems has different courts to deal with petty crimes, serious crimes, and appeals. Unlike the U.S. judicial system, however, other systems allow private claims for compensation (civil actions) to be heard during the same court proceeding as the criminal trial. These systems provide an opportunity for the victim and victim's counsel to be heard.

The nature of judicial discretion also varies from one country to another. In France and Saudi Arabia trial court judges do not interpret the law but simply apply existing law. Because other court systems have fewer evidentiary rules than the United States, judges in other countries hear a wider range of information. Judges then have the discretion to decide which evidence is trustworthy and which is not. As in the United States, both France and China provide for the participation of laypersons as triers of fact. Unlike the United States, however, these lay judges are given an opportunity to ask questions of witnesses and search out the facts.

Defendants in all three countries have an opportunity to be represented by counsel. France recognizes the right to counsel, but defense counsel works primarily to assure that the *dossier* is complete. China has few lawyers and no provision for appointed counsel. The laws may limit the ways in which counsel may participate and at what stage counsel may participate. In China, unlike the United States, counsel is required to inform the court if the defendant confesses. There is no attorney-client privilege. Saudi Arabian defendants formally possess a right to counsel, but hiring counsel is strongly discouraged.

Finally, each of these three countries illustrates a different perspective on the relative importance of substantive justice versus procedural justice. For example, China clearly stresses reaching substantive justice and resolving the "problem" that led to the violation of law in the first place. Saudi Arabia places great emphasis on the procedural rules relating to proof. These rules are based on the idea that it is worse to punish an innocent person than to let a guilty person go free.

Each system poses risks of convicting the innocent and freeing the guilty, but the source of these risks varies by country. By understanding how other judicial systems seek to attain substantive justice, we may be better able to understand our own system of justice.

◼ FOR FURTHER DISCUSSION

1. How does each system of criminal justice described in this chapter compare to the U.S. criminal justice system in terms of accessibility, reliability, and legitimacy? Are these the goals that are important in the cultures of these other countries?

2. What are the key differences between the adversarial process and the inquisitorial process? Historically, the inquisitorial process was linked to court procedures that were often cruel and subject to unfair manipulation. Is the inquisitorial process necessarily less fair than the adversarial process?

3. If you were accused of a crime, in which of the systems described here (French, Saudi Arabian, or Chinese) would you prefer to be tried? If you were the victim of a crime, in which of these systems would you prefer that the accused be tried?

4. One measure of the respect for human rights is the fairness of the trial provided to an accused person. Human rights organizations and the U.S. State Department attempt to judge whether the judicial systems of other countries adequately protect human rights by protecting the right to a fair trial. How would you judge the three systems described in this chapter? What additional information would you need to determine whether these countries protect the right to a fair trial?

5. The Chinese put great emphasis on mediation to resolve disputes, even serious disputes that would be called crimes in the United States. Some critics of the U.S. justice system have suggested that many cases that go to the criminal courts ought to be resolved instead through a form of mediation. What advantages and disadvantages do you see in using mediation to resolve disputes that now go through criminal courts?

■ REFERENCES

Baker, Beverly G. 1989. "Chinese Law in the Eighties: The Lawyer and the Criminal Process." In Ralph H. Folsom and John H. Minan, eds. *Law in the People's Republic of China.* Boston: Martinus Nijhoff.

Brand, Joseph L. 1986. "Aspects of Saudi Arabian Law and Practice." *Boston College International and Comparative Law Review* 9 (1): 1–29.

Cheng Yang. 1988. "Criminal Procedure in China: Some Comparisons with the English System." *International and Comparative Law Quarterly* 37: 190–207.

Cohen, Jerome Alan. 1982. "Chinese Criminal Code Symposium: Foreword—China's Criminal Codes." *The Journal of Criminal Law and Criminology* 73: 135–316.

Cottrell, Alvin J., ed. 1980. *The Persian Gulf States: A General Survey.* Baltimore: Johns Hopkins University Press.

David, Rene, and John E. C. Brierly. 1985. *Major Legal Systems in the World Today.* London: Stevens.

Epp, Todd D. 1989. "The New Code of Criminal Procedure in the People's Republic of China: Protection, Problems, and Predictions." In Ralph H. Folsom and John H. Minan, eds. *Law in the People's Republic of China: Commentary, Readings and Materials,* Boston: Martinus Nijhoff.

Fairchild, Erika. 1993. *Comparative Criminal Justice Systems.* Belmont, Calif.: Wadsworth.

Felkenes, George T. 1986. "Criminal Justice in the People's Republic of China: A System of Contradictions." *Judicature* 69 (April–May): 345–52.

Folsom, Ralph H., and John H. Minan. 1989. *Law in the People's Republic of China.* Boston: Martinus Nijhoff.

Frase, Richard S. 1990. "Comparative Criminal Justice as a Guide to American Law Reform: How Do the French Do it, How Can We Find Out, and Why Should We Care?" *California Law Review* 78 (May): 542–683.

Goldstein, Abraham S., and Martin Marcus. 1977. "The Myth of Judicial Supervision in Three 'Inquisitorial' Systems: France, Italy, and Germany." *Yale Law Journal* 87: 240–83.

Hagel, Gali. 1983. "A Practitioner's Introduction to Saudi Arabian Law." *Vanderbilt Journal of Transnational Law* 16: 113–77.

Hoyt, Robert S. 1957. *Europe in the Middle Ages.* New York: Harcourt Brace.

Johnson, Herbert A. 1988. *History of Criminal Justice.* Cincinnati: Anderson.

Kim Chin, trans. 1985. *Criminal Procedure Code of the People's Republic of China of 1980.* The American Series of Foreign Penal Codes. Vol. 26. Littleton, Colo.: Fred B. Rothman.

Knudten, Richard D. 1992. "The Saudi Arabian and Postrevolutionary Iranian Legal Systems." *Wisconsin Sociologist* 29 (Winter): 15–22.

Lehman, Edward E., and John R. Niemeyer. 1989. "The Bailiff Wore Sneakers: A Criminal Trial in China." *C.J. International* 5 (March–April): 4, 6.

Leng Shao-Chuan, and Chiu Hungdah. 1985. *Criminal Justice in Post-Mao China.* Albany: State University of New York Press.

Lippman, Matthew, Sean McConville, and Mordechai Yerushalmi. 1988. *Islamic Criminal Law and Procedure.* Westport, Conn.: Greenwood.

Lubman, Stanley. 1969. "Form and Function in the Chinese Criminal Process." *Columbia Law Review* 69 (April): 535–75.

Mayer, Ann Elizabeth. 1987. "Law and Religion in the Muslim Middle East." *American Journal of Comparative Law* 35: 127–184.

Merryman, John Henry, and David S. Clark. 1978. *Comparative Law: Western European and Latin American Legal Systems*. New York: Bobbs-Merrill.

"The Legal System of Saudi Arabia." 1990. *Modern Legal Systems Cyclopedia*. Buffalo: William Hein.

Moore, Richter H., Jr. 1987. "Courts, Law, Justice, and Criminal Trials in Saudi Arabia." *International Journal of Comparative and Applied Criminal Justice* 11 (Spring): 61–67.

Mueller, Gerhard O. W., and Fre Le Poole-Griffiths. 1969. *Comparative Criminal Procedure*. New York: New York University Press.

Newman, Graeme. 1982. "Khomeini and Criminal Justice: Notes on Crime and Culture." *Journal of Criminal Law and Criminology* 73 (Summer): 561–81.

Pipes, Daniel. 1983. *In the Path of God: Islam and Political Power*. New York: Basic Books.

Sanad, Nagaty. 1991. *The Theory of Crime and Criminal Responsibility in Islamic Law: Shari'a*. Chicago: Office of International Criminal Justice, University of Illinois.

Strachan, Gordon. 1986. "Justice in Shanghai." *Trial* (January): 66–71.

Terrill, Richard J. 1987. *World Criminal Justice Systems: A Survey*. Cincinnati: Anderson.

Vouin, Robert. 1970. "The Role of the Prosecutor in French Criminal Trials." *American Journal of Comparative Law* 18: 483–97.

ACTORS IN THE COURTS

CHAPTER **6**

 # JUDGES

The judge is the figurehead of the adversarial system and the voice of the court. It is through judges that society exercises the authority of the law. Because the judge serves as the guarantor of fairness and legality in the adversarial system, the character and competence of those who serve as judges influence the quality of justice the system produces. For this reason the methods used to select judges, the qualifications and character of those selected, and the training they receive are important considerations. This chapter describes the types of people who become judges, how they are selected to fill their positions, and the socialization and training of judges once they ascend the bench. It also describes the tasks of criminal court judges and considers the disciplinary actions that are available when judges fail to live up to community and professional standards.

☐ BECOMING A JUDGE

Being a judge is one of the most prestigious occupations in American society. Although judicial salaries are low compared to what judges could earn in a private law practice, the prestige and authority of being a judge attract people to the position. Being a judge can also be a stepping-stone to higher judicial office (the federal courts) and other powerful positions, such as attorney general or another high political office.

As a group the sorts of people who become judges are not representative of American society. Women and minorities are underrepresented, and men from privileged backgrounds are overrepresented. The elite characteristics of judges become even more pronounced in the upper levels of the judicial hierarchy, the appellate courts in the federal jurisdiction. The extent to which the relatively homogeneous backgrounds of judges influence judicial decision making remains unclear (Goldman 1975; Goldman and Lamb 1986; Ulmer 1973; Wice 1985, 97–98).

116

Most judges are lawyers. A law degree and some experience as a practicing attorney are the most common qualifications required of judges. All states require that those holding judgeships at the levels of court of general jurisdiction, intermediate appellate court, and court of last resort be licensed to practice law. Two main exceptions to the general requirement are the courts of limited jurisdiction and the U.S. Supreme Court. Many states do not require that judges in the courts of limited jurisdiction be trained or licensed to practice law (*North Carolina v. Russell* 1976; Silberman 1979, 24). Nonetheless, these positions usually are filled by lawyers. At the other end of the spectrum are justices of the United States Supreme Court, who also are not legally required to hold a law degree. However, all Supreme Court justices to date have had law degrees.

The Judiciary: A Traditional Status System

Although the judiciary has been responsible for some of the most controversial social changes in modern times—from school desegregation to the legalization of abortion—judges tend to come from backgrounds associated with conservative and traditional ideas. Judges are predominantly white and male and members of the upper middle class. According to extensive research (Wice 1985; Ryan et al. 1980; Silberman 1979), the typical criminal court judge is a

> man in his late fifties, white, upper middle-class who had a fairly successful law practice before reaching his current position on the bench, which he has held for approximately eight years.

> * * *

> Most of the judges . . . had middle-class parents who were typically either white-collar workers or skilled laborers. Only a very small percentage of judges had a parent who was a lawyer. . . . The ethnic and religious breakdown for white judges closely followed their city's respective demographic characteristics. (Wice 1985, 94–96)

Wice (1985, 95) found members of minority groups markedly underrepresented in trial courts in the urban areas he studied. Women and minorities comprised 12.6 percent of state court judges and 17.4 percent of federal court judges in the mid-1980s ("Merit Selection" 1986, 4).

Wice also reports that judges typically have fifteen to twenty years' experience practicing law before assuming a judgeship. Many—nearly one-third—have some experience as prosecutors (Wice 1985, 96). Although Wice observed that about one-third of the trial court judges seemed biased in favor of the prosecution, they were not necessarily the same judges who had served as prosecutors. In fact, some of those with prosecutorial experience were perceived as favoring the defense (Wice 1985, 97). This finding highlights the difficulty of attributing judicial attitudes and behavior to the background characteristics of judges.

The number of judges on state appellate courts is small, about 7 percent of all state court judges. Appellate judges tend to be a little older than their counterparts on the trial courts. Typically, they assume office after considerable experience as a practicing attorney and often with experience on the trial bench. Although more women and minorities are sitting on state appellate benches than ever before, their numbers are still vastly underrepresented, even in comparison to the number of women and African-Americans in the legal profession (Cook 1987, 9; "Merit Selection" 1986).

Federal judges represent an even more elite group. Even federal district court positions are sufficiently prestigious that only experienced and respected judges or attorneys attain these positions. More than half the appointees in the last twenty-five years have had prior experience as a judge or a prosecutor. Federal district judges are predominantly white, male, and nearly fifty years old at the time of their appointments. More than half of recent appointees attended private colleges for their undergraduate education (Carp and Stidham 1990, 201–3; see Figure 6–1).

About 15 percent of federal judges sit on the U.S. Courts of Appeals (Curran 1985, 16; Maguire and Pastore 1994, 69). Few in number (161 as of 1992, see Maguire and Pastore 1994, 69), these judges are among the most influential jurists in the country, second only to the justices of the U.S. Supreme Court. They occupy some of the most coveted and cherished legal positions in the country. The profile of the federal appellate judge is similar to that of the district judge, except that more of them have had previous judicial experience and more come from the ranks of law school faculty (Carp and Stidham 1990, 205–16). The underrepresentation of women and persons of color is even more pronounced at this level (see Figure 6–2).

The office of justice of the U.S. Supreme Court is without doubt the most revered judicial office in the land. The decisions made by the justices help shape the quality and nature of the freedoms and protections enjoyed by U.S. citizens. Most justices have come from the ranks of the federal judiciary or state supreme courts. A few have had experience as executives in federal or state government. Chief Justice Earl Warren, for example, had been state attorney general and later governor of California. A few others have earned their reputations as federal and state legislators. Only a handful have come from the ranks of law school faculty.

Until 1967 no African-American had ever been appointed to the Supreme Court. In that year Thurgood Marshall, who had argued *Brown v. Board of Education* (the 1954 school desegregation cases) before the Supreme Court, became the first justice of African-American descent. Sandra Day O'Connor became the first woman to serve on the Supreme Court in 1981. Although the nation's highest court is still comprised primarily of white Protestant males, significant incremental changes in gender and racial composition are obvious in recent years. The Court of the mid-1990s is also more religiously and ethnically diverse than ever, including the first Jewish justice since 1969 and the first Roman Catholic of Italian descent.

Some have criticized the extent to which ethnic and gender considerations have become a factor in recent Supreme Court nominations. Clearly, gender and ethnic considerations have always influenced the selection of justices. In the past only white Anglo-Saxon Protestants were considered for Supreme Court appointment. In recent years nominations have been made with greater consciousness of the lack of representation on the Court of women, African-Americans, and other minority ethnic and religious groups. In the future we will no doubt see the first Asian-American justice, the first Muslim justice, the first Latino-American justice, and so forth. The hope is that in time the ethnic characteristics of nominees will become unremarkable.

Rewards of the Job

Because judges are individuals with established and often distinguished careers, any number of well-paying and prestigious positions are available to them. Yet they choose to become judges. Salary is clearly not a motivating factor. At all levels judicial salaries are well below what most judges could make if they

FIGURE 6–1   Characteristics of Presidential Appointees to U.S. District Judgeships (by presidential administration, 1963–92[a])

SOURCE: Sheldon Goldman, "Reagan's Judicial Legacy: Completing the Puzzle and Summing Up," *Judicature* 72 (April–May 1989), pp. 320, 321, Table 1; and "Bush's Judicial Legacy: The Final Imprint," *Judicature* 76 (April–May 1993), p. 287; in Kathleen Maguire and Ann L. Pastore, eds., *Sourcebook of Criminal Justice Statistics 1993*, U.S. Department of Justice, Bureau of Justice Statistics (Washington, DC: U.S. Government Printing Office, 1994), p. 72. Reprinted by permission.

	President Johnson's appointees 1963–68 (N = 122)	President Nixon's appointees 1969–74 (N = 179)	President Ford's appointees 1974–76 (N = 52)	President Carter's appointees 1977–80 (N = 202)	President Reagan's first term appointees 1981–84 (N = 129)	President Reagan's second term appointees 1985–88[b] (N = 161)	President Bush's appointees 1989–92 (N = 148)
Sex							
Male	98.4%	99.4%	98.1%	85.6%	90.7%	92.5%	80.4%
Female	1.6	0.6	1.9	14.4	9.3	7.4	19.6
Ethnicity							
White	93.4	95.5	88.5	78.7	93.0	91.9	89.2
Black	4.1	3.4	5.8	13.9	0.8	3.1	6.8
Hispanic	2.5	1.1	1.9	6.9	5.4	4.3	4.0
Asian	0.0	0.0	3.9	0.5	0.8	0.6	0.0
Education, undergraduate							
Public-supported	38.5	41.3	48.1	57.4	34.1	36.6	44.6
Private (not Ivy League)	31.1	33.5	34.6	32.7	49.6	50.9	41.2
Ivy League	16.4	19.6	17.3	9.9	16.3	12.4	14.2
None indicated	13.9	0.6	0.0	0.0	0.0	0.0	0.0
Education, law school							
Public-Supported	40.2	41.9	44.2	50.5	44.2	41.0	52.7
Private (not Ivy League)	36.9	36.9	38.5	32.2	47.3	44.1	33.1
Ivy League	21.3	21.2	17.3	17.3	8.5	14.9	14.2
Occupation at nomination or appointment							
Politics or government	21.3	10.6	21.2	4.4	7.8	16.8	10.8
Judiciary	31.1	28.5	34.6	44.6	40.3	34.8	41.9
Law firm, large	2.4	11.2	9.6	14.0	11.6	22.4	25.7
Law firm, moderate	18.9	27.9	25.0	19.8	25.6	14.3	14.9
Law firm, small	23.0	19.0	9.6	13.9	10.8	9.9	4.7
Professor of law	3.3	2.8	0.0	3.0	2.3	1.9	0.7
Other	0.0	0.0	0.0	0.5	1.6	0.0	1.4

FIGURE 6–1   Characteristics of Presidential Appointees to U.S. District Judgeships (by presidential administration, 1963–92ᵃ)—continued

	President Johnson's appointees 1963–68 (N = 122)	President Nixon's appointees 1969–74 (N = 179)	President Ford's appointees 1974–76 (N = 52)	President Carter's appointees 1977–80 (N = 202)	President Reagan's first term appointees 1981–84 (N = 129)	President Reagan's second term appointees 1985–88ᵇ (N = 161)	President Bush's appointees 1989–92 (N = 148)
Occupational experience							
Judicial	34.4	35.2	42.3	54.5	50.4	43.5	46.6
Prosecutorial	45.9	41.9	50.0	38.6	43.4	44.7	39.2
Other	33.6	36.3	30.8	28.2	28.7	27.9	31.8
Religion							
Protestant	58.2	73.2	73.1	60.4	58.9	60.9	64.2
Catholic	31.1	18.4	17.3	27.7	34.1	27.3	28.4
Jewish	10.7	8.4	9.6	11.9	7.0	11.2	7.4
Political party							
Democrat	94.3	7.3	21.2	92.6	3.1	6.2	5.4
Republican	5.7	92.7	78.8	4.4	96.9	90.7	88.5
Independent	0.0	0.0	0.0	2.9	0.0	3.1	6.1
American Bar Association rating							
Extremely well/well qualified	48.4	45.3	46.1	50.9	50.4	57.1	57.4
Qualified	49.2	54.8	53.8	47.5	49.6	42.9	42.6
Not qualified	2.5	0.0	0.0	1.5	0.0	0.0	0.0

NOTE: See Note, Figure 6–2. Percent subtotals for occupational experience sum to more than 100 because some appointees have had both judicial and prosecutorial experience. Some figures have been revised by the Source and therefore will differ from previous editions of *Sourcebook*.
ᵃPercents may not add up to 100 because of rounding.
ᵇOne appointee classified as non-denominational.

FIGURE 6–2   Characteristics of Presidential Appointees to U.S. Courts of Appeals Judgeships (by presidential administration, 1963–92ᵃ)

SOURCE: Sheldon Goldman, "Reagan's Judicial Legacy: Completing the Puzzle and Summing Up," *Judicature* 72 (April-May 1989), pp. 323, 324, Table 3; and "Bush's Judicial Legacy: The Final Imprint," *Judicature* 76 (April-May 1993), p. 293; n Kathleen Maguire and Ann L. Pastore, eds., 1994. *Sourcebook of Criminal Justice Statistics 1993*. U.S. Department of Justice, Bureau of Justice Statistics (Washington, DC: U.S. Government Printing Office, 1994), p. 71. Reprinted by permission.

	President Johnson's appointees 1963–68ᵇ (N = 40)	President Nixon's appointees 1969–74 (N = 45)	President Ford's appointees 1974–76 (N = 12)	President Carter's appointees 1977–80 (N = 56)	President Reagan's first term appointees 1981–84 (N = 31)	President Reagan's second term appointees 1985–88 (N = 47)	President Bush's appointees 1989–92 (N = 37)
Sex							
Male	97.5%	100.0%	100.0%	80.4%	96.8%	93.6%	81.1%
Female	2.5	0.0	0.0	19.6	3.2	6.4	18.9
Ethnicity							
White	95.0	97.8	100.0	78.6	93.5	100.0	89.2
Black	5.0	0.0	0.0	16.1	3.2	0.0	5.4
Hispanic	0.0	0.0	0.0	3.6	3.2	0.0	5.4
Asian	0.0	2.2	0.0	1.8	0.0	0.0	0.0
Education, undergraduate							
Public-supported	32.5	40.0	50.0	30.4	29.0	21.3	29.7
Private (not Ivy League)	40.0	35.6	41.7	50.0	45.2	55.3	59.5
Ivy League	17.5	20.0	8.3	19.6	25.8	23.4	10.8
None indicated	10.0	4.4	0.0	0.0	0.0	0.0	0.0
Education, law school							
Public-Supported	40.0	37.8	50.0	39.3	35.5	42.6	29.7
Private (not Ivy League)	32.5	26.7	25.0	19.6	48.4	29.8	40.5
Ivy League	27.5	35.6	25.0	41.1	16.1	27.7	29.7
Occupation at nomination or appointment							
Politics or government	10.0	4.4	8.3	5.4	3.2	8.5	10.8
Judiciary	57.5	53.3	75.0	46.4	61.3	51.1	59.5
Law firm, large	5.0	4.4	8.3	10.8	9.6	14.9	16.2
Law firm, moderate	17.5	22.2	8.3	16.1	9.6	10.6	10.8
Law firm, small	7.5	6.7	0.0	5.4	0.0	2.1	0.0
Professor of law	2.5	2.2	0.0	14.3	16.1	10.6	2.7
Other	0.0	6.7	0.0	1.8	0.0	2.1	0.0

FIGURE 6–2   Characteristics of Presidential Appointees to U.S. Courts of Appeals Judgeships (by presidential administration, 1963–92[a])—continued

	President Johnson's appointees 1963–68[b] (N = 40)	President Nixon's appointees 1969–74 (N = 45)	President Ford's appointees 1974–76 (N = 12)	President Carter's appointees 1977–80 (N = 56)	President Reagan's first term appointees 1981–84 (N = 31)	President Reagan's second term appointees 1985–88 (N = 47)	President Bush's appointees 1989–92 (N = 37)
Occupational experience							
Judicial	65.0	57.8	75.0	53.6	70.9	53.2	62.2
Prosecutorial	47.5	46.7	25.0	32.1	19.3	34.0	29.7
Other	20.0	17.8	25.0	37.5	25.8	40.4	32.4
Religion							
Protestant	60.0	75.6	58.3	60.7	67.7	46.8	59.4
Catholic	25.0	15.6	33.3	23.2	22.6	36.2	24.3
Jewish	15.0	8.9	8.3	16.1	9.7	17.0	16.2
Political party							
Democrat	95.0	6.7	8.3	82.1	0.0	0.0	5.4
Republican	5.0	93.3	91.7	7.1	100.0	95.7	89.2
Independent	0.0	0.0	0.0	10.7	0.0	2.1	5.4
Other	0.0	0.0	0.0	0.0	0.0	2.1	0.0
American Bar Association ratings							
Extremely well/well qualified	75.0	73.3	58.3	75.0	64.5	55.3	64.9
Qualified	20.0	26.7	33.3	25.0	35.5	44.7	35.1
Not qualified	2.5	0.0	8.3	0.0	0.0	0.0	0.0

NOTE: These data were compiled from a variety of sources. Primarily used were questionnaires completed by judicial nominees for the U.S. Senate Judiciary Committee, transcripts of the confirmation hearing conducted by the Committee, and personal interviews. In addition, an investigation was made of various biographical directories including *The American Bench* (Sacramento: R. B. Forster), *Who's Who in American Politics* (New York: Bowker), *Martindale-Hubbell Law Dictionary* (Summit, NJ: Martindale-Hubbell, Inc.), national and regional editions of *Who's Who*, *The Judicial Staff Directory* (1992 edition), and local newspaper articles.

Law firms are categorized according to the number of partners/associates: 25 or more associates for a large firm; 5 to 24 associates for a moderate firm; and 4 or less for a small firm. Percent subtotals for occupational experience sum to more than 100 because some appointees have had both judicial and prosecutorial experience.

The American Bar Association's (ABA) ratings are assigned to candidates after investigation and evaluation by the ABA's Standing Committee on Federal Judiciary, which considers prospective Federal judicial nominees only upon referral by the U.S. Attorney General or at the request of the U.S. Senate. The ABA's Committee evaluation is directed primarily to professional qualifications—competence, integrity, and judicial temperament. Factors including intellectual capacity, judgment, writing and analytical ability, industry, knowledge of the law, and professional experience are assessed. Prior to the Bush administration, the ABA's Standing Committee on Federal Judiciary utilized four ratings: exceptionally well qualified, well qualified, qualified, and not qualified. Starting with the Bush administration, the ABA Standing Committee on Federal Judiciary dropped its "exceptionally well qualified" rating so that "well qualified" became the highest rating. Nominees who previously would have been rated "exceptionally well qualified" and nominees who would have been rated "well qualified" now received the same rating. The "exceptionally well qualified" and "well qualified" categories are combined for all six administrations' appointees and therefore will differ from previous editions of *Sourcebook*.

[a]Percents may not add up to 100 because of rounding.

[b]No ABA rating was requested for one Johnson appointee.

FIGURE 6-3   Judicial Salaries

Source: Kathleen Maguire and Ann L. Pastore, eds., 1994. *Sourcebook of Criminal Justice Statistics— 1993*. Washington, D.C.: U.S. Government Printing Office, pp. 68, 81; National Center for State Courts, 1994. *Survey of Judicial Salaries*. Williamsburg, Va.: National Center for State Courts.

Federal Judges (by judicial office)	
Federal Magistrates	$122,912
District Court Judges	$133,600
Circuit Court Judges	$141,700
Supreme Court Justices	$164,100
Chief Justice	$171,500

State Court Judges (salary ranges and national averages)	
Courts of General Jurisdiction	
North Dakota	$ 65,970
New York	$104,000
National average	$ 83,048
Intermediate Appellate Courts	
New Mexico	$ 73,388
California	$119,314
National average	$ 91,491
Highest Appellate Court	
Montana	$ 64,452
California	$127,267
National Average	$ 92,806

maintained a private law practice (see Figure 6–3). Being a judge does confer considerable prestige, however.

Although prestige is a traditional incentive to join the bench, judges in recent years have complained that prestige is poor compensation for low pay and sometimes dreadful work. Dissatisfaction among trial court judges is well documented. Complaints about salary are common, and many judges estimate that they could double their yearly income by returning to private practice. Other complaints center on the public's negative perception of urban criminal courts and the undesirable media attention that accompanies the job. Judges who work in courts with large caseloads complain about administrative tedium and stress. Some are unhappy with the physical working conditions and inadequate security of the criminal courts (Rosen 1987; Wice 1991, 291–302). As the challenges of being a judge increase, judges may become less willing to accept prestige as a substitute for salary. This is particularly true of those judges who work in the lower levels, where prestige may be more legend than reality.

GETTING THE JOB: JUDICIAL SELECTION PROCESSES

Because the legally mandated qualifications for becoming a judge are minimal, the selection process is critical in ensuring that only qualified and motivated individuals are selected for judicial positions. In the United States judges are selected through a wide range of processes. Some judges are appointed, others

FIGURE 6-4   **Methods of Selecting Judges for Courts of General Jurisdiction, Initial Selection**

Source: Adapted from Kathleen Maguire and Ann L. Patore, eds., 1994. *Sourcebook of Criminal Justice Statitistics—1993*. Washington, D.C.: United States Government Printing Office, pp. 85–86.

Nonpartisan Election	Nominating Commission	Partisan Election	Appointed by Governor	Elected by Legislature
California	Alaska	Alabama	Maine	South Carolina
Florida	Arizona	Arkansas	New Hampshire	Virginia
Georgia	Colorado	Illinois	New Jersey	
Idaho	Connecticut	Indiana	Rhode Island	
Kentucky	Delaware	Louisiana		
Michigan	District of Columbia	Mississippi		
Minnesota	Hawaii	Missouri		
Montana	Iowa	New York		
Nevada	Kansas	North Carolina		
North Dakota	Maryland	Pennsylvania		
Ohio	Massachusetts	Tennessee		
Oklahoma	Nebraska	Texas		
Oregon	New Mexico	West Virginia		
South Dakota	Utah			
Washington	Vermont			
Wisconsin	Wyoming			
N=16	N=16	N=13	N=4	N=2

are elected, and still others are appointed through a special nominating process and later must stand for general election to retain their positions. The selection process used is determined by the law for that jurisdiction and judicial position. Because the state and federal systems have quite different selection processes, we examine them separately.

Selection of State Court Judges

Methods of selecting judges vary from state to state and in some states vary with the level of court (see Figure 6-4). Also, the qualifications required of an appellate judge sometimes differ from those for trial court judge. It is common to require that appellate judges have more law experience, and the minimum age is sometimes a little higher for appellate positions. Once they have gained the office, appellate judges usually serve longer terms than their counterparts in the trial courts.

Appointments

appointment

The oldest method of attaining judicial office in the United States is through **appointment.** Following British practices the constitutions in the original thirteen colonies after independence provided for judges to be appointed (Swindler 1976, 31). In four states, all located in New England, judges are appointed to office by the governor. Two of these states (New Jersey and Maine) appoint judges for seven year terms, whereas Rhode Island appoints trial court judges for life and New Hampshire appoints them until age seventy.

Many states that rely on elections or merit selection have provisions for appointing a replacement when a vacancy occurs before a judge has completed the term of office. Many judges attain office through such interim appointments and subsequently stand for election or merit selection. This sort of interim appointment should not be confused with regular appointments in those states that rely on an appointment process to select judges for a full term of office.

Elections

election

More states rely on **election** than any other system for regularly selecting judges. In 1824 Georgia became the first state to adopt an electoral system for judges, with Mississippi following in 1832. New York abandoned appointment of judges in 1846, and within a few more years most states had embraced a system of electing judges (Winters 1976, 47–8). Twenty-nine of the fifty states now use popular election to select trial court judges (Maguire and Pastore 1994, 85–86). Judges elected to office typically serve terms of four, six, or eight years, with six-year terms the most common. Only sixteen states rely on a system of election for selecting appellate court judges (Maguire and Pastore 1994, 84), and twenty-two states elect judges for their highest courts (Maguire and Pastore, 1994, 82).

nonpartisan elections, partisan elections

Elections may be partisan or non-partisan. **Nonpartisan elections** are those in which the candidates for office run without party affiliation. **Partisan elections** are those in which judges running for office announce their affiliation with a specific party such as the Democratic, Republican, Libertarian, Communist, or Labor parties. Political parties, with their money, methods, and periodic scandals, sometimes detract from the dignity of judicial office. Nonpartisan elections were instituted as a reform to avoid party politics. In some states nonpartisan elections are held at a different time of year so that they are completely separate from partisan elections.

Whether partisan or not, judicial elections sometimes leave one or both candidates besmirched and belittled in the public eye, bringing out the base rather than the noble in the candidates. "Negative campaigning," which has proved both effective and controversial in recent years, does little to elevate the dignity of the office of judge in the public eye. Because the ugliness of some elections is seen as demeaning the judicial office, some states have attempted to curb abuses (McFadden 1990).

The notion that the public selects its judges, even in election states, is more an ideal than it is a reality. For example, in one state that holds partisan elections the local bar virtually fixes the nomination and the candidate is seldom challenged (Alfini 1981). In other states that hold popular elections for judgeships judges are more likely to first attain office through appointment than through popular election, although this is not universally true (Dubois 1980, 102–3, 109). When a vacancy occurs during a term of office the governor appoints someone to fill the vacancy until the next regular election. Commonly, the judge who has been appointed is then elected. Thus many judicial careers—in some places most judicial careers—are actually launched by executive action, not popular election. In short, in some states the electorate assumes a more passive role with respect to actually selecting the judges to sit on its courts.

Merit Plan

Amid harsh criticism of judicial election practices the American Judicature Society was established in 1913 to develop a nonpolitical judicial selection plan. In 1937 the American Bar Association endorsed the proposed plan, known as the merit plan, and in 1940 the state of Missouri became the first state to adopt such a plan. Today its popularity is evident in the fact that more than half the states use it in some form for at least some judgeships (Winters 1976, 48–9). Sixteen states use

CAMPAIGN GUIDELINES

One modern attempt to prevent and control abuses in judgeship compaigns is the campaign monitoring committee. These committees promulgate and enforce fair campaign guidelines. The committee is sometimes an arm of the local bar association and sometimes an independent citizen committee. The latter is thought to serve as a stronger deterrent for unscrupulous campaign tactics. The campaign monitoring committee also receives and investigates complaints of unfairness. Other recommended reforms include public campaign financing, voluntary limits on campaign spending, increased information disseminated to voters, and increased use of public debates by candidates. Here is an example of campaign guidelines:

COLUMBUS JUDICIAL ELECTION COMMITTEE CANDIDATE AGREEMENT (1988)

JUDICIAL ELECTIONS COMMITTEE
AGREEMENT TO
GUIDELINES FOR JUDICIAL CAMPAIGN
As a condition of having my name submitted for evaluation by the Columbus Bar Association's Judiciary Committee and the membership of the Columbus Bar Association, in either a primary election or general election campaign, I agree, irrespective of the recommendation made or action taken by the Association regarding my candidacy, to conduct my campaign in accordance with the following:

1. I agree to familiarize myself with all applicable laws and regulations regarding my campaign and to take such steps as are reasonably necessary to ensure that others involved in my campaign are familiar with and guided by them as well. I agree to conduct my campaign in accordance with said laws and regulations.
2. I agree that Canon 7 of the Code of Judicial Conduct contains minimal rules pertaining to types of campaign materials, including sample ballots, and advertisement on radio or television or in a newspaper or periodical, a public speech, press release, or otherwise, wherein the use of a title not currently held, the making or reference to a false statement is prohibited. I further agree that omission of information could make an otherwise truthful statement misleading.
3. I agree to personally be responsible for the approval of all types of campaign materials relating to my judicial campaign, which are released under circumstances which are or should be under the control of me or my committee. I further agree to publicly disavow any and all campaign material from any unauthorized source which would be in violation of this agreement, promptly upon notification of such material by the Committee.
4. I have read the attached materials, and have caused those managing my campaign to read same and I agree to abide by the terms thereof.
5. I understand that violation of these objectives by any candidate for a judicial position may result in public criticism and a deterioration of respect for the judiciary.
6. I agree that the Judicial Election Committee may act, in reviewing and attempting to eliminate unethical and/or illegal campaign materials, by public comment, and by referral of the matter to the Office of Disciplinary Counsel, the Columbus Bar Association, or other appropriate bodies.
7. I agree to be available or make a member of my committee available to meet at the request of the Committee.

WHEREFORE, I hereby set my name evidencing my agreement with the above.
Dated:
Signed:

SOURCE: Sara Mathias. 1990. *Electing Judges: A Handbook of Judicial Election Reforms*. Chicago: American Judicature Society, p. 92.

some form of merit plan to select judges at the trial level. Nominating commissions, the essential feature of the merit plan, are even more common at the appellate level, used by twenty-two states.

Merit plans for judicial selection take a variety of forms, but they are all designed to combine positive elements of appointment and election while avoiding the negative aspects. Merit selection retains an appointment component but avoids the appearance and pitfalls of political patronage. It retains an election component yet avoids a campaign that pits opponents against each other.

merit plan

In a typical **merit plan** a nominating commission, comprised of respected public figures such as prominent legislators and lawyers, identifies and recommends to the governor a slate of well-qualified candidates. From those recommended the governor appoints one to the judgeship for a period of one year. When the year has expired, the judge stands—unopposed—for a retention election. Rather than face an opponent, the judge stands on his or her record, and the electorate determines whether the incumbent will be retained in office or lose the seat. If the incumbent is retained, the term is typically a long one, such as ten or twelve years. If the judge loses the office, the nomination-and-appointment process is repeated, and a different individual is selected to serve until the referendum is held on that appointee. This method of selection avoids election campaign politics and scandals. It also gives the electorate a chance to see the judge in action before making a decision. In addition, this method involves not only the electorate but the two branches of government that serve as checks on the judiciary: legislators serve as members of the nominating commission, and the governor appoints from the list of nominees drawn up by the commission.

Although this method avoids public campaigns, the process can remain quite political. The nominating commission becomes the locus of political activity but out of the public eye. Some have criticized nominating commissions for being controlled too closely by the state bar association or by the dominant political party in the legislature. Studies of the merit plan indicate that the key to nonpolitical judicial selection rests with the composition of the nominating commission. Fewer politically motivated nominations result when nominating commissions are bipartisan and balanced, when recruitment is proactive, and when screening procedures are codified (Ashman 1974, 227–30).

Selection of Federal Judges

At the bottom of the federal judicial hierarchy are the federal magistrates. For two hundred years the federal system has employed judicial officers to perform functions similar to those of lower court judges in the states (Smith 1990, 15). Federal magistrates issue search and arrest warrants, conduct initial appearances, arraignments, and trials for petty offenses; and hear and decide motions and other preliminary matters (Director 1990, 26). The position requires a license to practice law and at least five years' experience as a member of the bar. Appointment as a U.S. magistrate is made by the chief judge of the district court, upon the advice of a citizen panel that helps to identify a slate of highly qualified candidates (Smith 1990, 32). The selection of federal judges becomes more political and more public above the level of federal magistrate.

An old lawyers' joke says that the best way to become a federal judge is to "have the foresight to be the law school roommate of a future United States senator; or, failing that, to pick a future senator for your first law partner" (Goulden 1974, 23). This old joke underscores the traditional influence of the Senate and political patronage in the nomination of federal judges. Judges at the U.S. District and appellate levels and justices of the Supreme Court are nominated by the president of the United States and confirmed by the Senate. In practice the nomination-and-confirmation process differs considerably from the district court level to the appellate and Supreme Court levels. The key issues in the selection process are how the president selects the nominee and the basis on which the Senate decides whether to confirm.

District Court Nominations

Nominations to the federal district courts receive relatively little public attention. Formally, the president nominates the district judges. Historically, presidents have

senatorial
courtesy

deferred to the wishes of senators from the state in which the judge is to serve, a practice known as **senatorial courtesy.** The president seeks nominees by consulting with the senator who is from the jurisdiction where the judge will serve and who belongs to the president's political party. The president allows the senator to exercise an informal veto over the president's choice (Ball 1987, 198). If the senator is unhappy with the president's choice, the president will generally defer to the senator's preference. Once the president and the senator have agreed on a nomination, it is screened by the Standing Committee on the Federal Judiciary of the American Bar Association (ABA) and the Senate Judiciary Committee; the full Senate votes on confirmation of the nomination.

The practice of senatorial courtesy has changed in recent years. In response to reforms introduced by President Jimmy Carter for appellate nominations, thirty senators from various states set up a commission to recommend nominees for vacancies on the district courts in their states. Many considered this to be an improvement over the old patronage system of senatorial courtesy. A task force of the Twentieth Century Fund, an organization that studies judicial and legal issues, has recommended the regular use of bipartisan nominating commissions, coupled with open hearings held in the locale of the position to be filled (O'Brien 1988; Twentieth Century Fund Task Force 1988, 7).

Courts of Appeals

Since 1891, when Congress created what was then known as the Circuit Courts of Appeals, the custom has been to nominate a replacement judge from the home state of the out-going judge. "In effect, if a judge, who came to the federal bench from a career in Mississippi politics and Mississippi legal experiences, retires, dies, or resigns (or is impeached and convicted in the Senate), the president is generally bound to choose a successor from the state of Mississippi" (Ball 1987, 200). Here too senatorial courtesy reigns; the president seeks the advice and consent of the senator from the nominee's state.

Traditionally, senators have exercised substantial influence in the selection of federal appellate judges. In contrast to past practice, President Carter established the U.S. Circuit Court Nominating Commission and charged it with screening and recommending nominees based on merit, not politics. Using the nominating commission, Carter appointed an unprecedented number of women and minorities to the federal appellate bench. This reform was short-lived, however. Soon after taking office President Ronald Reagan abolished the nominating commissions.

Regardless of the method used by the president to select nominees for appellate judgeships, the Senate maintains its constitutional role of providing "advice and consent" on judicial nominations. After the president nominates a candidate, the Senate Judiciary Committee conducts an investigation. Since 1948 the Senate Judiciary Committee also has consistently sought the advice of the ABA's Standing Committee on the Federal Judiciary in considering the qualifications of the nominee.

The ABA committee is comprised of fifteen members, appointed by the ABA president and representing all geographic regions of the nation. Aided by teams of legal scholars and practicing lawyers, this committee examines the qualifications of a nominee, reads the nominee's legal writings, and investigates the judicial behavior of the nominee by interviewing people with whom the nominee has worked. After assessing all the evidence, the ABA committee rates the nominee as well qualified, qualified, or not qualified (American Bar Association

1991; Maguire and Pastore 1994, 71). This rating is supposed to be based exclusively on the professional qualifications—not the political philosophy or ideology—of the nominee.

The Senate Judiciary Committee also holds public hearings on the nomination. After public hearings and the vote of the Judiciary Committee, the full Senate votes on the nomination. Typically, these hearings and votes receive little attention from the media or the public.

U.S. Supreme Court

The most visible judicial selection process occurs when the U.S. Supreme Court has a vacancy. Then the president's advisers, along with the attorney general and the deputy attorney general, begin to identify and evaluate potential nominees. After a routine check by the FBI the president settles on a single nominee and makes the choice public. The Senate Judiciary Committee then conducts a wide-ranging investigation that focuses on both the personal conduct and the legal skill and integrity of the nominee. As in appellate nominations, the committee consults the ABA Standing Committee on the Federal Judiciary.

After the Senate Judiciary Committee has completed its investigation, it conducts public hearings at which the nominee answers questions posed by the member senators. In recent years these hearings have been televised, and some have received enormous public attention. The confirmation hearings of Clarence Thomas, who was eventually confirmed, and Robert Bork, who was not confirmed, are two examples of high-profile and extraordinarily controversial hearings. After the Thomas hearings, which involved testimony concerning the propriety of Thomas's personal conduct toward a former employee, Anita Hill, the Senate Judiciary Committee changed its procedures. Now the portion of the Senate Judiciary Committee's hearings that bears on public conduct, such as legal opinions, decisions, and scholarly papers, is held in open session, whereas matters of personal conduct that relate to judicial qualifications are considered in closed session. When the Senate Judiciary Committee has finished its hearings, it makes a recommendation to the full Senate, which then takes a vote. If the majority vote to confirm the president's nominee, the appointment to the Supreme Court can proceed. In the history of the nation the Senate has refused to confirm about 20 percent of the presidential nominees to the Court. Confirmation is more likely when the nominee holds a centrist political ideology and when the president's political party controls the Senate (Carp and Stidham 1990, 224).

The selection process for Supreme Court justices is especially political. Recent presidents, most notably Ronald Reagan, have made no secret that the political ideology of the nominee is a key consideration. People favoring other political ideologies are quick to cry "foul" and claim that selection for the judiciary has been reduced to a litmus test, in which, for example, otherwise qualified people would be selected or rejected because they supported or opposed abortion rights, school prayer, or other controversial policy matters with potential constitutional implications. In deciding whether to vote to confirm, senators also take the candidates' ideological positions into consideration. Not surprisingly, those not pleased with the outcome of this process suggest that the Senate is not acting properly when it considers the nominee's political ideology (Tribe 1985).

Presidents tend to view Supreme Court nominations as a presidential prerogative; the Senate should confirm unless the nominee is clearly unqualified or unfit. The Senate has, not surprisingly, viewed its role more broadly: the Senate has the broad power to consent to the nomination before appointment, and that consent may rest as much on policy concerns as on qualifications (Ball 1987, 183–85). Since the 1930s the federal courts, and the Supreme Court in particular, have interpreted the Bill of Rights and the U.S. Constitution in far-reaching and prescriptive ways. Once the Court undertook what some criticize as "making law" rather than merely interpreting the law, the political ideology of its members became an even greater concern (Schwartz 1988, *xi–xii*). So long as courts render politically controversial decisions, the political ideology of nominees is likely to be a battleground.

☐ LEARNING THE ROPES

Anyone selected to be a judge faces myriad new challenges. In contrast to other countries (such as France, see Chapter 5), where judges attend specialized schools for several years to learn the job, the United States provides its judges with little formal training after their appointment or election. This practice assumes that experienced attorneys have sufficient courtroom experience to assume the position of judge. As the role of judge becomes more complex, this assumption becomes less and less reasonable. In recent years greater attention has been paid to providing training for judges.

Even so, judges receive most of their training informally and on the job. Some may spend a day or a week getting oriented by observing other judges in action (Carp and Stidham 1990, 243; Wice 1981, 163). Others receive even less training. For most judges the transition from an advocate who probably specialized in one area of law to a detached decision maker who may be required to be familiar with all areas of law can be difficult. The new judge confronts unfamiliar legal issues, baffling administrative issues, and unpleasant personal issues, such as social isolation.

Most help in grappling with these issues comes from other more experienced judges through informal socialization. More experienced judges and other members of the courtroom work group introduce the new judge to the norms and mores of work life (Alpert 1981; Carp and Wheeler 1972; Wice 1981, 154). Through informal socialization, judges gain an understanding of the pace of litigation expected in the local legal culture. Judges learn the norms for when to grant continuances or order hearings on motions. Judges learn when the caseload is getting too big and when cases are moving too slowly. Judges who never practiced criminal law before assuming the bench learn norms regarding judicial participation in plea bargaining and the "going rate" for bail and guilty pleas.

And more and more judges are participating in formal education. Since 1974 some states have required judges to participate in special continuing education. By the end of the 1980s twenty-two states and thirteen federal district courts had required continuing education for all licensed attorneys, including judges. A handful of organizations offer seminars and courses specifically for certain types of judges, such as criminal trial judges, appellate judges, juvenile court judges, and federal judges (Winters 1976, 58).

☐ THE WORK OF A JUDGE

In general, trial judges adjudicate cases, and appellate judges determine whether the procedures followed in the trial were legal and proper. Trial court judges work alone and make decisions quickly. Appellate judges work collegially with other judges on the appellate panel and may take weeks to review decisions that the trial court judge had to make in a few minutes. Finally, trial court judges must manage their caseloads. Administrative duties are a fact of life in trial courts and a painful one in courts with daunting caseloads.

Working in Trial Court

The foremost obligation of a trial court judge is to ensure that the defendant receives a fair trial. Part of ensuring a fair trial involves determining whether the actions taken by government agents before trial were fair and proper. Ensuring the fairness of the process typically requires a judge to make numerous decisions in each case, many on the spot with little time for reflection. In addition, judges have administrative responsibilities, including scheduling cases and making sure the caseload moves.

The Task of Adjudication

Judges must be good listeners. Most of the time that judges spend in adjudicating cases is spent listening: listening to testimony, listening to the arguments of counsel, listening to defendants and victims pleading for justice and mercy. To be effective, judges also need to be decisive. Decision making is the heart of the process. Aside from the central decision of whether the defendant is guilty, the judge makes dozens of related decisions concerning the admissibility of evidence and the proper procedures to be followed. These decisions are supposed to be based on existing constitutional and statutory law and related case law. Because case law is evolving, judges need to keep abreast of appellate decisions affecting the jurisdiction. They must make many decisions quickly and on the basis on minimal information. The ability to tolerate uncertainty and to make decisions based on limited information is probably an asset for judges in trial courts.

Legal decisions, like any others, are affected by the values, beliefs, perspectives, and personalities of the judge. The speed and uncertainty characteristic of trial court decisions increase the likelihood that personal values and beliefs will influence the decision. The degree to which a judge's decision reflects personal convictions depends a great deal on the kind of decision being made. Where the law is relatively clear and little discretion is allowed, personal beliefs play a minimal role. But when the judge is allowed broad discretion (such as deciding the amount of bail or the sentence to impose), the judge's personal values and beliefs are quite influential (Satter 1990, 184).

In the theory of the adversarial process judges are supposed to preside over the courtroom with detached neutrality. They are expected to apply the law to the facts in a given situation, without letting their personal opinions or prejudices influence their decisions. Nonetheless, judges are human, making decisions that can profoundly affect the lives of other people. Although judges are to be neutral and detached, they cannot completely put aside human feelings and prejudices. Judge Jerome Frank, a distinguished federal appellate judge, put it bluntly:

> No one who has had any dealings with the law would dispute that the personality and interests of the judge vitally affects the way in which he decides the case, as to style and as to substance. It is a dangerous myth that by merely putting on a . . . robe and taking the oath of office as a judge, a man [sic] ceases to be human and strips himself of all predilections, becomes a passionless thinking machine. (In re *J.P. Linahan* 1943, 652–3)

A judge must appreciate how judicial decisions affect the human beings involved. Judge Robert Satter, a trial judge reflecting on judicial decision making, concluded that "the true art of judging . . . is a judge using his mind to find valid ways to implement the stirrings of his heart" (Satter 1990, 51).

The judge has special responsibilities in dealing with laypersons in court. Judges are the voice of the court and the representative of government authority; their instructions to witnesses, jurors, and spectators hold particular importance. Judges may instruct witnesses to keep to the point and may urge jurors to continue to deliberate despite an apparent deadlock.

Finally, the judge serves as a symbol of justice to all those who observe the courts in action. Most judges behave with professional respect toward all those in the courtroom. Judges who show disrespect or indifference to witnesses and other members of the public may cast a shadow of disrespect on the entire court system. Spectators sometimes report their shock when they see a judge reading a newspaper, sleeping through testimony, or crudely berating witnesses.

The Task of Administration

Part of the judge's responsibility in overseeing the process is to make sure that cases continue at a steady pace toward resolution. A commonly recited maxim is: Justice delayed is justice denied. The judge has a heavy responsibility to assure that justice is not delayed because of poor administration. With the crush that faces the courts today moving cases is becoming an ever more important skill. Doing so requires not only learning in the law but having character traits that facilitate decision making and taking a leadership role.

A judge must be familiar with the law in order to move cases along without unnecessary delay. If a judge is not familiar with the rules of evidence, for example, to avoid error the judge will need time to research the issue before rendering a ruling. A judge who knows the law thoroughly is in the best position to make quick, decisive, and correct rulings.

A judge must be comfortable with quick decisions. The type of individual who mulls decisions and weighs them carefully will soon become a roadblock in a busy court system. In many courtrooms in urban settings, where most cases are processed, probable cause decisions at the initial appearance are made in a minute or less, and bail decisions are made about as quickly. The judge presiding over a trial makes rulings on the admissibility of evidence in a matter of seconds. Pondering the intriguing fine points of law is a luxury. Trial court judges simply have too little time.

Judges are leaders in the courtroom in a variety of ways that have an observable effect on the timely disposition of cases. Judges' reputations are based on their performance. Judges become known for being more or less prepared, more or less tolerant of delays, more or less familiar with the law, more or less hard working. In this way the judge sets standards in the courtroom that practicing attorneys come to expect and that shape the conduct of all involved. The judge who is familiar with the law will receive fewer frivolous objections and challenges; the judge who is well prepared sends a message that adversaries before the bench are expected to be well prepared. The judge who takes the bench at the stated hour can expect others to be present at the appointed time. The judge who does not tolerate unnecessary continuances will have fewer requests for them.

One of the most important ways a judge can exercise leadership is by controlling the court calendar, or schedule. In most jurisdictions judges maintain

DETERRING DISRUPTION AND ENFORCING
COMPLIANCE: CONTEMPT OF COURT

Judges have two weapons, civil contempt and criminal contempt, for maintaining courtroom propriety. Criminal contempt is a crime, punishable by a fine or a definite term of incarceration. A defendant who stands up, interrupts the proceedings, and shouts vulgarities and obscenities at a judge might receive a warning the first time. But if the defendant does it again, the judge might decide the defendant is guilty of criminal contempt and impose a fine or short jail sentence as punishment. A prosecutor who wonders aloud in open court, in a voice dripping with sarcasm, whether the judge ever attended law school might receive a fine or a day or two in jail for such a show of disrespect.

Civil contempt sanctions involve incarceration for an indefinite period of time. Incarcera-

tion for civil contempt is not for the purpose of punishment but to compel someone to comply with a court order. Recently, a woman who alleged that her daughter had been sexually molested by the father hid the child and refused to reveal to the court where she was. The court jailed the woman to persuade her to provide the information.

The indefinite status of the civil contempt incarceration is to impress upon the citizen that the only way to freedom is through compliance with the orders of the court. Some jurisdictions have elected to impose statutory limits on the duration of incarceration for civil contempt, but even in these jurisdictions the allowable period of incarceration is substantial, such as two years.

total control over their own court calendars. This means that a judge controls when trials are scheduled and for how long, when other hearings are scheduled and how much time is allowed. It means that a judge determines when the court day starts and when it ends. By setting a courtroom tone or style of getting down to serious business (or not), a judge affects the efficient movement of cases (or not). For example, when some judges set a trial date, it is firm, and the adversaries know exactly how long they have to reach a pretrial settlement if they wish to avoid a trial. In the case of other judges, attorneys know that a trial date can always be postponed and continuances are usually granted; they have no need to get down to business.

As managers of the courts judges sometimes make decisions that are tangential to the case but designed to maintain order and respect for the court. Judges have the authority to impose sanctions on any person in the courtroom or involved in the case whose conduct impedes adjudication or who is disrespectful to the court. For example, if a juror fails to appear for a trial as ordered, the consequence is delay. Similarly, if the presentence report is not filed on time, the sentencing hearing may be delayed. Anyone who shows open disrespect to the court, or attempts to halt or disrupt the proceedings, is a problem to which the judge may respond. In all such instances the court has the authority to take measures designed to gain compliance and cooperation with the process and to discourage the offending party and others from attempting to thwart the process in the future. These measures are known as citations for contempt. Research shows that judges rarely use such measures to maintain order and respect for the court (Dorsen and Friedman 1973, 6). Usually, a verbal warning about the consequences of continued disruption resolve the problem to the judge's satisfaction.

Chief Judge of the Trial Court. Trial courts in most urban jurisdictions are organized so that a chief judge serves as head administrator. The kinds of administrative matters that require the attention of the chief judge vary widely. Chief judges act in a quasisupervisory capacity over the trial court judges, they act as the final authority in policy-level decisions about running the courts, and they sometimes are the major administrators of the courts on a day-to-day basis, although this last task is often left to a professional court administrator. As supervisor the chief judge makes personnel management decisions. A chief judge is usually responsible for making the bench assignments, or deciding which judge will hear civil cases this year and who will hear criminal cases and how often the assignments will be rotated. The chief judge will assign the judges to the courtrooms as well. They also typically determine which judge will be the regular substitute for a specific judge if that judge is disqualified or a defendant requests a substitute. Chief judges sometimes must make the first-level decision when a complaint of misconduct is lodged against a judge.

The chief judge is the final authority about the actual operating procedures for the court system. For example, provided there are no restrictions from such external sources as the state supreme court or the legislature, the chief judge decides whether one judge hears preliminary hearings all day every day for a year or five years or whether each judge will hear the preliminary hearings in the cases assigned to them. The chief judge sets policy on the use of cameras in the courtroom. The chief judge also determines the exact procedures to be followed when summoning citizens for jury duty: whether potential jurors may call in to find out if they must report or whether all potential jurors have to appear in person every day for a set period. Obviously, many such decisions are linked to resources.

The chief judge must decide how to allocate the money in the operating budget and whether to ask the legislature for additional resources. Although a court administrator may be responsible for the daily operating budget, the chief judge of the trial court exercises final authority about allocating resources, especially when tough decisions have to be made. The court administrator works closely with the chief judge and on a daily basis implements the policies set by the chief judge. When the operating budget is running low, or when the courts need additional judgeships or equipment that cannot be absorbed in the operating budget, the chief judge presents those requests to the governmental body with the authority to allocate the court's budget. This is an important liaison role for the chief judge to play. The chief judge must justify the requests, and respond to criticism about the operations of the courts.

Managing the Courts: Support Personnel in the Trial Courts

Courts from early times required specialized staff to maintain the paperwork associated with a court case. As the workload of the courts has grown, the tasks associated with tracking cases and their associated paperwork have grown to include efforts to make the court process more efficient. Two key actors in the management of the courts are the clerk of courts and the professional court administrator.

Clerk of Courts

The clerk of courts can be viewed as the traditional forerunner of the modern court administrator. In most state courts the clerk is elected to office. In the federal system the clerk of courts is appointed. The clerk's primary function is to keep the official records of the court, both during the adjudication and indefinitely thereafter. This by itself is a mammoth job. The clerk of courts is also responsible for setting policy with respect to handling requests for files, access to files, providing copies of documents, and so on. Some policy decisions have little effect on the processing of cases, but others have a great effect. For example, attorneys need ready access to defendants' previous case files. If the clerk sets a policy that requires lawyers to make their requests days in advance, judges may have to delay hearings until the records become available.

Each case has a plethora of accompanying paperwork. Paper records, manually prepared, stored, and maintained, are still the norm in the nation's courts. Each court appearance must be recorded and dated, each motion filed must be received and stored, and the entire packet of paperwork must be maintained intact. Recording the proceedings, and maintaining, storing, and retrieving the files of criminal cases require a large staff. Typically, the clerk of courts assigns one or two people, in addition to the court stenographer, to each courtroom. These clerks create and file the paper that accompanies each case as it wends its way through the system.

Two key challenges to the management of files in the court system are misplaced files and slow access to files. Typically, the clerk of courts maintains only one copy of each file. Maintaining a paper-based case record is cumbersome and expensive. A file may be retrieved and opened seven or eight times, for each court appearance. Because each file may be pulled a number of times and may be checked out to a prosecutor or other court official, documents are sometimes lost or entire files misplaced. Paperwork foul-ups of this sort inevitably cause delays. A case may be called for trial or some other court hearing, only to be postponed because the clerk cannot locate the file.

Manual record keeping is antiquated. Modern data storage-and-retrieval technology could aid greatly in recording hearings, maintaining records, retrieving information quickly, and providing statistical descriptions of the court caseload. Attorneys could use a modem to look up information in court files from their offices. Statistics on court management, such as cases filed, cases disposed, appeals filed, cases pending, and so on, could be easily retrieved and reported. Yet most courts still base their records on a system of paper files. Bureaucratic inertia, lack of technical expertise, and technophobic mistrust of electronic records, along with the expense of installing new systems, seem to be the major impediments to the introduction of new technology. Even relatively inexpensive alternatives, such as video or audio recordings of hearings, have replaced the court stenographer only in a few locales.

Although the clerk of courts typically sets policies relating to record keeping and retrieval, in most jurisdictions the chief judge has authority to countermand policies that impede efficient case management and processing. In many jurisdictions both the chief judge and the clerk of courts are elected officials who share responsibility for court management. In most states, however, the state supreme court vests the chief judge of the trial court with the authority to establish local court rules for efficient and fair administration. Therefore, if a policy set by the clerk of courts proves counterproductive to efficient case processing, the chief judge has the power to establish alternative means of processing cases. Clearly, good communication, coordination, and cooperation between the clerk of courts and the chief judge, as well as a clear delineation of powers and responsibility, are important to the efficient administration of the courts (Hoffman 1991).

Court Administrators

As early as 1909 the American Bar Association acknowledged the need for better administration of the courts, but change was long in coming (Lawson and Howard 1991). But as courts grew more centralized, complex, and burdened with cases, and as procedural laws and their accompanying documents became ever more numerous and critical to case processing, the need for administrative coordination and efficiency increased accordingly. These changes forced chief judges to become more involved in administrative matters. In turn, the need to relieve judges of management oversight helped prompt the movement to establish an office of administrative expertise and long-range planning. The position of court administrator evolved in response. Since the early 1970s this position has become standard in the federal and state court systems. In the mid-1960s the United States had no more than thirty court administrators, whereas more than two thousand are working at the local or state level today (Hudzik 1991, 564). Court administrators are found at both the trial and appellate levels in the federal system. The federal system also has a centralized Administrative Office of the Courts, which maintains data relating to the entire federal court system.

The rapid development of this profession has paralleled the growing emphasis on professionalizing many functions in the criminal justice system and dates from the era of the federal government's "war on crime" and the federal Omnibus Crime Control and Safe Streets Act of 1968. One effect of that legislation was to earmark federal funds for developing educational and training programs to improve the quality of criminal justice administration. Today's court administrators are one result of that initiative. In many jurisdictions the court administrator is a lawyer with additional training in administration and management. Others hold master's degrees in judicial studies, court management, public administration, or related fields. A few graduate programs give certificates in court administration.

The distinction between the duties of the court administrator and the clerk of courts varies according to jurisdiction. In some jurisdictions the court administrator is replacing the clerk of courts. In other places the state constitution specifies the duties of the clerk of courts. In these states a court administrator may be hired to carry out some constitutional responsibilities of the clerk under the clerk's supervision or may assist the chief judge with administrative matters.

The court administrator is typically responsible for case-flow management. These duties include monitoring the case flow and making recommendations for optimizing case flow. Court administrators use management techniques, such as systems analysis and queuing theory, to identify trouble spots in case processing. The court administrator is reponsible for coordinating judges, courtrooms, clerks, jurors, and support personnel so that all resources needed to hear and decide cases are used efficiently (Berkson, Hays, and Carbon 1977).

Case-flow management involves a process of planning, feedback, and supervision designed to make court scheduling more predictable and certain (Solomon and Somerlot 1987). Court administrators try to match the number of cases scheduled at any particular time to the resources available. The difficulty in scheduling cases, however, is that "there are almost always more cases that theoretically could go to trial than it is possible to actually try" (Mahoney et al. 1988, 81). In addition, many cases are scheduled, but drop out at the last minute. Like airlines that overbook seats to ensure that the plane will be full despite last-minute cancellations, courts need to have extra cases scheduled because some will "fall out" because of continuances, plea bargains, or last-minute dimissals (Solomon and Somerlot 1987, 26). The problem for court administrators is knowing what proportion of cases is likely to fall out. If the court administrator guesses wrong, and fewer cases than expected fall out, attorneys, defendants, and witnesses will face long delays and may find their case being rescheduled because the judge could not get to it before the end of the day. On the other hand, if the court administrator guesses wrong and more cases than expected fall out, courtrooms and judges may sit unused.

Unfortunately for court administrators, successful case-flow management is not merely a set of techniques that can magically transform a backlogged court system into an efficient one. Although specific reforms, such as court unification and individual calendar systems, seem to offer simple solutions to case-flow management problems, research has not demonstrated that these techniques have a measureable effect on court performance (Dahlin 1986; Henderson et al. 1984; Lushkin 1987). The court administrator's success depends on the cooperation of others in the system. Judges must be committed to reducing the number of continuances they grant on frivolous grounds. Prosecutors and defense attorneys alike must come to court prepared rather than expecting to get a continuance (Mahoney 1987). The jail must cooperate by having defendants at court on time. The clerk of courts must make sure the necessary records are forwarded to the correct courtroom.

Achieving these outcomes requires that court administrators have strong skills for motivating people to cooperate. Consequently, the court administrator also acts as a liaison between the court and numerous other agencies whose cooperation and coordination are critical to a well-functioning court system. These duties sometimes include community relations and public information.

Fiscal administration is another of the court administrator's duties. Courts must request and justify their budgets to the state and local governments that fund them. Working with the chief judge, the court administrator assists in the preparation and justification of budgets. Finally, in some jurisdictions court administrators have major responsibilities for human resource management, space and equipment management, and even jury management.

The ability of judges, clerks, and court administrators to work together constructively has an inevitable effect on the pace and quality of the work of the criminal courts (Berg 1977, 201). Such cooperation can be difficult to achieve. Sometimes judges are reluctant to relinquish control over even minor administrative matters. Conversely, other judges are unwilling to devote any substantial time to understanding the administrative problems of the court and to work with the clerk and administrator to find solutions (Berg 1977, 201). The organizational and personal dynamics of these three court actors—judge, clerk, and administrator—are critical to the overall functioning of the court.

Working in Appellate Court

The work of the appellate judge is very different from that of the trial judge. Although the appellate courts make decisions in specific cases, they do so by focusing on the fairness of the process that the trial court used to reach the decision. The role of the appellate court is not to determine whether the defendant is guilty; rather, the appellate court's role is to determine whether the guilty verdict resulted from a fair trial that observed all the defendant's rights.

Defendants do not appear before appellate judges, and appellate judges do not listen to witnesses testifying to the facts. Appellate courts do not hold trials. Instead, the appellate judge examines the written court record and other relevant documents, reads the briefs submitted by the attorneys, and in some cases hears oral arguments from the lawyers who submitted the briefs. Oral arguments are by invitation of the court only and are severely restricted in time, only an hour or less. During oral arguments the justices ask probing and sometimes argumentative questions of the opposing lawyers in an exercise designed to explore the complexities of both positions.

opinion of the court

Appellate judges spend lots of time reading, thinking, discussing, and writing. The issues they consider must be carefully and completely researched to ensure consistency with prior decisions. Appellate court decisions are products of group decision making rather than individual judgments. The group decision, known as the **opinion of the court,** is often the product of self-education and compromise on complex and thorny legal issues. Compromise is a key element in reaching a decision that a majority of the group, or at least a plurality of the group, will support. But the process is far more than compromise. Because appellate decisions are written, members of the court must agree not only on the outcome of the decision but also on the reasons for that outcome. Judge Frank M. Coffin, a federal appellate judge, made this point based on his own experiences on the bench: "There is a difference between arriving at a yes or no decision through majority vote and working up an opinion on a close case so that three or more judges of different sensitivities, values and backgrounds can join not only in the result, but in the rationale, tone, nuances, and reservations" (1980, 59).

The writing of the opinion is a process that facilitates thinking and debate. Even when the judges think they agree, the first draft may highlight disagreements not previously recognized, or an individual judge may simply have second thoughts about the matter. Indeed, the writing of the opinion may convince the author of the draft to shift positions. According to Coffin,

> A remarkably effective device for detecting fissures in accuracy and logic is the reduction to writing of the results of one's thought processes. . . . Somehow, a decision mulled over in one's head or talked about in conference looks different when dressed up in written words and sent out into the sunlight. . . . The act of writing tells us what is wrong with the act of thinking. (1980, 57)

Appellate judges consider far fewer cases and far fewer issues than trial court judges, but they consider each matter for a much longer period of time. The nature of the work is scholarly and reflective. Arriving at the correct conclusion is more important than in a trial court, because the decision of the appellate court influences not only the present case but the way trial courts decide all similar cases in the future. Coffin stresses the importance of lengthy reflection on the issues before the court: "The quality of decision is enhanced by prolonged indecisiveness" (1980, 61). Contrast this comment to the quick decisions required of trial court judges. In short, reading, research, prolonged contemplation, and writing are the mainstays of appellate judges; these are activities for which trial judges are sorely pressed to find time.

Although appellate judges have more time to spend on each case, they do face time constraints. Recent increases in appellate caseloads have required appellate judges to think more about moving cases than they have in the past (see Chapter 18). Some appellate courts have shifted to support personnel, such as law clerks, tasks previously done by the justices themselves.

Law Clerks

law clerk

A **law clerk** is a legal research assistant. The traditional responsibility of law clerks is to research legal issues for appellate judges. As the appellate docket has become more crowded, law clerks have taken on additional responsibilities, including writing the first draft of opinions and screening cases for important legal issues before the judge looks at the case. In 1992 the federal courts employed more than seventeen hundred law clerks to serve about fourteen hundred judges at all levels (Maguire and Pastore 1994, 73).

These positions vary a great deal in the prestige they carry. For example, clerking for a federal appellate judge on an influential bench is a prestigious position for which the competition is quite stiff. Clerking for a state appellate judge is usually not as prestigious. Clerks at the federal appellate level are usually selected from the top graduates from the top law schools in the country. These positions are considered excellent training for future positions as law professors and judges (Marvell 1977).

MAINTAINING INTEGRITY

Judges are expected to epitomize justice, fairness, and propriety. "Fairness and justice in an adversary system are dependent upon the conduct of those who sit in judgment" (Lubet 1984, 5). Judges sometimes slip. Some judges are not very temperate. Some are arrogant or rude to those with business before the court. Some are lazy. Some do not know the law. Some once were good judges but have become burned out or senile. Some never were very good. Some are even corrupt. Judges have been guilty of murder, extortion, shoplifting, and pimping (Ashman 1973). The issues raised here encompass both professional competence and personal conduct.

Respect for the court may be damaged if judges bring disrespect upon themselves. Confidence in justice is undermined if judges are corrupt. To preserve dignity and respect for the court judges are often held to higher standards than the rest of us. Although society may tolerate rudeness and dishonesty in other occupations, judges can be disciplined for such conduct (Lubet 1984, 5, 37–41).

Many professions use salary as an incentive to promote positive behavior. Judicial salaries and fringe benefits, however, are not a direct method of controlling performance. Instead, they are a critical component of preventing judicial incompetence and misconduct. If the best and brightest of the nation's lawyers can be attracted to service on the bench, problems of incompetence and substandard conduct will be less. In other words, an ounce of prevention targeted at recruitment and retention of highly qualified lawyers is worth a pound of cure. More direct controls on judicial performance also are available. In state courts fixed terms of office and elections provide some control over judges. The public need not reelect incompetent or rude judges. But sometimes more immediate disciplinary action is warranted. The voters may petition for a recall election, or the legislature may move for impeachment. Judges who violate criminal laws can be prosecuted for their conduct. In addition, judges who violate the professional code of conduct are subject to the discipline of the bar.

Code of Judicial Conduct

Judges, as well as all other lawyers, are subject to a code of ethics. The American Bar Association influences the codes adopted by each state by formulating model codes and rules. The first set of broadly stated principles, called the Nine Canons of Ethics, was adopted by the ABA in 1908 (see Figure 6–5). Subsequently, more specific standards of conduct, called ethical considerations, augmented the canons to provide direction on the appropriate application of the canons in

FIGURE 6–5   The Nine Canons of Professional Ethics from the American Bar Association's Model Code of Professional Responsibility

SOURCE: American Bar Association 1986. *Model Code of Professional Responsibility and Code of Judicial Conduct*. Chicago: American Bar Association. Reprinted by permission of the American Bar Association. Copies of these publications are available from Service Center, American Bar Association, 750 Lake Shore Drive, Chicago, IL 60611.

Canon 1.   A lawyer should assist in maintaining the integrity and competence of the legal profession.
Canon 2.   A lawyer should assist the legal profession in fulfilling its duty to make legal counsel available.
Canon 3.   A lawyer should assist in preventing the unauthorized practice of law.
Canon 4.   A lawyer should preserve the confidences and secrets of a client.
Canon 5.   A lawyer should exercise independent professional judgment on behalf of a client.
Canon 6.   A lawyer should represent a client competently.
Canon 7.   A lawyer should represent a client zealously within the bounds of the law.
Canon 8.   A lawyer should assist in improving the legal system.
Canon 9.   A lawyer should avoid even the appearance of professional impropriety.

particular circumstances. After a comprehensive reevaluation of the ethical premises and problems of the legal profession, the ABA adopted a new code in 1983, called the Model Rules of Professional Conduct. The model rules embody and amplify the principles espoused in the original nine canons. By the early 1990s more than two-thirds of all U.S. court jurisdictions had adopted the model rules (ABA 1993, viii).

Judges are also governed by a special set of principles. In 1990 the ABA House of Delegates adopted a revised and expanded code, now called the Model Code of Judicial Conduct (Dilweg et al. 1992). The 1990 model code is comprehensive and addresses a wide range of topics with application to diverse forms of judicial service (Milford 1992, 61). Figure 6–6 provides the Seven Canons of the Model Code of Judicial Conduct. It is easy to see how these broad principles apply to the work of a judge and the requirements of the role. Nonetheless, the canons are broad and nonspecific. The mandatory standards elaborate on each canon to provide additional guidance to judges. Figure 6–7 shows some of the mandatory standards relating to Canon 3, "requiring judges to perform the duties of judicial office impartially and diligently."

Disciplinary Bodies and Judicial Conduct Commissions

Although most judges are conscientious, hard working, and ethical, some judges behave badly, violating the ethical standards of the profession and sometimes the law itself. Judges violate campaign laws, engage in sexual harassment, exercise favoritism, and even take bribes. If the judge's conduct constitutes a crime, it can be investigated and result in arrest, just like any other crime. There are obvious difficulties in carrying out such an investigation, however. At a conceptual level, having the police and prosecutor pursue criminal charges against a judge creates a potentially serious infringement on the independence of the judiciary. At a practical level police and prosecutors are unlikely to proceed against a judge unless the case is especially compelling.

Consequently, many states have established an alternative disciplinary structure. About seventy years ago, Albert Kale, the lead architect of the American

FIGURE 6–6   The Seven Canons from the American Bar Association's Model Code of Judicial Conduct

Source: American Bar Association 1986. *Model Code of Professional Responsibility and Code of Judicial Conduct.* Chicago: American Bar Association. Reprinted by permission of the American Bar Association. Copies of these publications are available from Service Center, American Bar Association, 750 Lake Shore Drive, Chicago, IL 60611.

Canon 1.   A judge should uphold the integrity and independence of the judiciary.

Canon 2.   A judge should avoid impropriety and the appearance of impropriety in all his activities.

Canon 3.   A judge should perform the duties of his office impartially and diligently.

Canon 4.   A judge may engage in activities to improve the law, the legal system, and the administration of justice.

Canon 5.   A judge should regulate his extra-judicial activities to minimize the risk of conflict with his judicial duties.

Canon 6.   A judge should regularly file reports of compensation received for quasi-judicial and extra-judicial activities.

Canon 7.   A judge should refrain from political activity inappropriate to his judicial office.

Judicature Society's merit plan for selecting judges, proposed a structure and process for imposing sanctions on wayward judges. He proposed that a duly constituted body of fellow judges who hold a position of power and authority be charged with investigating complaints and recommending disciplinary action. In 1947 New Jersey became the first state to authorize its supreme court to remove judges in trial courts for reasons specified by statute. In 1960 California established a misconduct commission composed of judges, practicing lawyers, and laypersons. The California commission has the duty to investigate complaints and resolve them unless the seriousness of the wrongdoing requires a hearing before the state supreme court, which has the authority to censure or remove judges. Since 1960 almost all states and the District of Columbia have established similar systems (Wheeler and Levin 1979, 14–24).

Many communities have been rocked by scandals relating to judicial misconduct of all kinds. Too often, when judicial misconduct has been reported or made public, the Code of Judicial Conduct has not been enforced by the judicial bodies authorized to discipline judges.

> Despite periodic scandals and persistent public criticism, there is little evidence that the legal profession has engaged in more effective regulation of misconduct or incompetence in recent years. It has revised the rules of professional conduct with increasing frequency, required law students to study them, and tested the knowledge of applicants for admission. (Abel 1989, 156)

Actually enforcing the code for specific offenses has been another matter. The notoriously lax self-regulation of the bar must be seen as a factor contributing to the low esteem in which legal ethics are viewed today. The lack of enforcement of standards extends to judges, and predictably judges complain about the low esteem the public has for the judiciary (Rosen 1987; Wice 1991).

The Judicial Conference of the United States sets conduct policies for federal judges. In 1973 it formally applied the ABA Code of Judicial Conduct to all federal

FIGURE 6–7   Selected Mandatory Standards Relating to Canon Three of the Code of Judicial Conduct

SOURCE: L. L. Milford. 1992. *The Development of the ABA Judicial Code*. Chicago: American Bar Association, Center for Professional Responsibility, pp. 74–75. Reprinted by permission of the American Bar Association. Copies of these publications are available from Service Center, American Bar Association, 750 Lake Shore Drive, Chicago, IL 60611.

B. Adjudicative Responsibilities.

(1) A judge shall hear and decide matters assigned to the judge except those in which disqualification is required.

(2) A judge shall be faithful to the law and maintain competence in it. A judge shall not be swayed by partisan interests, public clamor or fear of criticism.

(3) A judge shall require order and decorum in proceedings before the judge.

(4) A judge shall be patient, dignified and courteous to litigants, jurors, witnesses, lawyers and others with whom the judge deals in an official capacity, and shall require similar conduct of lawyers, and of staff, court officials and others subject to the judge's direction and control.

Commentary:

The duty to hear all proceedings fairly and with patience is not inconsistent with the duty to dispose promptly of the business of the court. Judges can be efficient and businesslike while being patient and deliberate.

(5) A judge shall perform judicial duties without bias or prejudice. A judge shall not, in the performance of judicial duties, by words or conduct manifest bias or prejudice, including but not limited to bias or prejudice based upon race, sex, religion, national origin, disability, age, sexual orientation or socioeconomic status, and shall not permit staff, court officials and others subject to the judge's direction and control to do so.

Commentary:

A judge must refrain from speech, gestures or other conduct that could reasonably be perceived as sexual harassment and must require the same standard of conduct of others subject to the judge's direction and control.

judges. Compliance with the Judicial Conference's ethical directives is voluntary, however (Wheeler and Levin 1979, 24–25). The disciplinary authority over federal judges is vested in regional judicial councils "composed of all active judges of the court of appeals in that circuit" (Wheeler and Levin 1979, 33). The council has the duty to compel the effective and expeditious administration of the business of the courts in its circuit. This duty is interpreted to include the avoidance of "stigma, disrepute, or other element of loss of public esteem and confidence in respect to the court system, from the actions of a judge or other persons attached to the courts" (Wheeler and Levin 1979, 35). The council does not have the authority to remove federal judges from office, however. The only means of involuntary removal is impeachment by the U.S. Senate. Federal judges are occasionally impeached for their misconduct in office, although a pending impeachment often prompts the judge to resign.

☐ SUMMARY

Judges are overseers of the adjudicatory process, ensuring fairness both for individuals and for the system as a whole. Trial court judges work quickly and decisively to dispose of their caseload, weighing evidence, applying law, and making bail and sentencing decisions. Although their duty is to make decisions from a neutral and detached perspective, trial judges are human beings whose values, perspectives, beliefs, and experiences shape their decisions.

Judges tend to come from middle or upper middle-class backgrounds. Women and members of minority ethnic groups have traditionally been, and continue to be, underrepresented in the ranks of judges. Judges attain office through appointment, election, or merit selection. Although judges are given little formal training for their job beyond the law degree and experience that qualify them for the position, judges experience informal socialization to the role.

Appellate court judges work slowly and deliberately, reading, thinking, researching, and writing. Appellate judges rely on group decision making, forging agreements not only on legal decisions but also on the reasons for those decisions. The work of appellate judges establishes in large part the parameters of justice in the trial courts.

Judges, like all lawyers, are supposed to comply with a code of ethics. The ABA Code of Judicial Conduct is tailored to the special ethical issues facing judges. Most states have established judicial disciplinary bodies to enforce ethical judicial conduct, but these bodies rarely discipline or remove judges from office.

■ FOR FURTHER DISCUSSION

1. Can you name any judges who serve in your local community? What do you know about them? Do you recall how you learned about these judges? What do your answers to these questions suggest about the visibility of the work of judges and the ways in which the public becomes aware of judges and what they do?

2. What does the task of administration in the courts entail, and who carries the responsibility for administration of the courts? How might poor court administration affect the outcome of cases in criminal courts?

3. How is the work of appellate judges different from the work of trial court judges?

4. Consider the following hypothetical case:

    A particular judge regularly calls women arrested for prostitution "honey" and "sweetie," and calls defendants arrested on drug charges "stupid" and "dopey" when addressing them. Is this a violation of the Code of Judicial Conduct? Do you think that such a judge should be disciplined? If so, in what way?

5. Are the justices on your state's highest court elected, appointed, or selected by the merit plan? Which method do you think is the best for this high judicial office? Why?

■ REFERENCES

Abel, Richard L. 1989. *American Lawyers*. New York: Oxford University Press.

Abraham, Henry J. 1992. *Justices and Presidents: A Political History of Appointments to the Supreme Court*. New York: Oxford University Press.

Alfini, James J. 1981. "Mississippi Judicial Selection: Election, Appointment, and Bar Anointment." In J. A. Cramer, ed. *Courts and Judges*. Beverly Hills, Calif.: Sage.

Alpert, Lenore. 1981. "Learning About Trial Judging: The Socialization of State Trial Judges." In J. A. Cramer, ed. *Courts and Judges*. Beverly Hills, Calif.: Sage.

American Bar Association. 1993. *Model Rules of Professional Conduct*. Chicago: American Bar Association.

————1991. *Standing Committee on the Federal Judiciary: What It Is and How It Works*. Chicago: American Bar Association

Ashman, Allan. 1974. *The Key to Judicial Selection: The Nominating Process*. Chicago: American Judicature Society.

Ashman, Charles R. 1973. *The Finest Judges Money Can Buy*. Los Angeles: Nash.

Ball, Howard. 1987. *Courts and Politics: The Federal Judicial System*. Englewood Cliffs, N.J.: Prentice-Hall.

Berg, Jerome S. 1977. "Judicial Interest in Administration: The Critical Variable." In Larry C. Bergson, Steven W. Hays, and Susan J. Carbon, eds. *Managing the State Courts*. St. Paul, Minn.: West.

Berkson, Larry C., Steven W. Hays, and Susan J. Carbon, eds. 1977. *Managing the State Courts*. St. Paul, Minn.: West.

Carp, Robert A., and Ronald Stidham. 1990. *Judicial Process in America*. Washington, D.C.: Congressional Quarterly Press.

Carp, Robert A. and Russell Wheeler. 1972. "Sink or Swim: The Socialization of a Federal District Judge." *Journal of Public Law* 21 (2):359–94.

Coffin, Frank M. 1980. *The Ways of a Judge: Reflections from the Federal Appellate Bench*. Boston: Houghton-Mifflin.

Cook, Beverly B. 1987. "Women as Judges." In B. B. Cook, L. F. Goldstein, K. O'Connor, and S. M. Talarico, eds. *Women in the Judicial Process*. Washington, D.C.: American Political Science Association.

Curran, Barbara. 1985. *The Lawyer Statistical Report: A Statistical Profile of the United States Legal Profession in the 1980s*. Chicago: American Bar Foundation.

Dahlin, D. C. 1986. *Models of Court Management*. Millwood, N.Y.: Associated Faculty Press.

Dilweg, V., and D. R. Fretz, T. Murphy, F. B. Rodgers, T. C. Wicker Jr. 1992. *Modern Judicial Ethics*. Reno, Nev.: National Judicial College.

Director of the Administrative Office of the Courts. 1990. *Report of the Proceedings of the Judicial Conference of the United States*. Washington, D.C.: U.S. Government Printing Office.

Dorsen, Norman and Leon Friedman. 1973. *Disorder in the Court*. New York: Pantheon.

Dubois, Philip L. 1980. *From Ballot to Bench: Judicial Elections and the Quest for Accountability*. Austin: University of Texas Press.

Goldman, Sheldon. 1975. "Voting Behavior on the Unites States Courts of Appeals Revisited." *American Political Science Review* 69 (June): 491–506.

Goldman, Sheldon, and Charles M. Lamb. 1986. *Judicial Conflict and Consensus: Behavioral Studies of American Appellate Courts*. Lexington: University Press of Kentucky.

Goulden, Joseph C. 1974. *The Benchwarmers: The Private World of the Powerful Federal Judges*. New York: Weybright and Talley.

Henderson, T. A., C. M. Kerwin, R. Guynes, C. Baar, N. Miller, H. Saisew, and R. Grieser. 1984. *The Significance of Judicial Structure: The Effect of Unification on Trial Court Operations*. Washington, D.C.: National Institute of Justice.

Henry, M. L. 1985. *The Success of Women and Minorities in Achieving Judicial Office: The Selection Process*. New York: Fund for Modern Courts.

In re *J. P. Linahan*, 138 F.2d 650 (2nd Cir. 1943).

Hudzik, J. K. 1991. "Voices from a Decade Ago: The First National Symposium on Court Management." *Justice System Journal* 15(2):563–579.

Lawson, H. O. and D. E. Howard. 1991. "Development of the Profession of Court Management: A History with Comment." *Justice System Journal* 15(2):580–604.

Lubet, Steven. 1984. *Beyond Reproach: Ethical Restrictions on the Extrajudicial Activities of State and Federal Judges*. Chicago: American Judicature Society.

Lushkin, M. L. 1987. "Social Loafing on the Bench: The Case of Calendars and Caseloads." *Justice System Journal* 12(2):177–195.

Maguire, Kathleen, and Ann L. Pastore, eds. 1994. *Sourcebook of Criminal Justice Statistics — 1993*. Washington, D.C.: USGPO.

Mahoney, B. 1987. "Attacking Problems of Delay in Urban Trial Courts." *State Court Journal* 11(3):4–10.

Mahoney, B., A. B. Arkman, P. Casey, V. E. Flango, G. Gallas, T. A. Henderson, J. A. Ito, D. C. Steelman, and S. Weller. 1988. *Changing Times in Trial Courts.* Williamsburg, Va.: National Center for State Courts.

Marvell, Thomas B. 1977. *Appellate Courts and Lawyers: Information Gathering in an Adversary System.* Westport, Conn.: Greenwood.

McFadden, Patrick M. 1990. *Electing Justice: The Law and Ethics of Judicial Campaigns.* Chicago: American Judicature Society.

"Merit Selection Found to Help Women, Blacks Win Judgeships." 1986. *Criminal Justice Newsletter* 17 (January 2): 4.

Milford, Lisa L. 1992. *The Development of the ABA Judicial Code.* Chicago: American Bar Association, Center for Professional Responsibility.

North Carolina v. Russell, 427 U.S. 328 (1976), 96 S.Ct. 2709.

O'Brien, David M. 1988. *Background Paper for Twentieth Century Fund Task Force on Judicial Selection.* New York: Priority Press.

Rosen, Ellen. 1987. "The Nation's Judges: No Unanimous Opinion." *Court Review* 24 (4): 4–9.

Ryan, John Paul, Allan Ashman, Bruce D. Sales, & Sandra Shane-DuBow. 1980. *American Trial Judges: Their Work Styles and Performance.* New York: Free Press.

Satter, Robert. 1990. *Doing Justice: A Trial Judge at Work.* New York: Simon & Schuster.

Schwartz, H. 1988. *Packing the Courts: The Conservative Campaign to Rewrite the Constitution.* New York: Scribner.

Silberman, Linda J. 1979. *Non-attorney Justice in the United States: An Empirical Study.* New York: New York University Institute of Judicial Administration.

Smith, Christopher E. 1990. *United States Magistrates in the Federal Courts: Subordinate Judges.* New York: Praeger.

Solomon, M., and D. K. Somerlot. 1987. *Caseflow Management in the Trial Court.* Chicago: American Bar Association.

Swindler, William F. 1976. "Seedtime of an American Judiciary." In Glenn R. Winters and Edward J. Schoenbaum, eds. *American Courts and Justice.* Chicago: American Judicature Society.

Tribe, Laurence H. 1985. *God Save This Honorable Court: How the Choice of Supreme Court Justices Shapes Our History.* New York: Random House.

Twentieth Century Fund Task Force on Judicial Selection. 1988. *Judicial Roulette.* New York: Priority Press.

Ulmer, S. Sidney. 1973. "Social Background as an Indicator of the Votes of Supreme Court Justices in Criminal Cases: 1947–1956 Terms." *American Journal of Political Science* 17 (August) 622–30.

Wheeler, Russell R., and A. Leo Levin. 1979. *Judicial Discipline and Removal in the United States.* Washington, D.C.: Federal Judicial Center.

Wice, Paul B. 1991. *Judges and Lawyers: The Human Side of Justice.* New York: Harper-Collins.

——— 1985. *Chaos in the Courthouse: The Inner Workings of the Urban Criminal Courts.* New York: Praeger.

——— 1981. "Judicial Socialization: The Philadelphia Experience." In J. A. Cramer, *Courts and Judges,* ed. Beverly Hills, Calif.: Sage.

Winters, Glenn R. 1976. "Two Centuries of Judicial Progress in America." In Glenn R. Winters and Edward J. Schoenbaum, eds. *American Courts and Justice* Chicago: American Judicature Society.

CHAPTER 7

PROSECUTORS

The modern prosecutor, sometimes described as the chief law enforcement officer of the jurisdiction, has the duty to represent the citizens of the jurisdiction in a criminal prosecution. Broadly stated, the function of the prosecutor in the adversarial process is to determine which cases will be prosecuted and then to prepare and present those cases to the court for judgment. Although the prosecutor's tasks can be stated rather simply, the role of the prosecutor is complex and full of inherent tensions. The prosecutor functions both as a quasijudicial officer in screening cases and determining whether to initiate prosecution and as an advocate in an adversarial proceeding. Despite the role as advocate, and despite the fact that the prosecutor belongs to the executive branch of government and is considered a law enforcement officer, as a representative of the people the prosecutor is expected to exercise authority in an even-handed and fair manner. Ideally, the prosecutor seeks more than a long list of convictions. The prosecutor seeks justice.

district attorney

Prosecutors (known variously as the **district attorney,** the county attorney, the state's attorney, the attorney for the commonwealth, and the prosecuting attorney) play a pivotal role in the processing of criminal cases. The authority of the contemporary prosecutor to issue charges is widely recognized as "the broadest and least regulated power in American criminal law" (Gershman 1993, 513). At one time the prosecutor's role in screening cases and initiating prosecutions was far less prominent. The prosecutor's office developed into a powerful force in the criminal justice system with the urbanization of the Unites States and the establishment of standing police forces (Jacoby 1980, 24).

This chapter describes the office of the prosecutor, how prosecutors are selected, the typical work of a prosecuting attorney, how prosecutors learn the work, and the constraints on the prosecuting attorney's authority.

■ The Office of the Prosecutor

The United States has more than 25,000 prosecuting attorneys, more than half of whom are employed full time. This army of prosecutors is comprised of 2,300 chief prosecutors practicing in state courts, aided by approximately 20,000 assistant prosecutors (Dawson 1992). The federal jurisdiction is much smaller, with 94 U.S. attorneys (Want's 1992) assisted by about 4,300 staff attorneys (Justice Management 1992). In addition, many city attorneys are responsible for prosecuting petty offenses in the lower courts, which are often branches of local government (see Chapter 10).

Prosecutors' offices, whether federal or state, vary greatly in size. The size, as well as the organization and standard operation of the prosecutor's office, is shaped primarily by the volume and complexity of criminal cases in that jurisdiction. The volume and nature of the cases in turn are shaped by the size and type of population served (Jacoby 1980, 47–77). In jurisdictions serving small populations the chief prosecutor serves only part time. In fact, more than half of the nation's chief prosecutors are part time officials (Dawson 1992, 1). At the other extreme, huge cities like Los Angeles, Chicago, and Houston and the counties of New York City each employ hundreds of full-time attorneys to process the criminal cases brought to them by citizens and police. Urban prosecutors' offices process most of the nation's crimes. For this reason this book focuses especially on the work of the urban prosecutor's office.

Prosecutors specialize in criminal lawsuits. In some jurisdictions the prosecutor works exclusively on criminal cases. In other jurisdictions the duties of the office include representing the government in noncriminal matters as well. For example, a prosecutor's office may have responsibility for nonsupport and paternity suits, consumer protection cases, extradition matters, mental commitments, environmental protection cases, and juvenile delinquency matters (Dawson 1992, 2). Sometimes these noncriminal matters account for a substantial segment of the caseload. In other jurisdictions noncriminal matters are the responsibilities of government lawyers who are not part of the local prosecutor's office.

In the United States the office of prosecutor possesses more power than its counterpart in other Western democracies, where the judiciary directly controls and supervises prosecutors (Cole, Frankowski, and Jertz 1987; see Chapter 5). Various origins have been assigned to the local prosecutor's functions, duties, and power in the United States. One scholar has described the modern prosecutor as a descendant of prosecutors from three European countries: the English attorney-general, the French *procureur publique,* and the Dutch *schout.* Powers of each of these three are vested in the modern local prosecutor in the United States. Specifically, the power of the English attorney-general to terminate prosecutions, the power of the French procureur to initiate prosecutions, and the local autonomy of the Dutch schout are combined in the prosecutor (Jacoby 1980, 3). Others have described the modern prosecutor as a combination of attorney general and justice of the peace (Nissman and Hagen 1982, 4). Whatever the exact characterization, it is widely agreed that the modern American prosecutor is a powerful official.

In the states the local prosecutor has great autonomy, both by design and by tradition. Judges have no greater authority over prosecutors than they have over any other attorney in court. Similarly, although the local prosecutor is part of the executive branch of government, the prosecutor is not an employee of the mayor or the governor or any other administrator in the executive branch of government. As an elected official, the local chief prosecutor answers directly to the voters.

attorney general

Typically, the state attorney general, although referred to as the chief law enforcement official in the state, is not a direct supervisor of local prosecutors. The state **attorney general** usually has the authority to initiate charges independently if a local prosecutor declines to prosecute, but this option is rarely exercised. In some states the power of the attorney general is more broad, allowing the state attorney general to terminate a prosecution when the local prosecutor wants to proceed. Authority to intervene in a local prosecution is frequently limited to those instances in which the local prosecutor requests assistance or when the governor directs the attorney general to intervene (National District Attorneys Association 1977, 24–26). The primary role of the attorney general with respect to the local prosecutor is to provide legal assistance and advice when asked. As a prosecutor the state attorney general is usually limited to cases involving regulatory offenses or special investigations, such as statewide drug distribution rings or public corruption.

U.S. attorney

In the federal system prosecution is conducted by **U.S. attorneys** located in each judicial district. The locally placed prosecutors work under the authority of the national chief prosecutor, the attorney general of the United States, who is the cabinet-level head of the U.S. Department of Justice. Consequently, U.S. attorneys enjoy somewhat less autonomy than local prosecutors. At the direction of the president, the attorney general sets the policy and the agenda for resource allocation for the U.S. attorneys across the country. The relationship between the U.S. attorney general and the various U.S. attorneys is stronger than the typical parallel relationship between a state's attorney general and local district attorneys, but the U.S. attorneys in the district offices still enjoy a fair amount of independence from the central authority in Washington, D.C. (Bell and Meador 1993, 248). For example, the attorney general does not require centralized supervision of all charging decisions by the U.S. attorneys' offices. The day-to-day work of charging and trying cases goes on with relatively little direct supervision or interference.

The attorney general does set priorities for the U.S. attorneys. Consequently, the crime control and prosecution policies of federal prosecutors tend to reflect the agenda of the administration to which the U.S. attorneys answer (U.S. Department of Justice 1980). For example, under President Jimmy Carter federal prosecutors turned their energies to white-collar crime investigations and prosecutions, whereas under President Ronald Reagan, they devoted more attention to drug investigations and prosecutions. These noticeable shifts in policy are possible because of the way in which U.S. attorneys are appointed and because they can be removed from office at any time by the president.

◼ BECOMING A PROSECUTOR

All prosecutors, whether state or federal, whether the head of the office or a rookie assistant, hold law degrees and are licensed to practice law in the jurisdiction in which they work. No other preparation is required of persons seeking jobs as prosecuting attorneys. In fact, prosecutors often recruit new lawyers right out of law school. Lawyers seeking careers as litigators view the prosecutor's office, with its unparalleled opportunity for trial practice, as an excellent training ground. As a consequence prosecutors' offices often have a fair amount of turnover in staff, as those who have gained the experience they seek move on to other more lucrative and comfortable positions in the legal community.

Chief prosecutors are more likely to be experienced attorneys, often with previous experience in political office. Historically, lawyers have used the position of chief prosecutor to gain a public reputation before running for higher political office. For example, New York Mayor Rudolph Guiliani attained public attention in his earlier position as U.S. attorney for the Southern District of New York, which includes New York City.

In contrast, chief prosecutors in several major cities have made careers in the prosecutor's office and have not treated the experience as a stepping-stone to some other public office. Such career prosecutors have become increasingly common in the past few decades. This trend is probably related to the rapid growth of crime and the resulting growth in prosecutorial staff and prestige of the office. Prosecutors' offices that are headed by career prosecutors typically experience less turnover among the assistant prosecutors. The relatively long tenure of assistant prosecutors means that the office benefits from more fully developed expertise and skills learned on the job. In turn, according to one of the few studies of attorneys practicing criminal law in different cities across the country (Wice 1978), the more highly respected the prosecutor's office, the more it is likely to attract highly skilled opposing defense counsel. In other words, the competence of the prosecutor's office defines in large part the general competence of the criminal bar in that locale. This research suggests that the trend toward career prosecutors holds substantial benefits for the justice system.

Selection

In most states prosecutors are locally elected officials who are responsive to the immediate community they serve. Only four states have prosecutors not directly elected by the local populace. In New Jersey the governor appoints local prosecutors. In Alaska, Connecticut, and Delaware, criminal prosecution is the responsibility of the state attorney general. The term of office for elected prosecutors ranges from two to eight years, with most jurisdictions (86 percent) providing four-year terms (Dawson 1992, 2). In case of a midterm vacancy in a state that elects prosecutors, the governor usually has authority to appoint an interim prosecutor until the next regular election.

In all but the most sparsely populated jurisdictions the chief prosecutor employs assistants who carry out most of the day-to-day operations of the office. *assistant prosecutor* **Assistant prosecutors** are either appointed by the elected prosecutor or are civil service employees. Assistant prosecutors who are civil service employees are hired on the basis of written exams and/or interviews and serve a probationary period. Satisfactory performance earns them a permanent position. Because these assistant prosecutors are protected by civil service, most of the staff remains after the chief prosecutor loses an election. This has the effect of ensuring continuity of expertise and consistency of standards, irrespective of election results.

In contrast, where assistant prosecutors are appointed by the chief prosecutor, appointments may be made for political or private purposes. Nepotism and favoritism are common complaints in offices that do not select assistant prosecutors through a civil service process. In addition, the office may undergo substantial turnover upon the defeat of the incumbent chief prosecutor. With the

OFFICE POLITICS

Former Queens County, New York, assistant prosecutor Alice Vachss describes how the chief prosecutor encouraged assistant prosecutors to support him in his election campaign:

In a bureau chiefs' meeting early on, Brown [the chief prosecutor] looked around the room preparing us for an announcement: We all knew he was running for election in September; he wanted us to know that we were all out of it. He didn't want us doing anything. He had plenty of people working on his campaign. Our job was to do our jobs, not get involved in politics. I only hoped he meant it.

*   *   *

[Sometime later] At one of Brown's weekly meetings he made an announcement. He knew he'd said that all of us were not to be involved in his campaign, he said. But so many of the bureau chiefs and executives had "begged" him to let them participate that

he didn't want to abridge our civic rights. He'd asked his legal counsel to research the situation. At the next meeting, Brown reported the results of that research. It turned out that despite the general prohibition against ADAs [assistant district attorneys] engaging in political activity, we *were* legally permitted to work on his campaign—so long as it wasn't fund-raising or on office hours.

*   *   *

I did as much for Brown's campaign as I had for Santucci's [the former chief prosecutor]: nothing.

*   *   *

Three days after the election, the chief assistant called me into his office. I was fired.

SOURCE: Excerpted from Alice Vachss, 1993. *Sex Crimes.* New York: Random House, pp. 269–71. Copyright © 1993 by Alice Vachss. Reprinted by permission of Random House, Inc.

newly elected prosecutor come a substantial number of newly appointed assistant prosecutors. The character of the office and the informal ways of doing business are likely to change. Such offices tend to be less consistent in the application of standards than offices that retain the bulk of the staff, regardless of election results. Offices with appointed assistants are susceptible to the prevailing political winds of crime control policy. Moreover, the assistants, whose jobs depend on the discretion of the chief prosecutor, are especially vulnerable to pressure to become involved in the election campaigns of their bosses, particularly through financial contributions.

U.S. attorneys are appointed by the president and confirmed by the Senate. Unlike federal judges, who serve lifetime appointments, the U.S. attorneys serve at the discretion of the president. Typically, when a new president is inaugurated, all U.S. attorneys submit their resignations, allowing the new president to appoint others, usually from the president's own political party. Senatorial courtesy plays a major role in the selection of the U.S. attorney's (Bell and Meador 1993, 249). In some states the nomination is the sole prerogative of the senators involved, and they rely only on their advisers in naming potential nominees. Other senators appoint citizen committees to aid in the process. The committee might include the district attorneys from urban areas in the state, deans of law schools, the president of the state bar association, and a private citizen or two. After a candidate emerges as the likely nominee the FBI conducts a thorough background investigation, a process that often takes several weeks or months. Eventually, the president announces the nomination, and the Senate is asked to vote to confirm. Because all U.S. attorneys serve at the pleasure of the president, U.S. attorneys may be asked to resign at any time, even if the attorney has done nothing wrong and is doing a good job.

TOO MUCH POLITICAL HEAT

David Marston was appointed United States attorney, eastern district, Pennsylvania (located in Philadelphia), by President Gerald Ford in July 1976. He was the fourth U.S. attorney in five years due to the dramatic political pressures on federal prosecutors in Pennsylvania. Marston was a 33-year-old lawyer who had been legislative counsel to Senator Richard Schweikert (R-Pa.) for three years. When the attorney's post opened up Marston indicated his interest and, on the basis of Schweikert's recommendation, got the job.

When he arrived in Philadelphia, Marston was confronted by a corruption-ridden political system complete with fraud, bribery, kickbacks, payoffs, and obstruction of justice by various public figures in local and state government. Given the politics of the area, Marston, a Republican, was soon prosecuting local Democratic leaders—and getting convictions. By this time, a new administration had come into the White House—the Democratic administration of President Jimmy Carter. Given Carter's pre-election campaign rhetoric (which called for the merit selection of federal judges *and* U.S. attorneys), given the fact that Marston had another three years left on his four year com-

mission, and given the fact that he was, after all, doing a good job, Marston felt that he would not be dismissed.

And for a time he was correct. Pleas to the Carter administration from Democratic congressional leaders to replace the Republican with a Democratic U.S. attorney were initially ignored by the attorney general and his assistants. The picture changed dramatically when Marston's staff began investigating the activities of two Democratic congressmen from Pennsylvania, Joshua Eilberg and Daniel Flood. A Philadelphia hospital had added a new wing, financed in part through federal funds. The U.S. attorney's office found out that Eilberg's Philadelphia law firm had been retained by the hospital as counsel and had received over $500,000 in fees—part of this money received by Eilberg. The firm worked with Congressman Flood to get a $14.5 million federal loan for new construction. (Flood was the chairman of the House Appropriations subcommittee on Labor, Health, Education, and Welfare.) Flood, in turn, convinced the hospital administrators to retain a Baltimore, Maryland, outfit, Capital Investment Development Corporation, to oversee the construction of the new wing for a fee of over $1 million.

The attorney general of the United States, who supervises the U.S. attorneys, is also appointed by the president with the consent of the Senate. The selection of attorney general attracts the same sort of media attention as other major cabinet appointments. U.S. attorneys supervise a staff of **assistant U.S. attorneys** who are not political appointees. Although these assistants are not civil service employees, their jobs are normally protected when the administration changes.

assistant U.S. attorney

Socialization

Except in the smallest offices, newly hired assistant prosecutors usually undergo some form of training before taking over their new responsibilities. In some jurisdictions the training consists of formal instruction in a classroom setting. In other offices the training consists of "structured observation"—the rookie shadows a more experienced assistant prosecutor for a week or two to develop a sense of how business is conducted (Heumann 1978, 93). A former prosecutor for the Manhattan district attorney's office describes the training he received as one in a group of fifty newly appointed assistant district attorneys (Heilbroner 1990, 1–22). First came a five-week formal course of lectures and readings to orient the *continued*

This information was gathered by Marston during the summer and early fall of 1977 and his staff was, in November 1977, seriously reviewing the possibility of criminal action.

On November 4, 1977, two days after the U.S. attorney's office asked the FBI to participate in the investigation, Congressman Eilberg called President Carter and asked Carter to get rid of Marston. Because of Eilberg's power in Congress (chairman of a House Immigration subcommittee), Carter immediately telphoned [sic] Attorney General [Griffin] Bell and instructed him to expedite the removal of Marston.

In mid-November, Marston was informed by Associate Attorney General Michael Egan that although "you're doing a good job, we may have to make a move on you next spring. When pressure comes from on high, it has to be relieved." At that point, Marston met with his immediate superior, Assistant Attorney General Russell Baker, Criminal Division of the Department of Justice, and informed his boss of the ongoing hospital investigation and the possible criminal linkage between the two congressmen, the hospital, the law firm, and the construction firm.

This was to no avail, however, because on January 20, 1978, Marston was summoned to Washington, D.C., and personally fired by Attorney General Griffin Bell. After an hour of discussion, Bell stated, simply, that "you're being fired because you're a Republican and we are Democrats." The "Marston Massacre," as it was labeled by Republicans who recalled the "Saturday Night Massacre" of October 1973 (when President Nixon fired Archibald Cox as Special Watergate Prosecutor) touched off a great outcry against the Carter administration. The White House received over 12,000 telephone calls and almost 25,000 letters in the next week. Over 99 percent of these communications condemned the Carter administration for the Marston firing. It mattered little; Marston was gone within days after the January meeting with Bell, and Congressman Jonathan Eilberg had a role in the selection of the replacement—a loyal Democratic party attorney.

Source: Excerpted from Howard Ball © 1987. *Courts and Politics: The Federal Judicial System*, 2d ed. Englewood Cliffs, N.J.: Prentice-Hall, pp. 97, 221–23. Reprinted by permission of Prentice-Hall, Englewood Cliffs, New Jersey.

recruits to the criminal code and the workings of the office. Then he was assigned to the Early Case Assessment Bureau (ECAB), which reviewed misdemeanor cases to determine what charges to issue. "By the end of my first week in ECAB I had drafted more than 100 complaints, interviewed as many police officers, and spoken with a half dozen victims" Heilbroner writes (1990, 13).

Even when a brief training period is offered, the prosecutor is expected to handle cases without direct supervision very soon after being hired. One scholar observes, "Within a few weeks after starting [the] job, the prosecutor[s] . . . are expected to handle cases on their own. Experienced personnel are still available for advice, and the newcomer is told that he can turn to them with his problems. But the cases are now the newcomer's" (Heumann 1978, 95). Through on-the-job training and socialization the new prosecutor learns the office norms of doing business. Supervisors, veteran assistant prosecutors, judges, defense attorneys, and police officers all contribute to this socialization process. Through their informal participation, sometimes implicit and sometimes explicit, sometimes solicited but often unsolicited, the new prosecutor learns expectations and limitations.

☐ THE WORK OF A PROSECUTOR

The basic work required to prosecute a case—investigation, determination of charges, preparation, and so on—is the same whether the case is prosecuted in a large office in New York City or a relatively small office in Cody, Wyoming. But the caseloads and resources of prosecutors' offices vary in significant ways. An armed robbery in New York and an armed robbery in Cody require the same preparation by the prosecutor, but the resources available to support the prosecutor's work vary widely. The experience of the prosecutor and workload constraints also vary dramatically. For example, the workload of federal prosecutors includes a higher proportion of drug cases and more complex cases that require significant investigation and resources to prosecute than the ordinary street crimes (robbery, burglary, and assault) common in local prosecutors' offices. These differences can help to explain differences in the ways in which prosecutors approach their work and differences in the outcomes they achieve.

Because the work of the prosecutor mirrors the processing of criminal cases, subsequent chapters describe each of these tasks in greater detail. This section provides an overview, focusing on the prosecutor's role at each stage.

Investigating the Crime

Prosecution depends on evidence to support the charge and conviction. In large part cases succeed or fail on the evidence. Obtaining evidence requires investigation, and the quality of the investigation affects the prosecutor's chance of obtaining a conviction. Prosecutors become involved in investigations in several ways. Some rely entirely on the police to conduct investigations. In other cases the prosecutor directs the police in special investigations or may conduct an investigation independent of that conducted by the police. How much or how little investigation the prosecutor conducts depends on a variety of factors: the nature of the criminal activity, the identity of the suspected offender, the complexity of the case, the competence and cooperation of the police investigators, the availability and expertise of the prosecutor's investigative staff, and how the crime comes to the attention of law enforcement officials. For example, prosecutors are frequently involved in the investigation of organized and white-collar crime. In the case of high-profile street crimes a prosecutor may direct the investigation once the police have identified a suspect.

Police-Prosecutor Interdependence

The relationship between prosecutor and police is a delicate and critical one of interdependence. Successful prosecutions depend on good police work. Most cases begin with the police detecting the crime and apprehending the suspect. For routine street crimes such as burglary, assault, retail theft, robbery, and disorderly conduct, police are the gatekeepers to the criminal court process; a case will not make it into the courts unless a police officer makes an arrest and refers that arrest to the prosecutor. The police also gather most evidence used to support prosecutions: they find weapons, they take statements from witnesses, they recover stolen property, and so on. Consequently, how the police do their jobs has an enormous effect on the types of cases the prosecutor receives and the quality of the evidence accompanying each case. The prosecutor also has an influence on the police. How the prosecutor treats police and how the prosecutor handles their cases influence how the police do their job in the future. When the prosecutor refuses to issue charges, the police assume that something went wrong. They may assume that what went wrong is that the prosecutor is a "bleeding heart" or corrupt. Frequently, however, they recognize that the kind of evidence the police need to make an arrest is less compelling than the evidence the prosecutor needs to get a conviction. If the police want their arrests to lead to convictions, they will strive to provide the prosecutor with the appropriate evidence.

This natural feedback from prosecutor to police has been characterized as an exchange relationship: prosecutors are dependent on the police to bring in clean arrests and solid evidence; police are dependent on prosecutors to turn their hard investigative work into convictions (Cole 1970). Given these interdependencies, friction can result when expectations are not met. Prosecutors may become annoyed when police bring them arrests not worth prosecuting or have done inadequate investigation. Police become resentful when prosecutors refuse to charge for reasons the police do not accept.

Working day to day with the police, some prosecutors begin to view the police, rather than the public, as their clients (Melilli 1992, 689). Some prosecutors are reluctant to criticize the work of the police, even implicitly. These prosecutors fear, often with good reason, that police will resent the prosecutor's decisions not to charge and will be less cooperative in the future. A prosecutor's reluctance to upset the relationship may result in the prosecutor charging cases that should not be charged, simply to satisfy the police. Unfortunately, overlooking sloppy police work or excessive charging by the police promotes neither justice nor efficiency.

Increasing the level of communication between the police and prosecutors can reduce these problems. Through close and complete communication each party may learn to appreciate the other's decisions and the unique role that each has to play in the criminal justice process. Working together in teams on specific tasks can help to overcome the tensions that arise when the police see their arrests do not lead to prosecution (Buchanan 1989).

Two additional prosecutorial roles help shape police performance and police-prosecutor relations: the prosecutor's role as trainer-adviser on legal matters and the prosecutor's duty to prosecute police misconduct. The prosecutor's role as legal adviser and trainer on matters of criminal procedure and policy can strengthen the police-prosecutor relationship. For example, when case law results in a change that affects police procedure, the prosecutor interprets the law and describes its application to police conduct. When police officers prepare search warrants or arrest warrants, in most jurisdictions it is routine procedure for a prosecutor to review the application and provide assistance to ensure the warrant is legally sufficient before taking it before a judge. Sometimes the police consult the prosecutor for advice on the legality of certain procedures before carrying out a search in unusual circumstances. Prosecutors often serve as instructors in formal in-service training for police officers. Preparing warrants, executing searches, and handling evidence are topics a prosecutor might discuss with police officers during in-service training.

Despite the best efforts to promote a good working relationship with the police, tensions inevitably arise when the prosecutor investigates crimes committed by police officers. Whenever a citizen is injured during an arrest, a prosecutor may review the event to determine whether the injury was the result of excessive force by the police. Every time an officer shoots a citizen, the prosecutor must review the facts to determine whether the shooting was justifiable. If the prosecutor finds no justification for the officer's actions, the prosecutor may file criminal charges. If an officer is suspected of stealing confiscated property or impounded drugs, the prosecutor may need to investigate to determine whether charges are warranted.

Investigations of police misconduct account for only a very small portion of the prosecutor's workload, but each is a point of friction with the police. Although many police officers appreciate the prosecutor's role in keeping the police accountable, some investigations of police misconduct result in deep resentment between the police and the prosecutor's office. These resentments can impede cooperation on routine cases.

Investigative Support

Large prosecutors' offices often employ civilian investigators to assist in special investigations or to conduct follow-up investigations to help the prosecutor prepare the case. The prosecutor's office, rather than the police, often takes responsibility for investigating white-collar and corporate crime. In addition, large prosecutors' offices often have specialized units to handle cases like domestic violence, sexual assault, organized crime, arson, and illegal gang activity. These investigations require special skills, such as accounting expertise or knowledge of victim psychology, and take a great deal of time. Sometimes the prosecutor's investigators work cooperatively with a task force of officers from several law enforcement agencies. For example, a drug task force might include officers from several local police departments and investigators from federal agencies as well as the local prosecutor's office.

Making the Charging Decision

Issuing charges against a defendant formally initiates prosecution. The prosecutor's office is the only one in the jurisdiction with the power to routinely initiate prosecutions. Although private prosecution is still practiced in Canada and Great Britain, and was practiced in the United States in earlier times, private prosecution is no longer permitted in the United States.

Deciding whether to issue charges is the most pivotal task of the prosecutor. The prosecutor is not required to charge in every case, and a third or more of the cases reviewed by many prosecutors' offices are not prosecuted (Jacoby 1982, 39). That this decision is effectively unregulated and practically unreviewable has been a point of concern for years (see Davis 1971, 188; Feeney, Dill and Wier 1983, 196–199; Gershman 1993, 513; Goldstein 1981; U.S. Department of Justice 1980, 14; Weimer 1980, 27).

In determining whether to issue charges the prosecutor is bound by the prosecutor's code of ethics to seek justice (Lezak and Leonard 1985). The decision is made in consideration of several factors. Primary among them is whether the evidence in the case is strong enough to meet the minimum legal requirement of probable cause. If probable cause does not exist, the prosecutor has no option but to decline to prosecute. Even when the evidence is strong enough to support issuing charges, other factors play a major role in the prosecutor's decision. As a representative of the citizens the prosecuting attorney takes into account the seriousness of the offense and public sentiment about such offenses. As a public employee mindful of the wise use of resources, the prosecutor also considers the likelihood of conviction, which requires proof beyond a reasonable doubt. The prosecutor also takes into account the probability of obtaining a disposition that will serve some useful purpose, whether it is imprisonment or some other outcome. Finally, the prosecutor considers humanitarian factors that affect common notions of blameworthiness.

The prosecutor makes the charging decision on behalf of the people of the jurisdiction, not as the personal attorney for the victim. The victim's wishes may play an important role in the decision, but they are only one of many factors a prosecutor must weigh (Miller 1969). This is a key distinction between public and private prosecution.

If a local prosecutor in the United States declines to issue charges based on the complaint of a victim, the victim has little recourse. The state attorney general has the authority to issue charges when the local prosecutor declines to do so, but this power is rarely exercised. The grand jury, where it is used, offers a check on a prosecutor's decision not to investigate or issue charges. A judge has the authority to convene a grand jury, which then has the power to investigate criminal matters and determine whether charges should be issued against a defendant. In the case of homicides a coroner's inquest may be used in a similar fashion. The coroner's inquest and the grand jury are not bound to follow the will of the prosecutor. As such, they serve as a check on a prosecutor's unwarranted leniency. In some states, if the prosecutor declines to issue charges, the victim may appeal to the court for a review of the decision. The court cannot force the prosecutor to issue charges. Instead, if the court determines that charges should be issued, it appoints a special prosecutor to oversee the case. Such extraordinary charging processes are rarely used, however. Absent extraordinary circumstances, the decision of the prosecutor not to charge means that the case will go no further in the criminal court process.

Case Preparation

work product

Evidence, which is the cornerstone of a prosecution, comes to the attention of the police and prosecutor in bits and pieces. The prosecutor must weave a credible fabric from the individual threads of evidence. This requires organizing the evidence and proposing credible inferences. The result of this part of the prosecutor's work is known as the **work product.** The work product is not part of the case itself; it is not evidence; it is not facts. It is the thinking and reasoning on the part of the prosecutor that make the pieces of evidence fit together in a single construction. Without this work many defendants would never be convicted.

Case preparation requires many activities: organizing the evidence and making sure that proof is adequate for each and every element of the charge, going over the testimony of witnesses to assess and maximize their credibility, anticipating defenses to the charges, and preparing explanations for why those defenses are not plausible. In sum, the prosecutor must make sure that the evidence is in a form that provides a convincing and complete picture to support a conviction on the charge.

ONE PROSECUTOR'S VIEW

My motives for becoming an assistant district attorney in the first place were mixed. I might have followed the majority of my law school class into a comfortable and lucrative corporate practice in Manhattan. At the time, however, I wanted something more interesting—something active, something that would get me into the "real world." The district attorney's office seemed to be the answer to these needs.

Moreover, I had known throughout law school that I wanted to be a real lawyer. I fancied the idea of courtroom drama, and in my mind's eye I had no difficulty envisioning myself doing great things. I was ambitious and impatient.

SOURCE: Excerpted from Steven J. Phillips, 1977. *No Heroes, No Villains: The Story of a Murder Trial.* New York: Vintage Books, p. 64. Copyright © 1977 by Steven J. Phillips. Reprinted by permission of Random House, Inc.

Court Work

The amount of time a prosecutor spends in court, and even the number of court appearances, varies greatly from case to case. In some cases, when the defendant pleads guilty and waives other hearings, court appearances may be limited to the initial appearance and the arraignment. In the case of some minor misdemeanors the defendant may make only one appearance before the court. In other cases a defendant may exercise the right to other hearings such as preliminary examination and trial. Still other cases include added court appearances for arguing motions. These hearings may be few or many, short or lengthy.

For many cases required appearances before the court are routine matters that take little preparation by the prosecutor. The initial appearance, for example, is such a routine matter that it requires virtually no thoughtful preparation. A misdemeanor sentencing hearing similarly consumes little of the prosecutor's time. Other court appearances require a great deal of preparation, as well as a great deal of time before the court. A complex trial may take months to prepare and weeks to present. A felony sentencing hearing may include a written brief from the prosecutor arguing that a harsh sentence is warranted.

Court work attracts many lawyers to the office of the prosecutor. Many urban prosecutors spend more time before the court in a year than other attorneys do in a lifetime. Still, trying a case and the related thrill of the courtroom contest is a comparatively rare event. In addition, court work often turns out to be less exciting than it sounds. Prosecutors complain about the time spent waiting in court and the frustration of repeated delays because of continuances granted to the defense.

Negotiation

Most criminal cases are resolved through guilty pleas. To facilitate guilty pleas the prosecutor engages in negotiation, or settlement of cases. Negotiation patterns vary widely. In addition, some chief prosecutors control negotiation through internal policies about the kinds of deals assistant prosecutors are allowed to make. Whatever the variations, one thing is consistent: negotiating criminal cases in the hope of reaching a settlement before trial is a routine aspect of the prosecutor's work.

Negotiations do not happen at a particular stage in the process, nor is it usually a particular task that the prosecutor sits down to execute. Negotiations unfold as the case unfolds and as the opportunities for settlement arise. For example, if the defense attorney is present when the prosecutor reviews the case for initial charging, negotiations may take place on the spot. Some cases are settled later, after arraignment, after the trial begins, or even later, while the jury is deliberating.

From the point of view of the prosecutor successful negotiation depends primarily on the evidence gathered, the case preparation, and the probability that the case can be proved in court. Paradoxically, the prosecutor who has a reputation for winning cases at trial does not have to; such a reputation encourages plea agreements from defendants. In that respect then, the very skills that make a prosecutor a good trial attorney will give the prosecutor leverage in plea negotiations. If the case is strong, the prosecutor works from an advantageous position in negotiations. If the case is weak, the defense has the advantage. Just as in trial work, solid evidence and good case preparation are the keys to a strong position in negotiations.

Organization of Work in Large Offices

Most criminal cases in this country are prosecuted in state prosecutors' offices in urban jurisdictions, staffed by scores, and perhaps hundreds, of assistant prosecutors (Dawson 1992). In these offices the chief prosecutor is responsible for managing the office, setting prosecutorial policy, and overseeing the work of all assistant prosecutors. Large offices with many employees are typically organized into specialized units for the efficient processing of cases. The most common division of labor is between misdemeanor and felony case processing. Felonies, being more serious cases, usually require more thorough investigation, more careful preparation, and are far more likely to go to trial than are misdemeanor cases. Because of these differences the prosecutor's staff typically is divided into felony and misdemeanor divisions, with the more experienced attorneys usually working in the felony division.

Another division of labor common in large offices involves the prosecutor's screening decision. In some jurisdictions the least experienced attorneys are assigned to screen cases, and case preparation and court work are left to those with more experience. This policy has long been the target of criticism (see Alschuler 1968, 64; Weimer 1980, 34). Good screening decisions promote both justice and efficiency. In a world of shrinking resources good judgments at this point become a high priority. Experienced prosecutors have greater experience in evaluating the merits of a case. Accordingly, some prosecutors' offices put experienced attorneys in charge of the screening function (Melilli 1992, 687).

Some large prosecutors' offices include special units devoted to the prosecution of certain kinds of cases, such as domestic violence, sexual assault, organized crime, white-collar crime, arson, illegal gang activities, and homicide. Special units are an advantage when caseload and staff resources permit, because the prosecution of certain types of cases requires special investigative skills and preparation or special sensitivity to the victims. Attorneys in the special units have a chance to develop the requisite skills and expertise through repeated handling of similar cases. Such special units often have investigative staff assigned to assist them.

Cases are assigned to attorneys within each organizational division. Two methods of assigning cases to assistant prosecutors are horizontal prosecution, sometimes referred to as the zone system, and vertical prosecution, sometimes referred to as the one-on-one system. In **vertical prosecution** the case is assigned to one prosecutor who sees the case through from beginning to final disposition. Vertical case processing is more common for felonies (Dawson 1992, 4), particularly in the special units (see Figure 7-1). Vertical case processing is the superior method, because one attorney is in charge of the case and accountable for the outcome. If the suspect is acquitted, the assistant assigned to the case cannot blame others for errors in the case.

vertical prosecution

The alternative is horizontal prosecution, which is more common in the processing of misdemeanor offenses. Under **horizontal prosecution** cases pass from attorney to attorney as the cases move through the court system. For example, one lawyer will handle the case at the initial appearance, a second attorney will represent the people at the preliminary hearing, and a third lawyer will attend the arraignment. Moreover, the first lawyer will represent the prosecution in all cases at initial appearance that day or perhaps that week. Similarly, the second attorney will handle all preliminary hearings for the prosecution that day, or that week, and so on. Thus the work in the office is not organized around individual cases but around stages in the adjudication process. Such an arrangement may allow more rapid processing of cases and require fewer attorneys. Horizontal prosecution simplifies scheduling. A prosecutor does not have to worry about being required to appear in two different courtrooms at the same time. If the public defender's office also operates on a horizontal system, waiting time for all participants can be significantly decreased.

horizontal prosecution

Despite the advantages to horizontal prosecution, efficiency comes at a high price. The lack of continuous consistent attention to and familiarity with the case invites problems. In this assembly-line style of case processing no one person is responsible for seeing the case through to the end. Because no one prosecutor is responsible for the case, individuals have less incentive to work on the case or to settle the case at the earliest point possible. An unsettled case passes on to the next person in the process (Melilli 1992, 688). For these reasons horizontal case processing is efficient in terms of lawyers' time but inferior to vertical processing in terms of case management and accountability (Jacoby 1982, 44–48).

Support for the Prosecution

Many urban prosecutors have initiated a variety of other programs that require additional staff to assist prosecutors in their day-to-day work. These programs include citizen complaint units, mental health screening programs, and victim-witness advocates.

Citizen Complaint Processors

One of many innovations in the modern prosecutor's office is the citizen complaint unit. Such units are designed to accept complaints directly from citizens. Citizen complain units are particularly useful when the police are unresponsive to certain kinds of offenses.

Domestic abuse is an example of the kind of complaint that is sometimes initiated through a citizen complaint unit. Police are sometimes unable or unwilling to make an arrest when called to the scene of a domestic assault. The

FIGURE 7-1   Use of Vertical Assignment of Felony Cases, by County Size, 1990

Source: Adapted from John M. Dawson, 1992. *Prosecutors in State Courts, 1990.* Washington, D.C.: U.S. Department of Justice, Bureau of Justice Statistics, p. 4.

Amount of cases assigned on vertical basis	All	75 largest counties	Elsewhere
None	12%	4%	12%
Some	18	69	16
Most or all	70	27	72

offender may have fled before the police arrived. State law may require an officer to witness the offense in order to make a valid arrest for misdemeanor assault. By the time the officer arrives, the assault is over and the officer has no legal grounds to make an arrest without a warrant. And sometimes police have not considered these assaults serious enough to make an arrest or to follow up on getting a warrant.

In each situation the citizen complaint process offers a solution. The victim may go to the citizen complaint unit, usually located in the prosecutor's office, which will prepare a complaint based on the victim's sworn statement describing the offense. The prosecutor may use that complaint as the basis for issuing criminal charges.

Although citizen complaint units do not give the victim of a crime as much control over the prosecution of a case as a system of private prosecution, they do bypass the normal gatekeeping function of the police. Even so, the police have not generally opposed the way in which these units have operated. In fact, police frequently inform victims of domestic violence of their option to go to the prosecutor and sign a complaint. However, the prosecutor is not obligated to issue charges for every complaint. The prosecutor still screens the charges.

Mental Health Screening

The mentally disabled are overrepresented among arrestees and are often arrested for offenses that are not serious (Hochstedler Steury 1991, 1993; Teplin 1984, 1990). Criminal prosecution and confinement to jail cause stress that, for mentally unstable people, can lead to a serious deterioration of their condition (Gibbs 1987). Unless detected and treated appropriately, the defendant with mental health problems poses a grave threat to order and safety in a setting such as an overcrowded jail. In addition, mentally ill defendants may be at a disadvantage in coping with the court process itself.

In recent years many courts have expanded their use of psychological and psychiatric services for criminal defendants. Some jurisdictions have set up screening units to divert the mentally ill from the criminal justice system and to arrange for treatment, usually medication, for those who need it while awaiting trial. Trained personnel in the jail or intake unit of the prosecutor's office may observe or interview defendants for signs of psychiatric distress or a history of psychiatric treatment. Defendants identified as having psychiatric problems may be treated differently from their mentally healthy counterparts. At the initial appearance the prosecutor may request that psychiatric treatment and medication be imposed as a condition of pretrial release. The mental health screening may result in a court-ordered psychiatric exam to determine whether the defendant is competent to stand trial. The prosecutor may use the findings of the screening to divert the defendant from the criminal process. For example, the prosecutor may persuade the defendant to seek voluntary treatment in lieu of prosecution. In other cases the prosecutor may seek involuntary civil commitment to a mental institution rather than pursue criminal prosecution.

Mental health screening units may be operated as part of the court itself, as a special unit of the prosecutor's office, or as an independent program on which the court, prosecutors, and defense counsel rely for information about a defendant's psychological health. The prosecutor is especially interested in this information because of the importance of psychological factors in determining the correct charge and whether criminal charges are an appropriate response at all.

Victim-Witness Advocates

Many scholars argue that the victim's satisfaction with the courts is the most critical component of the court's legitimacy in the eyes of the public (O'Grady et al. 1992). Victims and witnesses are key actors in any successful prosecution. Yet prosecutors often neglect to treat victims and witnesses with the sensitivity and even courtesy that these citizens reasonably expect. Increasingly, critics of the criminal courts have presented anecdotes about the neglect and abuse of victims and witnesses by the court process. Criticisms include the demands placed on victims and witnesses to make several court appearances, to tolerate long waits in uncomfortable and unsafe conditions, and to testify repeatedly. Shabby treatment of victims and witnesses raises obvious humanitarian concerns. In addition, the way in which victims and witnesses are treated can affect the success of a prosecution: when the hardships of testifying cause prosecution witnesses to fail to appear, the case is likely to be dismissed.

Many victims and witnesses are poor people who struggle in marginal jobs to earn enough money to make ends meet. Repeated trips to court are hardships. Simple things, like lack of transportation, the inability to take time off from a job without jeopardizing employment, parking fees, and child care problems, pose hardships and sometimes insurmountable barriers to cooperating with the prosecution. In addition, for some of the more traumatic and violent crimes victims and witnesses need emotional support to be able to repeatedly give statements about the event (Holmstrom and Burgess 1983).

Beginning in the late 1970s federal and state governments introduced legislation and policies to lessen the burdens on victims and witnesses in cooperating in the prosecution of crimes. Although most efforts designed to aid crime victims have focused on compensating victims for the physical and financial harms caused by crime, some efforts have sought to reduce the inconvenience and hardships on victims and witnesses associated with prosecution (see Figure 7-2). Some large prosecutors' offices also have initiated victim-witness assistance programs designed to improve the interaction between the prosecutor and victims and witnesses of crimes.

The goal of victim-witness services is to make the criminal justice system less onerous for those whose testimony is needed by the prosecution (see Finn 1986;

Figure 7-2   Assisting Victims and Witnesses

SOURCE: U.S. Bureau of Justice Statistics, 1983. *"Victim and Witness Assistance."* Bulletin.Washington, D.C.: U.S. Department of Justice; Case Continuance Advisory Board. 1986. *ABA Suggested Guidelines for Reducing Adverse Effects of Case Continuances and Delays on Crime Victims and Witnesses.* Washington, D.C.: American Bar Association.

Return of Seized Property:

Kansas has enacted legislation to more quickly return recovered property to victims of theft. Rather than keeping seized property in police custody until the offender is convicted, this program provides for prompt return of the property by photographing the property for later introduction in court.

Increased Witness Fees:

Witness fees in many states are too low to provide any real compensation for lost wages and other expenses associated with testifying in court (transportation, parking, child care). Several states have enacted legislation that significantly increases witness fees.

Employer Obligations to Victims and Witnesses:

A few states have passed legislation protecting victims and witnesses from being fired for absences caused by their participation in a prosecution. Other proposals require the employer to compensate employees for time lost due to court appearances.

Victim Notification and Participation Programs:

Various states have enacted legislation that requires victims to be notified of the progress of the case, such as the time of plea negotiations and sentencing. Other states provide for victim participation in sentencing, including in-court statements at the time of sentencing and victim impact statements. Other states provide victims with an opportunity to offer their views on a proposed plea bargain.

Depositions:

Several states have enacted legislation allowing depositions to be introduced as evidence rather than requiring courtroom appearances for certain victims and witnesses, particularly those who have suffered childhood abuse or who are mentally disturbed or seriously injured.

Reducing the Impact of Delay and Case Continuances:

The American Bar Association developed guidelines for police, prosecutors, defense counsel, and judges to reduce the number of continuances and to minimize the adverse impact of delays and continuances on victims.

Finn and Lee 1988; Webster 1988). Victim-witness support services have the broad objective of making participation in the process a more manageable ordeal. The advantages to the prosecution are obvious. These services help the victims and thereby improve their cooperation in the prosecution. Some victims need little assistance. For some people services might simply mean calling to remind them of their court appearances. For others it means giving them a bus ticket, providing ·cab fare, or sending a van to pick them up. For some it means providing child care for a few hours. For others it means intervening with unsympathetic or uncooperative employers. For those who have suffered a traumatizing crime it means counseling services and emotional support when they go to court. Flexibility in meeting the needs of victims and witnesses is a key ingredient, often missing from the more formal contacts between citizens and the prosecutor's office.

▪ MAINTAINING INTEGRITY, CONTROLLING DISCRETION

The Model Code of Professional Responsibility applies to prosecutors as it does to other attorneys (see Chapter 6). Canon 7 of the code, which states that "a lawyer should represent a client zealously within the bounds of law," has special application to the public prosecutor, as does Canon 5, which admonishes the lawyer to "exercise independent professional judgment on behalf of a client." Given that the prosecutor's client is the public, the question becomes what constitutes the right kind of zealous representation.

The prosecutor's duty to the public is far more complex than merely representing the individual victim in the instant case, and a prosecutor's judgment and conduct have implications that reach far beyond it:

> Although the prosecutor operates within the adversary system, it is fundamental that the prosecutor's obligation is to protect the innocent as well as to convict the guilty, to guard the rights of the accused as well as to enforce the rights of the public. Thus, the prosecutor has sometimes been described as a "minister of justice" or as occupying a quasi-judicial position. (American Bar Association 1993, 5)

This passage echoes the oft-quoted statement from the U.S. Supreme Court:

> The United States Attorney is the representative not of an ordinary party to a controversy, but of a sovereignty whose obligation to govern impartially is as compelling as its obligation to govern at all; and whose interest, therefore, in a criminal prosecution is not that it shall win a case; but that justice shall be done. As such, he is in a peculiar and very definite sense the servant of the law, the twofold aim of which is that guilt shall not escape nor innocence suffer. (*Berger v. United States, 88*)

The prosecutor is bound to give the criminally accused the "benefit of all reasonable doubt" and to make timely disclosure to the defense of all available evidence that tends to "negate the guilt of the accused, mitigate the degree of the offense, or reduce the punishment. Further, a prosecutor should not intentionally avoid pursuit of evidence merely because he believes it will damage the prosecutor's case or aid the accused" (Freedman 1975, 222). Finally, a prosecutor is not permitted to file charges against a suspect when the charges are not supported by probable cause (Freedman 1975, 212). Violations of these rules can result in the bar's imposing disciplinary sanctions against the offending attorney. Although rarely used, the bar's sanctions include revocation of the license to practice law. Consequently, the ABA Code of Professional Responsibility guides prosecutorial conduct but probably offers only a weak deterrent to any prosecutor motivated to violate these rules.

These mandates leave much room for the exercise of discretion. The formal stages of the criminal prosecution (preliminary hearing, grand jury, and trial) are designed to check the prosecutor's power to charge without sufficient evidence. Less regulated is the prosecutor's discretion to show lenience. The attorney general does have the power to initiate prosecution when the local prosecutor is unwilling to do so, and a judge may convene a grand jury or appoint a special prosecutor. However, these checks are used only rarely to curb abuse of the prosecutor's discretion to show leniency.

> **FIGURE 7-3   Limits on Plea Negotiations, 1990**
>
> SOURCE: Adapted from John M. Dawson, 1992. *Prosecutors in State Courts, 1990.* Washington, D.C.: U.S. Department of Justice, Bureau of Justice Statistics, p. 6.

	Counties:			Offices with assistant prosecutors:	
	Total	75 largest	Elsewhere	Yes	No
Percent of districts with explicit criteria controlling plea negotiations	36%	72%	35%	44%	8%

The converse of discretionary leniency is discretionary severity, specifically, the withholding of leniency when others in similar situations receive leniency. Judges are the main check on this kind of prosecutorial discretion, but they are virtually powerless to curb disparity in discretion except when prosecutors have acted so unjustly as to have abused their discretion or violated a law. For example, suppose the prosecutor routinely declines to prosecute first-time retail theft offenses when the value taken is less than $25. But one day the prosecutor is in a bad mood and issues a retail theft charge against a first offender who stole a compact disk priced at $15. So long as probable cause exists, and so long as there is no evidence of impermissible discrimination, a judge has no authority to question the decision.

Because the systemic checks on the prosecutor's exercise of discretionary authority are quite minimal, controls within prosecutors' offices are especially important. In large prosecutors' offices charging guidelines and negotiation guidelines are one means of ensuring control of discretion and consistency in the granting of leniency. However, internal guidelines that structure the exercise of discretion with respect to either charging or negotiating pleas are not yet a standard feature of prosecutors' offices (see Figure 7-3). Guidelines are found more frequently in offices in which the chief prosecutor seeks to reform prosecutorial practices. When the chief prosecutor is interested in maintaining the status quo, guidelines are less common (Flemming 1990, 40).

Finally, the public exercises control over the chief prosecutor through the ballot box. In the forty-six states that elect prosecutors, a displeased public has the power to elect someone else at the next general election. If public displeasure is aroused between elections, voters can force a recall election, which is a referendum on the incumbent. Impeachment by the legislature is an alternative to a recall election when there has been a serious breach of duty or when the prosecutor is appointed rather than elected.

■ SUMMARY

The prosecutor is a specialist in criminal law who represents the people in a criminal lawsuit. Specialization in criminal prosecution is gained primarily through experience; law schools offer only minimal preparation for this work.

Guided only by formal and informal office policies and norms and a professional code of responsibility, prosecutors investigate, screen, prosecute, and negotiate cases in the name of the people. Most crimes in this country are prosecuted by assistant prosecutors, who are employed in a local office headed by an elected official, known in many places as the district attorney. Autonomy is a remarkable feature of the position of prosecutor. The prosecutor is perhaps the most independent and powerful public official in the state criminal justice system and functions as both an advocate and a "minister of justice" in fulfilling the duties of the office. Local prosecutors have an interdependent and delicate relationship with the police, on whom they rely for investigation and arrests.

U.S. attorneys are appointed to their posts: the head of each district office is appointed by the president with the approval of the Senate. Federal prosecutions tend to reflect the agenda of the administration in office, and the criminal caseload in federal courts shows a concentration of efforts on certain types of criminal activities in any given time period. The U.S. attorney general sets the agenda and policies for the federal prosecutors across the United States.

■ FOR FURTHER DISCUSSION

1. What is the name of the chief prosecutor in your community? Do you know how long the chief prosecutor has been in office? What do you know about the chief prosecutor, and how do you know it? What do your answers to these questions tell you about the visibility of the office of prosecutor in your community?

2. The United States does not allow private prosecution. Consider all the likely consequences for the courts if private prosecution were allowed. What sorts of victims would be most likely to prosecute cases privately? What sorts of crimes would people be most likely to prosecute privately? How might the availability of private prosecution affect public prosecutors' charging decisions? All in all, would you expect private prosecution to be a positive reform of the justice system or not?

3. The residents of a community in which drug trafficking is widespread have worked with the police to clean up the streets. The police will arrest anyone known to be involved in the drug trade, even if the police have no probable cause for arrest on a particular occasion. The seriousness of the drug problem in the community, and community leaders' insistence that the criminal justice system respond, have persuaded the local prosecutor to cooperate. The prosecutor issues charges on all drug arrests brought by the police. Although many of these charges are later dropped for lack of evidence, the offender is off the streets for a time. A local defendants' rights group is protesting this policy and seeking an end to the practice of arresting and charging certain "known" drug offenders without probable cause. What options might be available for controlling the prosecutor's charging decisions?

■ REFERENCES

Alschuler, Albert W. 1968. "The Prosecutor's Role in Plea Bargaining." *University of Chicago Law Review* 36:50–112.

American Bar Association. 1993. *ABA Standards for Criminal Justice: Prosecution Function and Defense Function.* 3d ed. Washington, D.C.: Criminal Justice Section, American Bar Assocation.

Bell, Griffin B., and Daniel J. Meador. 1993. "Federal Judicial Selection: The Carter Years." In Henry J. Abraham, Griffin B. Bell, C. E. Grassley, E. W. Hickok, Jr., J. W. Kern III, S. J. Markham, and W. B. Reynolds, eds. *Judicial Selection: Merit, Ideology, and Politics.* Washington, D.C.: National Legal Center for the Public Interest.

Berger v. United States, 295 U.S. 78, 55 S. Ct. 629 (1935).

Buchanan, J. 1989. *Police-Prosecutor Teams: Innovations in Several Jurisdictions.* National Institute of Justice, Washington, D.C.: U.S. Department of Justice.

Cole, George F. 1970. "The Decision to Prosecute." *Law and Society Review,* 4: 331–42.

Cole, George F., Stanislaw J. Frankowski, and Marc G. Gertz. 1987. *Major Criminal Justice Systems: A Comparative Survey.* Newbury Park, Calif.: Sage.

Davis, Kenneth C. 1971. *Discretionary Justice: A Preliminary Inquiry.* Chicago: University of Chicago Press.

Dawson, John M. 1992. "Prosecutors in State Courts, 1990." *Bureau of Justice Statistics Bulletin.* Washington, D.C.: U.S. Department of Justice.

Feeney, Floyd, Forrest Dill, and Adrienne Wier. 1983. *Arrests Without Conviction.* Washington, D.C.: U.S. Department of Justice, National Institute of Justice.

Finn, Peter. 1986. "Collaboration Between the Judiciary and Victim-Witness Assistance Programs." *Judicature* 69 (December–January): 192–98.

Finn, Peter, and B. Lee. 1988. *Establishing and Expanding Victim-Witness Assistance Programs.* Washington, D.C.: U.S. Department of Justice, National Institute of Justice.

Flemming, Roy B. 1990. "The Political Styles and Organizational Strategies of American Prosecutors: Examples from Nine Courthouse Communities." *Law and Policy* 12: 25–50.

Freedman, Monroe H. 1975. *Lawyers' Ethics in an Adversary System.* Indianapolis: Bobbs-Merrill.

Gershman, B. L. 1993. "A Moral Standard for the Prosecutor's Exercise of Charging Discretion." *Fordham Urban Law Journal* 20: 513–30.

Gibbs, John J. 1987. "Symptoms of Psychopathology Among Jail Prisoners: The Effects of Exposure to the Jail Environment." *Criminal Justice and Behavior* 14 (3): 288–310.

Goldstein, Abraham S. 1981. *The Passive Judiciary: Prosecutorial Discretion and the Guilty Plea.* Baton Rouge: Louisiana State University Press.

Heilbroner, David. 1990. *Rough Justice: Days and Nights of a Young D.A.* New York: Pantheon.

Heumann, Milton. 1978. *Plea Bargaining: The Experience of Prosecutors, Judges, and Defense Attorneys.* Chicago: University of Chicago Press.

Hochstedler Steury, Ellen. 1991. "Specifying 'Criminalization' of the Mentally Disordered Misdemeanant." *Journal of Criminal Law and Criminology* 82: 334–59.

———— 1993. "The Psychiatrically Impaired in the Criminal Defendant Population: Prevalence, Probabilities, and Rates." *Journal of Criminal Law and Criminology* 84: 352–376.

Holmstrom, Lynda, and Ann Burgess. 1983. *The Victim of Rape: Institutional Reactions.* New Brunswick, N.J.: Transaction.

Jacoby, Joan E. 1980. *The American Prosecutor: A Search for Identity.* Lexington, Mass. D. C. Heath.

———— 1982. *Basic Issues in Prosecution and Public Defender Performance.* Washington, D.C.: U.S. Department of Justice, National Institute of Justice.

Justice Management Division. 1992. *Employment Fact Book.* Washington, D.C.: U.S. Department of Justice.

Lezak, Sidney I., and Maureen Leonard. 1985. "The Prosecutor's Discretion: Out of the Closet, Not out of Control." In C. F. Pinkele and W.C. Louthan, eds. *Discretion, Justice, and Democracy: A Public Policy Perspective.* Ames: Iowa State University Press.

Melilli, Kenneth J. 1992. "Prosecutorial Discretion in an Adversary System." *Brigham Young University Law Review* 1992 (3): 669–704.

Miller, Frank W. 1969. *Prosecution: The Decision to Charge a Suspect with a Crime*. Boston: Little, Brown.

National District Attorneys Association. 1977. *National Prosecution Standards*. Chicago: National District Attorneys Association.

Nissman, David M., and Ed Hagen. 1982. *The Prosecution Function*. Lexington, Mass.: Lexington Books.

O'Grady, Kevin O., Jeff Waldon, Wayne Carlson, Scott Streed, and Cassandra Cannizzaro. 1992. "The Importance of Victim Statisfaction: A Commentary." *Justice System Journal* 15 (3): 759–64.

Teplin, Linda A. 1984. "Criminalizing Mental Disorder: The Comparative Arrest Rate of the Mentally Ill." *American Psychologist* 39: 794–803.

———— 1990. "The Prevalence of Severe Mental Disorder Among Male Urban Jail Detainees: Comparison with the Epidemiologic Catchment Area Program." *American Journal of Public Health* 80: 663–69.

U.S. Department of Justice. 1980. *Principles of Federal Prosecution*. Washington, D.C.: U.S. Government Printing Office.

Want's Federal-State Court Directory, 1993 Edition. 1992. Washington, D.C.: WANT Publishing.

Webster, B. 1988. "Victim Assistance Program Report Increased Workloads." *NIJ Reports*. Washington D.C.: National Institute of Justice.

Weimer, David L. 1980. *Improving Prosecution: The Inducement and Implementation of Innovations for Prosecution Management*. Westport, Conn.: Greenwood.

Wice, Paul B. 1978. *Criminal Lawyers: An Endangered Species*. Beverly Hills, Calif.: Sage.

8

DEFENSE COUNSEL'S ROLE IN THE ADVERSARIAL SYSTEM

T he United States was the first nation in Western civilization to provide the right to counsel. Under English common law, defendants could be denied the assistance of an attorney, even if they paid for the attorney themselves. By the time of the American Revolution, however, more and more defendants were hiring counsellors who had been trained in the law, and in ordinary nonpolitical cases this right was not likely to be denied (see Chapter 4). The authors of the Bill of Rights recognized the potentially pivotal role of expert assistance in mounting a successful defense in an adversarial process. They guaranteed to all criminal defendants the right to the assistance of counsel. When it was adopted, the Sixth Amendment guarantee of counsel was understood to allow defendants to hire a lawyer of their choice and to prohibit the court from denying that assistance.

As the criminal court process evolved, the rules governing the criminal process became ever more formal, rigid, complex, and esoteric. These changes increased the need for expert assistance of counsel in the majority of cases. Just three decades ago, in 1963, the U.S. Supreme Court determined that the Sixth Amendment guarantee should be extended to all defendants charged with felonies, regardless of ability to pay for a lawyer. (For a more complete discussion of the defendant's right to counsel, see Chapter 3) Today the rule is that no defendant, regardless of ability to pay, may be imprisoned upon conviction unless she was offered the assistance of counsel. An important rationale for the Supreme Court decisions that resulted in this rule is that counsel is essential to protect the many other rights of defendants necessary to ensure a fair trial.

This chapter focuses primarily on the role of defense counsel in the adversary process, the attorney-client relationship, the tasks defense counsel performs, how defense services are organized, and controls on the performance of defense counsel.

☐ THE DEFENDER'S ROLE

Counsel for the defense is supposed to represent the defendant, protect the defendant's interests, and work to attain the best possible disposition for the defendant. This includes working to obtain an acquittal, a dismissal of all or some charges, and the least severe sanctions.

The defense attorney plays a critical role in ensuring that the defendant's rights are not violated. In most cases arrest and attempts to interrogate the suspect occur before counsel is involved. Although suspects are advised of their right to an attorney before questioning, counsel is not present when someone decides whether to talk to the police without a lawyer. As a result defense lawyers often find themselves representing clients who waived their Fifth Amendment rights and made incriminating statements to police. In these cases counsel needs to get an accurate idea of whether the defendant's rights were honored before counsel became involved in the case. Counsel may question the defendant about the way in which the interrogation was conducted—did the defendant request an attorney at any point? Did the police question the defendant after the defendant said he wanted the interrogation to stop? Did the police use any sort of coercion? Such information is critical in any attempt to have incriminating statements excluded from evidence at trial.

Because of the difficulties of reconstructing what happened during an interrogation or line-up, defense counsel prefer to be present at these events to make sure that they are conducted in a way that does not violate the rights of the defendant or the integrity and reliability of the investigative process. If present at an interrogation or line-up, the defense attorney can ensure that the defendant's rights are observed. In addition, defense counsel can make sure that any objections to the procedures followed by the police are recorded so that a court can review the legal issues raised without having to adjudicate factual disputes about what the police did and what the defendant said or did.

Although defense counsel's role in protecting the rights of defendants is critical to the integrity of the process, defense attorneys spend relatively little time litigating violations of due process through motions to suppress (Heumann 1978, 60). Police usually know the limits of their authority, and prosecutors frequently screen out cases in which the police have made obvious (indisputable) mistakes. If legal problems are pointed out to the prosecutor by defense counsel, charges may be dismissed without counsel's bringing a motion to exclude the evidence.

Defense counsel also offers information and advice so that the client can make informed decisions about key aspects of the case. Only the defendant can decide whether to waive a jury trial, to waive the Fifth Amendment protection against self-incrimination, or to enter a guilty plea. The defense attorney's role is to fully inform the defendant of the realistic consequences of waiving those rights and to discuss alternatives.

An attorney must exercise caution to ensure that realistic advice does not become undue pressure. For example, if the attorney believes a conviction is inevitable, but the defendant remains stubbornly and unrealistically optimistic about beating the charges, the defense attorney may not pressure or threaten the defendant to plead guilty. It would be unethical for the lawyer to threaten to withdraw from the case simply because the defendant was adamant about exercising his rights under the law. A defense attorney cannot ethically force a defendant to make the wise or shrewd choice; the attorney is ethically restricted

ADVISING CLIENTS

The excerpts that follow are the views of defendants interviewed by Jonathan Casper during the 1970s. These defendants were represented by privately retained counsel. Casper also interviewed defendants served by the public defender; he found they were less pleased with the level of communication with their attorneys.

He made a point always to see me either before or after court and explain. . . . If it was before court, he'd explain what was going to take place and what he was going to say and how he would present himself; and if he didn't get a chance to see me before court, after court he'd always come down and see me and say, Well, did you understand this, did you understand that; and if I said no, he'd explain it to me, you know, what went on.

Thinking back over your dealings with your lawyer, do you feel that he generally took instructions from you or told you what to do?

Think a little bit of both. He never dictated to me what to do, but I think he kind of used his knowledge and experience to kind of guide me along. And tell me where he thought I'd be making a mistake or help me plan a course of action.

Can you give me an example of that, of where he guided you along where you might be mistaken?

Where he advised me to plead guilty. He told me the reasons why he felt I should, but again he told me to do what I thought was right. I really think he was trying to help me. Because he told me that he didn't believe I could beat the case. So he said that he would try to mitigate the sentence as much as possible. He said he'd do anything in his power to

help me out. And the impression that he gave me was that he was doing just that. And you know, if I ever have any further dealings with the law—not necessarily criminal, I mean, if I ever want to file some sort of suit or anything—I think I'm going to look for him in the future.

*   *   *

He more or less told me what to do because for one thing I don't know too much about the law, to instruct a lawyer really—but no, I rather take that back. He didn't exactly tell me what to do. He laid things on the line. He told me this can happen, and this can happen; so what we got to do is make up our minds. What I would do if I don't understand what can happen, like you can say, "Well, you can get five-to-six because you sellin' narcotics." And I say, "Well, why do I have to take a five-to-six, because I know other cases where they been gettin' lesser time?" He explained to me how the law's working, and what they doing up there in Superior Court. So he didn't more or less tell me what to do. He explained what can happen and what couldn't happen, and I would make my judgment.

*   *   *

He suggested things, and I made the final decision. He did the talkin', and I told him what to do—what I wanted.

Source: Excerpted from Jonathan D. Casper. © 1972. *American Criminal Justice: The Defendant's Perspective*. Englewood Cliffs, N.J.: Prentice-Hall, pp. 116–17. Reprinted by permission of Prentice-Hall/A Division of Simon & Schuster.

to inform and advise. If the defendant rejects the advice of counsel, counsel is still obligated to provide the best defense possible under the circumstances.

Once the client has made the key choices in the case, the defense attorney takes control of the strategic decisions that, in the opinion of the attorney, are appropriate in light of the client's choices. For example, if the defendant decides to demand a jury trial, the attorney decides which witnesses to call, what questions to ask on direct examination and cross-examination, and what physical evidence to introduce. If an expert witness is needed, the attorney chooses the expert, although the selection may of course reflect the preferences of the client. In essence the attorney informs and advises the defendant; the defendant decides *what* to do, the attorney decides *how* best to accomplish what the client has chosen.

■ ATTORNEY-CLIENT PRIVILEGE

Defense attorneys have commented that they get more information about the case from what the prosecution discloses than they get directly from defendants.

Attorney-Client Privilege

Maintaining confidentiality is not always easy. The attorney-client privilege can be an ethical burden to counsel when a client reveals facts that become painful secrets. Sometimes defense counsel must uphold the ethical obligation to the defendant against the lawyer's personal sense of human sympathy. Consider this example:

A defendant, who was charged with one crime, confessed to his attorney that he had committed two other crimes: he had killed two young women. Law-enforcement authorities had not yet connected the defendant with the case of the missing women; law-enforcement authorities had no certain knowledge that the missing women were dead. The women's families continued searching for the women and offering rewards for information, not knowing for sure whether they were dead or alive. The defendant told the attorney where the dead bodies were located, and the attorney took photographs of the victims. Sometime after that, the attorney was asked by a family member of one victim whether he had any information about the missing women. The attorney said no.* (Freedman 1975)

This case stirred a great controversy in the legal, as well as lay, community. However, the prevailing legal opinion is that defense counsel acted properly in keeping the confidences of his client. The function of counsel is dangerously undermined, and perhaps rendered useless, if the defendant is not free to reveal anything and everything to the attorney, secure in the knowledge that the revelations will be held in strict confidence. Defendants cannot be put in the position of having to decide which facts are "safe" to share with their lawyers. Defendants should not have to worry that their own attorney will reveal information that could hurt them.

People in trouble often lie in the hope of protecting themselves. Specifically, defendants lie to their attorneys, especially at the beginning of the relationship (Heumann 1978, 59). Many defendants simply do not trust their lawyers, a problem affecting both public and private attorneys (Casper 1972; Wice 1978).

In many cases the defendant is both angry and scared. The defense lawyer is usually a stranger. Defendants mistakenly assume that an attorney will work hard on a case only if the client is innocent. As a result defendants give their own lawyers the same stories they give the police. These accounts may leave out a number of important facts. The defendant may believe that leaving out facts or shading the truth is a way to gain the sympathy and commitment of the attorney.

Unfortunately, clients who are not completely honest with their attorneys only put their lawyers at a tremendous disadvantage. To successfully defend, defense counsel needs to know as much as possible about the events that took place, and that includes everything that the defendant knows about it. If a defendant does not reveal everything about the event, even if it puts the defendant in a bad light, the defense attorney is undermined in devising an effective defense. Because defendants do not know the law, they do not understand that information that they believe is damaging could actually be helpful to their case. For example, a defendant may adamantly insist that he was not present at the scene of a crime (despite eyewitnesses that place him there), unaware that the facts of the situation might support a defense such as self-defense, diminished capacity, or the absence of intent. In other cases counsel may build a defense around the defendant's version of events, only to be surprised by contradictory evidence later on, which makes matters worse. Perhaps the defendant lies to counsel, altering key facts or even claiming innocence. Counsel in good faith allows the defendant to take the witness stand, and the prosecutor traps the defendant in the lie. The defendant is now in more jeopardy than before: she is now subject to criminal penalty for perjury even if she is not convicted of the original offense.

attorney-client
privilege

Given that they are in legal trouble, the law has a special provision to encourage defendants to tell all to their lawyers. This special provision is known as the **attorney-client privilege.** Basically, this privilege means that the client can tell the attorney anything and everything about past criminal conduct, because the attorney is ethically obligated to keep it all confidential. The purpose of the attorney-client privilege is to promote free and uncensored communication between defendant and attorney. The value placed on free communication between attorney and client in the U.S. system of justice contrasts with values in other countries. Recall the situation in China, where the lawyer is obligated to tell the court if the defendant confesses guilt.

The attorney-client privilege is not absolute, even in the United States, however. For example, an attorney may disclose client communications to the police in order to prevent a new crime from occurring (Ferguson and Stokke 1978, 59). The attorney-client privilege extends only to past criminal conduct and not to communication about planned or intended future criminal conduct. Because the destruction of evidence of crime is itself a criminal act (obstruction of justice), an attorney may also disclose communications in which the client reveals an intention to destroy or hide evidence.

■ THE WORK OF DEFENSE COUNSEL

In actual criminal cases the scope of the defense role varies greatly with each case. Because the presumption of innocence places the burden of proving guilt on the prosecution, the defense need not prove anything, and in some cases defense counsel may fulfill the role without appearing to do much. However, most clients expect their lawyers to actively and aggressively pursue an acquittal. Despite great differences in the amount of work required for each case, several basic tasks are common.

Many tasks of defense counsel mirror those of the prosecutor. This chapter focuses on the special nature of some of these tasks as they relate to the defense role. These tasks including making sure the charge is reasonable, attempting to obtain favorable bail terms for the defendant, investigating facts, exploring the parameters of a negotiated settlement, and preparing the defendant for sentencing. The defense attorney continues to protect the defendant's rights in relation to each of these tasks and to advise the defendant in relation to the key decisions the defendant must make about the case.

Getting the Right Charge

The defense would like to influence the initial charges in order to put the defendant in an advantageous position for later adjudication or negotiation. The charge determines how the case will be processed (whether in the lower court or in the court of general jurisdiction) and the range of potential penalties the defendant faces. The charge also determines the position from which all subsequent negotiations flow. Defense counsel might point out evidentiary weaknesses, legal problems, or extenuating circumstances in attempting to influence the charge.

In most jurisdictions, however, defense counsel has no routine opportunity to influence the initial charges. Charges are issued so early in the process that neither defendants nor defense attorneys have an opportunity to meet with the prosecutor beforehand. In some jurisdictions the prosecutor issues charges on the basis of the police report, without even interviewing the defendant. In these jurisdictions the defense attorney can only hope to get a reduction in charges later, in the plea negotiation process.

Obtaining Reasonable Release Terms

In most felony cases and many misdemeanor cases the defendant is arrested and can be detained in jail for weeks or even months unless granted pretrial release. Obviously, being free rather than in jail is desirable from the defendant's point of view. For a variety of reasons (discussed in Chapter 11) pretrial release is advantageous to the defense. One task of the defense attorney is to obtain terms of pretrial release that the defendant can meet.

If possible, defense counsel represents the defendant at the initial appearance and argues for release on recognizance or low bail. However, many defendants are not yet represented at the initial appearance. The Supreme Court has not held the initial appearance to be a "critical stage" of adjudication in relation to the right to counsel. Although counsel is probably extremely useful in persuading the court to impose less onerous conditions of release, and release pending trial is probably a factor influencing the outcome of the case, what happens at the initial appearance is not critical in obtaining the eventual release of the client. A motion to change the release conditions may be made later.

Defense arguments for reductions in bail and other conditions of release focus on the trustworthiness of the defendant, why the court need not be concerned that the defendant will flee, and the unreasonableness of the bail conditions imposed by the court in light of the defendant's financial means. Defense counsel will point out positive aspects of the defendant's record, employment and family responsibilities, and other personal factors. Defense counsel's goal is to counter the prosecution's representation of the defendant as shiftless, untrustworthy, or dangerous.

Investigating and Preparing the Defense

Investigation is a critical component of defense work, because defense investigation may uncover information that will create reasonable doubt and prevent the conviction of the defendant. Investigation is a time-consuming and expensive aspect of defense work. The investigative techniques available to the defense attorney are similar to those used by the prosecutor. The major and usually most critical investigative tool in virtually all cases is interviewing witnesses. The case may also require scientific tests or examination of the crime scene or physical evidence.

The main function of defense investigation is to find witnesses—whether the prosecution has interviewed them or not—who have information that might create reasonable doubt in the mind of the fact-finder. The prosecutor is legally obligated to share with defense counsel any exculpatory information arising from the police investigation. In addition, in most states the defense may obtain statements of any witnesses who will be called to testify against the defendant.

Rather than rely solely on the statements these witnesses made to police or prosecutors, defense counsel often wants to interview the witnesses personally. The answers witnesses give often depend on how the questions are posed. Defense counsel needs to know as much about what witnesses do not know about the crime as about what witnesses say they know. By interviewing the

Motions to Reduce Bail

The charges against Richardson were the most serious criminal charges envisioned in the Penal Law. The murder of a police officer was then a capital case, and if convicted on all charges Richardson faced the electric chair. Burton B. Roberts [the prosecutor] and his staff were quite prepared to argue—and did—that their case was strong, and the likelihood of conviction great. Therefore the prosecution demanded an astronomical bail far in excess of any amount that Richardson could conceivably raise. Faced with the People's demand, [William] Kunstler [the defense attorney] was not at a loss for words. Working with what he had, he stressed in moving terms Richardson's work record as a clerk at Lincoln Hospital, belittled his past criminal record as trivial, sneering at the marijuana conviction, and pointed out that his client helped to support five children.

Then, his anger growing, Kunstler moved on to his own version of the case. He asserted . . . that Patrolman Skagen "was shot to death by two New York City policemen," and that Richardson himself had been shot by these same arresting officers. . . As far as Kunstler was concerned, Richardson never possessed a gun

and fired no shots. His portrayal of Richardson was masterly.

Faced with these conflicting claims and bald assertions, Criminal Court Judge Louis A. Cioffi set Richardson's bail at $50,000. A week later, on July 18, before another judge, these arguments were repeated and the bail was reduced by $10,000 to $40,000.

By August 2 Richardson had been indicted, and the case had moved to the State Supreme Court [felony trial court in New York]. Here, once more, Kunstler summoned forth his anger and eloquence. His words had impact, for bail was reduced once again, this time to $25,000.

There matters stood for some five months. Then, in January of 1973, Kunstler tried again. He succeeded in chopping off another $10,000. Bail was set at $15,000. It never went lower.

*   *   *

Richardson was free on bail after February 13, 1973.

Source: Excerpted from Steven J. Phillips, 1978. *No Heroes, No Villains*. New York: Vintage, pp. 52–53, 61. Copyright © 1977 by Steven J. Phillips. Reprinted by permission of Random House, Inc.

state's witnesses the defense may find weaknesses or inconsistencies in the state's case. Moreover, the defense also interviews witnesses the prosecution does not plan to use. These witnesses may cast a different light on the facts or highlight inconsistencies and doubts that could be critical in reaching a verdict.

In most states defendants enjoy a right to know the results of scientific examinations or tests of physical evidence that the prosecution intends to use in the case against them. Defense counsel may obtain test results through a motion to discover. So long as the test results are not in dispute, the opportunity to discover means that the defense need not bear the cost for tests that would only duplicate the prosecution's information. Sometimes the defense may decide that additional tests are necessary or to consult other experts about the interpretation of results.

Negotiating Settlements

Like judges and prosecutors, new defense attorneys learn their role from lawyers with more experience. Judges, experienced prosecutors, and experienced defense attorneys all play important parts in socializing the newcomers. This socialization process replaces the erroneous expectations fostered by law school, with its emphasis on constitutional due process, motions, trial procedure, and appellate case law. Law school does not prepare the defense attorney for the reality of doing business in the criminal court. The defense attorney quickly learns that there are two ways to do business: cooperate or fight. Fighting, which consists of filing motions and insisting on going to trial, reaps hassles and a lack of cooperation and openness from prosecutors and judges. The message is clear: "We have to dispose of cases, and we can do this cooperatively or not. If you don't cooperate, chances are you will pay. If you are reasonable and cooperative, we will be reasonable and cooperative." The primary mode of doing business in the criminal court system is cooperation and negotiation, not fighting as adversaries. Virtually all research on plea bargaining documents the pervasive pressure on the defense attorney to negotiate cases rather than fight (see Heumann 1978; Maynard 1984; Rossett and Cressey 1976; Skolnick 1967; Sudnow 1965).

In the course of socialization the new defense attorney learns that many defendants do not oppose negotiated settlements. The newcomer begins to learn that most defendants have good reason to avoid trial, that most defendants are guilty of the crime charged, and that the prosecutor can prove the cases against them if they get to trial. Rather than ask the attorney, "Can you get me off?" a defendant is as likely to ask, "Can you get me a good deal?" The newcomer also learns that disputable issues concerning due process simply do not exist in most cases. According to one study of plea bargaining in the criminal courts, "Statistical estimates vary, but experienced defense attorneys agree that of the approximately 90 percent of the defendants who are factually guilty, most have cases devoid of any legally disputable issue. These cases, as one defense attorney phrased it, are "born dead" (Heuman 1978, 60). In short, the new defense attorney learns that in many cases the defendant has nothing to gain and a lot to lose by going to trial. In this context the defense attorney learns to become a negotiator and finally becomes a defender of the negotiation process (Heumann 1978, 84).

Although negotiation is the norm, the danger is that defense counsel will become so accustomed to bargaining (rather than fighting) and so cynical about the guilt of their clients that they avoid fighting and trial even when it is appropriate (Alschuler 1975). One of the few impediments to defense attorneys who want to negotiate when they should fight is the defendant who refuses to plead guilty. The defendant's refusal to accept an attorney's "strongly recommended" plea bargain is fraught with risks. Who would want to go to trial with an attorney who is so obviously reluctant to try the case?

Preparation for Sentencing

One important function of defense counsel is managing the defendant's image in court. In relation to sentencing, defense counsel tries to assist the defendant in creating a lawabiding image. If at all possible, defense counsel wants to be able to show the court that the defendant has a place to live, a way to earn money, and has accepted responsibilities. Defense counsel attempts to persuade the judge that the defendant will stay out of trouble in the future.

The defense attorney also prepares the defendant for the interview that is part of a presentence investigation. Counsel may warn the defendant about what information to volunteer, which facts to emphasize, which topics to avoid, and how to present a good impression. Presentence reports include conclusions and impressions by the investigator, and it is important that the defendant makes the best impression possible.

Very real limits constrain defense counsel's ability to influence the sentence through these efforts, however. A defendant who is in jail is unable to demonstrate responsibility and reform. Moreover, for serious offenses punitive considerations may diminish the extent to which a judge takes such factors into account.

■ THE ORGANIZATION OF DEFENSE SERVICES

Only a small segment of the nation's lawyers engages regularly in the practice of criminal defense. A study of lawyers in Chicago estimated that about 5 percent practiced criminal defense (Heinz and Laumann 1982). Traditionally, criminal defense attorneys have not enjoyed great prestige among their peers. Prestige seems to be associated with the social status of the clients served: lawyers who serve large corporations, banks, and wealthy individuals have traditionally enjoyed far more prestige than criminal defense attorneys. The Chicago study confirmed this impression. Of thirty specialties, criminal defense ranked twenty-third in prestige, close to the bottom (Heinz and Laumann 1982).

Anyone licensed to practice law may practice criminal defense. Defense counsel comes to the defendant in different ways. Defendants who can afford it hire their own attorneys. Defense services are provided to indigent defendants through appointment of counsel, government-financed public defender services, and contract defense services. Some jurisdictions rely more on one type of indigent defense service than another (see Figure 8-1), but in many jurisdictions appointed counsel, public defenders, and contract defenders coexist, with each taking a share of all cases coming through the criminal courts.

Privately Retained Counsel

privately retained counsel

Among defense counsel in private practice are few who are well paid hotshot criminal defense lawyers and have local or even national reputations. **Privately retained counsel** is paid by the defendant and can be fired by the defendant. The lawyers who take criminal cases for a fee make up a heterogenous group that defies simple description. At one end of the spectrum are a few criminal defense attorneys with national reputations. The "Dream Team" of Johnnie Cochran, F. Lee Bailey, and Alan Dershowitz that defended O.J. Simpson is representative of the elite of criminal defense work. Because they can command huge fees, they can reject uninteresting cases that represent only drudgery to them. They frequently attract media attention by representing the doctor who is charged with killing his wife, the corporate vice president charged with embezzling company funds, and wealthy organized crime figures pursued by the Justice Department. Although these criminal attorneys have a high profile in public, they are virtually inconsequential in the larger picture of criminal defense. The legendary attorneys usually command fees that put them out of the reach of the typical criminal defendant.

More typically, attorneys in the private practice of criminal defense work in anonymity. In fact, they tend to be the least prestigious sector of the bar. They often start their careers as government attorneys, as either a prosecutor or a public defender. Once they gain this experience, they open solo practices or join small law firms that specialize in criminal cases.

Because defense attorneys in private practice often represent clients who do not have a lot of money, making financial ends meet can be difficult. Therefore criminal defense attorneys often do other kinds of legal work to pay the bills.

FIGURE 8-1   Type of Indigent Defense Used in Majority of Counties in Each State

Source: U.S. Bureau of Justice Statistics, 1988. *Report to the Nation on Crime and Justice,* 2d ed. Washington, D.C.: U.S. Department of Justice, p. 75.

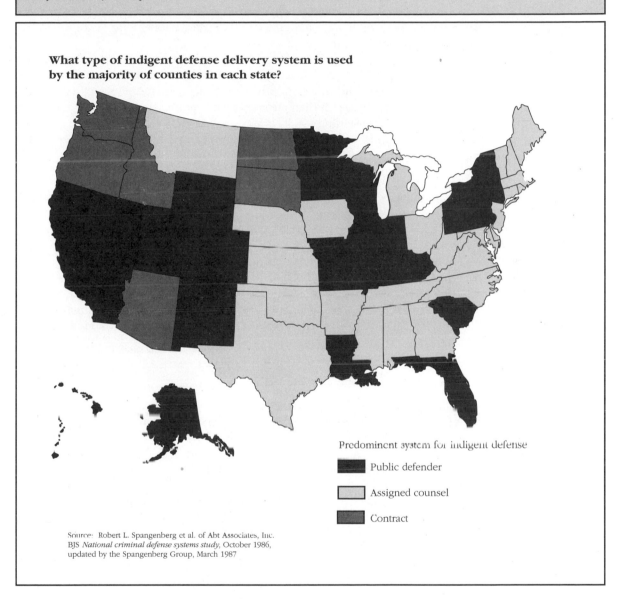

What type of indigent defense delivery system is used by the majority of counties in each state?

Predominant system for indigent defense

- Public defender
- Assigned counsel
- Contract

Source: Robert L. Spangenberg et al. of Abt Associates, Inc.
BJS *National criminal defense systems study,* October 1986,
updated by the Spangenberg Group, March 1987

Some supplement their income by accepting court-appointed assignments for indigent defendants.

Getting clients to pay legal fees in a timely manner is an additional challenge for private defense attorneys. If promises were golden, these lawyers would be rich. To pressure clients to pay their bills some attorneys refuse to work on the case until they are paid. Scheduled court appearances do not interfere with this tactic. Court workers in many parts of the country are familiar with the mysterious "Mr. Green." Defense counsel requests a continuance on the grounds that the defense has been unable to locate "Mr. Green," a code phrase that signals that the defendant has not paid and defense counsel is awaiting payment before doing more work in the case. Prosecutors and judges in some parts of the country routinely tolerate continuances requested on these grounds.

Some private attorneys are able to make a good living by maintaining a high volume of cases. In fact, some defense attorneys accept cases intending only to enter guilty pleas. These attorneys have been dubbed "quick pleaders" (Alschuler 1975). Their practice of entering guilty pleas for a reasonable fee is of questionable value to the client and of questionable ethics.

Although defendants perceive private attorneys to be more responsive to their concerns than public defenders or appointed counsel, there is no evidence that as a group defense attorneys in private practice are more competent, more zealous, or more successful than attorneys paid by the government to represent criminal defendants (Sterling 1983; Hanson et al. 1992). Nonetheless, the freedom to choose an attorney and the ability to pay that attorney clearly influence the attorney-client relationship. As one researcher put it,

> The nature of the transaction between attorney and client provides a context for *interpreting* the behavior of the attorney. In part because the defendant (or his family) was *paying* for the attorney, the whole tone of the relationship was altered. For example, insistence upon a particular course of action by a street lawyer (e.g., pleading guilty, commitment for observation to a hospital) is interpreted differently by his client. Similar "advice" from a public defender might well be interpreted as giving orders, as telling the client what to do rather than discussing it with him. With a street lawyer the insistent advice is only the lawyer's "proper" role and the exercise of expertise that he is supposed to possess. (Jonathan D. Casper *American Criminal Justice* © 1972, 117–18. Reprinted by permission of Prentice-Hall/A Division of Simon & Schuster.)

Indigent Defense Services

Indigent defendants are those who cannot afford to hire an attorney to defend them. Many defendants in criminal court cannot afford to hire an attorney to represent them. One study (Wice 1978) estimated that three of four criminal defendants were indigent. In 1988 the U.S. Department of Justice reported that the national Indigent Defense Survey found that 40 percent of all felony defendants were classified as indigent under varying state guidelines (Bureau of Justice Statistics 1988, 75). Another study in one midwestern state found that four of five misdemeanor defendants were indigent (Hochstedler Steury 1991, 343). Regardless of the exact proportion, no one disputes that a substantial majority of the nation's criminal defendants are indigent.

indigent defense services

Consequently, **indigent defense services** are critical in shaping the adjudicatory process and the quality of defense in any jurisdiction. The most common forms of providing indigents with defense counsel are the court-appointed attorney system, the public defender system, and the contract defense system. Each has its strengths and weaknesses. Some jurisdictions use one or the other system exclusively or predominantly. Other jurisdictions use a combination. In addition, it is not uncommon to find a public interest law group, such as the local legal aid society, providing supplemental support to one or more of the standard structures for indigent defense.

Court-Appointed Counsel

court-appointed counsel

The oldest form of providing representation to indigent defendants is through the system of **court-appointed counsel**. The legal profession accepts a collective *pro bono*

responsibility to provide free, or **pro bono**, legal counsel to clients in need of services they cannot afford. This collective professional obligation is not limited to criminal defense, but criminal defense is one of the most visible forms of pro bono work. For a long period U.S. courts customarily appointed attorneys to represent poor defendants as part of attorneys' professional obligations. Only a few states continue to rely primarily on pro bono appointments. More common today is for court-appointed attorneys to receive some financial compensation for their indigent defense services.

Although any attorney who has been admitted to the bar is eligible for appointment, courts usually appoint from a list of attorneys who have indicated a willingness to serve. The qualifications of appointed counsel are as widely varied as are the qualifications of privately retained counsel. Some courts require that court-appointed counsel provide evidence of experience and complete a court-sponsored training program, whereas others do not require even a résumé (Hanson et al. 1992).

Reimbursement practices for court-appointed attorneys also vary a great deal among jurisdictions. A few jurisdictions do not compensate court-appointed attorneys for their services at all, a situation that automatically raises serious questions about the effort these attorneys will put forth for their clients. In some places an appointed attorney is compensated on an hourly basis, although the hourly reimbursement often cannot exceed an upper limit, which in some jurisdictions is unrealistically low. Other places pay a flat fee for the case, with misdemeanor cases paying less than felonies. In still other places the pay depends not only on the seriousness of the offense but on whether the case goes to trial. Frequently, the compensation for court-appointed attorneys is criticized as inadequate to encourage zealous representation.

The court-appointed attorney system is only as good as its regulation and resources. Where the practice is to appoint only experienced attorneys and to provide them with reasonable compensation, the system can work well. Where it is unregulated, indigent defense appointments can become another means of securing clients and supplementing income for attorneys who may be incompetent or lack the commitment and experience to perform adequately. Where it is uncompensated, it invites inadequate representation and substandard performance. According to recent reports, some inexperienced counsel are being appointed without compensation as an emergency stopgap measure to shore up a failing system of indigent defense services.

Public Defenders

Most urban jurisdictions rely on public defender offices to provide the majority of defense work for indigent defendants. Public defender offices began to appear in the early 1900s in large metropolitan centers where the number of criminal cases with indigent defendants was great. The number of public defender offices grew after the U.S. Supreme Court mandated that all indigent defendants, if charged with a felony or if sentenced to imprisonment, be provided counsel at public expense. As of 1990 more than fourteen thousand full-time attorneys were employed in public defender offices (McGuire, Pastore, and Flanagan 1993, 24).

public defender

Public defender offices typically are organized either on a statewide or county basis. Attorneys in these public agencies are civil servants, neither elected nor appointed but hired on the basis of their credentials and apparent promise. Public defenders are lawyers who work exclusively in the practice of criminal defense and are full-time salaried employees of the government.

CRIMINAL CRASH COURSE
Knoxville's lawyers pressed into service for misdemeanor defense

What do Knoxville Mayor Victor Ashe, University of Tennessee law school professor Grayford Gray and mobile home magnate James Clayton have in common?

All three are non-practicing lawyers living in Knox County, Tenn. And all three have been ordered to represent an indigent client in court free of charge.

None has been singled out for special attention, either. The mayor, the professor and the mobile home maker just happen to be on a list of some 1,200 licensed lawyers in Knoxville who have been called into public service on behalf of the poor.

The draft, which began Jan. 7, 1992, was precipitated by a growing backlog of cases in the public defender's office and a looming shortfall in the state's indigent defense fund.

Last November, Knox County Public Defender Mark Stephens asked the courts for a 60-day suspension of new appointments to his office, citing a caseload that already exceeded more than 600 cases per lawyer, two to three times the recognized national standard.

Soon thereafter, the state announced that its indigent defense fund, which pays for the appointment of private lawyers in cases of conflict with the public defender's office, would run out of money by the end of January.

As a stopgap measure, the judges in General Sessions Court, which handles misdemeanors and preliminary appearances in felony cases, decided to spread the burden among every able-bodied attorney in the county.

Their decree recognized only three exceptions: lawyers who are retired, infirm or dead. And it warned the rest that no excuses would be countenanced.

The list of eligible lawyers includes people like Ashe, who hasn't practiced civil law in more than eight years and has never handled a criminal case; Gray, who teaches courses on such topics as appellate advocacy and legal research, but who has never fancied himself a litigator; and Clayton, who holds a law degree but runs one of the largest mobile home companies in the country.

Former White House Chief of Staff Howard Baker and Education Secretary Lamar Alexander also are on the list, although bar officials said that both are probably exempt from the order because they have homes outside the county.

The directive was wildly unpopular at first, although some, like the mayor, stepped forward and took their medicine without complaint. Ashe, who found out about the order in a phone call from his new client, quickly negotiated

The public defender's office is organizationally separate from the prosecutor's office. Unfortunately, in some places the public defender's physical office space is in the same building—sometimes on the same floor—as the prosecutor's office. The physical proximity of the offices, along with the fact that both officials are paid by the government, leads some defendants to doubt the independence of the public defender. To some the public defender appears to be simply another part of the same government that is seeking a conviction.

Newly hired public defenders, like newly hired prosecutors, may receive a short training course but do most of their learning by doing. A new hire usually begins to assume a full caseload of the least serious offenses shortly after hire. Although their training is either nonexistent or brief, public defenders learn quickly because of the volume of cases. Although trials account for only a small portion of their caseload, the caseload is large enough that they get plenty of trial practice, far more than most lawyers ever get. They quickly become experienced and knowledgeable about the system and the local way of doing business in the criminal courts.

a plea bargain to a criminal trespassing charge for which his client got thirty days in jail.

Bob McGee, one of the four judges who signed the order, said the initial reaction was mostly negative, but that most lawyers now understand how critical the situation has become and are cooperating with the judges to "get the job done."

ETHICAL DILEMMA

For some, though, the order posed more of a dilemma. Lawyers who don't normally do criminal defense work or appear regularly in court said the order created a conflict between their ethical duty to serve the poor and their professional obligations not to take a case for which they don't feel qualified.

"I don't see how the courts can justify putting a lawyer in that kind of a position," said Gray, who was assigned to represent a man facing a contempt charge for non-payment of child support. "Basically, I'm not competent to be a litigator. And there's not enough time to become competent before this case comes to court."

Others said they resented being ordered to do the work, although they based their objections on principle rather than money. "I'm not happy about it," said divorce lawyer Doug Toppenberg. "This seems to be the only vocational area where the government can step in and tell somebody that he has to work on something without compensation."

The harshest reaction so far has come from small firm lawyers and solo practitioners, who said the brunt of the extra workload would fall on their shoulders. Unlike the practice at some large firms, they can't assign their cases to a team of young associates or hire criminal lawyers outside as counsel.

Nobody is known to have died yet to get out of doing public service, but several lawyers feel so strongly about the decree that they have chosen to give up their licenses, said Bruce Anderson, who heads the Knoxville Bar Association. At least 400 others apparently have decided to wing it, signing up for three hastily arranged crash courses by the local bar on the nuts and bolts of criminal law, he said.

Left in limbo, though, are the private practitioners who used to make a living off of appointments to the indigent cases the public defender's office couldn't handle. The work, which they say never was financially rewarding, has suddenly become unprofitable.

"It was bad enough at $30-an-hour in court and $20-an-hour out of court, which was tied for the lowest rates in the nation," said Patrick Leonard, who is still putting in 30 to 40 hours a week on court-appointed cases for which he doesn't expect to get paid. "Doing it for nothing is impossible."

SOURCE: Excerpted from Mark Hansen, 1992. "Criminal Crash Course: Knoxville's Lawyers Pressed into Service for Misdemeanor Defense." *ABA Journal* 78 (April): 14. Reprinted by permission of the *ABA Journal*.

Because public defender offices handle such a great volume of cases, attorneys in these offices often specialize. Typically, offices have felony and misdemeanor units, with the newer attorneys assigned to the misdemeanors. Appeals are handled in a separate unit, because they require a different kind of work. Because misdemeanor cases typically require less attention than felony cases, defenders in the misdemeanor unit usually carry a heavier caseload—double or more.

Workload expectations vary widely and undoubtedly reflect the prevailing political sentiment in the jurisdiction. Where public defenders are required to open six hundred felony cases a year, the government's commitment to delivering quality defense services is less than in jurisdictions where they are required to open only two hundred felony cases. Evidence of erosion in the quality of defense services provided by the public defender's office is surfacing in many jurisdictions, where cost-saving mandates have increased caseloads by 100 percent or more. Critics decry these measures as not only penny wise and pound foolish, but as potential violations of constitutional rights (McWilliams 1993).

Contract Defense Services

contract defense

Contract defense means that the government unit responsible for providing indigent defense services contracts with a local organization to deliver the services. In some instances the local legal aid society or the local bar association is the contracting agency. Alternatively, the government might contract with a large law firm, several solo practitioners, or both. The contract might state that the firm will represent all indigent defendants for a year for a set fee, or the contract might be based on an hourly wage. In some cases the terms of the contract combine the two concepts: the first one hundred indigent defendants are represented for a set fee, and each case beyond the first one hundred is paid on an hourly basis at a prearranged fee. The various contractual terms undoubtedly influence the adequacy of the defense services provided.

Contract defense arrangements are the most recent innovation for providing indigent defense services. On the one hand they might be viewed as a sort of private alternative to a state or county public defender system. On the other hand they can be viewed as a more centralized and regulated alternative to court-appointed defense services. Small cities make the most use of contract defense systems as the primary means of providing indigent defense. Contract defense ensures a ready and reliable source of experienced attorneys to represent indigent defendants in those jurisdictions that do not need an office of full-time public defenders. In larger jurisdictions contract defense arrangements supplement the public defender system. For example, in Monterey County, California, the county government contracts with a consortium of six experienced criminal defense attorneys to accept cases that the public defender cannot represent because of conflicts of interest (Hanson et al. 1992, 24). Contract defense may also be relied on to handle overflow caseload for the regular public defense system.

Making the Indigent Pay

In many states free counsel may not be free after all. The U.S. Supreme Court has approved the recoupment or recovery of costs from convicted defendants for indigent defense services. Recovery is restricted to those who are convicted and can reimburse the state without economic hardship. Reimbursement is usually handled as one of several conditions of probation. Typically, the convict placed on probation is assessed a small sum each week or each month to help repay the cost of defense services.

This kind of reimbursement scheme, although approved by the U.S. Supreme Court, remains controversial. The primary question is whether such a plan "chills" the exercise of the Sixth Amendment right to counsel. The defendant is poor and may not understand the benefits of having an attorney. If the defendant is told, "We'll appoint an attorney for you, but you might have to pay for it later," the defendant may be reluctant to accept appointed counsel.

Comparison of Defense Services

Anecdotal evidence suggests that dissatisfaction with defense counsel is not uncommon. Defendants who hire their own attorneys and defendants represented by indigent defense lawyers tend to find fault with their attorneys. Typical complaints are that the attorney did not spend enough time with the client, the attorney did not work hard enough to get the client a good deal, the attorney did not believe the client, or that the attorney was too cozy with opposing counsel (Casper 1978; Wice 1978).

Differences in the organization of defense service suggest that attorneys face different incentives, different opportunities, and different levels of support services. These differences have led some researchers to explore whether there are any systemic differences in the quality of defense services provided by private counsel, appointed counsel, and public defenders. Aside from the problem of measuring "quality" (Worden 1991), studies suggest that measurable differences in outcomes are not pronounced or consistent from one study to another (Cohen, Semple, and Crew 1983; Hanson et al. 1992; Nagel 1973; Sterling 1983).

These studies, along with common sense, suggest that factors that cut across organizational structures are probably more powerful in explaining outcomes related to quality. Resources and experience seem to matter more than organizational structure. Resources determine the amount of time that an attorney can spend on a case. Whether the attorney is privately retained, a public defender, a contract defender, or a court-appointed attorney, time is money. Each may find for different reasons that the number of cases demanding attention exceeds the time available. For the public defender the lack of time results from caseload sizes mandated by managers of the public defender's office. Private attorneys who accept more cases than they can adequately represent create similar time pressures. Appointed attorneys find that the criminal cases compete with other cases they are handling at the same time. Any system of providing defense services will fail to provide quality services if resources are inadequate.

The second factor influencing the quality of defense services is experience and familiarity with local courtroom actors and norms. An experienced attorney knows the norms of the courtroom and can use that knowledge to the client's advantage. The attorney who represents three defendants a year will be less familiar and less experienced than the attorney who represents three hundred defendants a year. Experience and familiarity are not necessarily associated with any particular structure of defense services.

In sum, the quality of defense varies greatly and depends heavily on the competence and commitment of the individual defender and the resources available. No one structure of providing defense services is superior. From an administrative perspective some structures make more sense in some jurisdictions than others. A combination in a single jurisdiction tends to prevent the abuses that come with monopolies.

■ SUPPORT FOR DEFENDANTS AND THEIR COUNSEL

Defense counsel do not work without substantial assistance from others, both in their own firms or public agencies as well as from other organizations with related missions. Defense counsel and defendants use investigative services, social services, pretrial release services, and diversion programs.

Investigators

Although the prosecutor can rely on the police to do much of the routine investigation needed for case preparation, defense lawyers need independent investigators. Public defender offices typically have a small staff of investigators. Privately retained counsel may employ a private detective agency. These investigators do what any investigator does: ferret out and verify facts that bear on the case. Defense investigators locate and interview witnesses on behalf of the defendant. Whereas a defendant who is free on bail or ROR can sometimes assist with pretrial investigation, the defendant who is detained in jail cannot physically assist in the investigation. And in many situations it would be inappropriate for the defendant to contact witnesses before trial or search for other evidence.

Defendant Services

People who work with criminal defendants soon realize that defendants often have more trouble in their lives than the pending criminal charges. Defendants often have no job, no high school education, no special training, and even no home. Defendants may have emotional, mental, physical, or family problems that interfere with proper social functioning. Defendants often come from a situation that holds little promise for the future.

Defendant services are usually provided by either a public or private agency that is separate from the public defender's office, but a shrewd defense lawyer will use these services to the defendant's advantage. Defendant services staff attempt to ameliorate some of the problems plaguing defendants. They determine whether defendants are eligible for entitlement programs, such as welfare or social security disability. They arrange for housing. They facilitate enrollment in educational or training programs. They may help to find the defendant a job if the defendant is released pending trial. Very simply, they connect the needy defendant with social service programs that can address the defendant's specific needs.

Defendant services are supported by the government on the premise that for some defendants, involvement in the criminal justice system will recur unless the defendant's other problems are addressed. Defendant services offer rehabilitative support *before conviction for a crime*. Defense counsel can use defendant services to help defendants demonstrate to the court that they are worthy candidates for lenient sentences. A defendant who remains unemployed and unemployable, who has made no apparent effort to conform to societal expectations between the time of arrest and trial, is a less sympathetic subject at sentencing. By using defendant services and other social services, defense counsel shapes the defendant's image into one deserving of a second chance.

Defense Advocacy Programs

Some public defender offices have instituted advocacy programs that offer a range of services both before trial and at sentencing. Advocacy services are concerned with achieving a disposition for the defendant that avoids incarceration. Whereas defense counsel focuses primarily on the legal aspects of defense, including negotiating a plea and preparing for trial, the defense advocate assists by searching for alternatives to conviction and incarceration that would be acceptable to the prosecutor and the judge.

diversion

A defense advocate may look for diversion options. **Diversion** involves the suspension of charges in exchange for the defendant's participation in some special activity or program. Diversion programs are often administered by the prosecutor's office or a nonprofit organization and usually are set up for special purposes, such as dealing with first-time shoplifters or drunk drivers or diverting drug offenders into treatment. By using defense advocates defense counsel seeks to persuade the prosecutor that the defendant is an appropriate candidate for the program. Defense advocates may investigate the defendant's family and social relationships in order to show that the defendant needs services rather than punishment.

If diversion is not possible, the defense advocate may focus on developing a sentencing plan that relies on community resources rather than incarceration. Again, the goal is to convince the prosecutor and/or the judge that the defendant can be safely and appropriately sentenced to a community treatment center or other community-based program instead of jail or prison. Although defense counsel often attempt to make such arguments on their own, the use of specialized staff to make the necessary contacts and arrangements with community programs is more effective.

◼ MAINTAINING INTEGRITY

Criminal defense attorneys are governed by the same code of ethics that governs all other lawyers. Of the original nine canons, Canons 7 and 4 may have the most direct relevance to the functions performed by the criminal defense attorney. Canon 7 admonishes that "a lawyer should represent a client zealously within the bounds of the law." Canon 4 provides that "a lawyer should preserve the confidences and secrets of a client." Both canons limit what lawyers can and can not do with respect to their clients.

To represent a client zealously means that the defense attorney has an ethical obligation to vigorously defend even those whom the defense attorney knows to be guilty. An attorney cannot decide to vigorously defend only those clients whom the attorney believes to be innocent. An attorney's job is to zealously defend every client.

A parallel example might make this point more understandable. A doctor's job is to save lives. If a convicted murderer suffers life-threatening wounds from a brutal knife attack while in prison, the surgeon does not stop to consider whether, from a moral point of view, this is a person worth saving. In the same vein, defense counsel zealously defends a client because that is the lawyer's job. An attorney's professional obligations are not dependent on the strength of the evidence, the weakness of the defense, or the heinousness of the crime. Just as a doctor does not stop to ask whether the person on the operating table "deserves" to be saved, the defense attorney does not ask whether the defendant "deserves" a competent defense. A defendant is entitled to a competent defense. The defense attorney's role is not to judge the defendant; that is the role of judges and juries.

The injunction to zealously defend is limited, however. The attorney's zeal must yield to the "bounds of the law." At a minimum this means that defense counsel is obligated to obey the procedural law, both statutory and constitutional. The bounds of the law also constrain the attorney's conduct in relation to the truth and lies.

A defense lawyer in the adversary system is not obligated to reveal the truth or to accurately reflect the truth. In fact, in many cases the obligation to provide a zealous defense requires that defense counsel cast doubt on the truth. If this means attempting to lead the jury or judge to an erroneous conclusion regarding the facts, that is the defense attorney's duty. If that means making it appear that the prosecution's witness is lying when the defense knows he is telling the truth, that is also part of the criminal defense attorney's job. The defense attorney has a duty to draw an interpretation of the evidence that presents the defendant in the best light possible. Zealous representation must stop short of actual lying, however. As an officer of the court, the attorney is forbidden to tell lies or to **suborn perjury**, which is to knowingly allow others to tell lies under oath.

*suborning
perjury*

The Crisis in Indigent Defense Representation

A forthcoming ABA Criminal Justice Section report, "The Indigent Defense Crisis," by Richard Klein, concludes that the constitutional right to effective assistance of counsel is, in some states, in jeopardy.

A poor person charged with a crime may find that he or she is held in jail for three to six months without the assistance of counsel. . . .

Last June, the federal government ran out of money to pay counsel appointed under the Criminal Justice Act; there was a shortfall of $40 million.

In New Orleans, a public defender who had represented 418 clients in just the first seven months of 1991, obtained a court ruling that the excessive caseload precluded him from being effective. . . .

In Atlanta, where the daily law newspaper characterized indigent defense representation as "slaughterhouse justice," the average yearly felony caseload was 530 per public defender in 1990.

SOURCES: J. Michael McWilliams. 1993. "The Erosion of Indigent Rights." *ABA Journal* 79 (March):8. Reprinted by permission of the *ABA Journal*.

Canon 4 preserves the attorney-client relationship, but this obligation is also limited. Defense attorneys have a duty to keep the confidences of their clients. For example, if a client tells her attorney where stolen goods are hidden, the attorney cannot ethically reveal that fact to the police or prosecutor (or anyone else) without the permission of the client. To do so would be tantamount to admitting the involvement of her client. At the same time the defense attorney may not actively assist the client in concealing evidence. An attorney would become an accessory after the fact if she hid the stolen goods for the client.

Beyond the ethical obligations of the legal profession are constitutional mandates. The Sixth Amendment to the Constitution guarantees the right to "assistance of counsel." The Supreme Court has interpreted this to mean that representation must be effective if it is to be real assistance. Effective assistance is a concept that has not been clearly defined. Defendants who believe that counsel has been ineffective may bring a civil malpractice suit for damages against the attorney or may seek reversal of their conviction on the basis of ineffective assistance of counsel. The latter is by far the more common.

The traditional standard for showing ineffective assistance required a showing that "the proceedings were a farce and a mockery of justice" (*Diggs v. Welch* 1945, 669). Since the 1970s courts in many places have adopted new language to define incompetence of counsel, but the operational standard appears to have changed little (see Goldblatt 1983). More modern phrasing tends to make reference to reasonable or standard or customary performance. Despite the change in language, the test is still widely recognized as setting only the absolute minimum standard of competence. The test does not require that a defense be thorough or excellent, or even zealous, which is required by the ABA Code of Ethics. The test requires only that the defense not be egregiously substandard. Courts have refused to second guess defense counsel. There are several reasonable ways to defend a client, and the courts do not want to decide which strategy might have been better.

Moreover, despite attempts by some judges to change the law, the burden of proving ineffective assistance of counsel rests with the defendant who takes the appeal, and the presumption to overcome is great:

A convicted defendant making a claim of ineffective assistance of counsel must identify the acts or omissions of counsel that are alleged not to have been the result of reasonable professional judgment. . . . At the same time, the court should recognize that counsel is strongly presumed to have rendered adequate assistance and made all significant decisions in the exercise of reasonable professional judgment. (*Strickland v. Washington* 1984, 690)

Pressing caseloads in some jurisdictions have led defense lawyers themselves to charge that the system prevents effective assistance. If these conditions persist, the courts may be forced to take a closer look at the question of ineffective assistance of counsel.

■ SUMMARY

The role of defense counsel is to serve as adviser and personal representative of the accused. In practice this usually involves seeking acquittal or obtaining the most lenient sanction available. Defense counsel protects the rights of the defendant and advises the defendant about key decisions in the course of the prosecution. Communication between an attorney and a criminal defendant is protected by the attorney-client privilege. This privilege is necessary to promote trust between the attorney and client; nonetheless, many clients are reluctant to be completely candid with their attorneys.

Defense counsel attempts to shape the charges against the defendant and argues for the most lenient pretrial release conditions. Defense counsel investigates the facts of the case, looking for evidentiary and legal weaknesses that may be used to the client's advantage. Because going to trial is often not in the best interests of the client, defense counsel engages in negotiations with the prosecutor.

The attorneys who regularly practice criminal defense are only a very small fraction of all attorneys. Criminal defense work does not attract attorneys who are interested in a lucrative job advising influential people. Private criminal defense attorneys, who are available for hire by defendants who have enough money to pay legal fees, account for only a small segment of all criminal attorneys. Defendants who are indigent may be represented by court–appointed counsel, a public defender, or a contract defender. There is no evidence that one type of counsel is more effective than another. Instead, the crucial factors in the quality of criminal defense are resources and experience.

Attorneys are accountable to their profession through the ABA Code of Professional Responsibility. If the conduct of an attorney falls far below the acceptable standard, a defendant may be able to successfully secure a reversal of the conviction.

■ FOR FURTHER DISCUSSION

1. Laypeople often question how a defense lawyer can defend someone who has confessed to have committed a crime, sometimes horrible crimes. Based on what you have learned so far about the criminal courts and defense counsel's role in the court process, how would you answer this question? How do you think a defense lawyer would answer this question?

2. Consider the case in which a client tells his attorneys the location of victims' bodies and the attorneys do not reveal these facts to the police. Did the attorneys act ethically? Why or why not?

3.   Attorneys often know that their clients have little to gain, and much to lose, by going to trial. Yet defendants view attorneys with suspicion, particularly public defenders or appointed counsel. These lawyers appear to their clients to be too eager to persuade them to cop a plea. How can defense counsel persuade a client to take a good deal without appearing to be selling out?

4.   Because of the large number of guilty pleas, much of a defense lawyer's job involves getting the most lenient sentence for the defendant. Compare this role of the defense attorney in the United States to that of attorneys in France, Saudi Arabia, and China.

5.   One common criticism of public defender systems is that public defenders are paid less and required to handle a larger caseload than prosecutors in the same jurisdiction. What would you think of a policy of maintaining parity (or equivalence) in pay and workload for public defenders and prosecutors?

 # REFERENCES

Alschuler, Albert W. 1975. "The Defense Attorney's Role in Plea Bargaining." *Yale Law Journal* 84: 1179–1314.

Casper, Jonathan. 1978. *Criminal Court: The Defendant's Perspective*. Washington, D.C.: U.S. Government Printing Office.

———— 1972. *American Criminal Justice: The Defendant's Perspective*. Englewood Cliffs, N.J.: Prentice-Hall.

Cohen, Larry J., Patricia P. Semple, and Robert E. Crew, Jr. 1983. "Assigned Counsel Versus Public Defender Systems in Virginia." In William F. McDonald, ed. *The Defense Counsel*. Beverly Hills, Calif.: Sage.

Diggs v. Welch, 148 F.2d 667, cert. denied 325 U.S. 889, 65 S.Ct. 1576, (D.C. Cir. 1945).

Ferguson, Robert W., and Allen H. Stokke. 1978. *Legal Aspects of Evidence*. New York: Harcourt Brace & Company.

Freedman, Monroe. 1975. *Lawyer's Ethics in an Adversary System*. Indianapolis: Bobbs-Merrill.

Goldblatt, Steven H. 1983. "Ineffective Assistance of Counsel: Attempts to Establish Minimum Standards." In W. F. McDonald, ed. *The Defense Counsel*. Beverly Hills, Calif.: Sage.

Hanson, Roger A., Brian J. Ostrom, William E. Hewitt, and Christopher Lomvardias. 1992. *Indigent Defenders Get the Job Done and Done Well*. Williamsburg, Va.: National Center for State Courts.

Heinz, John P., and Edward O. Laumann. 1982. *Chicago Lawyers*. New York: Russell Sage and American Bar Foundation.

Heumann, Milton. 1978. *Plea Bargaining: The Experiences of Prosecutors, Judges, and Defense Attorneys*. Chicago: University of Chicago Press.

Hochstedler Steury, Ellen. 1991. "Specifying 'Criminalization' of the Mentally Disordered Misdemeanant." *Journal of Criminal Law and Criminology* 82: 334–359.

Maguire, Kathleen, Ann L. Pastore, and Timothy J. Flanagan. 1993. *Sourcebook of Criminal Justice Statistics, 1992*. Washington, D.C.: U.S. Government Printing Office.

Maynard, Douglas W. 1984. *Inside Plea Bargaining: The Language of Negotiation*. New York: Plenum.

McWilliams, J. Michael. 1993. "The Erosion of Indigent Rights: Excessive Caseloads Resulting in Ineffective Counsel for Poor." *American Bar Association Journal* 79 (March):8.

Nagel, Stuart S. 1973. "Effects of Alternative Types of Counsel on Criminal Procedure Treatment." *Indiana Law Journal* 48: 404–426.

Phillips, Steven. 1978. *No Heroes, No Villains*. New York: Vintage.

Rossett, Arthur, and Donald R. Cressey. 1976. *Justice by Consent*. Philadelphia: Lippincott.

Skolnick, Jerome. 1967. *Justice Without Trial: Law Enforcement in a Democratic Society.* New York: Wiley.

Sterling, Joyce S. 1983. "Retained Counsel Versus the Public Defender: The Impact of Type of Counsel on Charge Bargaining." In W. F. McDonald, ed. *The Defense Counsel.* Beverly Hills, Calif.: Sage.

Strickland v. Washington, 466 U.S. 668, 104 S.Ct. 2052 (1984).

Sudnow, David N. 1965. "Normal Crimes: Sociological Features of the Penal Code in a Public Defender Office." *Social Problems* 12: 209–215.

U.S. Bureau of Justice Statistics. 1988. *Report to the Nation on Crime and Justice*, 2d ed. Washington, D.C.: U.S. Department of Justice.

Wice, Paul B. 1978. *Criminal Lawyers: An Endangered Species.* Beverly Hills, Calif.: Sage.

Worden, Alissa P. 1991. "Privatizing Due Process: Issues in the Comparison of Assigned Counsel, Public Defender, and Contracted Indigent Defense Systems." *Justice System Journal* 14–15: 390–418.

PROCESSING CASES

CHAPTER **9**

THE PROSECUTOR'S INITIAL CHARGING DECISION

Most criminal cases are brought to the attention of the prosecutor by the police. Thus, police can be viewed as gatekeepers to the criminal courts. That is, if the police do not bring a suspect to the courts, chances are the suspect will not be prosecuted. When police arrest someone, their report is the official document that refers the arrest to the prosecutor. In the absence of an arrest report a complaining witness—either a police officer or a citizen—may provide the prosecutor with written or oral information about the crime and the suspect.

Historically, since the middle of the 19th century when standing police departments were established in most large cities, police controlled the inititial charging decisions. Virtually every arrest resulted in the filing of charges. Typically, a judge reviewed the case before the prosecutor had an opportunity to review the evidence. If the case was particularly weak or otherwise unfit for prosecution, the judge would reject the case at the initial appearance. This situation persisted into the late 1960s in some jurisdictions but in other jurisdictions had already given way to early prosecutorial screening by the 1920s (McIntyre 1968; McDonald 1979).

Today most urban prosecutors' offices exercise a great deal of control over the initial charging decision. The prosecutor reviews the arrest report and other available information. In some jurisdictions the prosecutor briefly interviews victims or other witnesses at this point. Then the prosecutor decides whether to issue a criminal charging instrument, the **criminal complaint**, which is signed by the complaining witness and affirms that the information in the complaint is true.

criminal complaint

The criminal complaint describes in plain words the facts and events known to the complaining witness that constitute the evidence for the charge against the suspect. The degree of detail in the criminal complaint varies by jurisdiction. In some courts the criminal complaint is extremely brief, stating little more than the name of the accused, the exact offense, and the time and place of the offense. In

192

other courts a typical criminal complaint contains two or three paragraphs of descriptive information, outlining the criminal event, naming witnesses, and summarizing statements made by witnesses. Whether short or long the criminal complaint is not meant to represent all details known about the criminal event. Often the last sentence of the criminal complaint states, "This does not exhaust complainant's knowledge of the facts in this case."

Once a criminal complaint is signed, the case is transmitted to the clerk of courts and receives a case number. At this point it is a "live" case in the court system. The criminal complaint operates as the document that moves the case to the next step, the initial appearance before the court. In misdemeanor cases the complaint may be the only official charging instrument. In a felony case a formal charging document (either an information or an indictment) is issued later to bind the case over for trial.

statute of limitations

In most cases the prosecutor issues the criminal complaint shortly after the arrest. The **statute of limitations** sets the outer limits of time that may elapse between the commission of an offense and the filing of criminal charges. If charges are not filed within the period prescribed by the statute of limitations, the state loses its authority to charge for that crime.

In most states the statute of limitations requires that misdemeanor charges be filed within three years of the date of the offense and felonies within seven years. Because homicide offenses are so serious, there is no statute of limitations; homicide charges may be filed whenever there is probable cause, regardless of when the offense occurred. The statute of limitations for crimes is generous and only rarely places law enforcement agents under pressure to investigate and charge. Occasionally, however, a prosecutor may race against the calendar to file charges. For example, catching a serial rapist can take years. Once a suspect is arrested, semen samples may link him to sexual assaults that occurred many years earlier. If some of these offenses are just inside the statutory limit, the prosecutor may have to move quickly to get the case charged within the statute of limitations.

Once a suspect is in custody, the police and prosecutor complete their investigation and issue charges as quickly as possible. An arrestee must be given an initial appearance shortly after arrest, at most a few days, usually less. Although the defendant could be sent to the initial appearance on the arrest charges, in many cases the prosecutor would rather complete the initial investigation and decide upon charges before giving the defendant an opportunity to be released from custody. Once defendants are released on bail, they may be able to conceal evidence, talk with confederates about a plausible excuse or alibi, or intimidate potential witnesses. Consequently, the prosecutor tries to gather the essential evidence and issue charges before the initial appearance.

Whether to issue charges or not (and which charges to issue) is perhaps the greatest exercise of discretion in the criminal justice system. Prosecutors really are not expected to prosecute every case to the fullest extent of the law. Instead the prosecutor must determine which cases, of all those that *could* be prosecuted, *should* be prosecuted. The initial charging decision can be seen as the convergence of three related or overlapping considerations: the strength of the evidence, the interests of justice, and the resources available. For the most part these are decisions that require subjective judgment on the part of the prosecutor. This chapter explores how prosecutors use their charging discretion and the factors they consider.

■ CHARGING AND ITS ALTERNATIVES

Stated most simply, the decision to charge is a decision to prosecute or not prosecute a suspect. In fact, the decision is more complex. The prosecutor may decide to defer prosecution, delaying the imposition of charges. Moreover, in all but the most straightforward cases the prosecutor must decide which charges and how many charges to issue.

nolle prosequi

Typically, 25 to 50 percent of the cases reviewed by prosecutors in a given jurisdiction are not prosecuted, a situation that has persisted for decades (see Boland et al. 1982; Boland, Mahanna, and Sones 1992; Graham and Letwin 1971; Hochstedler 1987; McDonald 1979; Neubauer 1974). The decision not to issue charges is known by a variety of names that stem from the Latin term, **nolle prosequi**, meaning to not prosecute. This term has been abbreviated to *nolle pros, nol pros*, and no process. All these terms refer to the prosecutor's decision to decline prosecution. Some observers consider the prosecutor's discretion to show leniency to be the most unregulated exercise of discretionary decision making in the system. Judges do not have authority to issue charges, so when the prosecutor declines to charge, the decision is virtually unreviewable (Becker 1988).

Deferred Prosecution and Diversion Programs

deferred prosecution

diversion program

Sometimes, rather than deciding not to prosecute at all, the prosecutor may decide on a middle ground—deferred prosecution. In **deferred prosecution** the initiation of charges is indefinitely postponed to give deserving defendants (often first-time offenders) a second chance. Frequently, deferred prosecution is used in conjunction with a diversion program. **Diversion programs** attempt to resolve the problems that led to an individual's criminal involvement. In exchange for the defendant's agreement to participate in some positive activity (such as voluntary drug treatment, placement in a residential treatment center, enrollment in a job training program, or completion of a high school equivalency degree and employment), the prosecutor agrees to defer prosecution. Diversion protects the defendant from the stigma of criminal prosecution and requires the participation of the defendant in rehabilitative treatment. Some diversion programs are informal, whereas others are formal and have explicit criteria for participants.

In informal diversion the conditions might be fashioned on a case-by-case basis by the prosecutor, and the suspect's compliance with the conditions is not monitored regularly. The prosecutor learns whether the defendant has failed to comply with the condition only if the suspect is arrested again. The most informal of the prosecutor's "diversion" alternatives is to agree that no charges will be issued for the instant offense if the offender is not arrested for any other offenses within a certain period of time, such as six or twelve months.

Other prosecutors participate in more formal diversion programs. In these, special staff may conduct a needs assessment to determine whether the defendant is a good candidate for diversion. Once in a diversion program the defendant is required to participate in specific rehabilitative activities, and the defendant is monitored for compliance. The prosecutor or court is informed regularly of the offender's participation and progress. The prosecutor can reinstitute criminal prosecution if the defendant performs poorly in the diversion program. Formalized diversion programs are less common than informal diversion arrangements because of the added staff needed to monitor compliance.

Selecting the Level and Number of Charges

criminal code

The prosecutor also decides which charge and how many charges to issue. In most jurisdictions the **criminal code**, the statutory law defining crimes, is quite extensive. Consequently, more than one statute may be applicable to any single act. That is, one fairly simple set of facts may support several different criminal charges. Consider the following example:

> A person, face covered by a mask, walks into a liquor store, pulls a gun from a jacket pocket, points it at the cashier, cocks the trigger, and demands all the money in the cash drawer. When the money is turned over, the thief tells the cashier to lie down on the floor and count slowly to one hundred before moving. The victim complies. The offender walks out the door and down the street with $2,000 in cash.

This fact situation is not particularly complicated. To most members of the public this looks like an armed robbery, nothing more and nothing less. To a prosecutor the possibilities go far beyond armed robbery. Along with armed robbery the defendant can be charged with the lesser included offenses of robbery and theft, as well as several other offenses.

lesser included offenses

Lesser included offenses are less serious offenses that involve some but not all the factual elements of the most serious offense charged. If armed robbery is defined as taking another's property by force or threat involving the use of a weapon, and robbery is defined as taking another's property by force or threat, robbery is a lesser included offense of armed robbery. The defendant could be convicted of either crime, although in most states a defendant cannot be convicted of both the primary offense and lesser included offenses. Lesser included offenses provide a range of possibilities, both to the judge or jury at trial and to the attorneys in plea negotiations. If a jury is not convinced of all the elements of the primary offense, it may find sufficient evidence to convict on a lesser included offense, if the troublesome element is not required to prove the lesser crime. Lesser included offenses also offer a range of possibilities for arriving at a plea bargain that is satisfactory to both sides.

In addition to lesser included offenses, other charges might be brought in the robbery case described above that are not lesser included offenses. Depending on the law in a particular jurisdiction, other offenses that might be charged in this armed robbery case include concealing identity while committing a crime, carrying a concealed weapon, reckless use of a dangerous weapon, and endangering safety by conduct regardless of life. These offenses are not lesser included offenses because they include additional elements that are not included in armed robbery (see Figure 9-1). The defendant might be charged and convicted of all these offenses simultaneously. Further, an offender with previous felony convictions might be liable for additional charges of habitual criminality or violating the felony firearm law, which prohibits convicted felons from owning firearms.

As this example demonstrates, one simple criminal transaction may support several charges. A prosecutor must decide whether to issue one charge, multiple charges, the more serious charges, the more lenient charges, or all charges supported by the facts. In selecting which and how many charges fit, a prosecutor is restricted by what the evidence will support. Within those evidentiary boundaries, however, the prosecutor is free to be as punitive or as lenient as justice requires. If leniency is deserved, the prosecutor may select a charge that is less serious and carries a lesser penalty than the facts might support. If the prosecutor

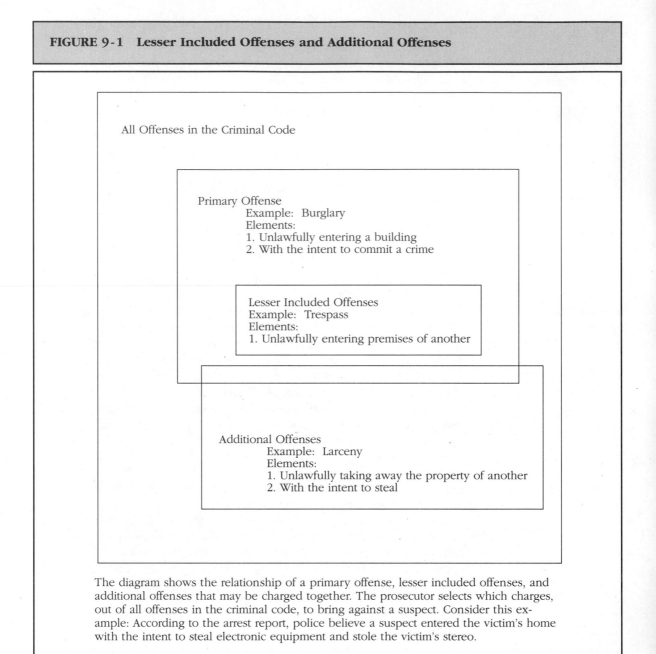

FIGURE 9-1   Lesser Included Offenses and Additional Offenses

All Offenses in the Criminal Code

Primary Offense
      Example: Burglary
      Elements:
      1. Unlawfully entering a building
      2. With the intent to commit a crime

Lesser Included Offenses
Example: Trespass
Elements:
1. Unlawfully entering premises of another

Additional Offenses
      Example: Larceny
      Elements:
      1. Unlawfully taking away the property of another
      2. With the intent to steal

The diagram shows the relationship of a primary offense, lesser included offenses, and additional offenses that may be charged together. The prosecutor selects which charges, out of all offenses in the criminal code, to bring against a suspect. Consider this example: According to the arrest report, police believe a suspect entered the victim's home with the intent to steal electronic equipment and stole the victim's stereo.

believes punishment is deserved, she may seek more punitive charges, such as those brought under habitual criminal statutes.

◻ KEY CONSIDERATIONS IN ISSUING CHARGES

The charging decision requires that the prosecutor weigh the evidence in light of the interests of justice and available resources. The prosecutor (1) weighs the evidence and determines which charges are legally possible, (2) decides what outcome is desirable, and (3) considers what outcome is acceptable, given the prosecutor's limited resources. Prosecutors make these decisions sequentially, moving up a decision ladder.

At the first rung the prosecutor weighs the evidence. Is there sufficient evidence to pass a formal probable cause screening? To move through the first phases of the court process the prosecutor must have, at a minimum, sufficient evidence against a defendant to demonstrate probable cause to a judge or grand jury. Thus the prosecutor's initial assessment of the case is likely to focus on this narrow issue. This assessment also involves a prediction of about whether prosecution can be successful. If the evidence is so weak that success is doubtful, prosecution may be a waste of precious resources.

Once the prosecutor has decided on legally appropriate and feasible charges, the prosecutor must decide whether the circumstances warrant conviction and punishment. Although sufficient evidence may exist to support a criminal charge, under a variety of circumstances prosecutors may not wish to charge without more—either more evidence or more compelling circumstances. The prosecutor's assessment of the seriousness of the crime is a subjective judgment influenced by the local political context. In making charging decisions in politically sensitive cases (such as charges against police officers or well-known members of the community) or demanding cases (for example organized crime or corporate crime), prosecutors may want more evidence than that required to show probable cause.

Prosecutorial priorities also influence the charging decision. These priorities shift over time in response to changing community sentiments. For example, before the 1970s prosecutors generally considered domestic violence a low priority. The circumstances of the crime—between family members in an ongoing relationship—persuaded prosecutors that domestic violence was not the sort of crime that deserved criminal prosecution and punishment. Consequently, unless the crime was particularly vicious or there were other unusual circumstances, most such cases were not charged, even though the probable cause requirement could be met.

In response to increasing pressure from women's groups and changing perceptions of the seriousness of spousal assault, prosecutors in many communities have changed the way they assess these cases. Similar shifts have occurred in relation to white-collar and corporate crime, drug offenses, date rape, drunk driving, and child abuse. At one time prosecutors viewed many of these offenses as not warranting prosecution. Prosecution, they believed, would not serve the interests of justice. As community sentiments change, prosecutorial practices also change.

The workload and available resources of the prosecutor's office and the courts also influence the charging decision. In a world of unlimited resources many more cases might be charged. Given real constraints on time and resources, prosecutors make choices about whether the case merits charging in comparison to other cases in the pipeline. Some kinds of cases may be informally defined as junk, resulting in quick decisions to forego criminal charges. Again, the kinds of cases that are labeled junk can change with shifting social and political trends. In most instances, however, limited resources affect only the level of charges and do not result in a decision to not prosecute at all. Low priority cases are charged, but the prosecutor may charge only a misdemeanor count or engage in plea bargaining to obtain a conviction with minimal expenditure of resources.

system efficiency model

Some prosecutors place primary emphasis on conserving scarce resources in making the charging decision. This pattern of prosecutorial decision making has been called the **system efficiency model** (Jacoby 1977). Prosecutors whose charging practices fit the system efficiency model are acutely aware that resources used to process any case necessarily use up resources that could be used to prosecute other more worthy cases. Although all prosecutors are influenced by resource concerns, the system efficiency model refers to prosecutorial decision making in which the efficient use of limited time and money becomes a central factor in the charging decision.

Finally, prosecutors assessing the appropriateness of charges consider whether they feel certain the suspect is guilty. Personal doubts can persuade prosecutors not to charge a suspect, even if they have enough evidence to do so (Gershman 1993, 524; Melilli 1992, 685; Schneider 1993, Stanko 1981–1982, 229). The prosecutors' responsibility to seek justice requires them to consider this. For example, if the prosecutor believes a suspect's explanation, even if nothing corroborates the suspect's story, the prosecutor may decide to forego prosecution. Rather than rely on a heartless and mechanical assessment of the evidence, prosecutors must satisfy themselves that defendants are guilty.

When a prosecutor has concluded that there is sufficient evidence to charge (and convict), that the case merits prosecution, and that the defendant is in fact guilty, the case is ripe for prosecution.

Meeting Probable Cause Requirements

At a legal minimum, criminal charges require supporting evidence that meets the standard of proof known as probable cause. Statute, case law, and the prosecutor's code of ethics all require that probable cause be established at the outset of the prosecution. In all states a court, a grand jury, or both review the evidence to determine whether the probable cause standard has been met. Probable cause is required because it is widely recognized that a criminal charge is a serious matter that is likely to have a pronounced negative effect on the defendant's life and prosperity. To ensure that individuals are not put through a prosecution unless there is good reason, the law requires that the state offer evidence meeting the probable cause standard early in the process. Probable cause exists if, considering all the evidence available at the time, a reasonable person has sound reason (probable cause) to believe that the suspect is guilty. Probable cause is not a precise standard and has been given different interpretations by different courts. Probable cause has been described as something more than a mere suspicion of guilt; how much more is unclear.

Because the probable cause standard is imprecise, the amount of evidence required to meet the standard appears to vary from place to place and even across decision points within a single jurisdiction. At any point in the process, however, an experienced prosecutor has a fairly good idea of the amount of evidence needed to convince a judge or grand jury that probable cause exists. Prosecutors make their charging decisions accordingly. If a prosecutor is fairly certain that a case will be dismissed for lack of probable cause, there is little point in preparing the formal charging documents, and the prosecutor is likely to reject the case on the spot or continue the investigation, hoping to develop sufficient evidence.

Developing Evidence

Evidence is the key to a criminal case. Without evidence there can be no prosecution. There are two basic kinds of evidence: real evidence and documentary evidence. Real evidence includes **direct evidence**, which directly proves a disputed fact, or **circumstantial evidence**, which requires the trier of fact to make a deduction or inference from the evidence presented. A case based heavily

direct evidence, circumstantial evidence

testimonial evidence, physical evidence, documentary evidence

on circumstantial evidence is more difficult to prove because the benefit of the doubt goes to the defendant if more than one reasonable inference can be drawn from the circumstantial evidence (Ferguson and Stokke 1978, 23–24). Both direct evidence and circumstantial evidence may take the form of testimonial, physical, or documentary evidence. **Testimonial evidence** exists in the form of words; it is someone's statement. **Physical evidence** includes objects (weapons, bullets, clothing, stolen property), blood stains, fingerprints, voice prints, fibers, and other evidence collected from the crime scene, suspect, or witnesses. **Documentary evidence** is written evidence such as business records, tax returns, or corporate memoranda and includes such "written evidence" as recordings and photographs. Police officers and other criminal investigators routinely develop and gather testimonial, physical, and documentary evidence in criminal cases. Prosecutors frequently interview suspects and key witnesses to develop testimonial evidence.

By the time a case crosses a prosecutor's desk some evidence against the suspect already exists. In most cases the evidence is presented to the prosecutor in either oral or written form by the arresting officer or by a liaison officer assigned to the court to stand in for arresting officers. This oral or written statement provides the basis for the criminal complaint. In many cases evidence sufficient to convict the suspect is already known to the police at this point; the police often have collected and cataloged all the physical evidence and recorded all the testimonial evidence needed before the prosecutor ever reviews it. In this situation additional investigation or development of evidence is unnecessary or minimal.

In some cases additional investigation is needed or desired by the prosecutor before issuing charges. The prosecutor may simply advise the police of what additional investigation is needed or refer the investigation to an investigator on the prosecutor's staff. In other cases the prosecutor may hold a charging conference to learn more about the case. Finally, in special situations the prosecutor may use an investigative grand jury to develop evidence to support the charges.

Investigative Resources

Rather than issue charges on the information provided by the police, the prosecutor may decide that additional evidence needs to be gathered before charges are issued. The prosecutor usually must rely on the police to conduct any further investigation.

The relationship between police investigators and the prosecutor is a delicate one. It contains the seeds of resentment and conflict. The police and prosecutors work in separate organizations with different priorities. Nonetheless, the police and prosecutors depend on each other to control crime in the community. Police need prosecutors to turn arrests into convictions. Prosecutors need police to bring cases forward and to develop the evidence needed to convict. A relationship of mutual respect and cooperation between the police investigator and the prosecutor sets the stage for more successful prosecutions. Achieving such a relationship can be a challenge.

Status differences between police and prosecutors create the backdrop for misunderstanding against which police and prosecutors play out their complementary but distinct roles. The amount of evidence police need to arrest is less than what is needed to convict. In addition, police are often more concerned about the immediate crisis and the need to make an arrest to maintain order than they are with determining whether a conviction can be obtained. Once the arrest is made, however, police usually want to see a conviction.

DIRECT AND CIRCUMSTANTIAL EVIDENCE

DIRECT EVIDENCE:

Defendants were caught a few blocks from the scene of a liquor store holdup. In their possession were various denominations of currency and checks that had been endorsed to the liquor store manager. The checks found in their possession are being offered as direct evidence that the defendants robbed the liquor store.

CIRCUMSTANTIAL EVIDENCE:

Hearing a loud scream, the banging of furniture and cries for help, hotel residents ran to the door of the victim's room. They heard nothing more. Suddenly, people from the street rushed up the stairwell towards the victim's room shouting, "She jumped" or "she fell." Breaking in the door, they saw the defendant standing near the open window. At the trial, the witnesses' statements as to the sounds they heard and the pedestrians' observations of the victim's fall were introduced. The prosecution sought to prove by this "pure" circumstantial evidence that the defendant argued and fought with the victim, and finally pushed her to her death.

Source: Excerpt from Robert W. Ferguson and Allan H. Stokke. Copyright © 1978. *Legal Aspects of Evidence*. New York: Harcourt Brace and Company, 1978, pp. 22 and 23. Reprinted by permission of the publisher.

Police officers sometimes resent a prosecutor's request for additional investigation. They may interpret the prosecutor's request as second guessing the arresting officer's judgment and even questioning the officer's credibility. Resentment is probably heightened when prosecutors are impatient and fail to communicate their goals and needs clearly.

Most large prosecutors' offices employ their own staff of investigators, but these investigators are not readily available for routine investigations. Rather than duplicate the functions of police, staff investigators are usually assigned to special projects that the police do not normally investigate. For example, prosecutor's investigators may be assigned to organized or white-collar crime projects or to investigate police or government corruption.

Charging Conference

charging conference

In some jurisdictions the prosecutor seeks additional information about the crime through a charging conference (Melilli 1992, 689). A **charging conference** is an informal meeting held with the suspect and key witnesses, including the police. The primary purpose of the charging conference is to assess the strength of the evidence by viewing it from different perspectives. The prosecutor interviews all parties involved. Each party has an opportunity to explain the facts from his or her perspective. After hearing each party's version of the facts, the prosecutor is in a better position to weigh the strength of the evidence and the appropriateness of prosecution than by relying on the police perspective alone.

The prosecutor has no authority to require that either the suspect or any key witnesses come to the charging conference or speak to the prosecutor. At the charging conference, as in any interrogation, the suspect is protected by the Fifth Amendment and the *Miranda* rule. At the beginning of the charging conference the suspect is informed of the right to remain silent and the right to have an attorney present. Even so, most suspects, victims, and witnesses are willing and even eager to talk to the prosecutor.

From a defendant's perspective the charging conference presents an opportunity to help shape the prosecutor's understanding of the circumstances of the offense and therefore influence the charges the prosecutor issues. The suspect's explanation of the circumstances might reveal persuasive mitigating factors or a valid excuse or justification for the suspect's actions.

Investigative Grand Jury

In unusual cases the standard methods for developing evidence may be inadequate. In that event the prosecutor has access to another mechanism: the investigative grand jury. Sometimes witnesses refuse to talk to police or other investigators about what they know. An uncooperative witness may be trying to protect someone from prosecution or may be fearful of retaliation if he cooperates with the government. In these situations a reluctant witness can be forced to answer questions if called to testify before a grand jury. When the grand jury summons witnesses, they must appear and answer questions or face being jailed for contempt. A witness may still be evasive and uncooperative, feigning memory loss or lying, but the threat of jail and perjury charges compels a greater degree of cooperation from reluctant witnesses than police or prosecutors can get on their own. Investigative grand juries are used most often to investigate conspiracies and on-going criminal activities, such as organized crime or police corruption. Because the **investigative grand jury** is similar to a charging grand jury except that it functions as an investigative body in addition to a charging body, it will be discussed in greater detail in Chapter 12.

investigative grand jury

Assessing the Evidence

The first rung of the decision ladder is deciding whether there is sufficient evidence to charge. In some prosecutors' offices the practice is to issue as many charges as can be legally supported by probable cause. This practice has been described as the **legal sufficiency model** of charging (Jacoby 1977; Mellon, Jacoby, and Brewer 1981).

legal sufficiency model

Although legally sufficient for issuing charges, probable cause is inadequate to support a conviction. If a case goes to trial, the evidence must meet the standard of proof beyond a reasonable doubt. Some prosecutors' offices screen cases on the basis of the higher standard of proof required for conviction at trial. This model has been called the **trial sufficiency model** (Jacoby 1977; Mellon et al. 1981). Under this model the prosecutor tries to select for charging only those cases that are likely to result in conviction. If it is clear from the outset that evidence sufficient for conviction has not been and will not be developed, no charges are issued, even though the evidence meets the lower standard of probable cause. Under this model the prosecutor is more likely to pay attention to the admissibility of evidence at trial. The prosecutor is also likely to assess the "jury appeal" of the case, whether jurors are likely to find key witnesses credible, for example. A case in which the victim and key prosecution witness is a convicted drug dealer is unlikely to have much jury appeal, and a prosecutor may alter the charging decision in light of this assessment.

trial sufficiency model

Compared to the trial sufficiency model of charging, the legal sufficiency model is likely to result in more suspects being charged and more charges being issued for each suspect. However, more charges will be dismissed later in the process because of weak evidence. In addition, because more charges will be issued against a defendant under the legal sufficiency model, more charges are eventually dropped in plea negotiations. Local norms about the "going rate" are influenced by the charging practices of the prosecutors in the jurisdiction.

Charging in accord with the legal sufficiency model is a style of prosecution that delays screening of weak cases. Charging under the trial sufficiency model screens out weak cases earlier in the process.

No matter what values and preferences underlie the prosecutor's charging decision (whether the prosecutor's practices fit the legal sufficiency, trial sufficiency, or system efficiency model), the prosecutor must weigh and evaluate evidence with respect to its strength and reliability. In most cases evidence is strongest at the time charges are issued. From that point on time erodes evidence: sentiments change, pain and anger fade, evidence is lost, witnesses lose interest and fail to appear, memories fade. If evidence is weak or scanty at the time of charging, it is unlikely to get stronger or more complete later.

Physical evidence often requires some scientific testing in order to link it to a crime. Scientific tests vary in accuracy, reliability, and usefulness. Some tests of evidence are more reliable, some results more conclusive, and some types of evidence more likely to yield information than others. For example, in some homicide cases a coroner can determine the precise cause of death, whereas in other cases the coroner can offer only a probable cause of death. In matching fingerprints some matches are exact and some are not. Sometimes ballistics tests of weapons can provide conclusive proof linking a bullet to a particular gun. In other cases, if the bullet was badly misshapen on impact, ballistics tests may be inconclusive or useless.

In addition to variation in the accuracy and usefulness of tests of physical evidence, in most criminal cases physical evidence does not tell the whole story. In fact, most criminal cases depend on testimonial evidence. The assessment of testimonial evidence depends on its **credibility**, or believability. In the daily parade of witnesses and suspects a prosecutor hears conflicting versions and interpretations of almost every crime. Is someone lying? Who has the most to gain from lying? Did a witness make an honest mistake? Could a witness be drawing inferences about the suspect's motives that are incorrect? Did events happen so fast that a witness is confused about what happened and when it happened? (Gershman 1993). Prosecutors possess no magic formula for assessing credibility; inevitably, assessing credibility relies on human judgment, subject to human prejudices and guided by human instincts. However, prosecutors do gain skill in analyzing witnesses' statements and identifying weaknesses and inconsistencies.

credibility

Among other things, a prosecutor might consider the plausibility of the testimony. A bizarre outlandish story is harder to believe than a more probable one. An account of a witness's actions that seems illogical or contrary to common sense is likely to be considered less than credible. If the explanation offered by the witness seems inconsistent with other things the witness related, the witness's credibility is undermined. Conversely, if the witness's statements remain constant and internally consistent during several repetitions, the witness's story becomes more credible. The reputation of the witness, if known, is also a factor to be considered.

In weighing testimonial evidence the prosecutor also considers obvious motives for dishonesty. A witness who gains something—whether money, power, or freedom—by lying about the events in question is a less credible witness. Conversely, a witness who has nothing to gain, or who may even be testifying despite personal loss, is credible. The accusation of a codefendant, when that accusation comes only in exchange for a plea bargain, is not as strong as an accusation made by someone who has nothing to gain by making an accusation. When Jeff Gillooly (now Stone) implicated Tonya Harding in the attack on Nancy

Kerrigan before the 1994 Olympics, his statement was not very credible on its own because he obtained a lenient sentence in exchange for providing evidence against Harding.

corroboration

Corroboration improves credibility. **Corroboration** is additional evidence that tends to confirm the accuracy of the testimonial evidence. Corroboration may come from either physical evidence or from the testimonial evidence of other witnesses. For example, in a homicide case a witness's testimony that the deceased had a knife is corroborated if a knife is found at the crime scene or by the testimony of other witnesses who also saw the knife.

Finally, prosecutors predict the likelihood that the witness will prove to be reliable over the course of the prosecution. Frequently, a trial will occur several months after the offense. In that time witnesses and victims sometimes lose interest in cooperating with the prosecution. Sometimes, especially for minor offenses, meeting with the prosecutor before trial and appearing to testify become a burden that the witness tries to avoid. In the case of offenses involving family members or friends, prosecutors come to expect witnesses to back down and become uncooperative. Shortly after the offense prosecution seems like a last hope for a situation spiralling out of control. During the months between the offense and tentative court date the situation may change dramatically. Wounds, both physical and emotional, heal. The conflicts that resulted in the crime may appear to be resolved. Cultural and familial pressures to be loyal and to forgive become more powerful than the prosecutor's exhortations to the witness to cooperate in convicting the offender. If the witness's testimony is critical to the prosecution, a strong case may be weakened beyond hope. Because any experienced prosecutor will have had cases in which witnesses became uncooperative because of their relationship to the offender, prosecutors become wary of pursuing such cases vigorously from the outset.

During the 1970s and 1980s battered women's groups criticized prosecutors for making calloused and stereotyped assessments when deciding whether to charge domestic violence cases. If prosecutors assume that battered women will become uncooperative, prosecutors will be unenthusiastic when these women seek charges against their abusers. To respond to these criticisms some prosecutors' offices initiated pro-charging policies. Like pro-arrest policies in police departments, pro-charging means that prosecutors are instructed to charge so long as there is probable cause. Considerations such as the prosecutor's prediction about whether the witness will cooperate later are not to be considered (Schmidt and Hochstedler Steury 1989).

Interests of Justice

Once the prosecutor has a relatively clear sense of the facts and has decided that the evidence is sufficiently strong to justify criminal charges, the prosecutor must consider whether charges are appropriate under the circumstances. In deciding whether a defendant should be prosecuted, and on what charges, the prosecutor is guided by a legal obligation to seek justice (American Bar Association 1970, 43). Seeking justice is broader than simply convicting the guilty. Even if the evidence of guilt is strong, legitimate reasons may justify a nol pros. The prosecutor possesses the discretion to charge or not.

The charging decision can forever alter the lives of those involved. For this reason charging is rarely a mechanical application of the law to the facts. Prosecutors can and do take human factors into account. David Heilbroner,

AMERICAN BAR ASSOCIATION STANDARDS FOR CRIMINAL JUSTICE: THE PROSECUTION FUNCTION

STANDARD 3-3.9   DISCRETION IN THE CHARGING DECISION

(a) A prosecutor should not institute, or cause to be instituted, or permit the continued pendency of criminal charges when the prosecutor knows that the charges are not supported by probable cause. A prosecutor should not institute, cause to be instituted, or permit the continued pendency of criminal charges in the absence of sufficient admissible evidence to support a conviction.

(b) The prosecutor is not obliged to present all charges which the evidence might support. The prosecutor may in some circumstances and for good cause consistent with the public interest decline to prosecute, notwithstanding that sufficient evidence may exist which would support a conviction. Illustrative of the factors which the prosecutor may properly consider in exercising his or her discretion are:

    (i)   the prosecutor's reasonable doubt that the accused is in fact guilty;

    (ii)   the extent of harm caused by the offense;

    (iii)   the disproportion of the authorized punishment in relation to the particular offense or the offender;

    (iv)   possible improper motives of a complainant;

    (v)   reluctance of the victim to testify;

    (vi)   cooperation of the accused in the apprehension or conviction of others; and

    (vii)   availability and likelihood of prosecution by another jurisdiction.

(c) A prosecutor should not be compelled by his or her supervisor to prosecute a case in which he or she has a reasonable doubt about the guilt of the accused.

(d) In making the decision to prosecute, the prosecutor should give no weight to the personal or political advantages or disadvantages which might be involved or to a desire to enhance his or her record of convictions.

(e) In cases which involve a serious threat to the community, the prosecutor should not be deterred from prosecution by the fact that in the jurisdiction juries have tended to acquit persons accused of the particular kind of criminal act in question.

(f) The prosecutor should not bring or seek charges greater in number or degree than can reasonably be supported with evidence at trial or than are necessary to fairly reflect the gravity of the offense.

(g) The prosecutor should not condition a dismissal of charges, nolle prosequi, or similar action on the accused's relinquishment of the right to seek civil redress unless the accused has agreed to the action knowingly and intelligently, freely and voluntarily, and where such waiver is approved by the court.

SOURCE: American Bar Association. 1993. *ABA Standards for Criminal Justice: Prosecution Function and Defense Function*, 3d ed. Washington, D.C.: Criminal Justice Section, American Bar Association, pp. 70–72. Reprinted by permission of the American Bar Association. Copies of these publications are available from Service Center, American Bar Association, 750 Lake Shore Drive, Chicago, IL 60611.

former assistant district attorney in Manhattan, describes the instructions he received upon joining the district attorney's office. In an orientation and talk to all new attorneys in the office a seasoned prosecutor spoke of the factors to consider when using discretion:

"Now, I want to remind you, right from the start, that you have been hired to do justice, to exercise discretion—not just to win cases and seek the maximum penalty. For example, what about the lady caught shoplifting meat from a super-market to feed her family? . . . Under these circumstances, of course, leniency should be shown. You could plea-bargain the case. . . . A lot will depend on her rap sheet and her attitude in court. But you are going to have to learn to make these judgments, judgments that will determine whether a person goes to prison." (1990, 18)

Human factors are considered in the context of the goals that prosecution is intended to achieve. A principal purpose of prosecution is to gain conviction and thereby gain authority to impose punishment. Consequently, the goals of retribution, deterrence, incapacitation, and rehabilitation figure into each decision to prosecute, as they relate to the specifics of each offense, offender, victim, and the public. For example, the seriousness of the offense and the motivation of the offender figure prominently in considerations of retribution. A long or serious criminal record may persuade the prosecutor of the need for severe punishment to deter and incapacitate the suspect. If the offender admits responsibility and shows genuine remorse, the prosecutor may conclude that the defendant is a good prospect for rehabilitation, perhaps through diversion rather than prosecution. In the case of a serious crime that receives a lot of publicity the prosecutor might consider the value of general deterrence even if the offender poses no danger to the community and is unlikely to commit a crime again. The public has to be shown that such conduct is not tolerated and will be punished. If the offender is dangerous, incapacitation may be the overriding factor. These goals will have different weights in different cases.

Obviously, the seriousness of the offense carries much weight when considering the interests of justice. All other mitigating and aggravating circumstances are viewed in relation to the seriousness of the offense. For minor offenses prosecutors often decline to issue charges if it is a first offense. Criminal prosecution in these cases would often do more harm than good: the offender would get a criminal record, which would probably affect employment opportunities and make the situation worse. For more serious offenses the lack of a prior record may not be an important consideration. For example, a homicide suspect with no record is unlikely to be shown leniency in charging.

Prosecutors consider a wide range of other factors in determining what is just under the circumstances: if the offender was provoked by the victim; if the offender is contrite; if the offender is youthful or elderly; if the offense resulted from a misunderstanding; if the offender cooperates with another investigation; if the offender acted out of financial hardship; if the offender was in a state of emotional or psychological strife at the time of the offense; if the offender offers restitution; or if the offender succumbed to the pressure of others involved in the offense. In the right set of circumstances, any one of these factors (and many others) might be a mitigating factor deserving leniency.

Serving the interests of justice is a flexible goal that allows the consideration of a variety of factors. The concept has its limits, however. The interests of justice should not include such things as inconvenience for the prosecutor, personal dislike for the offense or offender, or other feelings stemming from personal bias. The code of professional responsibility specifically prohibits the prosecutor from issuing charges based on improper motives. Issuing charges against a former political enemy when the same behavior would not result in charges against someone else, or issuing charges because the suspect filed a complaint of police brutality, is improper and outside the scope of the prosecutor's legitimate range of discretion. When a prosecutor's charging decision is based on such factors, the prosecutor is abusing the discretion of the office.

STANDING IN THE PROSECUTOR'S SHOES

The two vignettes presented here illustrate what prosecutors must consider in deciding the "right" thing to do. In each case the offense is misdemeanor battery. If you were the prosecutor reviewing these cases, would you charge these cases the same?

CASE A

The prosecutor has before her a criminal complaint for misdemeanor battery signed by the arresting officer, who is present at the charging conference. The suspect is present, without an attorney. The suspect's wife is present, looking concerned. The complaint states that the officer responded to a 911 phone call from a bartender reporting that a fight had broken out between two patrons and one had been hurt. The complaint further states that the bartender informed the officer that the victim had been telling crude jokes and the offender had become annoyed and told him to shut up. The victim then made an insulting remark about the offender's mother, and the offender punched the victim in the nose. The victim appeared to have no broken bones but suffered a profuse nosebleed and reported feeling some dizziness. He was taken by ambulance to a nearby hospital emergency room for first aid treatment.

The prosecutor asks the suspect if he wants a lawyer and informs him of his Miranda rights. The suspect indicates a willingness to talk, and the prosecutor asks him to explain what happened. The suspect, seeming quite subdued, embarrassed, and contrite, says that he had been feeling bad because he had been laid off his job and didn't know how he was going to support his wife and three kids. He had been arguing with his wife about money and had walked down the street to the corner bar to cool off a bit. He knows by sight and first name the man he hit; it is a neighbor who spends many evenings a week in the corner bar. The suspect says he just lost control.

The suspect's wife intervenes. She tells the prosecutor that this is the first arrest for her husband. This isn't like him. He is not a fighter; he is not a habitual drinker. His worries about her and their three children must have made him lose control at the moment. She says she doesn't know how they will be able to afford to pay the victim's out-of-pocket medical expenses for the ambulance and the emergency room treatment, but that if that makes a difference, they will figure out a way.

The neighbor is not present at the charging conference. There is no additional information about the extent of the injury sustained. The police have verified that this thirty-three-year-old suspect, married father of three, has no record as far as they can determine.

CASE B

The prosecutor reviews the misdemeanor battery complaint that was signed by the arresting officer. The complaint is based on the officer's interview with the victim at the crime scene. According to the complaint, the suspect had gone to his ex-wife's place of work at 9 P.M.,

■ RESEARCH ON CHARGING: STEREOTYPES AND PROSECUTORIAL DISCRETION

A number of studies have explored how prosecutors weigh the various factors in making real charging decisions. The studies reveal that the decision is based primarily on the seriousness of the offense and the evidentiary strength of the case. The record of the defendant affects the decision to a lesser extent (Adams and Cutshall 1987; Jacoby, Mellon, Ratledge, and Turner 1982; Miller 1969; Vera Institute of Justice 1981). This seems appropriate and consistent with basic notions of justice.

found her alone on break in the employee lounge, and threatened to punch her out if she didn't keep her boyfriend away from his kids. He punctuated his threats by roughly shoving her; the last shove caused the victim to lose balance, fall, and hit her head on the corner of a table and then on the floor. Fearful for her safety, she began shouting for help. The supervisor rushed in at that moment and immediately summoned the police. When the police arrived, the victim was bleeding from the laceration to the head and said she felt a little dizzy, or at least "shaken up." She had a big lump on her head and complained of a headache. She identified her assailant for the police and gave his address. The police arrested the suspect later that night, when he returned to his room in a boarding house.

The prosecutor informs the suspect of his *Miranda* rights. The suspect is willing to talk without defense counsel present. Upon questioning, the suspect acknowledges that he had consumed "five or six" beers in a couple of hours just before confronting the victim. The prosecutor notes that the computerized records show an outstanding warrant for the suspect's arrest for failure to appear at a court hearing on charges of nonsupport of his children. The suspect explains that he knew he was supposed to show up, but he didn't have a job, and he didn't have any money. He had been on welfare for the past eighteen months, after losing his job. The records also indicated that the suspect had violated a no-contact order (orders by the court to stay away from someone

or someplace) and that on two previous occasions battery charges had been issued but then dismissed because the victim, cooperative at first, later refused to testify. The victim was not present at the charging conference, although she had been notified of the time and place.

Stand in the prosecutor's shoes and review the questions that should be asked before issuing charges in a case:

1. Misdemeanor battery is defined as "Whoever causes bodily harm to another by an act done with intent to cause bodily harm to that person or another without the consent of the person so harmed." Is there probable cause to charge each of these battery defendants? Is it likely that the cases can be proved beyond a reasonable doubt if they go to trial?
2. What charges would best serve the interests of justice in these two cases? Is this a decision for you to make as prosecutor, or would you leave this determination to a jury at trial? How might your decision be influenced by the number and characteristics of other cases in line waiting to be prosecuted?
3. Do you as prosecutor have any personal doubts as to the guilt of the suspects?
4. Should these two cases be treated the same? What options are available? What are the ramifications of exercising your discretion? What facts about the cases influence your decision?

On closer examination, however, research also shows that prosecutors assess the strength of the evidence in relation to personal characteristics of the defendant, victim, and witnesses in ways that may bring improper biases into the decision to prosecute. Specifically, research findings indicate that after the legal variables (seriousness and prior record) are taken into account, race, gender, and age are powerful influences (Adams and Cutshall 1987; Albonetti 1986, 1987, 1992; Radelet and Pierce 1985; Spohn, Gruhl, and Welch 1987). Victim-offender relationships appear to influence the decision as well (Vera Institute of Justice 1981, 19).

These factors act like distorting lenses that influence the prosecutor's assessment of the credibility of witnesses and suspects. Moreover, even if the prosecutor is aware of the distortions, the prosecutor is equally aware that the judge and jury will be influenced by similar stereotypes in judging credibility at trial. Experiments confirm that the public uses stereotypes in attributing criminality to individuals based on facial characteristics that identify race, ethnic heritage, and sex (Fishman, Rattner, and Weimann 1987). Consequently, even if the prosecutor believes the witness's story, if the prosecutor believes that the judge or jury will not believe the witness, the prosecutor may still decline to prosecute (Miller 1969, 173, 186; Stanko 1981–1982, 229). According to one study,

> Social class, sex, race, and life style are factors often taken into account in the application of the law. . . . But the implicit (never explicit, of course) use of such attributes in the charging process is not—or at least not only—a measure of outright prosecutorial bias. More often, it emerges as the pragmatism of a prosecutor intent on maximizing convictions and using organizational resources efficiently. Convictions are maximized when only solid cases are brought to trial. . . . A victim must be credible not only in the eyes of the prosecutor, but also to the judge and the jury. Thus an essential element of the charging decision is the determination of perceived victim credibility. (Stanko 1981–1982, 226, 237)

In sum the assessment of the credibility of the victim and witnesses—which is part of the assessment of the evidentiary strength of the case—is related to the personal attributes and social class of the primary parties to the offense.

■ CHARGING IN ANTICIPATION OF NEGOTIATION

Charging clearly influences plea bargaining. The greater the number of charges brought against the defendant, the more likely it is that some of those charges will be dropped in exchange for some form of cooperation with the prosecution— whether by pleading guilty or by providing information related to other crimes and criminals. For the typical criminal suspect the major component of cooperation is the willingness to plead guilty.

In some jurisdictions prosecutors manipulate the charging decision to create the appearance of leniency. The prosecutor knows that the defendant is going to expect some leniency in return for pleading guilty. Anticipating this, the prosecutor adds some charges that can later be traded for the guilty plea, leaving untouched the charges the prosecutor would have charged in the first place. In an armed robbery the prosecutor might charge armed robbery, lesser included offenses, and one or more additional offenses, such as carrying a concealed weapon and reckless use of a dangerous weapon. Even at the time of charging the prosecutor might expect to drop the additional offenses, focusing on obtaining a conviction on the armed robbery charge alone.

This practice is known by a variety of names, including "piling on charges," "issuing throw-away charges," and "bed sheeting" (Lindquist 1988, 171). In studying prosecutors' practices in plea bargaining Milton Heumann documented this:

> I examined the files of 88 defendants in one superior court public defender's office and found that only 12 of these defendants were charged with a single count of a single offense. The remaining 76 defendants had a total of 288 charges leveled against them. This piling on of charges . . . . provide[d] ample years for the state's attorney to 'play with' in negotiations. (1978, 1942)

The following report describes piling on in the federal jurisdiction:

Two now common charging practices provide a potent incentive for defendants to plea bargain. Prosecutors regularly overcharge in both the number of counts *and* the severity of offenses in an indictment. It is not uncommon for federal prosecutors to charge scores of counts, even up to 100 in an indictment. (Glanzer and Taskier 1987, 7)

overcharging

Another way to allow room for plea bargaining is to overcharge. **Overcharging** is the practice of charging a more serious offense than would be sought under other circumstances. Frequently, when a prosecutor overcharges, the evidence supporting the higher charges is weak or nonexistent. For example, attempted homicide charges might be filed in the case of an aggravated battery, even though the evidence of intent to kill is weak or nonexistent.

Piling on and overcharging are practices that are common in some jurisdictions but not others. Overcharging is less likely to occur in jurisdictions in which formal screening processes (grand jury or preliminary hearing) are rigorous, providing a real screen of the evidence. In some jurisdictions, however, the formal screening processes are weak, amounting to little more than a rubber stamp of the prosecutor's charging decision. In these jurisdictions overcharging is a much greater possibility. Jurisdictions that follow the legal sufficiency model of charging would be more likely to pile on and overcharge. In addition, piling on and overcharging are more common in jurisdictions in which the prosecutor maintains sole discretion to reduce charges up to the point of conviction. This situation maximizes prosecutorial leverage and allows adjustment by prosecutors when it is most advantageous. In these jurisdictions prosecutors build bargaining chips into their charging decisions. In other jurisdictions piling on and overcharging are not common practices. In jurisdictions that operate under the trial sufficiency model, and in jurisdictions in which the charges cannot be amended or reduced without court approval, these practices are less likely to flourish. In these latter jurisdictions the plea-bargaining style is more akin to "You can take or leave my offer; if you don't take it, I can—and will—prove the charges in court."

CONTROLLING CHARGING DISCRETION

Clearly, exercising judgment is a big part of a prosecutor's job—especially in charging. Judgment calls inevitably vary from one prosecutor to the next. The circumstance that one prosecutor may consider as mitigating the defendant's guilt another may view as largely irrelevant. To channel this discretion many large prosecutors' offices have guidelines for making charging decisions (see Chapter 7). In some offices the guidelines are in the form of written policies; in other offices the guidelines are informal, learned on an ad hoc basis and passed on by word of mouth. More and more prosecutors' offices are adopting written guidelines in an effort to reduce disparity, a measure encouraged by the National District Attorneys Association (Lezak and Leonard 1985, 48). These measures increase the degree of centralized managerial control over the charging decisions of individual prosecutors in a single office.

charging guidelines

Where they exist in written form, **charging guidelines** may state fairly broad comprehensive policies or relatively specific ones. A broad guideline, for example, might require that the prosecutor state reasons for nolle prosequi. Another broad guideline might prohibit issuing throw-away charges. At the other extreme specific charging guidelines might prohibit a prosecutor from charging an armed robbery as a simple robbery or an armed burglary as a simple burglary. Such guidelines are relatively easy to supervise. In large offices supervisors may monitor charging decisions to ensure that individual prosecutors are complying with the guidelines.

This trend toward channeling charging discretion results in part from widespread and intense criticism of plea-bargaining practices. One way to control the great variability in bargaining is to control the great variability in charging, from which all negotiations proceed. If the charge is fair and appropriate to the facts and can be proved, and if the defendant knows the charge is a reasonable one, the prosecutor will be able to negotiate from a position of strength, to stand firm and exact a guilty plea with very little concession.

One study compares three jurisdictions with a high degree of managerial control over charging and plea bargaining to three jurisdictions that allow individual prosecutors great flexibility in charging and plea bargaining (LaFree 1985). The study found that prosecutors not subject to guidelines and managerial oversight tend to bring more charges and more serious charges against defendants initially. They also grant greater charge reductions during plea bargaining. In jurisdictions operating under tighter managerial control, case characteristics such as severity and evidence more closely predict sentencing outcome (LaFree 1985, 307–8). Decision making in jurisdictions with low managerial control are more idiosyncratic and less closely related to case characteristics, such as seriousness and strength of the evidence. Based on these results, the study concluded that "the attempt to increase centralized managerial control . . .was an important and justifiable reform." (LaFree 1985, 308).

Such guidelines, whether broad or specific, whether formal and written or informal and unwritten, exist to reduce disparity, the unequal treatment of equal cases. Even formal written charging guidelines will not eradicate all disparity in charging decisions. Charging decisions are based in part on a personal interpretation of justice and fairness, as applied to each individual case. Nonetheless, charging guidelines are meant to reduce disparity, without making charging a purely mechanical application of the law to the facts.

■ SUMMARY

The prosecutor's job is to determine whether evidence is sufficient to support a successful prosecution and whether prosecution will serve the legitimate interests of justice. In making this decision the prosecutor must use judgment informed by experience. The exercise of prosecutorial discretion is powerful in shaping outcomes in the criminal justice process.

Adequate supporting evidence is a prerequisite for issuing charges against an individual. Most often the prosecutor relies heavily on police detectives for developing evidence, but the prosecutor often takes part by interviewing witnesses or conducting a charging conference. In unusual cases evidence will be developed by special investigators in the prosecutor's office or through investigation by a grand jury.

Given the facts as they are presented at the time of charging, the prosecutor determines whether the evidence is sufficient to support any criminal charges and whether criminal charges are appropriate in light of the interests of justice and limited resources. The prosecutor considers the strength of the evidence, including the credibility of the accusing witnesses, the seriousness of the offense, the character and criminal record of the offender, the wishes of the victim, and the interests of the public, and weighs them in light of the legitimate goals of punishment, retribution, deterrence, incapacitation, and rehabilitation. Within ethical bounds the prosecutor is free to use discretion to be lenient and nol pros a case. Sometimes prosecutors engage in a practice called overcharging, in which the prosecutor issues charges that the evidence cannot really support. The extent to which prosecutors engage in this ethically questionable practice seems to vary from jurisdiction to jurisdiction.

Research suggests that the seriousness of the offense and the strength of the evidence are the most important factors influencing the charging decision. The prosecutor's assessment of the strength of the evidence is sometimes influenced by the characteristics of the offender, victim, and witnesses in ways that introduce bias into the charging process. Further, research shows that charging guidelines can be effective in reducing disparity in charging decisions within a jurisdiction.

When initial charging occurs early in the process, the case moves forward to the first formal stage of the court process; the initial appearance. For misdemeanor offenders the initial appearance is often the defendant's only appearance in court. For both misdemeanor and felony defendants the initial appearance often takes place in the lower courts (courts of limited jurisdiction). The next chapter examines the lower courts and the processing of misdemeanor cases. Chapter 11 examines the initial appearance in relation to felony cases, with special attention to the issue of bail.

■ FOR FURTHER DISCUSSION

1. In 25 to 50 percent of the cases reviewed by prosecutors no charges are issued. What are some reasons that prosecutors decide not to issue charges?

2. What are the goals of diversion, and how is diversion accomplished?

3. After a verbal confrontation between two groups of men, the three men in one group took off in their car. The two men in the other group dashed to their car and took off after the first group. The men in the second car followed the first, eventually pulling alongside. The man on the passenger side of the second car reached out the car window and started swinging a tire iron, causing dents on the roof, hood, and rear of the car. At one point the two cars struck each other. On reaching an intersection the men in the second car (who had been swinging the tire iron) sped off, were spotted by police, and apprehended. The prosecutor charged the driver of the car with failure to comply with the conditions of pretrial release, reckless endangerment while armed with a dangerous weapon, disorderly conduct, and criminal damage to property. The man on the passenger side of the car was charged with reckless endangerment while armed with a dangerous weapon, disorderly conduct while in possession of a dangerous weapon, criminal damage to property, and obstructing an officer. The maximum sentence faced by both men under these charges is a fine of $31,000 and sixteen years in prison.

   Analyze these charges in terms of the concepts of lesser included offenses and additional offenses. What is the significance of lesser included offenses and additional offenses to the potential outcome at plea bargaining or trial for each defendant? Would you consider this an example of overcharging or piling on charges? Why or why not?

4. One study establishes three different models of prosecutorial charging: system efficiency, legal sufficiency, and trial sufficiency. What patterns of

prosecutorial charging define each model? Which model is likely to result in the greatest number of criminal charges being filed, all else being equal?

5. Direct physical evidence probably is the strongest kind of evidence for proving charges. Many criminal cases rely on circumstantial evidence and on testimonial evidence, in which the credibility of the witness is a key factor in assessing the strength of the evidence. How might stereotypes influence the assessment of both circumstantial and testimonial evidence?

■ REFERENCES

Adams, Kenneth, and Charles R. Cutshall. 1987. "Refusing to Prosecute Minor Offenses: The Relative Influence of Legal and Extra-legal Factors." *Justice Quarterly* 4: 595–609.

Albonetti, Celesta A. 1992. "Charge Reduction: An Analysis of Prosecutorial Discretion in Burglary and Robbery Cases." *Journal of Quantitative Criminology* 8: 317–33.

——— 1987. "Prosecutorial Discretion: The Effects of Uncertainty." *Law and Society Review* 21: 291–313.

——— 1986. "Criminality, Prosecutorial Screening, and Uncertainty: Toward a Theory of Discretionary Decision Making in Felony Case Processing." *Criminology* 24: 623–44.

American Bar Association. 1970. *Project on Standards for Criminal Justice*. Chicago: American Bar Association.

Becker, Samuel. 1988. "Judicial Scrutiny of Prosecutorial Discretion in the Decision Not to File a Complaint." *Marquette Law Review* 71: 749–68.

Boland, Barbara, Elizabeth Brady, H. Tyson, and J. Bassler. 1982. *The Prosecution of Felony Arrests, 1979*. Washington, D.C.: Institute for Law and Social Research.

Boland, Barbara, Paul Mahanna, and Ronald Sones. 1992. *The Prosecution of Felony Arrests, 1988*. Washington, D.C.: U.S. Department of Justice, Bureau of Justice Statistics.

Davis, Kenneth C. 1971. *Discretionary Justice: A Preliminary Inquiry*. Chicago: University of Illinois Press.

Ferguson, Robert W., and Allan H. Stokke. 1978. *Legal Aspects of Evidence*. New York: Harcourt Brace Jovanovich.

Fishman, Gordon, Arye Rattner, and Gabriel Weimann. 1987. "The Effect of Ethnicity on Crime Attribution." *Criminology* 25: 507–24.

Gershman, Bennett L. 1993. "A Moral Standard for the Prosecutor's Exercise of the Charging Discretion." *Fordham Urban Law Journal* 20: 513–530.

Glanzer, Seymour, and Paul R. Taskier. 1987. "The Fine Art of Plea Bargaining." *Criminal Justice* 2 (Summer): 6–7, 40–44.

Graham, Kenneth, and Leon Letwin. 1971. "The Preliminary Hearing in Los Angeles: Some Field Findings and Legal Policy Observations." *University of California Los Angeles Law Review* 18: 635–757.

Heilbroner, David. 1990. *Rough Justice: Days and Nights of a Young D.A.* New York: Pantheon.

Hochstedler, Ellen. 1987. "Twice-Cursed? The Mentally Disordered Defendant." *Criminal Justice and Behavior* 14: 251–67.

Heumann, Milton. 1978. *Plea Bargaining: The Experience of Prosecutors, Judges, and Defense Attorneys*. Chicago: University of Chicago Press.

Jacoby, Joan. 1977. *The Prosecutor's Charging Decision: A Policy Perspective*. Washington, D.C.: U.S. Department of Justice, Law Enforcement Assistance Administration.

Jacoby, Joan, Leonard R. Mellon, Edward C. Ratledge, and S. H. Turner. 1982. *Prosecutorial Decision-Making: A National Study*. Washington, D.C.: Department of Justice, National Institute of Justice.

LaFree, Gary D. 1985. "Adversarial and Nonadversarial Justice: A Comparison of Guilty Pleas and Trials." *Criminology* 23 (May): 289–312.

Lezak, Sidney I., and Maureen Leonard. 1985. "The Prosecutor's Discretion: Out of the Closet, Not out of Control." In Carl F. Pinkele and William C. Louthan, eds. *Discretion, Justice and Democracy: A Public Policy Perspective*. Ames: Iowa State University Press.

Lindquist, J. H. 1988. *Misdemeanor Crime: Trivial Criminal Pursuit*. Newbury Park, Calif.: Sage.

McDonald, William F. 1979. "The Prosecutor's Domain." In W. F. McDonald, ed. *The Prosecutor*. Beverly Hills, Calif.: Sage.

McIntyre, Donald. 1968. "A Study of Judicial Dominance of the Charging Decision." *Journal of Criminal Law, Criminology, and Police Science* 59: 463–90.

Melilli, Kenneth J. 1992. "Prosecutorial Discretion in an Adversary System." *Brigham Young University Law Review* 1992 (3): 669–704.

Mellon, Leonard R., Joan E. Jacoby, and Marion A. Brewer. 1981. "The Prosecutor Constrained by His Environment: A New Look at Discretionary Justice in the United States." *Journal of Criminal Law and Criminology* 72: 52—81.

Miller, Frank W. 1969. *Prosecution: The Decision to Charge a Suspect with a Crime*. Boston: Little, Brown.

Neubauer, David W. 1974. "After the Arrest: The Charging Decision in Prairie City." *Law and Society Review* 8: 495–517.

Radelet, Michael L., and Glenn L. Pierce. 1985. "Race and Prosecutorial Discretion in Homicide Cases." *Law and Society Review* 19: 587–621.

Schmidt, Janell, and Ellen Hochstedler Steury. 1989. "Prosecutorial Discretion in Filing Charges in Domestic Violence Cases." *Criminology* 27 (August): 487–510.

Schneider, Thomas P. 1993. Interview with author. Milwaukee, Wisconsin, 23 March 1993.

Spohn, Cassia, John Gruhl, and Susan Welch. 1987. "The Impact of the Ethnicity and Gender of Defendants on the Decision to Reject or Dismiss Felony Charges." *Criminology* 25: 175–191.

Stanko, Elizabeth Anne. 1981–1982. "The Impact of Victim Assessment on Prosecutors' Screening Decisions: The Case of the New York County District Attorney's Office." *Law and Society Review* 16: 225–39.

Vera Institute of Justice. 1981. *Felony Arrests: Their Prosecution and Disposition in New York City's Courts*. White Plains, N.Y.: Longman.

10

PROCESSING LESSER OFFENSES IN LOWER COURTS

The experience of lesser offenders in the courts is often dramatically different from that of felons. The distinct stages of the felony criminal process (which occupy the remainder of this book) are telescoped into just one very brief appearance. In many cases involving petty offenses the initial appearance becomes at once the arraignment, during which the final plea is taken, and the sentencing hearing, during which the judge pronounces sentence. Moreover, studies report cases being processed in about two minutes on average (Dash 1951, 251; President's Commission 1967, 313). The label "assembly-line" justice aptly describes the swift and routine processing of nonfelony offenses.

Typically, less serious offenses are adjudicated in courts of limited jurisdiction. In some places the lower courts process only noncriminal municipal ordinance violations, and all criminal offenses are heard in courts of general jurisdiction. In other places some lower courts have broad jurisdiction to process noncriminal infractions and misdemeanors, and to conduct preliminary proceedings in felony cases. A few are even authorized to accept guilty pleas in some felony cases.

The lower courts process more than twice as many criminal cases as courts of general jurisdiction (Ostrom 1994, 6, 8; see Figure 10–1). Even so, the lower courts are the least studied segment of the courts. Consequently, some research that this chapter draws upon is dated. Nonetheless, the observations of researchers in the 1950s and 1960s are not too different from those of researchers working in the 1970s and 1980s. Despite periodic reform efforts, the assembly-line nature of case processing in the lower criminal courts appears to have remained largely unchanged.

This chapter describes the functions and operations of the lower courts, particularly in relation to the norm of "moving cases." Assembly-line processing in lower courts makes them a frequent target of criticism. This chapter assesses the lower courts in relation to their historic role in the system of justice, recent reforms, and prospects for the future.

> **FIGURE 10-1   Volume of Cases in Courts of Limited and General Jurisdiction**
>
> SOURCE: Brian J. Ostrom 1994. *State Court Caseload Statistics: Annual Report 1992.* Williamsburg, Va.: National Center for State Courts, pp. 6, 8.

	Limited Jurisdiction	General Jurisdiction
Criminal	9,237,705	4,007,838
Juvenile	579,888	1,150,833
Traffic/Ordinance Violations	51,031,260	8,071,601
Domestic Relations	1,112,873	3,326,059
Civil	9,044,000	6,224,442

A LEGACY FROM THE PAST: JUSTICE OF THE PEACE COURTS

justice of the peace (JP)

In the early days of our nation local justice was typically provided by **justices of the peace**, casually known as **JPs**. In the days when communication and travel were slow and expensive, these local magistrates were the backbone of law and order in isolated communities and rural areas. Citizens relied on the local JP for protection and justice long before police departments and public prosecutors' offices became common features of the criminal justice system. Justice of the peace courts provided ready access to a magistrate who was a local official, usually elected. The JP issued warrants for search or arrest to the town constable or to the sheriff in rural areas. Once a suspect was apprehended, the local justice presided over the disposition of the case.

JPs were the embodiment of justice for and by the common people. Traditionally, JPs were not required to hold law degrees or to be formally trained in law at all. They were supposed to be local citizens of good judgment and maturity who enjoyed the confidence of the people who elected them. They disposed of cases in an informal manner based on their common sense notions of justice and community sentiments.

The justice of the peace remained an important component of the court structure throughout the nineteenth century and into the beginning of the twentieth century. In 1928 all states authorized local communities to employ local justices. By the middle of the twentieth century, however, a combination of reformist pressures and changing circumstances heralded the end of the era of local justices of the peace. Many states abolished or severely restricted the authority of the JP. By 1964 eight states had eliminated the office, three more were preparing to eliminate it, and others had limited its authority (Vanlandingham 1974, 40). By 1987 only thirteen states still maintained courts called either justice or justice of the peace courts (National Center for State Courts [NCSC] 1988).

Among the principal factors associated with this change were the abuses associated with the JPs. The informality of JP courts invited abuse. JPs could be imperious and arbitrary, which conflicted with a law-based system of justice. One tangible sign of the lack of deference to the written law was the inadequate training of JPs in substantive and procedural law (Vanlandingham 1974, 42). Good judgment from a layperson is no longer widely accepted as an adequate substitute for knowledge of the rules of procedure or the rules of evidence.

fee system

The decline of the JP also was undoubtedly hastened by the notorious **fee system**—JPs were paid according to the amount of business they conducted. Rural JPs rarely received regular salaries. Instead they were paid on a fee-for-service or case-by-case basis. In some places the JP's fees were paid by the defendant if the defendant was convicted and by the town if the defendant was acquitted. This fee system created a mild conflict of interest by providing an incentive to try cases rather than dismiss them (Vanlandingham 1974, 44). Moreover, as a member of the local political elite, a JP may have felt pressure to protect the local treasury from having to absorb fees. Too many acquittals could be expensive for the community.

In some states, however, the inherent conflict of interest in the fee system was greater and far more objectionable. Several states provided for the JP to receive fees for services only if the defendant was found guilty. Upon conviction fees would be assessed against the defendant, and the fees went directly to pay for the JP's services. If acquitted, the JP received no compensation for time spent on the case.

In 1927 the U.S. Supreme Court ruled in *Tumey v. Ohio* that a judge in a misdemeanor case is disqualified from presiding if the judge's fee depends on the conviction of the defendant. *Tumey* did not find all fee-for-service payment arrangements unconstitutional. If the judge was paid only for the number of cases tried, whether the verdict was guilty or not guilty, the Court did not hold such arrangements unconstitutional. The fee system, in both constitutional and unconstitutional forms, persisted in many states for the next few decades (Vanlandingham 1974, 44–45).

As the JP courts were becoming more and more out of tune with changing twentieth century legal values, the circumstances that originally gave rise to the need for local lay justices also changed. Advances in communication and transportation reduced the need for local courts in every village and hamlet. With the invention of the telephone and automobile prisoners could be quickly transported to the county seat to appear before a judge.

Together these changes resulted in the decline of JP courts as a major institution of justice for most people living in the United States. The states that continue to operate JP courts are primarily sparsely populated states and are mostly in the West (Arizona, California, Louisiana, Mississippi, Montana, Nevada, Oregon, Texas, Utah, and Wyoming). Only three eastern states—Delaware, Pennsylvania, and New York—still use JP courts. In vast rural areas the very needs that gave rise to the JP in the early days of this nation persist and perpetuate the office. In the words of one judge from Montana, "In rural Montana, some counties are lucky to have even one lawyer. That makes the nonlawyer justice of the peace an essential provider of speedy justice" (Brownlee 1975, 373).

In urban areas the lower courts have also been subject to criticism and reform. The qualifications and training of lower-court judges has been a particularly important concern. As legal procedures and the rights of defendants have become more and more pronounced, the rough-and-ready justice offered by nonlawyer judges has become less acceptable. For example, where nonlawyers are allowed to serve in the lower courts, judges are now required to receive instruction in substantive and procedural law (Brownlee 1975; see also Ashman and Chapin 1976; Green, Russell, and Schmidhauser 1975; NCSC 1988; and Ryan and Guterman 1977). In addition, the fee system has been eliminated in most jurisdictions, eradicating another objection to this traditional lower-court official (Brownlee 1975; and Green, Russell, and Schmidhauser 1976).

◻ MODERN-DAY COURTS OF LIMITED JURISDICTION

Despite the decline of the JP court, courts of limited jurisdiction flourish. In urban settings courts of limited jurisdiction handle the great volume of minor crimes and noncriminal violations. In rural areas, where the volume of offenses is not so great, this work has been absorbed into the courts of general jurisdiction or countywide courts with limited jurisdiction.

As a consequence of the court reform movement some states have moved to limit the jurisdiction of the lower courts so that only the most trivial offenses are heard there. These efforts are constantly interrupted, however, by the need to relieve the courts of general jurisdiction and by local interest in using the courts to raise revenue.

Relieving Felony Courts

When courts of general jurisdiction become overcrowded and overworked, policymakers often seize upon the lower courts as a relief mechanism. By transferring the more routine work to the lower courts, felony courts are able to focus on those cases requiring more intensive attention because of their seriousness or complexity. By design the lower courts have been assigned the less "serious" types of cases and the more routine sorts of tasks.

The lower courts also relieve courts of general jurisdiction through the process of decriminalization.

exclusive civil jurisdiction

Decriminalization may take one of two forms. One form of decriminalization provides **exclusive civil jurisdiction** over an act that used to be, but no longer is, a crime. In such a case the criminal statute prohibiting the act is repealed in order to decriminalize the proscribed behavior. In its place the state may enact a noncriminal infraction, or local communities may opt to pass noncriminal ordinances relating to the behavior that formerly was defined as a crime. Traffic offenses, disorderly conduct, and public drunkenness are examples of behaviors that have been decriminalized in many places. Although jurisdictions pursue decriminalization of these offenses for a variety of reasons, one consequence is to relieve the courts of general jurisdiction from having to process these cases. Instead the lower courts become the exclusive forum for adjudicating these offenses.

concurrent jurisdiction

The second form of decriminalization simply provides an alternative to criminal processing; decriminalization is a matter of practice rather than of law. In this situation the proscribed act remains a crime, but the legislators enact a noncriminal prohibition of the conduct, such as a municipal ordinance. This results in **concurrent criminal and civil jurisdiction** over the proscribed conduct. For example, littering or disorderly conduct might be prohibited by both a criminal statute and an ordinance. Similarly, speeding or driving without a license might be both a crime and a violation of a traffic regulation. Where concurrent criminal and civil jurisdiction exists in regard to the same act, police and prosecutorial discretion are paramount in determining which arrests are labeled civil violations and which are labeled crimes.

This second form of decriminalization is frequently used to shift the burden of cases between the courts of limited and general jurisdiction. How the behavior is

TRAFFIC OFFENSES

Traffic offenses constitute a large proportion of the minor offenses entering the court process. Most of these cases (approximately 87 percent) are processed through the lower courts, either as noncriminal infractions or as misdemeanors.

Seventy-one percent of all criminal and civil case filings in courts of limited jurisdiction in 1992 were traffic cases (Ostrom 1994, 8). In addition to contested tickets for moving violations, these courts process cases involving driving without a license and driving while a license is suspended or revoked. In some jurisdictions traffic offenses are overwhelming the misdemeanor courts.

Traffic cases can be big revenue producers for local communities but only if the costs of processing these cases are relatively low. When these traffic offenses are processed as misdemeanors, the costs rise, especially in jurisdictions that provide indigent defense counsel and jury trials for these cases.

The costs of processing traffic cases are affected by a variety of factors. State law determines whether traffic offenses are exclusively criminal, exclusively civil, or whether there is concurrent criminal and civil jurisdiction. Local ordinances may create concurrent jurisdiction even if the state has only a criminal provision. Finally, for cases of operating without a license, particularly repeat offenses, police and prosecutors may conclude that a civil fine is an inadequate deterrent.

charged provides a measure of control over the criminal caseload of the courts and the associated costs of processing criminal offenses. A criminal defendant must be afforded a law-trained judge, an attorney for defense, and a jury of peers. When offenses are decriminalized many of the criminal defendant's due process rights do not apply, and the cost of observing those rights can be avoided. As the caseload of the criminal courts increases, so does the pressure to relieve the system by treating the least serious offenses as noncriminal matters.

Making Money the Old-Fashioned Way

Just as the early kings of England found that courts offered a revenue source, many municipalities find that it is in their economic self-interest to operate a local court. In most states fines collected by the courts of general jurisdiction go to the state treasury, but fines collected by locally funded courts go into the local treasury. Even when the state funds local courts in whole or in part, the state may share some revenue with the local government. By collecting fines for traffic and parking violations, and by handling minor criminal matters as petty offenses in the lower courts, municipalities can actually make money from their court systems.

Processing offenses that are not serious can indeed be a lucrative business. Minor offenses can move rapidly through the system, and fines are widely viewed as an appropriate sanction. The stakes are low enough that defendants often prefer to admit guilt and pay a fine than to fight the matter with a lawyer and additional court appearances. Noncriminal offenses in particular are relatively inexpensive to process because the jurisdiction need not provide free counsel to the indigent defendant. Prosecution is not a complex matter in many of these cases. A police officer often is assigned to act as prosecutor, further reducing the costs of prosecution. So long as the collection of fines and court costs exceeds the costs of operating the court, courts of limited jurisdiction will feed the local treasury and are likely to flourish.

However, local courts can serve as revenue producers only if the costs of adjudication are kept low. In the court as in the factory, routinization and standardization are tools for maintaining speed at a low cost. In contrast to the ideal of individualized justice, the lower courts, more than any other part of the court process, deliver assembly-line justice.

■ MOVING CASES: EVERYBODY'S BUSINESS

By design lower courts can and must process more cases more quickly than felony courts. Lower courts can deal with cases more rapidly because on the whole these cases are less complex and more routine. In addition, lower courts must deal with cases more quickly because so many cases must be heard. To be cost-effective, lower courts must dispose of cases rapidly.

Each morning a new queue of arrestees waits in the holding cell adjacent to the courtroom. The courtroom work group must process all the cases in the queue before day's end. Consequently, courtroom actors share a common goal: moving cases. Together they devise strategies for achieving their common goal while fulfilling the mandates of their individual positions. The judge must maintain a high court clearance rate. The public defender seeks to get the best deal for the defendant. The prosecutor tries to maintain a high conviction rate. The clerks need to complete paperwork (Lipetz 1984 48). To meet these goals courtroom participants develop shared understandings of the "worth" of a case. These norms in turn facilitate guilty pleas as a prime vehicle for moving cases (Knab and Lindberg 1977).

Moving cases efficiently entails being able to size up a case quickly, to establish its "worth" (Feeley 1979, 159; Mileski 1971, 73). Although the same thing occurs in felony cases, in misdemeanor cases the assessment occurs more rapidly and is unlikely to be reviewed at a later point (Nardulli, Eisenstein, and Flemming 1988; Sudnow 1965). "Case-typing" involves learning which cases are worth arguing about, what factors (mitigating and aggravating circumstances) make a difference in relation to the outcome, and knowing the going rates for the various offenses. For example, the prosecutor might size a case up as a basic first-offense shoplifting. Based on this classification, the prosecutor offers a standard plea, for example, a $50 fine in exchange for a guilty plea. Individualized negotiations between the prosecutor and defense are limited to the more serious or unusual cases in the lower courts.

Each major courtroom participant—police, prosecutor, judge, defendant, and defense counsel—benefits by cooperating in ways that keep the docket moving. Although the defense is often seen as benefiting from delay, even the defendant and the defense attorney may have a keen interest in swift processing. Athough delay can sometimes provide a strategic advantage to the defense, delay is costly for most defendants in lower courts. Delay means additional court appearances, and time is money. For the defendant additional court appearances may mean paying additional fees to a private defense attorney. For the public defender time is a precious commodity, not to be spent without good reason. Delay also may mean that a defendant sits in jail awaiting trial.

Prosecutors operate in much the same way but from a different position. Time, energy, and office resources are allotted according to the worth of the case. Leniency is the currency that moves cases through the system more quickly. Unless the case is worth the fight, leniency is a lever to persuade defendants to plead guilty quickly.

ASSEMBLY-LINE JUSTICE

Pofessor Malcolm Feeley provides an excellent description of the typically hurried and perfunctory initial appearance before a lower court, often the defendant's only appearance in court:

A clerk mumbles out a name and a long series of numbers (identifying numbers for relevant sections of the criminal code) and someone else (a defense attorney) springs forward. At the same time someone else (a prosecutor) peers up at the judge as he begins shuffling through a set of papers which has just been thrust into his hands by the clerk, and announces to the judge what he is going to do with the case—whether he will continue it for another week, nolle the charges, or urge the accused to plead guilty.

This preliminary business is completed at just about the same time the defendant has finished moving forward from the gallery and crossing the courtroom floor, until he arrives in front of the bench between the prosecutor and his defense attorney.

He might arrive just in time to hear the resolution of the case. If it is a continuance, either the prosecutor or the defense attorney instructs him to show up again at the same time and place a week later. If it is a nolle, they point to the door and tell him he is free to go. If it is to be a plea of guilty, he makes the plea and the clerk recites the charges anew, after which the prosecutor interjects his sentence recommendation to the judge, usually a fine of $10 or $25 or a suspended sentence. If it is a suspended sentence, the judge tells the defendant not to get in trouble again. If it is a fine, the prosecutor points out the bailiff who will instruct him [the defendant] as to how to pay the fine. If the defendant has any questions, it is unlikely that they will be answered because the prosecutor and the defense attorney have already turned their attention to the next case.

Source: Malcolm Feeley. © 1979. *The Process is the Punishment: Handling Cases in Lower Court*. New York: Russell Sage Foundation. p. 156.

Judges encourage defendants to accept the standard plea and keep cases moving in other ways as well. They can limit the time allotted to a case in court. The judge may cut short the explanations of a defendant or impose negative sanctions on defendants who take up more time than the judge considers appropriate. Judges have the authority, within the limits of reasonableness, to permit or deny continuances and adjournments. When a judge wishes to bring a case to an end, she denies continuances, sets a trial date, and forces the defense to either go to trial or settle. In these ways the judge maintains control over the scheduling of cases and ensures that cases are disposed of within a reasonable period of time.

The worth of a case is a value that evolves over time in any given system. The rates go up (or down), much like prices in the supermarket, in response to shifting trends and perspectives. Feeley describes how the going rate for marijuana offenses shifted in response to growing numbers of college students arrested for this crime in the early 1970s:

Within the past few years, marijuana and heroin have become "familiar" to the court and the community, and tolerance of drug use, especially marijuana, has increased. One result is that the court has become progressively more lenient in its handling of these cases, and in essence the "worth" or "going rate" of this type of case has declined.

This decline has been precipitated by changing social mores, but it received impetus in the court from the occasional actions of defense attorneys who . . . have threatened trial. . . .Other . . . attorneys for college students vigorously pressed for "better" deals for their clients, whom they argued would face a lifetime of lost opportunity if they were convicted for possession of marijuana. But once such exceptions were made, then attorneys for other defendants began to press for the same treatment, and eventually a new lower price for this type of case was established. (Malcolm Feeley, *The Process is the Punishment*, © 1979, 188–89, Russell Sage Foundation)

In this way leniency becomes routine, part of the process. It does not have to be specifically negotiated in every case. This sort of standard leniency keeps things moving with a minimum of information exchanged and time spent. In some courts such leniency apparently is available primarily to those in the know. In these courts a defense attorney is a valuable asset (Feeley 1979). In other courts this standard leniency is available to unrepresented defendants as well (Ryan 1980–1981, 93). For example, one study (Lipetz 1984) reports an exchange between court personnel when a new assistant state's attorney (ASA) did not consider the defendant a first offender because of a charge dismissed just eighteen days earlier. The ASA recommended a sentence of two days in jail in exchange for a guilty plea, the routine sentence for repeat offenders in this court. The court sergeant, the police liaison to the court, the judge, and the ASA engaged in the following exchange:

Sgt.:   Supervision on first conviction!

Judge: That's the way we do it here.

ASA: But she was arrested eighteen days ago.

Judge: No convictions. We do supervisions.

ASA: OK. (Lipetz 1984, 76)

The defense attorney, if there was one in this case, was not even a participant in the conversation. The norms of the courtroom were enforced by the judge and police officer.

DEFENSE COUNSEL IN THE LOWER COURTS

The sparse literature on the lower courts does not clearly indicate whether represented defendants typically fare better than unrepresented defendants or whether using a defense attorney is worthwhile. Clearly, risks and costs are associated with either using or not using defense counsel. If only those defendants who are represented by counsel receive the going rate, being represented by counsel is clearly advantageous. On the other hand, if the court is intent on moving cases as rapidly as possible, and if the use of counsel interferes with rapid processing, the defendant may be penalized for exercising the right to counsel. That is, the defendant may get something worse than the going rate for wasting the court's time.

Defense attorneys may also persuade clients to forego lengthy court proceedings. The defense attorney establishes the worth of the case in relation to court norms and pursues a realistic course to move the case. Defendants who do not take the advice of counsel and suggest pursuing unrealistic strategies often find themselves being "persuaded" to enter a guilty plea by the very person who is supposed to be acting as their advocate for leniency and freedom (see, for example, Alschuler 1975; Casper 1972; Feeley 1979; Sudnow 1965).

The literature suggests that the presence of defense counsel increases the focus and time spent on plea negotiations (Alfini and Passuth 1981, 108–9; Ryan 1980–1981, 87). Increased attention to negotiations does not necessarily result in a higher rate of guilty pleas, however. Instead, defense counsel may be successful in obtaining a dismissal after the initial appearance (Alfini and Passuth 1981, 108–9). In any event, studies of the lower courts that were conducted after the Supreme Court's 1972 *Argersinger* decision, which requires appointed counsel in any misdemeanor case in which a jail sentence is imposed, show regular use of defense counsel in lower courts. Feeley's study (1979) indicates that defense counsel is commonplace, and another (Ryan 1980–1981, 107) reports that almost all defendants in the sample (92 percent) were represented by counsel. *Argersinger* may have had only a minimal influence on the use of counsel, however. Most defendants in the second study (Ryan 1980–19981) were represented by privately retained counsel.

Formal Stages in Processing Lesser Offenses

The informality of the lower-court process and the norm of moving cases are evident at every stage. Moreover, in most cases in the lower courts the stages of the criminal process are merely different aspects of a single court appearance. Only in exceptional lower-court cases do these stages become distinct.

Initial Appearance

Most cases in the lower courts are referred to the courts by police. Many misdemeanants are not in custody at the time of the initial appearance and appear in court pursuant to a summons written by the officer in lieu of arrest. If the defendant fails to appear, the court issues a bench warrant. The next time the police have contact with the person, they will arrest the person to stand for the original charges.

Following any arrest, the arrestee-defendant is transported to a local precinct house or to the appropriate holding facility for processing. In the case of minor offenses defendants may be allowed to post bail at the police station. Standard bail schedules are used to determine the amount of bail required by the arrest charge. The defendant who posts bail at the police station is released with an order to appear at the next court session, often the next morning. Some defendants may decide to forfeit the bail, accepting the forfeited bail as a fine for the offense charged. Some jurisdictions tacitly allow this practice. In other jurisdictions, depending on the seriousness of the offense, the court will issue a bench warrant for any defendant who fails to appear. The bail is forfeited, and the defendant may again be arrested.

The arrestee unable to make stationhouse bail, may be required to spend the night in jail to await an initial appearance in the morning. At court many defendants are willing, and even eager, to plead guilty and take the consequences—especially when the consequences are a small fine or a sentence to time served. Consequently, setting bail at the initial appearance is uncommon in most misdemeanor cases. The court is authorized to accept guilty pleas and impose sentences on the spot, without additional proceedings.

If the defendant chooses not to plead guilty at the initial appearance, the court must decide the conditions of pretrial release. When the defendant has appeared in court in response to a summons, the court will usually release the defendant on recognizance. Indeed, most defendants whose cases are held over are released on recognizance. However, defendants who believe they will be held in jail have a strong incentive to waive the right to a trial. Available trial dates are often several weeks or months away. The possibility of pretrial detention serves as an additional prod to pleading guilty quickly. Samuel Dash reports the following statement by a prosecutor to a defendant "Don't be a fool—if you buck us you will wait six months in jail for your trial. Now if you take a plea, you'll get six months and at the end of that time you will be a free man" (1951, 253–54).

Initial Charging

The charge against the defendant is read at the initial appearance. Sometimes this function is executed by the prosecutor, sometimes by a clerk or the judge, and sometimes by a police liaison officer, serving as police prosecutor (Bing and Rosenfeld 1974; President's Commission 1967, 313). This is a hurried business, with an urgency to move one case right after another; sometimes the pace is so quick that in the confusion the wrong defendant is before the court for the reading of charges:

> Often . . . a new case . . . [is] called with the defendant in the prior case being presented to the court. After the police testify as to the facts of the case, the misplaced defendant is asked what he has to say for himself. He denies the story which is absurd and strange to him. He receives a strong rebuke from the judge for lying to the court and he is about to be threatened by the prosecutor when the police officer discovers that he [the defendant] is not the man he arrested. (Dash 1951, 250).*

Notification of Rights

Notifying defendants of their rights is similarly hurried. At this first appearance before the court defendants are supposed to be informed of their rights. In-court observers have long faulted the courts for making a mockery of this important role (Dash 1951, 251). Maureen Mileski offers the following description, based on her observations:

> In a quarter (26%) of the lower court cases, the judge does not apprise the defendant of his constitutional rights at all. . . . Moreover, defendants are warned in groups . . . in half (52%) of the cases. The judge warns a defendant of his rights as he stands alone before the bench in only 22% of the cases. Thus, of those who are apprised, most are apprised in groups. . . . In minor misdemeanor cases, the judge fails to apprise 35% of the time. (1971, 68–69)

Studies of lower courts since *Argersinger* (1972) find that the disregard for notifying defendants of their rights is far less egregious than it once was. It is important to note that in the two courts described here, defense lawyers were rarely present. Both studies are fairly old by now. Reports of such flagrant disregard for informing defendants are absent from more recent case studies.:

> However perfunctory the attention they give their clients' cases, their [defense counsel] very presence in the court has altered the relationship between the accused and the prosecution in a way that makes them more nearly equal. If instituting public defenders has not created a court which operates according to the ideal norms of the legal profession, it has definitely contributed to the elimination of the more gross displays of arbitrariness and favoritism that once were commonplace in the court. (Malcolm Feeley, *The Process is the Punishment*, © 1979, 60, Russell Sage Foundation)

Still, where offenses are less serious, due process rights are not only less protected but more likely to be regarded casually or disregarded entirely by court personnel. Defendants are as likely as court personnel to be unconcerned about formality and being informed of their rights when the stakes are low (Feeley 1979, 186–87; Mileski 1971, 79). Defendants in many instances are just as eager as the court to get it over with and get back to work.

---

* Although Dash wrote more than forty years ago, his descriptions seem to reflect the same features of lower courts that more recent studies describe. We use Dash here to illustrate the way in which real court actors talk and act in the lower courts.

Entering a Plea

Having heard the formal charges and been informed of their rights, defendants are asked to enter a plea. Entering a not guilty plea means that a trial must be scheduled and a decision made about the conditions of pretrial release. Entering a guilty plea means that final disposition of the case may be only seconds away. Several reports from observational studies show that defendants are often pressured to enter a guilty plea at this point. Feeley describes it this way:

> On . . . first appearance he [the prosecutor] will announce charges to the court and "expect" the defendant to plead guilty. This is implied in the standard question the prosecutor addresses to the accused: "Do you want to get your own attorney, make application for a public defender, or dispose of your case today?" The implications are clear: If the defendant wants to get an attorney, it will be complicated for him, but if he pleads guilty the whole matter will be over within a few minutes. The prosecutor is clearly communicating his preference and it is up to someone else—the defendant or his attorney—to suggest *another* course of action. (Malcolm Feeley, *The Process is the Punishment,* © 1979, 178, Russell Sage Foundation)

Reports of pressure from prosecutors, judges, and even defense attorneys to plead guilty at the initial appearance are not uncommon (Ryan 1980–1981, 87; Dash 1951, 253). In contrast, some judges routinely advise unrepresented defendants to consult with the public defender in the courtroom before entering a guilty plea (Ryan 1980—1981, 94).

If a misdemeanor defendant indicates a willingness to plead guilty early in the process, the case is typically disposed of in a single court appearance. Feeley (1979, 157) reports that most cases he observed were disposed of in one or two court appearances. Likewise, another researcher (Ryan 1980–1981, 107) found that 60 percent of the cases in his sample were disposed of at the first appearance and another 30 percent were disposed of at the second appearance. In a survey of jurisdictions across the nation researchers found that cases were less likely to be disposed of at the initial appearance in big city courts and in cases in which a defense attorney was involved (Alfini and Passuth 1981, 110–11).

Pretrial

pretrial conference

Unlike felony cases, misdemeanor cases are not usually subjected to formal screening of the charges (preliminary hearing or grand jury). However, in some jurisdictions, if a misdemeanor is not disposed of at the initial appearance, it is automatically scheduled for an informal **pretrial conference**, often simply called a pretrial, between the prosecutor and defense attorney. The major purpose of the pretrial is to engage in plea negotiations, although other business may be accomplished at this point as well. Often pretrials are held when a judge is available nearby, so that if a settlement is reached, the guilty plea may be entered and the case disposed of promptly. This is a relatively new development in misdemeanor cases, aimed primarily at convenience and scheduling efficiency for the attorneys.

Trial

Defendants charged with misdemeanors are at least entitled to a trial before a judge. Many, but not all, are entitled to a trial before a jury. Jury trials are rare in these courts, however. In fact, some lower courts do not conduct jury trials at all.

In these jurisdictions, if a defendant has a right to a jury trial and requests one, the case will be physically moved to a different court—and a different judge—that offers jury trials, usually the court of general jurisdiction.

Only a small percentage of misdemeanor defendants exercise their right to trial. In one sample of 1,640 cases in a New Haven, Connecticut, court, not a single trial was held (Feeley 1979, 9, 127). Another study (Ryan 1980–1981, 87–88) reports them as rare in a Columbus, Ohio, court, occurring in 2.7 percent of the cases studied. In addition, the provision of appointed counsel does not appear to increase the number of trials in misdemeanor cases (Alfini and Passuth 1981, 114). According to the Conneticut study (Malcolm Feeley, *The Process is the Punishment,* © 1979, 186–87, Russell Sage Foundation), "The time, effort, and expense of going to trial are overwhelming. A private attorney may charge $200 a day to conduct a trial; yet few fines exceed $50. . . . For the overwhelming majority of defendants . . . trial is simply not a viable alternative."

In fact, defendants sometimes see that going to trial would be a distinct disadvantage. Whether actual or perceived, the "trial penalty"—the increased severity of sanction imposed on defendants who go to trial—is a salient factor in deciding to request or waive trial. If defendants don't see this, a court actor may point it out to them, as Dash reports: "You had better plead guilty to petty larceny, or we'll make sure that you are sent up for ten years in the penitentiary. With the record you have nobody will believe your story, and it's a sure thing we'll get you found guilty of robbery at the trial" (1951, 254).

The Ohio Study (Ryan 1980—1981, 104) concludes that a trial penalty actually existed in the Columbus court and that attorneys were well aware of it. Courtroom regulars in Columbus observed wryly that "rent is charged for the use of the courtroom."

On those few occasions when trials are held, they are typically very brief affairs, lasting only several minutes or an hour at most (President's Commission 1967, 313). Of course there are exceptions—if the case is unusually complex, a misdemeanor trial might last several days. More typical is the description of a trial in the Recorder's Court of Detroit:

> A few defendants went to trial, but the great majority of them did so without counsel. In these cases the judge made no effort to explain the proceedings to the defendants or to tell them of their right to cross-examine the prosecution's witnesses or of their right to remain silent. After the policeman delivered his testimony, the judge did not appear to make any evaluation of the sufficiency of the evidence but turned immediately to the defendant and asked, "What do you have to say for yourself?" Where counsel appeared at trial, the procedure was slightly more formal, but the judge conducted most of the questioning himself. (President's Commission 1967, 313)

Sentencing

Often the court knows little about the offender to be sentenced in misdemeanor cases. In most cases the misdemeanant has pled guilty, spending few minutes at most with the prosecutor, defense attorney, or judge. Moreover, misdemeanor defendants are not usually the subject of presentence investigations. With so little information about the defendant the court makes the punishment fit the crime rather than the criminal.

The defendant has usually pled guilty with the expectation that something close to the going rate will be imposed, and judges rarely disappoint. Predictability is a critical element in maintaining the fast-paced, assembly-line processing style of the lower courts. If a defendant can enter a guilty plea based on a fairly reliable prediction of the sentence, the system is more likely to get its guilty plea. Unpredictability would encourage defendants to fight the charges. In addition, a court that responds to specific, individualized information invites such information. Taking such information into consideration takes time. Standard punishments discourage individualized approaches to case processing.

A substantial proportion of misdemeanor offenses is punished by a fine rather than imprisonment. Three studies (Mileski 1971, 78; Feeley 1979, 138; Ryan 1980–1981, 94) report that a fine was the most common sanction in the courts they examined. Other studies also have found fines to be the prevailing method of sanction (Ragona and Ryan 1983). The use of probation appears to vary widely from court to court (compare Bing and Rosenfeld 1974, 279; Feeley 1979, 138; Glaser and Gordon 1990; and Ryan 1980–1981, 99). Fines are usually quite low. Judges know that if the standard fine was relatively high, a substantial number of poor defendants would be unable to pay it. Given an "option" of $500 or seven days in jail, the poor defendant might have no choice but to opt for the jail time. In addition, because the standard fine is set so low, the deterrent on those defendants who are not poor is quite minimal.

day-fine

Recognizing these problems with the traditional operation of fines in the lower courts, some courts have been experimenting with **day-fines,** in which the amount of fine is adjusted to the income of the defendant, as well as other creative sentences, such as community service (see Chapter 17 for a more detailed discussion of these options). These new approaches seek to reduce the disparate effect of fines on low-income defendants while offering a meaningful deterrent to all defendants, whatever their economic means. These newer alternatives also alleviate the routine aspect of lower-court sentencing, making sentences fit the individual circumstances of the offender.

Appeals

Convicted misdemeanants may appeal their convictions. As described in Chapter 2, an appeal is a review of the propriety of the actions taken in the trial court, based on the record of the trial court. Appeals on the record are possible only when a record of the proceedings has been made. Traditionally, trials of defendants in lower courts were not recorded. The seriousness of the offense did not justify the expense of paying a court stenographer to record the proceedings. Appeals from courts that do not record their proceedings are provided by a trial *de novo.*

The phrase "*de novo*" is Latin meaning, literally, of new. Unlike an appeal on the record, a trial de novo is a new trial on the facts. It proceeds as if the first trial never happened. A trial de novo is akin to wiping the slate clean and starting over. The difference between the first trial and the trial de novo is that the new trial takes place in a court of record, usually a court with jurisdiction superior (court of general jurisdiction) to the court in which the case originated. Because a record of the proceedings is made in the trial de novo, if the defendant is again found guilty, the defendant may appeal on the record to the appellate court for the jurisdiction.

With the advent of sensitive and inexpensive recording equipment many jurisdictions electronically record misdemeanor trial proceedings. Therefore, in jurisdictions in which the trial proceedings for lesser offenses are recorded, direct criminal appeals to the appellate courts are taken from misdemeanor convictions just as they are from felony convictions (see Chapter 18.)

■ THE AFTERMATH OF REFORM: THE LOWER COURTS IN THE 1990S

As the case study examples suggest, lower courts have been viewed as far less than exemplary. In 1967 the President's Commission on Law Enforcement and the Administration of Justice singled out the lower courts as the most disquieting of the problems it found in the administration of justice in this nation (1967, 128). For nearly a century one investigative commission after another has criticized these lower courts for the inefficiency, injustice, indignity, and incompetence associated with them. More than one national commission has recommended the abolition of these lower courts as distinct entities, yet the lower courts persist (Alfini and Doan 1977).

The ills of the lower courts are often blamed on inadequate financial resources: courtroom facilities are poorly designed and in bad repair; judges in urban jurisdictions are paid salaries that do not attract competent lawyers; and record keeping is minimal and disorganized because of staffing problems. In turn, continues the argument, the quality of personnel willing to work in such an environment exacerbates the problems and is manifested in the disregard for correct procedure and lack of concern for justice. To cure these ills the President's Commission recommended abolishing the lower courts and establishing a unified court system, funded by state, not local, taxes (President's Commission 1967, 35–36). In the 1970s two major types of reforms changed the landscape of the lower courts. First, by the end of the 1970s at least half the states had elected to reorganize their court systems (Alfini and Doan 1981; see Chapter 2). Reorganization in turn affected the staffing and jurisdiction of the lower courts. The second major reform was dictated by the Supreme Court through its decision in *Argersinger* (1972). The effect of *Argersinger* was to funnel defense attorneys into the lower courts, where they had once been a rarity.

State court reorganization took many forms and had various effects. Court reorganization often dictated corollary changes in the operations of the lower courts A few jurisdictions completely abolished lower courts. Other states redrew jurisdictional boundaries so that part-time judgeships became full time. In connection with this, fee systems (in which judges were paid according to the fines they imposed) were replaced with salary systems. Record keeping was introduced, altering the nature of appeals taken from lower-court judgments.

Some jurisdictions changed their laws to require judges to hold law degrees. Still, a 1988 assessment reveals that only a little more than half (57 percent) of the judges in courts of limited jurisdiction actually held law degrees (NCSC 1988, 10). In 1976 the Supreme Court approved the use of lay judges for presiding over minor matters and declined to interpret the constitutional right to a trial as a right to a trial presided over by a law-trained judge (*North Carolina v. Russell*).

The increased use of defense attorneys has also altered the operations of the lower courts. Their mere presence shines light on the operations and reduces the chances that unfair procedures will go unnoticed and unchanged. Their involvement has produced changes: fewer guilty pleas, fewer guilty pleas at initial appearance, and an increase in the incidence of plea negotiation (Alfini and Passuth 1981).

Reforms have affected the operations of the lower courts, and changes in some jurisdictions are obvious and pronounced. Despite these improvements, however, the lower courts remain a low political priority. The tangible benefits of providing the lower courts with greater resources are few. Overcrowded, uncomfortable, and chaotic as they may be, the lower courts remain a lower priority than providing health care, hiring more police, and providing better services to abused and neglected children. Whereas the felony courts gain public attention because of the serious nature of the crimes they deal with every day, the lower courts work in relative obscurity. Those people who come into the lower courts may be dismayed at the conditions they find there, but their contact is brief and quickly forgotten. For these reasons lower courts likely will continue to be the poor stepchild of the criminal court system.

◼ BEYOND LOWER COURTS: MEDIATION

Another reform that could affect the lower courts is alternative dispute resolution. Some reformers have suggested that many cases that now go to the criminal courts, and especially to the lower courts, might be resolved through alternative mechanisms to formal adjudication. Alternative dispute resolution has been offered as a means of resolving disputes that otherwise will clog overcrowded court dockets.

Proponents of alternative dispute resolution observe that the church, the family, and the community have lost much of their power to serve as dispute resolution mechanisms. According to this theory, civil and criminal courts have filled the growing void (Sander 1982, 27; Merry 1982, 172). This greater reliance on adjudication, rather than more informal dispute resolution mechanisms, has contributed to overcrowded court dockets. The problem, however, is not one that is easily resolved simply by creating more courts, because the legal process is too complex and unresponsive to effectively resolve the everyday conflicts of ordinary people. As a result conflicts fester until in some cases they erupt in disorderly and sometimes violent confrontations (Tomasic and Feeley 1982). Thus, many proponents of alternative dispute resolution view the increase in crime as a symptom of the lack of effective dispute-resolving institutions in modern society.

History and Philosophy

The first formal alternative dispute resolution programs were developed during the late 1960s and 1970s. In 1975 fewer than a dozen such programs operated throughout the United States. By 1985 the American Bar Association Directory of Dispute Resolution Programs listed 182 nationwide (McGillis 1986, 7). Many of these programs seek to make the courts more efficient by handling cases that are not particularly amenable to court resolution. Another goal is to make the justice system more accessible to citizens. For example, alternative dispute resolution programs frequently are located in shopping areas adjacent to residential areas rather than in downtown courtrooms. In addition, many programs stress accessibility by holding sessions during evenings and weekends. Finally, some reformers hope that alternative dispute resolution will improve the quality and stability of resolutions, reducing the overall level of conflict between the parties (McGillis 1986, 20–21).

In some programs the emphasis is on noncriminal disputes that might escalate into more serious disputes if not resolved promptly. Other programs focus on disputes that have already resulted in one party's being charged with a crime. Two-thirds of dispute resolution programs are sponsored by either the courts or prosecutors' offices (National Institute of Justice 1986, 2). Participation is voluntary but with a coercive element: if the accused does not participate in the dispute resolution process, prosecution may commence.

Other dispute resolution programs rely on referrals from other community agencies, as well as self-referrals by the disputing parties (McGillis 1986, 20, 24). These programs are usually sponsored by nonprofit community agencies. Although a dispute might not require immediate court attention, preventing the escalation of conflict may preserve court resources down the road: "A minor assault among acquaintances today can result in a felonious assault or homicide next month or next year if the dispute is allowed to fester" (McGillis 1986, 25).

The most common dispute resolution technique used in all these programs is mediation. A neutral third party discusses the problem with both parties, trying to find common ground and a mutually satisfactory resolution. Although the mediator often inquires about the facts of the case, what has happened in the past is less important then reaching a resolution and getting the parties to focus on how they will get along in the future. The goal is to achieve a fresh start, with both parties beginning a new relationship on a more equal footing.

Evaluating Alternative Dispute Resolution

Some observers suggest that the initial promise of alternative dispute resolution has given way to pessimism because preliminary evaluations have shown mixed results. Although disputing parties are more satisfied with the fairness and ultimate solution of the conflict obtained through alternative programs, many disputes in alternative programs are never resolved because of a high rate of no-shows and failure to reach a disposition (McGillis 1986; Matthews 1988). Frequently, one or both parties fail to appear at the mediation session. In addition, it is unclear whether the resolutions are stable over time. Although disputants express satisfaction with the process, evaluations of the programs have not determined whether they avert future conflicts (McGillis 1986; Merry 1982).

The research does suggest that alternative dispute resolution is better at resolving some kinds of disputes and worse at others. According to one study (Merry 1982), disputes that focus on concrete issues like payment for damages or return of property are more amenable to mediation than conflicts arising out of relationships and focusing on issues like insults, rivalry, abuse, and other emotional issues. Ironically, alternative dispute resolution was originally proposed because the courts seemed ill-equipped to resolve disputes arising out of relationships.

Others criticize alternative dispute resolution for widening the net of formal social control, diverting simple cases to alternative dispute resolution that otherwise would have been dismissed. In other words, people who once would have been left alone are now being encouraged, pressured, or even coerced to use alternative dispute resolution (Abel 1982; Matthews 1988, 8). This criticism is especially pertinent in relation to the majority of programs that are run as adjuncts to the courts. Where community mediation programs are established separate from the courts, these options avoid formal social control and strengthen the institutions of informal social control.

Many school systems, especially in urban areas, are instituting mediation programs for resolving student disputes. Alternative dispute resolution has also gained popularity in areas of civil litigation that are otherwise quite costly. For alternative dispute resolution to become a major alternative to the lower courts, parties need to believe that alternative dispute resolution is better than going to court. In light of all the faults of lower courts, demonstrating that alternative dispute resolution is preferable might seem an easy task. The counterpoint, however, is the swift resolution that can be obtained in many lower courts.

Alternative resolution may require a greater investment of effort by all parties than does assembly-line adjudication.

▪ SUMMARY

The roots of urban lower courts are to be found in the rural justice of the peace. Although much maligned during the mid-twentieth century, these officers of justice were important during much of U.S. history and represented an important ideal: people's justice based on commonsense understandings of community mores. Arbitrary and unprofessional decision making by JPs during the twentieth century brought bad repute.

In urban areas courts of limited jurisdiction became the gateway to the court process. In addition to adjudicating noncriminal offenses and many misdemeanor offenses the lower courts issue search warrants, conduct initial appearances, and set bail in felony cases. These courts have been the targets of criticism during the middle of this century. Although much improved in recent years, the lower courts still represent rough and assembly-line justice. Actors in the system know the going rate for various offenses, and individualized deviations from the norm are discouraged. The style of operation in the lower courts is informal. In addition, the stages of criminal court processing, which can take months and numerous court appearances in a felony case, are condensed. Many cases are resolved at the first court appearance.

The rights of defendants are also more limited in the lower courts. As a result more defendants in the lower courts are not represented by counsel than in courts of general jurisdiction. Although some jurisdictions offer counsel for indigents in all criminal cases, other jurisdictions offer free counsel to indigents only if the defendant is actually going to jail, as required by *Argersinger* (1972). Trials are infrequent (even more infrequent than in felony cases), and the right to a jury trial is limited to the more serious misdemeanors. Usually, lower courts have no authority to conduct jury trials, so those cases are referred to the court of general jurisdiction. Following conviction in lower court, the most common sentence is a fine. Day-fines have been introduced in some courts to bring fines more in line with the defendant's ability to pay. Short jail sentences, often simply time served in jail since arrest, are also common. Because many lower courts are not courts of record, appeal from a conviction in lower court often takes place through a trial de novo, a new trial in a court of record.

Because these courts deal with minor crimes, they remain a low priority. Much greater attention and concern are placed on the courts of general jurisdiction that process felonies. Reforms directed at the lower courts since the 1970s have resulted in some positive changes in the operations of these courts. Better trained personnel, a wider availability of counsel, and increased financial support have eliminated some of the worst practices of thirty and forty years ago. Some jurisdictions are experimenting with alternative dispute resolution mechanisms, such as mediation, to reduce the burden on the lower courts and offer a more effective way to resolve the types of disputes that lead to minor offenses of all sorts. The actual effectiveness of these programs remains unclear.

▪ FOR FURTHER DISCUSSION

1. What lower courts exist in the county and city in which you live? What is the jurisdiction of these courts? Visit one of these courts. Describe the physical

setting. What kinds of cases were before the court during your visit? Did the processing of these cases resemble the process described in this chapter? In what ways was it similar, and in what ways was it different?

2. Police frequently have discretion to determine whether to arrest on state criminal charges or municipal ordinance violations. This decision may determine the court that has jurisdiction to try the case. From the perspective of the police what are the advantages of writing an ordinance violation rather than charging a crime? How do the decisions police make influence the composition of the caseloads in the courts?

3. Of the thirteen million criminal filings in state courts in 1992, more than nine million (or almost 70 percent) were filed in courts of limited jurisdiction (Ostrom 1994). Yet lower courts are relatively underfunded, and practices in the lower courts continue to resemble an assembly line more than the ideal of adversarial justice. If sufficient resources were funneled to the lower courts (more courtrooms, judges, prosecutors, and so on), how do you think case processing would be affected? In other words, if caseload pressures on court participants were reduced, would these courts change the way in which they handle cases?

4. Consider the two misdemeanor battery cases presented in Chapter 9 (Case A and Case B). Could alternative dispute resolution have helped to avoid these incidents? Would either case be appropriate for referral to a mediation program by the prosecutor reviewing the case?

◼ REFERENCES

Abel, Richard. 1982. *The Politics of Informal Justice*. New York: Academic Press.

Alfini, James J., and Patricia M. Passuth. 1981. "Case Processing in State Misdemeanor Courts: The Effect of Defense Attorney Presence." *Justice System Journal* 6:100–16.

Alfini, James J., and Rachel N. Doan. 1977. "A New Perspective on Misdemeanor Justice." *Judicature* 60(April): 425–434

Alschuler, Albert W. 1975. "The Defense Attorney's Role in Plea Bargaining." *Yale Law Journal* 84: 1179–1314.

Argersinger v. Hamlin, 407 U.S. 25, 92 S.Ct. 2006 (1972).

Ashman, Allan, and Pat Chapin. 1976. "Is the Bell Tolling for Nonlawyer Judges?" *Justice System Journal* 59(9): 416–21.

Bing, Stephen R., and Stephen S. Rosenfeld. 1974. "The Quality of Justice in the Lower Criminal Courts of Metropolitan Boston." In John A. Robertson, ed. *Rough Justice: Perspectives on Lower Criminal Courts*. Boston: Little Brown.

Brownlee, E. Gardner. 1975. "The Revival of the Justice of the Peace in Montana." *Judicature* 58 (8): 372–79.

Casper, Jonathan D. 1972. *American Criminal Justice: The Defendant's Perspective*. Englewood Cliffs, N.J.: Prentice-Hall.

Dash, Samuel. 1951. "Cracks in the Foundation of Criminal Justice." *Illinois Law Review* 46: 385–406. Northwestern University School of Law.

Feeley, Malcolm. 1979. *The Process is the Punishment: Handling Cases in a Lower Court*. New York: Russell Sage Foundation.

Glaser, Daniel, and Margaret A. Gordon. 1990. "Profitable Penalties for Lower Level Courts." *Judicature* 73 (5): 248–52.

Green, Justin, Ross Russell, and John Schmidhauser. 1975. "Iowa's Magistrate System: The Aftermath of Reform." *Judicature* 58 (8): 380–89.

Knab, Karen Markle, and Brent Lindberg. 1977. "Misdemeanor Justice: Is Due Process the Problem?" *Judicature* 60 (9): 416–24.

Lipetz, Marcia J. 1984. *Routine Justice: Processing Cases in Women's Court.* New Brunswick, N.J.: Transaction Books.

Matthews, Roger. 1988. *Informal Justice?* Beverly Hills: Sage.

Merry, Sally Engle. 1982. "Defining 'Success' in the Neighborhood Justice Movement." In Roman Tomasic and Malcolm Feeley, eds. *Neighborhood Justice: Assessment of an Emerging Idea.* New York: Longman.

Mileski, Maureen. 1971. "Courtroom Encounters: An Observation Study of a Lower Criminal Court." *Law and Society Review* 5: 473–533.

Nardulli, Peter F., James Eisenstein, and Roy B. Flemming. 1988. *The Tenor of Justice.* Urbana, Ill.: University of Chicago Press.

National Center for State Courts (NCSC). 1988. *State Court Organization 1987.* Williamsburg, Va.: National Center for State Courts.

National Institute of Justice. 1986. "Toward the Multi-Door Courthouse—Dispute Resolution Intake and Referral." *NIJ Reports* (July). Washington, D.C.: U.S. Department of Justice, National Institute of Justice.

North v. Russell, 427 U.S. 328, 96 S.Ct. 2709 (1976).

Ostrom, Brian J. 1994. *State Court Caseload Statistics: Annual Report 1992.* Williamsburg, Va.: National Center for State Courts.

President's Commission on Law Enforcement and the Administration of Justice. 1967. *Task Force Report: The Courts.* Washington, D.C.: U.S. Government Printing Office.

Ragona, Anthony J., and John P. Ryan. 1983. "Misdemeanor Courts and the Choice of Sanctions: A Comparative View." *Justice System Journal* 8 (2): 199–221.

Tomasic, Roman, and Malcolm Feeley, eds. 1982. *Neighborhood Justice: Assessment of an Emerging Idea.* New York: Longman.

Ryan, John P. 1980-81. "Adjudication and Sentencing in a Misdemeanor Court: The Outcome is the Punishment." *Law and Society Review* 15 (1): 79–108.

Ryan, John Paul, and James H. Guterman. 1977. "Lawyers Versus Nonlawyer Town Justices." *Judicature* 60: 272–80.

Sander, Frank E.A. 1982. "Varieties of Dispute Processing." In Roman Tomasic and Malcolm Feeley, eds. *Neighborhood Justice: Assessment of an Emerging Idea.* New York: Longman.

Sudnow, David N. 1965. "Normal Crimes: Sociological Features of the Penal Code in a Public Defender's Office." *Social Problems* 12: 209–15.

Tumey v. Ohio, 273 U.S. 510, 47 S.Ct. 437 (1927).

Vanlandingham, Kenneth E. 1974. "The Decline of the Justice of the Peace." In John A. Robertson, ed. *Rough Justice: Perspectives on Lower Criminal Courts.* Boston: Little Brown.

CHAPTER **11**

INITIAL APPEARANCE: SETTING BAIL AND OTHER CONDITIONS OF RELEASE

The first court appearance after arrest of the defendant is called the initial appearance. Most states require that an arrestee be brought before a judge or other designated court official, such as a magistrate or court commissioner, within a short time after arrest. Some states set this time limit by statute. For example, Minnesota requires that arrestees be brought before a judge within thirty-six hours, not counting the day of arrest, Sundays, and legal holidays. Others establish time limits through case law. In general, these requirements call for a court appearance within a day or two of arrest. Typically, the initial appearance is held in a court of limited jurisdiction.

The defendant is brought in from the bullpen, the detention area adjacent to the court. The judge reviews the arrest report, perhaps asking a question of the prosecutor or defense counsel. The judge then states for the record, "I find probable cause." The judge may then ask whether the prosecutor or the pretrial services agency has a pretrial release recommendation. After a brief review of the defendant's record and bail evaluation form, the judge decides whether and under what conditions the defendant may be released from jail pending trial. In routine cases the whole proceeding may last no more than a few minutes.

This chapter takes a closer look at the processing of felony cases in the criminal courts. Defendants charged with felonies are on the whole alleged to have engaged in serious criminal conduct, frequently have serious criminal records, and are entitled to substantial rights under both the U.S. Constitution and state laws. This chapter reviews the functions of the initial appearance and the options for pretrial release, including a special look at bail bonding. Concerns with pretrial release have spawned two bail reform movements—one during the 1960s and 1970s that was concerned with increasing the opportunities for pretrial release for less serious offenders and a second movement during the 1980s to allow courts to detain dangerous offenders. Current pretrial release decisions reflect the consequences of these reform movements.

◼ FUNCTIONS OF THE INITIAL APPEARANCE

The initial appearance serves a number of purposes in the criminal court process. The requirement that the initial appearance be held shortly after arrest is intended to prevent the police from holding someone indefinitely without filing charges. The first court appearance after arrest serves to officially inform the defendant of the charges. In addition, because most arrests are made without an arrest warrant, the initial appearance offers an opportunity for a judge to review the evidence supporting the charges to ensure there is probable cause. Because of the expansion of the right to counsel for indigent defendants many courts also use the initial appearance as an opportunity to determine the eligibility of the defendant for appointed counsel. Finally, the judge at the initial appearance is responsible for deciding whether and under what conditions the defendant will be released while the case is processed.

Being Informed of the Charges

complaint

At the initial appearance, the judge formally notifies the defendant of the exact charges. In addition, some states require that judges inform defendants of their rights, particularly the right to trial and the right to remain silent. Although a defendant is likely to have some information about the charges before the initial appearance, the defendant may be unclear about the precise charge brought by the state, whether the charge is a misdemeanor or felony, and the number of charges being brought. The **complaint** informs the defendant of the specific charges. In misdemeanor cases the complaint may be the only charging document. In felonies the charges listed in the complaint may be amended when the prosecutor draws up the information or indictment.

Probable Cause Determination

In some jurisdictions the intake court routinely makes a probable cause determination for all cases at the initial appearance. Other jurisdictions make a probable cause determination at the initial appearance only if the arrest was made without a warrant, which is often the case. In *Gerstein v. Pugh* (1975, 113) the Supreme Court held that the Fourth Amendment requires the determination of probable cause by a neutral and detached magistrate whenever possible. Although requiring an arrest warrant before any arrest would provide "maximum protection," the Court recognized that such a requirement would be "an intolerable handicap for legitimate law enforcement."

Once arrested, the suspect's need for a neutral determination of probable cause does not disappear, however. To balance the competing goals of law enforcement and Fourth Amendment rights, the Court held that "the Fourth Amendment requires a judicial determination of probable cause as a prerequisite to extended restraint on liberty following arrest" (*Gerstein v. Pugh* 1975, 114).

The Court went on to hold that the determination of probable cause does not require an adversarial hearing. Instead, an informal procedure in which the judge bases the decision on written information provided by the police is sufficient to determine whether there is probable cause to believe that the suspect committed the crimes charged. The only limitation the Court placed on the procedure is that it must be made by a judicial officer either before or promptly after arrest (*Gerstein v. Pugh* 1975, 120). Subsequently, in *Riverside County v. McLaughlin*

(1991) the Court clarified that this determination should generally take place within forty-eight hours after a warrantless arrest. This probable cause determination should not be confused with the probable cause determination at the preliminary hearing. At the initial appearance the probable cause determination is typically made on the basis of the police report and attached documentation, unlike the preliminary hearing at which witnesses must testify in court to establish probable cause.

Indigency and Early Appointment of Counsel

early representation

The availability of defense counsel at the initial appearance varies considerably from one locale to another. Some defense services agencies have a policy of **early representation** of counsel. A lawyer from the public defender's office or legal aid society is on hand at the initial appearance to represent any defendant who needs legal services. Because of the loss of liberty associated with pretrial detention, along with the greater likelihood of conviction and more severe sentences for those detained before trial, defense counsel at the initial appearance tries to convince the court to impose conditions that will allow the defendant's release. Early representation also decreases the number of motions for reduction of bail later in the court process.

indigency determination

Whether the public defender provides early representation or not, the initial appearance often is used as an opportunity to make an **indigency determination** and, if necessary, to appoint counsel. Jurisdictions vary in how they determine a defendant's financial means. In some jurisdictions a defendant's assertion of inability to pay for an attorney is sufficient to cause the judge to appoint counsel. Other jurisdictions collect and assess information about defendants' financial means to determine their eligibility for the services of the public defender or legal aid society (see Figure 11-1).

Determining Pretrial Release

Another function of the initial appearance is to determine whether the defendant will be released pending further court action and, if released, under what conditions. The government has a substantial interest in ensuring that the defendant appears for trial. Consequently, the government may place various restrictions on defendants to compel their appearance at subsequent court proceedings. At one time judges had few options and routinely ordered defendants to provide either cash bail or a bond in order to be released. Today most jurisdictions provide for a range of options designed to maximize the opportunities for release while protecting the government's interest in ensuring the appearance of the accused at trial.

◼ OPTIONS FOR PRETRIAL RELEASE

Judges have several options in determining whether and under what conditions to release the defendant before trial (see Figure 11-2). Jurisdictions differ widely in which options are available to judges and the extent to which judges use them. The judge's choice affects the likelihood that the defendant can gain release pending trial as well as the restrictions placed on defendants who are released.

One option at the initial appearance is to deny release on any condition. Many states allow judges to deny release to any defendant charged with a capital crime

FIGURE 11-1   Indigency Determination

SOURCE: Wisconsin, Office of State Public Defender.

MILWAUKEE COUNTY   **OFFICE OF STATE PUBLIC DEFENDER--TRIAL DIVISION**
(Revised 4/10/95)

If you want an attorney appointed for you, I must ask you for complete and accurate information about your income, assets, liabilities and expenses. You must certify that the information you give me is true. This financial information is not protected by the attorney/client privilege. It may be provided to the court and become available to the public in the future. If you lie about your finances and an attorney is appointed because of the lie, the prosecutor could charge you with a felony crime. Do you understand? Do you have any questions?

Applicant's Name _____   Applicant's Address _____

AFFIDAVIT OF INDIGENCY   Date of Birth _____   Social Security Number _____
    INCOME AND ASSETS

1. Take-home income from all sources. Please circle sources of income: Wages, general relief, AFDC, SSI, SSDI, SSIE, RNIP, Social Security, unemployment compensation, veterans, pension, child support, other.
   (Monthly amount x6 for felony, x2 for mental commitments, and x4 for all other cases.)

   ☐ a.   Applicant's and spouse's sole income is AFDC, RNIP, SSI(E), or general relief   AUTOMATICALLY ELIGIBLE
                                                                                                    Verification
         ☐ Verified with medical assistance card or other verification
      b.   Applicant
      c.   Spouse
   (Least allowable take home pay for full time minimum wage job: $134/wk or $536/mo.)
   If neither the applicant or spouse is employed full time (and neither receive unemployment compensation):
      d.   How do you support yourself?_____
      e.   Name of last employer?_____   Date of last employment? _____
2. Liquid assets of applicant and spouse.   Verification
      a.   Cash
      b.   Savings/Checking account   Bank name?_____
     *c.   Cash value of life insurance/Retirement account
     *d.   Stocks and bonds/Trust funds
      e.   Funds owed applicant/spouse
      f.   Bail posted by applicant/spouse on current offense
      g.   Other --Specify: _____
3. Non-liquid assets of applicant and spouse valued at 1/4 of equity
   (Only include those assets valued at $500 or more.)   Value - Owed = Equity   1/4 of equity
     *a.   House or other real estate
     *b.   Car - Yr/Make: _____
      c.   Other vehicle (truck, snowmobile, boat, etc.)
      d.   Valuable household goods/collections
      e.   Other--Specify: _____

TOTAL INCOME AND ASSETS _____

ESSENTIAL EXPENSES (If claiming over $200/400/600 depending on case type, then ALL expenses must be verified.)
Use only monthly payment amounts. If no monthly payment schedule has been established, establish one, not to exceed $100/month. Most expenses require payment on debt before including per 7.016 (P&P). For monthly expenses, use 6 mo for felony, 2 mo for commitments, and 4 mo for other cases.   **Monthly Amount** |Verification

	Monthly Amount	Verification
Child Support		
Outstanding fines and forfeitures		
Restitution and court ordered obligations		
Ch 11, 13 payments		
Child care (work related only)		
Health insurance		
High-risk auto insurance		
Huber		
Income taxes		
Med./Dent./Soc. Svc bills		
Outstanding civil judgments		
Rent/mortgage arrearages		
Student loans		
Utility arrears-no phone or cable		
TOTAL ESSENTIAL EXPENSES		

---

or, in some states, a crime carrying a life sentence. One rationale for these laws is that the sentence is so great that no amount of money can reasonably ensure that the defendant will cooperate in the prosecution by returning for trial. A defendant might be willing to forfeit any amount of money to avoid such serious sentences. Recent changes in federal and state laws, discussed at the end of this chapter, also allow judges to deny release if the defendant is believed likely to commit

FIGURE 11-1 Indigency Determination—continued

TOTAL INCOME AND ASSETS (from page 1) _____

TOTAL ESSENTIAL EXPENSES (from page 1)

COST OF LIVING (effective September 1, 1987)

Fam Size	Felony	Other	Commit	Fam Size	Felony	Other	Commit
1	$1488	$ 992	$ 496	6	$4596	$3064	$1532
2	2640	1760	880	7	4974	3316	1658
3	3102	2068	1034	8	5274	3516	1758
4	3702	2468	1234	9	5520	3680	1840
5	4248	2832	1416	10	5658	3772	1886

Name and age of dependents: _____

Use these special cost of living amounts for anyone who is blind, 65 or older or disabled (i.e. receiving SSI, SSDI or SSIE)

(Effective 1/1/95)	Monthly	Felony	Other	Commit
Single	$542	$3252	$2168	$1084
Single & SSIE	638	3828	2552	1276
Disabled Couple	819	4914	3276	1638
Disabled Couple with SSIE	1164	6984	4656	2328

TOTAL EXPENSES _____

AMOUNT AVAILABLE FOR COUNSEL (Total Income/Assets minus Total Expenses) _____

Indigency Determination

1. Cost of retaining counsel in this case _____

1st degree intent. hom.	$6600	Commitment	$565
Other Class A/B felony/TPR	$3400	Paternity	$800
Any other felony	$1900	Juvenile	$500
Traffic misdemeanor	$ 400	Parole/probation revoc.	$500
Other misdemeanors	$ 500	Special proceedings	$400

2. Applicant is: (Check one only)
   ____ **INDIGENT** (Amount available for counsel is $100 or less.)
   ____ **PARTIALLY INDIGENT** (Amount available for counsel is more than $100, but less than or equal to the amount on Line 1.)
   ____ **NOT INDIGENT** (Amount available for counsel is greater than Line 1.)

I have not sold or disposed of any assets for less than fair market value to qualify for public defender representation. I certify that this financial statement is true to the best of my knowledge and belief.

☐ I-Form was completed by phone

_____   _____
Applicant's Signature   Date Signed

_____   _____
Indigency Evaluator's Signature   Date Signed

_____   _____
First Assistant or Designee Signature*   Date Signed

You must promptly inform the SPD or your appointed attorney of any material change in your finances. If an attorney is appointed for you, the State of Wisconsin may seek reimbursement from you for the cost of counsel. The court may also order your payment of attorney's fees if you are placed on probation. If you are a juvenile, the court may order that your parents pay attorney's fees.
***First Assistant or Designee will review, approve, and sign off on each required I-Form.**

PARTIAL INDIGENCY (To be completed if Partially Indigent line is checked)

AMOUNT AVAILABLE FOR COUNSEL _____

-100.00

TOTAL AVAILABLE FOR COUNSEL _____

	Cost	First Payment		Cost	First Payment
1st degree intentional murder	$1320	$150	Civil Commitment	$112	$60
Class A or B Felonies	$ 680	$100	Paternity	$160	$50
Other Felonies	$ 380	$ 50	Juvenile	$100	$25
Traffic Misdemeanor	$ 80	$ 25	Revocation	$100	$25
Other Misdemeanor	$ 100	$ 25	Specials	$ 80	$25

Total Amount Owed:
(Enter cost of retaining counsel from chart, or "Total Amount Available", whichever is less.) _____

First Payment Amount:
(Enter amount from chart, or reasonable adjustment) _____

I agree to pay the costs of representation in the amount of $_____.
I also understand that the judge may order payment of attorney fees. If so, any partial indigency amount owed will be reduced accordingly.

_____
Applicant's Signature

additional crimes if released in the community. In most cases, however, defendants are given at least some opportunity to gain release pending trial.

Nonmonetary Conditions of Release

Money has been used to ensure the appearance of the defendant at trial since the founding of the United States. In recent decades, however, courts have experimented with a variety of nonmonetary conditions of release to reduce the

---

FIGURE 11-2   Release Options

Citation	Arrestees are released pending their first court appearance on a written order issued by law enforcement personnel. Eliminates even short-term detention to await the initial appearance. Reduces jail overcrowding.
Release on Recognizance	The court releases defendants on the promise that they will appear in court as required.
Conditional Release	The court releases defendants on the condition that they comply with various conditions that may be imposed by the court, such as appearing for periodic drug testing, maintaining employment, and attending counseling.
Unsecured Bond	Also called a signature bond, defendants pay no money to the court but are liable for the full amount of bail should they fail to appear in court.
Cash Bail	The defendant posts the full bail amount in cash with the court. The cash is returned to defendants who make all court appearances. If the defendant fails to appear in court, the cash is forfeited (retained by the court).
Ten Percent Alternative	Also known as a deposit bond. The defendant deposits a percentage (usually 10 percent) of the full bail amount with the court. The full amount of the bail is required if the defendant fails to appear in court. The percentage bail is returned after the disposition of the case, but the court often retains 1 percent for administrative costs.
Surety Bond	Also known as bail bonding. A third party, usually a bail bondsman, signs a promissory note to the court for the full bail amount and charges the defendant a fee for the service (usually 10 percent of the full bail amount). If the defendant fails to appear, the bondsman must pay the court the full bail amount. Frequently, the bondsman requires the defendant to post collateral in addition to the fee.

---

number of defendants held in jail before trial and to reduce the role of money in determining which defendants remain in jail.

Citation in Lieu of Arrest

citation

Some states rely on citations as a means of avoiding arrest and the related detention. In these jurisdictions police may issue a citation or summons requiring the individual to appear at court on a specific date. Like the recipient of a traffic ticket, the individual who receives a **citation** merely has to appear on that date to comply. Citations are frequently used instead of arrest for municipal ordinance violations and less serious misdemeanors. The use of citations eliminates the need to determine whether the defendant can be released before trial and saves jail space (Feeney 1982).

Release on Recognizance

release on recognizance (ROR)

If the defendant has been arrested, the least restrictive condition is **release on recognizance,** or **ROR.** ROR allows defendants to be released from custody pending further court action simply by agreeing to return for all court appearances. Some states restrict ROR to misdemeanors and less serious felonies, whereas other states leave it to the judge's discretion to determine whether ROR is appropriate, even for serious felonies. In making this decision judges attempt to predict whether a defendant can be trusted to return to court. Some courts rely on the services of a pretrial services agency to gather relevant information about defendants, such as their employment, family and community ties, and other information and to make a recommendation to the judge regarding the appropriateness of ROR for the defendant.

signature bond,
unsecured bond

A variation of ROR is a **signature bond,** or **unsecured bond.** A signature bond allows the defendant to be released without posting money but by agreeing to pay the court a sum of money upon failure to appear for trial. For the defendant this option operates much like ROR. The defendant is released without having to post money, so long as the defendant returns to court as required. If the defendant fails to appear, the court may collect the money promised by the defendant. Because most defendants who fail to appear eventually return to court, the court will then collect on the debt.

Conditional Release

In some instances the judge may be willing to release the defendant on ROR but requires the defendant to comply with additional conditions. For example, a judge might require a drug-dependent defendant to undergo drug treatment and submit to periodic urinalysis to ensure that the defendant remains drug free. Release pending trial is conditional on the defendant's accepting these conditions. In addition, if the defendant fails to comply with the conditions, pretrial release may be revoked. Such special conditions may be imposed because the judge believes that addressing the defendant's underlying drug problem makes the defendant less likely to **abscond,** or fail to appear. Some states also allow judges to impose such conditions in order to decrease the probability that the defendant will commit new crimes while released pending trial. Among the most common nonmonetary conditions are

abscond

- Requiring pretrial supervision by a pretrial services agency, similar to probation supervision.
- Placing the defendant in the custody of another person or an organization; for example, the court may require that the defendant live with a responsible family member or enter a residential treatment facility pending trial.
- Restricting the defendant's travel and social activities.
- Prohibiting the possession of weapons or alcohol.
- Requiring periodic drug testing.
- Requiring employment or registration in an education program.
- Requiring participation in drug or alcohol treatment or other counseling and treatment programs.
- Requiring "house arrest" or detention in jail in the evening or on weekends. (Goldkamp 1985, 13)

The judge must decide which of these conditions are necessary and whether any of these conditions can ensure the defendant's appearance at trial or prevent pretrial crime.

The use of nonfinancial conditions of release, such as those cited, is a relatively new development. It is not clear whether imposing these conditions has increased the ability of defendants to obtain release before trial.

Although defendants released on conditions avoid pretrial detention, many conditions do involve a significant deprivation of liberty (urine testing, participation in treatment, house arrest). This may be unfair if defendants could have been released on recognizance or on a nominal cash bail without significant risk of flight or crime. Some critics have questioned whether such conditions violate the presumption of innocence and require the defendant to participate in rehabilitation

PRETRIAL DRUG TESTING

Research on the relationship between drug use and crime consistently finds that individuals who use drugs are more likely to be involved in criminal activity than those who do not use drugs. Given these consistent research findings, one potentially rational policy would be to test arrestees for drug usage, use this information in the pretrial release decision, and then require periodic drug testing of those drug using arrestees who are released before trial, in order to deter them from using drugs (and committing crimes) during the pretrial period. Such policies were encouraged by the federal government during the late 1980s and early 1990s. The National Drug Control Strategy announced by President Bush in 1989 required that states receiving federal funds adopt drug testing programs and use the results of drug testing in making decisions relating to bail and pretrial release conditions, as well as in sentencing, early release, and probation and parole decisions. By 1990, 72 such programs were operating across the country, usually at the pretrial stage.

The value of these programs has been the subject of some research, with some surprising results. This research examined two questions: (1) Does urine testing of arrestees *improve predictions* of pretrial misconduct (defined as being rearrested for a new crime or failing to appear at trial) of released defendants? and (2) Does periodic drug monitoring of those defendants released before trial *reduce pretrial misconduct?*

While the logic of testing defendants for drug usage and then making decisions based on that information seems unassailable, the results of these efforts have been surprisingly weak. Urine testing is not completely accurate. Some people who have taken drugs shortly before arrest are missed by the tests, and others who have not used drugs incorrectly test positive for drugs. In addition, in several studies, predictions of rearrest and failure-to-appear rates were not improved substantially by urine test results. Since predictions of pretrial misconduct were almost or as good without the drug test information, conducting pretrial drug testing may not be cost effective.

Results of the drug monitoring were also disappointing. In only two jurisdictions did periodic drug testing have any measurable impact on pretrial misconduct. While about a third of those assigned to periodic drug testing abstained from drug use during the pretrial period, it is not clear that it was the drug-testing that produced this result. These defendants may have abstained from drugs during this period in any event.

Results of an assessment of pretrial drug testing programs conducted in 1992 should be available soon. If the results of this latest research turn out the same as the earlier evaluation studies, pretrial drug testing and monitoring may become a policy of the past rather than the wave of the future.

SOURCE: Reprinted from Christy A. Visher. 1992. *Pretrial Drug Testing*. Washington, D.C.: U.S. Department of Justice, National Institute of Justice, Office of Justice Programs, p. 5.

before trial. Another drawback to the use of nonmonetary conditions is the cost associated with pretrial supervision, drug testing, and other special programs. Many jurisdictions are willing to pay for these additional services because jail overcrowding makes pretrial detention increasingly impractical. One study (Austin, Krisberg, and Litsky 1985) found that pretrial supervision could decrease costs if it cut the jail population and related jail operating costs or if it allowed the jurisdiction to avoid the cost of expanding jail facilities. Frequently, however, funds for pretrial supervision and services must be added to an already strained criminal justice budget, at least in the short term. For this reason such programs remain small and are not widely available.

Monetary Conditions of Release

Despite the development of nonmonetary alternatives, many defendants still are required to post either cash or a monetary bond to obtain release. Monetary bail has three main variations.

Cash Bail

In the simplest variation of monetary bail the judge sets the amount of bail, and the defendant simply pays that amount in cash. If the defendant appears for trial, the money is returned in full to the defendant, much like a deposit on a bottle.

bail schedules

Some states allow courts to establish **bail schedules** that specify an amount of bail for each offense in the criminal code (Lynch and Patterson 1991, 39). When a person is arrested, the police determine the appropriate bail amount by checking the bail schedule. If the defendant is able to pay the bail immediately, the defendant is released without having to wait to go before a judge to have bail set. Bail schedules can help to minimize the time defendants spend in jail, thereby reducing jail populations.

Ten Percent Alternative

In some cases the judge may allow the defendant to obtain release merely by posting some percentage of the face amount of bail, usually 10 percent. This option is referred to as a **deposit bond,** or the **10 percent alternative,** which is an alternative to bail bonding. Some jurisdictions leave it to the judge to decide what percentage of the face amount of the bail to require in cash. The defendant may also be required, at the discretion of the judge, to post collateral for the full amount in addition to the cash deposit.

deposit bond,
10 percent
alternative

As with cash bail, if the defendant appears for court, the money posted is returned to the defendant. Some courts deduct a small handling fee when returning deposit bonds but not cash bail. If the defendant absconds, the defendant forfeits the percentage deposited, and the court may confiscate other property to collect the full bail amount.

Surety Bonds

bail bonding,
surety bond

Bail bonding, also known as a **surety bond,** was the most common release option before the 1960s. Although the bail reform movement has been instrumental in reducing the role of the bondsman in many court systems across the country, bondsmen still operate in most jurisdictions (Toborg 1983, 141). In bail bonding the judge sets the cash bail amount. The defendant, or defendant's family, may then seek the assistance of a professional bail bondsman, a private businessperson. The bondsman provides a surety bond in exchange for a fee for services. The defendant, the bondsman, and the court enter into an agreement. The defendant pays a fee to the bondsman, usually 10 percent of the face amount of the bond, although bondsmen may charge more, for example, 20 or 30 percent of the face amount. The bondsman also may require that the defendant's family and friends cosign the bond and post additional collateral. The bondsman in turn agrees to pay the court the full face amount of the bond if the defendant fails to appear at future court sessions. The court releases the defendant under these conditions. If the defendant fails to appear, the bondsman may seize the defendant, bring the defendant back to court, and seize any property offered as collateral.

The money paid to the bondsman is the bondsman's fee and is retained by the bondsman, regardless of the defendant's cooperation in returning to court. Unlike cash bail or the 10 percent alternative, a defendant released on a surety bond gets no money back for appearing at court as required.

■ BAIL BONDING: A CONTINUING DEBATE

The history and functions of bail bonding are important in understanding bail reform since the 1960s. Bail-bonding businesses arose during the nineteenth century, and professional bail bondsmen were a regular feature in courts in major American cities by the 1920s. Some jurisdictions, such as Wisconsin and Kentucky, have abolished bail bonding. In other jurisdictions bondsmen have simply withered away as courts released more and more defendants on ROR and other alternatives (Toborg 1983). Nonetheless, despite decades of criticism and the introduction of reforms and alternatives to surety bonds, bail bonding continues in many jurisdictions.

Because of the special nature of the relationship between these private businesses and the courts, bail bonding warrants a closer look. In addition, recent studies suggest that the reforms of the 1960s have altered the business environment of bondsmen, resulting in some defendants having a harder time than before in gaining pretrial release. This unanticipated consequence of bail reform is especially important in those jurisdictions in which bondsmen still are active.

The goal of bail bondsmen is simple: to make a profit. Nonetheless, in the course of pursuing their own economic goals bail bondsmen fulfill a number of functions that benefit the court system. The value of these functions, perhaps combined with the power of money to influence court policymakers, has resulted in the persistence of bail bonding despite three decades of reform.

Functions of Bondsmen

Studies of bail bonding suggest that bondsmen perform services that are valued by defendants and other court actors, including judges, prosecutors, and jailers. Bondsmen can help to maintain social control over defendants released on bond. The bondsman has an economic stake in the defendant's appearance in court, just as an auto insurance company has an interest in the good driving habits of the drivers it insures. Bondsmen try to decrease their risks by stressing to defendants the importance of appearing for court dates. In addition, by requiring family members to be cosigners of the bond agreement and provide collateral, the bondsman essentially recruits the family to make sure the defendant appears on time at court (Toborg 1983, 142). Bondsmen sometimes contact defendants to remind them of court dates. These practices increase the likelihood that the defendant will appear at trial, which is beneficial for the court.

Defendants and their families may also perceive the bondsman as a source of additional assistance. Because bondsmen are familiar with court routines, they guide people through the court process, explaining procedures and options and even giving advice on plea bargains (Gambitta and Hitchings 1983).

If a defendant fails to appear, the bondsman may try to locate the individual, saving police agencies' time and resources. Defendants are usually easy to find, especially because most defendants who fail to appear either forgot or have legitimate reasons for not appearing and are not trying to hide. Even most of those who deliberately miss court dates are easily found and persuaded to appear. Only rarely do defendants truly abscond, leaving town and trying to disappear.

Bondsmen may try to locate those defendants who abscond and leave the jurisdiction, especially if the bond is large and the court is demanding that the bond be paid. Some states allow bondsmen to hire bounty hunters to search for fugitive defendants. Law enforcement agencies may rely on bondsmen to provide this service to the courts, because bondsmen and their bounty hunters frequently have greater arrest powers than the police. The authority of the bondsman to seize a fugitive stems from the bond contract itself. Consequently, if the bondsman locates a fugitive defendant, the bondsman may simply take the defendant into custody, without a warrant and without having to worry about extradition (Toborg 1983, 143).

Finally, bondsmen insulate court officials from accountability for their decisions to release defendants. Judges set bail high to satisfy public demand for stern treatment of criminals. Even so, defendants are able to secure release through the services of the bondsman. Moreover, if a dangerous defendant absconds or commits a heinous crime while released on bond, the judge escapes full blame. The judge can point to the high bail and shrug off responsibility for the defendant's release.

The advantages to the court and court officials of relying on bondsmen to arrange the release of defendants solidify the bondsman's place in the court process. In addition, because of their constant presence in the courthouse, other court officials come to know and trust them. The political, social, and functional connections between bondsmen and the court help to explain the persistence of bail bonding in the face of periodic efforts at reform.

Criticism of the Bonding System and the Bail Reform Movement

Several studies of criminal justice administration in the early part of the twentieth century criticized the operations of bondsmen. Investigations revealed that bondsmen were engaging in corrupt business practices, such as giving bribes, kickbacks, and gifts to jailers, judges, and other court employees. In exchange for these corrupt payments court personnel would steer defendants and their families to a particular bondsman. Judges, who often were the recipients of such largesse, frequently waived forfeiture of the bond when defendants absconded, allowing bondsmen to collect fees while rarely paying the bonds of defendants who failed to return to court. Through such practices bonding remained highly profitable.

Despite periodic efforts to regulate bondsmen and curb abuses, the surety bonding system persisted with few changes. The same abuses described in the 1920s and 1930s were again cited by investigators in the 1960s. Investigations during the 1980s and 1990s suggest that little has changed. Court clerks and jail guards continue to receive gratuities and gifts of liquor and food in exchange for steering business to bondsmen and supplying bondsmen with information about defendants. Bondsmen are heavy contributors to elections of judges, prosecutors, court clerks, and sheriffs. In exchange, judges and prosecutors reduce forfeiture amounts or dismiss charges in order to release the bondsman from forfeiture obligations (Gambitta and Hitchings 1983; Klaidman 1990).

Critics of bail bonding continue to call for the abolition of surety bonding by private profit-oriented businesses. The profit goal of the bondsman encourages the kickbacks and other forms of corruption that are regularly found in relation to bail-bonding practices. Critics also point out that surety bonding discriminates against the poor. Any system of release that relies exclusively on the amount of money a defendant can raise to determine whether the defendant will be released before trial puts poor defendants at a disadvantage. Moreover, defendants with enough money to pay cash bail, bypassing the services of the bondsman, get a full refund upon completion of the trial. Defendants who must use the bondsman's services to gain release pay a nonrefundable fee to the bondsman (Feeley 1983, 43).

■ THE BAIL REFORM MOVEMENT

bail reform movement

The concerns about bail bonding, combined with overcrowded conditions in local jails, spurred the **bail reform movement** of the 1960s. In some places bail reform meant simply checking the worst abuses of bail bonding. In other situations the goal of the reformers was to revamp the methods by which defendants are released before trial. The goal was to provide information to judges that would encourage them to release low-risk defendants without requiring money bail. Reformers claimed that bail decisions were often arbitrary. Judges frequently made decisions in a vacuum, with little information about the defendant or the defendant's ability to pay bail. Judges were observed setting bail high in order to punish defendants (give them a taste of jail) or to detain defendants that judges considered dangerous (Goldkamp 1985, 3). In particular reformers were concerned about large numbers of indigent defendants jailed before trial, often on minor charges, simply because they could not afford even small amounts of cash bail or bail-bonding fees (Goldkamp 1984, 2).

The origins of the bail reform movement have been traced to an experiment conducted by a private foundation in New York City in the early 1960s. The Vera Institute, founded by a philanthropist working with an energetic social worker, launched an experiment in bail reform known as the Manhattan Bail Project. The goal was to obtain release for defendants who might otherwise remain in jail because they were unable to make bond.

Volunteers interviewed arrestees for information about employment, community ties, residence, and so on, verified the information, and then recommended release on recognizance if the person appeared to be a good risk. The Vera Institute evaluated the program after the first year of operation and concluded that it was a success (Feeley 1983, 45). Those released on ROR appeared for trial more reliably than those released on money bond (Feeley 1983, 46).

At the same time Attorney General Robert Kennedy directed U.S. attorneys to recommend release on recognizance to as many defendants as practicable. The federal Bail Reform Act, passed in 1966, became a model for state bail reform (Feeley 1983, 46). The act institutionalized ROR by creating a presumption that defendants be released on recognizance unless the judge finds that such release would not ensure the defendant's appearance at trial (Goldkamp 1985, 14). By 1969 eighty-nine courts had instituted local pretrial release projects modeled after the Manhattan Bail Project.

In general, these projects are set up as independent agencies that contract with the local court to provide services. Like the volunteers in the Manhattan Bail Project, agency personnel interview arrestees shortly after arrest to obtain information about their background, financial means, and community ties. Bail workers then verify the information by calling family members, employers, landlords, and others. Some agencies also provide follow-up services such as sending reminders of court dates or even requiring that the released defendant report at regular intervals to the bail agency (Feeley 1983).

Evaluating Bail Reform

Like most criminal justice reforms, bail reform has achieved dramatic successes in some jurisdictions, while barely affecting longstanding practices in others. In some jurisdictions bail reform ended the bail-bonding system, reduced pretrial detention, and resulted in the creation of a range of pretrial services designed to ensure the appearance of defendants at trial. In other jurisdictions bail bondsmen continue to operate, often in the same disreputable ways that have been criticized for decades.

Benefits of Bail Reform

Bail reform has brought about a number of positive changes for the criminal justice system. Before the bail reform movement defendants were jailed because they were unable to pay for the services of a bondsman. The Vera Institute demonstrated that large numbers of defendants could be released into the community without increasing failure-to-appear (FTA) rates. Moreover, of those defendants who missed court appearances, only a small proportion were true fugitives (Feeley 1983, 48). This evidence of the success of ROR has resulted in increased use of ROR nationwide. As a result a defendant's pocketbook plays less of a role in determining whether the defendant is released before trial. This reduction in economic discrimination is clearly a positive outcome of the bail reform movement.

Pretrial release agencies also generate improvements in the bail process. Follow-up services, such as regular contact with defendants and calling defendants to remind them of court dates, can reduce failure-to-appear rates (Feeley 1983, 71; Austin et al. 1985). In other words, greater contact with defendants before trial increases the likelihood that these defendants will appear for trial. More important, pretrial release agencies are successful in reducing arbitrariness and racial discrimination in the use of ROR. Because pretrial release agencies base their recommendations on standard criteria, judges are less likely to engage in blatant discrimination against nonwhite defendants. Several studies have found that pretrial release agencies reduce disparity and arbitrariness in bail decision making (Feeley 1983).

Criticisms of Bail Reform

Bail reform has not been an unqualified success, however. It has not completely eliminated the abuses associated with bail bonding. In fact, where bail bonding has continued, the availability of alternatives to the bond may have made it more difficult for some defendants to be released, even though they are relatively good risks for pretrial release. One researcher (Toborg 1983) studied surety bonding in four cities that had introduced reforms such as ROR and stricter rules requiring bond forfeiture for failure to appear. Since the introduction of reforms, defendants who do not gain release through alternatives to surety bonds may find it more difficult to gain release than before the reforms were introduced. The study found that defendants with relatively low bail amounts were being detained because bondsmen refused to bond these defendants, even though they offered their services to defendants with high bail amounts. Because the courts already have released the lowest-risk defendants on ROR or other nonmonetary conditions, bondsmen now face a different mix of low- and high- risk defendants. Although a judge may have imposed a relatively low bail, such as $500, bondsmen may perceive that decision as indicating some risk of flight because the defendant was not released on ROR. In addition, the fees that bondsmen can collect from these somewhat risky bonds do not make these contracts profitable. Because the gross profit on a bond of $500 is only $50, many bondsmen choose not to risk forfeiture for such a small potential profit (Toborg 1983, 154). This study's findings suggest that reforms have not eliminated bondsmen in many jurisdictions but have changed their business environment in ways that result in the detention of defendants despite relatively low risk of absconding and low bail amounts. Because reforms have decreased the overall profitability of the bonding business, bondsmen are less willing to take risks that they would have taken in a more profitable business climate. The result is relatively high rates of detention of relatively low-risk defendants. Consequently, detention rates—and the associated costs of keeping these defendants in jail—actually increase.

Other criticisms of the bail reform movement focus on the problem of unnecessary bureaucracy. Professor Malcolm Feeley has been especially skeptical about the effect of pretrial release agencies in expanding pretrial release and reducing FTA rates. Reviewing evaluations of bail reform, Feeley finds that jurisdictions with no pretrial release agency use ROR just as successfully as jurisdictions with pretrial release agencies. In addition, some pretrial release agencies are conservative in recommending ROR, for fear of creating bad publicity if the FTA rate increases (Feeley 1983).

Despite considerable evidence that pretrial release agencies are of questionable value in expanding pretrial release or reducing FTAs, the agencies have become a symbol of bail reform. Feeley concludes that judges and prosecutors use pretrial release agencies to deflect accountability for release decisions, just as they once used bail bondsmen to deflect accountability and criticism. In addition, according to Feeley, the work of pretrial release agencies has been wrapped in a veneer of scientific expertise. Agencies construct elaborate predictive scoring systems for assessing the likelihood that a defendant will appear for court. The reliability of these predictions has not been adequately tested, however. Feeley suggests that ROR can be practiced just as effectively without large staffs and elaborate prediction instruments.

Although the bail reform movement has clearly been less than a total success, most experts agree that it has reduced the role of money in the pretrial release decision, increased the opportunities for defendants to be released before trial, and decreased the arbitrary nature of pretrial decisions. In short, the bail process is more fair and equitable as a result of bail reform.

■ BAIL DECISION MAKING

bail decision

Determining the conditions of release before trial is routinely referred to as the **bail decision.** This decision is usually made by a lower-court judge, although in some jurisdictions a special court officer, such as a court commissioner, may be authorized to make bail decisions. And a number of other actors—most notably the police and prosecutor—influence the bail decision.

The police, for example, can influence the bail decision through the arrest charge and other information in the arrest report. A decision to arrest for misdemeanor assault rather than felony assault can translate into greater chances for ROR or lower monetary bail. In addition, some jurisdictions have bail schedules for misdemeanors that allow the police to release defendants immediately on cash bail according to a standardized schedule (Walker 1993, 58, 66). Finally, information included in the arrest report or offered by the police at the initial appearance—such as the cooperativeness of the defendant at the time of arrest—can also influence the judge's decision.

The prosecutor has substantial influence on the bail decision. Typically, the prosecutor makes a bail recommendation based on the information provided by police and other sources. In jurisdictions that have pretrial release agencies the recommendation of bail evaluators becomes an important piece of information for prosecutor and judge alike. By seeking consensus among these actors concerning an appropriate bail decision, a judge can share some of the responsibility for making the bail decision (Walker 1993).

Defense counsel, if present, may respond to the recommendations of the prosecutor or pretrial release agency. Typically, defense counsel will argue for lower bail, pointing out mitigating factors or personal characteristics that suggest that the defendant can be trusted with minimal restraints on liberty.

The judge formally determines the conditions of release but is clearly influenced by information from other actors and local norms about the appropriate conditions of release for various kinds of offenders. One early study of bail found that the judge, prosecutor, and defense counsel disagreed about the decision in only 12 percent of the cases reviewed (Suffet 1966).

The bail decision can be understood as a multistage decision process (Nagel 1983). First, the judge considers whether the defendant is an appropriate candidate for ROR or other nonfinancial release conditions. If not, the judge decides on an appropriate bail amount. Finally, if the jurisdiction allows a deposit bond, such as the 10 percent alternative, the judge must decide whether to offer this option to the defendant.

Many states specify by statute a number of factors that judges are to consider in making these decisions. Figure 11-3 presents the factors that judges in Montana are supposed to consider when setting bail. Although such statutes tell judges which factors to consider, they do not tell judges how to weigh the various factors in comparison to each other. For example, how should the judge weigh the defendant's criminal record in relation to family ties? Which factor should be counted as the stronger in making the bail decision?

Research on bail decision making suggests that in practice judges place the most emphasis on the current charges and the defendant's record (Goldkamp and Gottfredson 1985). Data from thirteen federal districts also showed that seriousness of the current charge and defendant's record were important influences on judges' pretrial release decisions (U.S. Bureau of Justice Statistics [BJS] 1985). Judges place importance on these factors because they view the charge and prior record as indicators of the likelihood that the defendant will commit serious new crimes if released. This suggests that bail decision making is more strongly influenced by judges' guesses about the dangerousness of offenders than concerns about the defendant's likelihood of appearing for trial. A number of bail studies conclude that "considerations of public safety dominate decisions, and 'dangerousness' is defined in terms of the seriousness of the pending charge and the criminal record of the defendant" (Walker 1993, 60).

Because judges are given minimal guidance, bail decisions can be inconsistent from one judge to another (Goldkamp and Gottfredson 1985; Nagel 1983). Judges are fairly consistent in their decisions regarding ROR but they vary significantly on the appropriate amount of cash bail and in relation to less commonly used

---

FIGURE 11-3   Statutory Factors for Bail Decisions

Many states specify by statute the factors that judges are to consider in making the bail decision. Although such statutes attempt to guide judicial discretion, they fail to inform judges about the weight to be attached to the various factors. The Montana statute reproduced here is typical of how legislatures attempt to guide judicial discretion in the bail decision.

Montana Code Annotated 46-9-301

Determining the amount of bail. In all cases that bail is determined to be necessary, bail must be reasonable in amount and the amount shall be:

(1) sufficient to ensure the presence of the defendant in a criminal proceeding;
(2) sufficient to assure compliance with the conditions set forth in the bail;
(3) sufficient to protect any person from bodily injury;
(4) not oppressive;
(5) commensurate with the nature of the offense charged;
(6) considerate of the financial ability of the accused;
(7) considerate of the defendant's prior record;
(8) considerate of the length of time the defendant has resided in the community and of his ties to the community;
(9) considerate of the defendant's family relationships and ties;
(10) considerate of the defendant's employment status; and
(11) sufficient to include the charge imposed in 46-18-236.

---

alternatives, such as the decision to offer the defendant release on a deposit bond (Goldkamp 1984, 11; Nagel 1983; Sviridoff 1986).

Race and Gender Bias

An issue of special concern is whether the race or gender of the defendant influences judges' decisions. The defendant's race may influence bail in two distinct ways. First, nonwhite defendants may be less likely to receive leniency or the benefit of a doubt than white defendants because of stereotypes about nonwhite defendants' characters and lifestyles. Second, because of economic disparities between whites and other racial groups, nonwhite defendants may be less able to make bail, even if judges are not racially biased in their decisions. To the extent that race affects bail outcomes even marginally, the effect of race may be magnified through later criminal justice decisions. Defendants who are detained before trial are more likely to be convicted and more likely to receive a sentence of incarceration than those defendants who gain release before trial.

Whether criminal justice decision making is influenced by the defendant's race has been the subject of much research. Early studies conducted between the 1930s and the 1960s found clear and consistent evidence of race bias in criminal justice decision making, including the bail decision. Nonwhite defendants were more likely to be detained before trial than white defendants. Research conducted during the late 1960s and 1970s contradicted these earlier findings, however. These studies found no direct effects of race on bail and other criminal justice decisions. Instead these studies concluded that legal factors, such as the current charges and defendant's prior record, accounted for the harsher treatment of racial minorities by the criminal justice system.

A third wave of research on the effects of race reanalyzed data originally collected during the 1960s and 1970s. Using still more sophisticated methods of statistical analysis, research during this period found that race influenced criminal justice outcomes but primarily indirectly. In particular, researchers found that small differences in the treatment of nonwhite defendants accumulate over several criminal justice decisions. Consequently, a study of race bias at only one point in the criminal process is likely to find that race effects are minimal. Small biases at each decision point, however, can add up to significant differences in the outcomes for nonwhite defendants compared to whites. Bias at early points in the process, such as arrest and bail, may disadvantage defendants in later decision making (Zatz 1987; Lynch and Patterson 1991).

The magnitude and nature of the effect of racial bias on criminal justice decisions is difficult to measure, and research results reflect this difficulty. Part of the confusion hinges on the definition of racial bias. Narrowly defined, racial bias refers to direct discrimination by a criminal justice decision maker. Broadly defined, racial bias includes the indirect effects of prior societal discrimination on factors that are appropriately taken into consideration by criminal justice decision makers. In between are the unconscious and subtle differences in assessments that are made by decision makers who are part of a culture with a long and pervasive history of discrimination and prejudice. Consider, for example, two defendants who are before the judge for a bail hearing. If the two defendants are virtually identical on all legally relevant factors—crime charged, prior record, education, employment history, living arrangements, and so on—and the judge sets high cash bail for the nonwhite defendant but permits the white defendant to gain release on ROR, then the judge has directly discriminated against the nonwhite defendant. These sorts of situations are rare. Real life is more complex. Suppose that the nonwhite defendant is unemployed and the white defendant is employed. If the judge then sets different conditions of release, is this racial bias? It is entirely appropriate for the judge to consider current employment in making a pretrial release decision. But nonwhites have higher unemployment rates than whites, due at least in part to the effects of prior and continuing race based discrimination. Many nonwhites are socially and economically disadvantaged in many ways because of the long and pervasive history of racial prejudice and discrimination in the United States. Thus, when social and economic factors are considered by criminal justice decision makers, societal racial bias indirectly influences the outcome, even if the individual criminal justice decision maker is scrupulously non-biased in making the decision.

Between these two extremes—where racial bias by the individual decision maker is clearly present or clearly absent—are the intuitive judgment calls that are routinely made by criminal justice decision makers. Negative stereotypes shape decisions, even among the most conscientious and well-intended individuals. The judge makes very subjective assessments to reach a bail decision: the defendant's dangerousness and willingness to cooperate, the seriousness of future offenses and the need to protect potential victims. These intuitive judgments are made through personal filters that are shaped by society's stereotypes. Although it would be virtually impossible to measure the impact of stereotypes on such decisions, it would be absurdly naive to conclude they do not have an effect.

Another question concerns gender and bail, specifically, why women are treated more leniently than men in the bail decision. Here, as with race effects, the question that has puzzled researchers is whether it is gender per se that results in this more lenient treatment or other characteristics commonly associated with gender. Early work on this topic hypothesized that chivalrous and paternalistic attitudes toward women resulted in leniency for women in bail decisions (Moulds 1980). According to this view, judges' desire to protect women from the rigors of jail causes them to set bail low or release women on recognizance more often than men. Later theorists argued that although this may be true for the majority of women, a small subset of women who deviate from traditional sex roles and commit unfeminine types of crimes such as armed robbery and burglary may actually receive harsher treatment than men (Visher 1983).

Research by Kathleen Daly (1987) suggests that neither hypothesis accurately depicts the nature of bail decision making in relation to women. Daly found that women receive lenient treatment in bail decisions because judges are trying to protect family life and the defendant's children. Defendants (whether male or female) who are responsible for taking care of their children are more likely to receive lenient bail decisions. But defendants who are mothers receive an extra dose of leniency. According to Daly, mothers are perceived as being more responsible for the care of children and as playing a more critical role in their social development. Because of gender roles women with children are treated more leniently than men with children because "(1) gender divisions of labor define women, not men, as the primary caregivers; and (2) the court attaches more importance to caregiving than breadwinning in maintaining family life" (Daly 1987, 282). Consistent with this reasoning, women who are perceived as bad mothers become ineligible for this leniency and are treated like other defendants (Daly 1987).

■ PRETRIAL RELEASE OUTCOMES

In recent years the federal government has gathered data from the seventy-five largest counties in the United States regarding the pretrial release of felony defendants (BJS 1991, 1992, 1994). These data show that two-thirds of defendants obtain release before the final disposition of their cases (see Figure 11-4). Of the one-third who are unable to obtain release, the majority have a bail amount set but are unable to gain release. These defendants may have been unable to raise sufficient funds to meet the monetary conditions of release or they may have had a "hold" placed on them because of a probation or parole violation or because they were wanted in another jurisdiction. Six percent of all felony defendants in these counties are held without bail.

In general, if the defendant is not released on ROR or some other nonfinancial conditions, the lower the amount of bail, the more likely the defendant is to be able to obtain release. Of those defendants who obtain release, 52 percent are released on the day of arrest or the day after (BJS 1994, 7). Seventy-seven percent of felony defendants are released within a week of arrest, and 91 percent within a month of arrest.

The reforms of the past thirty years have changed bail outcomes. In general, the availability of ROR and other nonmonetary conditions of release have increased the ability of defendants to gain release before trial. For a portion of the defendant population, however, reforms (or partial reforms) may actually have made it more difficult to obtain release before trial (Toborg 1983).

Failure to Appear

Because the main purpose of bail is to ensure appearance at trial, the number of defendants who fail to appear is an important indicator of the quality of pretrial

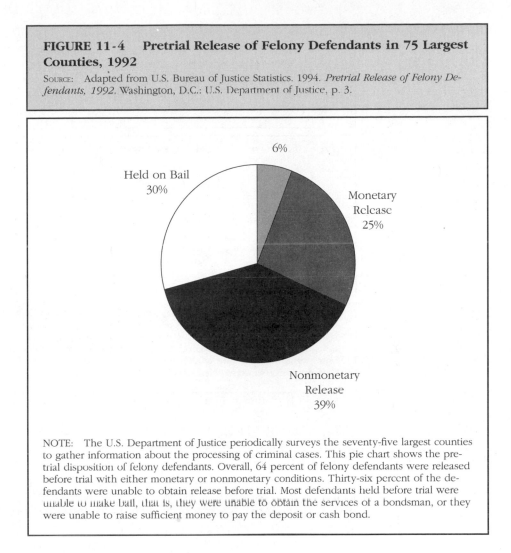

FIGURE 11-4   Pretrial Release of Felony Defendants in 75 Largest Counties, 1992

SOURCE: Adapted from U.S. Bureau of Justice Statistics. 1994. *Pretrial Release of Felony Defendants, 1992.* Washington, D.C.: U.S. Department of Justice, p. 3.

Held on Bail
30%

6%

Monetary Release
25%

Nonmonetary Release
39%

NOTE: The U.S. Department of Justice periodically surveys the seventy-five largest counties to gather information about the processing of criminal cases. This pie chart shows the pretrial disposition of felony defendants. Overall, 64 percent of felony defendants were released before trial with either monetary or nonmonetary conditions. Thirty-six percent of the defendants were unable to obtain release before trial. Most defendants held before trial were unable to make bail, that is, they were unable to obtain the services of a bondsman, or they were unable to raise sufficient money to pay the deposit or cash bond.

release decisions. All major studies have found relatively low FTA rates. That is, when defendants are released, only a small proportion of them fail to appear for their court dates. The Lazar Institute (1981) found that 87 percent of defendants appeared for all court appearances. In a study of pretrial release in Philadelphia 12 percent of defendants failed to appear (Goldkamp 1984, 11). In the BJS study of the seventy-five largest counties, three-fourths of defendants released before trial appeared for court as required (see Figure 11-5). According to BJS, only about 8 percent of all defendants remain fugitives a year after missing a court date (BJS 1994, 10).

Effect of Pretrial Release on Case Outcome

For the approximately one-third of defendants who are unable to gain release before trial, remaining in jail has obvious negative consequences. Defendants are separated from home and family, suffer loss of income, and may even lose their jobs because they are in jail. For defendants already too poor to afford bail, the economic effect of pretrial detention can be devastating. Although many of these defendants are not employed full time, they do manage to provide some income

FIGURE 11-5   Felony Defendants in 75 Largest Counties Released
Before Case Disposition, Failure to Appear by Type of Release,
1992.

SOURCE: Adapted from Bureau of Justice Statistics. 1994. *Pretrial Release of Felony Defendants, 1992.* Washington, D.C.: U.S. Department of Justice, p. 10.

Type of Release	Failure to Appear		
	Total	*Initially FTA but Returned to Court*	*Remained a Fugitive*
Surety Bond	15%	12%	3%
Deposit Bond	21	15	6
Cash Bail	22	14	8
ROR/Citation	26	18	9
Signature Bond	42	23	19
All Types of Release	25	17	8

NOTE: Previous studies of failure to appear have found little or no relationship between the type of release and failure to appear rates. The differences here suggest that non-monetary conditions of release may result in a somewhat greater chance that the defendant will fail to appear. Given the less serious offenses of the defendants released on recognizance, citations, or signature bonds, fewer efforts may be made to ensure the appearance of these defendants at trial.

to their families (Miller 1986). Local jails are frequently overcrowded, under-staffed, run down, and offer few diversions to help pass the time.

In addition to these obvious pains of pretrial imprisonment, detained defendants are treated more harshly at subsequent stages of prosecution (see Figure 11-6). As early as the mid-1960s researchers found that defendants who were detained before trial were more likely to be convicted and more likely to receive severe sentences. More recent research has come to the same conclusion (Walters 1982; Hagan and Bumiller 1983; Kruttschnitt and Green 1984). One study (Wheeler and Wheeler 1982) reviewed fourteen studies of pretrial release and found mixed results in relation to the effect of pretrial release on case disposition. Although only five of the fourteen studies found that detained defendants were more likely to be convicted, eight found that detained defendants were definitely more likely to receive a sentence of imprisonment. More recently, research (Austin et al. 1985) using a randomized experiment found that defendants not released pending trial were less likely to have charges dropped, more likely to be convicted, and more likely to be sentenced to prison than those released on ROR or supervised pretrial release.

The correlation between pretrial detention and conviction and sentencing outcomes is not surprising. Defendants experience a number of handicaps when behind bars. Defendants in jail have a more difficult time communicating with defense counsel and are not able to help prepare their defense. This isolation increases their anxiety. Jailed defendants want to know what is happening to their case but feel severely handicapped in making sure that their attorney is diligent. Defendants who are jailed before trial feel added pressure to accept plea bargains. In fact, detained defendants may be eager to plead guilty in order to gain release on probation or to be transferred to prison (Casper 1972, 66). Because poor defendants are more likely to be detained, and because detention creates

FIGURE 11-6   Effect of Pretrial Release on Case Outcome

Source: Adapted from U.S. Bureau of Justice Statistics. 1994. *Pretrial Release of Felon Defendants, 1992.* Washington, D.C.: U.S. Department of Justice, p. 14.

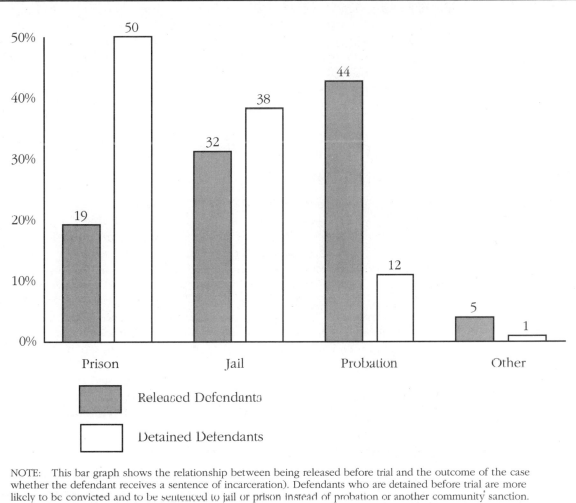

NOTE: This bar graph shows the relationship between being released before trial and the outcome of the case whether the defendant receives a sentence of incarceration). Defendants who are detained before trial are more likely to be convicted and to be sentenced to jail or prison instead of probation or another community sanction. This relationship may be partially explained by such factors as the seriousness of the charge and the record of the defendant. Nonetheless, studies that control for such factors suggest that being locked up before trial affects the likelihood of conviction and influences the sentence a defendant receives.

disadvantages that result in harsher dispositions, poor defendants are more likely to suffer the disadvantages associated with the bail system.

Rearrests for Pretrial Offending

Pretrial release policy has shifted in recent years to a concern about the likelihood that defendants will commit new crimes while awaiting trial. In the Philadelphia study 16 percent of defendants released before trial were rearrested for a new crime during a 120-day follow-up period (Goldkamp 1984). The risk of pretrial misconduct increases as the length of time on release increases (BJS 1985). A 1982 review of existing bail studies found a range of 3 to 20 percent of released defendants rearrested before trial; 5 to 8 percent of released defendants were rearrested for a serious crime (Hansen 1987). The most recent BJS data from the seventy-five largest counties found 14 percent of defendants rearrested while on pretrial release, but defendants with more serious prior records of conviction were more likely to be rearrested than those with less serious records (BJS 1994, 11). For example, 38 percent of defendants with 10 or more prior convictions were rearrested while on pretrial release, compared to 9 percent of defendants with no prior convictions. During the 1980s concern about pretrial crime prompted legislators to create laws allowing for preventive pretrial detention. This controversial trend led to a second generation in bail reform.

■ BAIL REFORM IN THE 1980s: PROTECTING THE PUBLIC

The bail reform movement of the 1960s and 1970s was concerned primarily with eliminating abuses associated with bail bonding and reducing the number of defendants detained before trial. The success of this movement, combined with rising fear of crime, prompted a second generation of bail reform, this time focused on protecting the public from new crimes committed by defendants while on pretrial release (Goldkamp 1985, 1). State and federal laws were enacted giving judges the authority to deny pretrial release to defendants who are considered dangerous. This **preventive detention** is based on the assumption that a "small but identifiable group of particularly dangerous offenders" can be prevented from endangering the public only by detaining them before trial (Goldkamp 1985, 1).

preventive detention

Preventive detention raises a variety of legal and empirical issues. Disagreements about constitutional requirements and the interpretation of research evidence have made preventive pretrial detention a highly controversial issue.

Justifications for Preventive Detention

The desire to detain defendants who might commit crimes, especially dangerous crimes, while on pretrial release is not new. Judges have always worried about the political repercussions of releasing a defendant who then commits some new horrible crime while out on bail. Judges can release thousands of defendants who commit no serious crimes; only the "mistakes" make headlines. Release of a single defendant who then commits a serious crime can ignite a scandal that may threaten a judge's career.

Some defendants pose such an apparent risk of danger that judges are strongly motivated to prevent their release pending trial. The case of Roosevelt Daniels illustrates the point and makes a strong case for preventive pretrial detention. Daniels was charged in 1985 with running a drug operation. His record would suggest to anyone that he would be likely to commit additional crimes if released on bail. The U.S. District Court described Daniels's record in reviewing a magistrate's decision to deny pretrial release:

> In 1970 he was convicted of battery and unlawful use of a weapon, in 1971 of armed robbery. He served five years on these convictions. In 1976 he was convicted of aggravated kidnapping—abducting two people at gunpoint and stuffing them in the

trunk of a car. . . . This affair cannot have come long after his release. He also was convicted of a separate incident in 1976 of murder; he bludgeoned a person to death in a dispute about $60. . . . Perhaps aggravated kidnapping and murder are not viewed as serious crimes these days, for by 1982 Daniels was at liberty once more, this time facing charges of unlawful use of a weapon. He was returned to jail. By 1984 he was out again. When arrested on drug charges in September 1984 he was wearing a holster for one of six guns thrown out of the window of a front for selling drugs. This led to the revocation of his parole in November 1984. But even that did not last. He was out again when arrested on April 15, 1985, and charged with running a drug operation. (*United States v. Daniels* 1985, 382–83)

Without preventive detention laws a judge faced with a defendant like Daniels has two options: allow the release of the defendant on bail, ROR, or other conditions, risking potential danger to the community, or set bail so high that the defendant can never raise enough money to gain release. This last practice has been called *sub rosa* preventive detention, because the judgment that the defendant is dangerous is hidden within the bail decision and never explicitly addressed by the court. Bail is set impossibly high for the hidden reason of preventing new crimes rather than for the stated reason of preventing flight. The legality of sub rosa preventive detention has been a point of debate for decades.

In the 1951 decision of *Stack v. Boyle* the Supreme Court appeared to hold that the only constitutional justification for setting bail high is to ensure the appearance of the accused at trial. Consequently, the practice of setting bail high for potentially dangerous defendants was widely understood as an illegal infringement of a defendant's Eighth Amendment rights.

Historical evidence suggests that judges frequently violated this principle, however. Prosecutors would request and judges would impose high bail for defendants who posed little risk of flight but appeared likely to commit new crimes while released. Under the bail-bonding system, in which high bail was fairly routine, judges could set high bail on presumably dangerous defendants without having to provide justification. Following the reforms of the 1960s, however, defendants were expected to be released unless they posed a risk of flight. With many defendants being released on recognizance or other alternatives, using high bail to deny release became both more visible and more difficult to justify.

By the beginning of the 1980s a number of influential people, including Chief Justice Warren Burger, Senator Edward Kennedy, and President Ronald Reagan, were calling for reforms that would allow judges to legally deny bail and preventively detain defendants without the pretext of preventing the flight of the defendant (Wheeler and Wheeler 1982, 229). By the mid-1980s most states, as well as the federal jurisdiction, had revised their bail statutes or constitutions to allow or even require judges to take future dangerousness into account in making pretrial release decisions (Goldkamp 1985).

Overview of Preventive Detention Laws

A review of existing laws in 1985 showed that a majority of jurisdictions had enacted preventive detention measures of one type or another (Goldkamp 1985). Thirty-five states and the District of Columbia had bail or preventive detention statutes that allowed consideration of potential danger in making pretrial release decisions. The laws are not uniform, of course.

Some states exclude certain offenders from the right to pretrial release. Traditionally, defendants charged with capital offenses could be denied bail.

PREDICTING DANGEROUSNESS

With preventive detention we encounter the prediction problem for the first but not the last time. The policy works only if we succeed in identifying and detaining the dangerous repeaters *and only those offenders*. Mistakes take two forms. First there are defendants whom we detain unnecessarily. We label them dangerous when in fact they will not commit violent felonies while they are out on bail. These people are referred to as "false positives." Then there are those people who slip through our net. We fail to identify them as potentially dangerous when in fact they do commit more violent crime while they are out on bail. These are the "false negatives." In both cases the social costs are high. . . .

Two studies of preventive detention independently found that only 5 percent of the criminal defendants who were potentially eligible to detention (that is, had committed a violent crime) would be rearrested for a violent crime while out on bail. The National Bureau of

Standards study found that between 15 percent and 25 percent of those eligible under the Washington, D.C., law would be rearrested but only 5 percent of those rearrests would be for a violent crime. A similar study in Boston found that 14.5 percent of the potentially eligible would be rearrested but only 5.2 percent for another violent crime. Identifying the small dangerous group within the original group is difficult, if not impossible. Remember, all of the original group qualify by having committed a violent crime. One obvious solution is to cast a broad net and lock up people just to be safe. The Boston study concluded that in order to hold all of the actually dangerous people, we would have to detain nineteen nondangerous people for every dangerous one. In other words, there would be nineteen false positives for every dangerous person we correctly detained. The cost of such mistakes would be threefold. Not only would we violate the rights of those individuals needlessly detained, but

Consistent with *Stack v. Boyle* (1951), detaining defendants charged with capital offenses is justified because no amount of money can ensure that the defendant whose life is at stake will appear at court. In recent years, some states have enlarged the group of defendants who may be denied bail to include all those who may be imprisoned for life if convicted or who are charged with certain serious violent offenses such as armed robbery. In other states, judges are permitted to take dangerousness into account in deciding whether to release the defendant on ROR or unsecured bond. Still other states have simply added dangerousness to the list of factors that judges should consider in determining the conditions of pretrial release.

The procedures that courts must follow in determining dangerousness vary substantially. Only a handful of jurisdictions provide full due process safeguards for defendants, including an adversarial evidentiary hearing to establish that the defendant is dangerous. In contrast, most states do not provide special hearings on the issue of dangerousness and do not require a review of decisions that result in detention. While many states have expanded judges' authority to consider future dangerousness in making pretrial release decisions, comparatively few have expanded procedural safeguards to minimize the risk of error in these critical decisions.

Criticism of Preventive Detention

Aside from questions of procedural fairness, critics of preventive detention argue that such laws are ineffective and unnecessary. "If trial judges are unable to predict the jail experience would encourage many of them toward more antisocial attitudes and behavior. Finally, the dollar cost of locking up so many people would be enormous.

The truth is that we simply can't tell who is dangerous and who is not. Human behavior is too unpredictable and past behavior is not necessarily the best guide. Many people think they can spot the dangerous repeaters. The concept of the "career criminal" is, in many respects, very misleading. The people we call "chronic" offenders commit crimes in spurts. They go through periods of very active criminality, followed by periods of inactivity. They are not like white-collar workers who go to the office on time week in and week out. In short, it is impossible to predict what one convicted offender will do in the next few weeks or months. Judge Charles Halleck of the District of Columbia Court of General Sessions, an advocate of preventive detention, did think he could make successful predictions. The D.C. bail agency had the impertinence to compare Judge Halleck's track record with that of another

judge of the same court. Halleck granted pretrial release to only 49 percent of the 200 defendants in his sample, while Judge Alexander released 80 percent of his defendants. The rearrest rates for the two judges were virtually identical: 8 percent of those released by Judge Halleck and 9 percent of those released by Judge Alexander were rearrested. In other words, while Judge Halleck detained two and a half times as many people as Judge Alexander, he was no more successful in spotting the truly dangerous. . . .

Preventive detention is not a reasonable criminal justice policy. Most prosecutors and judges will simply avoid using the law and try to achieve the same ends by covert means. If the law were implemented, it would fail in one of two costly ways: detention of too many, at great dollar cost, or detention of too few, and failure to reduce crime effectively.

SOURCE: Excerpted from Samuel Walker. 1989. *Sense and Nonsense About Crime: A Policy Guide,* 2d ed. Pacific Grove, Calif.: Brooks/Cole, pp. 68–69.

dangerous behavior, pretrial detention may not be rationally related to the goal of reducing pretrial crime," one critic points out (Eason 1988, 1065). Both psychiatric and statistical predictions of dangerousness are highly unreliable (Ewing 1985). Only 20 percent of defendants predicted to be dangerous actually commit a violent crime if released. And there is little reason to believe that judges' predictions of dangerousness are any better. Consequently, many defendants are detained who are not dangerous, and many others are released, only to commit new crimes.

Critics advocate other strategies for reducing pretrial crime. Because the risk of pretrial crime increases in relation to the length of the release (National Institute of Justice 1985), scheduling high-risk defendants for earlier trials prevents crime almost as effectively as holding these defendants in jail. In addition, pretrial supervision of bailed defendants may offer the social control needed to prevent crimes that might be committed by an unsupervised high-risk defendant (Himsell 1986).

Despite Supreme Court rulings to the contrary (*Salerno v. United States* 1987, *Bell v. Wolfish* 1979), some legal scholars continue to argue that pretrial preventive detention violates the Constitution. The constitutionality of preventive detention statutes hinges on a range of questions, among them, whether the U.S. Constitution guarantees a right to bail and whether pretrial preventive detention constitutes "punishment before trial." If there is a constitutional right to bail, pretrial preventive detention statutes may be unconstitutional. If pretrial preventive detention is punishment before trial, critics argue that it violates the right to a fair trial and the presumption of innocence.

Is There a Constitutional Right to Bail?

Some historians read the Eighth Amendment and early American history as granting a right to bail to all defendants in noncapital cases who do not pose a risk of flight. Opponents of pretrial preventive detention often take this position. Other historians read American legal history as granting no constitutional right to bail. According to these scholars, the Eighth Amendment bail clause means what it says and no more: excessive bail shall not be required. When a judge decides to set bail, the bail may not be excessive, but judges have the discretion to deny the opportunity for pretrial release. Finally, the courts have articulated a middle ground between the two positions. According to this view, the Eighth Amendment bail clause grants a limited right to bail that excludes those defendants "who pose either a serious risk of flight or a substantial danger to the community if released" (Verrilli 1982, 334). Both the "no right to bail" and the "limited right to bail" interpretations allow for pretrial preventive detention under at least some-circumstances. Based on the historical record, no conclusive resolution is possible (Verrilli 1982).

Punishment Before Trial

Because the historical record regarding congressional intent in framing the Eighth Amendment is unclear, additional arguments against preventive detention rest on due process grounds. Opponents argue that pretrial preventive detention is really punishment before trial, violating the right to trial and the principle of the presumption of innocence. The principle authority for the proposition that a right to bail is implied by the presumption of innocence is found in *Stack v. Boyle* (1951). The majority opinion noted that the presumption of innocence would "lose its meaning" if bail were set higher than that amount necessary to ensure the appearance of the accused at trial. According to this view, a defendant is as innocent on the day before trial as on the day after acquittal. If confining a person solely for dangerousness after an acquittal is an unconstitutional infringement on liberty, confining a person solely for dangerousness before trial is similarly unjustified because of the presumption of innocence. Many commentators read the *Stack* decision as recognizing a constitutional right to bail in order to preserve the presumption of innocence. If a person is presumed innocent until convicted at trial, what basis is there for confining an individual before trial, except to ensure appearance at trial?

Preventive Detention and the Supreme Court

By the early 1980s it was clear that the Supreme Court would be called upon to decide these issues once and for all. The first indication of the Court's position on pretrial preventive detention came in *Schall v. Martin* (1984), approving pretrial preventive detention of juvenile offenders. The Supreme Court decision in *Salerno v. United States* (1987), upholding the preventive detention provisions of the 1984 federal Bail Reform Act, resolved the longstanding legal debate regarding the legality of pretrial preventive detention statutes.

According to the Court, protecting the community from dangerous persons is a legitimate regulatory goal of government. Therefore the goal of detention under the act is regulatory, not punitive. Consequently, defendants detained under the provisions of the act are not being punished before trial, because the purpose of the law is not to punish. Although the Court recognized that protecting the trial process by ensuring the appearance of the defendant at trial is the primary purpose of bail, the Court held that the Eighth Amendment does not prohibit the government from pursuing other goals through the regulation of pretrial release. The Court also decided that the assertion of *Stack v. Boyle,* that the only constitutional purpose in setting bail is to ensure appearance, was not part of the Court's holding in that case. In short, *Salerno* held that pretrial preventive detention under the Bail Reform Act is constitutional because it is reasonably related to the government's interest in protecting the community (Eason 1988, 1055).

Critique of *Salerno*

The dissenting opinions in *Salerno* (1987), as well as subsequent legal commentary, were harshly critical of the majority opinion. As one critic has stated, "In approving the Bail Reform Act, the Court abandoned common sense, strained precedent, and ignored the great weight of sociological data that dooms the fair and effective use of pretrial detention" (Eason 1988, 1060). Opponents of pretrial preventive detention view the *Salerno* decision as a grave mistake that undermines traditional concepts of due process.

The dissent argues that the only constitutional purpose of pretrial detention is to protect the trial process. This may mean setting bail high enough to ensure the appearance of defendants who might otherwise be tempted to abscond, denying pretrial release to defendants charged with capital offenses, and even preventively detaining defendants who have threatened to subvert the trial process by threatening witnesses or jurors. According to the dissenters, it is unconstitutional to lock up defendants for the sole purpose of protecting the community from *future* crimes that *might* be committed by those *accused* of "crimes as yet unproved."

After *Salerno*: The Future of Preventive Detention

Although the *Salerno* decision establishes the constitutional basis for pretrial preventive detention, not all provisions adopted by the states in recent years are constitutional. Some critics of pretrial preventive detention laws concede that the Constitution may allow the consideration of danger in making pretrial release decisions but find current provisions unacceptable (Eason 1988; Ewing 1985; Goldkamp 1984). These critics argue that the laws are unconstitutional because they lack adequate due-process protections. Specifically, the laws that have been passed in most states provide only vague definitions of dangerousness, allow the detention of defendants with no specific finding of danger, and do not afford sufficient procedural safeguards to protect defendants from erroneous findings of dangerousness. Moreover, even if a pretrial detention statute is constitutional on its face, it may be unconstitutional in the way it is applied in specific cases. Consequently, a number of legal issues remain open after *Salerno*. State and federal provisions may be challenged in the future for being overbroad, because they result in the detention of individuals who do not pose a danger to the community or who pose a risk of danger that is insufficient to justify a denial of liberty. Given the enormous difficulties in predicting dangerousness, such challenges may eventually prove successful.

◼ NEW DIRECTIONS

Bail reform in the 1960s was primarily concerned with reducing pretrial detention and the influence of money in determining pretrial release. Bail reform in the

1980s was primarily concerned with creating new authority for judges to deny release to defendants who pose a risk of committing serious new crimes while awaiting trial.

Concerns today appear to be focusing on the inconsistency of judicial decisions in setting bail and other conditions of release. Although most states provide a list of factors that judges should consider in setting bail, they give judges little guidance about how these factors should be weighted. Judges vary enormously in their bail decisions (Rhynhart 1985; Nagel 1983; Goldkamp 1984).

Disparity in bail decisions is likely to be the target of policymaking during the next decade. Consequently, the next wave of bail reform is likely to involve the creation of bail guidelines. Modeled after parole and sentencing guidelines that were developed during the 1970s, **bail guidelines** are designed to guide judicial discretion by giving judges feedback about how other judges decided similar cases in the past. The goal is to improve judicial decision making by making it more consistent and less arbitrary.

bail guidelines

Bail guidelines were introduced in Philadelphia in the 1980s. Using research that informed judges about the factors associated with bail decisions, judges developed a set of guidelines—"ballpark" ranges—that they were then expected to follow in most cases. The pretrial services agency completed worksheets on each defendant, gathering information regarding the defendant's current charge and other factors associated with FTA risk or the risk that the defendant would commit a new crime before trial. From this information judges could determine whether the guidelines suggested ROR or cash bail and, if cash bail, the amount.

Judges followed the guidelines about 75 percent of the time. The amount of cash bail required under the guidelines was lower than what was required when judges made decisions on their own. The number of defendants detained and the length of pretrial detention did not change. Rates of defendant failure to appear and rearrest were also unchanged (Goldkamp 1984). Bail guidelines did foster more consistent bail decision making, however. Consequently, bail guidelines hold promise as a means of reducing inequities in the bail process.

Some cautions about bail guidelines may be in order, however. Researchers (Lynch and Patterson 1991) studied the effects of bail guidelines in one Florida county. Florida's guidelines were substantially less detailed than those created in Philadelphia. The researchers found that guidelines alone did not completely eliminate racial bias in the bail decision. They found that racial bias sometimes was a factor in judges' decisions to deviate from the guidelines. Although judges did not require bail amounts higher than the guidelines for nonwhites any more often than for whites, they were less likely to impose bail amounts below the guidelines for nonwhite defendants.

The use of bail guidelines appears to be a promising strategy for bail reform. Bail guidelines require careful construction and monitoring of their effectiveness, however. Extremely broad guidelines may offer the symbols of reform without substantive results.

■ SUMMARY

The initial appearance takes place within a few days after arrest, providing an opportunity to inform the defendant of the charges, to make a probable cause determination as required by *Gerstein v. Pugh* (1975) and various state laws, and to determine whether and under what conditions the defendant will be released pending trial. Since the bail reform movement of the 1960s, judges have a wider array of pretrial release options available to them. Release on recognizance, signature bonds, nonmonetary conditions, pretrial supervision, and the 10 percent deposit alternative were created to reduce the role of money and bail bondsmen in determining whether a defendant is released before trial.

The purpose of any of these conditions is first to ensure the defendant's appearance at trial and second, in a limited number of cases, to prevent new crimes while the defendant awaits trial. As measured by failure to appear and rearrest rates, pretrial release decisions are generally successful. More than two-thirds of defendants are released before trial. Of those released, 75 percent return for court appearances as required and less than 20 percent are rearrested for new crimes. Defendants detained before trial may suffer greater chances of conviction and receive more severe sentences.

Concern about crime in general has contributed to efforts to consider future dangerousness in making pretrial release decisions. The Supreme Court's decision in *Salerno v. United States* (1987) has opened the door to continued use of pretrial preventive detention. The next wave of reforms is likely to focus on disparity in bail decision making and the adoption of guidelines like those developed in Philadelphia.

■ FOR FURTHER DISCUSSION

1. In *Riverside County v. McLaughlin* (1991) the dissenting justices argued that judicial determination of probable cause should be made within twenty-four hours rather than the forty-eight hours allowed by the majority opinion. The majority noted that it is not unreasonable to wait up to forty-eight hours for the probable cause determination in order to combine it with the initial appearance. The dissent argued that twenty-four hours should be ample time to complete the booking process and that it is reasonable to expect police to bring an arrestee before a magistrate within twenty-four hours, absent extraordinary circumstances.

    Both the majority and the dissent expressed disapproval of delaying the probable cause determination solely for the purpose of allowing police additional time to gather evidence supporting probable cause—whether through additional investigation or interrogation of the suspect. Why are all Supreme Court justices concerned about preventing this use of the delay between arrest and the probable cause determination? How might police abuse the delay? Is the likelihood of abuse increased if the time limit is forty-eight hours rather than twenty-four hours? Explain.

2. The options for monetary conditions on pretrial release vary widely from one jurisdiction to another, especially with respect to the operation of bail bondsmen and alternatives such as the 10 percent alternative. The options available in your community may differ from the general outline of options presented in this chapter. Find out what options are available in your jurisdiction and, if possible, the proportion of defendants released under each type of monetary condition.

3. Do you consider the FTA rates shown in Figure 11-5 to be about right or too high? If they are about right, how do you come to this conclusion? If you consider them too high, how would you propose to decrease FTA rates? Would you target your efforts? How?

4. Consider the research on the relationship of race and gender and pretrial release outcomes. In what ways do these results support or refute the hypothesis that pretrial release decisions are racist and sexist?

5. Review the statistics on crimes committed by defendants while on pretrial release. Recall that many states enacted provisions allowing judges to take dangerousness into account in pretrial release decisions. Do the statistics suggest that these new laws are effective? Do they suggest, as some researchers caution, that it is not possible to predict which defendants will be dangerous while on release?

■ REFERENCES

Austin, James, Barry Krisberg, and Paul Litsky. 1985. "The Effectiveness of Supervised Pretrial Release." *Crime and Delinquency* 31 (October): 519–37.

Bell v. Wolfish, 441 U.S. 520, 99 S.Ct. 1861 (1979).

Casper, Jonathan. 1972. *American Criminal Justice: The Defendant's Perspective.* Englewood Cliffs, N.J.: Prentice-Hall.

Daly, Kathleen. 1987. "Structure and Practice of Familial-Based Justice in a Criminal Court." *Law and Society Review* 21 (2): 265–90.

Eason, Michael J. 1988. "Eighth Amendment—Pretrial Detention: What Will Become of the Innocent?" *Journal of Criminal Law and Criminology* 78 (4): 1048–1979.

Ewing, Charles Patrick. 1985. *"Schall v. Martin:* Preventive Detention and Dangerousness Through the Looking Glass." *Buffalo Law Review* 34: 173–226.

Feeley, Malcolm. 1983. *Court Reform on Trial.* New York: Basic Books.

Feeney, Floyd. 1982. *Police and Pretrial Release.* Lexington, Mass: Lexington Books.

Gambitta, Richard A., and Barry P. Hitchings. 1983. "Bail Bond Forfeiture Enforcement— The Mechanism and the Mirage." *American Journal of Criminal Law* 11 (November): 233–92.

Gerstein v. Pugh, 420 U.S. 103, 95 S.Ct. 854 (1975).

Goldkamp, John S. 1985. "Danger and Detention: A Second Generation of Bail Reform." *Journal of Criminal Law and Criminology* 76 (1): 1–74.

———— 1984. *The Development and Implementation of Bail Guidelines: Highlights and Issues.* Washington, D.C.: U.S. Department of Justice, National Institute of Justice.

Goldkamp, John S., and Michael R. Gottfredson. 1985. *Policy Guidelines for Bail: An Experiment in Court Reform.* Philadelphia: Temple University Press.

Hagan, John, and Kristin Bumiller. 1983. "Making Sense of Sentencing: A Review and Critique of Sentencing Research." In Alfred Blumstein, Jacqueline Cohen, Susan E. Martin, and Michael H. Tonry, eds. *Research on Sentencing: The Search for Reform.* Washington, D.C.: National Academy Press.

Hansen, Keith Eric. 1987. "When Worlds Collide: The Constitutional Politics of *United States v. Salerno."* *American Journal of Criminal Law* 14 (Spring): 155–225.

Himsell, Scott D. 1986. "Preventive Detention: A Constitutional but Ineffective Means of Fighting Pretrial Crime." *Journal of Criminal Law and Criminology* 77 (Summer): 439–76.

Klaidman, Daniel. 1990. "Hustling for Bail Bonds." *Legal Times* 13 (December 10): 1, 20.

Kruttschnitt, Candace, and Donald E. Green. 1984. "The Sex-Sanctioning Issue: Is It History?" *American Sociological Review* 49 (August): 541–51.

Lazar Institute. 1981. *Pretrial Release—A National Evaluation of Practices and Outcomes: Summary and Policy Analysis.* Rockville, Md.: National Institute of Justice, National Criminal Justice Reference Service.

Lynch, Michael J., and E. Britt Patterson. 1991. *Race and Criminal Justice.* New York: Harrow and Heston.

Miller, Eleanor. 1986. *Street Woman.* Philadelphia: Temple University Press.

Moulds, Elizabeth. 1980. "Chivalry and Paternalism: Disparities of Treatment in the Criminal Justice System." In Susan K. Datesman and Frank R. Scarpitti, eds. *Women, Crime, and Justice.* New York: Oxford University Press.

Nagel, Ilene. 1983. "The Legal/Extra-Legal Controversy: Judicial Decisions in Pretrial Release." *Law and Society Review* 17 (3): 481–515.

National Institute of Justice. 1985. *Pretrial Release and Misconduct: Federal Offenses and Offenders.* Rockville, Md.: National Institute of Justice, National Criminal Justice Reference Service.

Rhynhart, F. 1985. "Judicial Discretion in Pretrial Release." In Carl F. Pinkele and William C. Louthan, eds. *Discretion, Justice, and Democracy.* Ames: Iowa State University Press.

Riverside County v. McLaughlin, 500 U.S. 44, 111 S.Ct. 1661 49 (1991).

Salerno v. United States, 481 U.S. 739, 107 S.Ct. 2095 (1987).

Schall v. Martin, 467 U.S. 253, 104 S.Ct. 2403 (1984).

Stack v. Boyle, 342 U.S. 1, 72 S.Ct. 1 (1951).

Suffet, Frederic. 1966. "Bail Setting: A Study of Courtroom Interaction." *Crime and Delinquency* 12: 318–31.

Sviridoff, Michele. 1986. "Bail Bonds and Cash Alternatives: The Influence of 'Discounts' on Bail-Making in New York City." *Justice System Journal* 11 (2): 131–226.

Toborg, Mary A. 1983. "Bail Bondsmen and Criminal Courts." *Justice System Journal* 8 (2): 141–226.

U.S. Bureau of Justice Statistics. 1994. *Pretrial Release of Felony Defendants, 1992.* Washington, D.C.: U.S. Department of Justice.

——— 1992. *Pretrial Release of Felony Defendants, 1990.* Washington, D.C.: U.S. Department of Justice.

——— 1991. *Pretrial Release of Felony Defendants, 1988.* Washington, D.C.: U.S. Department of Justice.

——— 1985. *Pretrial Release and Misconduct: Federal Offenses and Offenders.* Washington, D.C.: U.S. Department of Justice.

United States v. Daniels, 772 F.2d 382 (7th Cir. 1985).

Verrilli, Donald B., Jr. 1982. "The Eighth Amendment and the Right to Bail: Historical Perspectives." *Columbia Law Review* 82: 328–62.

Visher, Christy A. 1992. *Pretrial Drug Testing.* Washington, D.C.: U.S. Department of Justice, National Institute of Justice, Office of Justice Programs.

——— 1983. "Gender, Police Arrest Decisions, and Notions of Chivalry." *Criminology* 21: 5–28.

Walker, Samuel. 1993. *Taming the System.* New York: Oxford University Press.

Walters, Michael J. 1982. Sequential Decision-Making in the Criminal Court: The Influence of Prior Court Outcomes on Sanctioning and Their Relationship to Discrimination. Doctoral dissertation, University of Cincinnati.

Wheeler, Gerald R., and Carol L. Wheeler. 1982. "Bail Reform in the 1980s: A Response to the Critics." *Criminal Law Bulletin* 18 (May–June): 228–40.

Zatz, Marjorie. 1987. "The Changing Forms of Racial/Ethnic Bias in Sentencing." *Journal of Research in Crime and Delinquency* 24 (1): 69–92.

CHAPTER 12

THE PRETRIAL PROCESSES

Once defendants have made an initial appearance in court, criminal cases move through a series of formal and informal processes that lead to the ultimate disposition of the case. The formal processes during this period include screening for probable cause through the grand jury or preliminary hearing, hearings on pretrial motions, and formal discovery. The attorneys begin to prepare the case, a process that includes an assessment of the evidence in terms of admissibility at trial and sufficiency to prove the charges beyond a reasonable doubt. This preparation is necessary whether the case is ultimately disposed of by guilty plea or trial. Because of variations in local practices and the circumstances of any particular case, these pretrial processes go forward in no particular order. Ordinarily, discovery and disclosure of evidence begin almost immediately after arrest. Within a few days or weeks of the initial appearance the case goes to the grand jury or to a preliminary hearing. Throughout these early stages the attorneys continually assess the evidence. Pretrial motions may be filed early or late in the process; their outcome influences the attorneys' assessment of the likelihood of success at trial and their interest in plea bargaining.

ASSESSING THE EVIDENCE

Once the initial charges have been issued by the prosecutor, both attorneys turn their attention to the challenges of proving the charges in court. The first step is to assemble all available information about the case. Ideally, this would include all discoverable information from opposing counsel (police reports, witness statements, defendant statements, physical evidence, forensic test results, and so on). Additional understanding of the crime may be obtained by visiting the scene of the crime. Once attorneys have investigated the information available, they can assess that information in relation to its admissibility as evidence and its sufficiency for proving (or disproving) the charges.

Few studies have been conducted on the extent to which criminal defense attorneys actually investigate the facts. It is safe to assume wide variation in the amount of pretrial investigation, especially when such factors as the seriousness of the offense and the caseload pressures on the attorney are taken into account. Information about typical practices is largely unavailable. The information that is available comes from a series of studies (Lieberman 1981, Steiner 1981) in a single jurisdiction (Phoenix, Arizona), and may not generalize to other jurisdictions. Nonetheless, the Phoenix results give an indication of the issues that arise in relation to investigation of the facts. The researchers interviewed 173 criminal defense attorneys and asked them to describe their case preparation in four recent cases.

Researchers found that defense lawyers conduct a less thorough investigation in cases that are plea bargained rather than decided at trial (Lieberman 1981). This suggests that attorneys postpone a thorough examination until they are certain that a case is going to trial. As a consequence defense counsel engage in plea bargaining without a full understanding of the potential strengths and weaknesses of the evidence. Interestingly, the lawyers in the Phoenix study agree that investigation is just as important in plea bargaining, but in practice they do not follow their own advice. The study also found that lawyers who interview victims in cases involving violent crimes are able to obtain better plea bargains for their clients than attorneys who do not interview victims (Lieberman 1981).

Another study conducted the same year examined the information available to the defense before trial. This study found that more than 50 percent of defense attorneys wait more than three days after becoming the attorney of record to interview their clients. In virtually all cases (96.3 percent), however, defense counsel interview the defendant at least thirty days before trial. The study does not report whether a similarly high percentage interview the defendant before engaging in plea bargaining. Slightly more than half the attorneys in the study visit the scene of the crime, but fewer than a third interview all prosecution witnesses (Steiner 1981).

The attorney who does a thorough job of investigating the facts is clearly in a better position to be an advocate for the defendant. The Phoenix study concluded that attorneys appear to prepare sufficiently to avoid a finding of ineffective assistance of counsel. In other words, attorneys in Phoenix prepare enough so that their preparation was not a "sham, farce, or mockery." This is not saying much, of course. Given the lack of complete investigation of the facts in a sizable proportion of cases, many attorneys proceed to plea bargaining or trial primarily on the basis of information from the defendant and from the prosecution.

Whatever information defense counsel acquire about the case, they must assess that information in relation to its value as evidence. Roughly speaking, evidence is composed of facts, but not all facts are evidence. Only those facts that are **trial admissible** are evidence. Both the prosecutor and defense counsel analyze the available information to determine what evidence is admissible in court and to assess its strength.

Admissibility is determined by the **rules of evidence,** which govern the kinds of information that may be considered as proof in court. Some rules of evidence derive from longstanding practice under English common law. Other rules of evidence are based on the Constitution as interpreted by the courts. Yet other rules of evidence originate in special statutory provisions. For example, many states have created statutes that bar evidence about a sexual assault victim's prior sexual conduct, except under narrow circumstances. The rules of evidence that apply at the formal screening of charges often are more relaxed or permissible

trial admissible evidence

rules of evidence

than the rules of evidence that apply at trial. Where this is the case, the prosecutor's initial charges may be based on information that cannot be admitted at trial.

An intricate body of rules has evolved to provide guidelines concerning when and for what purpose evidence may be considered. The rules of evidence are designed to ensure that the only evidence admitted in court is that which is relevant, trustworthy, and reliable and does not jeopardize the fairness of the process. The concern with promoting fairness and reliability is greatest at trial. This is why trial rules of evidence tend to be more strict than those at other stages of the court process, such as pretrial screens, hearings on pretrial motions, and sentencing.

Counsel (referring to both prosecutor and defense counsel) assess the evidence in light of these rules. The only "real" facts of the case are those facts that can be submitted at trial under the rules of evidence. The results of a polygraph test may convince the prosecutor that the defendant is truly guilty, but that information is not useful in court if the rules of evidence make polygraph results inadmissible. Instead the prosecutor must find trial-admissible evidence to convince the judge or jury. In addition, the attorneys must consider the strength of the evidence that will be admitted. Some evidence is highly credible and highly relevant, whereas other evidence is legally admissible but is not much help in proving the facts needed to convict.

evidence advocacy

Counsel engage in evidence advocacy to shape the evidence that will be admitted at trial (Goldberg 1982, 361). **Evidence advocacy** involves using the rules of evidence to get harmful evidence excluded and helpful evidence admitted at trial. The primary means of attaining these rulings is through pretrial motions, described toward the end of this chapter. The rulings on these motions can make the difference between winning or losing. In other situations rulings on admissibility must wait until trial. Whether conducted before trial or during trial, the goal of evidence advocacy is to shape the evidence that is placed in the record.

General Principles of Admissibility

material evidence, probative evidence

The threshold issue in determining the admissibility of evidence is relevance. Relevance is determined in relation to materiality and probity of the evidence in question. Evidence is **material** if it relates to what must be proved. Evidence is **probative** if it can establish, at least in part, the truthfulness of an allegation. If the evidence is being used to prove a point that is material to the case, and if the evidence offered can establish that point, the evidence is probably relevant (Waltz 1975, 50–51).

Again, evidence is material if it relates to what must be proved. Materiality does not depend solely on the elements of the offense, however. As a case unfolds, it may be necessary to prove other facts in order to make a case for or against the defendant. Consider, for example, a doctor who is charged with filing a fraudulent Medicaid claim—billing the government for medical services that the doctor did not actually provide. Essentially, the doctor is accused of lying on the claim form. Several witnesses may be available who are willing to testify that the doctor frequently lied in a variety of circumstances—about his golf score, about his availability for social engagements, about his faithfulness to his wife, and so on. This testimony would not be admissible to prove the charge of fraud, even though fraud involves lying. A habit of lying is not directly related—is not material—to the elements that must be established to prove Medicaid fraud.

If, however, the doctor takes the witness stand during the trial and denies the fraud, the prosecution could use his reputation as a liar to undermine the doctor's credibility as a witness. In general, this means that a defendant's character is considered immaterial as proof of a crime, but the character of a witness is material to that witness's credibility.

Probity is related to the issue of reliability. Evidence is probative if it is capable of establishing the truthfulness of an allegation. Unreliable evidence cannot establish the truthfulness of a claim. Evidence that is highly unreliable may be excluded entirely because it is not sufficiently probative. Some kinds of scientific evidence, like polygraph results, may be excluded because they are unreliable; therefore they do not offer probative evidence. Testimonial evidence can also be excluded for lack of probity. Circumstantial evidence is less probative than direct evidence, in which the witness directly observed the criminal act. At trial, the judge decides whether particular evidence is sufficiently probative to be admitted. During pretrial preparation by the attorneys, each side assesses the likelihood that the evidence will be admitted by the judge.

Admissibility of Scientific Evidence

Reliability is a major concern in the introduction of scientific evidence, such as fingerprint analysis, ballistics analysis, voice prints, handwriting analysis, polygraph analysis, and DNA identification. Because probity is considered a matter of degree, the judge must decide whether the evidence is sufficiently probative to improve the reliability of the fact-finding process. For some types of scientific evidence, such as fingerprints, the technology is widely accepted and is not decided for each case coming before the court. Whenever a new kind of scientific analysis is used, however, the trial judge must decide whether to admit the results of this new test into evidence.

For example, DNA identification techniques have been developed in recent years. DNA identification involves analyzing samples, usually of blood or semen, to determine whether the genetic material in the sample from the defendant matches the DNA recovered from the scene of the crime. DNA techniques are still controversial, and some courts continue to question the reliability of DNA identification. The determination of reliability, and therefore probity, depends in part on the techniques used in the lab conducting the test. Reliability also depends in part on the purposes for which the test is being used. Specifically, the reliability of DNA identification is more questionable when used by the prosecution to prove that the defendant is guilty than when used by the defense to prove the defendant is not guilty.

DNA analysis involves analyzing samples of blood, hair, or semen for specific genetic patterns that have a known probability in the population. This analysis results in a finding about how rare a particular DNA pattern is. If the pattern is sufficiently rare, and if the sample from the crime scene and the sample taken later from the accused match, the implication is that the DNA recovered from the crime scene also came from the accused.

For example, the DNA analysis may reveal that only 1 in 100 million individuals has the DNA pattern found in the two samples. If the crime took place in a city of 7 million that receives 20 million visitors each year, the DNA evidence is only partially probative (able to prove that the defendant is the one who left the blood at the scene). Somewhere in the country may be another person with the same DNA pattern, and that person could be the one who committed the crime and left the DNA sample at the scene. Although DNA is important circumstantial evidence, it cannot directly prove that the defendant left the blood, semen, or tissue sample at the scene. If the DNA does not match, however, that evidence is highly probative in relation to the defendant's claim of innocence. Unless the prosecution can show that the test was done improperly and that the results are therefore invalid, the lack of a match is direct evidence that the defendant was not the source of the DNA sample found at the scene.

The probity of DNA evidence can be compared to testimonial evidence relating to the identification of a getaway car. Consider the testimony of a witness who states that the getaway car was a blue sedan with a license plate number beginning with the letter *H*. If 5,000 cars match that description, the testimony of the witness who saw the car is only partially probative for proving that the defendant's blue sedan with license plate number HJ-4235 was the car seen leaving the crime. The car the witness saw could have been any of the other 4,999 automobiles that matched the description. If the defendant's car is a blue sedan with license plate number SB-1899, the witness's testimony is highly probative in proving that the defendant's car was not involved in the crime.

In fact, much identification evidence—anything short of a positive identification of the defendant as the alleged criminal—poses the same problem as DNA analysis in relation to probity. For example, if a witness testifies that the assailant had a mustache or walked with a limp, the defendant may also have that feature but certainly is not the only person who possesses the characteristic. However, DNA evidence is considered much more probative than this sort of testimonial evidence.

If the testimony of a witness may be admitted, even though it is only partially probative, why would DNA evidence be excluded? The problem with DNA evidence is that it is potentially prejudicial. Courts have been concerned that juries will give DNA evidence undue weight because it is "scientific," even though it is not completely reliable in making a positive identification. Jurors may not understand that the DNA patterns used to make these identifications are not unique markers. This scientific aura may cause jurors to overlook the limitations of the technology in proving who could have left DNA samples at the scene.

Ironically, DNA analyses have also demonstrated the unreliability of eyewitness identifications. Several prisoners have obtained release after DNA tests proved conclusively that they could not have been the assailant. The convictions of these prisoners originally had been based on the victim's positive identification.

Hearsay

Hearsay is a type of evidence that is considered so generally unreliable that a whole set of evidentiary rules relates just to hearsay. Hearsay is secondhand testimony. Susan Carlisle tells Jane Dickson that she was robbed by a man wearing a blue jogging suit. If Carlisle later refuses to testify, the prosecution may not substitute the secondhand testimony of Dickson as to what Carlisle saw. Because her only knowledge of the crime and the description of the assailant are hearsay, they are inadmissible at trial. Dickson can testify only about what she observed personally.

Hearsay is the subject of many exceptions, however. One common exception is the excited utterance. Suppose Carlisle ran out of her house, grabbed Dickson as she was getting out of her car, and screamed, "I've been robbed!" In this situation Dickson would be allowed to testify to what Carlisle said to her because it is an **excited utterance.** Excited utterances are thought to be more probative than statements made thoughtfully at a later time.

excited utterance

Another exception to the hearsay rule is the declaration of a dying person. Suppose, for example, that Peter Wilson is dying and tells the nurse at the hospital that he killed his wife. The police had previously arrested a local troublemaker who had been walking in the neighborhood shortly after Wilson reported his wife's death. The prosecutor's theory was that the troublemaker had broken into the Wilson home to commit a burglary, was caught in the act by Rita Wilson, and hit her over the head with a fireplace poker. If the dying confession of Peter Wilson was insufficient on its own to cause the prosecutor to dismiss the charges against the other man, the defense could call the nurse to testify at trial regarding Wilson's dying confession. Because Wilson is dead, the nurse's hearsay testimony is the only testimony available. Because Wilson was unlikely to lie as he lay dying, the law allows such statements to be admitted in court.

Another exception to the hearsay rule involves the spontaneous admissions of a defendant. If Helen Snyder tells her friend Otto Cobb that she beat her child, and Snyder later is tried for child abuse, Cobb's testimony regarding Snyder's admission of child abuse is admissible. Again, although the testimony about the abuse is secondhand, the law allows it. Snyder's confession to Cobb is likely to be truthful, because people are rarely motivated to admit to crimes they did not commit.

Exclusions of Evidence to Protect Other Rights

The exclusion of evidence because it is irrelevant, immaterial, or unreliable constitutes a large portion of the law of evidence. Other rules of evidence are less concerned with truthfulness and reliability and more concerned with maintaining the overall fairness and reliability of the criminal justice process.

One example is evidence that is so inflammatory or prejudicial to the defendant that it cannot be admitted, even though it is material and probative. In fact, sometimes the most probative evidence is excluded because it is so potentially prejudicial. For example, pictures of homicide victims are commonly excluded as prejudicial and inflammatory. The court fears that the jury's sympathies might be so inflamed by the shocking pictures of the deceased that it will be unable to give the defendant a fair trial. Moreover, only rarely would pictures of the deceased offer information that could not be submitted through testimonial evidence of the medical examiner or the investigating officers. Demonstrations are also frequently excluded. For example, to show that the defendant could not have had time to fire all the shots, the defense might want to have a demonstration in court to show how long it takes to reload the gun alleged to be the murder weapon. Although popular in TV court dramas, demonstrations are often not allowed in real trials because the demonstration may impress the jury in a way that goes beyond the probative value of the evidence (Goldberg 1982). For similar reasons the introduction of evidence that disrupts the regularity of the court proceedings, such as visiting the scene of the crime, is often ruled inadmissible.

Evidence obtained in violation of the defendant's rights is also not admissible at trial. The Supreme Court has ruled that evidence obtained as a result of an illegal search or interrogation, for example, must be excluded. Again, although such evidence may be both material and probative, the law excludes it in order to protect other values, in this case the integrity of police and judicial procedures. Some evidence may be excluded in order to protect a relationship when society has an interest in protecting such relationships in general. For example, communications between a husband and wife, attorney and client, and physician and

privileged   patient are examples of **privileged communications,** although the privilege
communications   can be waived by consent (Ferguson and Stokke 1978, 52–55).

Assessing the Strength of the Evidence

Evidence that is admissible is not necessarily sufficient to meet the standard of
evidence. In addition to assessing the admissibility of evidence the attorneys need
to assess the strength of the evidence in order to predict the likelihood of
conviction or acquittal. In deciding whether to issue charges and what charges to
issue the prosecutor assesses the credibility of the witnesses and the strength of
physical and scientific evidence that supports the charges (see Chapter 9).
Initially, the prosecutor's main concern may be whether the evidence can
establish probable cause in the formal screening process. However, even early in
the process the prosecutor will be anticipating the strength of the evidence in
relation to the standard of evidence at trial: proof beyond a reasonable doubt. As
the case progresses, both attorneys continue to assess the strength of the
evidence, particularly the reliability of scientific evidence and the credibility of
testimonial evidence offered by witnesses. These assessments can be critical in
shaping plea negotiations and the overall strategy in the case.

■ FORMAL PRETRIAL SCREENS OF EVIDENCE: THE GRAND JURY AND PRELIMINARY HEARING

After arrest and the initial appearance many cases are subjected to a formal screen
of the evidence. Unless waived, all felony cases are formally screened, through
either a grand jury or a preliminary hearing and sometimes through both.
Misdemeanors may be screened by a grand jury or a preliminary hearing but often
are not screened at all after the initial appearance.

    The purpose of the formal pretrial screen is to test the evidence to determine
that prosecution is warranted. Nominally, the standard of proof required for the
pretrial screen is the same at both the grand jury and preliminary hearing reviews:
probable cause. Probable cause is an indistinct standard, subject to varying
interpretations and applications. Because of the differing procedures governing
the grand jury and preliminary hearing, probable cause undoubtedly has a
different meaning and application in the two types of reviews. In addition,
jurisdictions vary with respect to the rigor of the review undertaken.

Standard of Evidence: Probable Cause

Probable cause has been defined in different ways in different jurisdictions. The
practical meaning of the probable cause standard at the pretrial screen varies
between jurisdictions and even between courts within a jurisdiction (Kamisar,
LaFave, and Israel 1986, 952). In some jurisdictions the standard is interpreted as
nothing more than a strong suspicion. In others probable cause is met only if
there is evidence that, if unexplained or uncontradicted, would warrant conviction of the defendant. Judges sometimes explain the standard in other terms, such
as the balance of the evidence being more than fifty-fifty in favor of probable
guilt. Most simply defined, probable cause is established whenever "evidence
which, when viewed by a person of reasonable caution, in light of the person's

training and experience, would permit the person to conclude that a fact probably exists" (Subin, Mirsky, and Weinstein 1993, 11).

Although the arrest standard is also probable cause, it is widely acknowledged that the probable cause standard applied at the grand jury or preliminary hearing is a higher standard of evidence. There are two important differences. First, probable cause for arrest is concerned merely with the question of whether the officer at the moment of the arrest is justified in making the arrest. That is, is there sufficient evidence to justify a brief infringement of the person's liberty? In contrast, the grand jury and preliminary hearing reviews are forward looking, assessing the evidence used to justify putting the defendant through the substantial and long-term burdens of a criminal prosecution. Second, by the time the grand jury or magistrate at a preliminary hearing reviews the evidence, a few days and sometimes weeks have passed since arrest. In that period, the prosecutor has contacted and interviewed witnesses, experts have examined physical evidence, and the statements of some witnesses may have been corroborated by scientific tests of physical evidence. Given these different circumstances, the demand of a bit more to meet probable cause at the pretrial screen is understandable.

Although both the grand jury and the preliminary hearing use the probable cause standard, these procedures arose from different historical contexts and offer strikingly different procedures for accomplishing the same result. Given these differences, a question that continues to haunt would-be reformers is whether one procedure is better than the other.

The Grand Jury

The modern grand jury evolved from the English grand jury of the twelfth century (see Chapter 4 for a discussion of the development of the grand jury). In its early days the grand jury operated primarily as a tool for identifying citizens who might be guilty of wrongdoing. This investigative function of the grand jury reflects the original use of the grand jury for uncovering crime. Over the centuries grand juries acquired a second function, operating as a shield to protect citizens from unfair criminal accusations by the government. These dual functions earned the grand jury the reputation of being both a sword and a shield.

By the time the colonies separated from England, grand juries in both America and Britain had become established as bodies quite independent of the government. Grand juries occasionally refused to indict citizens whom the government wanted to prosecute. Because of the grand jury's independence and power it acted as a shield, or buffer, between the government and citizen. Between the individual and the government stood the grand jury, representing the fair judgment of twenty-three good and common citizens:

> Historically, this body [the grand jury] has been regarded as a primary security to the innocent against hasty, malicious and oppressive persecution; it serves the invaluable function in our society of standing between the accuser and the accused, whether the latter be an individual, minority group, or other, to determine whether a charge is founded upon reasons or was dictated by an intimidating power or by malice and personal ill will. (*Wood v. Georgia,* 1962, 390)

When the federal and early state constitutions were drafted, the grand jury was viewed as an important protection from government persecution. The Fifth Amendment to the U. S. Constitution prohibits prosecution of infamous crimes, known today as felonies, unless a grand jury returns an indictment. This portion

FIGURE 12-1   States Requiring Grand Jury Indictments

SOURCE: Sigmund G. Popko. 1987. "Arizona's County Grand Jury: The Empty Promise of Independence." *Arizona Law Review* 29: 667–88.

States	Capital Crimes (only)	Felonies	Misdemeanors
Alabama		X	
Alaska		X	
Delaware		X	
Florida	X		
Kentucky		X	
Louisiana	X		
Maine		X	
Massachusetts		X	
Mississippi		X	
New Hampshire		X	
New Jersey		X	X
New York		X	
North Carolina		X	
Ohio		X	
Rhode Island	X		
South Carolina		X	X
Tennessee		X	X
Texas		X	
West Virginia		X	X

of the Fifth Amendment has never been imposed on the states and is considered applicable only to the federal jurisdiction. Several states, referred to as grand jury states, adopted their own constitutional requirement that felonies be indicted by a grand jury. Today sixteen states (see Figure 12-1), primarily in the eastern half of the country, and the federal jurisdiction require grand jury approval of all felony prosecutions. Some of those states also require grand jury indictments in misdemeanors. Another three states require grand jury approval only in prosecutions of capital crimes (Popko 1987, 674–75). All other states have provisions for grand juries but use them only when a special investigation is needed and do not require their routine involvement in prosecutions.

Structure and Process in the Grand Jury

The grand jury is something of a paradox in the adversarial system of criminal adjudication. Unlike most other formal proceedings in the criminal process, the grand jury is not an adversarial procedure. The nonadversarial procedures of the grand jury are best understood in the context of its earliest historical roots. Traditionally, the grand jury was used to identify criminals. No defendant was officially identified prior to the grand jury proceeding. An individual became a defendant as a *result* of a grand jury decision, not before the grand jury considered the evidence. Because there was no named defendant during the grand jury proceeding, no one acted as the state's adversary. This tradition persists with few changes.

Traditionally, grand juries were composed of twenty-three reputable members of the community. Today the size of the grand jury varies, because jurisdictions have sought to reduce costs by reducing the number of jurors. In urban jurisdictions grand juries are convened on a regular basis, allowing cases to proceed to the grand jury without delay. The grand jurors are required to serve for a set period of time. A typical term is three months, but jurisdictions vary considerably in the amount of business the grand juries must conduct. The busier the grand jury, the shorter the term the jurors must serve. In some jurisdictions the grand jury meets daily to review the evidence in support of felony charges; in other jurisdictions, where the volume of cases is less, the grand jury is in session only once or twice each month.

The grand jurors conduct business in secret and consider evidence presented to it by the government, represented by the prosecutor. The grand jury is free to call anyone within its jurisdiction as a witness. The court that convenes the grand jury can compel witnesses to testify or to produce documents or other objects. Testimony before the grand jury is taken under oath. Hearsay and other evidence generally inadmissible in a court of law can be considered by the grand jury (*Costello v. United States* 1956). Witnesses before the grand jury have a right to refuse to answer questions that might be self-incriminating, but the exclusionary rule does not apply; that is, any statement obtained outside the grand jury in violation of the Fifth Amendment protection may be presented to the grand jurors and serve as the basis for the indictment (*United States v. Calandra* 1974).

People who appear before the grand jury to give testimony are witnesses. Although some witnesses may be suspected of wrongdoing, they are nonetheless only witnesses. Because there is no defendant, the rights of the accused do not apply in the grand jury context. Grand jury witnesses, even if they are the target of the investigation, do not have a right to cross-examine and confront other witnesses, do not have a right to be present at the grand jury proceedings, and do not have a right to offer a statement or witnesses of their own. In addition, waiver of a grand jury hearing is impossible in many jurisdictions. Traditionally, grand jury witnesses are not permitted to have counsel with them at the grand jury hearing. The U.S. Supreme Court has held that witnesses before a grand jury have no constitutional right to counsel, even if the witness is the target of the investigation (*United States v. Mandujano* 1976). In recent years, however, several states have changed their laws to allow grand jury witnesses to be accompanied by counsel, and the consensus is that the presence of counsel has not interfered with the grand jury's ability to conduct its business (Bayless 1981, 571).

Once it collects or has heard sufficient evidence, the grand jury votes to determine whether the evidence is sufficient to justify a formal accusation. If a majority of the grand jurors find that the evidence is sufficient, they return an **indictment,** also known as a **true bill.** This decision by the grand jury binds the defendant over for trial and authorizes the prosecutor to proceed with the prosecution. If the grand jury finds no true bill, the case is not necessarily closed. The prosecutor is free in most jurisdictions to try again to get an indictment before a new grand jury.

indictment, true bill

Functions of the Grand Jury: Investigation and Charging

The original function of the grand jury as an investigative body has diminished but continues to be an important use in special kinds of cases. Today, however, most grand juries are summoned to fulfill the pretrial screening function. A defendant has been identified and an investigation completed; the prosecutor presents evidence to the grand jurors. These functions are discussed separately here because a grand jury that is convened as a charging grand jury will not generally be involved in the investigation of crimes. An investigative grand jury both investigates and issues indictments against any criminals it finds in the course of its investigation.

Investigative Grand Juries

When the U. S. Constitution was adopted, the grand jury's investigative function played a more central role in the processing of routine cases than it does today. Municipal police departments staffed by trained detectives did not exist. Instead the grand jury gathered evidence to determine whether a crime had occurred and who should be charged in connection with it.

Today the investigative function of the grand jury is exercised infrequently. In routine cases the grand jury need not conduct an investigation because law enforcement agents have already investigated by the time the grand jury considers the evidence. For some types of criminal activity, however, the investigative grand jury is valuable in obtaining information.

Although it is used only rarely for investigative purposes, the grand jury is a powerful tool when other means of investigating crimes are not suitable. Grand juries typically investigate complex organized crime, government wrongdoing, corruption in government agencies, and other crimes that are difficult to investigate through normal means available to the police. In some states the grand jury is limited by law to investigating matters that affect the whole community, such as government corruption (Schimizzi 1980). The grand jury is not available to the prosecutor who runs into a snag in the investigation after formal charges have been issued.

Because the grand jury is independent of any branch of government, it is free to investigate without regard to pressure or retaliation from superiors or from the electorate. Even the prosecutor who requests that an investigative grand jury be convened cannot control the grand jury if the jurors resist. This independence can take the investigation in a direction not anticipated by the prosecutor. These grand juries, known as runaway grand juries, are exceedingly rare but symbolize the importance of the investigative grand jury's independence.

In most cases, however, the grand jury operates in cooperation with and under the guidance of the prosecutor. Laws in some jurisdictions give the prosecutor the right to be present at grand jury proceedings, to name witnesses that the grand jury must call, and to serve as legal adviser to the grand jury. When an investigative grand jury is convened, the prosecutor most often is seeking the special powers associated with the grand jury, not the advice or interference of laypeople.

*compulsory
process*

contempt

These special powers relate to the grand jury's power to compel testimony and the production of physical and documentary evidence, known as **compulsory process.** This is a power reserved for the courts, and the court lends its power to the grand jury. If a person refuses to comply with the grand jury's subpoena, a judge may find the person in **contempt** of the grand jury and detain the person in jail (see discussion of contempt in Chapter 6). Similarly, a person who appears but refuses to answer questions or to produce documents requested by the grand jury may be jailed for contempt. Police and prosecutors do not have such power. Anyone is free to refuse to answer questions when being interrogated by the police or prosecutor. The witness before a grand jury cannot merely refuse to cooperate. Unless the witness can point to a legally protected privilege, the witness must answer. One such privilege is the Fifth Amendment right against self-incrimination.

The Fifth Amendment guarantees that no person "shall be compelled . . . to be a witness against himself." Under the Fifth Amendment even the grand jury cannot force someone to provide information that would be self-incriminating. But the Fifth Amendment applies only if the information could be used to prosecute the witness. Witnesses may be reluctant to testify against friends or family members, but the Fifth Amendment privilege offers no protection under these circumstances. Testifying about other people's crimes is not *self-incrimination.*

immunity from prosecution

When a grand jury witness invokes the Fifth Amendment protection and refuses to answer a question, the grand jury may decide to offer the defendant **immunity from prosecution.** Immunity is a promise by the government that any self-incriminating evidence offered under the immunity grant will not be admissible in court in a prosecution of the witness who received immunity. So long as the information will not be used to prosecute the witness, the protection provided in the Fifth Amendment has been honored, and the witness is compelled by law to respond to the grand jury's questions. Today the most common form of immunity is called **use and derivative use immunity.** This form of immunity guarantees that neither the information provided in the answer nor any additional evidence developed (or derived) from that answer will be used to prosecute the witness. For example, if the witness's testimony leads the grand jury to call another witness, and that witness further incriminates the witness who received immunity, the additional evidence is also inadmissible in court because it is covered by the grant of immunity. The witness who is granted immunity may still be indicted and tried for the crimes to which the witness testified, but the evidence in support of the indictment and conviction must be developed entirely independently of the information provided by the witness.

use and derivative use immunity

Once granted immunity, the witness who refuses to testify may be cited for contempt of the grand jury. A witness sometimes would rather go to jail for contempt than answer the questions. Reporters have sometimes been jailed for contempt when they have refused to reveal their sources. Individuals involved in organized crime are often more fearful of retaliation than they are of going to jail for contempt.

When an investigative grand jury has completed its investigation, it may issue criminal charges. Thus the investigative grand jury both investigates and conducts the formal screen for probable cause.

The Charging Grand Jury: Effectiveness of the Screening Function

Almost all cases reviewed by a grand jury today involve an individual who has already been arrested, taken into custody, accused as an offender in a criminal complaint, and had an initial appearance before a judge. The grand jury review sometimes precedes the arrest, but a suspect has been clearly identified by the prosecutor before going to the grand jury. Practically speaking, then, a defendant already exists in most cases presented to the grand jury. In such cases the grand jury does not exercise its investigative powers; it functions merely as a **charging grand jury.** The distinction between a charging grand jury and an investigative grand jury is not a legal one but simply a description of the kind of business a grand jury is conducting.

charging grand jury

When a prosecutor presents a routine case to the grand jury for review, the aim is to present enough evidence to convince the grand jurors that probable cause exists and to accomplish this as quickly and with as little trouble as possible. The prosecutor sometimes is the only "witness" to appear before the grand jury.

Because hearsay is admissible before the grand jury in many jurisdictions, the prosecutor merely testifies about information reported to her by police investigators and other witnesses. The prosecutor may stand before the grand jury and read the criminal complaint, perhaps supplemented by other notes on the case. This is a quick and inexpensive way to satisfy the requirement of presenting the case to a grand jury. It saves the time and trouble of requiring the presence of police officers or citizen witnesses. David Heilbroner, a former Manhattan prosecutor, reports that assistant district attorneys were instructed, "If your case is typical, keep it short. Besides, witnesses' memories invariably change over time, and the less a person says on the record, the harder it is to impeach him with trivial inconsistencies later on. . . . So try to get it over within fifteen minutes" (1990, 199). Describing a typical grand jury hearing for a robbery, Heilbroner notes that for a second-degree robbery charge he called two witnesses and instructed the grand jury on the robbery statute. The grand jurors asked no questions. In a mere thirty seconds the grand jurors deliberated and returned a true bill. The whole process had taken less than fifteen minutes (Heilbroner 1990, 207–8).

This rapid and seemingly perfunctory review of the evidence has caused some critics to call the grand jury process a rubber stamp for the prosecutor. With the prosecutor controlling the evidence the grand jury hears, and with the deliberation taking only seconds to complete, the grand jury does not seem to offer any real independent review of the evidence. Because the grand jury often does not provide an independent screening function, it has been criticized as a waste of taxpayers' money (Blank 1993; Cantwell 1989; Wachtler 1990).

Grand Jury Reform

Because of such criticisms the grand jury has been the target of reform in many states in recent decades. Some reforms are aimed at streamlining the process and making the system less costly. Others are designed to ensure that the grand jury serves as more than a mere rubber stamp for the prosecutor.

To reduce the costs associated with the grand jury some jurisdictions now allow the defendant to waive the grand jury hearing (Kamisar et al. 1986, 976). Defendants are willing to waive because they often have nothing to gain from the grand jury review. This reduces the caseload of the grand jury and the number of grand jury sessions needed to process the caseload. Another reform has been to reduce the size of the grand jury. Grand juries of sixteen and twelve members are no longer uncommon, and smaller grand juries have been suggested (Sullivan and Nackman 1984, 1068).

Many lawyers, judges, and legal scholars have supported reform of the grand jury to enhance its independence of the prosecutor and the rigor of its screening function. The American Bar Association has endorsed reform proposals that would make significant changes in the grand jury process. Some states have adopted at least some reforms, including

1. Granting the target of the grand jury hearing the right to testify
2. Forbidding the use of evidence that is constitutionally inadmissible at trial
3. Severely limiting the use of hearsay evidence
4. Allowing the review of the grand jury transcript by a neutral magistrate for a review of procedural correctness
5. Requiring the prosecutor to present all exculpatory evidence known to the state at that time. (Aranella 1980, 1981; New Jersey Law Journal 1986)

SITTING AMONG THE JUDGERS

I was a grand juror, condemned to sit on a hard chair in a stuffy room with 22 other good citizens while cops spoke of "perps" and "buy and busts" and assistant district attorneys too untried to dare paraphrase tangled themselves in clauses and "Did there come a time when you . . ."

During the testimony we were all business. Indicting drug dealers was our game, and we did. By the dozen, I think.

In they came and out they went, the attorneys in suits that were the sartorial equivalent of starter homes (unless they were female, in which case they were sober in skirts and blouses) and the officers with their shields slung around their necks and their jeans clinging to their every inch.

Not for them the blow-dries and close shaves of the legal profession. These were cavaliers, with hair that curled around their collars or rose in Grace Jones skyscrapers, and upper lips scrolled with mustaches. Most of them worked undercover. . . .

And their language! Their language was as colorful as their coiffures, their facial foliage and their wardrobes.

They'd bought "controlled substances" like "Public Enemy," "Murder," "Extra Power," "Brainbuster," "Obsession," and "Miami Vice," brand names for heroin, from people they called "J.D. Blue Shoes" and "J.D. Suede Jacket" and "J.D. Female Voice."

A backup was a "ghost," a transaction a "set." When they wanted to make a buy, they said "Who's working?"

We sat there on our hard chairs, we 23 good citizens, raising our hands as regularly as automatons.

Indict, indict, indict. "Alleged crack cocaine" was indeed crack cocaine; "alleged heroin" was indeed heroin: The police lab said so. Five dollars for crack, 10 bucks for heroin, and here a vial, there a vial, everywhere a vial. . . .

That's what happens when you sit on a hard chair in a stuffy room day after day hearing about the two pounds of cocaine somebody was toting through Penn Station in a shopping bag, and the two vials of "Redcaps" some office worker bought on her lunch hour, and the 12-year-old up at the north end of town who's a conduit for "Miami Vice."

Indict, indict, indict.

"This is a waste of time," a fellow juror said during a corridor prowl. . . .

SOURCE: Excerpted from Mary Cantwell. © 1989, Daily Journal Corp. "Sitting Among the Judgers and Not the Judged, Purely by Chance." *Los Angeles Daily Journal*, May 10, p. 6.

Some jurisdictions allow the defendant and other witnesses to be represented by counsel before the grand jury.

These proposed changes, although few, are sweeping. For example, although the proposed reforms would not absolutely exclude hearsay evidence, the prosecutor would have the responsibility to present the best readily available evidence. This makes the grand jury more cumbersome and changes the nature of the grand jury deliberation. If the grand jurors receive information directly from the victim or even the arresting officer instead of receiving a summary of the evidence from the prosecutor, the credibility of the witness becomes an additional factor for the grand jurors to consider. Clearly, these reforms provide a better opportunity for grand jurors to weigh evidence.

Some states have required the prosecutor to inform the grand jury of evidence that is substantially exculpatory. Nonetheless, the U.S. Supreme Court has held that such disclosure is not required by due process. In *United States v. Williams* (1992) a bare majority of the justices held that a prosecutor in a federal case is under no obligation to inform the grand jurors of evidence that is substantially exculpatory. The decision was based on the notion that the grand jury is designed to determine whether the basis for bringing a criminal charge is adequate, not to determine guilt or innocence. The Court reasoned that if the prosecutor is required to present exculpatory evidence, the role of the grand jury would shift toward judging guilt rather than probable cause (*United States v. Williams* 1992, 1744). It remains unclear whether the states will continue to move toward disclosure of exculpatory evidence in light of *Williams*. Certainly, if a jurisdiction seeks to have the grand jury screen out cases that do not warrant prosecution, disclosure of exculpatory evidence would be a sensible policy.

The Preliminary Hearing

The alternative process for formally screening evidence before trial is the preliminary hearing. The preliminary hearing predominates in the United States. The purpose of a preliminary hearing is to "prevent hasty, malicious, improvident, and oppressive prosecutions, to protect the person charged from open and public accusations of crime, to avoid both for the defendant and the public the expense of a public prosecution, and to discover whether or not there are substantial grounds upon which a prosecution may be based" (*Thies v. State* 1922, 103). In short, the purpose of the preliminary hearing is the same as the purpose of the grand jury. Because of its structure the preliminary hearing serves additional informal functions in the criminal court process.

Despite the grand jury's deep historical roots, by the middle of the nineteenth century the prevailing opinion in the United States was that the grand jury was too awkward and ineffective for routine use. In 1859 Michigan became the first jurisdiction to provide an alternative to indictment by grand jury by allowing the charges to be reviewed at a preliminary hearing. Other jurisdictions quickly echoed Michigan's change, and the prevailing pattern today is to use the preliminary hearing rather than the grand jury. Jurisdictions that use the information as the primary charging instrument are known as **information jurisdictions.**

information jurisdictions

Information is the name given to the formal charging document prepared by the prosecutor to accompany the case to court for prosecution. The information is based on the criminal complaint, the sworn statement of the complaining witness. The information names the crimes alleged, the suspect, and the potential penalty, and it refers to the criminal complaint as a supporting document. The prosecutor presents the information to the court at a preliminary hearing or preliminary examination. For purposes of accusation the information is the equivalent of an indictment, the document issued by the grand jury. Both the information and the indictment are formal charging documents in a criminal case.

The constitutionality of the preliminary hearing as a screening device equivalent to the grand jury was considered and approved by the Supreme Court in *Hurtado v. California* (1884), a position it reaffirmed in several subsequent cases. In *Hurtado* the Court reasoned that fairness of the process, rather than the exact style of the process, is the overriding concern. The Court concluded that a defendant is treated no less fairly if the evidence is screened by a judge than if the evidence is screened by a group of laypersons. Although the two hearings serve the same purpose and are considered legal equivalents, there are important differences in the way they work. Today many observers believe that the preliminary hearing is more protective of the defendant than the grand jury (Kamisar et al. 1986).

PRELIMINARY HEARING IS A CRITICAL STAGE

In its decision in *Coleman v. Alabama* (1970) the Supreme Court explained why the preliminary hearing is a critical stage in the prosecution of a criminal defendant. According to the Court, important trial rights are at stake at the preliminary hearing. To protect these rights a defendant needs to have the assistance of counsel:

Plainly the guiding hand of counsel at the preliminary hearing is essential to protect the indigent accused against an erroneous or improper prosecution. First, the lawyer's skilled examination of witnesses may expose fatal weaknesses in the State's case that may lead the magistrate to refuse to bind the accused over. Second, in any event, the skilled interrogation of witnesses by an experienced lawyer can fashion a vital impeachment tool for use in cross-examination of the State's witnesses at trial, or preserve testimony favorable to the accused of a witness who does not appear at the trial. Third, trained counsel can more effectively discover the case the State has against his client and make possible the preparation of a proper defense to meet that case at the trial. Fourth, counsel can also be influential at the preliminary hearing in making effective arguments for the accused on such matters as the necessity for an early psychiatric examination or bail. (*Coleman v. Alabama*, 399 U.S. 1, 8 (1970)

Procedural Rules Governing the Preliminary Hearing

In stark contrast to the grand jury, the preliminary hearing is an adversarial proceeding, open to the public and held before a judge (or magistrate), who is the sole decision maker. The prosecutor presents evidence for the judge to consider. The prosecutor does not have to present all the evidence against the defendant at this point but must reveal enough to convince the judge to find probable cause. The defense may cross-examine and present evidence of its own. All testimony is taken under oath. A verbatim record is made, so that a transcript of the hearing can be produced if it is needed at a later time. If, after hearing all the evidence presented, the judge is convinced that probable cause exists, the judge binds the defendant over for trial. If the evidence is not sufficient, the judge dismisses the case for lack of probable cause.

Because it is designed as an adversarial hearing, the defendant enjoys important rights at a preliminary hearing. The defendant has a right to be present to hear the accusation and the supporting evidence. Furthermore, the defendant has a right to be represented by counsel. The U.S. Supreme Court held that the preliminary hearing is a critical stage in the prosecution. Consequently, the Court held that due process requires that the defendant have a right to an attorney at the preliminary hearing and that indigent defendants have the right to a free attorney (*Coleman v. Alabama* 1970). The preliminary hearing is a critical stage because what happens at the preliminary hearing can affect the defendant's rights at trial.

Variations in Practice

At the preliminary hearing many jurisdictions allow the introduction of evidence that would be inadmissible at trial. In most cases the preliminary hearing is held before the court has ruled on motions that challenge and seek to suppress evidence. Similarly, in some jurisdictions the credibility of the prosecution's witnesses cannot be explored at the preliminary hearing. For example, the defense may be prevented from exploring motives for lying. Thus, although the defense has a right to cross-examine and challenge the evidence, the right is restricted in ways that effectively limit the hearing so that it does not become a minitrial.

However, some states require more rigorous rules of evidence at the preliminary hearing. For example, some jurisdictions maintain the same rules concerning hearsay that they apply at trial. This means that eyewitnesses may be required to appear; the prosecutor is not allowed merely to repeat what eyewitnesses reported to the police. Similarly, a medical examiner would appear to provide expert testimony about the cause and time of death; the prosecutor would not be allowed to relate the findings or conclusions of the medical examiner. In jurisdictions that prohibit hearsay at the preliminary hearing, a hearing typically involves at least the arresting officer, the victim, and key witnesses.

Even under these circumstances the preliminary hearing is usually a brief one-sided affair. The defense often chooses to make no rebuttal, to introduce no evidence, and to offer no witnesses. Frequently, the defense declines even to cross-examine the witnesses.

Preliminary hearings in states that allow hearsay evidence tend to be even less adversarial and time consuming. In these jurisdictions usually only the arresting officer and/or the investigating officer testify. They state what key witnesses told them, usually referring to notes in order to refresh their memories and keep the details straight. Although the defense attorney may cross-examine them, many do not.

Given the differences in practice in preliminary hearing states, the rigor of the probable cause screen probably varies widely. In general, the more streamlined the procedures, the more likely the judge will have little basis for rejecting any charges brought by the prosecutor.

Although the preliminary hearing is meant to fulfill the same function as the grand jury with respect to screening charges, the different procedures followed in the preliminary hearing create some additional benefits and liabilities for both the prosecution and the defense. Because the defendant has a right to be present at the preliminary hearing, the defense can learn the outline of the prosecutor's case. Before the liberalization of formal discovery this was an important benefit for the defense. For both defense and prosecution the preliminary hearing is a dress rehearsal for trial, providing an opportunity for the attorneys to see how their witnesses come across on the witness stand and how they hold up under cross-examination. Whatever weaknesses and strengths are present will likely be equally apparent to both adversaries, and both sides will have the opportunity to prepare to take advantage of, or counter, weaknesses and strengths.

Perhaps the most important unintended effect of the preliminary hearing is the impression it makes on the defendant. Before the preliminary hearing many defendants harbor hopes that the prosecutor cannot prove the charges. But the preliminary hearing often demonstrates the futility of contesting the charges. After observing the strength of the prosecution's case against them in court, defendants sometimes become more interested in exploring the possibility of a plea agreement.

Many states allow defendants the opportunity to waive the preliminary hearing. Studies show that a substantial number of defendants waive this right. In some jurisdictions one-quarter to one-third of all defendants entitled to a preliminary hearing waive it (Miller, 1969). In other jurisdictions as many as half the defendants charged with felonies waive the preliminary hearing (Kamisar et al. 1986, 940). The most common reason that defendants waive preliminary hearings is to show cooperation. If the defendant plans to enter a guilty plea, or has already negotiated a plea agreement with the prosecutor, the preliminary hearing serves little purpose. In cases heading to trial the preliminary hearing has become less useful as a discovery tool in states that have expanded the opportunity for formal discovery. The defense often already knows the strength and nature of the prosecution's evidence before the preliminary hearing. In a high-profile case, the preliminary hearing may only intensify media attention, which can be prejudicial to the defendant. To avoid any additional negative publicity the defense may waive the preliminary hearing.

Probable Cause and Pretrial Screens

attrition rate

Criticism of both processes often focuses on the case **attrition rate,** that is, the proportion of cases in which probable cause is not found and the case is rejected from the system. Low attrition rates give rise to concerns that the screening process is flawed and ineffective. Unfortunately, the attrition rate is not a useful measure of the quality of the formal pretrial screening processes in different jurisdictions. First, attrition rates in information jurisdictions vary dramatically, from 80 percent in some jurisdictions to 10 percent in others (Greenwood et al. 1976; McIntyre 1968; Neubauer 1974). Given this wide variation, it is difficult to make generalizations about the effectiveness of the preliminary hearing as a pretrial screen, let alone compare it to the grand jury screen.

In addition, pretrial screen attrition rates are a poor measure of effectiveness of the screening function because they tell only half the story. Prosecutorial charging practices influence the attrition rate at least as much as the rigor of the formal pretrial screen, whether it is the grand jury or the preliminary hearing. The attrition rate is likely to be lower in a jurisdiction in which prosecutors charge under a trial sufficiency model rather than a legal sufficiency model (see Chapter 9). In jurisdictions in which the case proceeds to the grand jury or preliminary hearing on the police charges, with no opportunity for initial screening by the prosecutor, the attrition rate is likely to be higher than in jurisdictions in which the prosecutor informally screens the charges first. The standards applied in the formal screening of charges undoubtedly influence the prosecutor's informal screening decisions. As prosecutors learn how much evidence they need to meet the probable cause standard, they adjust their initial charging decisions accordingly and reject weak cases before they get to court. The cases rejected at the preliminary hearing and grand jury also shape the prosecutor's initial charging decision. Thus, the attrition rate offers no independent indication of the stringency of the probable cause standard.

Whether the probable cause standard is relatively tough or easy also affects the attrition rate. Local practice and tradition influence the stringency of the probable cause standard, and the rules of evidence affect the amount of evidence that is needed to show probable cause. A jurisdiction that admits hearsay at the grand jury or preliminary hearing is likely to experience a lower attrition rate than one that excludes hearsay. When a police officer or prosecutor offers hearsay testimony, the judge or jury is unlikely to question the credibility of the witness. When other witnesses testify, judgments about credibility play a much greater role in assessing the strength of the evidence and whether it meets the probable cause standard.

Attrition rates, which focus on cases rather than on charges, do not reveal the extent to which formal pretrial screens weed out inappropriate charges while permitting the case to survive on other, well-supported charges. This is an important function in jurisdictions where prosecutors follow a practice of piling on charges.

refiling

In information jurisdictions the attrition rate also depends on the willingness of the judge to reject the case, which in turn is influenced by rules on refiling charges. **Refiling** refers to the prosecutor's option to file charges a second time if the preliminary hearing results in no bindover. In some jurisdictions, if the judge at the preliminary hearing finds no probable cause, the prosecutor is severely restricted in refiling the charges. In other jurisdictions the prosecutor is allowed to refile the case, to present the case at a preliminary hearing again. If charges can be easily refiled, judges are more willing to uphold a more rigorous probable cause standard. Where refiling is difficult, judges are apt to allow prosecutors a bit more leeway in demonstrating probable cause. These rules have predictable effects on rates of case attrition.

Despite wide variation, some general conclusions apply equally to both processes. In general, the more formal, complex, and regulated the process (either process), the tighter the probable cause screen is likely to be. The more formal and regulated the process, the more likely it is to become protracted and tedious. On the other hand, more relaxed procedures, ungoverned by technical rules and requirements, result in less stringent screening.

If states adopted the grand jury reforms endorsed by the American Bar Association, the grand jury process would begin to resemble the preliminary hearing more than it does now. Although the structures of the two processes likely will continue to be distinct, the rules of practice—particularly in relation to the kinds of evidence that may be submitted—are converging.

◼ DISCOVERY

discovery

Discovery is the formal process through which one party obtains certain kinds of information from the opposing party. The rules of discovery in criminal cases have traditionally provided for only limited discovery by defendants. Common law provided no right of discovery in criminal cases. The prosecutor was allowed to maintain a great deal of secrecy about the evidence against the defendant and the proof that would be offered at trial. The likely rationale for this practice was to prevent defendants from fabricating exculpatory explanations of the evidence. After all, a defendant need only raise a reasonable doubt. If the defendant can fabricate a plausible and innocent explanation of the prosecution's evidence, a jury is likely to acquit. The more advance notice the defense has of all the evidence, the more opportunity the defendant has to make up such a plausible explanation. On the other hand, unless some kinds of evidence are disclosed in advance, the defense is unable to adequately prepare its case.

In recent decades the rules governing disclosure of evidence have become more favorable to the defense. The U.S. Supreme Court and state supreme courts have ruled that some disclosure by the prosecutor is required as a matter of due process. In *Brady v. Maryland* (1963) the Supreme Court held that due process requires that the prosecutor disclose exculpatory evidence. In addition, if the prosecution is aware that a state witness has committed perjury, the prosecution must notify the defense (*Alcorta v. Texas* 1963).

Many states have established even more liberal discovery rules. Much pretrial discovery is reciprocal, that is, the sides exchange information. For example, in requesting the prosecutor's list of proposed witnesses the defense must offer to provide a list of all witnesses the defense intends to call. Some evidence must be disclosed on demand, whereas other items can be discovered only by filing a motion with the court. For example, in Wisconsin the defense can obtain, simply by asking, written or recorded statements of the defendant related to the crime. However, to obtain access to physical evidence for inspection or scientific testing, the defense must file a motion with the court. The court is required to order the production of such evidence but can specify the conditions under which the evidence will be made available.

work product

The work product of either attorney generally is not subject to discovery. **Work product** refers to the materials prepared by an attorney or the attorney's agents, such as the police or a private investigator working for the defense, that reflect the attorney's training, analysis, or strategy. Work product includes the attorney's outline of the evidence, the list of witnesses in the order they will be presented, or other notes and materials created in the course of reviewing and organizing the evidence for trial. The work product is not evidence and therefore is not subject to discovery rules.

Prosecutors differ in the extent to which they cooperate with defense counsel in disclosing evidence. Some prosecutors maintain an "open file" policy, by which they allow the defense to review the entire file, including work product. Other prosecutors reveal only the minimum required by law. If the prosecutor refuses to disclose information that the defense asserts a right to see, the defense may pursue the matter through a motion requesting that the prosecutor turn over the information sought.

Disclosure puts the parties on a more equal footing. In addition, disclosure probably increases the likelihood of guilty pleas. With full disclosure the prosecutor cannot bluff. Either the evidence is in the record or it is not. With the evidence laid out the defense is in a better position to judge the risks associated with trial.

■ PRETRIAL MOTIONS

As Chapter 3 noted, pretrial motions are one way to protect the rights of the defendant, by requesting an order from the court to apply a rule of procedure or a rule of evidence. Although motions are an important tool for protecting the rights of defendants, the prosecution may also make motions to obtain rulings from the judge in regard to procedures or evidence. In general, motions can be made at any time, before and even during the trial. In most cases, however, some motions are filed before trial to resolve questions relating to the admissibility of evidence or the procedures to be followed at trial.

Pretrial motions are usually made in writing, although motions also can be made orally during the court proceedings. Usually, the attorney making the motion drafts a short brief that states the grounds for the request and provides a short legal analysis, citing relevant case law and applying the law to the facts of the present case. Opposing counsel is given an opportunity to respond by brief. In some cases the judge may decide the issue by reading the briefs, without hearing oral arguments. In other cases, especially if the issue is important to the case and the law is unclear, the judge can order oral arguments. The party making the motion bears the burden of convincing the judge that the law and fairness require the ruling requested.

Some motions also require a fact-finding hearing. For example, on a motion to suppress illegally obtained evidence a fact-finding hearing is held to determine the circumstances under which the evidence was obtained. A hearsay objection that involves the exception for excited utterances may require a hearing to determine the circumstances under which the utterance was made.

The outcome of pretrial motions related to the admissibility of evidence can make an enormous difference in the prospects for conviction or acquittal. A strong case can be weakened, sometimes fatally. Consequently, stalled plea negotiations may move forward after pretrial motions resolve evidentiary issues.

SUMMARY

Attorneys in a criminal case must continually assess the evidence in the case, both in terms of its admissibility at trial and its reliability and credibility in proving the charges. In the weeks and months between the initial appearance and trial (or guilty plea), felony cases are subjected to a formal screen of the evidence through either a grand jury or a preliminary hearing. The grand jury is a nonadversarial secret proceeding; a group of lay jurors reviews the evidence in support of the charges. In general, grand juries serve two functions: investigation and screening. Investigative grand juries conduct hearings to develop evidence and, if crimes are uncovered, issue charges against specific individuals. Charging grand juries do not investigate crime. Instead they review the evidence presented by the prosecutor. Although the grand jury is a powerful body, in most cases it follows the prosecutor's lead and does not act independently.

An alternative process for screening charges is the preliminary hearing. This is an adversarial hearing conducted before a judge as the sole decision maker. In both the grand jury and the preliminary hearing the standard of evidence is probable cause, although the precise meaning of that phrase varies from place to place, depending on local tradition, rules of evidence, and procedure. The adversarial procedures and more trial-like rules of evidence in many preliminary hearing jurisdictions suggest that the probable cause standard in these jurisdictions is more rigorous than in most grand jury jurisdictions. Attrition rates tend to be quite low for both pretrial screns. Attrition rates are a poor indicator of the effectiveness of the formal screening process, however.

During the pretrial period motions are filed and the attorneys engage in the discovery process. The prosecutor is required to disclose certain kinds of evidence to the defense. This disclosure has been expanded in recent decades. The result of greater disclosure is less uncertainty for the defense in assessing the risks of pursuing the case through trial.

Once the defendant is bound over for trial and most of the preliminary procedural and evidentiary matters have been considered through pretrial motions, the stage is set for the adjudication phase. Traditionally, this has meant preparing for and going to trial. Today it is more likely to mean preparing for and entering into negotiations.

FOR FURTHER DISCUSSION

1. One study of investigation by defense counsel found that those attorneys who interviewed the victims of violent offenses obtained more favorable terms in guilty pleas for their clients than attorneys who did not conduct such interviews. What hypotheses can you generate to explain this relationship?

2. Many judicial systems, such as the inquisitorial systems of Europe, do not have the elaborate rules of evidence found in the adversarial system. Instead the fact-finders (professional judges or a panel of lay jurors and professional judges) are allowed to hear all relevant evidence. During deliberation the trier

of fact decides how much weight to place on the various pieces of evidence, based on such concerns as reliability and fairness. Which of these systems do you think is most likely to achieve substantive justice? Could the rules of evidence be eliminated (or weakened) under our system of trial by lay jurors without subverting substantive justice?

3. When the U.S. Supreme Court created the exclusionary rules under *Mapp v. Ohio* (1961) and *Miranda v. Arizona* (1966), the Court cited two primary rationales. First, the exclusion of evidence is intended to deter improper police procedure. Second, at least some members of the Court were concerned that judges not become accessories after the fact to police misconduct by admitting illegally obtained evidence. These justices believed that the value of maintaining judicial integrity is more important than attaining a conviction in any individual case. This assessment might be compared to the balancing of values in excluding privileged communications. The exclusion of privileged communication (for example, between husband and wife) is based on the belief that the value of safeguarding open communication within marriage is more important than obtaining a conviction in any particular case. How would you assess the various values involved in these situations? What might be the undesirable consequences of admitting each of these kinds of evidence?

4. The grand jury is an anomaly in the U.S. court system. In a system that values openness and adversarial procedures the grand jury is highly secretive and nonadversarial. How does the historical evolution of the grand jury explain its unusual characteristics?

5. In *U.S. v. Williams* (1992) the Supreme Court declined to require prosecutors to present exculpatory evidence to the grand jury, reasoning that this would transform the grand jury into a forum for judging the guilt of the defendant rather than a mere screening body to ensure that the prosecution is not totally without grounds. Although the Constitution undoubtedly requires merely a screen for probable cause, would justice be enhanced by a grand jury process that considers exculpatory evidence? Would efficiency be enhanced? What additional costs might such a role impose on the courts and on society as a whole?

6. In *Hurtado v. California* (1884) the Supreme Court held that any fair process for screening evidence against the accused must meet the requirements of due process. Both the grand jury and the preliminary hearing use substantial resources. Perhaps a more efficient screen for probable cause would be a panel of three law-trained court commissioners that reviews the complete investigative record and determines whether the evidence shows probable cause. This would save police time (because officers would not have to appear as witnesses), as well as the time of prosecutors and public defenders. Would such a process provide a fair screen of the evidence? As a defendant, what advantages and disadvantages would you experience under this alternative screening process?

■ REFERENCES

Alcorta v. Texas, 355 U.S. 28, 78 S. Ct. 103 (1957).

Arenella, Peter. 1981. "Reforming the State Grand Jury System: A Model Grand Jury Act." *Rutgers Law Journal* 13: 1–57.

————— 1980. "Reforming the Federal Grand Jury and the State Preliminary Hearing to Prevent Conviction Without Adjudication." *Michigan Law Review* 78: 463–585.

Bayless, H. Jeffrey. 1981. "Grand Jury Reform: The Colorado Experience." *American Bar Association Journal* 67: 568–72.

Blank, Blanche D. 1993. *The Not So Grand Jury: The Story of the Federal Grand Jury System*. Lanham, Md.: University Press of America.

Brady v. Maryland, 373 U.S. 83, 83 S. Ct. 1194 (1963).

Cantwell, Mary. 1989. "Sitting Among the Judges, Not the Judged, Purely by Chance." *Los Angeles Daily Journal,* May 10, p. 6.

Coleman v. Alabama, 399 U.S. 1, 90 S. Ct. 1999 (1970).

Costello v. United States, 350 U.S. 359, 76 S. Ct. 406 (1956).

Ferguson, Robert W., and Allan H. Stokke. 1978. *Legal Aspects of Evidence*. New York: Harcourt Brace Jovanovich.

Goldberg, Steven H. 1982. *The First Trial: Where Do I Sit? What Do I Say?* St. Paul, Minn.: West.

Greenwood, Peter, Sorrel Wildhorn, Eugene Poggio, Michael J. Strumwasser, and Peter DeLeon. 1976. *Prosecution of Adult Felony Defendants in Los Angeles County: A Policy Perspective*. Lexington, Mass.: D. C. Heath.

Heilbroner, David. 1990. *Rough Justice: Days and Nights of a Young D.A.* New York: Pantheon.

Hurtado v. California, 110 U.S. 516, 4 S. Ct. 111 (1884).

Kamisar, Yale, Wayne R. LaFave, and Jerold H. Israel. 1986. *Modern Criminal Procedure*. St. Paul, Minn.: West.

Lieberman, Marty. 1981. "Investigation of Facts in Preparation for Plea Bargaining." *Arizona State Law Journal* 1981 (2): 557–83.

McIntyre, Donald. 1968. "A Study of Judicial Dominance of the Charging Decision." *Journal of Criminal Law, Criminology, and Police Science* 59: 463–90.

Miller, Frank. 1969. *Prosecution: The Decision to Charge a Suspect with a Crime*. Boston: Little Brown.

Neubauer, David W. 1974. *Criminal Justice in Middle America*. Morristown, N.J.: General Learning Press.

New Jersey Law Journal. 1986. "ABA Calls for Reform of Grand Jury System." *New Jersey Law Journal* 117 (January 9): 28.

Popko, Sigmund G. 1987. "Arizona's County Grand Jury: The Empty Promise of Independence." *Arizona Law Review* 29: 667–88.

Schimizzi, Richard W. 1980. "Investigative Grand Juries: A Comparison of Pennsylvania's Judicially and Legislatively Created Bodies." *Duquesne Law Review* 18: 933–55.

Steiner, Margaret L. 1981. "Adequacy of Fact Investigation in Criminal Defense Lawyer's Trial Preparation." *Arizona State Law Journal* 1981 (2): 523–56.

Subin, Harry I., Chester L. Mirsky, and Ian. S. Weinstein. 1993. *The Criminal Process: Prosecution and Defense Functions*. St. Paul, Minn.: West.

Sullivan, Thomas P., and Richard D. Nachman. 1984. "If It Ain't Broke, Don't Fix It: Why the Grand Jury's Accusatory Function Should Not Change." *Journal of Criminal Law and Criminology* 75: 1047–69.

Thies v. State, 178 Wis. 98, 189 N.W. 539 (1922).

United States v. Calandra, 414 U.S. 338, 94 S. Ct. 613 (1974).

United States v. Mandujano, 425 U.S. 564, 96 S. Ct. 1768 (1976).

United States v. Williams, 504 U.S. 36, 112 S. Ct. 1735 (1992).

Wachtler, S. 1990. "Grand Juries Are Wasteful and Pointless." *Los Angeles Daily Journal,* January 23, p. 6.

Waltz, Jon R. 1975. *Criminal Evidence*. Chicago: Nelson-Hall.

Wood v. Georgia, 370 U.S. 375, 82 S. Ct. 1364 (1962).

13

TRADING FOR TIME: PLEA NEGOTIATIONS

The vast majority of cases charged by the prosecutor are resolved by a guilty plea. With some variation between jurisdictions defendants plead guilty in 90 percent or more of criminal cases (Flanagan and Maguire 1990, 500, 510). Historical research indicates that guilty pleas have predominated in our system for a century or more. Many, if not most, guilty pleas are the product of either implicit or explicit plea agreements.

Negotiating is a time-honored skill in civil litigation. The judge encourages the parties to a civil suit to negotiate a settlement, and negotiation is viewed as an appropriate practice for a civil litigator. In contrast, negotiation (or plea bargaining) in the criminal process is highly controversial. Only recently have the courts recognized plea bargaining as a legitimate practice in criminal cases, and some commentators remain flatly opposed to it.

Some controversy over plea bargaining stems from stereotypical images of the practice that are inconsistent with the actual practices described by the term *plea bargaining*. The stereotypes often represent the worst aspects of plea bargaining as it is actually practiced. One goal of this chapter is to show the enormous variations in how plea negotiations take place and the nature of the deals that result. However, some controversy arises from conflicting views of the propriety of any form of plea negotiation in the criminal court process. This chapter explores these fundamentally different perspectives.

◼ HISTORICAL DEVELOPMENT OF PLEA BARGAINING

By all accounts plea bargaining is a widespread practice today. Some experts believe the system is so dependent on the practice that justice would grind to a halt if all cases had to go to trial. In fact, the origins of plea bargaining are often blamed on rising caseload pressure.

This explanation seems reasonable, except for some contradictory evidence. Plea bargaining today prevails both in jurisdictions where the caseload is heavy and where it is light (Heumann 1975; Feeley 1979, 244–277). This has caused some scholars to question the common assumption that plea bargaining originally developed in response to caseload pressures. Other factors, related to changes in how cases are initially brought into the court process and how they are pursued within the courts, appear to be at least as important as caseload pressures.

Although negotiations between the state and the accused criminal go back several centuries, plea bargaining as we know it arose during the nineteenth century (Sanborn 1986). Historical court documents show isolated instances of negotiated pleas before the Civil War, and that they became more common after the war (Alschuler 1979, 221–223). Evidence from one county in California shows the steadily increasing use of both explicit and implicit plea agreements from the end of the nineteenth century through the twentieth century (Friedman 1979). Other studies have confirmed that in the early part of the twentieth century negotiated guilty pleas supplanted trials at ever greater rates (Moley 1928).

Modern reliance on plea agreements can best be understood in light of the dramatic changes in our system of justice over the past two hundred years. By the time the British colonized North America, the jury trial had become firmly established as an important right of English subjects. However, eighteenth-century jury trials differed substantially from modern trials (see Chapter 4). The urban court in London held twelve to twenty felony trials per day, and English rural courts operated similarly in the 1700s. Jury trials were conducted rapidly (Langbein 1979, 262), and defendants were not represented by counsel. In most cases a layman (the complaining witness or a police officer) acted as prosecutor and presented the case to the jury. Jurors were not subject to questioning. Lay prosecutors and unrepresented defendants were in no position to make motions and use other delaying tactics. The law of evidence was as yet undeveloped. In short, the typical trial in eighteenth-century England, the period during which the United States established its independence, involved a layman who used a commonsense approach to present evidence to persuade a jury that had not been screened and a judge who had broad powers to comment on the evidence and influence the jury. The adversarial party was an untrained defendant (Langbein 1979, 263–65). Evidence consisted of physical evidence, plain to the untrained eye, and the uncoached testimony of both witnesses and the accused. Technology and science had not yet elevated evidence to a specialty, and expert testimony was not yet commonplace. Under these circumstances the jury trial was an efficient way to dispose of cases.

In addition, as long as prosecution was the responsibility of the victim, victims and offenders probably negotiated outside the court process before any charges were filed. Only if the offender refused to make satisfactory restitution or if the victim insisted on criminal retribution would the case go to court. Because of the difficulty and expense of prosecuting a criminal case victims were likely to have thought long and hard before seeking an indictment. Consequently, victims had little reason to change their minds between indictment and trial.

When the United States adopted its trial-centered adversarial system of justice, the political, social, and demographic features of this country were also very different than they are today. In 1776 the United States was still primarily a rural agrarian society. Standing police departments, professional prosecutors' offices, a law-trained judiciary, public defenders, prisons, and probation were unknown. All these factors changed and in turn altered the pace and balance in the processing of criminal cases.

One significant change during the nineteenth century was the creation of municipal police departments. Because of industrialization the populations of cities grew rapidly—New York's population nearly doubled between 1790 and 1800—and municipalities established standing police departments. The mission of these new professionals was to contain the real and imagined threats to the social order posed by the "dangerous classes," immigrants and freed slaves. The advent of professional policing permanently changed the criminal court process.

Where previously a part-time constable would be asked to arrest a suspect after indictment by the grand jury, police now took a more proactive role in detecting and investigating crimes and initiating court action against suspects. Where previously the court maintained some control over the number of suspects indicted, professional police brought ever greater numbers of suspects to the courts for processing. Victims relinquished control over their own cases in exchange for the professional assistance of police and government prosecutors.

Another important change was the shift to imprisonment instead of physical punishment. Unlike physical punishment, which requires few resources to deliver, prison space is limited and expensive. With the shift to imprisonment as punishment the courts lost their capacity to impose punishment without concern for resource limitations. Plea bargaining appeared at the same time that courts needed to alleviate the problems posed by the growing number of cases fed into the courts by police and the limited space available in prisons (Haller 1979). In short, plea bargaining does seem to have developed as an adaptation for managing scarce resources. This supports the view that plea bargaining arose in response to caseload pressures.

Other changes supported this development. As the supply of lawyers increased, especially in urban areas, judges and prosecutors were more likely to be trained in the law. In earlier centuries the economic burdens of initiating a court case meant that once an indictment was obtained, the victim/prosecutor was unlikely to drop the charges. The professional prosecutor did not have an emotional or financial stake in pursuing the case. Instead professional prosecutors became bureaucrats interested as much in conserving their resources as they were in any particular outcome. The role of the victim in the criminal process was greatly diminished.

For decades plea bargaining was practiced widely but almost furtively. Bargains were not recorded in court documents or acknowledged in appellate decisions or legal treatises on criminal court process. After World War II, however, plea bargains finally became the subject of scholarly discussion and scrutiny (see Newman 1966). The lower appellate courts slowly confronted the reality of plea negotiations. Plea bargaining finally gained a measure of legitimacy when in 1970 the U.S. Supreme Court acknowledged the importance of defense counsel during explicit plea negotiations (*Brady v. United States* 1970). The next year, in *Santobello v. New York* (1971) the Supreme Court gave its approval to the practice of plea bargaining, referring to it as "highly desirable" and "an essential component of the administration of justice."

Today guilty pleas are entered in 85 to 90 percent of criminal cases (see Figure 13-1), and most of those pleas, perhaps all of them, are the result of either explicit negotiations or implicit understandings that a guilty plea will bring leniency.

FIGURE 13-1   Guilty Pleas

SOURCE: Reprinted from Barbara Boland, Paul Mahanna, and Ronald Sones, 1992. *The Prosecution of Felony Arrests, 1988.* Washington, D.C.: U.S. Department of Justice, Bureau of Justice Statistics, p. 6.

Statistics on guilty pleas can be presented in a variety of ways with varying results. The proportion of cases resolved by guilty plea depends on what one counts as a case. The guilty plea rate is higher if it is calculated on the basis of all convictions than if it is calculated on the basis of all indicted cases or all arrests, since many cases are rejected by the prosecutor or dismissed and result in neither a guilty plea nor a conviction at trial. In addition, statistics of guilty pleas can not be equated with explicit plea bargaining. Many defendants are persuaded to plead guilty by the desire to come clean and get it over with, and by the hope that a guilty plea will earn some lenience.

The table below shows the percentage of all felony arrests resulting in a guilty plea. What percentage of convictions were resolved by guilty plea?

Disposition of All Felony Arrests Presented for Prosecution
Percentage of felony arrests resulting in

Jurisdiction	Number of arrests	Diversion or referral	Rejection or dismissal			Guilty plea	Trial	Percentage of trials resulting in	
			Rejection	Dismissal	Total			Conviction	Acquittal
Brooklyn	35,816		3%	38%	41%	56%	2%	60%	40%
Los Angeles	89,302		36	10	46	54	..	..	..
Manhattan	38,601	–	2	42	44	54	3	70	30
Miami[b]	41,181	5%	30	6	36	56	2	63	37
Minneapolis[c]	3,943	7	31	12	42	46	3	79	21
Portland	10,281	6	28	15	43	42	10	87	13
Queens	19,122		1	32	33	63	3	77	23
Rhode Island	7,039		0	39	39	58	3	57	43
Riverside	11,751		25	17	42	56	1	80	20
San Diego	30,234	10	21	10	31	57	2	82	18
Seattle	9,368	4	20	11	31	57	8	85	15
Washington, D.C.	15,283	2	18	26	44	49	6	70	30
Jurisdiction mean		6%	18%	21%	39%	52%	3%	74%	26%

NOTE: In jurisdictions in which diversions and referrals are not reported as such, cases diverted or referred are included with rejections and dismissals.

.. Data not available.

– Insufficient data to calculate.

[a] Trial convictions are included with guilty pleas, and acquittals are included with dismissals.

[b] In Miami, diversions or referrals include pretrial diversions, restitution cases, transfers to other jurisdictions, and miscellaneous dispositions.

[c] Rejections in Minneapolis include some arrests referred to the city prosecutor for misdemeanor prosecution.

■ DEFINITIONS AND BASIC VARIATIONS

quid pro quo

All plea agreements have a common thread: a defendant enters a guilty plea, and because of that an official decision maker extends some measure of lenience to the defendant. This lenience is sometimes referred to as the *quid pro quo* for the defendant's willingness to plead guilty. **Quid pro quo** refers to a trade of "this for that," an exchange of one thing for another or, alternatively, an offering of one thing in compensation for something given up by the other. In exchange for the defendant's giving up the right to trial the government offers some measure of lenience, either as an inducement to waive trial in the first place or as a reward or compensation for waiving trial and admitting criminal responsibility.

explicit negotiation, implicit agreement

Beyond this basic definition plea agreements and plea negotiation (or bargaining) vary tremendously in how the negotiation is conducted and the concessions included in the agreements themselves. First, plea agreements may be the end result of individualized and **explicit negotiation** between the prosecution and the defense. In other cases no negotiation occurs at all; concessions are made through an **implicit agreement** based on past practice or local norms. The defense knows from past practice that defendants who plead guilty receive a more lenient sentence. Because of this knowledge the defendant is persuaded to plead guilty, even though the prosecutor makes no explicit promises. Second, although plea agreements by definition involve lenience in exchange for a guilty plea, the prosecutor may seek additional concessions from the defendant, such as testifying against co-defendants or cooperating in other ways with ongoing investigations. Another variation concerns the official who grants the concessions: the prosecutor or the judge. Concessions may be granted by the prosecutor in the form of fewer charges, less severe charges, or some particular **sentence recommendation** to the judge or an agreement to make no recommendation regarding the sentence. In some cases defendants have even agreed to plead guilty in exchange for lenient treatment of a co-defendant. When the judge grants concessions, the lenience usually relates to the sentence, although it may involve dismissals or acquittals on multiple charges.

sentence recommendation

Sometimes the defendant is represented by counsel in negotiations, and sometimes the defendant negotiates directly with the prosecutor or the judge. Explicit negotiations may occur early in the process, before initial charging by the prosecutor, or late, even after the trial has started and the jury has begun to deliberate. The plea discussion may take place as part of a pre-arraignment or pretrial conference that is routinely scheduled for each case in anticipation of a negotiated plea (Nimmer and Krauthaus 1977). Alternatively, plea discussions may occur almost in passing, during a chance encounter in a courtroom anteroom, for example.

Both petty and serious crimes can be resolved through a plea agreement. From traffic offenses to capital murder cases defendants and prosecutors engage in plea negotiations. In some cases the plea agreement is part of a more complex deal involving other promises on the part of the government or the defendant. For example, the prosecutor may agree to drop a felony charge in exchange for a guilty plea to a lesser included misdemeanor *and* the defendant's testimony against a co-conspirator. The prosecutor or judge can be generous or stingy in granting lenience, depending on the seriousness of the charges, the strength of the case, and a host of other factors. In some cases the defendant is clearly guilty of the charges dropped by the prosecutor. In other cases the defendant may claim to be innocent of the charges but pleads guilty.

INDIVIDUALIZED NEGOTIATIONS
PEOPLE V. HENRY

Philip Henry, a twenty-seven-year-old defendant, is charged with first-degree sexual assault—using a weapon to force his victim into sexual intercourse—an offense carrying a maximum penalty of twenty years' imprisonment. Five years ago he was convicted of second-degree sexual assault, essentially the same offense without use of a weapon, punishable by up to ten years' imprisonment. He was sentenced to three years in prison but was paroled after two years.

In the current case Henry is represented by a seasoned public defender known for vigorous and effective defense. Henry entered a plea of not guilty and demanded a jury trial. The prosecutor's case is based almost entirely on the victim's testimony. Although the victim reported that she was attacked with a knife, the police found no weapon when they arrested Henry. Also, hospital personnel who examined the victim after the attack had not been adequately trained to collect physical evidence of a sexual assault. Consequently, the only trial-admissible evidence from the hospital is staff members' testimony about abrasions and bruises in the victim's genital area. The prosecution's case rests heavily on the victim's positive identification. The victim is confident in her identification, and her story is consistent and logical. The prosecutor is confident that a jury will find her credible.

Nine months pass. The twenty-four-year-old victim was a newlywed at the time of the assault, but the psychological trauma of the assault has caused the marriage to founder. She is now legally separated from her husband, living at home with her parents, and receiving psychiatric care on a regular basis. One month after the offense, around the time that she was to testify at the preliminary hearing, she experienced nightmares and recurring nausea. As the trial date approaches, the nightmares return, even though the scheduled trial is still two months off. Concerned about his daughter's welfare, her father approaches the prosecutor, pleading with him to offer a deal and spare his daughter the trauma of testifying at trial.

The prosecutor reviews the situation. The judge assigned to the case does not tend to be lenient with sex offenders, especially repeaters. The judge would know the original charge and the factual circumstances of the case. Moreover, any argument from the defense for lenience would be pretty weak in light of the defendant's record. A guilty plea to second-degree sexual assault would allow the judge to sentence the defendant to a maximum of ten years in prison. Even after conviction on first-degree sexual assault at a jury trial, the defendant probably would not receive more than a fifteen-year sentence. So reducing the charge to a crime that carries a maximum of ten years in prison does not give up much.

The prosecutor considers the evidence. Because the only evidence about the use of a weapon is the victim's testimony, getting a conviction on the first-degree charge is risky. And there is always the possibility that the jury will acquit the defendant on all charges. That would be unacceptable. This repeat offender is likely to rape again if a jury frees him.

The prosecutor decides that getting the defendant to plead guilty to second-degree sexual assault is more acceptable. Given the judge's

■ STYLES OF NEGOTIATION

Plea bargaining conjures an image of bartering between the prosecutor and defense counsel, almost like the haggling involved in buying a car. The prosecutor suggests a price, and the defense responds, "Throw in a dismissal of the weapons charge, and you've got a deal!" Although such stereotypical plea bargaining does occur in some cases, a 1988 study suggests that such individualized negotiations are not the norm. The study of plea negotiations shows that sentencing history, the prosecutor decides to sweeten the offer by promising to make no recommendation as to sentence. This judge will know the right thing to do, and the added concession might be enough to make the offer more agreeable to the defense. With any luck at all the defendant will receive a long sentence, something close to ten years. It seems there is really not that much to lose by reducing the charge and making no sentence recommendation. And there is much to gain: a certain conviction and sparing the victim the ordeal of trial. The public defender might not go for it, smelling the potential for an acquittal at trial, but it is worth a try, provided the victim really wants to avoid trial.

The prosecutor discusses the strengths and weaknesses of the case with the victim and outlines his reasons for making the offer: in return for a guilty plea the state would reduce the charge to second-degree sexual assault and agree not to counter the defense attorney's sentence recommendation. The victim agrees, and the prosecutor calls the public defender to make the offer.

A meeting is not necessary. These two professionals know each other well and can conduct business over the phone. The prosecutor offers a take-it-or-leave-it deal: guilty to second-degree sexual assault and no sentence recommendation. The prosecutor says he will not haggle or accept counteroffers. The public defender says she will check with her client.

Now the public defender weighs the pros and cons. She has seen these deals before. They aren't great, but they are better than nothing and often all that is available. Realistically, the chances of a full acquittal at trial are not at all promising. The victim is credible and likely to evoke the jury's sympathy, despite the lack of physical evidence in the case. The state must have a lot of confidence in the victim's credibility to charge on a count that requires proof of a weapon even though no weapon has ever been recovered. On the other hand, if the victim is beginning to fall apart. . . . What to do, what to do? Not taking the deal is risky. The prosecutor specializes in prosecutions of sex offenses, and he is good with a jury. The judge will not be sympathetic to the defendant if he pleads guilty, but he would be even less sympathetic if the defendant is convicted after the trial. The victim's testimony would certainly extinguish any impulses toward lenience that the judge might have. Moreover, if they go to trial, the maximum sentence is twenty years, not ten. What more might she get out of the prosecutor? Anyone can predict an eight- or ten-year sentence after a guilty plea, especially from this judge. Asking the prosecutor to recommend a five-year sentence would be futile. Besides, when this prosecutor says no haggling, he means it. Even if the prosecutor would agree to recommend a five-year or even a seven-year sentence, the judge is unlikely to go for it.

She thinks her client won't be very happy about the offer, but the public defender sees the deal as the surest way to the most lenient sentence. The prosecutor does not have a dead bang case, especially on the weapon element, but an acquittal in this case is an unrealistic hope too. She decides to advise her client that, all things considered, this is a good offer and a better bet than going to trial. It reduces the maximum sentence from twenty years to ten years, and the judge is not exposed to a half-day of seeing the victim's anguish and pain. The defense lawyer heads to the jail to consult with her client.

"concessions and explicit bargaining have a role to play, but they are restricted to a small subset of cases involving lengthy sentences, evidentiary deficiencies, or some other type of problem" (Nardulli, Eisenstein, and Flemming 1988, 206). Serious cases, such as those involving violent or deadly felonies, as well as cases that have unusual features fall into this category, cases that are likely to involve individualized negotiations and explicit bargains.

Far more common is the practice of routinely granting standardized lenience to defendants willing to plead guilty, without explicit discussion. Standardized lenience is commonly shown to defendants who have very little bargaining leverage and who adopt a reasonable, or even remorseful, posture. Many times these cases would be very easy for the prosecutor to prove in court, and the defendant knows it. So, to avoid the trouble of a trial, the prosecutor offers a standard reduction. **Standardized lenience** reflects the "going rate" for routine cases. Defendants who take unreasonable positions—from the prosecutor's perspective—such as denying guilt when caught redhanded or claiming police brutality when there is no evidence of any, are denied standardized lenience. This mode of operation has been aptly described as a **consensus model** (Nardulli et al. 1988, 207–211) that has emerged in response to normal crimes (Sudnow 1965).

standardized lenience

consensus model

A consensus develops among the decision makers in the criminal court process about a suitable punishment for the typical case. Normal crimes are those that roughly fit the profile of a typical retail theft, an ordinary burglary, or a standard domestic assault, and so on. What prosecutors, defense lawyers, and judges mean when they talk about **normal crimes** is that the main features of the crime, relating to the victim-offender relationship, the amount of force used, the motive, the context in which the crime occurred, and other factors, are pretty much like most other crimes of the same type. For example, the typical or normal domestic assault occurs at home between a husband and wife or boyfriend and girlfriend. This is a normal crime. If the assault occurs in an expensive restaurant or between a couple on their second date, it may not be viewed as a normal domestic assault. A house burglary is normal if it involves the theft of such household items as small electronic equipment, jewelry, and cash. Normally, a burglary does not involve driving a truck up to the door, stripping the home of all furnishings, and vandalizing the interior. This would *not* be a normal burglary.

normal crime

An additional feature of a normal crime is a willingness to plead guilty (Sudnow 1965). Prosecutors, defense attorneys, and judges expect that "most defendants should plead guilty and [should] be rewarded for their guilty plea" (Heumann 1978, 158). If the defendant appears reluctant or unwilling to plead guilty, the court actors cannot easily handle the crime as a normal crime, even if the characteristics of the offense in all other respects fit the normal profile.

Normal crimes have a going rate. The going rate of lenience might be a standard charge reduction; for example, first-offense burglary might routinely be reduced to receiving stolen property, provided the defendant pleads guilty. Alternatively, the prosecutor may offer a standard sentence recommendation; for example, the state may routinely recommend probation in first-offense drug possession cases, provided the defendant pleads guilty. Regardless of its form, the standard grant of lenience reflects a consensus among court actors—prosecutors, defense attorneys, and judges—about the appropriate punishment for a particular normal crime when the defendant accepts responsibility (Nardulli et al. 1988, 207–211).

For the defendant who is prepared to plead, lenience is available for the asking and often even without asking. The attorneys need little time to reflect on the facts of the case and even less time to discuss the plea agreement. When standardized lenience is so entrenched in the system, individual cases often do not require discussion. Defendants who are represented and those who are not represented usually receive the same going rate (Feeley 1979, 189–191).

The lenience received by defendants who are willing to plead guilty to normal crimes is known as implicit plea bargaining. Implicit plea bargaining means that the prosecutor and defense do not specifically discuss concessions in exchange for a guilty plea. Instead concessions are granted as a routine matter in those

STANDARDIZED LENIENCE
STATE V. ROJAK

Sue Rojak is mortified and very worried. The twenty-year-old arrestee declined the prosecutor's offer to contact an attorney or a public defender. She doesn't want to fight this; there is no basis on which to fight. She just wants it to go away as quietly and quickly as possible. If only there were some way to get through this without her parents finding out.

She had been working at a summer job in an ice cream store. For weeks she had admired a $69 sweater in the department store next door. She had thought about it for some time. The sweater cost more than half a week's pay. She had worked so hard. She deserved something special. She "scoped" out the store and thought she could get away with it. On her last day of work for the summer she did it. She looked around, saw the clerk occupied with another customer, and stuffed the sweater in her bag. As soon as she stepped out the door, a plain-clothes security guard approached her, and she knew she had been caught. She did not deny she had stolen it. She told the security guard how embarrassed she was, that she had never done anything like this before. She offered to pay for the sweater. The guard told her that store policy is to fully prosecute all shoplifters. She would have to see the state's attorney.

Now facing the prosecutor, her mind is racing with questions and possibilities. Before the prosecutor left her in this room, he asked whether she would be willing to answer a few questions. She had nodded in agreement. Now she wonders. The prosecutor has told her she can talk to an attorney. She wonders whether she really does need a lawyer.

She saw the security guard talking to the prosecutor. Obviously, the prosecutor already knew everything that has happened. How serious is this? she wonders. Could she go to jail?

She doesn't even know whether shoplifting is a misdemeanor or a felony or the difference between the two. She has no record. Maybe the prosecutor will give her a break and wipe the slate clean.

She is willing to make restitution; she has already returned the property. This is her first offense. This isn't like her; she has never before been in trouble this way.

The prosecutor interrupts her thoughts. He comes into the room, looking stern and serious. He tells her that the offense she is alleged to have committed is known as retail theft, a misdemeanor punishable by up to nine months in jail and/or a fine of $500. He tells her that if the sweater were worth less than $50, she would have been charged with a less serious offense, one that carries a lesser maximum penalty.

He lets the news sink in for a few very long seconds and then asks her if she is willing to admit responsibility for the crime. She is. Well, in that case the prosecutor will reduce the charge from the higher retail theft charge to the lower one, of retail theft under $50, which is usually punished by only a small fine. He speculates that she probably will be fined $150 to $200 for her crime. Of course, he warned her, he can't guarantee what the judge will do. But he is willing to recommend a fine of $100.

What a relief, she thinks. It will hurt, but she can handle that without letting her parents know. The prosecutor seems ready to terminate the interview. Before ushering her toward the court, he comments on his reasons for being lenient. He is comfortable doing this because the offense is minor, it is her first offense, and she is willing to admit responsibility. If she had not owned up to being responsible, he adds, he would have gone for a conviction on the more serious charge.

cases in which the defendant is willing to plead guilty. This willingness to plead may come about because of the defendant's desire to come clean. In other cases the defendant's willingness to plead may result from defense counsel's advice that a guilty plea will result in lenience, even though the defense lawyer has not specifically discussed this with the prosecutor. The defense lawyer simply knows from experience that this is how a guilty plea will be rewarded.

Implicit bargaining is likely to predominate in courts that give few cases individualized attention. Because defendants are more willing to plead guilty to minor crimes, implicit bargaining is especially common in the lower courts and in misdemeanor processing. Although implicit bargaining occurs in felony cases as well (normal burglary, normal assault, and so on), as the stakes (potential sentence) increase, the defendant may seek more explicit promises of lenience from the prosecutor.

THE PARTIES AND THEIR PARTS

Judges, prosecutors, defense attorneys, and defendants all play key roles in establishing and maintaining a system based primarily on plea agreements, whether explicit or implicit. Despite variations, without the acquiescence or active support of each of these players, the system of plea agreements would collapse.

Judicial Participation in Plea Bargaining

The judge is intended to be a symbol of neutral, detached, and even-handed justice. A judge has an overriding duty to protect the public interest, including ensuring fairness in the administration of justice. More specifically, judges are charged with examining the facts to determine whether the guilty plea has a factual basis, and with examining the defendant to establish that the plea was made knowingly, intelligently, and voluntarily. Whether judges can fulfill these duties while participating in plea negotiations is a matter of some controversy.

The extent to which judges actively participate in the give and take of plea bargaining varies greatly between jurisdictions. Most defendants' primary objective in negotiating a plea agreement is to limit the punishment. From the defendant's point of view, then, the person with the trump card is the judge, because only the judge is empowered to determine the punishment. Defendants' uncertainty about the sentence is reduced if defendants can negotiate directly with the judge or get the judge to agree to a specific sentence in exchange for a guilty plea.

However, many states forbid judges to actively engage in plea negotiations. For example, the federal rule does not allow judges to "participate" in plea discussions in order to maintain the appearance, if not the reality, of judicial neutrality. When the judge becomes involved in securing a guilty plea instead of remaining detached the balance of power between the two adversaries tilts. First-hand detailed knowledge of failed plea negotiations is likely to destroy the impartiality of the judge as fact-finder if the case proceeds to trial. How can the judge be impartial if the judge was present during negotiations in which the defendant's guilt was taken as a given? Perhaps most important, judicial involvement invites judicial vindictiveness. Whether explicitly stated or not, when a judge participates in plea bargaining, defendants may sense that the judge will hold it against them if they refuse to plead, especially if the judge is encouraging an agreement. The defendant may fear that the judge will impose a trial penalty to punish the defendant for not cooperating. A **trial penalty** is the added severity of sentence that defendants receive when they go to trial rather than plead guilty. Finally, the judge who has actively engaged in inducing the defendant to plead guilty loses an objective perspective from which to determine whether the plea was entered voluntarily or whether the inducements were coercive.

trial penalty

Despite these arguments in favor of barring judges from the negotiating process, some experts support judicial involvement. Paradoxically, some of the most vocal opponents of plea bargaining argue that if plea bargaining is going to be allowed to persist, judges should be allowed to participate (Alschuler 1976; Odiaga 1989). These commentators suggest that allowing judges to openly participate would be more honest and would offer defendants greater certainty in the outcome. Without judicial involvement defendants may know that they will receive a trial penalty, but they cannot be sure how big that penalty will be. Judicial involvement would give defendants the information they need to make a more informed choice about waiving their right to a trial. In other words, so long as the trial penalty is real, judges may as well make it explicit.

Some jurisdictions permit judges to take a more active role. Illinois, for example, does not allow judges to initiate plea negotiations, but Illinois judges participate in plea discussions after the defense requests a conference for that purpose (Alschuler 1976, 1087–91). North Carolina also permits judges to engage in plea discussions (Anderson 1989, 43). Beyond legal prohibitions, however, some judges simply are more willing than others to become involved in actual negotiations. Three published studies have examined the level and type of judicial participation in plea discussions. These studies reflect the willingness of some judges and the reluctance of others to be involved, even when the law permits involvement.

Albert Alschuler (1976) studied judges in ten major urban jurisdictions in the 1960s. He provides many examples of judicial involvement in plea negotiations and reports that direct involvement was uncommon in only one city. In most cities "there were at least one or two judges who regularly offered specific sentence commitments in advance of trial" (Alschuler 1976, 1090–91). The opposing attorneys and the judge often met in the judge's chambers in an effort to come to some plea agreement. Alschuler's observations led him to estimate that the majority of judges in his study influenced plea negotiations by making hints before the arraignment was held:

> Many judges would tell defense attorneys of their "current inclinations" or their "willingness to consider" particular sentences that they would not promise to impose. . . . Still other judges apparently believed that, although it was improper to promise a specific sentence to a guilty-plea defendant, they could properly promise that the sentence would fall within a specified range or that it would not exceed a specified figure. (1976, 1093)

Surveys of judges present a somewhat more conservative picture of judicial involvement in plea negotiations. One survey, conducted by John Paul Ryan and James Alfini (1979), asked judges from across the country about their involvement in plea negotiations (see Figure 13-2). Ryan and Alfini categorized the judges' responses according to four levels of participation:

- Actively engaged in forging the plea agreement
- Was present during negotiations but only to review agreements
- Attended the plea discussion but made no comment
- Was not present during the negotiations and only accepted or rejected the plea based on the agreement in open court

According to judges' self-reports, more than two-thirds of the judges surveyed (69 percent) described their participation as passive, which is the fourth category of judicial involvement. One-fifth of all judges reported that they indirectly involved themselves in plea agreements, through reviewing agreements reached by the

FIGURE 13-2   Judicial Involvement in Plea Bargaining

Level of Judicial Participation	Ryan and Alfini Study*	Anderson Study*
Actively participated plea negotiations	7%	> 50% at least sometimes
Present during negotiations	—	46%
Reviewed and commented on plea agreements	20%	—
Not present during negotiations; only accepts or rejects pleas in open court	69%	42%

*NOTE: J.P. Ryan and J.Alfini. 1979. "Trial Judges' Participation in Plea Bargaining: An Empirical Perspective." *Law and Society Review* 13: 479–507.
A. F. Anderson. 1989. "Judicial Participation in the Plea Negotiation Process: Some Frequencies and Disposing Factors." *Hamline Journal of Public Law and Policy* 10: 13–57.

adversaries and advising them about the acceptability of the agreement before the plea is announced in open court. Only a small percentage of judges (7 percent) reported active participation in the give and take of plea negotiations (Ryan and Alfini 1979, 486).

Another survey of judges examined the behavior of judges in North Carolina, where the law permits judges to participate in plea negotiations (Anderson 1989). More than half the judges in this study said they participated in plea discussions at least sometimes (Anderson 1989, 45). Almost half (46 percent) said their habit was to attend the plea discussions and review the agreements. Slightly fewer (42 percent) said they did not attend plea discussions and only accepted or rejected them in open court (Anderson 1989, 47).

These two more recent studies of judicial participation indicate that judges generally take a passive role in plea negotiations, even when they are legally permitted to take an active role (Ryan and Alfini 1979; Anderson 1989). But judges may be disinclined to report active involvement in response to survey questions. Alschuler's observational study of plea negotiations (1976) suggests that at least some judges do actively participate in most cases, and many judges actively participate in some cases, even when the law does not allow it.

Judicial Role in Perpetuating Bargaining

Whether their participation is active or passive, judges' participation is critical if the practice of disposing of cases by exchanging lenience for guilty pleas is to be maintained. The systemic pressure to support at least an implicit system of bargaining is strong. New judges quickly learn the norm—that defendants who plead guilty expect lenience, and that prosecutors also expect these defendants will receive lenience: "A plea bargain normally comes before [the judge] as a fait accompli. Experienced prosecutors and defense attorneys have reached an agreement, and all that remains is for the judge to grant his imprimatur. The temptation for the new judge to accept the decision worked out by the 'adversaries' is great" (Heumann 1978, 134). When confused or uncomfortable with the decision they have to make, new judges often seek the advice of senior judges and even prosecutors (Heumann 1978, 135). In this way the new judge establishes patterns that are consistent with already established norms in the court. Although the judge's personal imprint may be evident in a penchant for harsher or more lenient sentences in certain cases, overall the judge's sentencing comes to look like that of most other judges.

Even judges who remain aloof from direct bargaining exert substantial influence over plea bargains. Judges provide feedback to both prosecutors and defense attorneys that helps shape the terms of the agreements. For example, a judge who routinely declines to follow a prosecutor's recommendation for probation for first-offense drug offenders is in fact shaping the bargaining process. Eventually, both defense attorneys and prosecutors learn that the recommendations are not followed. Accordingly, defense attorneys cease to settle for such a concession (because it doesn't turn out to be a concession), and the prosecutor is forced to offer some other kind of concession in order to secure a guilty plea.

Prosecutors

charge bargaining, sentence bargaining

Because most judges adopt a reactive posture with respect to plea bargaining, the prosecutor is usually the only representative for the state in explicit plea negotiations. Prosecutors may negotiate the severity and number of charges, called **charge bargaining**. In addition, the prosecutor can offer to make a specific sentence recommendation or no recommendation at all. This practice, although dependent on the judge's passive cooperation, is called **sentence bargaining**.

The prosecutor can engage in charge bargaining without having to rely on the cooperation of the judge to ratify the agreement. The charging decision rests solely with the prosecutor. A judge who believes the prosecutor has been too lenient in the charging decision can do little about it beyond attempting to persuade the prosecutor to reconsider.

Case law illustrates the governing principle that the prosecutor rightfully controls the charging decision, whether that decision is part of a plea agreement or not. The issue posed in *United States v. Ammidown* (1973) was whether a judge may refuse to accept a guilty plea to a lesser charge because the judge thinks a higher charge is more appropriate. The appellate court acknowledged that the judge has a duty to protect the public interest but concluded that unless the public interest is violated, the charging decision rests solely within the discretion of the prosecutor. The appellate court found that "the question is not what the judge would do if he were the prosecuting attorney, but whether [the judge] can say that the action of the prosecuting attorney is such a departure from sound prosecutorial principle as to mark it an abuse of prosecutorial discretion" (622).

Where a jurisdiction has created mandatory sentencing provisions, the prosecutor's charging decision is indistinguishable from the sentencing decision. In these cases the prosecutor's willingness to drop a charge that carries a mandatory sentence is a substantial concession and one that evades the original intent of the mandatory sentence. In general, the less discretion that judges have in sentencing under the sentencing laws of the jurisdiction, the greater the prosecutor's control over the sentence a defendant actually receives. This means that the prosecutor's promise to drop certain charges gives the defendant a fairly certain outcome in terms of the sentence that actually will be imposed.

In jurisdictions that allow judges wide discretion in imposing sentences the prosecutor can agree to recommend a particular sentence or to make no recommendation at all. Compared to charge bargaining, bargaining over a sentence recommendation represents a weak position for the prosecutor. From a defendant's perspective sentence recommendations are risky and therefore less desirable. They guarantee only the prosecutor's recommendation, not the actual sentence. The prosecutor's sentence recommendation is not binding on the judge; sentencing is exclusively within the judge's authority, and the range of options may be broad—from probation to many years in prison. Although judges normally cooperate in the process, the judge is free to reject the prosecutor's recommendation in any case at any time.

hollow promise

For these reasons banking on a sentence recommendation is risky. If the defense is aware of the judge's sentencing history, the risk may be a calculated and safe one. If a judge invariably makes first-offense drug offenders do time, a prosecutor's offer to recommend probation is not worth much. Of course the prosecutor's intention may be to offer only the appearance of a concession, hoping (and perhaps even knowing) that the judge will not concur. Such an offer is known as a **hollow promise**. Unrepresented defendants and inexperienced defense counsel may be misled by such offers, thinking they are getting something of value in exchange for the guilty plea when the prosecutor knows that the sentence recommendation is largely worthless. Hollow promises are perfectly legal, but some scholars have criticized them as unethical, because the defendant receives nothing in exchange for the guilty plea. In a system characterized by exchange a hollow promise is the ethical equivalent of false advertising. In a system of plea bargaining a defendant needs to respect the maxim of "buyer beware."

Limits on Prosecutorial Discretion

The prosecutor does not possess total discretion in negotiating plea agreements. The duty of the judge to examine the voluntariness of the plea and its factual basis helps to keep negotiations within reasonable bounds. More important in practice, however, are a variety of practical, legal, and ethical restrictions on the prosecutor's discretion.

One important practical restraint is the participation of defense counsel. Experienced knowledgeable defense attorneys are in a position to evaluate the strength of the case and to advise clients about the real value of apparent concessions by the prosecutor. An experienced attorney is unlikely to be taken in by a hollow promise or a threat of charges that cannot be proved.

A second constraint is the defendant's right of discovery and the widespread prosecutorial practice of disclosure. When a prosecutor discloses the state's evidence to the defense, the defense can realistically assess the strength of the case. Disclosure reduces uncertainty about the likelihood of conviction at trial. This sharing of evidence effectively restrains the prosecutor from threatening to convict on charges unsupported by the evidence. The defense can see that the prosecutor is bluffing. Without disclosure prosecutors could bluff defendants into pleading guilty to higher charges.

Ethical standards also restrain prosecutors. The American Bar Association's (1968) *Standards Relating to Pleas* stress that "similarly situated defendants should be afforded equal plea agreement opportunities." Where this admonition is taken seriously, attempts to minimize disparity in plea agreements serve to establish standards, or going rates, which keep negotiations within predictable bounds. In some prosecutors' offices the concern for equality of offers has resulted in internal written policies to guide negotiations.

Although the legal constraints on plea bargaining are few, the law does restrain some of the more obvious potential prosecutorial abuses. By law prosecutors are limited to making only those promises that they can fulfill as part of their legitimate authority. If the prosecutor were to promise, for example, that the defendant would receive early parole (a decision made by the parole board over which the prosecutor has no control), the bargain exceeds the prosecutor's authority. In other words, a prosecutor is not free to make promises that are unfulfillable or to make "promises that are by their nature improper as having no proper relationship to the prosecutor's business" (*Shelton v. United States* 1957, 115). To do so would be the ethical equivalent of selling the Brooklyn Bridge. In other words, the prosecutor may not "sell" a concession that does not belong to the prosecutor in the first place.

Prosecutors also must keep the promises they make. In *Santobello v. New York* (1971) the Supreme Court upheld this simple but important principle. Once the defendant pleads guilty, the prosecutor must follow through by dropping the remaining charges or making the sentence recommendation as promised. In addition, the entire prosecutor's office is bound by the promise. For example, if a prosecutor agrees to offer a recommendation of probation, and another colleague is assigned to the case when it goes to court for sentencing, the colleague may not disregard the promise and recommend a jail sentence or make no recommendation at all. According to the Court in *Santobello*, if a prosecutor breaks a promise, the court may enforce the earlier promise (for example, by dismissing the remaining charges) or allow the defendant to withdraw the guilty plea.

Playing Hardball

Although *Ammidown* (1973), *Shelton* (1957), and *Santobello* (1971) set constitutional limits on plea bargaining, the limits do not prevent prosecutors from driving hard bargains, even to the point of threatening severe punishment if a defendant refuses to plead guilty. In *Bordenkircher v. Hayes* (1978) a defendant complained that the prosecutor had retaliated because he exercised his right to trial. The defendant had been charged with forgery. The prosecutor agreed to offer a sentence recommendation of five years in prison if the defendant pled guilty. The prosecutor also warned the defendant that if he demanded a trial, the prosecutor would seek an additional indictment under the habitual criminal statute, which carried a mandatory sentence of life imprisonment without parole. The defendant pled not guilty, and the prosecutor followed through with the habitual criminal charge.

vindictive prosecution

The defendant argued that the prosecutor's conduct in this case amounted to retaliation for exercising his rights, a practice known as **vindictive prosecution**. In an earlier case (*Blackledge v. Perry* 1974) the Supreme Court had held that when a defendant's conviction is overturned on appeal, it is unlawful for a prosecutor to issue *more serious* charges against the defendant when retrying the case. Unless new evidence has come to light, any increase in the charges after a successful appeal is presumed to stem from vindictiveness on the part of the prosecutor. The defendant in *Bordenkircher v. Hayes* argued that the logic that prevents vindictive prosecution also should prevent a prosecutor from issuing more serious charges in retaliation for pleading not guilty. In both cases the defendant is being punished for exercising constitutional rights.

The U.S. Supreme Court found no fault with the conduct of the prosecutor in *Bordenkircher*. The majority opinion identified two critical differences between the conduct of the prosecutor in *Bordenkircher* and the prosecutor in *Blackledge*. First, in *Bordenkircher* the prosecutor announced his intentions before the defendant chose to exercise his constitutional rights. Thus, the Court reasoned, the defendant had made a fully informed choice. Second, the Court drew a distinction between the give and take of plea bargaining, where the prosecutor has an admitted—and constitutionally accepted—interest in inducing a guilty plea, and retaliation by the state against a defendant who appeals a conviction.

The dissent considered these distinctions to be unfounded. The dissenting justices noted that merely announcing an intention to act vindictively beforehand, as was the case in *Bordenkircher*, does not mitigate the vindictiveness. Furthermore, they pointed to the irrationality of drawing a distinction between rights that are exercised to avoid a conviction in the first place and rights that are exercised to attack a conviction after the fact.

The Roles of Defense Counsel and Defendant

Some defendants go through the court process without benefit of counsel, and in most states prosecutors are free to enter into plea agreements with unrepresented defendants. Unrepresented defendants navigate plea negotiations at their own risk. Except in simple cases involving implicit bargains, most defendants are too ignorant of both law and local conventions to assess the value of the prosecutor's offer. Defendants cannot evaluate the legal and evidentiary strengths and weaknesses of their own cases. In addition, a defendant may be impressed with the prosecutor's offer to drop a charge, when the normal concession or going rate includes the dropped charge and a recommendation of probation. Consequently, although the plea decision belongs to the defendant, the advice of counsel can be valuable in making that decision.

Defense counsel has an ethical duty to give advice that will assist the defendant in weighing the advantages and disadvantages in pleading guilty or not guilty. According to the Code of Professional Responsibility, defense counsel is required to "advise his client of the possible effect of each legal alternative. . . . He may emphasize the possibility of harsh consequences that might result from assertion of legally permissible positions" (1969, Ethical Consideration 7-9). In short, the defense attorney is charged with giving informed, realistic, and strategic advice to the client. Given certain circumstances, then, a defense attorney might ethically advise a guilty client to plead not guilty or even advise an innocent client to plead guilty. The advice depends on the attorney's assessment of the client's best interests in light of the prosecution's case. The value of defense counsel's advice comes from the lawyer's ability to accurately predict an outcome for the case, which is based on both legal knowledge and practical experiences with the judge and prosecutor.

Defendants tell tales of defense attorneys who pressure them to plead guilty (Casper 1972). Although defendants undoubtedly feel pressure, their distrust of their own attorney may reflect a desire to "kill the messenger." In the context of defense counsel's duty, if the attorney's best judgment is that contesting the charges will result only in more severe sanctions for the client, advising the client to plead guilty is the ethical thing to do. Flatly informing the defendant that "you can't win this one" may feel like pressure, but it is the attorney's ethical duty if it is the attorney's honest best judgment.

Ironically, doing what is ethical only helps to perpetuate the system of bargain justice and trial penalties. Essentially, defense counsel helps the defendant get the best bargain, given the realities of a system of justice in which defendants are penalized more harshly when they go to trial. From the defendant's perspective defense counsel is the source of this pressure, but the pressure in fact is inherent in the system.

Defense attorneys say their clients often are the first to mention the possibility of a deal. Defendants are often much more interested in the concessions they can get than they are in fighting the case in court. Consequently, defendants also perpetuate plea bargaining.:

JUSTICE AND ETHICS IN A BARGAINING SYSTEM

Ethical questions can be raised about the propriety of the bargaining that takes place. Plea bargaining generates controversy, primarily controversy related to the conflicting views of the ethical nature of plea bargaining. Opposition to plea bargaining is based on several grounds, among them that:

- Plea bargaining induces innocent defendants to plead guilty in order to avoid a harsh punishment.
- Plea bargaining allows guilty defendants to escape full punishment for their crimes, because some charges are dropped and sentences are mitigated in order to induce a guilty plea.
- Plea bargaining creates a trial penalty; defendants who stand firm and exercise their right to trial are penalized, an especially troubling result for those innocent defendants who are erroneously convicted. (Scott and Stuntz 1992)

To counter these criticisms the defenders of plea bargaining offer three contrary propositions:

- Truly guilty defendants who plead do not really get a reduced sentence; they get the same punishment they would have received if they had not bargained. There are no concessions and there is no trial penalty.
- From the public's perspective half a loaf is better than none. That is, obtaining a conviction on some charge is better than risking acquittal of someone who is guilty of serious crimes.
- There is nothing inappropriate about concessions and a trial penalty. Pleading guilty deserves a reward.

These positions represent the heart of the plea-bargaining controversy.

Hollow Promises and Just Deserts

Opponents of plea bargaining complain that it grants lenience to guilty defendants who plead guilty by allowing them to escape full responsibility and full punishment for their crimes. Defenders of plea bargaining counter that guilty pleaders actually receive the same punishment they would have received had they not made the plea agreement—that plea bargaining achieves the same results that would have been obtained had the case gone to trial but without the time and expense of trial. For example, in a particular case, the prosecutor and defense counsel both use their experience to judge the merits of the case. They may in fact agree. Both may conclude that in all probability the jury would convict on the lesser charge and acquit on the higher charge because of lack of sufficient evidence. They strike a bargain that simply mirrors the outcome that would have resulted.

Opponents of plea bargaining reason that if defendants who plead guilty receive the same punishment they would have received had they gone to trial, they have been victimized by a hollow promise. Defenders of plea bargaining assert that there is no hollow promise. Defense counsel advises the defendant of the probabilities of the various results. Defendants know that they are not receiving lenience, but only the same result they probably would get from trial. Yet defendants do receive something of value to them: certainty of the result and quick resolution of the case. According to the defenders of plea bargaining, defendants are not victimized by a hollow promise because these are real benefits.

Bargaining for Half a Loaf

Another argument offered in favor of plea bargaining is that it allows the prosecutor to get half a loaf—conviction on some charges—in difficult cases in which the risk of full acquittal is great. The half-a-loaf argument is based on the difference between factual guilt and legal guilt. Because of evidentiary or legal problems, legal guilt sometimes is impossible to prove, even when factual guilt is not in doubt. Physical evidence may be lost; witnesses may lose interest. Procedural error might render key evidence inadmissible. In each instance the prosecutor is certain of the defendant's factual guilt, but the evidence required to prove it in court is not available. The half-a-loaf argument recognizes that procedural justice allows the state to punish only those who are legally guilty, whereas substantive justice demands the punishment of the factually guilty. There is a distinction between the proof a prosecutor has and what can be offered in court.

Those who defend the practice of plea negotiations argue that it is often the only practical means to any conviction at all. According to the defenders of plea bargaining, those who would ban the practice fail to recognize this important function. For example, if some of the evidence in a case is potentially inadmissible because a search warrant is defective, a prosecutor might be able to get a conviction through plea bargaining even though the case would be dimissed if it went to trial (Curridan 1992, 18). Seeing guilty (and potentially dangerous) defendants go free is a powerful incentive to bargain in tough cases. The question here is whether that is a valid justification for the practice of negotiating pleas. Is it justifiable to convict (by guilty plea) for offenses that could not be proved if the accused exercised their rights under the law? Is it appropriate to pursue weak or shaky cases, cases that do not meet trial standards? What should justify legal punishment—factual guilt or legal guilt? Are we satisfied that the prosecutor who goes for half-a-loaf knows that the defendant really is guilty?

Rewarding Guilty Pleas

Another argument offered in favor of plea bargaining is that the act of pleading guilty deserves a reward. By waiving trial rights the defendant saves the state time, trouble, and resources. This, the argument goes, is worth some consideration by the state. In addition, pleading guilty is an admission of responsibility that merits consideration in sentencing.

Reward for Saving Time and Money

The American Bar Association's *Standards Relating to Pleas* (1968) hint that rewarding guilty pleas is justified. The standards note that a guilty plea makes "a public trial unnecessary when there are good reasons" for not having a public trial and avoids "delay in the disposition of other cases." Opponents of plea bargaining question how far this reward for enhancing efficiency should go. Would it be fair to reward defendants for accommodating in other ways that increase system efficiency? Would we offer lenience as a reward for waiving other rights that save time and money? Would we consider it proper to grant concessions to those who waive counsel, for example? The limits on offering lenience in exchange for saving the state money are unclear because such lenience is completely unrelated to any notion of just desserts. Therefore, offering lenience in exchange for a guilty plea on the grounds that it saves time and money is similarly unprincipled.

Moreover, opponents of plea bargaining say that rewarding defendants for waiving their rights is the same thing as imposing a trial penalty on those defendants who plead not guilty. If defendants who plead guilty are punished less severely than other defendants, defendants who exercise their trial rights are worse off in comparison.

In this view the trial penalty exists only because the state grants concessions (or rewards) to defendants who waive trial rights. The state's participation in plea bargaining creates a penalty for, or imposes a burden on, the exercise of constitutional rights. This, opponents of plea bargaining argue, is inconsistent with constitutional standards of due process.

Time and again, courts have prohibited government practices, policies, and statutes that would discourage defendants from exercising constitutional rights. For example, the Supreme Court ruled that a prosecutor may not issue more serious charges against a defendant on retrial after a defendant successfully appeals the conviction (*Blackledge* 1974). The rationale for this ruling is that vindictive prosecution following appeal would chill the defendant's exercise of the right to appeal. Similarly, statutes that permit the death penalty to be imposed only after a jury trial discourage the exercise of the right to jury, and are therefore unconstitutional (*United States v. Jackson* 1968). Plea bargaining discourages the exercise of these same rights, but the courts have not found this to be illegal. Opponents of plea bargaining argue that rewarding the waiver of constitutional rights is always unfair, whether the reward comes about through plea bargaining or other practices. The courts, however, have held that rewarding the waiver of constitutional rights is acceptable only in situations involving plea bargaining.

Defendants are free to make the choices facing them. But is it proper for the state to make one of those choices—the exercise of constitutional rights—distinctly more unattractive? Although these constitutional questions are inherent in the practice of plea bargaining, the U.S. Supreme Court has avoided a discussion of them. According to some legal scholars, the Court's tortured reasoning in relation to plea bargaining has left it in a "constitutional black hole" (Becker 1988, 760). Constitutional objections to the practice of plea bargaining have been dismissed by the Court on the ground that the defendant makes a free choice. The Court has held irrelevant the substantial penalties some defendants may pay for "freely choosing" whether to plead guilty.

Reward for Accepting Responsibility

Another justification for rewarding guilty pleas is the defendant's acceptance of responsibility for the crime. This justification attempts to tie the lenience into some notion of deserts, that is, what the offender deserves. Many scholars and practitioners take the position that an admission of responsibility is deserving of lenience. This position is echoed in the American Bar Association's justification of the differential treatment of those who plead guilty and in federal sentencing guidelines. The guidelines allow a "sentence discount" for a guilty plea if the defendant sincerely accepts responsibility. The discount can reduce the sentence by as much as 67 percent for a relatively minor offense and as little as 14 percent for a serious one (Sands and Coates 1991).

Opponents of plea bargaining acknowledge that a reward is at least consistent with notions of just deserts. As plea bargaining is practiced, however, the size of this reward appears to fluctuate widely, unrelated to the depth and sincerity of remorse and dependent primarily on the strength of the evidence and other factors unrelated to the sincerity of the defendant's admission. In addition, it is not clear why the reward for admitting guilt is offered only to defendants who waive trial. Why is a defendant who is convicted at trial and who accepts responsibility at sentencing not eligible for the same reward? Is there any difference in the sincerity of their admissions? The only difference is that the one who pleads guilty saves the state the time and trouble of proving guilt. If this is the only difference, the reward for pleading guilty is really a reward for saving resources and not for accepting responsibility.

Another argument against treating the admission of guilt as deserving of lenience is the dilemma such a situation creates for wrongly accused defendants (Kipnis 1976; Scott and Stuntz 1992). A system of plea bargaining presumes that all defendants are guilty—how else is it possible to justify a trial penalty? But we know that not all defendants are guilty, even after careful and responsible screening by prosecutors. Errors occur. The trial process is designed to minimize those errors, but even so the trial process results in some unknown number of erroneous convictions. Defendants who are erroneously convicted are punished more severely than if they had falsely admitted guilt.

Plea bargaining is difficult to defend from the perspective of justice and ethics. The arguments in favor of it hinge largely on expedience and efficiency. The ethical limits on these justifications are unstated and leave unclear whether other rights also could, or should, be compromised in favor of efficiency (Harvard Law Review Note 1970). Because plea bargaining conflicts with the ideals of justice, many advocate the abolition or drastic reform of plea bargaining. Here too controversy abounds (Smith 1986). Defenders of plea bargaining argue that reform will fail and plea bargaining will continue, even if it is driven underground, or that if reforms succeed and plea bargaining is in fact abolished, the court system will collapse as the pace of litigation grinds to a halt.

■ THE PROBABILITY OF SUCCESSFUL REFORM

Several jurisdictions have attempted to abolish plea bargaining, either in all cases or for specific kinds of crimes. Alaska's attorney general prohibited plea bargaining statewide for all offenses in 1975 and that ban remains in effect today (White Carns and Kruse 1992). In 1977 Michigan banned plea bargaining in firearms cases and imposed mandatory sentencing for those offenses (Heumann and Loftin 1979). El Paso, Texas, prohibited plea bargaining in late 1975 (Weninger 1987). In Black Hawk County, Iowa, the prosecutor banned all plea bargains in 1974 (Iowa Law Review Note 1975). Similar policies have been instituted in Maricopa County (Phoenix), Arizona, and in the federal jurisdiction in the Southern District of California. In 1991 judges in Tyler, Texas, banned plea bargaining in all cases (Curriden 1992). Did those reforms work? Did they effectively limit or eradicate plea bargaining? Did the demand for trials overwhelm the system?

Eliminating Plea Bargaining

Studies of efforts to eliminate plea bargaining have uniformly found that the ban caused some alteration in the normal style of doing business. Typically, research suggests that banning plea bargaining merely shifts bargaining to other points in the process. This phenomenon is sometimes likened to hydraulic displacement (Miethe 1987). Discretion to show lenience is usually available to both the prosecutor and the judge at a variety of points in the process. When one decision maker's discretion is limited at one decision point, discretion shifts to other points. When the prosecutor is prevented from exchanging lenience for guilty pleas, the decisions of the judge at conviction and sentencing (as well as the police at arrest) become all the more powerful in the final disposition of the case. If judges exercise their sentencing discretion in a manner that clearly rewards guilty pleas, plea bargaining—at least implicit bargaining—continues, despite controls on the prosecutor.

Early abolition attempts seemed to produce exactly this result. Researchers in Alaska, for example, initially found that implicit bargaining persisted in the face of the ban, although it eliminated explicit bargaining (Rubenstein and White 1979, 373–4). Similar conclusions were reached by those who evaluated abolition efforts in Maricopa County (Phoenix), Arizona (Berger 1976), the Southern District of California (Parnas and Atkins 1978), and Black Hawk County, Iowa (Iowa Law Review Note 1975). These findings have caused many observers to conclude that implicit plea bargaining is impossible to eradicate in our system of criminal case processing (see Schulhofer 1984, 1046).

However, more recent studies suggest that implicit bargaining may not be inevitable. The early efforts to abolish plea bargaining targeted the behavior of prosecutors and left judicial discretion in sentencing unchecked. This approach permits the maintenance of a trial penalty and allows a system of implicit bargaining to prevail. If judicial sentencing practices can be altered to eliminate a trial penalty, even implicit bargaining will diminish. Alaska's abolition experiment again proves illustrative. Two years after the ban on prosecutorial bargaining in 1975, Alaska instituted controls on sentencing practices. An evaluation of the combined effects of these policies indicates that implicit bargaining is no longer the norm. Sentencing data show that defendants who plead guilty in Alaska cannot expect more lenient sentences than defendants who go to trial (White Carns and Kruse 1992, 54).

Real Offense Sentencing

real offense sentencing

Since the mid-1980s, new efforts have been made to curtail bargaining. These are best described as backdoor policies designed to reduce the incentives for bargaining. **Real offense sentencing**, an approach to controlling judicial and prosecutorial discretion reflected in the federal sentencing guidelines, requires that the sentence imposed be based on the real offense, regardless of the offense charged by the prosecutor. For example, an armed robber might agree to enter a guilty plea in exchange for a reduced charge of robbery. However, at sentencing the judge is obligated to sentence the defendant on the facts in the record. Although the maximum sentence may be reduced, aggravating factors associated with the more serious offense (such as the use of a weapon) are given explicit weight in the sentencing decision. Under this scheme the incentives for the defendant to plea bargain are greatly diminished.

Plea bargaining is not prohibited under the federal sentencing guidelines; on the contrary, real offense sentencing was designed in the expectation that bargaining will occur and that it needs to be restricted. Real offense sentencing reduces the reward for pleading guilty. The guidelines do allow a small credit that reduces the sentence marginally for defendants who accept responsibility for their crime, but this credit is much smaller than the sentence reduction otherwise received through plea bargaining (Hochstedler Steury 1989). Early analysis of the effects of the federal sentencing guidelines suggests that the reward for entering a guilty plea is restricted in most cases to that allowed by the guidelines, a major change in the practice of plea bargaining in the federal system (Schulhofer and Nagel 1989, 285).

Rigorous Case Screening

Rigorous screening by prosecutors can also dramatically influence the amount of plea bargaining. If prosecutors do not issue charges in weak cases, those cases are not in the system, and prosecutors cannot be tempted to bargain to get half a loaf. A recent finding in regard to prosecutorial screening practices in response to Alaska's ban underscores this point. A second evaluation of the bargaining practices in Alaska found an important adaptation by prosecuters in response to the ban: before the ban prosecutors screened out about 8 percent of the cases as unworthy of prosecution; after the ban this proportion rose to 30 percent (White Carns and Kruse 1992, 42). The implication is clear: weak cases in Alaska are no longer viable in a system that does not allow prosecutors to bargain in the hope of obtaining half a loaf. The logical implication of course is that in some jurisdictions weak cases are plea bargained, and in other jurisdictions they are not prosecuted at all. One actual result of eliminating plea bargaining is to forego entirely the prosecution of relatively weak cases.

The Demand for Jury Trials

Defenders of plea bargaining have often predicted that the court system would grind to a halt without plea bargaining. That is, if a ban on plea bargaining is actually successful, the system will be overwhelmed by defendants seeking trial. Former Supreme Court Chief Justice Warren Burger reflected this view when he commented, "If every criminal charge were subjected to a full-scale trial, the States and the Federal Government would need to multiply by many times the number of judges and court facilities" (*Santobello* 1971, 260).

This prediction rests on an unproved assumption: that defendants will not enter guilty pleas unless the state offers an incentive to do so. Although the evidence is far from definitive, studies of abolition efforts suggest that this prediction is simply not borne out. Researchers and practitioners agree on this point: when plea bargaining is eliminated, demands for jury trials sometimes increase and sometimes do not; in any case the increase is marginal and does not overwhelm the system or threaten the financial solvency of the jurisdiction. For example, in the first three years after the Alaska ban was imposed, demand for jury trials increased from 7 percent to 10 percent, and then fell back again to 7 percent (White Carns and Kruse 1992, 52). Judging from the abolition experiments, it is reasonable to expect a marginal increase in demand for trials when bargaining is banned, but fears of the system grinding to a halt appear to be unfounded.

Additional evidence in support of this view comes from comparison of the proportion of cases that go to trial in different jurisdictions. For decades certain jurisdictions have experienced unusually low rates of guilty pleas. These jurisdictions raise obvious questions about the necessity of plea bargaining.

After examining several of these jurisdictions, researchers concluded that trials in the jurisdictions with low guilty plea rates are not the full-blown trials Chief Justice Burger may have had in mind. Rather, many of the cases recorded as trials were so quick and informal that researchers dubbed them slow pleas (Levin 1977; Mather 1973; Eisenstein and Jacobs 1977; Heumann and Loftin 1979). **Slow pleas** involve the brief, relatively informal, and uncontested presentation of evidence against the defendant, after which the defendant is found guilty by the judge.

slow pleas

Several researchers have characterized slow-plea court appearances as more akin to the plea-bargaining process than the full-blown trial we have come to associate with modern adversarial processes. The goal of the defense in slow plea trials is not to vigorously contest guilt but rather to introduce factors that might justify lenience for the defendant. However, another researcher has questioned whether even this characterization of slow pleas is accurate. Stephen Schulhofer and his research assistants observed hundreds of bench trials characterized as slow pleas in Philadelphia's felony and misdemeanor courts (Schulhofer 1984; 1985). He concluded that, while not elaborate or protracted, many of these bench trials were adversarial proceedings that dealt with contested matters of fact or law.

The evidence from a variety of studies leads to the conclusion that slow pleas vary in the extent to which they differ in any real way from plea agreements. One researcher described slow pleas in one jurisdiction that sometimes included "the same kinds of bargains as to charge and sentence as in a guilty plea" and sometimes were a "semi-adversary proceeding" (Mather 1973, 195), and other researchers describe similar variations in other jurisdictions (Heumann and Loftin 1979, 417–420).

Whatever the variations, slow pleas clearly are not signed and sealed bargains between the prosecutor and the defendant that never undergo judicial scrutiny in open court. They are not the wholesale explicit exchange of lenience for all trial rights, the Fifth Amendment protection against self-incrimination, and any right to appeal. In short, all available evidence indicates that several major urban jurisdictions in this nation—jurisdictions with serious crime and huge caseloads—have not become as reliant on the practice of plea bargaining as have others. These jurisdictions still rely heavily on the trial process to arrive at a disposition, although a fair number of these trials take only fifteen or thirty minutes (Levin 1977, 80). Perhaps the most interesting aspect of slow pleas is their resemblance to the rapid summary kinds of trials so prevalent in eighteenth-century England. If this type of trial were to become more common as a way to eliminate plea bargaining, would this be a positive reform? What answer could be given to critics who would complain that these quick trials are another form of assembly-line justice?

The lesson to be drawn here is that plea bargaining, implicit or explicit, is not inevitable. In the absence of plea bargaining the system adapts to handle the volume of cases presented. Prosecutors may institute more rigorous case screening. Cases that go to trial may be handled with an abbreviated process. The policy question that these results raise is whether the adaptations are preferable to plea bargaining.

SUMMARY

Plea bargaining appears to be the primary mode of disposing of cases in many jurisdictions. For it to prevail as a system it needs the implicit or explicit support of three parties: the prosecutor, the defense (defense counsel and defendant), and the judge. Plea bargaining is the unplanned adaptation to drastic legal, structural, and social changes that affect the courts' ability to manage the cases in the system. More cases were flowing into the system as the courts were evolving in ways that slowed the pace of trials. Interestingly, however, studies of jurisdictions that have a relatively large number of trials suggest that those trials today look much like the fast-paced trials of a bygone era.

Despite its acceptance by the courts and most practitioners, and its widespread use and institutionalization, the practice of plea bargaining presents troubling ethical problems that may conflict with the very premises of our system of justice. Consequently, several jurisdictions have attempted to abolish or reform plea bargaining. These efforts have had mixed results but offer reason to believe that reforms can produce positive and real results. Furthermore, some studies show that plea bargaining can be abolished without creating tremendous backlogs in the system. Many defendants are motivated to plead guilty even without concessions, although they are unlikely to do so if they expect concessions to be forthcoming if only they wait long enough. With a more comprehensive understanding of the dynamics of the players and more comprehensive reforms designed to control discretion at several decision points and that reduce the incentives to bargain, plea bargaining can be drastically reduced and transformed.

FOR FURTHER DISCUSSION

1. Look at the hypothetical case of *People v. Henry* presented in this chapter. From the perspective of attaining substantive justice, make a list of the advantages and disadvantages of the plea bargain offered by the prosecutor in this case. Do you think that the defense lawyer acted ethically in deciding to persuade the defendant to accept the prosecutor's plea offer? Discuss how the ethics of the defense counsel's action depend on how she presents the options to the defendant.

2. Put yourself in the position of the judge in *State v. Rojak*. Would you accept the prosecutor's sentence recommendation, or would you substitute a different sentence? Explain the considerations that would go into your decision.

3. How are case preparation and the skill of the attorney important in shaping the outcome of plea bargaining? Are these factors equally important in explicit and implicit bargaining?

4. Consider plea bargaining from the perspective of (1) the crime control model and (2) the due process model. Which of these models is more likely to be a source of criticism of plea bargaining?

5. What do you know about the way in which plea negotiation is practiced in your community? Map a research strategy that could tell you how plea negotiations are carried out in your community and with what consequences.

■ REFERENCES

Alschuler, Albert W. 1979. "Plea Bargaining and Its History." *Law and Society Review* 13: 211–245.

——— 1976. "The Trial Judge's Role in Plea Bargaining: Part I." *Columbia Law Review* 76: 1059–1153.

American Bar Association. Commission on Minimum Standards for Criminal Justice. 1968. *Standards Relating to Pleas.* Chicago: American Bar Association.

American Bar Association. Special Committee on Evaluation of Ethical Standards. 1969. *Code of Professional Responsibility, Final Draft, July 1, 1969.* Chicago: American Bar Association.

Anderson, Allen F. 1989. "Judicial Participation in the Plea Negotiation Process: Some Frequencies and Disposing Factors." *Hamline Journal of Public Law and Policy* 10: 39–57.

Becker, Loftus E., Jr. 1988. "Plea Bargaining and the Supreme Court." *Loyola of Los Angeles Law Review* 21: 757–841.

Berger, Moise. 1976. "The Case Against Plea Bargaining." *American Bar Association Journal* 62: 621–624.

Blackledge v. Perry, 417 U.S. 21, 94 S. Ct. 2098 (1974).

Bordenkircher v. Hayes, 434 U.S. 357, 98 S. Ct. 663 (1978).

Brady v. United States, 397 U.S. 742, 90 S. Ct. 1463 (1970).

Casper, Jonathan. 1972. *American Criminal Justice: The Defendant's Perspective.* Englewood Cliffs, N.J.: Prentice-Hall.

Curriden, Mark. 1992. "Banning Bargaining: Tyler, Texas, Judges Order a Stop to Plea Agreements." *American Bar Association Journal* 78: 18.

Eisenstein, James, and James Jacobs. 1977. *Felony Justice: An Organizational Analysis of Criminal Courts.* Boston: Little, Brown.

Feeley, Malcolm M. 1979. *The Process Is the Punishment: Handling Cases in a Lower Criminal Court.* New York: Russell Sage.

Flanagan, Timothy J., and Kathleen Maguire, eds. 1990. *Sourcebook of Criminal Justice Statistics—1989.* Washington, D.C.: U.S. Government Printing Office.

Friedman, Lawrence M. 1979. "Plea Bargaining in Historical Perspective." *Law and Society Review* 13: 247–59.

Haller, Mark H. 1979. "Plea Bargaining: The Nineteenth Century Context." *Law and Society Review* 13: 273–79.

Harvard Law Review Note. 1970. "The Unconstitutionality of Plea Bargaining." *Harvard Law Review* 83: 1387–1411.

Heumann, Milton. 1978. *Plea Bargaining: The Experiences of Prosecutors, Judges, and Defense Attorneys.* Chicago: University of Chicago Press.

——— 1975. "A Note on Plea Bargaining and Case Pressure." *Law and Society Review* 9: 515–28.

Heumann, Milton, and C. Loftin. 1979. "Mandatory Sentencing and the Abolition of Plea Bargaining: The Michigan Felony Firearm Statute." *Law and Society Review* 13: 393–430.

Hochstedler Steury, Ellen. 1989. "Prosecutorial and Judicial Discretion." In D. J. Champion, ed. *The U.S. Sentencing Guidelines: Implications for Criminal Justice.* New York: Praeger.

Iowa Law Review Note. 1975. "The Elimination of Plea Bargaining in Black Hawk County: A Case Study." *Iowa Law Review* 60: 1053–71.

Langbein, John H. 1979. "Understanding the Short History of Plea Bargaining." *Law and Society Review* 13: 261–72.

Levin, Martin A. 1977. *Urban Politics and the Criminal Courts.* Chicago: University of Chicago Press.

Kipnis, Kenneth. 1976. "Criminal Justice and the Negotiated Plea." *Ethics* 86: 93–106.

Mather, Lynn M. 1973. "Some Determinants of the Method of Case Disposition: Decision Making by Public Defenders in Los Angeles." *Law and Society Review* 8: 187–216.

Miethe, Terrance D. 1987. "Charging and Plea Bargaining Practices Under Determinate Sentencing: An Investigation of the Hydraulic Displacement of Discretion." *Journal of Criminal Law and Criminology* 78: 155–76.

Moley, Raymond. 1928. "The Vanishing Jury." *Southern California Law Review* 2: 97–127.

Nardulli, Peter F., James Eisenstein, and Roy B. Flemming. 1988. *The Tenor of Justice: Criminal Courts and the Guilty Plea Process*. Urbana: University of Illinois Press.

Newman, Donald J. 1966. *Conviction: The Determination of Guilt or Innocence Without Trial*. Boston: Little, Brown.

Nimmer, Raymond T., and Patricia A. Krauthaus. 1977. "Plea Bargaining: Reform in Two Cities." *Justice System Journal* 3: 6–21.

Odiaga, Ursula. 1989. "The Ethics of Judicial Discretion in Plea Bargaining." *Georgetown Journal of Legal Ethics* 2: 695–723.

Parnas, Raymond I., and Riley J. Atkins. 1978. "Abolishing Plea Bargaining: A Proposal." *Criminal Law Bulletin* 14: 101–22.

Rubenstein, Michael L., and Teresa White. 1979. "Alaska's Ban on Plea Bargaining." *Law and Society Review* 13: 367–83.

Ryan, John Paul, and James Alfini. 1979. "Trial Judges' Participation in Plea Bargaining: An Empirical Perspective." *Law and Society Review* 13: 479–507.

Sanborn, Joseph B. 1986. "A Historical Sketch of Plea Bargaining." *Justice Quarterly* 3:111–38.

Sands, Jon M., and Cynthia A. Coates. 1991. "The Mikado's Object: The Tension Between Relevant Conduct and Acceptance of Responsibility in the Federal Sentencing Guidelines." *Arizona State Law Journal* 23: 61–108.

Santobello v. New York, 404 U.S. 257, 92 S. Ct. 495 (1971).

——— 1985. "No Job Too Small: Justice Without Bargaining in the Lower Criminal Courts." *American Bar Foundation Research Journal* 1985 (3): 519–98.

Schulhofer, Stephen J. 1992. "Plea Bargaining as Disaster." *Yale Law Journal* 101:1979–2009.

——— 1984. "Is Plea Bargaining Inevitable?" *Harvard Law Review* 97: 1037–1107.

Schulhofer, Stephen J., and Ilene H. Nagel. 1989. "Negotiated Pleas Under the Federal Sentencing Guidelines: The First Fifteen Months." *American Criminal Law Review* 1989: 231–88.

Scott, Robert E., and William J. Stuntz. 1992. "Plea Bargaining as Contract." *Yale Law Journal* 101: 1909–68.

Shelton v. United States, 242 F.2d 101 (5th Cir. 1957).

Smith, Douglas. 1986. "The Plea Bargaining Controversy." *Journal of Criminal Law and Criminology* 77: 949–57.

Sudnow, David N. 1965. "Normal Crimes: Sociological Features of the Penal Code in a Public Defender's Office." *Social Problems* 12: 209–15.

United States v. Ammidown, 497 F.2d 615 (D.C. Cir. 1973).

United States v. Jackson, 390 U.S. 570, 88 S. Ct. 1209 (1968).

Weninger, Robert A. 1987. "The Abolition of Plea Bargaining. A Case Study of El Paso County, Texas." *University of California, Los Angeles Law Review* 35: 265–313.

White Carns, Teresa, and James Kruse. 1992. "A Reevaluation of Alaska's Ban on Plea Bargaining." *Alaska Law Review* 8: 27–69.

CHAPTER **14**

ARRAIGNMENT: PLEADING TO THE CHARGE

Arraignment is the formal court appearance at which the defendant is required to plead to the charges. The word *arraignment* is commonly used to refer to the initial appearance. This usage may have come about because of the many misdemeanor cases resolved by guilty pleas at the initial appearance after arrest. As a consequence in many misdemeanor cases the initial appearance is the arraignment as well. However, in felony cases the defendant generally is not allowed to enter a guilty plea in the lower court. Consequently, felony arraignments typically occur in the court of general jurisdiction a few weeks or even months after the initial appearance (LaFave and Israel 1985, 801).

In the few cases in which the defendant pleads not guilty the main business of the arraignment is to receive the not guilty plea and schedule the case for trial. When the defendant pleads guilty at arraignment the court must determine whether the guilty plea is voluntary and appropriate under the circumstances.

■ THE ARRAIGNMENT PROCEEDING

In felony cases the arraignment is a separate court proceeding at which the defendant appears and is asked to plead to the charges. If the defendant is not already represented by counsel, the defendant will be informed of the right to an attorney. If the defendant is indigent, an attorney is provided.

The first step in the proceeding is the reading of the formal charging document, the indictment or the information. Defendants often waive this reading in order to expedite the proceeding and avoid the degradation of listening to a public recitation of the charges. If the charging document is defective in any way, such as an omission of an essential element of the offense charged, defense counsel may challenge the charging document at this point.

Next, the judge asks the defendant, "How do you plead?" The defendant has four major options: to enter a plea of not guilty, guilty, or no contest (sometimes

313

referred to as *nolo contendere*), or to stand mute and say nothing in response to the charges.

■ PLEAS THAT WAIVE THE RIGHT TO TRIAL

guilty plea

In most cases the defendant simply pleads guilty, which amounts to a confession to the crime and a waiver of the right to a jury trial and all other trial rights. In addition, a **guilty plea** is an admission of guilt that waives the defendant's Fifth Amendment right against self-incrimination. However, the defendant could waive the trial without admitting guilt by pleading no contest or by entering an *Alford* plea. In a no contest plea and an *Alford* plea the defendant waives the right to trial but does not waive the Fifth Amendment right against self-incrimination and does not admit to having committed the crimes charged.

No Contest Plea

no contest plea

A **no contest plea** means that the defendant has chosen not to contest the charges at trial but does not admit to having committed the crime. In a no contest plea the defendant neither admits nor denies the truthfulness of the allegations. Instead the defendant merely waives the right to have the state prove guilt at trial. The main purpose of a no contest plea is to avoid a confession that could be used against the defendant in a civil trial stemming from the circumstances that led to the criminal charges.

In a variety of circumstances a defendant might be facing court action in both the criminal and civil courts. For example, if a person is accused of wrecking someone's car with a sledgehammer, the state might charge that person with criminal damage to property, and the owner of the car might bring a civil suit requesting monetary compensation for the damage. The victim of a vicious assault might bring a tort action in civil court against the defendant at the same time that the government brings criminal assault charges. A regulatory agency might pursue criminal charges against a toxic waste dumper and bring a civil suit or administrative action against the defendant to order cleanup of the hazardous materials. In each case, if the defendant were to plead guilty to the criminal charge, the guilty plea would be an admission that could be submitted as evidence against the defendant in the pending civil action, a possibility the defendant may wish to avoid. At the same time the defendant may wish to avoid trial in the criminal case. For example, the defendant may be seeking to gain lenience from the prosecutor or judge by waiving trial.

The judge must decide whether to accept or reject the no contest plea. In some cases the prosecutor recommends that the court reject the plea; a prosecutor may bargain with a defendant over this issue. If the judge refuses to accept the no contest plea, the only alternatives are to plead guilty, thereby admitting guilt, or to plead not guilty and go to trial.

Alford Plea

Alford plea

Like the no contest plea, the ***Alford* plea** is used to waive the right to trial without admitting guilt. In this plea defendants waive the right to trial but continue to maintain their innocence. The *Alford* plea is used when the evidence against the defendant is strong, making trial risky, particularly given the concessions offered by the prosecution in exchange for a guilty plea. The *Alford* plea is named for the defendant in the case of *North Carolina v. Alford* (1970), the case in which the U.S. Supreme Court approved this plea. Alford had been indicted on first-degree murder charges, which carried the death penalty under North Carolina law. Alford gave his defense lawyer a list of witnesses who would support his claim of innocence. When his attorney questioned these witnesses, however, they all gave statements that pointed to Alford's guilt. Because there was no corroboration for Alford's claim that he was innocent, his attorney recommended that Alford accept the prosecutor's plea bargain offer and plead guilty to second-degree murder, which carried a maximum sentence of thirty years' imprisonment.

At the arraignment Alford pleaded guilty to the reduced charge. However, in response to questions by the judge Alford stated that he had not committed murder but was pleading guilty because he faced the threat of the death penalty if he went to trial. The judge continued to question him regarding the voluntariness of his decision and concluded that Alford was aware of the consequences of pleading guilty and accepted Alford's plea.

In considering the facts of this case on appeal the Supreme Court noted that in the case of a no contest plea the defendant waives the right to trial even though there is no admission of guilt. The Court held that an express admission of guilt is not a constitutional requirement for accepting a guilty plea and concluded that, "In view of the strong factual basis for the plea demonstrated by the State and Alford's clearly expressed desire to enter it despite his professed belief in his innocence, we hold that the trial judge did not commit constitutional error in accepting it" (*North Carolina v. Alford* 1970, 38). Since this decision, the term *Alford* plea has been used to refer to defendants who want to plead guilty but at the same time maintain that they are really innocent.

The *Alford* plea continues to be controversial, despite the Supreme Court's approval of it. Some defense attorneys will not allow their clients to plead guilty if they continue to profess their innocence. Judges also may be reluctant to allow defendants to plead guilty under these circumstances. A study of the use of the *Alford* plea found that, although the *Alford* plea was raised in only 2 percent of the cases studied, half the judges stated that they did not accept *Alford* pleas (McDonald 1987, 212–13). This reluctance may stem in part from uncertainty about the strength of the factual basis for the plea. Where the facts all point to guilt and there is virtually no chance of acquittal, a judge might more readily accept an *Alford* plea than in a case in which the evidence is less certain. Federal law and the laws in some states caution judges not to accept *Alford* pleas unless there is a factual basis for the plea (Miller et al. 1986, 948).

Consequences of Pleading Guilty

The criminal consequences of a simple guilty plea, a no contest plea, and an *Alford* plea are the same. If the judge accepts the plea, the defendant has waived the right to trial. In the case of a simple guilty plea (as opposed to a no contest or *Alford* plea) the defendant also has waived the Fifth Amendment protection against self-incrimination and a number of other constitutional rights: the rights to trial by jury, to confront accusers, and to have the state prove guilt beyond a reasonable doubt (*Boykin v. Alabama*, 1969). In most cases a guilty plea also waives the right to object to defects in the state's case, such as an illegal search or a confession obtained in violation of the *Miranda* requirements (Miller et al. 1986,

906). The right to appeal is extremely limited in cases in which the defendant pleads guilty (LaFave and Israel 1985, 806).

knowing, intelligent, and voluntary waiver

Because these important rights are waived by the guilty plea, the defendant is entitled to the assistance of counsel at the arraignment. In addition, the judge is required to question the defendant to ensure that the waiver is **knowing**, **intelligent**, and **voluntary**. This means that the judge must ensure that the defendant understands the nature of the charges and the consequences of pleading guilty and that the guilty plea has not been coerced. In addition, many states and the federal courts require that the judge determine the accuracy of the plea by inquiring into the **factual basis** for the charges to which the defendant is pleading guilty. How judges fulfill these tasks, and how well they do them, varies widely, however. "The most carefully worded, required inquiry can be made into an unintelligible rattle of words when read off like a tobacco auctioneer—as was observed in some courts" (McDonald 1987, 205). Determining the voluntariness, knowledge, and understanding of the defendant, and ascertaining the factual basis for the charge, can be accomplished in more than one way, but these tasks require some effort by the judge if the examination is to be more than a formality.

factual basis

Voluntariness

By questioning the defendant the judge is supposed to determine whether the defendant has been coerced to plead guilty through threats or promises. The judge is required to ascertain whether the guilty plea has been freely chosen from the alternatives available to the defendant. Judging the voluntariness of the plea may be difficult when the prosecutor has made threats or promises in the context of plea bargaining. Several Supreme Court cases have highlighted the dilemmas judges face in determining voluntariness.

In the *Alford* decision, the Supreme Court noted that, "confronted with the choice between a trial for first-degree murder [a capital offense] on the one hand, and a plea of guilty to second-degree murder on the other, Alford quite reasonably chose the latter and thereby limited the maximum penalty to a 30-year term" (1970, 37). The Court found nothing coercive in the inherent pressure to plead guilty that is created in such a choice, even though Alford continued to maintain his innocence. The Court has also ruled that guilty pleas are voluntary even if they are entered in order to avoid additional charges threatened by the prosecutor. In *Bordenkircher v. Hayes* (1978) the defendant argued that the prosecutor threatened to charge him as a habitual criminal unless Hayes pleaded guilty to a forgery charge. Hayes contended that the threat of additional penalties coerced his guilty plea. The Court held that this was not coercion:

> While confronting a defendant with the risk of more severe punishment clearly may have a "discouraging effect on the defendant's assertion of his trial rights, the imposition of these difficult choices [is] an inevitable"—and permissible—"attribute of any legitimate system which tolerates and encourages the negotiation of pleas." It follows that, by tolerating and encouraging the negotiation of pleas, this Court has necessarily accepted as constitutionally legitimate the simple reality that the prosecutor's interest at the bargaining table is to persuade the defendant to forgo his right to plead not guilty. . . . We hold only that the course of conduct engaged in by the prosecutor in this case, which no more than openly presented the defendant with the unpleasant alternatives of forgoing trial or facing charges on which he was plainly subject to prosecution, did not violate the Due Process Clause of the Fourteenth Amendment. (364)

The general conclusion that can be drawn from these cases is that the Supreme Court finds no coercion when the prosecutor pressures the defendant to plead guilty, unless that pressure involves improper conduct on the part of the prosecutor or other court officials. Absent evidence of direct coercion, any inducements to plead guilty that are part of the statutory structure under which the defendant pleads are to be considered part of the normal give and take of bargaining. So long as the defendant is able to rationally weigh the pros and cons of pleading guilty, and the prosecutor has done nothing illegal, the waiver of the right to trial has not been coerced. These Supreme Court cases show that the Court views a guilty plea as voluntary—no matter how distasteful the defendant's options—so long as the defendant freely chooses from among the alternatives available. Even statutory structures that encourage guilty pleas by authorizing more serious penalties for defendants convicted at trial have not been interpreted as coercive within the meaning of the Constitution (*Brady v. United States* 1970).

Understanding the Charges

Before accepting a guilty plea a judge must ensure that the defendant understands the nature of the charge to which the defendant is pleading guilty. For the decision to plead guilty to be knowing and intelligent the defendant must understand what facts the prosecution would need to prove if the defendant had pleaded not guilty (LaFave and Israel 1985, 805). In most cases judges simply rely on defense counsel to advise the defendant about the nature of the charge to which the defendant is pleading.

Knowledge of Consequences

By advising the defendant of the consequences of pleading guilty the judge ensures that the defendant understands what the guilty plea means. The judge must advise the defendant about the sentence that may be imposed following conviction on a guilty plea. In most cases this simply requires that the judge inform the defendant of the maximum penalty allowed by statute. In federal prosecutions and in most states the judge is also required to inform the defendant of any mandatory minimum sentence requirements related to the charge. Some courts also require that the court advise the defendant who is pleading guilty to more than one charge that the court may sentence the defendant to serve the sentences consecutively rather than concurrently or simultaneously. In some instances the judge must also inform the defendant if the guilty plea makes the defendant eligible for increased or "enhanced" penalties for being a repeat or habitual offender. Finally, the judge may also be required to inform the defendant of the rights that are waived in the act of pleading guilty (LaFave and Israel 1985, 805–7).

Factual Basis

In most jurisdictions the judge is also required to inquire about the accuracy of the plea, making certain that the charge to which the defendant is pleading is supported by the facts of the case. The judge may do this by reading the case file, particularly the criminal complaint, and asking questions of the defendant and prosecutor (LaFave and Israel 1985, 808). In some cases the judge may take the case under advisement, until after the presentence investigation has been completed, because it may shed more light on the facts underlying the charge (Remington et al. 1969, 572).

Requiring that the judge find some factual basis for the charge serves several purposes. First, it may prevent the conviction of the innocent. Second, it puts information about the charges on the record, preserving that information for later proceedings if the defendant later seeks to challenge the conviction. Finally, the information about the circumstances of the offense is useful to the judge in sentencing.

Disclosure of Plea Agreements

Because many guilty pleas are the result of plea bargaining, the judge may also be required by statute to inquire about the terms of the bargain and to have the bargain put on the record. Any promises that have been made to the defendant become a matter of record. Disclosure of the terms of the plea bargain creates a clear factual record if the defendant challenges the conviction at some later point. In particular, disclosure insulates the conviction from later claims by the defendant that the prosecutor made specific promises and then broke them.

If the prosecutor has agreed to recommend a particular sentence to the judge, the judge must inform the defendant that the judge is under no obligation to follow the prosecutor's recommendation and may impose a more severe penalty. If a judge decides that the prosecutor's recommendation is too lenient, the judge sometimes informs the defendant of this decision. The defendant is then free to either change the plea to not guilty or to continue with the guilty plea, knowing that the judge will not follow the prosecutor's recommendation.

The Ideal Versus the Real

Although judges are supposed to actively supervise guilty pleas, some evidence raises questions about the quality of their supervision. Researcher William F. McDonald (1987) studied felony and misdemeanor arraignments in six jurisdictions and found substantial variation in practice (see Figure 14-1). According to McDonald, the judge's role remains "fluid and uncertain."

McDonald found a general relationship between the length of the arraignment proceeding and the overall quality of the judge's participation in it. On average the arraignment lasted less than eight minutes. Felony arraignments lasted just under ten minutes (McDonald 1987, 206). Judges asked whether the defendant understood the charges in fewer than two-thirds of the cases. In just over half the cases the judge noted for the record that defense counsel had explained the charges to the defendant. In less than half the cases the judge advised the defendant of the maximum sentence for the charge; in only 4 percent of cases did the judge inform the defendant of other rights waived in the process of pleading guilty. In 55 percent of cases the judge asked whether the defendant had been threatened, coerced, or pressured to plead guilty. Sometimes judges were careful to word this question so that defendants would understand that the inducements to plead offered by the prosecutor should not be understood as pressure. In 71 percent of cases the judge had the plea agreement read into the record (McDonald 1987, 207–9).

Three states studied by McDonald require an inquiry into the factual basis for the charge. In 59 percent of the cases the judge simply asked the defendant whether he had committed the offense. In about half the cases the prosecutor reported evidence underlying the charge (McDonald 1987, 211).

Upon interviewing defendants McDonald found that some did not understand some or all of what the judge and lawyers said during the arraignment. Defendants reported that their attorneys had advised them how to answer the

FIGURE 14-1 Establishing "Knowing" and "Intelligent" Guilty Pleas by Jurisdiction (June–August 1977)

Source: William F. McDonald. 1987. "Judicial Supervision of the Guilty Plea Process: A Study of Six Jurisdictions." *Judicature* 70 (December–January):208. With permission of William F. McDonald.

Method/type of charge	El Paso (N = 106)	New Orleans (N = 120)	Seattle (N = 138)	Tucson (N = 110)	Delaware Co. (N = 131)	Norfolk (N = 106)	Total* (N = 711)**
Waiver of rights							
One or more rights mentioned as waived?							
Yes	68.2%	95.8%	46.0%	98.2%	87.8%	67.9%	76.8%
Three or more rights?							
Yes	15.1	55.0	29.7	85.5	64.1	16.0	44.7
Five or more rights?							
Yes	0.0	24.2	8.0	0.0	51.1	0.0	15.0
Which rights were verbally specified as being waived?							
Trial by jury	67.9	94.2	46.7	97.3	67.2	56.6	70.0
Remain silent	12.3	0.0	7.2	0.9	0.0	0.0	37.9
Confront witnesses	15.1	50.0	33.3	80.9	64.2	8.6	44.4
Appeal	0.0	81.8	37.0	0.0	78.6	60.9	43.0
Counsel (at no cost)	10.4	0.8	1.4	40.0	68.0	11.3	22.4
Who recited rights waived?							
Judge	22.9	94.1	30.4	98.2	8.5	66.0	51.9
Defense counsel	0.0	0.0	12.3	0.9	73.6	0.0	16.0
None	30.5	5.9	53.6	0.9	14.7	32.1	23.6
Other	46.6	0.0	3.6	0.0	3.1	1.9	8.6
Who asked defendant if he understood rights he was waiving?							
Judge	19.0	96.7	56.5	91.8	24.8	65.1	58.8
Defense counsel	0.0	0.0	0.0	0.9	45.7	0.0	8.5
None	47.6	3.3	42.0	7.3	25.6	33.0	26.6
Other	33.3	0.0	1.4	0.0	3.9	0.9	6.1
Was it noted that defense counsel had explained the defendant's rights to him?							
Yes	8.6	95.0	56.9	18.2	91.5	54.9	56.3

FIGURE 14-1   Establishing "Knowing" and "Intelligent" Guilty Pleas by Jurisdiction (June–August 1977)—continued

Method/type of charge	El Paso (N = 106)	New Orleans (N = 120)	Seattle (N = 138)	Tucson (N = 110)	Delaware Co. (N = 131)	Norfolk (N = 106)	Total* (N = 711)**
Explaining the charges							
Who explained charges?							
No one							
Felony charge	4.3	59.1	40.0	15.9	3.8	18.7	26.1
Misdemeanor charge	2.4	75.5	68.4	63.4	1.9	45.2	36.6
All cases	2.9	66.4	47.8	33.6	3.1	26.4	30.6
Who asked if defendant understood the charges?							
No one	56.2	19.3	51.1	34.5	46.2	36.8	40.9
Was it noted that counsel had explained charges to defendant?							
Yes	10.5	93.3	18.7	9.1	19.8	55.8	34.4
Explaining the consequences							
Defendant notified of the maximum possible sentence?							
Yes	35.8	75.8	56.6	80.0	6.1	39.1	48.5

*Percentages that do not total to 100 are due to rounding.
**The sizes of the respective Ns vary slightly due to item non-response.

judge's questions. Moreover, McDonald observed that standardized forms, used in some courts to advise defendants of their rights, were even less likely to give defendants real understanding of the charges or the consequences of pleading guilty.

Based on these observations McDonald concluded that, although defendants are probably better informed than they once were,

> the use of plea-acceptance forms with minimal additional questioning of the defendant; establishing the factual basis in ways designed to minimize the possibility of a discrepancy between what the defendant believes happened and what the state says happened; and the use of other measures designed to meet the mandate of appellate courts in a streamlined manner bring today's plea-taking close to being a new kind of "pious fraud." (1987, 214)

Rejecting Guilty Pleas

In most cases the process of accepting the guilty plea is brief, perfunctory, and uncomplicated. Nonetheless, a variety of issues may arise that cast doubt on the voluntariness of the defendant's guilty plea, the factual guilt of the defendant in relation to the offense charged, or the defendant's understanding of the consequences of pleading guilty. One study found that:

> The defendant may be emotionally disturbed; he may be motivated by desire to protect someone else or to cover up more serious conduct; he may think it preferable to take a lesser penalty rather than risk the possibility of conviction for a major crime even though he is not guilty. Or he may misconceive the elements of the crime with which he is charged and plead guilty even when under the law's definition his conduct does not constitute the offense he thinks it does, or even though he may have a valid defense. (Remington et al. 1969, 570)

A judge who has any such doubts about the appropriateness of the plea may reject a guilty plea. In McDonald's sample, judges rejected the guilty plea offered in 2 percent of cases (McDonald 1987, 213).

Rejecting a guilty plea is a serious decision that may create a dilemma for the judge. In rejecting the guilty plea the judge in effect forces the defendant to undergo a trial that the defendant had chosen to avoid, often for good reasons. Appellate court opinions differ in regard to the situations in which the trial judge may refuse to accept a guilty plea. These decisions seek to balance the fair treatment of the accused, the authority of the prosecutor over the charging decision, the authority of the judge over the sentencing decision, and the protection of the public interest in seeing that justice is done.

Withdrawing the Guilty Plea

Once the judge has accepted the guilty plea, the defendant may not withdraw it except with the approval of the judge and then only under limited circumstances. Generally, the defendant needs to show some good reason that he should be allowed to withdraw the guilty plea. Once the judge has imposed sentence, a guilty plea can be withdrawn only by showing that not allowing it to be withdrawn would cause a "manifest injustice" or by appealing the conviction (LaFave and Israel 1985, 811).

At one time it was virtually impossible to appeal if the defendant had pleaded guilty. Today some jurisdictions allow a defendant to bring a direct appeal of a

conviction based on a guilty plea if the defendant claims that improper procedures were followed. Such actions typically relate to promises and threats made
in plea bargaining or the ineffective assistance of counsel. Supreme Court cases
discussing the situations under which it is possible to challenge a conviction
obtained through a guilty plea are contradictory and confusing. Generally, the
Court appears to have signaled that if the defendant was deprived of constitutional or other rights, and because of that deprivation the defendant was
persuaded to plead guilty, the conviction may be challenged, despite the
admission of guilt through the guilty plea.

☐ Not Guilty Pleas

stands mute

If the defendant pleads not guilty, a trial date is usually set. If the defendant
stands mute, saying nothing in response to the charges, the court enters a not
guilty plea for the defendant and proceeds as though the defendant had pleaded
not guilty.

Notice of Affirmative Defenses

affirmative
defense

Ordinarily, the burden of proof rests with the prosecution, and the defendant
does not have to offer an active defense. The defendant is entitled to a
presumption of innocence and does not need to prove it. In certain circumstances, however, it may be to the defendant's strategic advantage to offer proof
of innocence in an **affirmative defense**. Insanity, alibi, justifiable homicide, and
diminished capacity are all considered affirmative defenses (see Chapter 15). In
affirmative defenses the defense accepts the burden of producing evidence that
the defendant did not commit the offense or should not be held criminally
responsible. In most jurisdictions, a defendant who is going to raise an affirmative
defense must provide advance notice of this intention. Typically, this notice
would be given at the arraignment or earlier and is necessary to allow the
prosecution time to prepare a case that counters the defense claims.

☐ Special Issues Relating to the Plea: Incompetency and Insanity

The mental capacities of the defendant may come to hold special significance at
the arraignment, if not before. Defendants who are severely mentally disabled or
mentally ill may be unable to understand the proceedings in court and may not
have the mental capacity legally required to waive the right to trial. In addition,
the arraignment is the proceeding at which a defendant may plead "not guilty by
reason of insanity" (the insanity defense). These issues, incompetence and
insanity, are frequently misunderstood.

Concerns about the mental health of defendants have increased in recent
decades. Following deinstitutionalization of the mentally ill during the 1970s
many urban centers were flooded with large numbers of former mental patients.
Because many states and localities failed to provide appropriate community and
outpatient treatment for these individuals, and because of changes in civil
commitment laws, police arrest many mentally ill people whose sometimes erratic
behavior is viewed as a nuisance or a cause for fear or concern. As a result

mentally ill defendants have become more common in courts across the nation. Although mental illness on its own does not render an individual incompetent or insane, issues related to mental illness are raised with increasing frequency. Some studies suggest that the incompetence and insanity procedures of the criminal courts have been used increasingly to institutionalize mentally ill individuals.

◼ COMPETENCY TO PLEAD OR STAND TRIAL

incompetence

Because the guilty plea constitutes a waiver of many important rights, and because all waivers must be knowing, intelligent, and voluntary to be constitutionally valid, the judge must exercise extreme care in accepting a guilty plea from a defendant who appears to be confused. Defendants who are mentally retarded or seriously mentally ill may not be able to understand what they are waiving or the consequences of doing so. In such cases the defendant may be **incompetent** to plead guilty or to stand trial.

Because of the concern for a valid waiver of the right to trial, the standard for competence to plead guilty is even higher than the standard for competence to stand trial in a few states. However, in most states a single competency standard applies to defendants who plead guilty and to defendants who plead not guilty and anticipate standing trial (LaFave and Israel 1985, 802).

Definition of Incompetence to Stand Trial

The prototypical standard for assessing competence to stand trial was announced by the U.S. Supreme Court in *Dusky v. United States* (1960). In that case the Supreme Court held that a defendant's competence to stand trial depends on whether the defendant "has sufficient present ability to consult with his lawyer with a reasonable degree of rational understanding—and whether he has a rational as well as factual understanding of the proceedings against him" (402). This standard has two overarching components: the ability to communicate rationally and the ability to understand what it means to be criminally charged, prosecuted, and punished. Both concerns relate to the defendant's present mental condition, that is, the defendant's condition at the time of court proceedings. The defendant's mental condition at the time of the crime is irrelevant to the issue of competence.

A variety of conditions might render a defendant incompetent to stand trial. The defendant may be mentally retarded and unable to comprehend the meaning of being in a courtroom and charged with a criminal offense. Or the defendant may be suffering from hallucinations or psychotic delusions. Memory loss caused by senility or brain injury may make it impossible for the defendant to assist in preparing a defense. A defendant may be so physically weak or debilitated that communication is not possible.

Some defendants will be incompetent for only short periods of time—given proper treatment they may regain competence. In other cases successful treatment of the mental or physical infirmity is unlikely or impossible. Other defendants may drift in and out of legal competence. Because competence concerns the defendant's present mental condition, it is entirely possible for a defendant to be competent one week, incompetent the next, and competent again the third week.

INCOMPETENCE

The following is a prosecutor's perspective on the attempt of a defendant to use incompetency proceedings to delay trial and buy time. Clearly, this prosecutor viewed the defendant's claim of incompetence as a manipulative ploy.

Santana [a rape defendant facing a potentially long sentence if convicted] tried claiming he was too crazy to go to trial, that he was not mentally fit to assist in his own defense. Even if he were successful in convincing the courts of this, it wouldn't get him off the hook, but at least it would buy him some time—and maybe save him a lot of it. His attorneys requested court-ordered mental examinations. . . . The psychiatrists disagreed with each other. . . . Queens [County court] . . . found Santana fit. . . .

   The trials were approaching, and Santana was running out of options. He swallowed a razor blade. It was a standard jailhouse ploy: File the edges down to dull them, coat the blade with Vaseline, swallow it, then have it show up on an X ray. It worked.

. . . Queens ordered a new hearing and did an about-face. According to the Queens judge, Santana was so depressed over the prospect of spending so many years behind bars that he was too despondent to assist in his defense. Santana had what he wanted—findings . . . that he was unfit.

The judge's ruling was a stretch of the usual definition of incompetence. Queens County prosecutors had believed that "no judge was going to find anyone unfit based on depression." Nonetheless, the defendant got what he apparently was hoping for—a delay in the prosecution. Three and a half years later he was found psychiatrically fit to proceed. He was convicted on all charges.

SOURCE: Alice Vachss. *Sex Crimes.* ©1993 by Alice Vachss. New York: Random House, p. 157. Reprinted by permission of Random House, Inc.

Motion for Incompetency Examination

Often a defendant's potential incompetence is noticed early in the adjudication process by either the defense attorney or the prosecutor, the two lawyers having contact with the defendant. Either party may bring the matter to the attention of the court and ask for an examination of the defendant. In some cases the claim of incompetence may be a tactic to avoid prosecution. In other cases the prosecutor becomes aware of the mental limitations of the defendant and brings a motion for an examination of the defendant's competence, even though doing so will postpone the processing of the charges. Finally, a judge may order an incompetency examination even if neither attorney raises the issue. The U.S. Supreme Court has ruled that a judge's responsibility to ensure a fair trial necessitates an inquiry into competence whenever there is some doubt about the defendant's mental status (*Pate v. Robinson* 1966).

   When a defendant's competence is questioned, whether by defense counsel, the prosecutor, or the judge, the court must order that the defendant submit to a mental status examination. The place and duration of this examination vary greatly between jurisdictions and between cases. In some places defendants are usually examined for a few hours in a doctor's office. In other places defendants are typically hospitalized in a psychiatric facility for several days or weeks of observation. In either case the examination is for the purpose of allowing experts—psychiatrists and psychologists—to form an opinion about the mental status of the defendant.

   After the examination and observation, the examining doctor writes a report, an **expert opinion** on the issue, that is filed with the court. Next is a hearing at which evidence is presented that relates to the defendant's ability to communicate with counsel and participate in the defense and the defendant's ability to

expert opinion

understand the court proceedings at trial. In most cases the defense does not contest the challenge to the defendant's competence although it may. Sometimes the defendant prefers to go to trial and may challenge expert opinion that the defendant is incompetent. In other cases the defense may be seeking an incompetency finding that is opposed by the prosecution. Psychiatric experts may testify and give their opinion about the defendant's competence, but the final decision rests with the judge or, in a few states, the jury.

Consequences of Incompetency Finding

If the defendant is found to be competent, the court process continues as though it had never been interrupted by the competency motion and proceedings. If the defendant is found to be incompetent, the court must make an additional determination of the likelihood that the defendant will regain competence. If the psychiatric experts present information to the court that with treatment the defendant is likely to regain competence, the court may order the defendant to receive treatment, often in an institution. If the defendant's condition improves, the court reviews the defendant's condition and determines whether the defendant is competent. If the defendant is found competent, the trial again proceeds as though it had never been interrupted by the defendant's incompetence.

If the defendant is not eventually restored to competence, or if at any time it becomes obvious that the defendant is unlikely to ever become competent to stand trial, the charges against the defendant must be dismissed (*Jackson v. Indiana* 1975). The period of time during which the state is allowed an opportunity to restore a defendant's competence varies greatly between jurisdictions and across cases. The U.S. Supreme Court has declined to set "arbitrary time limits" on the allowable period of confinement for treatment of incompetent defendants, and most states operate under the standard of a "reasonable" period of time.

Some states and the federal jurisdiction have adopted absolute limits on the duration of confinement for these defendants. Limits of six, twelve, or eighteen months are typical. In a few states the duration of the commitment for incompetence is not permitted to exceed the maximum penal sentence that could be imposed if the defendant had been convicted of the charges. In other words, if a defendant is charged with disorderly conduct with a maximum sentence of thirty days, an incompetent defendant accused of disorderly conduct could be hospitalized for treatment for only thirty days, no longer.

Competence and Fairness

The purpose of the incompetency proceedings and confinement can be summarized in fairly simple terms: it is unfair to try a defendant who does not understand what is going on or who cannot communicate sufficiently with counsel to assist in her or his own defense. Therefore trials are halted if the defendant is in such a disadvantageous mental or physical state. Because the state has an interest in bringing the accused to trial, the state may attempt to improve the condition of incompetent defendants so that they may become competent, even if this requires confinement and treatment in a psychiatric hospital. At some point, if the defendant has not regained competence to stand trial, the state must cease its efforts and forego the prosecution.

◼ INSANITY AND DIMINISHED CAPACITY DEFENSES

The mental state of the defendant also becomes an issue if the defendant raises impaired mental capacity as a defense to the crime through diminished capacity defenses or the insanity defense. Although the question of competence to stand trial focuses on the *present* capacity of the defendant, both the diminished capacity defense and the insanity defense concern the defendant's mental state *at the time of the crime*, regardless of the defendant's current mental condition. In addition, whereas incompetence concerns the ability of the defendant to understand the proceedings and participate in the defense, diminished capacity and insanity both concern criminal responsibility and blameworthiness.

Diminished Capacity Defenses

diminished capacity defense

If a defendant is charged with a crime that requires proof of a particular mental state (such as intent, malice aforethought, or other mental elements), the defendant may not be found guilty of that particular offense if, "as a result of mental disease or defect, [the defendant] lacked the state of mind required as an element of the crime charged" (Dix and Sharlot 1987, 624). This is known as the **diminished capacity defense**. These individuals might be considered blameworthy with respect to a lesser offense or one that does not include a particular mental state, but may show diminished capacity with respect to any offense requiring a mental state. For example, because first-degree homicide requires a mental state of malice aforethought, someone incapable of malice aforethought could be convicted of some lesser degree of homicide that does not require malice aforethought. If there is no lesser offense, the defendant may be acquitted entirely because of diminished capacity. Unlike an insanity finding, acquittal as a result of a diminished capacity defense is not followed by confinement in a mental institution or treatment of the mental illness.

Insanity Defense

insanity defense

The insanity defense has been the target of debate and reform in recent years. Much of the debate concerns the appropriate definition of insanity. The problem with defining insanity arises in drawing the boundary between mad and bad. "The law must make a distinction between those who *would* not and those who *could* not conform their conduct to the requirements of law," write Rita Simon and David Aaronson (1988, 174). The **insanity defense** is designed to excuse from both punishment and the stigma of conviction those individuals whose mental condition is such that they cannot be held to answer for the conduct. Excusing those who do not deserve to be blamed reinforces the general notion of responsibility under the criminal law.

The definition of insanity is ultimately concerned with the issue of free will. The criminal law assumes that people are responsible for their acts because they possess free will. If the defendant lacked free will at the time of the crime because of mental disease or defect, the defendant is considered not responsible. Clearly, the insanity defense is important symbolically to our sense of justice and our notion of blameworthiness. At the same time the definition of insanity must be crafted carefully so that truly blameworthy defendants cannot manipulate the defense and literally get away with murder.

DIMINISHED CAPACITY DEFENSE

The defense called a neurologist. . . .

The neurologist was eminently qualified to make his diagnosis. He had studied Robert Roudabush [the defendant] and confirmed his findings through interviews with the family. The defendant had a history, from birth complications through childhood epilepsy, that together with a lifelong propensity toward sudden violence, led to a diagnosis of "episodic dyscontrol." The doctor conceded that the attempted murder being tried was not an isolated incident—there had been a long and escalating course of domestic violence. Because of a brain malfunction, Roudabush had "fits" during which he could not control his anger. Some people called this "limbic rage." The popular media was starting to write articles about it.

According to the doctor, Roudabush did not "intend" his crime. His episodic dyscontrol meant he had irresistible urges to commit violence— episodic rages beyond his own control. . . .

What the doctor had said sounded logical, but its consequences were devastating. Roudabush wasn't pleading "not guilty by reason of insanity"—he was challenging the "intent" element of the crimes of assault and attempted murder. If he convinced a jury, he simply went free, the Not Guilty verdict carrying with it a built-in defense to any murder he might later commit. . . .

Monday morning I cross-examined the neurologist for several hours. Then I delivered the payload question. If Roudabush suffered episodic dyscontrol, how come the only victim of his violence was his wife? How come he never had these fits at work or driving his car, but only when he was in the safety (for him, not his victims) of his own home?

The jury convicted. Roudabush did ten years of a six-to-eighteen-year sentence before being paroled out of state. He hasn't had any incidents of "episodic dyscontrol" since the trial.

SOURCE: Exerpted from Alice Vachss. © 1993 by Alice Vachss. *Sex Crimes.* New York: Random House, pp. 80–81. Reprinted by permission of Random House, Inc.

Courts have considered the mental capacities of the accused since Roman times. Some mechanism for excusing the profoundly mentally disturbed from criminal responsibility has been recognized for centuries under English common law. Before the Norman conquest in England, the Church urged that the kin of a mad killer be allowed to pay *wergeld* rather than be put to death (Walker 1985, 26–27). Examples of courts acquitting obvious lunatics can be found as early as the medieval period (Walker 1985, 27). By the eighteenth century the insane were routinely acquitted on the ground that they did not act voluntarily in committing the criminal act. According to one legal historian, "Prior to the beginning of the nineteenth century, persons acquitted on a plea of insanity were legally entitled to their release. The criminal law had no direct power over them. If the court believed that they were too dangerous to be given their freedom, a separate civil commitment hearing had to be conducted before they could be confined as dangerous lunatics" (Moran 1985, 32). During the seventeenth and eighteenth centuries, acquittals of the insane were not uncommon. Another historian relates that "in a case in 1688, for example, the jury found that 'Elizabeth Waterman, the prisoner at the Barr being distracted and not of sound mind did kill Mary Waterman, her daughter, with a razor and that she came by her death by no other means.' She was acquitted, as was a man some years later who had been indicted for murdering his father, and she was found by the jury to be 'a Lunatick person and Non Compos Mentis,'" (Beattie 1986, 84). The historical accounts provide ample evidence that the insanity defense is not a modern invention. Nonetheless, the definition of insanity was not authoritatively established until the middle of the nineteenth century in relation to the prosecution of Daniel M'Naghten.

Development of the Insanity Rule

Daniel M'Naghten was charged in the death of Edward Drummond, secretary to Sir Robert Peel. Drummond was killed in an apparent assassination attempt against Peel, who was then prime minister of England. At trial M'Naghten's lawyer argued that M'Naghten suffered from delusions and sincerely believed that people wanted to kill him and were pursuing him for that purpose. When the jury acquitted M'Naghten, the public outcry caused the House of Lords (functioning as the equivalent of the U.S. Supreme Court) to consider the definition of insanity (Dix and Sharlot 1987, 616). The issues the House of Lords considered are the same issues that plague lawyers, judges, and legislators today in defining insanity:

> [T]he jurors ought to be told in all cases that every man is presumed to be sane, and to possess a sufficient degree of reason to be responsible for his crimes, until the contrary be proved to their satisfaction; and that to establish a defense on the ground of insanity, it must be clearly proved that, at the time of committing the act, the party accused was labouring under such a defect of reason, from disease of the mind, as not to know the nature and quality of the act he was doing; or, if he did know it, that he did not know he was doing what was wrong.

*   *   *

> For example, if under the influence of his delusion he supposes another man to be in the act of attempting to take away his life, and he kills that man, as he supposes, in self-defence, he would be exempt from punishment. If his delusion was that the deceased had inflicted a serious injury to his character and fortune, and he killed him in revenge for such supposed injury, he would be liable to punishment. (quoted in Dix and Sharlot 1987, 616, 617. Reprinted by permission from *Basic Criminal Law: Cases and Materials, 3rd. ed.* by Dix and Sharlot. Copyright © 1987 by West Publishing Co. All rights reserved.)

M'Naghten rule

The **M'Naghten rule,** often referred to as the "right/wrong rule," was quickly adopted by courts and legislatures in the United States as an authoritative and sound definition of insanity. The chief advantage of the M'Naghten rule was that it set forth in clear language the findings required of the jury to acquit a defendant as insane.

Irresistible Impulse Test

Experience with the M'Naghten rule demonstrated that in some situations defendants, although suffering from mental illness, knew the conduct was wrong but could not control their actions. Such situations prompted the promulgation of

irresistible impulse

a new insanity rule that included the so-called **irresistible impulse** test, first enunciated in *Parsons v. State* (1886). This addition to the older M'Naghten test resulted in a "two-pronged" insanity test: one component of the test focused on the defendant's ability to distinguish right from wrong, or to know the difference between the two; the other component focused on the defendant's ability to control his or her actions, or the voluntariness of the action. Together, the two components of the insanity test formed a new definition of criminal blameworthiness: to be considered criminally culpable, the act had to be both knowing and voluntary.

Durham Rule

Yet a third definition of insanity was briefly considered after the 1954 federal court ruling in the case of *Durham v. United States,* in which the appellate court adopted a definition of insanity announced in an earlier New Hampshire case. The new rule allowed acquittal by reason of insanity if a crime was the product of a mental disease or defect. The new rule was quickly dubbed the "product rule" and proved to be broader than either the right/wrong or irresistible impulse tests.

Durham rule

The focus in the **Durham rule** was on the causal connection between the mental disease and the criminal offense. For example, under the M'Naghten rule the man who killed another man in the delusional belief that the other man had ruined his reputation and fortune (the example offered by the House of Lords in the *M'Naghten* opinion) would not be acquitted. In contrast, that same defendant might be acquitted under the Durham rule if the jury was convinced that the mental disease caused the criminal act, even though the defendant may have known that it was wrong to kill a man out of revenge and could have controlled his impulses. If the cause of the desire for revenge was the mental illness, the jury could legally acquit the defendant under the Durham rule.

Model Penal Code Definition

The U.S. Circuit Court for the District of Columbia's adoption of the Durham rule in 1954 raised a new flurry of public and scholarly interest in the appropriate definition of insanity. This renewed focus on the issue led to a study of the issue by the American Law Institute (ALI) in its development of the Model Penal Code. In 1962 the Model Penal Code set forth the following definition of insanity:

> A person is not responsible for criminal conduct if at the time of such conduct as a result of mental disease or defect he lacks substantial capacity either to appreciate the criminality [wrongfulness] of his conduct or to conform his conduct to the requirements of law. (Model Penal Code 1985, 61)

This definition is essentially a restatement of the combined right/wrong and irresistible impulse rules. About half the states use the ALI insanity rule, with most of the other states maintaining the M'Naghten formulation or the combined M'Naghten and irresistible impulse rules (ABA Criminal Justice Mental Health Standards 1989, 333).

Recent Reforms of the Definition of Insanity

In 1981 John Hinckley attempted to assassinate Ronald Reagan, then president of the United States. The subsequent insanity trial and Hinckley's acquittal led to public outcry and reexamination of the meaning and operation of the insanity defense. The National Commission on the Insanity Defense was formed to study the legal and moral dilemmas presented in insanity acquittals. In its report the commission concluded that:

> Through its investigation, public hearings, and supplemental analysis the Commission discovered that much of the clamor for change in the insanity defense is based on myths and misplaced frustration in the wake of the Hinckley verdict. These myths characterize the insanity **defense** as an overused plea, used for easy acquittal and to

escape punishment, and causing major problems for the criminal justice system. These myths characterize all insanity **defendants** as dangerous criminals who commit random acts of violence and repeat those crimes after being in treatment for only a short period of time.

The Commission unanimously concludes that these myths have no basis in fact. (National Commission 1983, 1)

Nonetheless, in 1984 Congress adopted an insanity rule—the first federal insanity statute—that incorporated the right/wrong test and rejected the irresistible impulse test.

It is an affirmative defense to prosecution under any Federal statute that, at the time of the commission of the acts constituting the offense, the defendant, as a result of severe mental disease or defect, was unable to appreciate the nature and quality or wrongfulness of his acts. Mental disease or defect does not otherwise constitute a defense. (18 U.S.C. §17(a))

Similarly, several states revised their insanity provisions to eliminate the irresistible impulse component of the defense. The controversy over the insanity defense engendered by the Hinckley case also led a few states—Idaho, Montana, and Utah—to abolish the insanity defense, leaving only a diminished capacity defense for dealing with cases in which the defendant's mental state at the time of the crime is at issue (Simon and Aaronson 1988).

Finally, some states have enacted "guilty but mentally ill" provisions. Although some of these states abolished the traditional insanity defense, in most cases the "guilty but mentally ill" option operates as an alternative finding when the defendant raises an insanity defense. Where law provides, a defendant may be

guilty but mentally ill

found **guilty but mentally ill** if the trier of fact (judge or jury) finds beyond a reasonable doubt that the defendant is guilty of an offense, the defendant was mentally ill at the time the crime was committed, and the defendant was not legally insane at the time the crime was committed (Dix and Sharlot 1987, 627). Such a defendant may be sentenced to prison but may be transferred to another facility for psychiatric treatment if necessary. In some states a "guilty but mentally ill" verdict requires the state to provide psychiatric treatment as part of the penal sentence.

The guilty but mentally ill formula has also been criticized. Some have called it an easy way out for jurors who may be reluctant to acquit a defendant charged with a heinous crime, despite ample evidence of mental illness (Finkel 1988, 45). Ironically, research suggests that states with the guilty but mentally ill option have not experienced a reduction in insanity acquittals (Steadman 1985, 68). Finally, although the apparent purpose of the "guilty but mentally ill" option is to ensure that mentally disturbed defendants receive treatment while in prison, 75 percent of those found guilty but mentally ill receive no treatment while in prison (Simon and Aaronson 1988, 192).

Insanity Defense: Procedures

When a defendant pleads not guilty by reason of insanity, the adversaries as well as the court are entitled to seek expert opinion on the issue of mental status. Each expert files a written report to the court, stating expert conclusions based on examination of the defendant. These psychiatric examinations may be done on either an outpatient or inpatient basis and may last a few hours, several days, or even several weeks.

Procedures for determining insanity vary between jurisdictions. The typical insanity defense requires that the defense offer evidence sufficient to show by a preponderance of the evidence that the defendant was insane at the time of the crime. There is wide variation in procedural requirements, however. In all states a defendant has a right to a jury trial, and the jury decides the insanity question, unless the defendant has waived the right to a jury trial and chosen a bench trial instead. In either case expert testimony is important, but the experts are not the ultimate decision makers; the insanity decision is made by nonmedical personnel, the judge or jury.

Consequences of a Successful Insanity Plea

Most defendants who raise an insanity defense are convicted. Even the few who are acquitted by reason of insanity rarely walk out the courtroom door a free person. In virtually all cases of insanity acquittal the defendant is committed to a mental institution.

Some states allow automatic confinement of insanity acquittees. Laws in these states presume that a defendant who was insane at the time of the crime is still mentally ill and potentially dangerous after the trial. Such procedures were approved by the U.S. Supreme Court in 1983 (*Jones v. United States*). The majority of states require an independent and specific finding that the acquitted defendant is mentally ill and dangerous before the court may commit the individual to a mental institution. A substantial number of states use the same standards for committing a defendant acquitted by reason of insanity as are used to civilly commit any individual who is mentally ill and dangerous (Robinson 1984, 306).

If institutionalized, insanity acquittees are entitled to periodic examinations to determine whether their condition justifies continued confinement. In all states defendants found to be no longer mentally ill and dangerous must be released. In a few states the insanity acquittee may not be confined for longer than the maximum sentence that would apply if the defendant had been found guilty (Hochstedler Steury and Rotter 1991).

The Insanity Defense in Perspective

The concept of insanity has been recognized in the Anglo-American legal tradition for centuries. Nonetheless, defining the concept in operational terms that excuse the blameless and convict the blameworthy has proven difficult and contentious. Highly publicized insanity cases periodically spark a new round of redefinition and reform. The current trend is to create alternatives to acquittal by insanity for those defendants who are mentally ill, but not so mentally ill that they deserve no condemnation whatsoever.

These reforms appear to be premised on the belief that a significant number of defendants use the insanity defense to successfully escape punishment by pleading insanity. Public opinion polls indicate that the general public thinks the insanity defense is used, and used successfully, much more frequently than it actually is (see Dix and Sharlot, 1987, 615). On average the insanity defense is raised in less than 1 percent of all felony prosecutions, although that figure is as high as 5 percent in some jurisdictions and less than 0.5 percent in other jurisdictions. Insanity pleas are successful about one-quarter of the time (Callahan et al. 1991). Finally, the overwhelming majority of defendants who are acquitted by reason of insanity are confined in a mental institution for a substantial period of time, often longer than the maximum sentence for the offense.

■ SUMMARY

Arraignment is the proceeding in felony court at which the defendant is required to plead to the charges. It is typically short and uncomplicated. In the majority of cases the defendant pleads guilty. The judge in these cases must ensure that the guilty plea is voluntary, knowing, and intelligent and that the charge to which the defendant is pleading is supported by the facts. By way of ensuring that the plea is knowing and intelligent the judge must ascertain that the defendant is competent to enter a guilty plea; that is, that the defendant understands the nature of the proceedings and the consequences of the plea. After the judge accepts the guilty plea, the case proceeds to the sentencing stage of the court process.

In a small proportion of cases (as few as 10 percent of all cases) the defendant pleads not guilty and the case is scheduled for trial. The case can proceed to trial only if the defendant is competent to stand trial. If the defendant's competence is in question, the proceedings are delayed, the defendant's mental condition is examined, and a hearing is held before a judge or a jury to decide whether the defendant is competent to proceed. If the defendant is not competent and never becomes competent to stand trial, the defendant is never tried for the offense. In less than 1 percent of all cases the defendant pleads not guilty by reason of insanity and is examined with respect to mental condition at the time of the offense. Insanity concerns the mental state of the defendant at the time of the crime. Most states have adopted the ALI definition of insanity that combines the M'Naghten right/wrong test with the irresistible impulse test. Insanity is a matter decided at trial by a judge or a jury, and therefore only competent defendants are ever tried on an insanity defense. Most insanity pleas are unsuccessful.

■ FOR FURTHER DISCUSSION

1.   Chapter Five describes several foreign systems of justice. In each of them a civil action for compensation to the victim was part of the criminal court action. In the United States, a victim must file a separate civil suit in a separate court to seek compensation. If the defendant pleads no contest, the victim may still be required to prove the defendant's responsiblity for the victim's injuries at the civil trial. Even a conviction in criminal court does not mean that the victim will prevail in the civil action. What advantages can you see in adopting the practice followed in other countries of joining the civil action with criminal prosecution, rather than having two completely independent actions in separate courts? What disadvantages can you anticipate if such a reform were adopted in the United States?

2.   What is the difference between a no contest plea and an Alford plea?

3.   The Supreme Court has held that strong inducements to plead guilty do not make the decision to plead guilty less than voluntary. Only if the defendant is coerced is voluntariness undermined. If you were a judge, where would you draw the line between strong inducements by the prosecutor (which are permissible) and coercion (which is impermissible)? What kinds of inducements by the prosecutor would you consider coercive? What effect would your rulings be likely to have on the practice of plea bargaining in cases before your court?

4. Put yourself in the position of a judge at arraignment. The prosecutor announces a plea bargain. You question the defendant. The defendant's waiver of the right to trial appears to be knowing, intelligent, and voluntary, but you are concerned that the factual basis for the charge is quite weak. Although there is evidence in support of each element of the offense, some is scientific evidence of questionable reliability. Although a jury certainly might convict on the evidence, you have a reasonable doubt about its accuracy. Because the state's identification of the defendant depends on this evidence, the doubt undermines the factual basis for the conviction. Do you accept or reject the guilty plea? What considerations would enter into your decision? What would you expect to happen after rejecting the guilty plea?

5. Again, waiver of the right to trial must be knowing, intelligent, and voluntary. Explain why a defendant who is incompetent to stand trial would be unable to make a knowing, intelligent, and voluntary waiver of the right to trial.

6. The diminished capacity defense (or closely related defenses) has been used in recent years to obtain acquittals of defendants claiming battered spouse and other post-traumatic stress syndromes. Some people have expressed outrage that defendants who commit violent acts can be acquitted under the diminished capacity defense, facing neither imprisonment nor mandatory mental health treatment. Would you support legislation to abolish the diminished capacity defense in your state, thereby forcing defendants to either plead not guilty by reason of insanity or forego making mental capacity an issue at trial? What are your predictions about the consequences if such a law were passed?

REFERENCES

ABA Criminal Justice Mental Health Standards. 1989. Washington, D.C.: American Bar Association.

Beattie, J. M. 1986. *Crime and the Courts in England, 1660–1800.* Oxford, England: Clarendon Press.

Bordenkircher v. Hayes, 434 U.S. 357, 98 S. Ct. 663 (1978).

Boykin v. Alabama, 395 U.S. 238, 89 S. Ct. 1709 (1969).

Brady v. United States, 397 U.S. 742, 90 S. Ct. 1463 (1970).

Callahan, Lisa A , Henry J. Steadman, Marge A. McGreevy, and Pamela Clark Robbins. 1991. "The Volume and Characteristics of Insanity Defense Pleas: An Eight-State Study." Working Paper. Delmar, N.Y.: Research Policy Associates, Inc.

Dix, George E., and M. Michael Sharlot. 1987. *Basic Criminal Law: Cases and Materials,* 3d ed. St. Paul, Minn.: West.

Durham v. United States, 214 F.2d 874 (D. C. Cir. 1954).

Dusky v. United States, 362 U.S. 402, 80 S. Ct. 788 (1960).

Finkel, Norman J. 1988. *Insanity of Trial.* New York: Plenum.

Hochstedler Steury, Ellen, and Francis J. Rotter. 1991. "Raising the Insanity Defense: A Comparison of Rates in Jurisdictions with Differing Insanity Commitment Release Laws." *Criminal Justice Policy Review* 5 (4): 307–21.

Jackson v. Indiana, 406 U.S. 715, 92 S. Ct. 1845 (1972).

Johnson, Herbert A. 1988. *History of Criminal Justice.* Cincinnati: Anderson.

Jones v. United States, 463 U.S. 354, 103 S. Ct. 3043 (1983).

LaFave, Wayne R., and Jerold H. Israel. 1985. *Criminal Procedure.* St. Paul, Minn.: West.

McDonald, William F. 1987. "Judicial Supervision of the Guilty Plea Process: A Study of Six Jurisdictions." *Judicature* 70 (December–January): 203–15.

Miller, Frank W., Robert O. Dawson, George E. Dix, and Raymond I. Parnas. 1986. *Prosecution and Adjudication,* 3d ed. Minecla, N.Y.: Foundation Press.

Model Penal Code. 1985. Official draft and explanatory notes. Complete text as adopted May 24, 1962. Philadelphia: American Law Institute.

Moran, Richard. 1985. "The Modern Foundation for the Insanity Defense: The Cases of James Hadfield (1800) and Daniel McNaughtan (1843)." *Annals of the American Academy of Political and Social Science* 477 (January): 31–42.

National Commission on the Insanity Defense. 1983. *Report of the National Commission on the Insanity Defense.* Arlington, Va.: National Mental Health Association.

North Carolina v. Alford, 400 U.S. 25, 91 S. Ct. 160 (1970).

Parsons v. State, 81 Alabama 577, 2 So. 854 (1886).

Pate v. Robinson, 383 U.S. 375, 86 S. Ct. 836 (1966).

Remington, Frank J., Donald J. Newman, Edward L. Kimball, Marygold Melli, and Herman Goldstein. 1969. *Criminal Justice Administration: Materials and Cases.* Indianapolis: Bobbs-Merrill.

Robinson, Paul H. 1984. *Criminal Law Defenses.* St. Paul, Minn.: West.

Simon, Rita J., and David E. Aaronson. 1988. *The Insanity Defense: A Critical Assessment of Law and Policy in the Post-Hinckley Era.* New York: Praeger.

Steadman, Henry J. 1985. "Empirical Research on the Insanity Defense." *Annals of the American Academy of Political and Social Science* 477 (January): 58–71.

Walker, Nigel. 1985. "The Insanity Defense Before 1800." *Annals of the American Academy of Political and Social Science* 477 (January): 25–30.

CHAPTER  **15**

PREPARING FOR TRIAL

For every one hundred felony arrests fewer than five are resolved through trial (Boland, Mahanna, and Sones 1992, 3). As we have seen, many of those arrested for felonies are not charged by the prosecutor or have their cases dismissed before trial. Of those remaining, the overwhelming majority are resolved through a guilty plea. Clearly, trials are the exception rather than the expected outcome for most cases in the felony courts.

Although trials are relatively rare, some cases are more likely to result in a trial than others. Homicide and sexual assault charges are more likely than other types of charges to go to trial. Even in these crimes, however, most defendants plead guilty rather than go to trial (see Figure 15-1). Those more likely to go to trial are cases in which either the facts or the law are unclear.

Because the possibility for trial exists up to the point at which the prosecution dismisses the charges or the defendant pleads guilty, preparation for trial begins as soon as the defendant enters the criminal court process. As Chapter 12 describes, the attorneys interview potential witnesses and review physical evidence to learn all they can about the situation leading to the defendant's arrest. The initial investigation and preparation are as important in influencing the outcome of a settlement as they are in winning at trial. However, once a settlement appears unlikely, the attorneys turn their attention to the presentation of the case at trial. This chapter describes the major issues that the prosecutor and defense counsel must consider in preparing for trial.

In all but the simplest cases the attorneys face a mountain of evidence: stacks of paper and documents, witnesses' statements, police reports, defendant's statements, forensic lab reports, physical evidence, photographs, and so on. Some evidence is irrelevant or unnecessary to make the case. Some evidence is inconsistent with other evidence, some pieces of evidence are more helpful, and still other pieces are potentially damaging or even damning.

FIGURE 15-1   Likelihood of Trial by Type of Offense

Source: Adapted from Barbara Boland, Paul Mahanna, and Ronald Sones. 1992 *The Prosecution of Felony Arrests, 1988.* Washington, D.C.: U.S. Department of Justice, Bureau of Justice Statistics, pp. 30–34.

In all jurisdictions the more serious cases are more likely to go to trial, but the proportion of cases going to trial varies widely by jurisdiction. For example, in St. Louis homicide cases are twenty-three times more likely to be resolved by trial than drug possession cases, whereas in Los Angeles homicides are only four times more likely to go to trial than drug offenses. In San Diego only 7 percent of sexual assaults are resolved at trial. None of the drug possession cases in Manhattan or in Washington, D.C., are resolved by trial, but in Portland 22 percent of drug possession cases are resolved at trial.

What differences in police practices, prosecutorial case screening, and plea bargaining might account for such variations? What other factors might account for these differences between jurisdictions?

Percentage of indicted cases resolved by trial

Jurisdiction	Violent offenses			Property offenses		
	Homicide	Sexual Assault	Robbery	Burglary	Larceny	Drug Possession
Denver	38%	22%	6%	2%	2%	9%
Los Angeles	26	25	10	6	6	3
Manhattan	26	19	11	7	8	0
New Orleans	50	22	27	11	7	8
Portland, Oreg.	44	27	22	13	14	22
St. Louis	46	23	17	7	3	2
San Diego	26	7	9	4	2	1
Seattle	45	33	17	9	6	8
Washington, D.C.	53	36	24	11	4	0

The attorney's task in preparing for trial is to distill this mountain of information to the essential information and weave a story for the trier of fact that will be both understandable and believable. The attorney builds the story around a theme that summarizes the single idea that explains why the attorney's client (whether the state or the defendant) should prevail (Goldberg 1982, 62). The prosecutor creates a story that demonstrates the guilt of the defendant. The defense in turn creates a different story—one in which the defendant is not guilty or at least not *so* guilty. For example, the prosecutor's theme in a homicide case might be "Wife kills cheating husband in a vengeful rage." The defense theme for the same case might be "Battered woman snaps under stress of years of abuse and betrayal and kills husband in desperate attempt to escape his fury." Each lawyer then organizes the available evidence to elaborate on this theme (Bennett and Feldman 1981, 41). Each side presents its story in the opening statement and emphasizes it with the examination of each witness.

If a jury is to be the trier of fact, the attorneys must also prepare for the selection of jurors. In routine cases preparing for jury selection is a small part of trial preparation. In some cases, however, this task can be enormous, consuming as much time and resources as are available.

Time is a critical factor in case preparation. The amount of time devoted to it depends on a variety of factors, including the temperament of the attorneys involved, the time available, and the seriousness of the case. In some cases attorneys may have little opportunity to prepare for trial. A crushing caseload may mean that only the most serious cases receive more than cursory inspection before trial. In other cases an attorney may receive a case only days or hours, or even minutes, before it is scheduled for trial (Marcus 1989, 3). In these cases the prosecutor or defense attorney may have had only enough time to read the police report and other documents in the case file and to hastily outline the points that need to be established during the trial.

The description that follows presumes that the attorney has both the time and the inclination to carefully prepare for trial. Actual preparation is often much more limited.

ANTICIPATING THE DEFENSE

Although much preparation for trial is similar for the prosecution and the defense, their different roles at trial mean that there are some differences. The prosecutor must be especially careful to analyze the evidence and plan for its introduction at trial so that the prosecutor presents credible and persuasive evidence in court for each element of the offense.

Although prosecutors construct a story that becomes the state's case, they also must anticipate the sort of story that the defense might weave to convince the jury to acquit. The prosecutor looks at the evidence from the perspective of the defense. Are the witness identifications of the defendant shaky or contradictory? If so, the prosecution anticipates a mistaken identity defense. Did the victim of a rape know the defendant? If so, the prosecution may expect the defense to argue that the victim consented to have sex.

The prosecutor also searches for other clues to potential defense strategies. For example, statements the defendant made to the police, especially exculpatory statements, may provide a hint of the direction a defense may take. Questions asked by defense counsel at the preliminary hearing may tip off their strategy. For example, if the defense focuses at the preliminary hearing on the certainty of an eyewitness's identification of the defendant, the prosecutor can guess that this may be a central issue for the defense at trial. Statements made by the defense in arguing for a reduction in bail and in plea bargaining may also provide insights to the defense view of the weaknesses of the prosecutor's case. In cases that receive media coverage defense counsel may present the defense theme in statements to reporters. These clues give the prosecutor an opportunity to plan how to weaken the defense story and bolster the prosecution's case.

THE DEFENSE PLAN

Like the prosecutor, defense counsel analyzes the strengths and weaknesses of the case as measured against the elements that must be proved. Weaknesses in the evidence might lead the trier of fact to acquit the defendant or at least acquit on some of the more serious charges in the complaint.

Deciding on a Defense Strategy

Selecting a defense strategy is not usually a simple matter of identifying the one weak point in the prosecution's case and hoping that the evidence will fall like a house of cards once that one weak point is attacked. Instead the defense frequently has several potential strategies. The difficulty is in choosing among them, especially when raising one defense eliminates the possibility of using another, and the relative chances of success of the two approaches are unknown.

For example, if the victim's identification of the defendant is uncertain, a mistaken identity theme might work. If the victim's identification is corroborated by DNA identification, this strategy becomes more risky. DNA evidence is still sufficiently new that some judges refuse to admit it, and jurors may view the results as doubtful. In the same case the defense may also be able to pose a plausible self-defense story. However, if the defense argues self-defense, it clearly cannot also argue mistaken identity. To do so would be the same as saying, "I didn't hit him, but if I did, I was justified because he hit me first." Because of the risks involved in selecting a defense strategy from several options, the defendant is usually briefed on potential defenses and the risks and advantages of each. Sometimes the strategy chosen depends on how the judge rules on pretrial motions. For example, if the judge grants a defense motion challenging the admission of DNA evidence, the defense would choose the mistaken identity strategy. If the judge denies the motion, a mistaken identity defense would become more risky, and defense counsel might decide to go with the self-defense strategy.

In general, there are two main types of defense strategy at trial. One strategy is to undermine the credibility of the prosecution case, which involves chipping away at the credibility of the witnesses and other evidence and putting a different interpretation or "spin" on the facts. For example, if police contend that the defendant approached an undercover officer and tried to buy drugs, the defense strategy may be to persuade the jury that the police misunderstood the defendant's actions. The other general strategy is to raise an **affirmative defense,** by which the defense actively tries to prove that the defendant did not commit the crime, was justified in the act, or should be excused from criminal responsibility. For example, in the case of an undercover drug buy, the defense may try to prove the affirmative defense of entrapment.

affirmative defense

Undermining the State's Case

Michael D. Marcus, deputy district attorney for Los Angeles County for seventeen years, summarizes the tactics used by defense attorneys to undermine the credibility of the state's case. Frequently, the defense strategy focuses on one element of the crime and tries to show that the prosecutor is unable to prove that element (Marcus 1989). If the defense can raise a doubt about the prosecutor's proof of any element, the judge or jury should not convict on that charge. A defendant charged with unarmed robbery might argue that he got into a fight with the victim but did not intend to rob the victim. However, feeling bruised and self-righteous after the fight, he stole the victim's jacket. The defense here is that the defendant did not commit a robbery, because he did not assault *with the intent to steal* the jacket. Instead the defendant committed a simple larceny, a much less serious crime. If the defense can successfully raise a doubt about the defendant's intention to steal before the struggle began, the defendant may win an acquittal. To convince the jury of the reasonableness of this alternative story the defense might present evidence of a longtime relationship between the victim and the defendant and evidence that the victim is a bully and a thief. By presenting evidence that supports the defense story that the jacket was stolen only after a fight between acquaintances, the defense hopes to raise a reasonable doubt about a critical element of the robbery charge.

WITNESSES WITH A RECORD

David Heilbroner, a former Manhattan prosecutor, describes a case in which the victim and a key witness had records of crack dealing and how this undermined his case against the defendant. Quintana [the defendant] was accused of stealing Keith's jacket.

Mookie [a key witness] testified that morning, but with two convicted crack-sellers accusing another convicted crack-seller of robbery, and with inconsistent stories, the case became a farce. Quintana [the defendant] also took the stand and gave Davidson [the judge] his own version of events. He claimed that Keith [the victim] had sold him bad drugs earlier in the evening. When he returned to complain about the "product" Keith said that he had already spent the money, so they struck a deal. "Give me your jacket as collateral," Quintana said. "I'll hold it until you get me my money."

Because Keith and Mookie had criminal records, the story Quintana told was at least plausible. The judge had little reason to consider Keith and Mookie more credible than the defendant in these circumstances. Quintana's story must have seemed a plausible account of what happened between the defendant and the "victim." The judge acquitted Quintana of the charges.

SOURCE: Excerpted from David Heilbroner. 1990. *Rough Justice: Days and Nights of a Young D.A.* New York: Pantheon, p. 271.

Another way to undermine the state's case is to attack the credibility of the state's witnesses (Marcus 1989). As part of the discovery process defense counsel may obtain criminal histories for all prosecution witnesses. If a defense witness has a criminal record, especially a recent conviction or charges pending, the defense is in a good position to undermine the witness's credibility. By stressing the witness's prior criminal involvement the defense portrays the state's witness as involved in nefarious dealings, a person not to be trusted. The prosecution's case is undermined to the extent that the defense can cast doubt on the innocence and credibility of the victim.

If the witness is facing charges, the defense can cast doubt on the witness's testimony by suggesting that the witness is being rewarded with lenience for providing evidence against the defendant. The witness's credibility is doubly undermined. First, the defense argues the witness is a "known criminal" and cannot be trusted. Then the defense argues that the witness stands to gain from testifying to whatever the prosecutor wants her to say.

Even the credibility of police officers can be undermined. Sometimes police officers make less than credible witnesses because of their demeanor in court. A defense attorney who knows that a particular officer comes off as arrogant or lazy may plan to capitalize on this characteristic in court. In other cases the defense may try to paint police actions as corrupt or unlawful. For example, the defense may try to show that undercover agents encouraged the defendant to commit the crime. The defense might argue that the police were "out to get" the defendant, regardless of whether the defendant committed a crime. In cross-examining the police witnesses the defense may try to get the police officer to acknowledge that police had been desperate to solve a highly publicized crime and were under pressure from the media and local politicians to arrest someone, perhaps anyone. If the defendant confessed to the crime, the defense may try to show that the interrogation was coercive and the confession not believable.

If the witnesses for the state appear trustworthy and are not easily maligned, undermining the state's case may involve suggesting that the witness made an

DEFENSE STRATEGY: OVERBEARING INTERROGATION

The excerpt here is from a book about the Central Park jogger rape trial. Defense counsel Mickey Joseph sought to undermine the state's case by showing that his client's confession was the result of unfair pressure by the police officers interrogating him.

As he opened the defense case on Friday, July 27, Mickey Joseph's task was to answer the one essential question raised by his client's videotape. Why would Antron McCray [the defendant] confess to crimes he hadn't committed?

McCray's parents were present, after all, throughout his interrogation. Would they have let the detectives force their son to falsely incriminate himself? Joseph's answer was that they would, if the cops had promised to let the boy go if he agreed to incriminate himself and testify against the other suspects. Now Joseph had to convince the jurors that such a deal had been made, despite the denials they had already heard from detectives Hildebrandt and Gonzalez.

Joseph's cross-examination had done considerable damage to the credibility of the detectives, highlighting important contradictions between their accounts of the interrogation.

*   *   *

Joseph had prepared his witness well. [Bobby] McCray's [the defendant's father] answers were consistent, delivered without hesitation. He told a story that followed the structure of the testimony given by detectives Hildebrandt and Gonzalez. There had been three parts to the interrogation, interrupted by two hallway discussions among himself and the detectives. Before the third session his wife asked to leave the room and only then did Antron incriminate himself regarding the female Jogger.

Beyond that outline McCray and the policemen differed on all the crucial points. In the father's testimony the boy said he witnessed the assaults on "some gentlemen" in the park but had not participated. He had insisted he knew nothing about any woman. The boy had been yelled at and badgered until he and his mother were in tears. His wife was told to leave the room, not to relieve Antron's shame but because she was trying to shield her son from this coercion.

Joseph asked McCray whether he had objected when Detective Gonzalez asked Linda McCray to leave. "I didn't have no right to say anything," he replied matter-of-factly. "I was in the precinct."

*   *   *

Eventually, said McCray, he ordered his son to incriminate himself in the reservoir assaults and the rape because the detectives had persuaded him that Antron would not be a credible witness against the others unless he admitted some involvement.

Bobby McCray described his private conversation with Antron. "I said, 'I know you're telling me the truth. You tell these people what they want to hear and you'll go home.'"

"What did your son say?" asked Joseph.

"'I wasn't there. I'm not going to lie,'" answered McCray.

"What happened next?"

"I got upset and angry, and threw a chair across the room, because I was trying to get my son to tell a lie," he replied. (The detectives had said they heard a loud noise, like furniture moving, when McCray and his son were alone in the youth room).

When the interrogation resumed, said McCray, the detectives questioned his son repeatedly about the rape. The cops were yelling, "Stop bullshitting! Stop bullshitting!" stretching their arms across the table to point their fingers into Antron's face.

The boy continued to assert that he knew nothing about any woman, despite his father's urging, now in the presence of the detectives, that he cooperate. "I kept insisting," said McCray, "'if you don't tell them what they want to hear, you are going to jail.'"

Finally, said McCray, his son, in tears, capitulated to the combined pressure from himself and the cops. "He said, 'Okay . . . . forget it.'"

[McCray then explained why he and Linda McCray had consented to have their son's confession videotaped, despite the fact that they now claimed in court that they believed he was innocent.] "Because I already told the police my son was going to cooperate and be a witness," said McCray.

After the taping, McCray added, he was surprised to learn that his son was not free to go.

Joseph asked McCray what he had said to the detective he'd made the deal with.

"I said, 'What the fuck is this? You told me we can go home. . . . We have been here a long time.'"

"What did he say?" asked the lawyer.

"Just sat there looking at me like I was crazy."

Antron McCray was convicted on all charges: rape, several counts of assault, and robbery.

SOURCE: Excerpted from Timothy Sullivan. 1992. *Unequal Verdicts: The Central Park Jogger Trials.* New York: Simon & Schuster, pp. 181–4. Copyright © 1992 by Timothy Sullivan. Reprinted by permission of Simon & Schuster, Inc.

honest mistake. The attorney may emphasize the difficulties of making a positive identification when the witness identifies a stranger as the person who committed the alleged crime. The defense will emphasize the conditions under which the witness had an opportunity to observe the defendant. Poor lighting, failing eyesight, stress, and having only a brief time to observe—all will come under the scrutiny of the defense.

Affirmative Defenses

affirmative defense, justification

In addition to undermining the state's case by highlighting inconsistencies and other problems with the evidence, the defense may raise an **affirmative defense**. Affirmative defenses frequently are based on a defendant's claim of justification or excuse. **Justification** means that even though the acts carried out by the defendant would ordinarily constitute a crime, *under the circumstances* the defendant was justified in acting in that way and should not be held criminally liable. Examples include self-defense, duress, and necessity. **Excuse**, in contrast, means that although the defendant may have violated the law, the circumstances in which she committed the crime are such that she should be excused, in whole or in part, from criminal liability. An example of a defense based on the concept of excuse is the insanity defense (see Chapter 14). Some of the novel defenses raised by criminal defendants in recent years, including the battered spouse syndrome and posttraumatic stress disorder, are based on the concept of excuse for criminal conduct. Another affirmative defense is to prove that the defendant could not have committed the crime because the defendant was somewhere else at the time. This is an **alibi** defense.

excuse

alibi

Unlike other defense strategies, affirmative defenses require that the defense bring forward evidence in support of its account of what happened. Typically, state law requires that the defense bear the burden of proof to successfully raise an affirmative defense. The standard of evidence may be a preponderance of the evidence, clear and convincing evidence, or by proof beyond a reasonable doubt, depending on the requirements of state law. A preponderance of the evidence is the lowest standard of the three; clear and convincing evidence is an intermediate standard. No matter what standard of evidence the defense must meet to establish its affirmative defense, the prosecution must still prove each element of the crime beyond a reasonable doubt. Even if the prosecution meets its burden, the defendant is acquitted if the defense can prove the elements of an affirmative defense. Consequently, when an affirmative defense is raised, the prosecutor must plan to undermine the defense case in addition to proving the elements of the offense charged.

Defenses of Justification

self-defense

Statutory and common law interpretations vary, but all states justify the use of force in **self-defense**—when it is used to protect oneself or others from serious bodily injury. In general, the defense must prove that the defendant reasonably believed that he or she was in imminent danger of serious bodily harm and that the amount of force used by the defendant was reasonable under the circumstances. Defense of others involves using force to protect someone else. In planning a defense on these grounds defense counsel must consider whether evidence in support of a claim of self-defense exists. For example, did the

Affirmative Defenseses

Most affirmative defenses relate either to justifications or excuses for the defendant's actions. *Justification* means that conduct that otherwise would be a crime is justified under the circumstances, and the defendant is acquitted. An *excuse* means that the defendant may be excused from criminal liability, often on the grounds that the defendant lacks the necessary mental capacity to form criminal intent and to be held blameworthy for his or her actions.

Professor Sue Titus Reid summarizes the traditional affirmative defenses as well as novel defenses that have been tried in some cases.

IGNORANCE OR MISTAKE

Generally, ignorance of the law is no excuse for criminal liability. In rare cases, ignorance of the law may be a valid defense, however. Specifically, if the state does not provide reasonable notice of a legal requirement, violation of that requirement may be held to excuse criminal liability. A mistake of fact may also excuse a person of criminal responsibility. For example, if a person takes someone else's coat from a public coat rack, mistaking it for his own, that mistake may excuse the person from criminal liability for the crime of theft.

INSANITY

A defendant may be excused entirely from criminal liability if the defendant was so mentally disturbed at the time of the crime that he or she cannot be held blameworthy for his or her conduct. A related defense is the diminished capacity defense. Both these defenses are discussed in greater detail in the special section at the end of Chapter 14.

SELF-DEFENSE (JUSTIFIABLE HOMICIDE)

A person is justified in using force in order to protect him or her self from an imminent threat of death or great bodily harm. If the defendant can prove that the victim created such an imminent threat just prior to the defendant's actions, the defendant may be found not guilty.

DURESS OR NECESSITY

Similar to the justification of self-defense, a person is justified in committing a crime, including the use of force, if such action is necessary in order to prevent an imminent threat of death or serious injury. A necessity defense might be raised by a defendant who had broken into someone's home in order to call the police to the scene of an emergency. If a defendant was coerced by the threat of force into committing a crime, the defendant may claim that the crime was committed under duress.

BATTERED WOMAN SYNDROME

In some cases, women have successfully argued that they should be excused from criminal responsibility for assault or homicide because they suffered a history of violence at the hands of the person they later assaulted. Courts have been deeply divided about whether to allow this type of defense to be presented at all.

STRESS DEFENSES

Post-traumatic stress disorder is the psychological distress that many victims of severe trauma experience for some time, often years, after the original traumatic stress. Some Vietnam War veterans have raised this defense when charged with a variety of offenses. Victims of severe physical abuse who commit violent acts themselves may also try to raise a stress defense. The Battered Woman defense often involves elements of the stress defense as well.

LAW ENFORCEMENT

Police officers, and in some cases private citizens, may be justified in using force or committing other acts that would ordinarily be crimes, if such acts are necessary in order to enforce the law. The defense of the four Los Angeles police officers charged in the beating of Rodney King involved the law enforcement defense.

ENTRAPMENT

A defendant who raises an entrapment defense must prove that a government agent induced the defendant to commit the crime and that the defendant was not otherwise disposed to commit the crime. Entrapment defenses are commonly raised in cases where undercover officers have attempted to engage in a criminal transaction (such as prostitution or drug sales) with the defendant.

ALIBI

An alibi defense asserts that the defendant cannot be the guilty culprit because the defendant was someplace else at the time the crime took place. To be successful, the defense must prove the time and place of the offense and prove the impossibility of the defendant being at that place at that time by proving that the defendant was elsewhere. Unlike most other affirmative defenses, alibi is neither a justification for the conduct nor an excuse. Alibi asserts that the defendant was not present at all.

SOURCE: Sue Titus Reid. 1992. *Criminal Law*, 2d ed. New York: Macmillan.

---

defendant suffer any injuries, or was the victim armed in some way? Did the victim make verbal threats while moving toward the defendant in a menacing way? Are witnesses available who can testify that they believed the defendant was in danger? Would the defendant make a credible and persuasive witness?

In the case of a battered woman who kills her husband, for example, defense counsel must consider how the trier of fact will assess the situation if the battering husband had his back turned when the woman stabbed him with a kitchen knife. The prosecution in such a case may be trying to prove that the defendant intended to kill her husband to get out of an unhappy marriage. The defense in turn will try to prove that the defendant believed that her husband was preparing to renew his attack against her and that she struck in self-defense as the only way to avoid a brutal and perhaps fatal beating. To prove the case defense counsel may need to present evidence regarding the defendant's state of mind at the time of the crime, including evidence about other beatings she suffered and expert testimony regarding the battered spouse syndrome.

necessity defense

The **necessity defense** involves a situation in which the forces of nature would have injured or killed someone had the defendant not intervened. For example, if a homeless person is arrested for trespassing after being found sleeping in a warehouse, the defense might argue that the danger to the defendant of freezing to death created the necessity of trespassing and that the trespass is therefore justified.

duress

To claim **duress** the defense must prove that someone coerced the defendant into committing a crime by the use or threat of unlawful force. Defense counsel's client might be a sixteen-year-old caught committing burglaries with older companions. The defense might argue that the older co-defendants actually threatened to harm the young defendant unless he agreed to participate in the burglaries. The success of the defense might hinge on defense counsel's ability to convince the trier of fact that the younger child feared serious injury if he refused to cooperate.

Alibi

In an alibi defense, counsel attempts to prove the defendant was somewhere other than at the scene of the crime when the crime took place. The defense must produce witnesses who will testify that they can vouch for the defendant's whereabouts at the time of the crime. This defense is frequently raised when the evidence connecting the defendant to the crime is circumstantial, when the victim's identification of the defendant is doubtful, or the defense can suggest that the victim has reason to lie about the defendant's involvement. Many states require that the defense notify the prosecution if it plans to raise an alibi defense at trial (Miller et al. 1986, 776). This requirement gives the prosecution an opportunity to investigate the credibility of the witnesses who support the defendant's alibi and to search for other witnesses who might refute the defense witnesses' story. For example, if the defense witness claims to have been at a movie with the defendant at the time of the crime, the prosecutor might interview employees of the theater. In addition, the prosecutor might interview other people who may have seen the defense witness alone or with someone else at the time of the crime.

■ PREPARING WITNESSES: REVIEWING THE EVIDENCE AND PREVIEWING THE TRIAL

Much evidence at trial is testimonial evidence, presented through the testimony of witnesses. Lawyers for both sides create lists of the witnesses who need to be called and determine the order in which they will be called to testify. They then prepare a subpoena for each witness and arrange through the court to have the subpoena served before trial.

During the initial preparation of a case (see Chapter 12) the witnesses prepare the lawyers by providing information about what happened leading up to the defendant's arrest and charge. By the time the attorneys begin to prepare for trial, they have interviewed important witnesses at least once, perhaps more. As preparation turns specifically to preparation for trial, the focus of attorney-witness interaction shifts. Now the attorney begins to prepare the witness for trial.

The attorneys try to maintain contact with witnesses, to make sure that they are still cooperative and to meet any needs or concerns the witnesses might have related to the case. The prosecutor may obtain assistance in this task from victim-witness services personnel. Before trial the attorney meets with each witness—sometimes individually, sometimes in groups—to review what the witness knows and can testify to. Inadequate pretrial preparation with witnesses can mean awkward surprises on the witness stand.

Reviewing the Witness's Testimony

A lawyer first needs to have a clear idea of what the witness does and does not know and will or will not say. Frequently, the attorney provides the witness with copies of the witness's prior statements, such as statements the witness made to the police, transcripts of earlier interviews with the attorney, and the witness's statement at the preliminary hearing. Providing these statements refreshes the witness's memory, and gives the witness an opportunity to react to statements that may not accurately reflect his recollections (Goldberg 1982). The attorney also may point out any ambiguities or conflicts with other evidence in the case, asking the witness to explain.

Previewing the Trial Appearance

In addition to reviewing the information offered by a witness, the attorney prepares the witness for the appearance in court. The attorney teaches the witness how to be a "believable player on the trial stage" (Goldberg 1982, 104), often rehearsing parts or all of the direct examination. In addition, the lawyer might prepare the witness for cross-examination by playing the role of opposing counsel. The main purpose of this preparation is to ease the witness's anxiety about testifying and about cross-examination in particular. Sometimes attorneys will videotape the rehearsal so that witnesses can see how they come across (Goldberg 1982, 122). The attorney may offer pointers and general feedback about the witness's testimony. For example, if a witness makes a statement during an interview that is particularly striking and persuasive, the attorney can suggest that if asked that question at trial, the witness answer in just that way (Marcus 1989, 72). If a witness gets angry and defensive during mock cross-examination, the attorney can caution the witness that getting angry will not make a good impression on the jurors.

The attorney may make suggestions to witnesses about appropriate dress and demeanor at trial. Witnesses are advised not to discuss the case with strangers in the court hallways and to act serious and reserved both in and out of the courtroom, because a witness never knows when a juror might be watching or listening.

The defense attorney also must prepare the defendant for trial. Even if the defendant is not going to testify, defense counsel may need to warn the defendant to avoid making any facial expressions or noises while other witnesses are testifying. Some defendants think they should use facial expressions or groans to convey that a prosecution witness is lying. Most defense lawyers believe that a jury finds such distractions annoying, especially if the defendant is unwilling to testify (Goldberg 1982, 134). Generally, counsel suggests that the client write comments on a sheet of paper in order to inform counsel when a witness is lying or to suggest questions for cross-examination.

■ PREPARING PHYSICAL AND DEMONSTRATIVE EVIDENCE

The attorneys also need to review the physical evidence to be used at trial and to interview any expert witnesses needed to interpret the physical, psychological, or other evidence (see Figure 15-2). The prosecutor in particular must ensure that all physical evidence needed to prove the crime is available and ready for trial. If evidence has been lost or tampered with or has deteriorated over time, it is better to find out sooner rather than on the morning of trial. Physical evidence, such as weapons, clothing, documents, betting slips, or other items, help the prosecutor prove the offense. Demonstrative evidence, such as photographs, diagrams, maps, charts, and even computer simulations and reenactments of the crime, help the attorneys to present the evidence in court. Photographic experts may be needed to create blow-ups of photographs and documents for presentation to the jury. Graphic artists may be needed to draw maps of the crime scene or diagrams of the results of ballistics tests. An artist may even be asked to draw a series of pictures depicting the events in the crime. These are used by both attorneys to make the crime more understandable to the judge and jury.

FIGURE 15-2   Subjects for Expert Testimony

SOURCE: Michael D. Marcus. Copyright © 1989. *Trial Preparation for Prosecutors*. New York: Wiley, pp. 148–49. Reprinted by permission of John Wiley & Sons, Inc.

Analysis of gang values and graffiti
Interpretation and analysis of financial data
Toothmark identification
Toolmark identification
Paint chip and glass fragment analysis
Cause of death
Age and sex of bones
Manner in which firearms operate
Manner in which destructive devices function
Handwriting analysis and identification
Fingerprint identification
Physical condition of the victim or defendant
Blood analysis
Sperm analysis
Hair analysis
Analysis of breath results for blood alcohol content
Description of radar operation
Description of magnetometer operation
Quantitative and qualitative analysis of narcotics and dangerous drugs
Purpose for which drugs were possessed
Explanation of certain fraudulent schemes such as advance fee operation, bait and
    switch, and pigeon drop
Linguistics analysis
Analysis and interpretation of bookmaking paraphernalia
Pornography surveys to establish community standards
Analysis of mental disease or defect, diminished capacity, insanity, and compe-
    tency to stand trial
Analysis of child abuse trauma
Description of the child abuse accommodation syndrome
Description of rape trauma syndrome
Description of posttraumatic stress disorder
Age of documents
Estimating the reasonable or fair market value of property
Accident reconstruction

The appropriateness of demonstrative evidence can be a contentious issue at trial. Opposing counsel may object that a particular diagram or photograph is misleading or prejudicial. When demonstrative evidence is to be used, the attorney may need to seek a stipulation from opposing counsel or file a motion requesting that the judge rule on the admissibility of the demonstrative evidence before trial.

☐ TO WAIVE OR NOT TO WAIVE: JURY TRIAL AND TRIAL STRATEGY

The right to a jury trial is commonly viewed as one of the fundamental protections of defendants and the cornerstone of the Anglo-American system of justice. In addition, a jury trial offers a variety of strategic advantages to the

DEMONSTRATIVE EVIDENCE

The exhibits were big, about four feet by six feet, and fancy, with black backgrounds and lettering in white, green, yellow and pink. They were divided into grids like giant sheets of graph paper, with lots of horizontal and vertical columns. Impressive and expensive, the charts were state of the art in the growing field of litigation support: exhibits designed by consultants to help trial lawyers make their cases more visually compelling to the jurors. And they scared the hell out of the defense lawyers.

The charts illustrated the results of tests conducted on blood samples, hair samples, semen samples and clothing seized from the suspects or found at the rape scene. In the extreme left column, for example, a slide with a smear from the Jogger's vagina was listed. Following the color coded boxes across the board, jurors could see when the sample was taken, when and where it was tested and by whom. On the far right, in the column labeled "Conclusions," were little magnetic covers. The intention was that a witness describing the results of a test performed on that slide at Metropolitan Hospital, for example, would remove the cover and the words, "positive for sperm" would be revealed.

The prosecutors had commissioned the charts to help the jury and themselves. There were so many tests done on so many items—some with conflicting results—that they were concerned the jurors would be confused about the evidence. For example, a slide containing a smear from Harris's [the jogger] rectum that was examined at Metropolitan Hospital tested negative for sperm. When that slide was tested again by the police lab, it came out positive for sperm. Expecting that the defense would attack the credibility of their scientific evidence, the prosecutors hoped the charts would reinforce their interpretation of the results.

While it was certainly true that the state had conducted hundreds of tests, the prosecutors were still left with a paucity of physical evidence. The best [Elizabeth] Lederer [the prosecutor] could do with respect to the three defendants was prove that there was semen on [Antron] McCray's underpants and mud on his clothes that might have come from the park, and semen on Raymond Santana's sweatshirt and underpants. These charts, however, would undoubtedly give the jury the false impression that the prosecutors had a virtual mountain of physical evidence.

At a bench conference, Joseph and Bobby Burns [defense counsel] expressed alarm at the prospect of the jury seeing the charts. . . . The defense lawyers conceded that the charts might be appropriate tools for the prosecutors to use during summation. They argued strongly, however, that there was no justification for bringing the charts in as evidence, in themselves, of anything. . . .

Joseph told the judge the exhibits could mislead the jury. "The bottom line is, it's not evidence. It's a summary. It does say 'positive for sperm' but cannot say whose sperm. . . . This chart merely attempts to take what a witness is saying and then boil it down to one word, and then allow the People to have that one word displayed before the jury. . . . That's improper and prejudicial," Joseph concluded.

[Judge Thomas] Galligan decided not to permit the charts in evidence "at this time," reserving judgment on whether they could be used later. Lederer never offered them again. The defense had won an important battle.

SOURCE: Excerpted from Timothy Sullivan. 1992. *Unequal Verdicts: The Central Park Jogger Trials.* New York: Simon & Schuster, pp. 128–29. Copyright © 1992 Timothy Sullivan. Reprinted by permission of Simon & Schuster, Inc.

defense. In a jury trial the defense needs to raise a reasonable doubt in the mind of just one or more of the jurors. Juries also increase the odds of raising a successful appeal. Although a judge is expected to be able to disregard prejudicial comments that may be made in the course of trial, such statements made before a jury may be grounds for reversing a conviction on appeal.

A jury trial is not always a blessing for the defense; situations do arise in which the defense is not interested in having a jury try the case. The defendant may waive the right to a jury trial subject to the state's right to request a jury (*Singer v. United States* 1965). Defense counsel advises the defendant about the risks of a jury trial compared to a bench trial, but the defendant must decide whether to waive a jury trial.

The defense tries to assess how the case will "play" to a jury as opposed to a judge. When the issues in a case are highly emotional, and the emotional reactions of the jurors are likely to prejudice the jury against the defendant, the defense might choose to try the case before a judge. Because judges hear case after case, day after day, they are more accustomed to hearing sordid and unsavory stories and might be expected to give a more dispassionate assessment of the evidence (Bailey and Rothblatt 1985, 167). For example, if a homicide involved particularly brutal and savage attacks that probably caused the victim to suffer a great deal before death, the jurors may become so outraged that they want to find someone guilty. In this situation the defense has to be concerned that the jury's wish to punish will cloud its ability to weigh the evidence.

The defense also is likely to waive a jury trial when the legal and factual issues involved in a case are highly technical or complex (Bailey and Rothblatt 1985, 167). In more routine cases some defense lawyers advise their clients to waive a jury trial in the belief that the judge will be more lenient in sentencing "because the defendant spared the bother and expense of a jury trial" (Bailey and Rothblatt 1985, 168).

When the defense waives a jury trial, some jurisdictions give the prosecution an opportunity to assert the state's right to trial by jury. That is, the prosecutor can request a jury trial (Bailey and Rothblatt 1985, 169). Some states have gone even further and allow the court to demand a jury trial even when both parties have waived a jury trial. The rationale for such a rule is that the state has an interest in ensuring a fair trial and that a jury trial is recognized as the fairest procedure for the resolution of factual disputes. The Supreme Court has held that the Constitution does not confer upon defendants the right to have trial held before a judge (*Singer v. United States* 1965).

When the prosecutor is faced with choosing between a jury and bench trial, the considerations are similar to those weighed by the defense in its decision to waive the jury. When the facts are complex or boring, as in a fraud prosecution, the prosecutor may decide that a judge would be a better trier of fact. On the other hand jurors are also believed to be more likely than judges to convict in certain cases, such as child molesting (Marcus 1989, 366).

Preparation for Jury Selection

voir dire

In routine cases preparing for jury selection involves a simple process of planning in advance the kinds of questions to be asked during **voir dire**, which is the questioning of jurors during the jury selection process. In more serious or nonroutine cases preparation for jury selection may be quite intensive. Before voir dire attorneys gather information about potential jurors from a variety of sources. They use this information to guide voir dire, looking for possible issues to raise with some jurors. The attorney uses this information and a prospective juror's responses during voir dire to decide whether to accept a juror or attempt to have the juror excused.

Using Information About Jurors

The first task in preparing for jury selection is to consider the kinds of people who would be unsympathetic to the story counsel is presenting at trial. In important cases the attorneys may consult psychologists who specialize in assessing jurors' predispositions and attitudes based on limited information. These consultants may advise the attorney on the kinds of questions to ask during voir dire and the nonverbal cues (such as posture and eye contact) that may offer insights to a juror's predisposition. In some cases experts may be employed at considerable expense to conduct surveys of representative samples of residents of the area in which the trial is to be held. The purpose of these surveys is to identify the sorts of people who are more likely to be sympathetic to the prosecution or the defense. In some cases they hold mock trials in order to observe the mock jurors as they deliberate and to assess the kinds of issues that were important in reaching their "verdict" (Gobert and Jordan 1990, 82–133). Mock trials give the attorney a dress rehearsal for the trial, and interviews with the mock jurors reveal whether certain types of jurors are likely to remain unpersuaded. This information can be used in selecting the actual jurors for trial.

Once the attorney has decided what characteristics are undesirable, the lawyer begins to study available information about the potential jurors to find out what sorts of people they are. Information that jurisdictions maintain about the individuals in the current jury pool include the cases on which they have served as jurors, the verdicts in those cases, and other data. Some jurisdictions ask jurors to complete a personal data sheet that provides at least each potential juror's name and address and sometimes such additional information as age, marital status, educational level, occupation, and jury service (Goldberg 1982, 168). From the address the attorney may be able to make inferences about a potential juror's socioeconomic status. The attorney can use the name and address to look up the juror in a city directory that provides information about residents' occupations. The attorney uses all this information to make rough predictions about the jurors' sympathies and prejudices.

Most jurisdictions also maintain a verdict form file that contains the names of jurors who supported a particular verdict in other cases. From this the attorneys can find out whether any prospective jurors have previously voted to acquit or convict a criminal defendant and other information about cases on which the juror may have served. Some defense attorneys believe that a juror who has voted to convict in one case is more likely to vote to convict in other cases. Some prosecutors' offices maintain information compiled by the prosecuting attorneys about their experiences with particular jurors. These information systems provide the prosecutor with information about why a prosecutor struck a juror in a previous case, whether the defense struck a juror and the likely reason, whether a juror was removed for cause in a previous case, and any other information that may have been obtained from posttrial interviews with the jurors (Marcus 1989, 381).

Relying on Stereotypes

In most cases counsel has neither the time nor the budget to do anything but prepare mentally for the task of jury selection. In addition, because the prosecutor and defense counsel usually have only a limited opportunity to question potential jurors about their attitudes and values, the attorneys try to guess jurors' predispositions by relying on stereotypes. They use stereotypes to predict the kinds of people who are likely to be sympathetic, prejudiced, or independent jurors. For

FINDING SYMPATHETIC JURORS: WILLIAM KENNEDY SMITH DEFENSE LAWYER REVEALS HIS TACTICS

As any member of the William Kennedy Smith defense team could tell you, the process of picking a jury may be the most important element of any trial.

They ought to know. The defense team spent nearly four weeks helping to select the Florida jury that acquitted Smith of rape last Dec. 12 [1991] after deliberating only 77 minutes.

Miami lawyer Roy Black, who defended Smith, said the choosing of a sympathetic jury was "absolutely critical" to winning the case. But finding the right jurors for the Smith trial was a lot harder than it looked, as he and a team of consultants proved during a program on jury selection at the ABA Midyear Meeting in Dallas. Demonstrating their techniques, husband-and-wife consultants Cathy Bennett and Robert Hirshhorn distributed copies of the questionnaires that they developed to pick a jury in the Smith trial. As the audience soon learned, some of the least promising prospects on paper went on to become some of the favorite candidates for the jury.

Take the 44-year-old married man who said he was a church-going Catholic with children the same age as the daughter of Smith's accuser, for example. On his questionnaire, the man also indicated that a member of his family was in law enforcement and his daughter had been the victim of a crime.

Based on his answers to the questionnaire, a majority of the audience said they would have quickly rejected the man as a juror for the defense in the Smith trial. But the consultants revealed how the man, who became an alternate juror, won them over during voir dire.

Under questioning, the man came across as sensitive, warm and caring, they said. He spoke softly and looked directly at Smith in a non-judgmental way. And he said he admired his own father because his dad "worked hard and never quit" on his family.

Black changed his mind on another juror, too, based on his consultants' advice. The man was a Vietnam War veteran who ended up as foreman of the jury.

"I thought there were things in his background that would be real damaging to us, but he turned out to be one of the best defense jurors and one of our strongest supporters," Black said.

HURDLES CLEARED

Black said the defense had to overcome two big obstacles in seating a jury for the Smith case. The first was the extent of pre-trial publicity the case had received. The second was the public's strong and sometimes negative preconceptions about the Kennedy family.

To expose any biases on potential jurors' part, Black said he questioned each member of the panel at length, asking open-ended questions that were designed to get them to reveal their deepest thoughts and feelings. He also operated without taking notes, which allowed him to concentrate completely on what the would-be jurors were saying.

"If you're open and honest with them and show them that you're human, they'll start to like you, and that's 50 percent of the battle," he said. "If you come in there with a big ego and act overbearing and supercilious, they'll cut your legs out from under you."

SOURCE: Reprinted from Mark Hansen. 1992. "Finding Sympathetic Jurors: William Kennedy Smith Defense Lawyer Reveals His Tactics." *ABA Journal* 78 (April): 29. Reprinted by permission of the *ABA Journal*.

example, many attorneys believe that politically conservative jurors are more likely to convict and that certain occupational groups are more likely to hold conservative political values. From a potential juror's occupation the attorneys make inferences that influence whether the juror will be retained.

Despite the widespread reliance on stereotypes, research on juror verdict preferences has found few generalizations that are reliable. Personal characteris-

---

JUROR SELECTION

The ADAs [assistant district attorneys] at SVB [Special Victims Bureau] already knew by heart the basic profile of the jurors that I wanted for sex-crimes trials: men in their forties to fifties who said they read the *New York Times* but really read the *Daily News*. I wanted people who had a veneer of sophistication about sexual assault, but who would still respond from the gut to ugly crimes. I wanted down-to-earth jurors, grounded in everyday realities of urban violence—not anyone who would ever consider falling asleep on the subway at night.

Ideally, I wanted jurors whose jobs required interaction with the public so that their perceptions were tested every day—bus drivers instead of housewives. And I wanted jurors who'd served on a jury before. Somehow they got better with practice. Mostly what I wanted to avoid was collaborators—anyone who would take a tolerance for rapists into the jury room and express it in a verdict.

SOURCE: Excerpted from Alice Vachss. © 1993 by Alice Vachss. *Sex Crimes.* New York: Random House, p. 198. Reprinted by permission of Random House, Inc.

---

tics, such as religion, ethnic background, political affiliation, and occupation, are actually poor predictors of whether jurors will be hardliners or bleeding hearts in the jury room. Research does consistently suggest that female jurors are more likely to convict in rape cases and that jurors who favor capital punishment are more likely to convict in all kinds of cases (Ellsworth 1993, 45).

Dealing with Pretrial Publicity

One key issue in any jury trial concerns the amount and content of pretrial publicity about the defendant, the victim, and the evidence in the case. Pretrial publicity has always been a problem. The spread of rumor and gossip about a pending criminal case in a small town during the nineteenth century was as potentially prejudicial as modern media coverage. The traditional remedy for *change of venue* protecting against pretrial publicity is a **change of venue**, that is, changing the location of the trial in order to seat jurors who have not been exposed to the pretrial publicity. In some states jurors simply are selected from a different jurisdiction and brought to the original court jurisdiction instead of moving the location of the trial. Such measures can be effective in ensuring the impartiality of the jurors if pretrial publicity has occurred only in the local media.

However, pretrial publicity in some cases is so widespread that moving the trial to another location would make little difference. For example, the arrest and investigation of the defendants charged in the bombing of the World Trade Center in New York was covered heavily in the national media; thus potential jurors in Omaha would be as likely to have been exposed to prejudicial coverage as any New Yorker. Furthermore, in highly publicized cases both the prosecution and the defense may try to shape the content of pretrial publicity in order to create an advantage at trial. This practice was seen most vividly in the public relations blitz conducted in relation to the O. J. Simpson trial.

However, simply hearing about a case and certain allegations does not necessarily disqualify a juror. A juror who has closely followed news coverage of a case may still be sufficiently impartial if the person has not formed a fixed opinion about the defendant's guilt or innocence (Bailey and Rothblatt 1985, 205–6). The problem for the attorneys is to plan their voir dire to be able to identify those jurors who have already formed an opinion about the likely outcome of the case. In a case that has received considerable media attention and public interest, the attorneys want to find out whether the prospective juror has heard others discussing the case, has participated in discussions of the case, and whether the juror has expressed any opinion about the defendant's guilt or innocence. The attorneys may plan to question jurors about the particular media sources they use, particularly if tabloid TV or newspapers have carried emotional and prejudicial coverage of the case. The attorneys might plan to ask the jurors whether what they have read or heard about the case gives them the impression that it is an open-and-shut case (Ginger 1969, 21).

■ SUMMARY

Ideally, the preparation for trial begins as soon as the case is referred to counsel. Each attorney needs to weave a story from the individual bits of evidence and testimony that will be presented at trial. Each attorney must know the strengths and weaknesses of both sides of the case.

The defense is not required to prove anything at trial and may choose to defend against the charges simply by undermining the state's case. However, in some circumstances the defense may wish to bring an affirmative defense, such as self-defense, insanity, or alibi. When the defense raises an affirmative defense, it bears the burden of proving certain facts.

In highly emotional or complex cases the defense may decide that a jury trial is more risky than having the case decided by a judge. If a jury trial is to be held, the attorneys need to prepare for jury selection, deciding what kinds of people are most likely to be sympathetic to their story and what kinds of questions are likely to help them decide whether a particular juror is likely to be sympathetic. In addition, if the defendant demands a jury trial and the case receives extensive pretrial publicity, one or both attorneys might move for a change of venue to obtain jurors less likely to have been exposed to prejudicial news coverage.

Trial preparation can be extremely time-consuming and detailed, if the attorneys are given unlimited time and resources. How extensively attorneys prepare depends on the stakes involved (generally, the seriousness of the charges) and the resources available to them. In a routine case prosecutors and public defenders are unlikely to have the time or money for elaborate preparations but instead make quick decisions based on experience. Even so, attorneys need to do their homework if they hope to be successful in the courtroom. The next chapter looks more closely at what happens when the case finally comes to trial.

■ FOR FURTHER DISCUSSION

1. A common strategy of the defense in sexual assault cases is to attempt to impugn the character and credibility of the victim. Many states have imposed limits on the information that may be admitted at trial concerning victims' private lives (such as previous sexual experiences). Find out what your state law is in relation to restricting such evidence. In the face of such laws, what sorts of defense strategies are left? Are there other ways to undermine the credibility of the victim? If you were the prosecutor, how would you plan to counter the defense efforts?

2. The federal case against former Panamanian dictator Manuel Noriega on drug-related charges relied heavily on the testimony of former drug-trade

participants who were offered deals in exchange for their testimony. According to news accounts, twenty-nine prosecution witnesses received reduced charges or sentences in exchange for their testimony against Noriega (Doppelt 1993, 56–59). Although the government succeeded in convicting Noriega, placing such heavy reliance on former drug dealers who testify only to save their own necks certainly offers the defense ample opportunity to undermine the government's case. Such witnesses, the defense can point out, are motivated to lie in order to get a better deal from the government. The honesty and integrity of such witnesses are also brought into question. Why should jurors believe witnesses who have cheated and broken the law as a normal part of their business—especially when such witnesses stand to improve their own situations by exaggerating the criminality of the defendant? How would you weigh the testimony of such witnesses?

3. Pretrial publicity and the prospects for obtaining impartial jurors have become an increasing concern as the media have discovered the entertainment value of crime news, particularly outlandish crimes, and crimes involving famous people. Consider a recent case that has received substantial coverage in the local and/or national media. What do you know about this case? Do you think that you would be able to be an impartial juror if called for jury service? Do you think both the prosecution and the defense would consider you impartial after completing their voir dire?

REFERENCES

Bailey, F. Lee, and Henry B. Rothblatt. 1985. *Successful Techniques for Criminal Trials,* 2d ed. Rochester, N.Y.: Lawyers Co-Operative Publishing.

Bennett, W. Lance, and Martha S. Feldman. 1981. *Reconstructing Reality in the Courtroom: Justice and Judgment in American Culture.* New Brunswick, N.J.: Rutgers University Press.

Boland, Barbara, Paul Mahanna, and Ronald Sones. 1992. *The Prosecution of Felony Arrests, 1988.* Washington, D.C.: U.S. Department of Justice, Bureau of Justice Statistics.

Doppelt, Jack. 1993. "No Longer News: The Trial of the Century That Wasn't." *ABA Journal* (January): 56–59.

Ellsworth, Phoebe C. 1993. "Some Steps Between Attitudes and Verdicts." In Reid Hastie, ed. *Inside the Juror: The Psychology of Juror Decision Making.* New York: University of Cambridge Press.

Ginger, Ann Fagan. 1969. *Minimizing Racism in Jury Trials.* Berkeley, Calif.: National Lawyers' Guild.

Gobert, James J., and Walter E. Jordan. 1990. *Jury Selection: The Law, Art, and Science of Selecting a Jury,* 2d ed. Colorado Springs, Colo.: Shepard's–McGraw Hill.

Goldberg, Steven H. 1982. *The First Trial: Where Do I Sit? What Do I Say?* St. Paul, Minn.: West.

Marcus, Michael D. 1989. *Trial Preparation for Prosecutors.* New York: Wiley.

Miller, Frank W., Robert O. Dawson, George E. Dix, and Raymond I. Parnas. 1986. *Prosecution and Adjudication.* Mineola, N.Y.: Foundation Press.

Singer v. United States, 380 U.S. 24, 85 S. Ct. 783 (1965).

CHAPTER **16**

THE DRAMA OF TRIAL

Few public events epitomize the ideals of the U.S. Constitution like a criminal trial. If the Constitution stands for the protection of individual liberty against the power of government, the criminal trial is a graphic expression of that ideal. Moreover, a trial encapsulates all the drama of a good mystery. Who is lying? Who do we trust? Is the meek-looking defendant really vicious? The drama and mystery of trial have been of public interest for centuries—people always find trials fascinating.

Part of the fascination stems from the gamesmanship that is so much a part of the adversarial process. Jury selection involves a gamble: which jurors will be more sympathetic? Examination of witnesses is a sort of verbal jousting. Both attorneys struggle to set the stage, even to the point of putting their witnesses in the right costumes and attitudes. The drama culminates in the verdict. No wonder we are fascinated—a trial combines all the excitement of a sporting match, a mystery, and a morality play.

Since the birth of television the courtroom drama has been a popular format for television series. In recent years, with television news cameras increasingly allowed in the courtroom, and even entire cable networks devoted to showing criminal trials, the drama of the courtroom has come into our homes and our awareness as never before (Marcotte 1990a, 19). After years of television depictions of criminal trials—from *Perry Mason* to *Equal Justice, Law & Order,* and *L.A. Law*—we are now seeing *real* trials that sometimes have us glued to our sets.

Unlike many courtroom dramas, real trials hardly ever end with the confession of the guilty. Instead the public is learning about the ambiguity and uncertainty that surround the trial and verdict. The verdict is not a statement of "truth" but only the judgment of fallible people operating in a fallible system. The verdict does not necessarily end uncertainty about the accuracy of the result. While waiting for the verdict, spectators may sense how easily the verdict might go either way.

Although perfect truth may be unattainable in any system of adjudication, it is worth asking whether our court procedures offer the most reliable methods for making these admittedly difficult judgments. Again, given the visibility of criminal trials, maintaining the legitimacy of the trial process is an important consideration. Unfortunately, to the casual observer the reasons behind the seemingly arcane procedures of the criminal courts often are a mystery.

This chapter seeks to demystify some trial processes. It begins by examining the rights of defendants at trial, followed by a chronological description of the major stages of the trial and the challenges that arise during the trial.

▪ TRIAL RIGHTS

The defendant's rights at trial include the right to a jury trial, the right to an impartial judge, and the right to confront accusers.

Right to a Jury Trial

The U.S. Bureau of Justice Statistics (BJS) has found that "most felony cases that reach trial are tried before a jury" (1988, 84). The right to trial by jury is a distinguishing feature of the Anglo-American criminal process. As Chapter Five notes, other judicial systems include lay representation as the trier of fact in criminal trials. Nonetheless, for both the British and Americans the jury has symbolized the liberal ideals of freedom from tyranny.

The jury is more than a symbol of justice in this country. To a large degree it serves as a symbol of democracy itself. Ordinary men and women sitting in judgment of their peers symbolize the participatory ideals of our democratic form of government. In contrast, trial by a judge smacks of authoritarianism, unless it is the choice of the defendant (Hyman and Tarrant 1975, 40).

Trial by jury is guaranteed by the Sixth Amendment. In addition, every state has constitutional provisions for trial by jury. Despite this widespread recognition of the right to jury, interpretations of what the "right to jury" means in practice vary widely. The U.S. Supreme Court sets the minimum standards for what is required by the due process clause of the Fourteenth Amendment. The Court today accepts a fair degree of diversity and experimentation among the states in their interpretations of what the right to jury means in state cases. Some key questions regarding the right to jury include:

1. Do all criminal defendants, regardless of the type of crime charged, have a right to jury trial?
2. How many jurors must agree in order to reach a verdict?
3. Who may serve as a juror?
4. How are impartial jurors to be identified and selected for jury service?

Scope of the Right to Jury

The Sixth Amendment appears to be quite explicit about the scope of the right to a jury trial in criminal cases. It states:

In *all criminal prosecutions*, the accused shall enjoy the right to a speedy and public trial, by an impartial jury of the State and district wherein the crime shall have been committed . . . [emphasis added].

The wording of the amendment makes no distinction between felonies and misdemeanors or serious and petty offenses. Moreover, the Supreme Court has held that the right to a jury trial is "fundamental" and must be recognized in both federal and state trials (*Duncan v. Louisiana* 1968).

Although it has applied a literal interpretation of the Sixth Amendment in federal cases, the Supreme Court has allowed the states greater latitude in determining whether due process requires a right to jury trial in *all* criminal cases. The Supreme Court has held that the Constitution, specifically the due process clause, does not establish a right to jury trials for petty offenses in *state* cases (*Duncan v. Louisiana*; *Baldwin v. New York* 1970; *Blanton v. City of Las Vegas* 1989). The Court reasoned that for such petty offenses, those carrying a maximum jail sentence of six months or less, the benefits of "speedy and inexpensive nonjury adjudications" outweigh the disadvantages to the defendant denied the right to jury for a petty offense (*Baldwin*).

Jury Size and Unanimity

Traditionally, trial juries in the United States, also called petit juries (from the French word for *small* as distinguished from grand [large] juries), are made up of twelve jurors. Additional people may be selected to serve as alternates in the event that one or more original jurors becomes ill or for any other reason is not able to serve for the duration of the trial. However, in an attempt to reduce the expense of juries and the inconvenience to the public, some states have introduced smaller juries. Connecticut, Florida, Louisiana, and Oregon allow many felonies to be decided by a jury of six. Eighteen states provide for juries of fewer than twelve in misdemeanor cases (BJS 1988, 86). Although the Supreme Court has approved juries of fewer than twelve members (*Williams v. Florida* 1970), some commentators have questioned "whether a jury of six substantively provides an adequately representative cross-section of the defendant's community, so that justice will be achieved" (Hyman and Tarrant 1975, 39). Small juries may decrease minority representation. A study conducted by the National Center for State Courts found that reducing jury size from twelve to eight jurors reduces the proportion of African-American and Latino jurors selected to serve (DeBenedictus 1990, 24). Because African-Americans and Latinos typically are underrepresented on juries, reducing jury size only exacerbates this problem.

The Court has clearly drawn the line at six jurors, however. In *Ballew v. Georgia* (1978) a plurality of the Court held that a five-person jury is too small to be constitutionally acceptable. The following year the Court ruled that when a state opts to use a six-person jury, the verdict must be unanimous; a majority verdict or even five votes out of six is not acceptable (*Burch v. Louisiana* 1979).

Although most states require unanimous verdicts, five states (Louisiana, Montana, Oklahoma, Oregon, and Texas) allow verdicts by majority vote (BJS 1988, 84). The Supreme Court has held that the Fourteenth Amendment requirement of due process in state criminal trials does not mandate that jury verdicts be unanimous (*Johnson v. Louisiana* 1972; *Apodaca v. Oregon* 1972). The Court has upheld convictions based on as few as nine out of twelve jurors voting for conviction (*Johnson v. Louisiana*). However, when the jury is composed of only six jurors, the Court has required a unanimous verdict (*Burch*).

A simulation study explored some ramifications of less than unanimous jury verdicts (Hastie, Penrod, and Pennington 1983). The study found no differences in the probability of conviction or acquittal. However, the researchers did find that requiring unanimity appears to be associated with longer deliberations. This would be expected and is probably the primary rationale behind state provisions that permit less than unanimous verdicts. The study also found that juries required to reach a unanimous verdict were more thorough in their examination of the evidence and the law.

Jury Composition

The U.S. Constitution makes no reference to a jury of peers. Yet the right to a jury of peers has been read into the concept of the jury through English common law and early American applications of it. The origins of the phrase "jury of peers" can be traced indirectly to the Magna Carta and the feudal notion that a person should be judged by feudal lords of a similar rank. The main thrust of the feudal requirement was to ensure that a noble was not judged by his social and political inferiors (Gobert and Jordan 1990, 46). Over time the idea of trial by a jury of peers has come to mean that a person has a right to be judged by other laypersons rather than by professional jurists. In modern times the common law notion of peers has been interpreted as requiring that jurors be selected from a representative cross section of the locale in which the crime occurred or the trial is taking place.

venire, talesmen, panel

The Supreme Court described this cross-section requirement most explicitly in *Duren v. Missouri* (1979). Each petit jury need not be representative of the community. Only the **venire**, or the group from which the jurors are selected (also called the **talesmen**, or **panel**), must be representative of the community in relevant respects.

In a finding that has come to be known as the *Duren* rule, the Court said that a defendant must establish three assertions to show a violation of the cross-section requirement:

> (1) that a group alleged to be excluded is a "distinctive" group in the community; (2) that the representation of this group in venires from which jurors are selected is not fair and reasonable in relation to the number of such persons in the community, and (3) that this under-representation is due to systematic exclusion of the group in the jury selection process. (*Duren v. Missouri* 1979, 364)

In *Carter v. Jury Commission* (1970) the Court further held that groups underrepresented on jury venires may sue to force the court system to address the problem. In other words, the lack of representativeness is not something about which only the defendant may complain; a member of an underrepresented group may sue to change jury selection procedures to be more inclusive. The Court subsequently held that in cases involving the lack of representation of racial groups in the venire, a defendant may object to the lack of racial representation even if the defendant is not a member of the underrepresented group (*Peters v. Kiff* 1972).

Impartial Jurors

Another constitutional requirement regarding the jury is that it be impartial. The Supreme Court has never defined *impartiality* precisely but has found some bases for finding jurors biased in one way or another. In general, the Court has held that a juror who holds an actual bias, which cannot be put aside by the prospective juror in considering the evidence, should be excused from serving on the jury. Biases must be uncovered during jury selection, but the Court has been less clear about the circumstances under which the defendant is entitled to inquire into potential biases that may influence the deliberation of the jurors.

One sort of bias is racial prejudice. The Court has ruled that when race might be relevant to the case, the defense must be allowed to question prospective jurors about their racial biases (*Ham v. South Carolina* 1973), but the Court declined to apply this rule to all cases involving interracial crimes (*Ristaino v. Ross* 1976). Although it upheld the rationale in *Ristaino,* the Court later distinguished capital and noncapital cases, holding that in a capital case a defendant charged with an interracial crime is entitled to have prospective jurors informed of the race of the victim and questioned on the issue of racial bias (*Turner v. Murray* 1986).

Pretrial publicity can also prejudice jurors. The Court's rulings on pretrial publicity underscore the Court's general rule that only bias that cannot be set aside by the juror renders the juror partial. In *Irvin v. Dowd* (1961) the Court noted that jurors need not be "totally ignorant" of the facts of the case, only that all jurors be sufficiently impartial that they can lay aside any prior knowledge or impressions in reaching a verdict. The Court has held that a defendant does not have a right to have jurors questioned about the content of news coverage they have read or heard, only whether the jurors have formed fixed opinions about the defendant's guilt or innocence (*Mu'Min v. Virginia* 1991).

The Court has also addressed a special problem of impartiality in relation to the death penalty. Because many people are morally opposed to the death penalty, prosecutors in death penalty cases worry that a juror may refuse to convict because of reluctance to play a role in authorizing the government to execute the defendant. The Court has faced this issue in several cases.

Witherspoon v. Illinois (1968) held that a death sentence could not be carried out if prospective jurors were excluded for cause simply because they voiced general objections to the death penalty. The current rule is that a juror may be excluded for cause in a death penalty case if the juror's views on capital punishment would "prevent or substantially impair the performance of his duties as a juror in accord with his instructions and his oath" (*Wainwright v. Witt* 1985, 424). Again, the Court appears to have drawn the line between partiality and impartiality at the point at which preconceptions, values, and beliefs would interfere with a juror's ability to assess the evidence as instructed by the court.

Other Trial Rights

Defendants possess a number of other rights at trial, including the right to an impartial judge, to have the state prove the charges by evidence beyond a reasonable doubt, to be present at trial, and to confront and cross-examine witnesses.

Judicial Impartiality

If the judge assigned to a particular case has a conflict of interest, is biased, or has formed an opinion about the guilt or innocence of the defendant, the judge should **recuse** (or remove) herself from the trial and have the case assigned to another judge. If either party believes that the judge is biased, a motion may be filed to request removal of the judge.

recusal

Some jurisdictions make it possible for either party to request the assignment of a different judge without having to show that the judge is actually biased. This may be called a motion for substitution of judge or an **affidavit of prejudice** (Marcus 1989, 278). In other jurisdictions the party requesting removal of the judge may have to show cause, giving a factual reason that the judge may be biased in the case. Whichever procedure is available, counsel must take care to

affidavit of prejudice

consider whether the next judge assigned to the case might be worse than the first judge. In those jurisdictions allowing one substitution without a showing of cause, counsel may be tempted to substitute a judge for reasons other than actual bias, such as the judge's sentencing practices or familiarity with the law. Counsel needs to weigh this decision carefully, because "it does no good to get rid of one judge and then get one who is worse" (Marcus 1989, 278). In cases of clear bias, of course, counsel should seek removal of the judge for cause without worrying about the next judge.

Right of Confrontation

The right to be present at trial is part of the Sixth Amendment right to confront accusers. In general, defendants have a right to be present, but this right is not absolute. Courts have upheld cases in which the trial proceeded in the absence of the defendant, so long as the defendant was notified of the time and place of trial and voluntarily decided to waive the right to be present. Nonetheless, trial courts make every effort to make sure that the defendant is present at trial. If the defendant fails to appear for the trial date, the trial is postponed until the defendant can be located.

If the defendant becomes disruptive in the courtroom, judges typically work to maintain order without infringing on the defendant's right to be present. A defendant whose behavior is out of control may be sequestered in a separate room and allowed to observe the trial via one-way mirror or closed-circuit television, or to listen through a loud speaker.

A special issue concerning the right of confrontation involves trials for crimes involving child victims, especially child sexual abuse cases. Testifying against an abusive adult can be a highly traumatic event for a child. In addition, the intimidating prospect of accusing the defendant, who may also be a parent or other adult with whom the child has had a dependent relationship, may cause child victims to be unwilling or unable to testify in court. To reduce the trauma to child victims, at least twenty-three states have passed laws allowing the child to testify on closed circuit TV or on videotape. In 1990 the Supreme Court approved a Maryland law allowing the trial court to accept the child's testimony over closed-circuit television if testifying in open court would result in "serious emotional distress such that the child cannot reasonably communicate" (*Maryland v. Craig* 1990).

■ TRIAL PROCEDURE

bench trial

Of the cases that go to trial, more than half result in a jury trial. In the other cases the defendant waives the right to a jury and opts for a **bench trial**, in which the judge serves as the sole trier of fact (Dawson 1992, 7). In many jurisdictions the prosecutor may demand a jury trial, even if the defendant waives the right. Unless a jury trial is waived, the first stage in trial procedure is jury selection.

Jury Selection

The jury selection process creates the procedural framework for ensuring the representativeness of jury venires and the impartiality of jurors selected to hear a particular case. Citizens are summoned to court and questioned. The answers jurors give to the questions determine whether they will serve on a jury.

Summoning Jurors

The jury selection process begins as a simple administrative process of periodically selecting at random a large group of community members to be called for jury service. The names of the individuals called for jury duty are placed on a list, called the **master jury list** or **jury wheel**. From this list panels of jurors are called to serve on particular cases. From that point the jury selection process focuses on the impartiality, character, and attitudes of the individual jurors.

master jury list, jury wheel

Different jurisdictions use a variety of sources for compiling the master jury list. In theory the master list should include the names of all members of the jurisdiction who have reached the age of majority. In practice master lists are often substantially incomplete. Sixteen states rely exclusively on voter registration lists. A few jurisdictions rely exclusively on the state driver's license list (BJS 1988, 86). Because some ethnic and age groups are less inclined to vote than others or less likely to hold valid driver's licenses, the lists tend not to be representative of the community as a whole. Because such lists tend to underrepresent minority groups, some jurisdictions supplement voter registration or driver's license lists with names from other sources, such as the telephone directory or city directory.

challenge to the array

If the master list does not represent a cross section of the community or has been improperly selected, either party may object with a **challenge to the array**. Such a challenge may be based on the *Duren* rule. For example, if the local jurisdiction is 7 percent Native American, but groups called for jury duty regularly include only 1 percent Native Americans, a defendant of any racial or ethnic group might challenge the array, claiming that the process for selecting individuals for jury duty is unconstitutionally biased against Native Americans.

Once the master list is compiled, the clerk of courts or another official summons people for jury service. Sometimes the summons includes a questionnaire that must be completed and returned before the summons date. As Chapter 15 notes, the information gathered through these questionnaires is sometimes used by the attorneys to prepare for jury selection. The questionnaire is designed to identify individuals who will be automatically excluded from jury service or who might be excused from jury service for a variety of reasons. For example, federal law excludes from jury service anyone who is younger than eighteen, not a citizen, unable to communicate in English, incapacitated by mental or physical infirmities, charged in a criminal offense, or who is a convicted felon whose civil rights have not been restored (Gobert and Jordan 1990, 153). In addition, certain occupations, such as fire fighter and police officer, are exempt from jury service. Courts may also excuse individuals from jury service if serving would pose an undue hardship or extreme inconvenience (Gobert and Jordan 1990, 155–156).

voir dire

Jurors on the venire may be required to report to court each morning to be available for a specific trial. When a jury trial is scheduled, a smaller group of jurors is called to be questioned. This is the **voir dire** process. The panel varies in size, from as few as twenty-four to one hundred or more, depending on the judge's estimate of the number of jurors likely to be excluded for cause (Goldberg 1982, 168). The minimum size of the panel, or venire, is determined by the size of the jury, plus alternates if it is to be a lengthy trial, and the total number of peremptory strikes, which permit the attorneys to dismiss jurors without giving reasons. Jurors' names are then drawn at random from the panel to participate in voir dire, either individually or in small groups.

Voir Dire

Voir dire, meaning "to speak the truth" is the process by which jurors are questioned to determine whether they are impartial as to the guilt or innocence of the defendant. Voir dire serves three broad functions within the trial process:

- It identifies jurors who should be excused for cause
- It identifies jurors who counsel may wish to peremptorily strike
- It presents counsel with an early opportunity to begin the process of persuasion.

Although state law sets broad parameters for voir dire procedure, judges have considerable discretion in determining the role and participation of counsel in voir dire. Some judges dominate the voir dire, doing all or most of the questioning or requiring counsel to submit questions for the judge's approval before questioning the jurors. In contrast, other judges take a minimal role, limiting their interaction with prospective jurors to introducing the attorneys and asking preliminary and broad general questions regarding the jurors' qualifications to serve, whether any juror wishes to be excused, and what knowledge and opinions each juror brings to the case.

Many questions asked by the judge will be asked of the venire as a group rather than the individual jurors. For example, the judge might ask whether serving on the jury would pose a substantial hardship to any juror. "Some judges will also excuse college students, those who have long-standing appointments that cannot be broken easily, and those who have made advance reservations that cannot be canceled without substantial penalty," one study notes (Myers and Pudlow 1991, 90–91).

When the attorneys are allowed to ask questions, local practices and individual judges differ with respect to the style of questioning allowed. Some judges require the attorneys to maintain a high degree of formality and to limit their questions to issues relating to the juror's fitness and partiality. Supreme Court cases have held that lawyers have no right to ask questions that will assist them in exercising their peremptory strikes. Opposing counsel may object to voir dire questions that address issues other than juror bias (Gobert and Jordan 1990, 336). Nonetheless, some judges allow a relatively open and wide-ranging dialogue with prospective jurors.

Challenging a Juror for Cause

Voir dire helps to identify those jurors who have already formed some opinion about the case that would prevent them from arriving at a decision based solely on the evidence presented at trial. Counsel seeks to eliminate these jurors through a challenge for cause. If a juror responds to a question in a way that indicates that the juror may not be completely impartial, one or both attorneys *challenge for cause* may challenge the juror. A **challenge for cause** may be raised if the prospective juror "has a preconceived idea of the defendant's guilt" or "appears to be prejudiced toward a particular class of people" (Myers and Pudlow 1991, 94). The judge must then decide whether a challenge for cause is legally warranted, given the views expressed by the prospective juror. If the judge finds that the juror is probably biased, the judge excuses the juror from service in the present case. The following excerpt from a trial transcript illustrates this procedure:

> THE COURT: Does anyone on the panel know any of the witnesses whose names were called off by Mr. Guarisco [a prosecutor] or Mr. Harper [a defense attorney]?

MR. PETERS [prospective juror]: Probably Major Campbell [from the sheriff's office], yes.

THE COURT: Probably Major Campbell? Do you feel that you would give his testimony more weight or less than you would any other witness?

MR. PETERS: Probably more.

THE COURT [Speaking to the attorneys]: You want to approach the bench?
(Whereupon a bench conference was held.)

MR. BAJOCZKY [a defense attorney]: Obviously, Your Honor, Mr. Peters has mentioned Major Campbell and has for the record indicated that he would probably give his testimony greater weight than any other testimony: he's prejudiced. And we would ask that he be struck.
(End of bench conference.)

THE COURT: Mr. Peters, I'm going to ask you to step down, if you will. Call the next juror. (Meyers and Pudlow 1991, 92)

The judge may, however, deny a challenge for cause if he is satisfied that the prospective juror can be fair and impartial in deciding the questions at hand, following the Supreme Court rulings on impartiality. Denying a challenge for cause may become the basis for an appeal after conviction at trial.

Exercising Peremptory Strikes

For the lawyers another goal of voir dire is to have an opportunity to shape the composition of the jury. Both the prosecution and the defense are trying to shape a jury that is biased in their favor. Neither side is trying to create an unbiased jury. The adversarial process assumes that if both sides are given equal opportunity to bias the jury and are supervised by a judge who is required to discharge any juror who is obviously biased, the result will be a jury that is not biased more in favor of one side than another.

peremptory strike

Counsel use peremptory strikes to shape the jury in line with their hunches about the kinds of people who will be most sympathetic or, perhaps more accurately, least unsympathetic (Goldberg 1982, 174). Unlike a challenge for cause, a **peremptory strike** may be used to excuse jurors without giving reasons and even without having a good reason. Peremptory strikes may be used because counsel did not like the expression on a juror's face when asked a particular question, or because the juror is a Protestant, or because the juror seems bored and annoyed with the prospect of jury duty.

In selecting a jury each side is given a specific number of peremptory strikes. The number is set by law and may vary according to the nature of the charges against the defendant. There is no constitutional right to peremptory strikes, so states may allow any number they choose (*Ross v. Oklahoma* 1987). In general, the more serious the charges, the greater the number of peremptory strikes given to both sides. For example, in a federal case the prosecution and defense are each allowed 20 peremptory strikes in a capital trial. In other felony cases the prosecution is allowed 6 peremptory strikes and the defense is allowed 10. In misdemeanor cases each side is allowed 3 peremptory strikes (Gobert and Jordan 1990, 273).

Because both sides have a limited number of peremptory strikes, they will first attempt to have "undesirables" excused by the judge on a challenge for cause (Bailey and Rothblatt 1985, 191). If no basis exists for excusing such a juror for cause, the attorney exercises a peremptory strike. Because the number of peremptory strikes is limited, counsel must use their strikes judiciously and sparingly to excuse only the worst prospective jurors.

Questioning of Jurors by Counsel

Through voir dire questioning counsel tries to get inside the head of each juror. Hearing from the juror's own mouth about predispositions and attitudes is obviously more reliable than guessing about these matters from stereotypes.

If the defense is planning to argue self-defense, counsel will want to inquire into the jurors' attitudes toward violence. If an insanity defense is to be used, both the prosecutor and defense counsel will want to learn the jurors' attitudes toward mental illness and toward psychiatrists as expert witnesses. In cases in which there has been a great deal of pretrial publicity, learning what the jurors already have heard about the case and whether media coverage has influenced them are key goals. Counsel may ask jurors whether they have formed an opinion and whether they would have difficulty overcoming that opinion.

Racial Bias

Finding racial bias among jurors is another important goal of voir dire. If the bias is sufficient, a juror may be challenged for cause. If the judge fails to sustain the challenge for cause, counsel may need to strike the juror through a peremptory challenge. In a trial involving racial issues, for example, if the victim is white and the defendant black, or in a case involving an allegation of police brutality and a black suspect, uncovering racist attitudes can be extremely important to both the prosecution and the defense, although for opposite reasons. It is an unfortunate fact that in some cases one side or the other might prefer to have racist jurors.

Because racist attitudes are not socially acceptable (that is, people generally believe that such attitudes are not supposed to be expressed in public), counsel may have difficulty getting prospective jurors to answer truthfully when asked about their racial attitudes. Consequently, the attorneys also watch for nonverbal cues in the juror's eye contact and body language when answering such questions.

Traditionally, peremptory strikes have been totally within the discretion of the attorneys. Attorneys have relied on specific information about the jurors as well as inferences based on stereotypes related to the jurors' social status, occupation, and other characteristics, including race and gender. Recent Supreme Court decisions have limited the freedom of attorneys to use their peremptory challenges in ways that discriminate against racial minorities and women.

In *Batson v. Kentucky* (1986) and *Powers v. Ohio* (1991) the Supreme Court held that the state's use of peremptory strikes to remove prospective jurors solely on the basis of race is a violation of the defendant's right to equal protection. If the defense can present evidence that suggests on its face that the prosecution excused the jurors solely on the basis of race, the prosecution must then show that it had reasons other than race for removing the jurors. The prosecutor may not strike jurors of the defendant's race on the assumption that they would be biased in favor of the defendant because of their shared race. The prosecutor must articulate some other attribute of the juror that prompted the peremptory strike (*Batson v. Kentucky* 1986, 97). In *Powers* the Court held that a prosecutor may not use peremptory strikes in a race-biased way even if the jurors are not the same race as the defendant. For example in a prosecution against a white defendant, the prosecutor may not strike all black jurors from the panel unless the prosecutor can show some reason other than race for removing them. In *Georgia*

SAMPLE VOIR DIRE QUESTiONS

The excerpt that follows is from a book that literally gives attorneys a script for voir dire. This example is designed for the defense in a grand larceny case in which the defendant, Bob, is African-American and his lawyer is concerned about the prejudices of white prospective jurors.

I know this whole process of jury selection seems a bit much to most of you, but I can assure you that if you were in Bob's position right now—if your life, your liberty, and your future were on the line—you too would want to learn something about the men and women who would decide your fate. Can you all understand how important all of this is to Bob? My purpose in voir dire is to talk to each of you about this case, to give you an idea of the issues you will have to deal with so we can decide if this is going to be the best case for you to sit in judgment of.

We all have opinions and attitudes. I do, the judge does, and you do. We would not be human if we didn't. I believe it is very difficult, if not impossible, for most of us to just clear our minds of any opinions or attitudes we have. I also believe that jurors want to give everybody a fair shake. So the purpose of voir dire is simply to talk about those experiences, opinions, and attitudes to see if they might make it difficult or uncomfortable for you to sit on this particular case, or if some of your opinions, attitudes, or experiences would make it tough for you—no matter how hard you try—to keep an open mind.

I once had a prospective juror tell me her daughter had been raped, and no matter how unfair it was, anyone accused of rape or who has a penis is guilty. She was excused from that jury but became the foreperson on a commercial case. Is there anyone here who feels that way about anyone charged with a crime or charged with car theft? When I said "penis" was anyone offended? On the videotape you'll be seeing you'll hear some pretty rough language. Is there anyone who believes that just because someone uses four letter words, he or she must be a criminal? Is there anyone, knowing just what you know now, who feels this is the kind of case you should not serve on as a juror?

I want you to know there are no tricks here. I will try my best not to embarrass anyone or put anyone on the spot. And, most important, this is not a quiz and there are no right or wrong answers.

RACIAL PREJUDICE

1. How long have you lived in Pierce County? (If less than two years:) Where did you live prior to that time? How long did you live there? What neighborhood did you live in?
2. How long have you lived at your current address?
3. What other areas of the country have you lived in? Why did you move? Have you or your family ever moved out of a neighborhood because people you didn't feel comfortable around were moving in? (Listen for phrases, words, or tone of voice revealing potential prejudice.)
4. Tell me something about your neighborhood—
   (a) What racial or ethnic groups live in your neighborhood?
   (b) What contact do you have with (list individually each group in juror's neighborhood)?
   (c) Has the racial composition of your neighborhood changed since you've lived there? If yes, how has it changed? How do you feel about this?
   (d) Tell me about crime and lawless behavior in your neighborhood. Has crime and lawless

v. *McCollum* (1992), the Court extended these rules to apply to the defense in the same way that it applies to the prosecution. The Court stated, "We hold that the Constitution prohibits a criminal defendant from engaging in purposeful discrimination on the ground of race in the exercise of peremptory challenges" (*Georgia v. McCollum* 1992, 2359).

Subsequently, the Court held in a civil suit for paternity that the Constitution prohibits attorneys from using peremptory strikes in a way that discriminates on the basis of gender (*J. E. B. v. Alabama* ex rel. *T. B.* 1994). The rationale of the Court in this case and the earlier cases concerning race suggests that striking jurors on the basis of gender stereotypes in criminal cases is also prohibited. The Court stated that these rulings do not prohibit attorneys from using stereotypes in exercising peremptory strikes; only stereotypes about racial and gender groups are prohibited. Attorneys may still draw inferences from stereotypes about occupational groups, economic status, and other factors because these have not been the basis for a long history of illegal discrimination.

behavior increased in your neighborhood? What concerns you most?

5. Have you completed any schooling beyond high school? If yes, what did you study?

6. (For those who have completed college work:) What were your major and minor during college?

7. (For those currently in school:) Are you planning to go into a particular kind of work?

8. What type of work do you do?
   (a) What other types of jobs or occupations have you held before this one? For how long?
   (b) Do you supervise other workers? If yes, how many people do you supervise? How long have you been employed as a supervisor? How do you feel about being a supervisor?
   (c) Describe the racial and ethnic make-up of the people you work with. (Listen for phrases, words, or tone of voice belying potential prejudice.)

9. What type of work does your spouse do?
   (a) What race or ethnic group is your spouse?
   (b) What other types of jobs or occupations has your spouse held before this one? For how long?
   (c) Does your spouse supervise other workers? If yes, how many people does he or she supervise? How long has he or she been employed as a supervisor?
   (d) Does your spouse work with people of a different race or ethnic group?

10. Do you have children? If yes, what are their ages?

11. What organizations or activities do you actively participate in? Do you belong to clubs, churches, or other organizations that have African-American members?

12. Do you believe the crime rate among African-Americans is higher than the rate of other racial groups?

13. What group of people do you believe is responsible for committing the greatest number of crimes in Pierce County? (If drug dealers, etc.:) How would you describe them to a friend?

14. Have you or has anyone close to you ever had a direct experience with racial, religious, or ethnic prejudice? If yes, what was that experience?

15. Have you ever had an unfortunate experience with an African-American?

16. When was the last time you had African-Americans in your home as guests?

17. What is your contact with African-Americans?

18. Do you believe that it makes a difference in America if you're white or white Hispanic rather than African-American?

19. Do you think your life would have been different if you had been born African-American? How so?

20. Some people say that most African-Americans are lazy and just want to stay on welfare. Do you think most white people believe that?

21. Would you say that you were raised in an atmosphere free of prejudice?

22. In school, did you learn about any of the great achievements of African-Americans in American history?

23. Do you believe that there will come a time in this country when race will have no more significance than hair color? If yes, how soon?

24. Do you think prejudice against African-Americans is on the increase or on the decline? In what ways do you think it is decreasing (increasing)? Can you give me any specific examples?

Source: Reprinted from V. Hale Starr. Copyright © 1993. *Jury Selection: Sample Voir Dire Questions*. Boston: Little, Brown, and Co., pp. 255–57.

Attitudes Toward the Death Penalty

When the prosecution plans to ask the court to impose the death penalty, much of voir dire will be spent exploring jurors' attitudes toward the death penalty and their willingness to convict a defendant who would then face a death sentence. The Supreme Court ruled in *Witherspoon v. Illinois* (1968) that jurors may be excused for cause if their opinions about the death penalty would prevent them from reaching a guilty verdict in a death penalty case. In addition to challenging jurors for cause because of their unwillingness to convict when the death penalty may be imposed, counsel may wish to explore jurors' attitudes toward the death penalty and use peremptory strikes to excuse some jurors.

The Persuasive Process Begins

A third purpose of voir dire has nothing to do with learning about the jurors. Rather the third function is to begin the process of persuading the jurors. This involves developing a rapport with the jurors, making them feel comfortable, and

CREATING DEATH-QUALIFIED JURIES

The Supreme Court's decision in *Witherspoon v. Illinois* (1968) allows prosecutors to obtain a so-called death-qualified jury. This means that all jurors must have expressed at least some willingness to impose the death penalty. Research shows that jurors who favor the death penalty are more predisposed to convict than jurors who oppose the death penalty. Given this finding, does the *Witherspoon* requirement give prosecutors an advantage at trial?

Here are some questions that might be asked in voir dire to assess jurors' attitudes toward the death penalty:

What are your feelings about the death penalty?

Are your feelings about the death penalty such that you could never, under any circumstances, bring back a verdict of death?

If you were convinced beyond a reasonable doubt at the end of this trial that the defendant was guilty and that his actions had been so shocking that they would merit the death penalty, would you have any conscientious scruples about capital punishment that would automatically prevent you from returning such a verdict?

SOURCE: Michael D. Marcus. Copyright © 1989. *Trial Preparation for Prosecutors*. New York: Wiley, p. 409. Reprinted by permission of John Wiley & Sons, Inc.

winning their trust. In addition, the voir dire offers attorneys their first opportunity to introduce the jurors to some evidence and issues that will arise at trial. Counsel attempts to "influence jurors to change their attitudes or values and to affect the way in which they will process the evidence they will hear" (Fried, Kaplan, and Klein 1975, 50). This may involve using the voir dire to introduce jurors to damaging facts and get the jurors on record as stating that such facts would not influence their ability to impartially decide the question of guilt or innocence. For example, if the defendant is charged with date rape, the prosecutor may wish to begin educating the jurors about date rape during voir dire.

Trial Begins

The trial officially begins when the jurors are sworn. They are required to take an oath that they will carry out their duties according to the law. The judge explains the jurors' role to them and the rules that they must observe during the trial, particularly in relation to speaking to one another or to other people about the facts of the case. Sometimes jurors are sequestered during the trial as well as during its deliberation. **Sequestration** means that the jurors are prevented from having contact with outside influences, including their families. The state arranges for the jurors to stay in a hotel, and the jurors are allowed only limited contact with people other than those on the panel. If the jurors are to be sequestered during the trial, the judge will explain how and where the jurors will be sequestered and why this is necessary. In a bench trial the trial officially begins with the swearing in of the first witness.

sequestration

Once the trial officially begins, jeopardy attaches. After the official start of trial a defendant who is charged again for the same conduct might be able to argue "double jeopardy," that is, that the defendant is being required to stand trial more than once for the same crime. However, numerous rules surrounding double jeopardy allow retrials under a variety of circumstances (see Chapter 3).

Opening Statements

Before either party begins to call witnesses, each has an opportunity to make an opening statement. Because the state presents its witnesses first, the prosecutor is

SHAPING JURORS' ATTITUDES

One author offers examples of questions that might be asked during voir dire to educate and persuade jurors that date rape is a real crime:

Q: In this case, there may be evidence that the defendant and the victim went on a date and that they kissed and petted but that she then told him to stop. What is your opinion as to whether she has the right to tell the man to stop at that point?

Q: If that should occur, do you understand and do you agree that it is no defense to the charge of rape that the defendant had an irresistible impulse to perform the act? Does anyone have any quarrel with the proposition that the law requires him to restrain himself at the time when the woman tells him to stop?

Q: Do you have any opinion as to whether a man who meets a flirtatious woman is entitled to believe that he has the right to have sex with that woman?

Q: What is your opinion as to whether a man who meets a flirtatious woman is entitled to believe that that woman wants to have sex with him?

Through this series of questions the prosecutor introduces some facts about which jurors are likely to have preconceived opinions. These questions also give the prosecutor an opportunity to educate the jurors about the requirements of the law regarding valid defenses to the crime. The questions require the jurors to state openly whether they (1) agree that the law requires a man to stop when a woman says no, and (2) disagree that flirting by a woman entitles a man to believe that she wants to have sex. Once on record during voir dire jurors may have a harder time adopting contrary views during deliberation. Finally, these questions also alert the prosecutor to any jurors who express views that would make them unsympathetic to the victim of date rape. Defense counsel would engage in a similar process of shaping the jurors' introduction to key facts and legal issues and molding the jurors' attitudes.

SOURCE: Michael D. Marcus. Copyright © 1989. *Trial Preparation for Prosecutors*. New York: Wiley, p. 413. Reprinted by permission of John Wiley & Sons, Inc.

the first to make an opening statement at trial. The defense may elect to make an opening statement immediately after the prosecutor's. In some cases the defense strategy depends on how well the prosecutor is able to present the state's case and how well the defense is able to undermine the credibility of the state's version of events. The defense may decide to wait until after the prosecutor rests to present its opening statement. Finally, the defense may choose not to make a statement at all, although this is uncommon.

The purpose of opening statements is to introduce the trier of fact to the evidence to be presented at trial. The opening statement prepares the jury for what is to come and puts the evidence into a perspective that lets the jury see the plausibility of the story counsel is weaving from the facts. By presenting the facts—sometimes highly selective facts—in a particular order the attorney produces "an image of events that encourages fair-minded jurors to do what the lawyer wants" (Goldberg 1982, 192). The opening statement also provides an opportunity to present weak spots in the story in their most favorable light.

The opening statement is considered an important part of the persuasion process at trial. Jury research concludes that 80 percent of jurors ultimately decide the case in favor of the party that was more persuasive in opening statements (Goldberg 1982, 193). Even though jurors are cautioned by the judge to avoid coming to any conclusions until after they have heard all the evidence, jurors almost inevitably reach some tentative conclusions after the opening statements.

Presentation of Evidence

Because the prosecution has the burden of proof, the prosecution presents its evidence first. This is an advantage for the prosecution. By going first the prosecution is able to set the tone of the trial and impress the jury with the evidence that points to the defendant's guilt. Presenting evidence involves calling witnesses to testify and introducing physical or documentary evidence to be examined by the trier of fact.

Witnesses typically are sequestered, that is, not allowed in the courtroom, during the presentation of other witnesses. By sequestering witnesses the court ensures that the testimony of one witness is not influenced by testimony that has come before. Questions are the attorneys' tools for producing the evidence they need. Questions take four general forms. First, open-ended questions ask the witness to provide a narrative account of the events the witness observed. For example, the prosecutor might ask the victim to recount events on the day he was mugged. A second type of question defines the subject of the witness's response. For example, "What can you tell us about the way the victim looked when you arrived at the scene?" A third type of question calls for a specific response from the witness. For example, the attorney might specifically ask the witness to a robbery, "What color was the getaway car?" Finally, some questions, called ***leading questions***, suggest a response through the way the question is phrased, for example, "The car was green, wasn't it?" (Goldberg 1982, 211–212).

leading question

The attorney who calls a witness to testify engages in **direct examination** of the witness. The opposing attorney then has an opportunity to **cross-examine** the witness. In general, direct examination will be composed primarily of open-ended questions of the first two types. This type of questioning gives the jurors the greatest opportunity to judge the credibility of the witness but gives the attorney the least control over what the witness says (Goldberg 1982, 212). Cross-examination is more likely to be composed of specific response and leading questions.

direct examination, cross-examination

Throughout the direct and cross-examinations both attorneys must abide by the **rules of evidence** (see Chapter 12). If a rule of evidence is violated, either in the way the question is asked or in the way the witness answered the question, the opposing side may **object**, stating the grounds for the objection. For example, "Objection, Your Honor, hearsay." The attorney who asks the question may then offer a brief justification or request a **sidebar conference** (out of hearing of the jury) to offer a more extended explanation of why the question or answer should be allowed by the judge. The judge then decides whether the rules of evidence have been violated. If the judge disagrees with the attorney who is objecting to a question or answer, the judge **overrules** the objection, and the witness proceeds to answer. If the judge agrees that the question or response violated the rules of evidence, the judge **sustains** the objection. The examining attorney must move on to a different question. If the objection was to the answer given by the witness, the judge will advise the jurors to disregard the answer. In some cases the answer of the witness may be so prejudicial to the outcome of the case that counsel moves for a mistrial. Figure 16-1 provides a list and description of some of the most common grounds for objections.

rules of evidence

objection

sidebar conference

overrule

sustain

Although impassioned objections by counsel are one dramatic element of a trial, attorneys are careful to object only as often as necessary. An attorney who objects too frequently may irritate the judge and jurors, or the jurors may conclude that the attorney does not want them to hear the truth (American Bar Association [ABA] 1989, 127; Bailey and Rothblatt 1985, 382).

REDIRECT EXAMINATION OF WITNESSES

During direct examinaton in a robbery case the prosecutor asked the witness to the robbery to describe the robber. The witness answered that among other characteristics, the robber had a scar on his cheek and several days' growth of beard. On cross-examination defense counsel brought out that nothing in the police reports indicated that the witness had mentioned a scar on the robber's cheek and several days' growth of beard. Defense counsel used these omissions to undermine the reliability of the witness's identification of the defendant as the robber. In this case the prosecutor might conduct a redirect to put the omission in context for the jury:

Q: Did you tell the officer about the scar and the three-day growth on the man who robbed the store?

A: I'm not sure if I did or not. Things happened so fast. I tried to tell him the things that I thought would help him to catch the guy. The scar was so small, and at night the fact that he was not shaven would not help if he wasn't in the light—I might not have mentioned them to the officer, but I really can't say for sure.

Q: Why did you mention the scar and the three-day growth here in court?

A: Well, you asked me to describe the man, and I wanted to be as complete as I could. I have had a lot of time to think about the face, and I am not likely to forget it. I thought I was supposed to tell you everything I could remember.

Q: Does the description that you gave on direct examination fit anybody in this courtroom?

A: Yes sir. Except for the three day growth that is gone now, it fits that man over there. (Pointing resolutely to the defendant.)

SOURCE: Steven H. Goldberg. 1982. *The First Trial: Where Do I Sit? What Do I Say?* St. Paul, Minn.: West, pp. 359–60. Reprinted with permisson of West Publishing Corporation.

Direct Examination

The goal of direct examination is to build up the pile of evidence in support of the account of the crime the lawyer provided in opening statements. Direct examination usually involves questioning witnesses who are sympathetic and cooperative with the attorney who called them to testify. For these reasons direct examination relies primarily on open-ended types of questions. The attorney examining the witness on direct has gone over the testimony with the witness and knows what the witness is likely to say.

hostile witness

Occasionally, a witness on direct examination is unfriendly or even hostile to the goals of the examining attorney. Examples of unfriendly or **hostile witnesses** would include the defendant's girlfriend who is called by the prosecution to testify as to the whereabouts of the defendant on the night of the crime or the mother of a homicide victim who is called by the defense to testify about her deceased daughter's drug habit. These witnesses have reason to avoid testifying about the matters asked by counsel. Because hostile witnesses are unlikely to volunteer information, attorneys usually ask specific response or leading questions when examining hostile witnesses.

Cross-Examination

Whereas the goal of direct examination is to build up the pile of evidence in support of the client's version of events, cross-examination is aimed at tearing down the opponent's pile of evidence. Although every attorney probably dreams about the knockdown cross-examination that catches a witness in a lie, the more usual cross-examination involves chipping away at the credibility and certainty of the witness.

FIGURE 16-1   Common Objections and What They Mean

Sources: F. Lee Bailey and Henry B. Rothblatt. 1985. *Successful Techniques for Criminal Trials*, 2d ed. Rochester, N.Y.: Lawyers Co-Operative, p. 385; American Bar Association. 1989. *Going to Trial: A Step-by-Step Guide to Trial Practice and Procedure*. Chicago: American Bar Association, pp. 125–27; Michael H. Graham. 1989. *Modern State and Federal Evidence: A Comprehensive Reference Text*, Vol. 1. South Bend, Ind.: National Institute for Trial Advocacy.

RELEVANCE:

Information that is not specifically connected to the issues at trial. Irrelevant evidence may mislead the jurors, causing confusion and undue delay.

COMPETENCE:

A witness may not testify to a matter unless evidence is introduced sufficient to support a finding that the witness has personal knowledge of the matter.

HEARSAY:

Information about which the witness has no direct knowledge but has only been told by someone else. In other words, rather than calling Person A, who directly observed the event or who made a statement originally, counsel wants to rely on Person B, who only heard about the event or statement from Person A. The hearsay rule requires that only the most reliable evidence be admitted at trial. In this example, Person A's direct observations are more reliable as an account of the event than Person B's account, since B did not even witness the event itself. After all, B cannot know that the event even occurred. Person B only knows that Person A said it occurred. The hearsay rule does have several exceptions, all of which relate to the primary purpose of admitting at trial only the most reliable evidence.

NON-RESPONSIVE ANSWER:

The witness's answer does not match the question asked by the attorney and quite possibly includes information the attorney did not want the jury to have. A witness's answer may also be ruled nonresponsive if the attorney appropriately asked a leading question and the witness attempted to provide more than a yes or no answer.

OPINION:

Witnesses, except for expert witnesses, are to testify only to facts, unless the witness offers an opinion that helps to clarify the witness's understanding of the facts or is an opinion within the experience of most people. Opinions requiring specialized knowledge require that the witness be admitted as an expert witness.

LEADING QUESTION:

The question is phrased as a yes or no question and in such a way that it presents the information and requires the witness to merely agree or disagree. A question is also leading when it suggests the answer desired or assumes a fact that is in controversy. Leading questions are not allowed on direct examination, unless a witness is found to be uncooperative, or hostile. Leading questions are allowed on cross-examination because of the presumed lack of cooperation from opposing witnesses.

Trial lawyer Steven Goldberg describes the attorney's goals in cross-examination. Goldberg's observations apply equally to civil and criminal trials:

> The touchstone for chipping away, changing emphasis, and diminishing effect [of the witness's direct testimony] is the realization that life is grey, and most testimony is black and white. Witnesses are not usually content to tell things as they are. They usually tell things as they are, plus a little added for how it would be best for them to be. This is not the conscious lie, nor even the big mistake. It is a matter of human

nature when a person is put under oath and placed in a courtroom. Each witness wants to be precise and knowledgeable as can be. The result is that facts that are eighty percent favorable to the other side are presented as ninety-five percent favorable. For example, if there was a very light rain on the day in question, the witness for the plaintiff or [prosecutor] may talk about a mist, and the defendant's witness may identify a rainshower. The plaintiff's witness is likely to describe a roadway that was barely damp, while the defendant's witness will talk about the slick wet road-bed. If a witness is a close friend of the plaintiff's, he may describe himself as a friend, or maybe answer the question about the relationship by saying, "we work together." Witnesses who view accidents from half a block away looking through a screened window are likely to say that they had a "clear view" of the accident. (Reprinted from *The First Trial: Where Do I Sit? What Do I Say?*, Steven Goldberg, 1982, with permission of West Publishing Corporation pp. 303–6.)

On cross-examination the attorney attempts to elicit information that may have been (conveniently) omitted during direct examination. The attorney tries to attack or undermine the witness's assertions about his opportunity to observe the incident or his ability to recall what she observed. In addition, cross-examination often attempts to draw attention to relationships between the witness and other parties to the crime in order to show that the witness has a stake in the result of the trial. Through cross-examination the attorney attempts to convey to the jurors that there is reason to be skeptical of a witness's testimony.

Redirect and Recross

redirect examination

"A skillful and dexterous cross-examiner may force a witness to answer questions out of context, or restrict the witness to 'yes' and 'no' answers in situations where the answer becomes misleading. It will frequently happen that the witness admits confusion or uncertainty when he is cross-examined on a certain point," note F. Lee Bailey and Henry B. Rothblatt (1985, 409). For these reasons the attorney who originally called the witness may engage in **redirect examination** to rebuild the pile of evidence that cross-examination successfully pulled apart. Questions on redirect are designed to put damaging testimony from cross-examination into context or perspective. "The successful redirect examination is that which explains and neutralizes the apparent contradictions, admissions, or apparently false statements developed . . . on cross-examination," Bailey and Rothblatt add (1985, 408). Following redirect, the opposition may again conduct further cross-examination of any points raised on redirect. Jurisdictions have rules about the scope of redirect and recross that limit the opportunity to engage in redirect or recross-examination.

The Prosecution Rests

directed verdict

When the prosecution has presented all its witnesses and testimony and believes that it has proved the crime as best it can, the prosecution rests. At this stage in the trial the defense routinely enters a motion for a **directed verdict**, which asks the judge to rule that the prosecution has not presented evidence supporting each element of the offense and that the only just verdict would be an acquittal (ABA 1989, 150). In some instances, either because of poor preparation by the prosecution, sloppy presentation of the evidence at trial, or real factual problems with a case, a motion for a directed verdict is granted. The result is that the defendant is acquitted, and the trial comes to an immediate halt. In most cases, however, these defense motions are denied as routinely as they are made.

The Defense

If the judge denies the motion for a directed verdict, the trial proceeds with the defense presentation. The defense may call witnesses to support its version of what happened. The defense may have located witnesses who have a different recollection of events than the prosecution witnesses'. If the defense is raising an alibi defense, witnesses must testify that they saw the defendant someplace else at the time of the crime. In some cases the defense may have little to do but bring character witnesses to testify that the defendant is not the sort of person who would commit the kind of crime charged.

One important decision of the defense is whether to have the defendant testify at trial. The defendant does not have to testify because the Fifth Amendment states that "No person . . . shall be compelled in any criminal case to be a witness against himself." Moreover, the jury will usually be instructed to draw no conclusions or inferences from the fact the defendant chose not to testify (Bailey and Rothblatt 1985, 416). Despite these warnings from the judge, jurors may conclude that the defendant who does not testify has something to hide.

For the defense the decision often hinges on the potential damage that might arise from the cross-examination of the defendant. For example, if the defendant has made previous statements about the crime that are not admissible, the statements may be admitted if the defendant makes contradictory statements at trial. For example, an otherwise illegal confession or statements made to a grand jury might be used to impeach the defendant's testimony at trial. A defendant with a criminal record is also a problem. So long as the defendant does not take the stand, the defendant's record is legally irrelevant. However, once the defendant takes the stand, the prosecution may use prior convictions to attack the credibility of the defendant (Bailey and Rothblatt 1985, 417).

Rebuttal

rebuttal witness

The prosecution may need to shore up its case at the conclusion of the defense presentation. It is allowed to do this by calling **rebuttal witnesses**. Additional evidence or witnesses the prosecution originally thought unnecessary may be called to bring additional facts to light. For example, if defense witnesses create some doubt about the honesty and truthfulness of a prosecution witness, the prosecution may need to bring forward additional witnesses on rebuttal to testify that the prosecution witness in question has a reputation for telling the truth (Marcus 1989, 177). In general, rebuttal is used to explain, qualify, or contradict the defendant's case (ABA 1989, 148). In some cases the prosecution may even plan its rebuttal, holding back some evidence in anticipation of the defense strategy at trial.

Following the rebuttal the defense may also call rebuttal witnesses. In any event the defense will typically renew its motion for a directed verdict. Again the motion for directed verdict is usually denied. So long as there is some evidence for each element of the offense, judges are reluctant to take the decision away from the jury.

Closing Arguments

closing argument, summation

Two final stages must be completed before the jury retires to deliberate its verdict: closing arguments and jury instructions. **Closing arguments**, also called closing statements or **summation**, are similar to opening statements in that the attorneys speak directly to the jury. Unlike opening statements, which stick primarily to the facts, closing statements are meant to provide an opportunity to argue why the jury should bring the verdict requested by the attorney. Closing arguments give attorneys the opportunity to persuade the jury that conviction (prosecution) or acquittal (defense) is the fair and reasonable verdict, given the evidence the jurors have heard.

Jury Instructions

charging the jury

When the defense and prosecution have completed their closing statements, the judge addresses the jury in a procedure sometimes called **charging the jury**. The judge must instruct the jury about the law and the jurors' legal responsibilities in reaching a verdict. These instructions define legal terms and concepts for jurors so that jurors can decide whether the evidence they have heard meets the legal requirements for convicting the defendant. Instructions tend to be phrased in fairly technical legal language, despite the goal of communicating with lay jurors. Consequently, jurors may be more confused about what they are supposed to do after instructions than before.

Preparation for jury instructions involves both the prosecution and the defense. Both sides have an opportunity to suggest instructions that they would like the judge to give to the jury. Jury instructions are usually selected from books that provide jury instructions on almost every issue that arises in a criminal trial. Figure 16-2 offers an example of jury instructions for the federal crime of assaulting a federal officer with a deadly or dangerous weapon. The instructions in these books have been approved on appeal and become the model for instructing juries in later cases.

Although jury instruction books reduce the amount of variation in instructions from one court to another and constrain judges' discretion in instructing jurors, the judge often has an opportunity to make important decisions about how jurors will be instructed in a particular case. Sometimes there is more than one choice for instruction on a specific point, and the choice may depend on particular facts introduced at trial or the specific allegations being made in the case. In these instances the judge must select the instruction that is most appropriate under the circumstances. In other instances the books may offer no accepted model for the circumstances of the particular case. Attorneys may refer to instructions given in previous cases and argue that the facts of the present case are sufficiently similar to warrant the same instructions.

Usually, both the prosecutor and defense counsel will submit proposed jury instructions to the judge sometime during the evidentiary phase of the trial (Bergman 1979, 294). Before the close of trial the judge will meet with counsel to discuss the instructions. Counsel will typically have an opportunity to argue for a particular wording. Some negotiation also takes place. Counsel may give up an unimportant instruction in order to persuade the judge to accept a more critical instruction on another issue. The judge will note for the official record of the trial what instructions were submitted by counsel and whether they were accepted, modified, or refused (Goldberg 1982, 97). The instructions that are accepted are then delivered orally to the jurors at the close of the trial.

Deliberation and Verdict

Once instructed, the jury retires to deliberate the verdict. In rare cases jurors may be sequestered throughout the trial to avoid communication with others,

FIGURE 16-2   Jury Instructions

SOURCE: Reprinted from Edward J. Devitt, Charles B. Blackman, and Kevin O'Malley. 1990. *Federal Jury Practice and Instructions, Criminal*, 4th ed. Vol. 2. St Paul, Minn.: West, pp. 34–37.

B. USING A DEADLY OR DANGEROUS
WEAPON
[18 U.S.C.A. 111(B)]

23.06 The Nature of the Offense Charged

Count __ of the indictment charges that on or about the __ day of _____ , 19 __ , within the _____ district of _____ , the defendant, _____ used a dangerous or deadly weapon to forcibly assault _____ , a [Special Agent of the Federal Bureau of Investigation], who was at that time engaged in the official duties of a [Special Agent of the Federal Bureau of Investigation].

23.05 The Statutes Defining the Offense Charged

Section 111 and 1114 of title 18 of the United States Code provide, in part, that:

> "whoever forcibly assaults, resists, opposes, impedes, intimidates or interferes with any person designated in Section 1114 of this title [as officers and employees of the United States] while engaged, in or on account of the performance of his [her] official duties, . . . [and] in the commission of any of such acts uses a deadly or dangerous weapon . . ."

shall be guilty of an offense against the United States.

23.06 The Essential Elements of the Offense Charged

In order to sustain its burden of proof for the crime of forcibly assaulting a federal officer using a deadly or dangerous weapon as charged in Count ____ of the indictment, the government must prove the following five (5) essential elements beyond a reasonable doubt:

One: The defendant _____ forcibly assaulted [the individual identified in the indictment];

Two: At the time of this forcible assault, _____ [the person identified in the indictment] was an officer or employee of the United States;

Three: _____ [the individual identified as an officer or employee of the United States] was engaged in official duties at the time of the assault;

Four: The assault was made whole using a deadly or dangerous weapon; and

Five: The assault was done in a voluntary and deliberate manner by the defendant _____ .

23.07 "Deadly or Dangerous Weapon"—Defined

The phrase "deadly or dangerous weapon" means any instrument or device capable of inflicting serious bodily injury or causing the death of a person.

Both the physical capabilities of the object and the manner in which the object is used may be considered by the jury in determining whether the object is a "deadly or dangerous weapon."

23.08 "Forcibly Assaults"—Defined

The term "forcibly assaults" means any deliberate and intentional attempt or threat to inflict physical injury upon another with force or strength when that attempt or threat is coupled with an apparent present ability to do so.

Although a "forcible assault" may be committed by a defendant without actually touching, striking, or doing bodily harm to another, the government must prove that the actions of the defendant _____ were of such a nature to put the person against whom they are directed in fear of immediate bodily harm.

exposure to media coverage of the case, or even pressure to vote a particular way. If the jurors have not been sequestered throughout the trial, they may be sequestered during their deliberations. In some cases the jurors may be put up at a hotel if they have not finished their work before nine or ten o'clock at night. In other cases jurors may be allowed to go home at night and return the next day to deliberate further.

How Juries Work: Research in Jury Deliberation

Research into the dynamics of jury deliberations reveals that the way in which the law supposes jurors carry out their role is different from the way in which they really do their job. Research has taken a variety of forms. Sometimes researchers interview jurors after real criminal trials. In other research mock trials are presented to research subjects who are then asked to reach a verdict as though they are jurors in the case.

Research suggests that jurors "do not spend a great deal of time trying to define the legal categories, evaluating the admissibility of evidence they are using, or testing their final conclusion against a standard of proof" (Ellsworth 1993, 47). In fact, some research indicates that jurors sometimes are confused by important legal concepts like burden of proof (Marcotte 1990b, 32). Instead jurors operate on stereotyped themes that summarize their individual views of the case. For example, one juror might summarize the case as "cold-hearted killer plots revenge," whereas another might view the case as "nice guy panics and overreacts" (Ellsworth 1993, 48). This characteristic of jury deliberation underscores the importance of presenting a coherent and believable theme. Based on these sketches of the offense, jurors "choose a verdict based on the severity of the crime as they perceive it" (Ellsworth 1993, 48).

The first ballot is usually not unanimous (Ellsworth 1993, 42). Jurors draw different conclusions about the correct verdict and often miss important pieces of evidence during trial. During hours of often boring testimony of unclear relevance, jurors' minds inevitably wander. Some facts stick in the mind of one juror and color that juror's perception of the whole event, whereas another juror may not even remember that testimony.

Jurors also differ in their judgments about the credibility of witnesses. Some patterns emerge, however. For example, jurors generally are likely to reject the testimony of expert witnesses who are viewed by jurors as hired guns but are persuaded by testimony of experts who are perceived to be independent or who seemed to use common sense (Marcotte 1990b, 32). Police witnesses, who traditionally were perceived as credible witnesses, seem to have lost this distinction.

Eventually, through a combination of persuasive discussion, review of the evidence, and blatant arm twisting, most juries reach their verdict.

Hung Jury

Because the jurors must reach a certain degree of agreement on the verdict (majority or unanimity, depending on state law), the jury may not always be able to come to a conclusion. If the jurors cannot reach the required unanimity or majority, the jurors send a message to the judge that they are unable to reach a verdict. Typically, the judge will exhort them to continue to try to reach a verdict, without putting too much pressure on them. If, despite a sincere effort, the jurors are irreconcilably divided in their findings, the judge declares a mistrial. Following

ACCUSED AND POLICE GIVEN EQUAL WEIGHT, POLL FINDS
By Shawn G. Kennedy

When faced with conflicting testimonies, jurors do not necessarily give more weight to the testimony of police officers than they do defendants, a national survey of jurors has found.

In a survey of 783 jurors serving on both criminal and civil cases, 51 percent of those questioned said they were as likely to believe defendants as they were police officers. Among black jurors, the poll found, 70 percent said the testimony of police officers would not carry more weight.

Of the jurors polled, 61 percent said they would have found the four Los Angeles police officers guilty in the beating of Rodney G. King. Unlike the jury in California, the jurors in the poll had the benefit of hindsight; the survey was conducted from Aug. 31 to Nov. 5, 1992, several months after the deadly rioting in Los Angeles that followed the acquittal of the four officers.

100 QUESTIONS IN POLL

The survey, sponsored by The National Law Journal and Lexis, the legal news and information service, was based on more than 100 questions. Doreen Weisenhaus, editor in chief of The National Law Journal, which formulated the questions, said the jurors polled were drawn from 40 urban, suburban and rural jurisdictions in 31 states and the District of Columbia; the margin of sampling error was plus or minus five percentage points.

The results will be published in today's edition of The National Law Journal.

Susan Hendricks, deputy director of litigation for the New York Legal Aid Society, said the findings on the testimony of police officers did not surprise her.

"People who live in communities that have close exposure to the police have always been somewhat distrustful of the police," she said. "But with expanded media coverage and video tape, police conduct is now more a part of what the public knows."

The results of the survey indicated that while jurors might not give special credence to the testimony of police officers, they did tend to respect the testimony of expert witnesses. Of those questioned, 70 percent said the testimony of experts influenced the outcome of the trial on which they served. But one in four said they thought the word of experts was shaded by which side was paying for the testimony.

a mistrial caused by a hung jury, the defense may move to have the judge order acquittal of the defendant. If this motion is denied, the prosecutor may either retry the case or decide that it is not worth the bother and move for dismissal of the charges (*Arizona v. Washington*, 1978).

Bench Trial Deliberations

findings of fact, conclusions of law

If the judge is the trier of fact, the judge must reach a verdict. The judge must do more than is required of a jury. Rather than simply render a verdict—guilty or not guilty—the judge must draft **findings of fact** and **conclusions of law** in support of the verdict. Surprisingly, because of this added work in bench trials, judges may be able to try a greater number of jury trials in less time than nonjury trials:

A jury trial is an easier trial for judges. It is easier to instruct on the law than it is to decide the facts and write Findings of Fact and Conclusions of Law. I also find I can try a greater number of jury cases than nonjury cases because, as a judge, I need more time to deliberate with myself and to prepare Findings of Fact and Conclusions

---

HUNG JURY

The jury was out a long time. After the first few hours of deliberation they sent back a note: "Time will not resolve our differences." It was the most poetic announcement of a hung jury I'd ever heard.

It was too soon to declare the jury deadlocked. The judge sent them overnight to a hotel and told them in the morning to resume deliberations. The next day, a Thursday, they got no further. Friday morning dragged.

Queens judges tend to declare a jury hung and a mistrial after three days of deliberation, and they rarely permit jurors to deliberate through a weekend unless the jurors themselves request it. The prospect of having to put Antoinette and Daisy Bayard [the victims] through this all over again in a retrial loomed over that third day.

[The jury returned a guilty verdict.]

SOURCE: Reprinted from Alice Vachss. © 1993 by Alice Vachss. *Sex Crimes*. New York: Random House, p. 106. Reprinted by permission of Random House, Inc.

---

of Law than it takes to pick a jury. Furthermore, I can start a second jury case when the first jury is deliberating. (Joiner 1975, 155)

A bench trial may not be a time-saving measure for judges.

Announcing the Verdict

When the judge or jury reaches a verdict, the parties are summoned to the courtroom for the announcement. The prosecutor, defendant, and defense counsel stand to hear the verdict. Everyone is a bit tense, especially if the charges have been serious. The tension is heightened by the ritual of announcing the verdict. The jury foreperson hands the verdict to the judge, who reads it and hands it back to the foreperson or to the clerk to read aloud. Either attorney may

polling the jury

ask the judge to **poll the jurors**, although this request is uncommon. In polling the jurors each juror is asked to affirm that the verdict read in court is the verdict given by each juror. The judge then thanks the jury for its attention and hard work and discharges the jurors.

If the verdict is not guilty, the judge informs the defendant that he or she is free to go. According to a study of twenty-six urban jurisdictions, only 27 percent of all cases that go to trial end in an acquittal (Boland et al. 1989, 5). Although the burdens of defending against the state's accusations are often enormous, especially if the defendant is in jail before trial, an acquittal does not entitle the defendant to any compensation from the state, despite loss of earnings, loss of job, and loss of reputation. For this reason, if for no other, pretrial screening procedures are important because they minimize such losses.

A guilty verdict does not quite end the defense's attempts to win an acquittal. If the jury returns a verdict of guilty, the defense may move to have the judge

acquittal notwithstanding the verdict

enter an **acquittal notwithstanding the verdict**, a motion that asks the judge to set aside the guilty verdict because the prosecution's evidence did not meet the burden of proof beyond a reasonable doubt. This motion is relatively routine but will likely be made only if the sufficiency of the evidence is going to be raised as an issue on appeal (Bailey and Rothblatt 1985, 734). Such motions are seldom granted. One reason that such motions are rarely successful is because the judge has had opportunites before this point (at the close of the prosecutor's case and before submitting the case to the jury) to dismiss the case for insufficient evidence or direct a verdict of not guilty.

judgment of conviction

Finally, the court enters a **judgment of conviction**. This is a written order of the court giving effect to the jury verdict. A defendant is not convicted until the judgment of conviction has been signed by the court. Following a conviction the prosecution may move for increased bail or the revocation of pretrial release. The trial judge must consider the likelihood that the defendant will disappear in order to escape punishment. In addition, if a presentence investigation is not automatic, the prosecutor may request such an investigation, or the judge may order it without a request from the prosecution. A date is set for sentencing, and court adjourns.

■ SUMMARY

Within the adversarial trial process the rights of defendants and the rules of procedure become critical factors in processing cases. The rights of defendants include the right to a jury trial, although the Supreme Court has been reluctant to extend this right to defendants in all state prosecutions. Although juries are typically composed of twelve impartial citizens selected from a representative cross-section of the community, the Supreme Court has allowed states to experiment with juries of less than twelve members. In addition, some states allow verdicts from less than unanimous juries.

A change of venue and careful jury selection are remedies for pretrial publicity that may cause prospective jurors to have already formed an opinion about the guilt of the defendant. Jurors who are actually biased, whether from prior acquaintance with the parties, pretrial publicity, racial prejudice, or other factors, are excused for cause. In addition, both sides have a limited opportunity to excuse jurors through peremptory strikes without having to offer a reason for excusing the juror.

Opening statements acquaint jurors with the facts of the case as alleged by both prosecution and defense. Through direct and cross-examination the jurors have an opportunity to assess the evidence and the credibility of witnesses offering testimony. Based on the evidence, which is presented according to the rules of evidence, the jury (or judge) reaches a verdict.

Throughout the trial process both sides use whatever tactics they can (usually within the limits of the law, sometimes not) to convince the judge or jury to convict (or acquit). The rules of procedure, including the rules of evidence, are tools the attorneys use to shape the evidence that will come before the court. The predispositions of the judge and jurors are raw materials to be shaped in the direction of the verdict sought. The success of their efforts is reflected in the verdict. The strength of the evidence is ultimately a subjective matter to be assessed by the judge or jury using their best efforts.

When the verdict is an acquittal, the defendant is released but is not compensated for the losses associated with the accusation by the state. When the verdict results in conviction, the criminal court process moves on to the next stage: sentencing.

■ FOR FURTHER DISCUSSION

1.   The testimony of confidential informants and undercover officers can be problematic for the prosecution. The prosecution frequently would prefer to keep the identity of these witnesses secret from the defense. What constitu-

tional right might be infringed by keeping their identity secret? How, consistent with the Constitution, might such witnesses testify without completely revealing their identities?

2. To have a statistically representative venire each adult member of the community should have an equal likelihood of being summoned for jury duty and of responding to the summons. If a jurisdiction uses voter registration lists to select the jury, what kinds of people are likely to be underrepresented in the venire? What additional selection devices might be used to increase the proportion of those groups that might otherwise be underrepresented? Contact your clerk of courts or jury commissioner to find out which lists are used to summon jurors.

3. In *Ross v. Oklahoma* (1987) the Supreme Court held that establishing the number of peremptory strikes allowed during jury selection is a state responsibility. Suppose that a state decided to allow fifty peremptory strikes for the prosecution but only five for the defense. Do you think such a law would be upheld by the Supreme Court? What principles of law or constitutional provisions might be important in deciding this issue?

4. In *The Jury: Trial and Error in the American Courtroom*, author Stephen J. Adler argues that jury trials are conducted in ways that confuse and bore jurors. Adler suggests that jurors would be better able to follow the evidence and understand its significance if jurors were instructed about the law before they hear the evidence. Why might this be preferable to the traditional practice of instructing jurors after they have heard all of the evidence? What problems might be created by instructing jurors before the evidence is presented?

5. Researchers have used a variety of techniques in attempting to better understand the workings of the jury during deliberations. One technique is to eavesdrop on the deliberations of an actual jury. Why might a researcher prefer to hear the deliberations of a real jury to those of a mock jury? What ethical and legal objections might be raised by "bugging" jury deliberations for the purposes of research? What precautions might a researcher take to avoid such ethical and legal problems?

■ REFERENCES

Adler, Stephen J. 1994. *The Jury: Trial and Error in the American Courtroom.* New York: Times Books.

American Bar Association. 1989. *Going to Trial: A Step-by-Step Guide to Trial Practice and Procedure.* Chicago: American Bar Association.

Apodaca v. Oregon, 406 U.S. 404, 92 S. Ct. 1628 (1972).

Arizona v. Washington, 434 U.S. 497, 98 S. Ct. 824 (1978).

Bailey, F. Lee, and Henry B. Rothblatt. 1985. *Successful Techniques for Criminal Trials,* 2d ed. Rochester, N.Y.: Lawyers Co-operative.

Baldwin v. New York, 399 U.S. 66, 90 S. Ct. 1886 (1970).

Ballew v. Georgia, 435 U.S. 223, 98 S. Ct. 1029 (1978).

Batson v. Kentucky, 476 U.S. 79, 106 S. Ct. 1712 (1986).

Bergman, Paul. 1979. *Trial Advocacy in a Nutshell.* St. Paul, Minn.: West.

Blanton v. City of Las Vegas, 489 U.S. 538, 109 S. Ct. 1289 (1989).

Boland, Barbara, Catherine H. Conly, Lynn Warner, Ronald Sones, and William Martin. 1989. *The Prosecution of Felony Arrests, 1986.* Washington, D.C.: U.S. Department of Justice, Bureau of Justice Statistics.

Burch v. Louisiana, 441 U.S. 130, 99 S. Ct. 1623 (1979).

Carter v. Jury Commission, 396 U.S. 320, 90 S. Ct. 518 (1970).

Criminal Justice Newsletter. 1990. "Supreme Court Allows Testimony by Video in Child Abuse Cases." *Criminal Justice Newsletter.* (July 7): 4–6.

Dawson, John M. 1992. "Prosecutors in State Courts, 1990." *Bureau of Justice Statistics Buletin.* Washington, D.C.: U.S. Department of Justice.

DeBenedictus, Don J. 1990. "Small-Jury Study." *ABA Journal* (March): 24.

Duncan v. Louisiana, 391 U.S. 145, 88 S. Ct. 1444 (1968).

Duren v. Missouri, 439 U.S. 357, 99 S. Ct. 664 (1979).

Ellsworth, Phoebe C. 1993. "Some Steps Between Attitudes and Verdicts." In Reid Hastie, ed. *Inside the Juror: The Psychology of Juror Decision-Making.* New York: Cambridge University Press.

Fried, Michael, Kalman J. Kaplan, and Katherine W. Klein. 1975. "Juror Selection: An Analysis of Voir Dire." In Rita James Simon, ed. *The Jury System in America: A Critical Overview.* Beverly Hills, Calif.: Sage.

Georgia v. McCollum, 505 U.S. 42, 112 S. Ct. 2348 (1992).

Gobert, James J., and Walter E. Jordan. 1990. *Jury Selection: The Law, Art, and Science of Selecting a Jury,* 2d ed. Colorado Springs, Colo.: Shepard's–McGraw-Hill.

Goldberg, Steven H. 1982. *The First Trial: Where Do I Sit? What Do I Say?* St. Paul, Minn.: West.

Ham v. South Carolina, 409 U.S. 524, 93 S. Ct. 848 (1973).

Hastie, Reid, Steven D. Penrod, and Nancy Pennington. 1983. *Inside the Jury.* Cambridge, Mass.: Harvard University Press.

Hyman, Harold M., and Catherine M. Tarrant. 1975. "Aspects of American Trial Jury History." In Rita James Simon, ed. *The Jury System in America: A Critical Overview.* Beverly Hills, Calif.: Sage.

Irvin v. Dowd, 366 U.S. 717, 81 S. Ct. 1639 (1961).

J.E.B. v. Alabama ex rel. *T.B.*, 114 S. Ct. 1419 (1994).

Johnson v. Louisiana, 406 U.S. 356, 92 S. Ct. 1620 (1972).

Joiner, Charles W. 1975. "From the Bench." In Rita James Simon, ed., *The Jury System in America: A Critical Overview.* Beverly Hills, Calif.: Sage.

Marcotte, Paul. 1990a. "Courts on Cable." *ABA Journal* (April): 19.

——— 1990b. "The Verdict Is . . . " *ABA Journal* (June): 32.

Marcus, Michael D. 1989. *Trial Preparation for Prosecutors.* New York: Wiley.

Maryland v. Craig, 497 U.S. 836, 110 S. Ct. 3157 (1990).

Mu'Min v. Virginia, 500 U.S. 415, 111 S. Ct. 1899 (1991).

Myers, Howard, and Jan Pudlow. 1991. *The Trial: A Procedural Description and Case Study.* St. Paul, Minn.: West.

Peters v. Kiff, 407 U.S. 493, 92 S. Ct. 2163 (1972).

Powers v. Ohio, 499 U.S. 400, 111 S. Ct. 1364 (1991).

Ristaino v. Ross, 424 U.S. 589, 96 S. Ct. 1017 (1976).

Ross v. Oklahoma, 487 U.S. 81, 108 S. Ct. 2273 (1987).

Turner v. Murray, 476 U.S. 28, 106 S. Ct. 1683 (1986).

U.S. Bureau of Justice Statistics. 1988. *Report to the Nation on Crime and Justice.* Washington, D.C.: U.S. Department of Justice.

Wainwright v. Witt, 469 U.S. 412, 105 S. Ct. 844 (1985).

Williams v. Florida, 399 U.S. 78, 90 S. Ct. 1893 (1970).

Witherspoon v. Illinois, 391 U.S. 510, 88 S. Ct. 1770 (1968).

CHAPTER 17

SENTENCING

Conviction, whether by a verdict or by guilty plea, transforms the defendant from a citizen entitled to a broad range of liberties to a convicted felon denied many rights of citizenship. Conviction gives the court the authority to order severe constraints on the convicted defendant's liberty and in some cases to deny the offender's right to live. This authority is formally vested in the judge, or in some cases the jury. Informally, however, prosecutors exert tremendous influence on the sentence through the charging and plea agreement process. In many cases the judge simply ratifies an agreement negotiated by the prosecutor and defense counsel.

Sentencing plays a critical role in maintaining (or eroding) the legitimacy of the criminal court process. A victim's satisfaction with the sentence has a major influence on the victim's satisfaction with the criminal justice system as a whole (Erez and Tontodonato 1992). Similarly, the public's satisfaction with the criminal justice system seems to be closely related to public perceptions of sentencing. Seeing convicted criminals punished commensurate with the seriousness of their crimes is an important element of substantive justice. The public perception that criminals do not get their just deserts has contributed to reforms of the sentencing process in many states.

This chapter describes the goals of sentencing, sentencing options, sentencing procedures in felony cases, and the statutory penalty structures that circumscribe judicial discretion in order to reduce sentencing disparity. In recent years lawmakers have sought to reduce sentencing discretion and make penalties for crime more certain. This chapter explores the effects of these changes and concludes with an examination of the death penalty.

■ THE GOALS OF SENTENCING

Conviction gives the government broad authority within statutory and constitutional limits to intervene in the life of the convicted defendant. The purpose is to protect the public and to see that justice is done. Within these broad parameters sentencing serves a number of specific goals.

Utilitarian Goals: Protecting the Public

utilitarian goals

Several goals of punishment are considered **utilitarian** because they justify punishment in relation to specific and tangible benefits to society that are expected to result from imposing the sentence. By doing something to the offender, whether it is described as punishment or treatment, the utilitarian goal is to reduce crime. The utilitarian justifications of punishment include deterrence, incapacitation, and rehabilitation. Although each justification is based on a different assumption about the most effective way to reduce crime, they share one goal: to use the sentence to reduce crime.

Deterrence

Our system of justice is founded on the idea that individuals are endowed with rationality and free will. Because people are rational, they are able to weigh the potential gains and risks of different choices and different courses of action. Adjusting the likely rewards or penalties that result from any act can influence behavior. This is the philosophy behind deterrence policies.

Jeremy Bentham, an English social philosopher of the late eighteenth century, was among the first to specify the characteristics of punishment that make it an effective deterrent. According to Bentham, punishment that is swift, certain, and severe is more likely to deter illegal acts than punishment that is delayed, highly unlikely, or insufficiently painful. When punishment occurs long after the crime, the individual has an opportunity to enjoy the fruits of the crime before being punished, which makes punishment less effective in deterring the crime. When punishment is highly unlikely, more people are willing to risk that they will never be caught and punished. If the punishment is not very painful compared to the enjoyment the criminal act brings to the offender (a slap on the wrist), even swift and certain punishment may not deter the offender.

general deterrence

specific deterrence

recidivism rate

Philosophers and scientists alike have drawn a distinction between general deterrence and specific deterrence. **General deterrence** refers to the deterrent effect on the general public when the government punishes a criminal. The punished criminal demonstrates to the rest of us that crime does not pay, thus making us less likely to commit a crime. **Specific deterrence** refers to the deterrent effect on the person who is being punished. Having experienced punishment as the consequence of one crime, the individual is less likely to commit a new crime in the future. One measure of specific deterrence is the **recidivism rate**, that is, the proportion of offenders who commit a new crime after they are punished.

Anyone who has ever spotted a patrol car in the rearview mirror knows that deterrence works. The questions that puzzle researchers concern the circumstances under which deterrence is effective and the limits of punishment in deterring crime. Studies of deterrence have found that the more certain the punishment, based on arrest and punishment rates, the lower the crime rate. This finding is consistent with the predictions of Bentham and other early deterrence philosophers. However, this finding can be interpreted in a number of ways, only some of which support deterrence theory (Gibbs and Firebaugh 1990). Much research suggests that fear of informal sanctions, such as loss of reputation, deters more effectively than fear of arrest and punishment. Overall, deterrence research has produced mixed results, and deterrence researchers have not been able to demonstrate that criminal behavior can be decreased by increasing the certainty and severity of formal punishment (Paternoster 1987). Consequently, the effectiveness of changing deterrence policies, such as by increasing penalties or enhancing the certainty of punishment through mandatory sentences, has not been substantiated.

Incapacitation

incapacitation

Incapacitation seeks to restrain criminals, usually by locking them up, so that they are physically unable to commit crimes. Unlike deterrence, incapacitation makes no assumption about the rationality of criminals or society's ability to deter crime. Incapacitation is based on the idea of social defense. According to the **social defense** philosophy, society has a right and a responsiblity to protect itself from those who would prey on others, namely, criminals.

social defense

selective incapacitation, high-rate offender

In recent years a policy of **selective incapacitation** has received a considerable amount of attention from policymakers and scholars alike. This policy is based on research that shows that a small number of **high-rate offenders** commit a disproportionate amount of crime. "It has been argued that, if prosecution resources and institutional and other treatment facilities could be used more effectively for these high-rate offenders, this might prevent a significant number of crimes" (Barnett, Blumstein, and Farrington 1987, 83). In other words, these high-rate offenders are singled out for more vigorous prosecution and longer sentences in order to selectively incapacitate them because they are responsible for such a large proportion of serious crimes. It is more economically efficient to target incapacitation resources on this select group than to impose longer sentences on all offenders. For example, prosecutors' offices have introduced screening policies to identify high-rate offenders. These defendants' cases are then handled by a special team of prosecutors that works to get them off the streets for as long as the law allows. Habitual offender laws that provide increased sentences for repeat offenders are also aimed at incapacitating high-rate offenders.

Selective incapacitation has many critics. After the initial flurry of optimistic research results (Blumstein et al. 1986; Cohen 1983; Greenwood and Abrahamse 1982), subsequent studies showed the near impossibility of predicting which offenders will continue to offend at high rates if they are released rather than sent to prison (Greenwood and Turner 1987; Haapanen 1990). Predicting high-rate offending appears to be just as impossible as predicting dangerousness for the purpose of pretrial detention. Moreover, even if we could predict perfectly which offenders will continue to offend at high rates, incapacitating them might reduce the overall crime rate only marginally, by less than 2 percent according to one study (Haapanen 1990, 142).

Rehabilitation

rehabilitation

Rehabilitation is based on the assumption that human behavior is malleable or changeable. The term refers to changing criminals into productive and law-abiding members of society by attacking the individual factors that cause their criminal behavior. Rehabilitation programs from psychotherapy to job training have attempted to address the underlying causes of criminal behavior.

Rehabilitation has gone through periods of waxing and waning popularity. In the late nineteenth century probation and parole programs were created, based in part on the idea of rehabilitation. In 1967 the President's Crime Commission recommended expanded use of community-based corrections as a more effective approach to rehabilitation. Prisons introduced job training programs to address the poor job skills of many convicts. Many institutions also introduced group therapy to address offenders' psychological problems in order to reduce their likelihood of committing crimes.

During the 1970s many observers of the U.S. penal system concluded that rehabilitation had failed. In 1974 Robert Martinson reviewed the research on the effectiveness of a wide range of rehabilitative programs. His conclusion: "With few and isolated exceptions, the rehabilitative efforts that have been reported so far have had no appreciable effect on recidivism" (1974, 25). Criminologists and policymakers alike quickly repeated the pessimistic refrain, "Nothing works." Some commentators recommended that correctional administrators abandon the goal of rehabilitation and focus instead on a more obtainable goal: punishment.

Rehabilitation made a modest comeback in the 1980s. Proponents of rehabilitation reminded their antirehabilitation colleagues that Martinson had not recommended that rehabilitation be abandoned. Rather Martinson had merely pointed out that "our programs aren't yet good enough [and] what our correctional system needs is simply more full-hearted commitment to the strategy of treatment" (Andrews et al. 1990, 371). The debate rages on today. Two reviews of rehabilitation studies published from 1974 to 1985 came to somewhat contradictory conclusions. John R. Whitehead and Steven P. Lab (1989) pessimistically concluded that little had improved since Martinson's 1974 review of the research and that few rehabilitation programs had been successful. Their findings were "far from encouraging for advocates of correctional intervention" (Whitehead and Lab 1989, 289). In contrast, D. A. Andrews and colleagues (1990) concluded that appropriately designed correctional services appeared to reduce crime more than criminal sanctions without rehabilitative services. The problem, according to these authors, is to design more effective rehabilitation programs. All these researchers agree that rehabilitation efforts have often been half-hearted and that the relative lack of success thus far should not cause researchers to abandon rehabilitation. A different question is whether judges should abandon rehabilitation in deciding on an appropriate sentence for individual offenders.

Doing Justice: Nonutilitarian Justifications

Given the limited success in demonstrating the effectiveness of sentencing policies based on deterrence, rehabilitation, and incapacitation, some argue that sentencing should focus simply on doing justice. Two goals of sentencing—retribution and restitution—have nothing to do with supposed utilitarian benefits to society. Instead these goals concern the problem of justice. One kind of justice concerns the need to punish wrongdoing in order to maintain the legitimacy and fairness of the law. The law promises punishment of criminals. Therefore criminals deserve punishment, and in fairness to those who obey the law the guilty must be punished. A second kind of justice concerns compensation for injury. If a person causes someone else harm, that person ought to compensate the injured person. Both justifications may be traced to the ancient admonition of *lex talionis,* "An eye for an eye, a tooth for a tooth." **Retribution** seeks to right a balance upset by the criminal act. The criminal owes a debt to society and deserves punishment. **Restitution** seeks to compensate the victim of crime in proportion to the injury suffered.

retribution

restitution

Just Deserts: The Goal of Retribution

Retribution has roots in the blood feud of ancient times. Unlike blind vengeance, however, retribution is not simply an emotional outlet for the anger of the victim. Retribution is carefully regulated to make sure that the punishment fits the crime. Scholars refer to this as **proportionality**. Retribution makes the community whole by redressing the unfairness created by a criminal act. The criminal law promises punishment. Law-abiding members of society are owed this debt of punishment when the criminal breaks the law. The sentencing reforms of the 1970s were often explicitly justified in terms of the goal of retribution, or "just deserts," that is, giving criminals what they justly deserve.

proportionality

Restitution: The Goal of Compensation

The U.S. criminal justice system has only recently adopted compensation as a goal in sentencing. As Chapter 5 describes, some countries provide an opportunity for victims to bring civil actions as part of the criminal prosecution against an accused criminal. The United States has always relied instead on separate civil suits to afford victims an opportunity for compensation.

During the 1970s many courts began to experiment with restitution as a sentencing option. The convicted criminal compensates the victim through cash paid either directly to the victim or to a victims' compensation fund that serves many victims. Alternatively, the criminal may be required to compensate the community as a whole through community service. Compensating victims through restitution orders became popular in many jurisdictions through the 1980s. The U.S. Bureau of Justice Statistics sponsors a National Judicial Reporting Program, which collects data on felony sentencing in a nationally representative sample of three hundred counties in the United States. In 1990, 16 percent of felony sentences reported through the National Judicial Reporting Program included restitution orders (Maguire and Pastore 1994, 541).

■ SENTENCING OPTIONS

The goals of sentencing have an obvious influence on the choice of sentence. That is, the sentence that seems appropriate under the circumstances will depend on what the sentencing judge hopes to accomplish by imposing that sentence. In addition, the popularity of specific goals affects the mix of sentences available for different offenses and offenders. Finally, even though a wide range of sentencing options is available to judges, sentencing structures, plea agreements, and community sentiments influence the choices judges make.

The death penalty, incarceration, and community-based sanctions are the three main categories of sentencing options. Courts have experimented in recent years with novel combinations of incarceration and community sanctions. They have combined short periods of incarceration with longer periods of community-based treatment. They have also experimented with house arrest, a sort of incarceration in the community.

Death

A sentence of death is one of the most ancient and dreadful punishments a government can impose. Before the seventeenth century all felonies in England carried the death penalty. Hangings were events that brought out crowds of

FIGURE 17-1   Jurisdictions with Death Penalty Provisions and
Number of Prisoners Executed, 1977–1991

Source: Adapted from Kathleen Maquire, Ann L. Pastore, and Timothy J. Flanagan, 1993.
Sourcebook of Criminal Justice Statistics— 1992. Washington D.C.: U.S. Government Printing
Office, p. 678; U.S. Bureau of Justice Statistics, 1992. *Capital Punishment 1991.* Washington,
D.C.: U.S. Department of Justice, p. 1.

State or Jurisdiction	Number Executed	Number Executed in 1991
Texas	42	5
Florida	27	2
Louisiana	20	1
Georgia	15	1
Virginia	13	2
Alabama	8	0
Missouri	6	1
Nevada	5	0
Mississippi	4	0
North Carolina	4	1
South Carolina	4	1
Utah	3	0
Arkansas	2	0
Indiana	2	0
Illinois	1	0
Oklahoma	1	0
Arizona	0	0
California	0	0
Colorado	0	0
Connecticut	0	0
Delaware	0	0
Idaho	0	0
Kentucky	0	0
Maryland	0	0
Montana	0	0
Nebraska	0	0
New Hampshire	0	0
New Jersey	0	0
New Mexico	0	0
Ohio	0	0
Oregon	0	0
Pennsylvania	0	0
South Dakota	0	0
Tennessee	0	0
Washington	0	0
Wyoming	0	0
Federal System	0	0
United States, Total	157	14

spectators (Newman 1978). Although executions are no longer public spectacles,
the United States continues to impose the penalty of death (see Figure 17-1). As
of April 1993 thirty-six jurisdictions, the federal government, and the U.S. military
had death penalty statutes in effect (Maguire, Pastore, and Flanagan 1993, 670).

Proponents of the death penalty have justified its use on three principal
grounds: retribution, deterrence, and incapacitation. Whether the death penalty

deters and whether the death penalty is needed to incapacitate offenders are questions of some controversy. Research on the deterrent effects of the death penalty has not demonstrated significant deterrent effects (Bedau 1982, 97). Although the death penalty clearly incapacitates (a dead person cannot kill again), opponents of the death penalty have suggested that such a draconian means of incapacitating offenders is not necessary for most of those who are sentenced to death. For example, researchers James W. Marquart and Jonathan R. Sorenson studied the behavior of inmates whose original sentences of death were commuted to a prison term after the Supreme Court ruled in *Furman v. Georgia* (1972) that death penalties cannot be applied capriciously:

> Thirty-one of the *Furman* group (including the 3 armed robbers) were eventually released into the free community. The data indicate that the majority of releasees did not recidivate. Four releasees committed new felonies—one murder, one rape, and two burglaries. To some, this second killing may be "too many" and beyond an "acceptable" level or rate of violence. (1988, 690)

However, others might conclude that the overwhelming majority of these offenders, who had been sentenced to death, posed no danger to society after their punishment and release from prison.

Although the utilitarian goals of deterrence and incapacitation may be elusive, the death penalty does serve other goals: retribution and the condemnation of outrageous acts of violence. Proponents of the death penalty argue that justice demands the death penalty for heinous murders, even if deterrent or incapacitating effects cannot be expected. Opponents of the death penalty point to the negative potential of the death penalty, particularly the risk of executing an innocent person. Legal scholars continue to debate the constitutionality of the death penalty, including the discriminatory application of the death penalty to African-Americans.

Incarceration

Before the seventeenth century, incarceration was rarely used as a punishment for crime. However, the courts evolved a variety of mechanisms for commuting the sentences of many felons who would otherwise be put to death. Those who were not executed often found themselves transported to colonies in distant lands or placed in bondage in a form of indentured labor that was hardly distinguishable from slavery.

During the seventeenth and eighteenth centuries liberal reformers argued that the death penalty was excessively severe. The eighteenth-century Italian reformer Cesare Beccaria argued that crime could be deterred with much less severe sentences. Influential American politicians of the time, such as John Adams and Benjamin Franklin, were familiar with the ideas of Beccaria and his English co-reformer, Bentham. The influential American statesmen expressed interest in substituting less severe punishments for many felonies (Shane-DuBow, Brown, and Olsen 1985, 1–2).

In 1790 the Pennsylvania Quakers built the first American penitentiary, and Pennsylvania cut back drastically on the use of the death penalty as a punishment (Shane-DuBow et al. 1985, 3). Virginia soon followed Pennsylvania's example when Thomas Jefferson introduced a bill "for Proportioning Crime and Punishments in Cases Heretofore Capital" (Shane-DuBow et al. 1985, 3). These actions marked the beginning of a national movement early in the nineteenth century to sharply curtail the use of capital punishment and substitute incarceration. In 1853 *jail*

prison

disposition

Wisconsin became the first of many states to completely abolish capital punishment. Other states limited the use of the death penalty to only the most serious felonies (murder, rape, robbery, and kidnapping, for example). Declining reliance on the death penalty resulted in an increased reliance on incarceration as punishment.

Sentences of incarceration are commonly served in a jail or a prison. **Jails** are usually locally operated institutions reserved for the punishment of offenders serving short sentences, typically less than a year. **Prisons** are usually state-operated institutions. In most states an offender must be convicted of a felony and serve a maximum sentence of at least a year in order to be sent to prison.

Jail sentences are usually considered more lenient than prison sentences. Paradoxically, however, the conditions of confinement in local jails are often worse than the standard found in prisons. Jails are often overcrowded and are less likely to offer prisoners opportunities for education, rehabilitation, and recreation. Jail inmates are more likely than prison inmates to spend long hours locked in cells with limited opportunity to move about the institution. Health care and mental health services are also less likely to be available to prisoners in jails. If a jail sentence is a more lenient sentence, it is only because a jail sentence is shorter, not because doing time in a jail is easier.

Prisons are usually larger, better staffed, and better equipped than local jails. Some prisoners serve their sentences in nineteenth-century stone fortresses with gun towers and razor wire around the perimeter. Others serve theirs on prison farms or boot camps with little security. Some prisons have large prison industry programs that offer prisoners opportunities to work. Others stress education and job training. Some prisons focus on reforming criminals through discipline, whereas others rely on drug treatment and group therapy. Despite the rhetoric of retribution and deterrence, the goals of which are simply to punish and not rehabilitate, few prisons have completely abandoned the idea of rehabilitation.

In 1990 incarceration was the most common **disposition**, or outcome, of sentencing in felony cases (Solari 1992; see Figure 17-2). In 1979 the National Council on Crime and Delinquency documented that the United States had the third-highest incarceration rate in the world, ranking behind only South Africa and the Soviet Union. By 1991 the United States had passed all other countries with the highest incarceration rate in the world. In 1991 the United States incarcerated 426 of every 100,000 people in the country, compared to incarceration rates of 333 per 100,000 in South Africa and 268 per 100,000 in the Soviet Union before its disintegration at the beginning of 1992. Moreover, incarceration rates in Western Europe range from a high of 120 per 100,000 to a low of 35 per 100,000 (Mauer 1991, 3).

The high incarceration rate in the United States is attributable to a variety of factors. First, the United States has higher rates of crime than other countries. For example, the homicide rate in the United States is about seven times the European homicide rate. Another reason is the harsher sentencing policies adopted since the mid-1980s. Mandatory minimum sentences, restrictive parole policies, and harsher sentencing structures have all contributed to the increase in incarceration in this country. As a result of these policies and the war on drugs, a higher proportion of offenders is being sentenced to prison than ten years ago. In 1980, 196 offenders were sentenced to prison for every 1,000 arrests for serious crime. In 1987 that number had jumped to 301 offenders (Mauer 1991, 8).

Two consequences of these sentencing policies are increased prison overcrowding and skyrocketing costs in the corrections system. As of 1987, researcher

FIGURE 17-2 Types of Felony Sentences Imposed by State Courts, 1990

Source: Reprinted from Patrick A. Langan and John M. Dawson. 1993. *Felony Sentences in State Courts, 1990.* Washington, D.C.: U.S. Department of Justice, Bureau of Justice Statistics, p. 2.

Most serious conviction offense	Total	Percent of felons sentenced to incarceration			Probation
		Total	Prison	Jail	
All offenses	100%	71%	46%	25%	29%
Violent offenses	100%	80%	59%	21%	20%
Murder[a]	100	95	91	4	5
Rape	100	86	67	19	14
Robbery	100	90	73	17	10
Aggravated assault	100	72	45	27	28
Other violent[b]	100	67	42	25	33
Property offenses	100%	66%	44%	22%	34%
Burglary	100	75	54	21	25
Larceny[c]	100	65	40	25	33
Fraud[d]	100	53	33	20	47
Drug offenses	100%	72%	43%	29%	28%
Possession	100	64	35	29	36
Trafficking	100	77	49	28	23
Weapons offenses	100%	62%	38%	24%	38%
Other offenses[e]	100%	66%	37%	29%	34%

NOTE: For persons receiving a combination of sentences, the sentence designation came from the most severe penalty imposed—prison being the most severe, followed by jail, then probation. Data on sentence type were available for 99.4% of the estimated total.
[a] Includes nonnegligent manslaughter
[b] Includes offenses such as negligent manslaughter, sexual assault, and kidnapping
[c] Includes motor vehicle theft
[d] Includes forgery and embezzlement
[e] Composed of nonviolent offenses such as receiving stolen property and driving while intoxicated

Joan Petersilia found, "Nine states [were] operating their entire prison systems under court order or consent decree concerning overcrowding or other conditions. Another 28 states [had] at least one major prison operating under court order" (1987, 2).

Critics of harsh sentencing policies argue that increased prison expenditures have not led to decreased crime rates:

Had the punitive policies of the past decade resulted in dramatically reduced crime rates, one could argue that their great expense was partially justified by the results. But as the 1990s begin, we are faced with the same problems as in the 1980s, only in

FIGURE 17-3   Annual Costs per Offender of Incarceration and Alternatives in Delaware, 1985

SOURCE: Reprinted from Marc Mauer. 1991. *Americans Behind Bars: A Comparison of International Rates of Incarceration.* Washington, D.C.: Sentencing Project, American Judicature Society, p. 15.

Prison	$17,761
Work release	11,556
House arrest	3,332
Intensive supervision	2,292
Regular probation	569

greater degree—overcrowded prisons, high rates of crime, a major national drug problem, and the public lack of confidence in the criminal justice system. (Mauer 1991, 11)

Such critics urge increased reliance on community sanctions for nondangerous offenders.

The pressures of overcrowding also have forced state correctional administrators to search for new options that keep offenders out of prisons while satisfying the public's demand for security and punishment. Consequently, during the 1990s policymakers have turned their attention to community alternatives to incarceration.

Community Alternatives

A variety of nonincarceration options is available in many felony cases and most misdemeanor cases. These alternatives include split sentences (sometimes called shock probation or shock incarceration), work release, house arrest and electronic monitoring, intensive supervision in the community, and traditional probation. Fines, restitution, and community service orders also allow the offender to remain in the community; sometimes these sanctions are combined with a sentence of incarceration.

One attraction of community alternatives is that they are much less costly to administer than jail and prison. As figures from Delaware illustrate (Figure 17-3), a prisoner can be held in house arrest for less than one-fifth the cost of housing and guarding the offender in prison (Mauer 1991, 15). Community alternatives, *intermediate sanction* also called **intermediate sanctions,** are not appropriate for dangerous offenders. States are exploring intermediate sanctions for habitual offenders sentenced to prison in property crime or minor drug offenses, who probably could be held safely in the community. Despite the financial advantages of intermediate sanctions, some people worry that they are insufficient to meet the deterrent and retributive goals of punishment. Their effectiveness in rehabilitating offenders is still unclear.

Split Sentences

A split sentence, by which an offender is sentenced to a short period of incarceration followed by a longer period of probation, has been used to keep offenders in the community and deliver a jolt of deterring reality that is greater *shock probation* than through a sentence of probation alone. Dubbed **shock probation**, the idea is to demonstrate to young offenders the realities of incarceration in order to motivate them to go straight and comply with the requirements of probation. The goal is a combination of rehabilitation and deterrence. In addition, the short jail sentence allows judges to deliver some retributive punishment without keeping the offender in jail for an extended period of time.

In recent years another variation of shock probation has been instituted in many states—boot camps. Like the original shock probation programs, boot camps are aimed primarily at young offenders, especially drug offenders. Usually, they are sentenced to a short prison term (three to six months) to be completed in the boot camp setting. The philosophy of boot camp programs is to provide military-like discipline and to provide punishment without long-term incarceration. As of July 1990 seventeen states had instituted boot camp programs, compared to only eleven states in 1989, and seventeen other states were in the process of planning or considering boot camp programs. Programs differ widely in relation to the amount of time spent on physical training and drilling as opposed to education and counseling activities. Although researchers have identified some benefits of boot camp programs, whether positive changes can be sustained once the offender returns to the community is unclear (MacKenzie 1990, 6–8). Researchers are looking for effective combinations of boot camp, drug abuse treatment, and aftercare programming (Gowdy 1993, 10).

Work Release

Like the split sentence, work release offers a way to combine deterrence, retribution, and rehabilitation. The offender remains confined but is released during the day to work in the community. A variation of work release is weekends in jail; the offender lives at home, goes to work or school during the week, and checks into jail for the weekend. Work release lowers the costs of imprisonment, because offenders are often required to contribute to the cost of room and board. In addition, through work the offender is able to contribute to the support of dependents who might otherwise be forced onto the welfare rolls.

House Arrest and Electronic Monitoring

A new approach to incapacitation is to order the offender incarcerated at home. This option is frequently combined with work release, so that the offender is expected to be at home except to go to work or to attend school or court-ordered treatment programs.

In order to ensure that the offender is at home, house arrest is frequently combined with some form of electronic monitoring. Electronic monitoring programs have grown tremendously in recent years (see Figure 17-4). Prisoners under house arrest are required to wear bracelets that emit electronic signals. Researchers estimate that by early 1992, forty thousand electronic monitors were in use (Gowdy 1993, 6). One type of monitor emits a continuous signal, immediately alerting a central monitoring station to an offender who has left home without authorization. Another type of monitor randomly telephones offenders to verify their presence at home (Friel, Vaughn, and del Carmen 1987, 3–4).

Early reports suggest that house arrest may be a viable means of diverting some offenders from jail and prison. Florida, for example, placed twenty thousand convicts under house arrest. Seventy percent would have gone to prison if the house arrest option had not been available, and an additional 15 percent would have gone to jail. Even with this "prison-bound" population, only 22 percent were eventually sent to prison before completing their sentence, most for technical violations rather than new crimes (Petersilia 1987, 38).

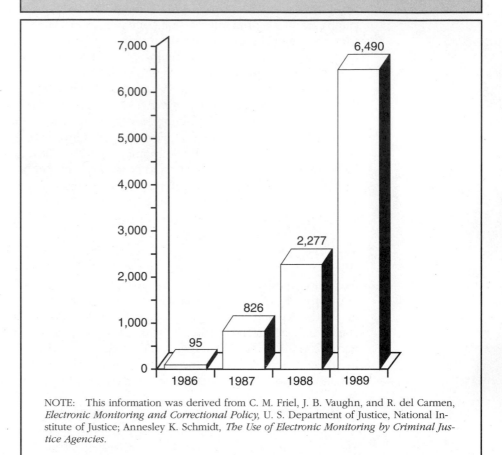

FIGURE 17-4   Estimated Daily Monitored Population in the United States, 1986–1989

SOURCE: Reprinted from Marc Renzema and David R. Skelton. 1990. "Use of Electronic Monitoring in the United States: 1989 Update." *NIJ Reports,* (November–December): p. 9.

NOTE: This information was derived from C. M. Friel, J. B. Vaughn, and R. del Carmen, *Electronic Monitoring and Correctional Policy,* U. S. Department of Justice, National Institute of Justice; Annesley K. Schmidt, *The Use of Electronic Monitoring by Criminal Justice Agencies.*

Offenders have reported that the curfew restrictions of house arrest are punishing (Petersilia 1987). In addition, house arrest may produce rehabilitative effects beyond those obtainable through probation. Confinement at home changes the individual's interactions with the peer group and makes offenders learn more constructive, noncriminal activities to fill their nonworking hours (Friel et al. 1987, 21). Some monitored offenders also reported that they used the monitor as an excuse to avoid participating in criminal activities with their friends (Gowdy 1993, 6). House arrest and electronic monitoring need further evaluation, but initial results appear promising.

These relatively new sanctions have stirred some controversy. Some commentators have wondered whether house arrest and electronic monitoring violate the rights of defendants or presage an era of greater government intrusion in the lives of citizens, criminal and noncriminal alike (see Berry 1985; Lilly, Ball, and Lotz 1986). Critics have noted that, instead of using the intermediate sanctions as alternatives to incarceration, they could be used to expand government control of offenders who otherwise would have been placed on probation (Tonry and Morris 1990). If this happens, intermediate sanctions will increase correctional costs instead of decreasing them. A survey conducted by the National Institute of Justice in 1989 suggests that this widening of the security net may be occurring. A 1993 study found electronic monitoring is being used to follow up on people paroled from incarceration, to control those sentenced to community corrections, and to monitor people before trial or sentencing (Gowdy 1993, 6).

Probation

conditions of probation

In large urban jurisdictions about a quarter of convicted felons receive a sentence of probation alone, with no incarceration (U.S. Bureau of Justice Statistics [BJS] 1993, 17). Usually, the judge imposes a sentence of incarceration and then orders that sentence suspended, indefinitely delaying the delivery of the offender to jail or prison. In lieu of incarceration the judge places the offender under the supervision of the probation department. Probation carries certain restrictions, called **conditions of probation,** which typically require that the offender report periodically to a probation officer and include other general conditions imposed on all probationers. In addition, the judge has discretion to order special conditions of probation tailored to the needs of the individual offender. For example, the judge might order a drug-dependent offender to participate in a drug treatment program as a condition of probation. The only limitations on a judge's authority to impose conditions are that the conditions not violate fundamental rights of the offender and that the conditions be reasonably related to some goal of sentencing (Czajkoski and Wollan 1986).

Originally, probation was conceived as lenient treatment for first-time or nonserious offenders. In addition, probation officers were expected to rehabilitate offenders through counseling. In practice probation caseloads have prevented officers from engaging in significant efforts to rehabilitate. Delivering counseling or even supervising treatment is often impossible. With a single probation officer being responsible for one hundred or more probationers, probation officers can do little but follow up on those offenders who have been arrested for a new crime. Not surprisingly, probation has failed to deliver on its rehabilitative promise. One study of felons released on probation found that 43 percent were rearrested for a felony within three years (BJS 1992b).

intensive supervision probation

Because of the need for more community sanctions to reduce prison overcrowding, many probation departments have experimented with **intensive supervision probation** (ISP) for those whose criminal tendencies are deemed too serious for a regular probation caseload. They are required to report frequently to a probation officer who has a smaller than normal caseload, perhaps thirty to fifty probationers (Gowdy 1993, 4; Maguire and Pastore 1994, 579–80; Petersilia 1987, 10). ISP programs operating in forty states typically include some attempt to predict whether an offender is at high risk for recidivism. Each probationer's treatment needs are assessed, and probationers are referred to community treatment programs for education, job training, and substance abuse problems. ISP probationers are subjected to more frequent surveillance by probation authorities, including curfews, house arrest, and periodic testing for drug and alcohol use. ISP probation officers frequently receive special training for dealing with these more difficult clients (Petersilia 1987, 12). Although initial evaluations are inconclusive, it appears to be possible to divert a significant number of serious felons from prison and maintain them on probation without increased danger to the community.

Fines

One of the oldest sentencing options is the fine. As Chapter 4 notes, English kings found that fines could provide a sizable revenue for the government. Today, more than $1 billion in fines is collected each year in the United States (BJS 1988, 96). Fines play an important role in sentencing petty offenders but are used less often in sentencing serious offenders (Hillsman et al. 1987, 2). For more serious offenses, only first offenders and those who have the ability to pay are likely to be fined. For example, fines are frequently used to sentence corporations and executives convicted of such crimes as securities violations and environmental crimes. Poorer offenders may not be able to pay fines imposed by the court and are incarcerated instead (Hillsman et al. 1987, 3). Fines may also be used in conjunction with other penalties, especially for offenders who have financial means. According to the National Judicial Reporting Program, fines were imposed on 16 percent of felons sentenced in the reporting jurisdictions (Maguire and Pastore 1994, 541).

In most U.S. courts judges tend to set informal fixed fine amounts that they impose on all defendants convicted of a particular crime. These fixed fine amounts are typically quite low so that even poor defendants can afford to pay them in most cases (Hillsman and Greene 1988, 39). As a result fines on offenders who are not poor are typically much lower than they could (or should) be. In addition, judges are reluctant to use fines for more serious misdemeanors and felonies (Hillsman et al. 1984, 43).

Prison and jail overcrowding is causing policymakers to take a closer look at the advantages and disadvantages of a revamped system of criminal fines. Proponents argue that fines serve as an appropriate punishment and deterrent, depriving offenders of ill-gotten gains. Fines can also be combined with other sentences to achieve the goals of sentencing. Finally, the amount of the fine can be adjusted according to the circumstances, including the seriousness of the offense and the offender's economic means (Hillsman and Greene 1988).

day-fine

A European variation, called day-fines, appears to be promising. The **day-fines** system encourages judges to fine on a sliding scale, roughly equivalent to an offender's daily wage (hence the term *day-fine*). Some U.S. courts have begun to adopt this idea. The court obtains information on the economic status of the defendant before sentencing and adjusts the amount of the fine accordingly.

A recent study of the implementation of day-fines in Staten Island found that the total dollar amount of fines collected increased by 14 percent. If statutory caps on fine levels had not been in effect, fines would have increased by 50 percent. In addition, although the courts imposed higher amounts, day-fines were collected in full as frequently as the traditional lower fixed fines had been (Gowdy 1993, 2).

Restitution and Community Service Programs

None of the sentencing options discussed thus far addresses the goal of compensation. Although the offender may be required to repay a debt to society by serving a prison sentence or paying a fine, the victim is not directly compensated for the injuries or property loss caused by the offender's conduct. Restitution and community service require that the offender pay compensation through monetary payments or work.

Restitution is money paid by the offender to the victim as compensation for harm suffered. In most states the judge can order restitution at sentencing. In some jurisdictions the judge may order the payment of restitution as a condition of probation. If the offender fails to pay the restitution, the probation is revoked

DAY-FINES

In practice, judges using a day-fine approach first sentence an offender to a certain number of fine units (e.g. 10, 50, 125 units) which reflects the degree of punishment the judge deems appropriate for the offense. To help ensure that decisions as to the number of fine units are systematic and consistent (within a judge's own sentencing activities and across a given court), the judges using day fines have tended to develop flexible, written guidelines. After determining the appropriate number of fine units, the judge calculates the monetary value of each unit according to the means of the particular offender being sentenced. To do so, the judge uses information routinely available from the police, the court, probation or the defendant (often the latter). In Sweden, for example, the process is guided by a uniform method of calculating ability to pay which has been pro-

mulgated by the Prosecutor General's Office. Through this two-step sentencing process, the total monetary penalty the judge imposes—the degree of punishment—is in proportion to the offense's seriousness but, at the same time, should cause an equivalent level of economic burden across offenders who have different means.

When European courts began using day-fine systems, fine amounts rose significantly, to reflect just punishment for more affluent offenders, and the fine's usefulness as a sanction was broadened. This took place, however, without increasing default rates, imposing costly demands on enforcement systems and without increasing re-offending.

SOURCE: Reprinted from Sally T. Hillsman, Vice President of the National Center for State Courts, and Judith A. Greene. 1988. "Tailoring Criminal Fines to the Financial Means of the Offender." *Judicature* 72 (June–July): 38–45.

and the offender sent to jail or prison. Some jurisdictions combine restitution with work release programs or prison labor programs, so that a portion of the offender's earnings is automatically sent to the victim as compensation. Another variation requires that the offender contribute to a victim compensation fund that is used to compensate victims of certain violent and property crimes.

community service

Community service compensates the community as a whole by requiring the offender to perform service for the community. Initially, community service was conceived as a way to allow poor defendants to work off their fine through service to the community. This sanction has been popular for individuals convicted of drunken driving, white-collar crimes (such as violations of environmental laws), and offenses that do not have identifiable victims. The offender is assigned to work as a "volunteer" in a community agency, for example, assisting in a hospital, doing maintenance in public parks, or serving meals at homeless shelters. The judge specifies the number of hours of service that the offender must work. A review of the Vera Institute's community service sentencing project concluded that "community service can be imposed in large numbers not only upon relatively well to do first time offenders who possess valuable skills, but also upon those chronic property offenders who are generally not violent, but who nonetheless present the courts with difficult problems" (Petersilia 1987, 75–76). In 1990, 4 percent of all felony sentences reported through the National Judicial Reporting Program included community service orders. The number of such orders for misdemeanors is probably somewhat higher.

■ THE SENTENCING PROCESS

Given the wide range of sentencing options, how do judges decide what sentence to impose? The sentencing decision is best understood as a series of decisions. The initial decision focuses on whether the offender requires incarceration. This is often referred to as the "in/out decision": will the offender be kept locked up in jail or prison or released back to the community with no immediate incarceration? If the judge decides that the offender may be immediately released to the community, the series of decisions that follows relates to the length of the probationary period, special conditions of probation, ordering restitution or community service, or imposing a fine. The judge who decides to impose a sentence of incarceration must then decide the length of incarceration. Research on sentencing practices has focused primarily on the in/out decision and the length of incarceration.

The sentence formally imposed by the judge is influenced by both formal and informal constraints. The statutory sentencing structure, which may set a minimum and a maximum sentence, is the principal formal constraint on the judge's decision. Informal constraints include any bargains related to the sentence negotiated by the prosecutor and local norms about the kinds of sentences given for certain kinds of crimes and offenders (the going rate). Although a judge may reject a sentence recommendation of a prosecutor, judges are reluctant to upset the set of expectations that allows plea negotiations to operate. Unless the recommended sentence appears wholly unreasonable, the judge is likely to defer to the prosecutor's recommendation.

When the prosecutor has not entered an agreement with the defendant on the sentence, the judge has more latitude. Nonetheless, the judge's decision is influenced by prevailing norms of the legal culture of the jurisdiction. Another influence on the judge's decision may be the presentence investigation.

Presentence Investigation

The presentence investigation has become a standard procedure in many courts. The purpose is to provide the judge with more detailed information about the offense and offender. In particular, judges frequently rely on presentence investigations to identify those offenders who are good prospects for a suspended sentence and probation. In most jurisdictions the probation department is responsible for conducting the presentence investigation and can exercise some influence in "selecting" the offenders to be placed under its authority.

Presentence investigations include a wide variety of information. Some information is relatively objective, whereas other information is nothing more than the subjective impressions of the investigating officer or others who are interviewed by the investigator. Most presentence investigations include a description of the current offense, including an assessment of the offender's culpability and remorse and the financial and emotional effect on the victim (Clear, Clear, and Burrell 1989, 15). Because the court is often looking for information regarding the risk involved in allowing the offender to remain in the community on probation, presentence investigations typically include the offender's record, including dispositions for previous offenses. Some courts also ask the investigator to include a risk assessment, which weighs the likelihood that the offender will commit a new crime if released in the community (Clear et al. 1989, 15). Many probation departments now use risk-screening instruments to predict future criminal involvement of offenders coming up for sentencing. These instruments base their predictions on a variety of characteristics, including the offender's record, substance abuse history, and age of first arrest. If appropriately constructed, these instruments can generally be helpful in identifying low-risk offenders but frequently are wrong about which offenders are likely to commit a crime if released in the community (Clear et al. 1989). In other words, if an offender is predicted to be low risk, chances are good that the offender will not commit serious new crimes if released. However, a prediction that an offender is likely to commit new crimes is much less reliable. Many offenders predicted to be dangerous or high risk do not commit serious new crimes upon release.

Another portion of the presentence report describes the offender's current circumstances, including educational attainment, current employment and employability, family circumstances, and other data. The probation officer conducting the investigation can use considerable discretion in deciding which circumstances to investigate, what sources to use for gathering information, and what information to include in the report.

Finally, some presentence reports may include information about the sentencing options available. In some jurisdictions the probation department evaluates the feasibility of nontraditional alternatives to incarceration or traditional probation. Although the inclusion of such information has been limited in the past, current emphases on employing intermediate sanctions and using alternatives to incarceration may make this a higher priority in presentence investigations.

The importance of plea bargaining in relation to sentencing has led to research on how the presentence report influences the sentences actually imposed. Research shows that judges tend to follow the sentence recommendations given in presentence reports (Carter and Wilkins 1967; Hagan 1975; Rosecrance 1988; Walsh 1985).

Researchers disagree, however, on why sentence recommendations are influential. Some researchers view the probation officer as a powerful factor in the sentencing process and the presentence report as influencing judges' decisions (Walsh 1985). Other researchers suggest that the probation officer is more a follower than a leader in the sentencing process, actually responding to the cues of others. For example, in cases where the sentence recommendation is part of the plea agreement, it is not surprising to find that the probation officer's recommendation matches the prosecutor's recommendation. Some departments conduct only minimal investigation in such cases and file a short form presentence report.

Even in other types of cases the probation officer's recommendation may be no more than a reflection of preconceived outcomes. One study found that early in the presentence investigation probation officers arrive at an initial recommendation based only on the current offense and the offender's prior record. Then information is gathered and interpreted to support the initial recommendation. Because the offense is critical in shaping the initial recommendation, the prosecutor's charging decision influences the outcome of the presentence investigation. The study concluded that the presentence investigation may be largely ceremonial, giving only the appearance of individualized justice (Rosecrance 1988).

The quality of the information included in the report is another controversial matter. Most probation officers are overworked. A normal caseload is about eighty probationers under supervision, and caseloads of 150 to 200 have become common in recent years (Gowdy 1993, 4). On top of this, the probation officer is expected to complete several presentence reports each week—as many as twelve in some jurisdictions (Clear et al. 1989). Working under the tight time constraints that these caseloads impose, probation officers often cannot verify information. As a result presentence investigation reports can be incomplete and contain factual errors. In addition, critics of presentence reports point out that they may include subtle biases that may not be apparent to the judge. For example, "A probation officer who was raised in a white, middle-class family may misinterpret a black street-wise youth's nervous behavior in an interview as hostility toward authority, and misinterpret the offender's behavior in the [presentence report]" (Clear et al. 1989, 21).

These problems are compounded by the confidentiality of most parts of the report. In most jurisdictions neither the defendant nor defense counsel is allowed access to the full report. They may be allowed to read the listing of the defendant's record but are usually not allowed to read those portions based on confidential interviews with the victim, the offender's employer, family, teachers, and others. The U.S. Supreme Court has upheld the confidentiality of the report except when the presentence report is used to justify imposition of the death penalty (*Gardner v. Florida* 1977).

Although the defendant rarely has a right to inspect the entire presentence report, in some jurisdictions the routine practice is to give the defense a copy of the report. This practice accords with the trend toward more disclosure and sharing of information. In jurisdictions where the defense is not granted access to the presentence report, errors will not be detected and challenged or corrected. Because of the possibility of error some defense lawyers recommend that a separate presentence report be prepared by an investigator in private practice (Rodgers, Gitchoff, and Paur 1984). In some cases legal aid associations or other charitable groups have offered this service to indigent defendants. In most places, however, the preparation of a defense presentence report is unusual and likely to be undertaken only by a well-to-do client (Rosecrance 1988).

Like the court-ordered presentence report, the defense presentence report is designed to provide information that will be useful to the judge in sentencing. Defense reports are more likely to seek out creative dispositions that use a wide array of community resources. For example, the defense report may include a probation plan that identifies special conditions that should be imposed and special programs for the offender. Defense presentence reports are likely to stress the feasibility of the least restrictive alternatives to incarceration. The defense presentence investigation continues the adversarial approach through the sentencing phase and offers the judge concrete suggestions and justifications for a more lenient sentence.

Victim Impact Statements

A new trend in many courts is the submission of victim impact statements to the court at the time of sentencing. The victim impact statement specifies the harm the victim or victim's family has suffered as a result of the offender's crime. Physical, economic, emotional, and psychological harm may be discussed in these statements (Erez and Tontodonato 1992, 394). In addition, victim impact statements have been promoted as a way to make the victim part of the court process and give victims an opportunity to publicly express the pain caused by the crime.

Victim impact statements help judges to gauge the seriousness of the offense. An aggravated assault that results in the loss of an eye might be considered more serious than a similar assault that results in no permanent damage to the victim. Nonetheless, critics of victim impact statements argue that the effect on the victim is often a matter of chance and not directly related to the intent of the offender.

Critics wonder why the offender whose victim was poor, and who therefore suffered greater relative harm from a theft, should receive a more serious sentence than an offender whose victim happened to have insurance or money in the bank.

The current trend toward increased participation of victims in sentencing has led to research on the effects of victim participation. Researchers Edna Erez and Pamela Tontodonato (1990) found that victim impact statements had only a marginal effect on the sentence imposed. Further, victims who fill out a victim impact report may have inflated expectations about the weight that will be placed on the information they provide. If such victims feel that their statement had no effect on the sentence imposed, they are likely to be dissatisfied with the sentence and with the criminal justice system as a whole (Erez and Tontodonato 1992).

Sentencing Hearing

The sentence is announced at the sentencing hearing, which may occur immediately after the verdict or acceptance of a guilty plea. However, counsel often requests time to prepare for the sentencing hearing, or the judge may wish to postpone sentencing to allow for completion of the presentence investigation. Generally, sentencing occurs within a month of conviction.

The sentencing hearing is formal and usually takes place in open court. However, the rules of evidence are not as strict as at trial, and information that was excluded (hearsay or prejudicial evidence) may be admitted for the purpose of sentencing. The defendant has a right to be represented by counsel, including appointed counsel if the defendant cannot afford a private lawyer (*Mempa v. Rhay* 1967). The court may take evidence and hear the testimony of witnesses, but the judge usually bases the sentence on the statements of counsel, the presentence report, and the statement of the offender.

Constitutional Protections at Sentencing

In addition to the statutory limits on judicial sentencing discretion, the Eighth Amendment to the U.S. Constitution prohibits judges in federal and state courts from imposing sentences that are cruel and unusual. The meaning of "cruel and unusual" has not been defined in any definitive or final way by the Supreme Court. In fact, the Court has explicitly noted that the meaning of cruel and unusual evolves over time (*Weems v. United States* 1910; *Trop v. Dulles* 1958). When the Bill of Rights was ratified in 1791, corporal punishments that were relatively common, such as whipping and confinement in the stocks, would be rejected today as shocking to the conscience. Similarly, punishments that are today held constitutional and not violations of the protection from cruel and unusual punishment might shock the consciences of future generations.

The Supreme Court has held that punishments may be found to be cruel and unusual if they violate any of three criteria:

- If the punishment exceeds the statutory maximum sentence;
- If the punishment, although authorized by state law, is disproportionate to the seriousness of the crime;
- If the punishment is inhumane and barbarous, such as torture.

disproportionate sentence

The Court has also specified three criteria for courts to use in deciding whether a sentence is **disproportionate:**

- If the sentence is excessively severe in light of the gravity of the offense;
- If the sentences imposed on other criminals in the same jurisdiction for more serious crimes are given the same penalty or less serious penalties;
- If the sentence imposed is excessive in comparison to the sentences imposed in other jurisdictions for commission of the same crime.

The Court's decision in *Solem v. Helm* (1983) illustrates how these criteria are applied. The defendant was sentenced under South Dakota's recidivist statute to life imprisonment without parole for passing a $100 bad check. In South Dakota life imprisonment explicitly denies the offender an opportunity for parole. The Court held that the sentence was unconstitutional because it was disproportionate to the offense. Specifically, the Court noted that the offender's offense was minor and the offender did not have a history of violent offenses. The Court also noted that in South Dakota life imprisonment without parole is otherwise reserved for only the most serious crimes: murder, treason, arson, and kidnapping. Therefore the sentence imposed for this offense of passing a bad check was equal to that otherwise imposed for much more serious offenses. Finally, the Court noted that only one other state imposed penalties as severe as South Dakota's for similar offenses.

■ DISCRETION AND SENTENCING DISPARITY

sentence disparity

Disproportionality in sentencing is the extreme form of a more prevalent type of unfairness in sentencing: **sentence disparity.** Disparity can exist in a number of ways, such as between states or between counties within a state. Convicted of the same crime, offenders in rural counties, for example, may receive more severe sentences than those in urban areas. Any jurisdiction may evidence disparity between judges, with some judges imposing more severe or more lenient sentences than their colleagues. This sort of sentence disparity means that the sentence a defendant receives depends largely on which judge handles the defendant's sentencing. Finally, disparity may occur when judges respond to differences between defendants that should be irrelevant to sentencing, such as race or gender.

Sentencing discretion and the disparity that often results were critical policy issues in criminal justice during the 1970s and 1980s. Research conducted in the 1960s and early 1970s suggested that indeterminate sentencing structures allowed judges too much discretion and gave judges too little guidance about sentencing norms. As a result the sentence a defendant received often depended on the judge doing the sentencing.

Researchers also pointed to sentence disparity between defendants, particularly between white defendants and black defendants. Although all researchers have noted that the seriousness of the current offense and prior record are the strongest influences on sentence severity, some researchers have found that black defendants receive harsher sentences than similar white defendants (Spohn and Cederblom 1991). Race appears to influence sentencing decisions for minor crimes more than for serious crimes. In serious cases the appropriate sentence is clear, and judges have little opportunity to be affected by the race of the offender. In less serious cases, however, the judge may be more uncertain about the appropriate sentence, and legally irrelevant factors, such as race, may have a greater influence on the sentence imposed.

Researchers Harry Kalven and Hans Zeisel (1966) dubbed this the "liberation hypothesis," arguing that when the facts are unclear or ambiguous, decision makers are liberated from the strict requirements of the law and rely on their own values (and prejudices) to reach a conclusion. Other researchers found support for the liberation hypothesis in relation to sentencing. They found that in less serious cases "judges have greater discretion in determining the sentence, and their biases and attitudes toward racial minorities may come into play" (Spohn and Cederblom 1991, 323).

■ SENTENCING STRUCTURES: STRUCTURING JUDICIAL DISCRETION

The outcome of the sentencing hearing depends on the type of sentencing structure in place in a given jurisdiction. The sentencing structure circumscribes sentencing discretion. Some sentencing structures give judges wide discretion, whereas others limit the choices available to judges in determining the sentence. Consequently, some sentencing structures maximize the potential for disparity in sentencing, and others greatly reduce the possibility of sentence disparity.

Indeterminate Sentencing

indeterminate sentencing

Indeterminate sentencing refers to sentencing structures characterized by broad discretion and the opportunity for wide variation in sentences served by individual offenders. Indeterminate sentencing allows wide variation in two ways. First, the legislature sets only broad ranges for sentencing, giving judges much latitude to impose a mild or a harsh sentence within the legislatively set range. Second, the judge imposes a sentence of indeterminate length, leaving it to the parole authorities to decide how long the offender will in fact remain in prison.

Many states classify offenses and then set a maximum and minimum sentence for all offenses in that level. For example, Texas law defines four classes of felonies—capital felonies, and first-, second-, and third-degree felonies. The punishment defined by Texas statute for a second-degree felony, whether voluntary manslaughter or bribery or any other second-degree felony, is "confinement in the Texas Department of Corrections for any term of not more than 20 years or less than 2 years." Between the maximum and minimum the judge has complete discretion to set the sentence. In some cases the statute may specify only the maximum sentence. Judges in turn impose only a minimum and maximum sentence rather than specify a specific sentence length to be served by the offender. The parole board decides whether and when the offender will be released within that broad range (Knapp 1988, 46). Under indeterminate sentencing the time served by defendants is substantially less than the maximum sentences allowed by the legislature and the maximum sentences imposed by judges.

Determinate Sentencing

determinate sentencing

Determinate sentencing structures are those that give judges little discretion in imposing the sentence and eliminate the parole board's discretion entirely. Determinate sentencing structures limit sentencing discretion in one or both of two ways. First, determinate sentencing may narrow the range within which judges may choose a sentence, usually allowing little, if any, discretion.

flat sentencing

good time

Second, determinate sentencing reduces discretion by reducing the role of the parole board or by eliminating the parole board entirely. This is known as **flat sentencing.** The sentence imposed by the judge is the sentence served by the offender, subject only to reductions for **good time,** time off the sentence for good behavior that is awarded on a formula basis. For example, for two days served without disciplinary infractions the sentence length may be reduced by one day.

Until the late nineteenth century determinate sentencing structures were the norm in the United States. Judges had little discretion. Their role in sentencing was limited to looking in the statute book to see what sentence was required by law. Parole boards did not exist. When many states experienced prison overcrowding toward the end of the nineteenth century, prison administrators and legislatures looked for mechanisms for controlling the prison population (Shane-DuBow et al. 1985, 4).

Pardons and the granting of good time helped to alleviate some overcrowding problems. Many states also began to adopt the English "ticket-of-leave" system, which became known as *parole* in this country. In 1870 the National Prison Association called for the adoption of indeterminate sentencing by judges to facilitate discretionary release on parole (Shane-DuBow et al. 1985, 5). By 1911 nine states had adopted indeterminate sentencing structures to replace the older fixed sentencing structures (Shane-DuBow et al. 1985, 6). By the 1960s every state in the nation had some form of indeterminate sentencing and parole.

Reducing Indeterminacy and Sentencing Discretion

Indeterminate sentencing, which began as a liberal reform in the 1870s, became the target of liberal and conservative critics alike during the 1970s. Indeterminate sentencing increased judicial discretion, which allowed judges to vary the sentence by the characteristics of the offender, a major goal of the movement toward indeterminacy. But judicial discretion could be both a blessing and a curse. Several major reports published during the 1970s suggested that judicial discretion in sentencing should be reduced or eliminated (American Friends Service Committee 1971; Von Hirsch 1976; Dershowitz 1976). Sentencing research in the 1960s and 1970s reported that the sentence handed down depended more on which judge imposed the sentence than on the crime committed by the offender. The critics of indeterminate sentencing felt that the unfairness inherent in disparity caused "considerable inmate anger and frustration which often caused unrest within the prisons" (Shame-DuBow et al. 1985, 7). Indeterminate sentencing also was blamed for increasing crime rates. Beginning in the mid-1960s conservative politicians called for increased "law and order" and promised to increase sentences (Cohen 1985, 91; Finckenauer 1978). Politicians and conservative scholars promoted "get tough" strategies (see, for example, van den Haag 1977; Wilson 1983). One way to get tough was to reduce judges' discretion (Link and Shover 1986).

presumptive sentencing

Dissatisfaction with indeterminate sentencing led to reforms of two types. One reduced the discretion of judges by narrowing the range set by the legislature, either through presumptive sentencing or sentencing guidelines. **Presumptive sentencing** is a form of determinate sentencing that narrows the range of potential sentences and reduces the range of judicial discretion without eliminating it entirely. In exceptional cases judges may sentence outside the "presumptive" range, so long as they provide a written justification. Most presumptive sentencing schemes also retain judicial discretion to decide whether to sentence an offender to prison or some form of community sanction (Knapp 1988, 46). In other states **sentencing guidelines** have been created to assist judges in their sentencing decisions. The difference between presumptive sentencing and sentencing guidelines lies primarily in how the sentencing structure is adopted. Legislatively created structures are usually referred to as presumptive sentencing, whereas structures devised by state court judges or a special commission are usually referred to as guidelines. Although the term "guidelines" sounds less binding, some sentencing guidelines, like those of the federal system, are extremely detailed and give judges little room for discretion. In contrast, some presumptive sentencing structures allow substantial discretion for judges to sentence outside the presumptive sentence imposed by statute.

sentencing guidelines

In some cases legislatures further reduce judicial discretion by creating mandatory sentences. **Mandatory sentences** typically require judges to sentence offenders convicted of certain crimes to a statutory minimum term of imprisonment, with no exceptions. Mandatory sentences have been advanced as part of a general "get tough" strategy of crime control. By imposing mandatory sentences the legislature is able to prevent judges from being "soft" on criminals. Mandatory sentences do not allow judges to reduce the sentence for mitigating circumstances or to tailor the sentence to the individual needs of the offender.

mandatory sentences

Many states have habitual offender statutes, often referred to during the early 1990s as "three strikes and you're out" provisions. Earlier forms of these laws allowed prosecutors to bring additional charges, sometimes called supercharges, against any defendant previously convicted of two felonies. On being convicted as a habitual offender, the sentence would be double the normal maximum sentence or life imprisonment. The more recent incarnation of habitual offender laws increases the stakes for defendants and removes the discretion of prosecutors and judges. These three-strikes provisions allow for automatic mandatory life imprisonment without parole upon conviction for a third serious felony. These laws typically list specific felonies that "count" as serious felonies under the law. Several states and the federal jurisdiction now have such provisions.

Another reform eliminates the discretion of the parole board by requiring flat sentences. Flat sentences reduce the uncertainty created by indeterminate sentencing in relation to the length of imprisonment. Indeterminate sentencing allows the calculation of a **parole eligibility date** and a **mandatory release date** (maximum sentence minus good time), but the difference between these two dates is often great. Neither the sentencing judge, nor the prisoner, nor prison authorities know when the prisoner will actually be released. The parole board makes this decision. Flat sentencing eliminates the parole decision. Although states that have adopted flat sentencing allow prisoners to earn good time, the lengths of sentences in those states are more certain from the moment they are imposed. Prisoners who follow the rules of the institution can figure out the date of their release.

parole eligibility date, mandatory release date

These reforms are not without critics. In particular many experts fear that (1) eliminating parole reduces prisoners' incentive to comply with prison rules and to participate in rehabilitation programs; (2) moving from an indeterminate structure to a determinate structure merely shifts sentencing discretion from the relatively visible position of the judge to the much less visible position of the prosecutor; and (3) that the practical effect of moving from indeterminate structures to determinate structures is to increase the actual time served by offenders instead of reducing sentence lengths as proposed by the reformers (Shane-DuBow et al. 1985, 9). Although the critics of determinate sentencing often sympathize with the reformers' goals, they consider the solutions—presumptive sentencing and elimination of the parole decision—unworkable and doomed to make matters worse rather than better.

Despite the critics, sentencing reform proposals appeal to a broad spectrum of policymakers. Liberal reform-oriented policymakers are attracted to the reduction in sentencing disparity promised by presumptive sentencing structures. In addition, liberal reformers view presumptive sentencing as more humane, because it allows prisoners to know their release dates with greater certainty. More conservative policymakers find in the reform proposals an ideology with which they are comfortable. The philosophy of retribution and the abandonment of the goal of rehabilitation fit well with conservatives' pessimism about rehabilitation and their concern that criminals are escaping punishment because liberal judges are too soft. The momentum for sentencing reform has resulted in sweeping changes in many states and adoption of at least partial reforms in many other states (Shane-DuBow et al. 1985, 279; Link and Shover 1986).

Variations in Determinate Sentencing Policies

Whether they are called determinate sentencing, presumptive sentencing, or sentencing guidelines, all these systems narrow the discretion of judges in setting sentences. Although most states have revised their sentencing policies in some way, not all states have adopted the same kinds of changes. Within the fifty states and the District of Columbia (included here as a "state"), the following changes occurred from 1971 to about 1981:

- Eleven states did not significantly alter their codes.
- Fifteen states adopted determinate sentencing proposals.
- Twenty-five states underwent major criminal code revisions.
- Fifteen states experienced piecemeal code revisions.
- Thirty-three states enacted or increased repeater or habitual criminal laws.
- Forty-nine states enacted mandatory sentencing laws for some offenses other than first-degree murder and drunken driving, which also carry mandatory sentences in many states.
- Twenty-seven states tightened parole eligibility criteria.
- Eight states eliminated parole altogether (flat sentencing).

Some states have opted to change the criminal code itself, whereas others have simply drafted guidelines. Some states make it difficult for judges to deviate from the established sentence, whereas others give judges substantial discretion to modify the sentence prescribed for the offender under the circumstances. Some states put most weight on the nature of the conviction charges and the record of the offender, and others consider the characteristics of the offender, such as employment history (Kramer, Lubitz, and Kempinen 1989). Some states precisely define aggravating and mitigating circumstances and how these are to influence the sentence; others give the judge more discretion to weigh aggravating and mitigating factors.

Consequences of Reform

Given the wide variation in sentencing reforms undertaken in the 1970s and 1980s, it is difficult to reach any simple conclusions about the consequences of reform. The success of sentencing reform has been highly uneven. One of the most widely hailed successes in establishing a determinate sentencing structure is Minnesota's sentencing guidelines. In 1980 Minnesota implemented sentencing guidelines developed by an independent commission that considered prior sentencing practices in developing them. However, rather than simply transfer past practices to new guidelines, the Minnesota Sentencing Guidelines Commission adopted the view that prison sentences should be reserved primarily for violent offenders, not property offenders. In other words, even if the commission found that many property offenders were being sentenced to prison, it deliberately avoided perpetuating this practice in drafting the guidelines (Miethe and Moore 1989, 2).

In the first two years after implementation Minnesota's guidelines substantially reduced sentence disparity and did not result in increases in prison populations, as had been the case in other states establishing determinate sentencing systems (Miethe and Moore 1989, 1). In conducting a follow-up on the effect of the guidelines researchers found that:

- Imprisonment rates crept up during the transition period but remained lower than they had been before implementation of guidelines. In marked contrast, other states have seen their incarceration rates increase after they implemented determinate sentencing.
- As time wore on, judges were more and more likely to depart from the guidelines. Nonetheless, four years after implementation, judges were staying within the guidelines in more than 90 percent of their sentencing decisions.
- Judges increased the proportion of cases in which they gave jail sentences as a condition of probation, from 44 to 66 percent. As a result, although the state prisons did not experience crowding problems, the local jails did have problems with managing increasing populations.
- Initially, the guidelines resulted in improvements in uniformity and proportionality of sentences, but these improvements declined in the later years.
- Prosecutors adjusted their charging and plea negotiation practices to circumvent the guidelines when they saw them as unreasonable. (Miethe and Moore 1989, 3–4)

The same study concluded:

Based on the criteria used in this study, the successes of Minnesota's experiment in sentencing reform are indisputable. Compared with preguideline practices, sentencing in Minnesota is more uniform, more predictable, and more socioeconomically neutral than it was before the guidelines. Findings show that violent offenders are more likely to be imprisoned now than before the guidelines. And these changes were accomplished without placing additional burdens on State correctional resources. (Miethe and Moore 1989, 5)

The experience with determinate sentencing in other states has been less positive, however. According to an analysis of the sentencing structures of all fifty states undertaken in the mid-1980s:

the commonality of the reforms indicates that when sentencing laws were changed, penalties, almost entirely, were increased, mandatory minimum terms were enacted, repeater or habitual criminal laws enacted [sic] or tightened or eliminated altogether. . . . An ancillary commonality . . . is that almost every state is facing grave

HARD TIME

Is time running out on mandatory sentences for certain federal crimes?

The ABA, in urging Congress to hold hearings to consider the impact of mandatory minimum sentencing on the nation's fight against crime, joins a growing list of groups questioning the merits of the tactic.

ABA policy opposing mandatory minimum sentencing, which dates back to 1974, is rooted in the belief that it imposes a rigidity on the sentencing process that can thwart justice, takes discretionary sentencing out of the hands of judges, and gives the public false expectations about mandatory minimums as a crime-fighting measure.

The debate over mandatory minimum sentencing is heating up. While Congress has addressed the nation's crime problem, particularly the increase in drug-related crime, by imposing mandatory minimum sentences for more than 100 federal crimes found in 60 statutes, the wisdom of such sentences is being questioned in light of a burgeoning prison population and seemingly marginal impact on criminal behavior.

The issue came to the fore in August 1991, when the U.S. Sentencing Commission released a report concluding that mandatory minimum sentences clash with the concept of sentencing guidelines, are not being applied appropriately, and have led to increased racial disparities in sentencing.

Sentencing guidelines developed by the commission went into effect in 1987 in an effort to reduce unwarranted disparities among sentences imposed by different judges for the same crime. The guidelines established sentencing ranges to be considered by judges.

But as guidelines were being incorporated into the federal judicial system, Congress enacted numerous statutes setting certain minimum sentences and mandating that they be incorporated into the guidelines structure. Such proposals also were included in proposed omnibus crime legislation pending at the end of the 102nd Congress last year.

The Sentencing Commission's 1991 study found that judges generally believe the mandatory minimum sentencing requirements are too harsh and eliminate judicial discretion. U.S. attorneys indicated that they hesitate to charge defendants with certain crimes carrying stringent mandatory minimums.

Sentencing disparities uncovered by the commission were based on factors such as race, gender, crime rates, caseloads, circuit, and prosecutorial practices.

Black defendants received the highest percentage of sentences at or above the mandatory minimum, followed by Hispanics and whites, the study found. White defendants received lesser sentences than black and Hispanic defendants convicted of similar crimes, and female defendants were less likely to be sentenced at

problems with overcrowding, and many states are building new penal institutions. (Shane-DuBow et al. 1985, 279)

Florida, for example, established statewide guidelines in 1983. The guidelines emphasized incapacitation of repeat offenders, increasing sentence severity for offenders with lengthy criminal records, even if their earlier offenses were relatively minor. As a result prison populations increased as persistent minor offenders were increasingly sentenced to prison under the guidelines (Griswold 1985). Mandatory sentencing provisions have created similar problems. Under the mandatory sentencing provisions enacted in Arizona more than 50 percent of the prison population was sentenced under a mandatory sentencing provision. Researchers estimated that the increased sentence lengths produced by mandatory sentencing would increase costs by 48.3 percent (Fischer and Thaker 1992).

Overall, the results of sentencing reform have been mixed. Judges tend to ignore voluntary guidelines, which results in continued disparity. Conversely, or above the mandatory minimum level than male defendants.

The commission also found that prison terms required by mandatory minimum sentences often outweigh the severity of the offenses and the culpability of the offenders. Non-violent first-time offenders often receive longer sentences than those with long criminal records who may have more information to offer in exchange for reduced sentences as part of the plea-bargaining process.

PACKING PRISONS

Mandatory minimums, the new guidelines and other factors have contributed to an increase in the federal prison population from 20,000 in 1980 to 80,000 in 1992. In 1992, federal prison costs were $2.3 billion.

The General Accounting Office (GAO) projected a total of 106,000 inmates by 1996, and the federal Bureau of Prisons is predicting federal prison population of 133,000 by 2000.

Inmates who have been convicted under drug statutes constitute 57 percent of all federal prisoners, and the GAO projects that, three years from now [1996], this segment of prisoners will comprise two-thirds of the federal inmate population. Many of these prisoners will be incarcerated under the mandatory statutes.

"Mandatory minimums have created huge new numbers of prisoners that our already overburdened prison system simply cannot accommodate," according to Rep. Don Edwards,

D-Calif., who sponsored legislation in 1992 that would repeal such sentences.

Edwards argues that the creation of mandatory minimums has been a primary cause of prison overcrowding because judges have little or no discretion to sentence certain offenders to noncustodial sentences. Mandatory minimums also burden the judicial system, he adds, by reducing the incentive of defendants to plead guilty in hopes of receiving lighter sentences.

The ABA, the Federal Court Study Committee created by Congress, the U.S. Judicial Conference, judges in 12 federal circuits and numerous criminal justice organizations all support legislation to repeal mandatory minimum sentences. A bill seeking their repeal is expected to be reintroduced by Edwards early this Congress.

The Department of Justice, however, is on record supporting mandatory minimum sentences.

Under Bush, the Justice Department viewed mandatory minimum sentences as a complement to sentencing guidelines that set baselines for sentences and reinforced predictability of punishment. At the time President Bill Clinton entered office, he had not stated a position on the issue.

SOURCE: Reprinted from Rhonda McMillion 1993. "Hard Time: Mandatory Minimum Sentencing Comes Under Congressional Scrutiny." *ABA Journal* 79 (March): 100. Reprinted by permission of the *ABA Journal*.

those jurisdictions that restrict judicial discretion only shift discretion to prosecutors, who adjust their charging decisions and plea agreements in light of sentencing guidelines. In addition, sentencing reforms have been blamed for the dramatic increase in prison populations during the 1980s.

■ SPECIAL ISSUE: THE DEATH PENALTY

The power to impose a sentence of death is one of the most momentous in the criminal court process. From 1977 to 1991 more than 150 sentenced offenders were executed, and more than 2,700 awaited execution on death row on April 20, 1993 (BJS 1992b, 12; Maguire et al. 1993, 670). Of the states authorizing the death penalty, only sixteen states actually carried out executions between 1977 and 1991 (BJS 1992b, 12). Just four states—Texas, Florida, Louisiana, and Georgia—executed more than two-thirds of the offenders put to death during the same period (Maguire et al. 1993, 678). Of the 130 prisoners removed from death row in 1991, fewer than 11 percent were executed, almost 60 percent had their sentences vacated by an appellate court, and about 22 percent had both their sentence and conviction vacated (Maguire and Pastore 1994, 673). Methods of execution authorized by state laws include lethal injection, electrocution, lethal gas, hanging, and firing squad. Although more states authorize execution by lethal injection than any other method, most actual executions are carried out by electrocution. Seventeen states authorize the death penalty for offenders younger than eighteen (BJS 1992b, 7).

Death and the Eighth Amendment

The Supreme Court has never held that the death penalty per se is a violation of the Eighth Amendment. However, it has held that the death penalty is disproportionate for some offenses and that the death penalty may violate the Eighth Amendment if it is applied in an arbitrary and capricious manner (*Furman v. Georgia* 1972). In addition, through the *Weems* doctrine of evolving standards, (*Weems v. United States* 1910), the Court has left the door open for some future Court to rule that the death penalty is not constitutionally tolerable in a civilized society.

The Court has found the death penalty to be disproportionate for some offenses and for some types of offenders. In its decision in *Coker v. Georgia* (1977) the Supreme Court held that the death penalty is disproportionately severe for the crime of rape. Before *Coker* several states authorized sentences of death for the crimes of robbery, rape, and kidnapping. The Court held that the death penalty is "grossly disproportionate and excessive punishment for the crime of rape and is therefore forbidden by the Eighth Amendment as cruel and unusual punishment" (592). On the other hand, the Supreme Court has declared the death penalty to be proportionate to the crime in cases of murder in which aggravating factors justify this most serious of penalties. The Supreme Court has approved of death sentencing procedures that guide discretion and require the sentencing authority to weigh aggravating and mitigating factors.

During the 1960s public opinion was evenly divided between those favoring the death penalty and those opposing it (White 1991, 24). Many believed that the Court's decision in *Furman v. Georgia* (1972) would bring the permanent abolition of capital punishment in this country. In *Furman* the Court held that the death penalty violated the Eighth and Fourteenth Amendments as it had been applied in the cases before the Court. The Court offered no single rationale for its decision; there were nine separate opinions filed, five in support of the decision and four in dissent. The clearest message from the Court in *Furman* was that the Constitution prohibits the imposition of the death penalty under statutes that allow jurors to impose the death penalty without any guidance, allowing arbitrary and capricious decisions. Two concurring justices argued that the death penalty should be held unconstitutional under all circumstances. Three justices invalidated Georgia's death penalty statute on more narrow grounds, leaving open the question of whether a state could fashion a death penalty statute that would avoid the arbitrary and capricious nature of Georgia's law.

Several members of the Court viewed the Georgia law as defective because it offered no guidance to courts regarding those situations in which the death penalty should be imposed. As a result some defendants received the death penalty in circumstances indistinguishable from those of other defendants sentenced to prison. Because many state death penalty laws allowed the same kind of arbitrary and capricious results complained of in the Georgia statute, states began to draft new death penalty laws that would pass constitutional scrutiny. Thirty-five states enacted death penalty statutes between 1972 and 1977. The solution adopted in a number of states, and later approved by the Court in *Gregg v. Georgia* (1976), was to provide legislative guidelines that allow individualized consideration of the crime and the offender in imposing the death penalty.

In a series of cases the Court clarified which procedures and considerations are permissible in determining who is to be sentenced to die and who is to be spared the death penalty. The Court approved a bifurcated trial process, in which the jury first decides the question of guilt and only later returns to hear additional evidence relevant to sentencing. Death penalty statutes must afford the offender an opportunity to establish mitigating circumstances to be considered by the sentencing authority. Mandatory death penalty statutes cannot meet this requirement. The sentencing authority must have discretion, but that discretion must be guided by statutory standards. Specifically, death penalty statutes must guide discretion by specifying the aggravating and mitigating factors to be considered in imposing the sentence (see Figure 17-5). Specific individualized evidence must be presented in support of finding aggravating circumstances in order to justify the death penalty. Finally, the state must provide for broad appellate review of the death sentence to ensure that the sentence is not being imposed unfairly in relation to other defendants convicted of similar crimes.

After the *Gregg* decision the focus of death penalty litigation turned to issues of due process and equal protection under the Fourteenth Amendment. The equal protection argument against the death penalty rests on the apparent association between race and imposition of the death penalty.

Racial Disparity, Equal Protection, and the Death Penalty

For many years research indicated that racial biases operate to make black defendants more vulnerable to the death penalty than white defendants. For example, black men who raped white women were much more likely to receive the death penalty than other criminals. In the *Furman* (1972) decision two concurring justices noted that racial discrimination in the application of the death penalty was a factor in their decision to hold the death penalty unconstitutional (White 1991, 135).

More recent research has not found the race of the defendant to be a factor in the imposition of the death penalty. Beginning in the early 1980s research showed that the discrimination against black defendants that was apparent before the *Furman* decision no longer appeared to be operating. However, the race of the victim does appear to influence the sentence. "A number of recent studies show that blacks who murder whites incur a greater risk of receiving the death penalty than blacks who murder blacks, or whites who murder whites or blacks," write Cassia Spohn and Jerry Cederblom (1991, 307). Another study (Baldus, Pulaski, and Woodworth 1983), using data from Georgia, found that the killer of a white victim was 4.3 times more likely to receive the death penalty than the killer of a black victim. A similar study in Kentucky found that "regardless of the seriousness of the homicide, Kentucky prosecutors and jurors were most likely to recommend a death sentence for blacks who killed whites" (Spohn and Cederblom

FIGURE 17-5   Aggravating and Mitigating Factors and the Death Penalty

SOURCE: Reprinted from Howard Myers and Jan Pudlow. 1991. *The Trial: A Procedural Description and Case Study*. St. Paul, Minn.: West, p. 167. Reprinted by permission. Copyright © 1991 by West Publishing Co. All Rights Reserved.

Aggravating Circumstances

1. The capital felony was committed by a person under sentence of imprisonment;
2. The defendant was previously convicted of another capital felony or felony involving the use of threat or [sic] violence to the person;
3. The defendant knowingly created a great risk of death to many persons;
4. The capital felony was committed while the defendant was engaged or was an accomplice in the commission of or attempt to commit flight after committing or attempting to commit a robbery, sexual battery, arson, burglary, kidnapping, aircraft piracy, or unlawful throwing, placing or discharging of an obstructive device or bomb;
5. The capital felony was committed for the purpose of avoiding or preventing a lawful arrest or affecting [sic] an escape from custody;
6. The capital felony was committed for pecuniary gain;
7. The capital felony was committed to disrupt or hinder the lawful exercise of any government function or the enforcement of laws;
8. The capital felony was especially heinous, atrocious, or cruel;
9. The capital felony was a homicide committed in a cold, calculated, and premeditated manner without any pretense of moral or legal justification;
10. The victim of the capital felony was a law enforcement officer engaged in the performance of official duties;
11. The victim of the capital felony was an elected or appointed public official engaged in the performance of his official duties if the motive for capital felony was related, in whole or in part, to the victim's official capacity.

Mitigating Circumstances

1. The defendant has no significant history of prior criminal activity;
2. The capital felony was committed while the defendant was under the influence of extreme mental or emotional disturbance;
3. The victim was a participant in the defendant's conduct or consented to the act;
4. The defendant was an accomplice in the capital felony committed by another person, and the defendant's participation was relatively minor;
5. The defendant acted under extreme duress or under the substantial domination of another person;
6. The capacity of the defendant to appreciate the criminality of his conduct or to conform his conduct to the requirements of law was substantially impaired;
7. Age of defendant at time of the crime;
8. Any other aspect of the defendant's character or record, and any other circumstance of the offense. Mitigating circumstance Number Eight includes such conditions as having been abused as a child, being an alcoholic, having experienced religious conversion, expressing genuine remorse, having been a model prisoner while awaiting trial, and having experienced extreme mental or emotional disturbance at the time the offense was committed.

1991, 308). Furthermore, consistent with the liberation hypothesis described earlier, the racial disparity in the imposition of the death penalty appears to be greatest in those cases in which the seriousness and culpability of the homicide are ambiguous (Barnett 1985).

The equal protection clause is meant to ensure that similarly situated individuals are treated similarly without regard to irrelevant factors such as race or religion. If killers of white victims are more likely to receive the death penalty than killers of people of other races, should the death penalty be invalidated on equal protection grounds? This was the issue raised in *McCleskey v. Kemp* (1987). In a 5–4 vote the Supreme Court held that Georgia's imposition of the death penalty did not violate the equal protection clause. Despite evidence of the effects of race provided by researchers (Baldus et al. 1983), the Court held that death sentencing in Georgia was not racially discriminatory (White 1991, 158). The Court held that in order to prove a violation of equal protection, the defendant needs to show discriminatory intent that actually has a discriminatory effect on the defendant's sentence. In addition, the majority held that statistical evidence is inappropriate in relation to the death penalty, arguing that the petit jury in capital cases considers innumerable characteristics of the individual and the particular facts of the crime (Erickson et al. 1992, 13–73). According to the Court, the study was unable to capture all the unique attributes of the offender and offense that might be considered by the jury in justifying the death penalty. The Court also rejected the defendant's claim that Georgia purposely discriminated against blacks in adopting and maintaining a death penalty statute. To prove discrimination the defendant would have to show that the "legislature enacted the [death penalty] statute *because of,* not merely in spite of, its adverse effects on an identifiable group" (Erickson et al. 1992, 13–74). This ruling sets a high standard of proof to show discrimination in capital sentencing. According to one author,

> After *McCleskey,* statistical studies showing bias in capital sentencing are not likely to have an impact in the litigation of capital cases. Unless a legislature addresses the problem of racism in capital sentencing, a capital defendant will be able to invalidate his death sentence only if he can show that "decisionmakers in his case acted with a discriminatory purpose." Barring the unusual situation in which the defendant can present evidence relating to the particular prosecution—a prosecutor's statement that he was charging the defendant because of the race of the victim, for example— establishing such a purpose will be extremely difficult. (White 1991, 159)

The Prosecutor's Role in Capital Sentencing

In most jurisdictions part of the prosecutor's charging decision in a homicide case is whether to request the death penalty. If prosecutorial discretion is arbitrary or capricious, the same concerns arise that led the Court to invalidate death penalty statutes in the *Furman* decision. The prosecutor's decision not to request the death penalty may be made on arbitrary or capricious grounds, but this decision is not subject to review. Further, the death penalty often becomes a major focus of plea negotiations in death penalty cases. One researcher (White 1991) describes the incentives of defense lawyers and prosecutors to engage in plea bargaining in relation to the death penalty. Although some prosecutors are reluctant to bargain with defendants facing the possibility of a death sentence, and some prosecutors' offices have guidelines to control such bargaining, bargaining in regard to the

BARGAINING FOR LIFE

[Sandra] Lockett was prosecuted for murder as a result of her involvement in the killing of a pawnshop owner. According to the state's evidence, Lockett, Al Parker, and two others discussed various ways of obtaining money. Lockett suggested the idea of a robbery and led the group to a pawnshop. There was never any talk about killing anybody. During the holdup, Parker held a gun on the victim, the victim grabbed for it, and the gun accidentally went off, killing the victim. Parker and his companions fled. Parker rejoined Lockett in the car, and the two of them drove away.

Before trial, Lockett was offered an opportunity to plead guilty to voluntary manslaughter and aggravated robbery if she would cooperate with the state. After the government had "prepared its case" (i.e., obtained the testimony of Parker in exchange for a plea bargain), it made Lockett a slightly less generous offer. She would be allowed to avoid any possibility of the death penalty by pleading guilty to aggravated murder. Both of these offers were rejected. Lockett subsequently went to trial, was found guilty of aggravated murder with two specifications, and was sentenced to death.

As Charles Black [legal scholar] has said, the Lockett case "spins off many problems." On the most obvious level, it seems anomalous that Lockett should be sentenced to death when her involvement in the killing was so minimal. She

did not fire the shot that killed the pawnshop operator, she did not intend that he should die, and she was not even present when he was killed. If the new system of capital punishment is designed to select only the most heinous criminals for execution, it seems ironic that Sandra Lockett was one of those selected.

The irony is heightened when Lockett's death penalty is considered in the context of the plea bargaining that took place in that case. Since Parker was the actual killer of the pawnshop owner, it would seem that if anyone should receive the death penalty it should be him. Yet Parker entered into a plea bargain under which he pled guilty to murder and testified on behalf of the government; in exchange, he received a life sentence. Lockett, on the other hand, went to trial and was sentenced to death.

[Lockett appealed her conviction and confinement. The U.S. Supreme Court set aside her death sentence on the grounds that Ohio's death penalty statute did not permit the judge to consider mitigating factors with respect to the defendant's character and record (*Lockett v. Ohio* 1978). See Chapter 18 for a description of the appeals in Lockett's case.]

SOURCE: Reprinted from Welsh S. White. 1991. *The Death Penalty in the Nineties: An Examination of the Modern System of Capital Punishment.* Ann Arbor: University of Michigan Press, pp. 60–61.

death penalty appears to be quite common. As with noncapital sentencing, when the plea agreement affects the sentence, sentencing discretion really resides in the office of the prosecutor rather than with the court. "Since plea bargaining is widely employed in capital cases, its effects on the selection of those sentenced to death will be pervasive, and it will dramatically skew the extent to which the death penalty is even-handedly applied" (White 1991, 62).

Conclusion: The Death Penalty in the Future

Social scientists have not been successful in persuading the Supreme Court that the death penalty does not deter and that it is imposed in a discriminatory way. Ironically, the Court has appeared to be responsive to social science surveys of public opinion indicating widespread and growing support for the death penalty. Surveys suggest that more than 70 percent of the public favors the death penalty (Bowers 1993).

However, a careful look at public responses to questions about the death penalty suggests that public support for the death penalty is soft. Specifically, public support for the death penalty declines precipitously when survey respondents are given a choice between the death penalty and life imprisonment without parole but with mandatory restitution to the victim's family (Bowers 1993, 163). Although the Supreme Court may continue to decline to find a prohibition of the death penalty in the Constitution, shifting public sentiments and the development of meaningful alternatives to the death penalty may lead states to abandon the death penalty. Finally, the *Weems* doctrine of evolving standards leaves open the possibility that the Court may one day find the death penalty to be cruel and unusual.

◼ SUMMARY

After conviction, the court imposes a sentence based on the justifications of retribution, deterrence, incapacitation, rehabilitation, and/or restitution. Courts today have a wide range of options, including death, incarceration, and community-based sanctions such as probation. Prison overcrowding has encouraged the development and use of intermediate sanctions such as shock probation and electronic monitoring. Most states continue to use an indeterminate sentencing system, which gives the sentencing judge broad discretion. Since the mid-1970s, however, a significant number of states have reformed their sentencing systems to reduce judicial discretion, by requiring more determinate sentencing, and to eliminate the parole decision.

Although formal authority for sentencing belongs to the judge, or in limited cases to the jury, the prosecutor possesses enormous influence over the sentence through the charging and plea-bargaining processes. The highest charge and the number of charges determine the maximum sentence. In addition, a plea agreement may include a specific sentence recommendation, which the judge accepts in accepting the plea agreement. Even in death penalty cases the prosecutor may agree not to pursue a capital charge or seek the death penalty in exchange for a guilty plea. Prosecutors may also be able to manipulate sentence lengths in determinate sentencing systems by controlling the type of information about aggravating and mitigating circumstances that is presented in court.

This prosecutorial influence on sentencing complicates the problem of measuring sentencing disparity. Disparity in judicial sentencing may be masked by the discretionary decisions of prosecutors made long before the sentencing hearing. Research on sentence disparity suggests that disparity is greatest for those offenses that present ambiguous circumstances. Cases that clearly merit lenience or severity tend to be treated on their merits. It is in the middle-range cases, where the "right" outcome is less clear, that defendant characteristics, including race and gender, are most likely to have an effect on the sentence imposed.

◼ FOR FURTHER DISCUSSION

1. What systemic pressures are driving innovation in the direction of intermediate sanctions? Which goals of sentencing are fulfilled by house arrest with electronic monitoring? How should the effectiveness of intermediate sanctions be judged?

2. Some people have objected to the use of victim impact statements on the ground that the effect on the victim is not relevant. The relevant issue is the harm intended by the defendant. Suppose two defendants are to be sentenced. Both committed the same crime, shooting a store clerk in the course of a robbery. In one case the bullet hit only soft tissue and did no permanent damage. In the other the bullet hit the victim's spine, causing permanent paralysis. Should the defendant in the second case receive a harsher sentence than the defendant in the first? Why? How should considerations of victim impact be balanced against considerations of sentence disparity?

3. Mandatory sentences and the relatively new three-strikes provisions seem to be premised on distrust of criminal justice professionals to exercise the sense of justice demanded by the public and legislators. If prosecutors and judges are out of touch with community sentiment in relation to sentencing, why does the public seem to prefer to reduce prosecutorial and judicial discretion rather than elect tougher prosecutors and judges?

4. According to the liberation hypothesis, the more clear and less ambiguous the facts, and the more serious the crime, the less disparity exists in sentencing. If this is the case, what additional function is served by three-strikes provisions?

5. Consider the armed robbery case, described above, in which Al Parker pled guilty, avoiding the death penalty, but Sandra Lockett, who was less culpable, pled not guilty, was convicted and sentenced to death. Do you think that imposition of the death sentence was fair in this case? Why or why not? If not, what remedies might prevent such injustices in the future?

■ REFERENCES

American Friends Service Committee. 1971. *Struggle for Justice.* New York: Hill and Wang.

Andrews, D. A., Ivan Zinger, Robert D. Hoge, James Bonta, Paul Gendreau, and Francis T. Cullen. 1990. "Does Correctional Treatment Work? A Clinically Relevant and Psychologically Informed Meta-analysis." *Criminology* 28 (August): 369–404, 419–426.

Baldus, David C., Charles Pulaski, and George Woodworth. 1983. "Comparative Review of Death Sentences: An Empirical Study of the Georgia Experience." *Journal of Criminal Law and Criminology* 74: 661–753.

Barnett, Arnold. 1985. "Some Distribution Patterns for the Georgia Death Sentence." *U.C. Davis Law Review* 18: 1327–74.

Barnett, Arnold, Alfred Blumstein, and David P. Farrington. 1987. "Probabilistic Models of Youthful Criminal Careers." *Criminology* 25 (February): 83–107.

Bedau, Hugo Adam. 1982. *The Death Penalty in America,* 3d ed. New York: Oxford University Press.

Berry, Bonnie. 1985. "Electronic Jails: A New Criminal Justice Concern." *Justice Quarterly* 2 (March): 1–22.

Blumstein, A., J. Cohen, J. Roth, and C. Visher. 1986. *Criminal Careers and "Career Criminals,"* Vol. 1. Washington, D.C.: National Academy Press.

Bowers, William. 1993. "Capital Punishment and Contemporary Values: People's Misgivings and the Court's Misperceptions." *Law and Society Review* 27 (1): 157–75.

Carter, Robert M., and Leslie T. Wilkins. 1967. "Some Factors in Sentencing Policy." *Journal of Criminal Law, Criminology, and Police Science* 58: 503–14.

Clear, Todd R., Val B. Clear, and William D. Burrell. 1989. *Offender Assessment and Evaluation.* Cincinnati: Anderson.

Cohen, J. 1983. "Incapacitation as a Strategy for Crime Control: Possibilities and Pitfalls." In Michael Tonry and Norval Morris, eds., *Crime and Justice: An Annual Review of Research,* Vol. 5. Chicago: University of Chicago Press.

Cohen, Stanley. 1985. *Visions of Social Control.* Cambridge, U.K.: Polity Press.

Coker v. Georgia, 433 U.S. 584, 97 S. Ct. 2861 (1977).

Czajkoski, Eugene H., and Laurin A. Wollan, Jr. 1986. "Opinion and Debate: Creative Sentencing: A Critical Analysis." *Justice Quarterly* 3 (June): 215–29.

Dershowitz, Alan. 1976. *Fair and Certain Punishment.* New York: McGraw-Hill.

Erez, Edna, and Pamela Tontodonato. 1992. "Victim Participation in Sentencing and Satisfaction with Justice." *Justice Quarterly* 9 (September): 393–415.

——— 1990. "The Effect of Victim Participation in Sentencing on Sentence Outcome." *Criminology* 28 (August): 451–74.

Erickson, William H., William D. Neighbors, and B. J. George, Jr. 1992. *United States Supreme Court Cases and Comments.* New York: Matthew Bender.

Finckenauer, James O. 1978. "Crime as a National Political Issue: 1967–76." *Crime and Delinquency* 24: 13–27.

Fischer, Daryl R., and Andy Thaker. 1992. *Mandatory Sentencing Study.* Phoenix: Arizona Department of Corrections.

Friel, Charles M., Joseph P. Vaughn, and Rolando del Carmen. 1987. *Electronic Monitoring and Correctional Policy: The Technology and Its Application.* Washington, D.C.: U.S. Department of Justice.

Furman v. Georgia, 408 U.S. 238, 92 S. Ct. 2726 (1972).

Gardner v. Florida, 430 U.S. 349, 97 S. Ct. 1197 (1977).

Gibbs, Jack, and Glenn Firebaugh. 1990. "The Artifact Issue in Deterrence Research." *Criminology* 28 (May): 347–67.

Gowdy, Voncile B. 1993. *Intermediate Sanctions.* Research in Brief, National Institute of Justice. Washington, D.C.: U.S. Department of Justice.

Greenwood, Peter, and A. Abrahamse. 1982. *Selective Incapacitation.* Santa Monica, Calif.: Rand.

Greenwood, Peter, and Susan Turner. 1987. *Selective Incapacitation Revisited: Why the High-Rate Offenders Are Hard to Predict.* Santa Monica, Calif.: Rand.

Gregg v. Georgia, 428 U.S. 153, 96 S. Ct. 2909 (1976).

Griswold, D. B. 1985. "Florida's Sentencing Guidelines—Progression or Regression?" *Federal Probation* 49 (March): 25–32.

Haapanen, Rudy A. 1990. *Selective Incapacitation and the Serious Offender: A Longitudinal Study of Criminal Career Patterns.* New York: Springer-Verlag.

Hagan, John. 1975. "The Social and Legal Construction of Criminal Justice: A Study of the Presentence Process." *Social Problems* 22: 620–37.

Hillsman, Sally T., and Judith A. Greene. 1988. "Tailoring Criminal Fines to the Financial Means of the Offender." *Judicature* 72 (June–July): 38–45.

Hillsman, Sally T., Barry Mahoney, George F. Cole, and Bernard Auchter. 1987. *Fines as Criminal Sanctions.* Washington, D.C.: U.S. Department of Justice.

Hillsman, Sally T., Joyce L. Sichel, and Barry Mahoney. 1984. *Fines in Sentencing: A Study of the Use of the Fine as a Criminal Sanction.* Executive Summary. Washington, D.C.: U.S. Department of Justice.

Kalven, Harry, Jr., and Hans Zeisel. 1966. *The American Jury.* Boston: Little, Brown.

Knapp, Kay A. 1988. "Structured Sentencing: Building on Experience." *Judicature* 72 (June–July): 46–52.

Kramer, John H., Robin L. Lubitz, and Cynthia A. Kempinen. 1989. "Sentencing Guidelines: A Quantitative Comparison of Sentencing Policy in Minnesota, Pennsylvania, and Washington." *Justice Quarterly* 6 (December): 565–587.

Lilly, J. Robert, Richard A. Ball, and W. Robert Lotz, Jr. 1986. "Electronic Jail Revisited." *Justice Quarterly* 3 (September): 353–61.

Link, Christopher T., and Neal Shover. 1986. "The Origins of Criminal Sentencing Reforms." *Justice Quarterly* 3 (September): 329–41.

Lockett v. Ohio, 438 U.S. 586, 98 S. Ct. 2954 (1978).

MacKenzie, Doris Layton. 1990. " 'Boot Camp' Programs Grow in Number and Scope." *National Institute of Justice Reports* (November–December): 21–28.

Maguire, Kathleen, and Ann L. Pastore. 1994. *Sourcebook of Criminal Justice Statistics— 1993*. Washington, D.C.: U.S. Government Printing Office.

Maguire, Kathleen, Ann L. Pastore, and Timothy J. Flanagan. 1993. *Sourcebook of Criminal Justice Statistics— 1992*. Washington, D.C.: U.S. Government Printing Office.

Marquart, James W., and Jonathan R. Sorensen. 1988. "Institutional and Postrelease Behavior of *Furman*-Commuted Inmates in Texas." *Criminology* 26 (November): 677–93.

Martinson, Robert. 1974. "What Works? Questions and Answers About Prison Reform." *Public Interest* 35: 22–54.

Mauer, Marc. 1991. *Americans Behind Bars: A Comparison of International Rates of Incarceration*. Washington, D.C.: Sentencing Project.

McCleskey v. Kemp, 481 U.S. 279, 107 S. Ct. 1756 (1987).

Mempa v. Rhay, 389 U.S. 128, 88 S. Ct. 254 (1967).

Miethe, Terance, and Charles A. Moore. 1989. *Sentencing Guidelines: Their Effect in Minnesota*. Washington, D.C.: U.S. Department of Justice.

Newman, Graeme. 1978. *The Punishment Response*. New York: Lippincott.

Paternoster, Raymond. 1987. "The Deterrent Effect of Perceived Certainty and Severity of Punishment: A Review of the Evidence and Issues." *Justice Quarterly* 4 (June): 173–217.

Petersilia, Joan. 1987. *Expanding Options for Criminal Sanctioning*. Santa Monica, Calif.: Rand.

Rodgers, T. A., G. T. Gitchoff, and I. Paur. 1984. "The Privately Commissioned Presentence Report." In Robert M. Carter, Daniel Glaser, and Leslie T. Wilkins, eds. *Probation, Parole, and Community Corrections*. New York: Wiley.

Rosecrance, John. 1988. "Maintaining the Myth of Individualized Justice: Probation Presentence Reports." *Justice Quarterly* 5 (June): 235–56.

Shane-DuBow, Sandra, Alice P. Brown, and Erik Olsen. 1985. *Sentencing Reform in the United States: History, Content, and Effect*. Washington, D.C.: U.S. Department of Justice.

Solari, Richard. 1992. *National Judicial Reporting Program, 1988*. Washington, D.C.: U.S. Department of Justice, Bureau of Justice Statistics.

Solem v. Helm, 463 U.S. 277, 103 S. Ct. 3001 (1983).

Spohn, Cassia, and Jerry Cederblom. 1991. "Race and Disparities in Sentencing: A Test of the Liberation Hypothesis." *Justice Quarterly* 8 (September): 305–27.

Tonry, Michael, and Norval Morris. 1990. *Between Prison and Probation*. New York: Oxford University Press.

Trop v. Dulles, 356 U.S. 86, 78 S. Ct. 590 (1958).

U.S. Bureau of Justice Statistics. 1993. *Felony Defendants in Large Urban Counties, 1990*. Washington, D.C.: U.S. Department of Justice.

——— 1992a. *Recidivism of Felons on Probation, 1986–89*. BJS Special Report. Washington, D.C.: U.S. Department of Justice.

——— 1992b. *Capital Punishment 1991*. Washington, D.C.: U.S. Department of Justice.

——— 1988. *Report to the Nation on Crime and Justice,* 2d ed. Washington, D.C.: U.S. Department of Justice.

van den Haag, Ernst. 1977. *Punishing Criminals*. New York: Basic Books.

Von Hirsch, Andrew. 1976. *Doing Justice—The Choice of Punishment*. New York: Hill and Wang.

Walsh, Anthony. 1985. "The Role of the Probation Officer in the Sentencing Process." *Criminal Justice and Behavior* 12: 289–303.

Weems v. United States, 217 U.S. 349, 30 S. Ct. 544 (1910).

White, Welsh S. 1991. *The Death Penalty in the Nineties: An Examination of the Modern System of Capital Punishment*. Ann Arbor: University of Michigan Press.

Whitehead, John T., and Steven P. Lab. 1989. "A Meta-analysis of Juvenile Correctional Treatment." *Journal of Research in Crime and Delinquency* 26: 276–95.

Wilson, James Q. 1983. *Thinking About Crime,* rev. ed. New York: Vintage Books.

Appeals and Other Post-Conviction Remedies

Despite the numerous safeguards and checks built into the adversarial process, errors occur. Sometimes the errors are so significant that they result in a miscarriage of justice. For this reason every state has procedures for reviewing criminal convictions. The purpose of these procedures is to supervise the trial courts by correcting errors in their rulings, by maintaining uniformity of practice in all courts in the jurisdiction, and by clarifying the law as it applies to a specific case and all future cases in the jurisdiction.

When errors are found, the reviewing court may reverse or modify the order of the trial court to amend the harm that may have been done, for example, by reversing the conviction or modifying the sentence imposed by the trial court. The reviewing court also affirms, modifies, or clarifies the rule of law to be applied in similar cases. Appellate decisions provide feedback to trial courts about the appropriateness of their decisions. Through this review process, appellate courts communicate the law to all courts and all court participants in the jurisdiction. This supervisory and policy role of the appellate courts is at least as important for the system of justice as their role in correcting errors affecting individuals.

direct appeal

Two broad categories of review are direct appeal and collateral review. **Direct appeals** are a continuation of the criminal case, appealing to a higher court. All states provide for some opportunity for direct appellate review. **Collateral**

collateral review

review is a separate civil proceeding in which a convicted defendant petitions a court for release on the ground that he or she is being detained illegally. The most

writ of habeas corpus

common remedy of this sort is the **writ of habeas corpus,** a civil action challenging the legality of a prisoner's detention.

■ Pathway of Appeals and Collateral Review

The appellate process involves a series of steps in which the case moves from the trial court to progressively higher levels of appellate review and collateral review.

The case of a defendant who takes advantage of every step possible would move in the following progression:

1. Motion to the trial-level court for a new trial
2. Direct appeal to the state intermediate appellate court
3. Discretionary review in the state supreme court
4. Discretionary review in the U.S. Supreme Court of issues involving alleged violation of U.S. constitutional rights
5. Petition for collateral review in state court
6. Appeal of collateral proceeding in the state intermediate appellate court
7. Discretionary review of the collateral proceeding in the state supreme court
8. Discretionary review of the state collateral proceeding in the U.S. Supreme Court
9. Federal habeas corpus petition in U.S. District Court
10. Appeal of habeas corpus decision in the U.S. Court of Appeals
11. Discretionary review of the decision on the federal habeas petition before the U.S. Supreme Court (Carrington, Meador, and Rosenberg 1976, 105)

Variations from this general outline are numerous. For example, in some cases no direct appeal of the conviction is taken, and the case moves directly from trial to state or federal habeas corpus proceedings. No single line must be pursued all the way to the end. For example, after an unsuccessful appeal to the state intermediate appellate court a prisoner may petition for release under state or federal habeas corpus. Moreover, even if a petition for habeas corpus has been denied and all appeals of the petition exhausted, a prisoner may continue to bring new petitions for habeas corpus on new allegations of improper confinement (see Figure 18–1).

Petitions for habeas corpus and other forms of collateral relief also are brought in a trial-level court. Whichever party loses at the trial level may appeal through the regular direct appeal process. Because of the differences between direct appeals and collateral attacks, we discuss them separately.

◼ DIRECT APPEALS

Chapter 2 describes the structure of the court system. Recall that most states have created a three-tiered court system, composed of trial-level courts, intermediate courts of appeal, and the court of last resort, or supreme court. A few states retain the more traditional two-tiered structure in which all appeals are heard by the supreme court. The appellate courts review what occurred in the trial court in order to determine whether the trial court violated rules of procedure or the constitutional rights of the defendant. Appellate review is based on the record, the written transcript of all that was said in the case before the trial court. The appellate courts do not hear testimony. They do not see witnesses. Often, they do not even concern themselves with the whole of the trial court proceeding, but only that portion related to the issues on appeal. The appellate court is not a fact-finding body. A trial court is best equipped to judge the credibility of witnesses and the plausibility of their testimony, whereas the task of the appellate court does not require such judgments. The appellate courts make findings of law

FIGURE 18-1   Pathway of Appeals and Collateral Review

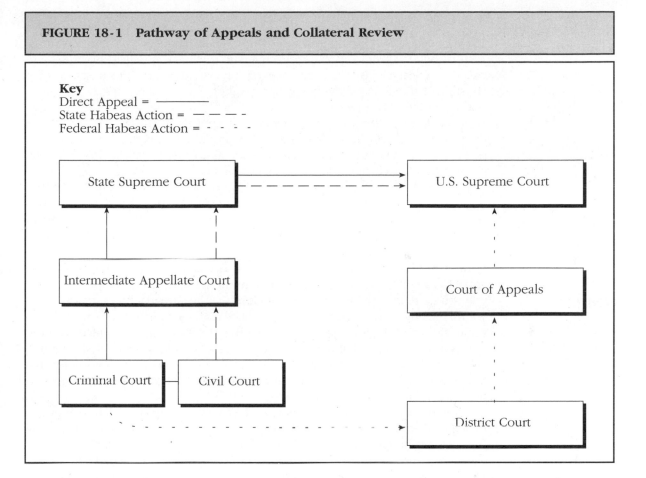

Key
Direct Appeal = ─────────
State Habeas Action = ── ── ── -
Federal Habeas Action = - - - -

based on the cold written record and the written (and sometimes oral) arguments of counsel.

A former U.S. solicitor general once commented, "There is nothing in the Constitution and nothing in common sense that says that decisions of an appellate court are more likely to be right than a district court" (Resnik 1985, 605). He was correct in pointing out that nothing in the Constitution makes appellate courts more likely to correctly interpret the law. However, common sense might suggest that decisions made by trial courts—under intense time pressure and without an opportunity for reflection and discussion with colleagues—are indeed more prone to error than the more deliberative decisions of appellate courts. Two distinguishing features of appellate decision making are the time allowed for deliberation and the collegial style.

Appellate decisions are usually made by a panel of at least three appellate judges. Unlike trial judges, who often must make decisions quickly and as they are raised in the course of the case, appellate judges have time to study the questions raised by both sides and weigh the most appropriate decision. In addition, unlike trial court judges, appellate judges can discuss the issues with one another, which sheds further light on the issues and their appropriate resolution.

Right to Appeal

There is no U.S. Constitutional right to appeal (*McKane v. Durston* 1984; *Pennsylvania v. Finlay* 1987). Consequently, the state appellate processes are created exclusively by state constitution or statute. Only fifteen states have constitutional provisions that recognize a right to appeal (Arkin 1992, 516). Most states provide for appeal under statutory law. Two states, Virginia and West Virginia, do not offer an appeal of right; all appeals in these states are at the discretion of the appellate court. Federal law provides for an appellate process for federal defendants and allows state defendants to appeal to the U.S. Supreme Court if they are claiming denial of a U.S. Constitutional right.

Because there is no constitutional right to appeal, states may limit the opportunity for appeal or restrict the rights of defendants in appellate processes. So long as the procedures do not deny defendants equal protection in seeking an appeal, the U.S. Supreme Court has found the procedures to be a matter of state discretion (Arkin 1992, 507).

appeal of right

In most states defendants have either a constitutional or statutory right to appeal to an intermediate appellate court. In these states this first appeal from the trial court is referred to as an **appeal of right**—if the defendant files for an appeal within the time period specified, the appellate court is obligated to consider it. In some states with intermediate appellate courts the initial appeal is filed with the state supreme court. That court screens the cases, decides which it will review, and refers the rest to the intermediate appellate court. Finally, in those states that have no intermediate appellate level, the first appeal after trial is made directly to the state's highest court (Meador 1991, 17).

Traditionally, defendants have not been allowed to appeal preliminary orders issued by the trial court. In general, states have allowed defendants to appeal only from the final judgment following the verdict. All objections to preliminary orders would be consolidated in a single appeal at the conclusion of the trial (Stern 1981, 52–55). This policy was designed to avoid "piecemeal adjudication" and to reduce the costs, delay, and court congestion that would arise if every intermediate decision of the trial court were subject to immediate appeal before the final decision in the case (Martineau 1987, 468).

interlocutory appeal

A major exception to the general rule of allowing appeals only after final judgment is the interlocutory appeal. An **interlocutory appeal** is an appeal initiated to obtain appellate review before the final judgment or verdict. In general, interlocutory appeals are allowed in order to correct errors that might cause irreparable damage to either party. For example, if the trial court rules an interrogation to be illegal and excludes the confession, the prosecution might seek an interlocutory appeal of the ruling, because exclusion of the evidence might seriously damage the state's case (American Bar Association [ABA] Commission 1977, 21). An interlocutory appeal may be taken when the issue involves a question of law where the proper finding of law is unclear, because good arguments can be made on both sides of the question, and when immediate review of the question will greatly influence the outcome of the case. Interlocutory appeals are one of the few situations in which the prosecution may appeal the decisions of trial courts.

Standing to Appeal

standing, appellant

Standing is a legal concept that refers to a party's eligibility to bring a matter to court. The general rule on standing to appeal is that the **appellant,** that is, the party bringing the appeal, must have "lost something" in the lower court (Stern 1981, 51). The winning party cannot appeal. This means that in a criminal case, with only some narrow exceptions, only a convicted defendant may appeal. Some jurisdictions allow a prosecutor who has lost a preliminary decision in trial court to bring an interlocutory appeal. In addition, a few states allow the prosecution to seek advisory rulings from appellate courts after the trial verdict. However, such prosecution appeals seek only a declaration of the law and do not result in the reversal of an acquittal. Consequently, in most appeals in criminal cases the **appellee,** the party responding to the appeal, is the state (Martineau 1987, 469).

appellee

Issues on Appeal

A general rule of appellate procedure requires that issues raised on appeal first must have been raised before the trial court. Trial courts must be given an opportunity to correct their errors (Stern 1981, 37). A criminal defendant cannot sit on issues, saving them for appeal in hope of obtaining a reversal from the appellate court. Errors are raised in the trial court by filing motions, raising objections, and noting exceptions to the rulings of the trial judge.

Despite this general rule, in limited circumstances an appellant may be able to raise issues not originally raised before the trial court. If the trial court's error was fundamental or plain to the reviewing court, the defendant may appeal even if the issue was not raised at the trial level. This exception is most likely to occur in the case of violations of constitutional rights. Another major exception occurs in those cases in which the defendant claims to have suffered the ineffective assistance of counsel at trial. In this situation the defendant argues that objections to improper procedures were not made during the trial because counsel was lazy or incompetent and failed to fulfill the minimal responsibilities of defense counsel. Consequently, the defendant requests that the appellate court review the errors of the trial court.

Although appeals following guilty pleas have become more common in recent years, most appeals follow convictions at trial and involve crimes against persons and sentences of five years or less (Chapper and Hanson 1989, 42). About 25 percent of appeals arise from nontrial proceedings, such as guilty pleas, revocation of probation, and denials of post-conviction relief such as habeas corpus (Chapper and Hanson 1989, 4). The issues raised on appeal vary by the type of appeal being taken. After jury trials the issues raised most frequently on appeal relate to the introduction of evidence or testimony, the sufficiency of the evidence supporting conviction, and the instructions given to the jury.

Appeals relating to the sentence may challenge an enhanced sentence, the imposition of consecutive rather than concurrent prison terms, procedural problems at the sentencing hearing, and the consideration of prohibited factors (such as a defendant's not guilty plea) in imposing the sentence (Chapper and Hanson 1989, 6). Sentencing appeals have been increasing in recent years, despite a long tradition of disallowing appeals of the sentence (Chapper and Hanson 1989, 8). A number of organizations and advisory bodies, including the American Bar Association and the National Advisory Commission on Criminal Justice Standards and Goals, have recommended the expansion of sentence review. When sentence appeals are allowed, they usually concern issues related to the reasonableness or excessiveness of the sentence or clear departures from sentencing standards (Carrington et al. 1976, 97).

Appellate Procedure

Some states require defendants to file a motion for a new trial before they can file a notice to appeal (Carrington et al. 1976, 105). Once the trial court rejects the motion for a new trial, the defendant must file the notice of appeal within a certain number of days, usually within thirty, of the trial court judgment or denial of the motion for a new trial. Failure to file within the legal time limit results in dismissal of the appeal, regardless of the merits of the appellant's case. Once the time limit is past, the only recourse is collateral review.

In many states the notice of appeal is filed with the trial court. Notice of appeal initiates preparation of the court transcript and other records that must be sent to the appellate court for consideration of the appeal. A typist transcribes the verbatim court record as recorded by the court stenographer. This is time consuming and expensive, costing several hundred dollars. When state law provides that an appeal is a right, indigent defendants have a right to receive a transcript at no cost so that their inability to pay for a transcript does not block their equal access to the appellate courts (*Griffin v. Illinois* 1956).

In addition, when the state provides a right to appeal, poor defendants have a constitutional right under the equal protection clause of the Fourteenth Amendment to obtain counsel for the appeal (*Douglas v. California* 1963). When the appeal is discretionary, however, the state is not required to provide counsel for the indigent (*Ross v. Moffitt* 1974).

Filing an appeal does not automatically stay (or postpone) the judgment of the trial court. A convicted defendant is usually taken to prison even though an appeal is pending. In some cases the trial court may grant a motion to stay the judgment pending appeal. Courts consider four factors in deciding whether to grant a stay: the likelihood that the appellant will prevail upon appeal, the probability that the appellant will suffer irreparable harm in the absence of a stay, the harm that the appellee may suffer if relief is granted, and the public interest (Martineau 1987, 471). In cases of serious crime the public interest typically is judged to outweigh the potential harm to the appellant, and stays are not routinely granted.

Briefing the Issues

Most appeals raise only one or two issues. Counsel for the convicted defendant must prepare an appellate brief outlining the issues on which the defendant is appealing the conviction, that is, the errors alleged to have occurred in the trial process. The brief alleges facts and cites statutory and case law in support of its assertion that the procedures followed in the case were illegal or improper. All errors must be in the trial court record. After the appellant's brief has been filed, the appellee submits a brief arguing that the appellate court should rule that the procedures followed in the trial court were lawful and fair.

amicus curiae brief

Other interested parties also may file briefs, known as **amicus curiae briefs** (often referred to simply as amicus briefs). *Amicus curiae* means friend of the court. Amicus briefs are usually filed by individuals or organizations that have a policy interest in the outcome of the case—police departments, the International Association of Chiefs of Police, prosecutors' organizations and attorneys general, bar organizations, the American Civil Liberties Union, or other voluntary associations concerned with criminal justice and civil liberties issues.

Usually, amicus briefs are submitted on the organization's own motion, although the reviewing court sometimes requests amicus briefs from appropriate interested parties. To submit an amicus brief the organization usually must obtain the permission of the reviewing court, the party whose side in the dispute the brief supports, or both (Marvell 1978, 80). Amicus briefs bring additional expertise before the court, providing a more complete analysis of the issues in question.

Oral Arguments

oral argument

After the briefs have been filed, the appellate judges study them and discuss the issues raised. Initial discussion of the case might lead the appellate court to decide that additional information is necessary before it can reach a decision. In this case the court will order **oral arguments.** British tradition carved out an important role for oral arguments. To this day British courts rely primarily on oral arguments, not written briefs (Carrington et al. 1976, 16). In the United States the importance of oral arguments has declined since the 1960s (Martineau 1987, 472). Nonetheless, the tradition of oral arguments remains deeply ingrained in appellate procedure.

Oral arguments help to focus on the most important issues raised by the appellant and appellee. In addition, they offer an opportunity for the judges to ask questions. Many justices have commented on the importance of oral arguments in reaching decisions in difficult cases. Supreme Court Justice William J. Brennan wrote,

> Oral argument is the absolutely indispensable ingredient of appellate advocacy. . . . Often my whole notion of what a case is about crystallizes at oral argument. This happens even though I read the briefs before oral argument; indeed, that is the practice now of all the members of the Supreme Court. . . . Often my idea of how a case shapes up is changed by oral argument. . . . Oral argument is a Socratic dialogue between Justices and counsel. (Stern 1981, 358)

Overburdened appellate courts are dispensing with oral arguments as a means of saving time. In the federal appellate courts 33 percent of criminal appeals are decided without oral arguments (Cecil and Stienstra 1987, 22). In some circuits as many as 55 to 65 percent of criminal appeals are decided without oral argument. Cases are likely to be decided without oral argument when the issues are clear, the case involves well-settled law, and the facts and legal arguments are well stated in the briefs (Cecil and Stienstra 1987). The trend toward less oral argument has been criticized (Stern 1981; see ABA Commission 1977, 55–56), but it is likely to continue.

When oral arguments are heard, they tend to be relatively short, perhaps fifteen to thirty minutes for each side in state appellate courts (Carrington et al. 1975, 5). Many judges complain of the poor quality of oral arguments, and some consider oral arguments to be a waste of time (Baker 194, 111; Carrington et al. 1975, 5; Stern 1981, 360).

Deciding the Case

concurring opinion

Immediately after oral arguments, if they are held, the judges hold a conference to discuss the issues and reach tentative conclusions on the case. One judge will be assigned to write a draft opinion of the majority position. The draft opinion will be circulated among the judges. Judges often meet in small groups to discuss their views of the draft. Sometimes judges shift their positions, or subtle differences of opinion emerge. Some judges may decide to write **concurring**

*dissenting
opinion*

opinions, which agree with the result ordered for the defendant but offer a different rationale or elaborate on a particular point of law. A judge may also write a **dissenting opinion,** which disagrees with the majority's ruling on the case and explains the judge's reasons for disagreeing.

Much of this work is conducted in absolute secrecy. Although the briefs of the parties, *amici* (plural for *amicus*), oral arguments, and final written opinions are public, the discussions and draft opinions of appellate judges are strictly confidential, even after the case is decided. This secrecy has been justified as necessary to ensure open discussion in the decision-making process, allowing judges to state tentative views and change their minds upon further reflection and discussion (Marvell 1978, 7–8).

The appellate court ultimately must decide whether the trial court erred in its resolution of the issue before it and whether the error is reversible or harmless error.

Reversible Versus Harmless Error

*reversible
error*

*harmless
error*

Reversible error is error that results in a reversal of the ruling of the trial court. At one time any error, no matter how minor or technical, would result in reversal of a conviction (Traynor 1970, 103). Today, however, the federal system and most state systems have passed **harmless error** statutes, which allow appellate courts to reverse a conviction only if the error violated a fundamental right of the defendant or actually affected the outcome of the case. The harmless error rule frees appellate judges to point out errors, even minor errors, without having to reverse a conviction for which evidence of guilt is sufficient. Without the harmless error rule appellate courts might hesitate to point out procedural errors if doing so would free an obviously guilty defendant. If the appellate court decides an error is harmless, its ruling helps to clarify the law, but the defendant's conviction is not reversed.

The harmless error rule puts appellate judges in the anomalous situation of having to decide whether a jury would have found the defendant guilty had proper procedures been followed. For example, if the illegal confession had been properly suppressed, would the other evidence presented by the prosecutor have been sufficient to convince the jury to convict? Requiring appellate judges to make such determinations seems to violate their traditional role. The harmless error rule requires appellate judges to weigh the evidence and decide whether it demonstrates guilt beyond a reasonable doubt, instead of merely examining the procedures followed. However, this weighing of the evidence is limited to those cases in which the appellate court has found error.

In most cases, even if the appellate court finds that the trial court erred, it finds that the error was harmless and does not warrant reversal of the conviction. The nature of the matter on appeal is related to whether the court is likely to view the error as harmless and, consequently, whether a reversal is likely (see Figure 18–2). Some issues are routinely raised on appeal, and they are routinely held to be harmless error. Evidentiary rulings, sufficiency of evidence, and jury instructions are among the most common matters raised on appeal. For example, a court may find no harm where evidence was improperly admitted because the remaining properly admitted evidence was sufficient to support the conviction. In contrast, an erroneous interpretation of a statute is less likely to be viewed as harmless error.

FIGURE 18-2   Reversible Error by Issue

SOURCE: Joy A. Chapper and Roger A. Hansen. 1990. *Understanding Reversible Error in Criminal Appeals, Final Report.* Williamsburg, Va.: National Center for State Courts, p. 7.

Issue	Percentage of All Error Associated with Issue	Success Rate
Admission/exclusion of evidence	20.6%	7.7%
Instructions	13.5	9.7
Procedural or discretionary ruling	13.1	7.8
Sufficiency of the evidence	12.0	5.8
Merger of offenses	10.5	51.9
Suppression of evidence, statements, or identification	10.5	8.4
Ineffective assistance/waiver of counsel	6.0	12.9
Other constitutional claims (double jeopardy, speedy trial)	4.9	11.5
Jury selection or deliberation	3.4	8.8
Statutory interpretation or application	2.2	19.4
Plea	2.2	15.0
Prosecutorial misconduct	1.1	1.9
	100 %	
	N = 267	

Remedies on Appeal

If the appellate court finds that an error was not harmless, it reverses the judgment of the lower court and remands the case to the trial court. The state may retry the defendant. Retrial after reversal by an appellate court is one exception to the general rule against double jeopardy.

Defendants who are retried or resentenced after a successful appeal are protected from judges who might wish to punish them for appealing the original conviction. In *North Carolina v. Pearce* (1969) the Supreme Court held that judges may not be vindictive in sentencing defendants after a successful appeal and reprosecution. A judge is permitted to impose a heavier sentence after a successful reprosecution only if it is justified on the basis of information brought to light subsequent to the original trial, such as evidence presented at the second trial, a new presentence investigation, the defendant's prison record, or other sources.

Appeals Beyond the First Appeal

The case is not necessarily ended at the conclusion of the first appeal. The losing party may move for a rehearing or reconsideration. If a panel of judges heard the first appeal, the appellate court might grant a rehearing of the appeal *en banc*, that is, by all the judges on the bench. Such a motion is likely to be granted if different panels have come to contrary conclusions on a question of law or if the issue being decided is especially important. To fulfill its role in clarifying the law the appellate court rehears the appeal to resolve the inconsistency without delay. The U.S. Supreme Court has shown great deference to the decisions of en banc proceedings, overturning such decisions much less frequently than decisions of three-judge panels (Ball 1987, 252).

If the first appeal was to the state supreme court, as in those states with a two-tier court structure, and a federal question is raised, the losing party may be able to take an appeal to the U.S. Supreme Court. If the first appeal was to an intermediate court of appeals, the losing party may appeal to the state supreme court and to the U.S. Supreme Court. This is the case regardless of which side prevails at the appellate level. In any case these subsequent appeals are almost always discretionary.

writ of certiorari

The first step is for the appellant, that is, the party seeking an appeal at the next higher level, to petition for a writ of certiorari. The request for a **writ of certiorari** is essentially an application petitioning the court to consider the appeal. If granted, the appellate court asks the lower court to send the record up for review. In the jargon of the appellate process the higher court "grants cert." Because the decision to hear the case at this level is entirely discretionary, only a small proportion of cases is accepted for consideration. For example, the U.S. Supreme Court grants fewer than 1 percent of the petitions for certiorari, meaning that it agrees to consider the appeal (Maguire and Pastore 1994, 554).

Because of the many applications for certiorari and the small number that can be accepted for hearing, these courts develop criteria for deciding whether to grant a certiorari petition. The merit of the particular case is only one factor the court takes into account. A petition that raises a legal principle of particular significance is more likely to be accepted for consideration. The higher court also is more likely to accept a case that presents an issue on which lower court decisions have been inconsistent (Martineau 1987, 474; Marvell 1978, 17). For example, if several circuits of the appellate courts have come to conflicting conclusions on a particular legal issue, the Supreme Court may accept the case in order to promote uniformity among the circuits (Arkin 1992, 509).

■ COLLATERAL RELIEF

Once the parties have exhausted their opportunities to petition for certiorari to the highest state court and, if a federal question is involved, to the U.S. Supreme Court, direct appellate opportunities end. Nonetheless, an aggrieved defendant may bring issues back into court through the mechanism of collateral attack. The most common collateral remedy is habeas corpus. In addition, collateral remedies may be pursued even if the defendant never took advantage of opportunities for direct appeal.

The Writ of Habeas Corpus

The writ of habeas corpus, sometimes referred to by legal scholars as "the Great Writ," has ancient origins. Literally translated, habeas corpus means "to have the body" (Duker 1980, 23). The writ was used historically to compel the appearance of a person in court. The first recorded case of the writ's use by a prisoner to request a court to examine the cause of imprisonment occurred in 1340 (Duker 1980, 23). During the seventeenth century legal developments in England resulted in the use of the writ of habeas corpus as a tool for protecting individual liberty, but the writ was generally unavailable to those confined as criminals (Duker 1980, 225).

The framers of the U.S. Constitution apparently considered the writ to be fairly important. The Constitution provides in Article I, section 9, that the writ of habeas corpus may be suspended only in case of rebellion or invasion. The Judiciary Act of 1789 was the first statute authorizing use of the writ of habeas corpus. This statute has been amended from time to time. Until the 1860s the federal writ of habeas corpus was available only to those individuals held under federal authority. In addition, convicted defendants found little help through the writ. No matter how erroneous and unfair the procedures in the trial court, so long as the defendant had been officially tried and sentenced, the writ offered no remedy.

This changed (or began to change) in 1867. Congress was concerned about the potential for discriminatory use of the criminal justice system against the freed slaves in the former Confederate states. It enacted a revised habeas corpus statute in 1867 that provided a remedy for state prisoners seeking to challenge the authority under which they were held. Although the 1867 act was amended the following year, once again contracting the scope of federal habeas corpus, the Supreme Court continued to take a more expansive view of the availability of habeas corpus (Duker 1980, 230). By 1915 federal habeas corpus was used as a means of collateral attack to challenge the confinement of a prisoner on the ground that the person's constitutional rights had been violated. Use of the writ of habeas corpus evolved so that any person held in custody in violation of the U.S. Constitution could challenge that detention through the writ of habeas corpus (*Peyton v. Rowe* 1968). About thirty states also have habeas corpus laws. These state laws may be used to challenge detention through the state courts (Sokol 1969).

Habeas corpus is a civil action and must be filed first in a trial-level court, rather than an appellate court; in a federal habeas action the writ is filed in the district court. Because it is a civil action, the Sixth Amendment right to counsel does not apply. Instead federal statutory law provides for the appointment of counsel for the indigent in any type of federal court action by allowing a person to proceed *in forma pauperis*. **In forma pauperis** means that the petitioner claims to be indigent and the court may assign counsel to represent the individual in court. In state habeas actions some states do not provide for a right to counsel. In these cases the petitioner is required to proceed pro se, that is, without an attorney (*Pennsylvania v. Finlay* 1987). This difference in procedure makes federal habeas action more attractive to many prisoners. Twenty-two percent of the more than twenty-eight thousand civil cases disposed of by U.S. magistrates in one year were state prisoners' petitions (Judicial Conference 1990, 283).

The petition for a writ of habeas corpus usually requests the release of the petitioner from custody. Typically, the respondent is the warden of the prison in which the petitioner is being held. The court receiving the petition orders the respondent to show cause why the relief requested should not be granted (Sokol 1969, 103). Typically, the state attorney general's office drafts a response, which may include relevant portions of the transcript from the petitioner's original trial and legal arguments in response to the allegations made in the petition. "If evidence is in existence, or can be brought into existence through the use of depositions or affidavits, which refute petitioner's allegations, that evidence should be incorporated into the return to the order to show cause" (Sokol 1969, 109–10). This is important, because any allegations not answered by the respondent are accepted by the court as factually true.

Once the court has received the respondent's answer, the court must decide whether a hearing is necessary to resolve disputed facts. This fact-finding hearing

in forma pauperis

is not like the oral arguments held in the case of a direct appeal. Oral arguments are for the purpose of explaining legal reasoning and the rationale for the positions advocated by the parties to the appeal. In a habeas corpus action the hearing is a fact-finding hearing in which witnesses are asked to testify under oath in order to allow the court to resolve any factual disputes presented in the petition and response. In almost all habeas actions the fact-finder is a judge rather than a jury. There is no right to a jury in habeas corpus proceedings.

If the facts and the law indicate to the judge that the petitioner's rights were violated, the court may order the relief requested. Release is not automatic, however. The protection against double jeopardy does not apply to a situation in which a prisoner petitions for release through habeas corpus. Consequently, the state is free to retry the prisoner after it loses a habeas action. In this case release of the prisoner may be postponed until the state says whether it intends to retry the defendant or appeal the decision of the judge in the habeas action. Again, because a habeas petition is a civil action, the state may appeal this decision if it loses at the trial-court level. In fact, habeas actions are routinely appealed, no matter which party loses.

Limitations on the Availability of Habeas Corpus

The federal habeas corpus statute requires that a state prisoner exhaust all state remedies before filing for a writ of habeas corpus in federal court. This means that if the time for filing a direct appeal has not yet expired, the prisoner should file a direct appeal with the state rather than bring a federal habeas action. Similarly, if the state provides a habeas option, the federal courts may require the petitioner to first exhaust the state remedy. The rationale for this requirement is that "if the doors of the state courts and the federal courts are both currently open, a state prisoner ought to try the state door first" (Sokol 1969, 163).

In addition, the Supreme Court has ruled in recent years that some issues are not the proper subject of a federal habeas action. The first instance of such a ruling came in the decision of *Stone v. Powell* (1976), in which the Court ruled that the federal district courts are not to review Fourth Amendment claims on habeas petitions from state prisoners if those claims already have had an opportunity for full and fair litigation in the state courts. In 1989 the Court went further, holding that the federal district courts must "refuse to hear claims in habeas review that are based on a state court's good faith interpretation of existing federal constitutional precedent even if those decisions do not accord with federal decisions handed down after the prisoner completes his direct appeal" (Arkin 1992, 512; *Graham v. Collins* 1993, 897–898). The practical effect of this decision is to limit the number of times a state prisoner may challenge a conviction. The Court has continued to constrict the discretion of the lower federal courts to hear federal habeas petitions from state prisoners (*McClesky v. Zant* 1991; *Coleman v. Thompson* 1991; *Herrera v. Collins* 1993).

Are There Too Many Opportunities for Review?

These rulings reflect the growing dissatisfaction with the lack of finality in criminal cases expressed by some members of the Court, members of Congress, and state court officials. The late former Chief Justice Warren Burger criticized federal habeas corpus policy, commenting that the policy allows convicted defendants repeated review, "unnecessarily delaying justice and taxing the judicial system beyond reasonable expectations" (Roper and Melone 1981, 136).

Unquestionably, the combination of appellate and other post-conviction remedies creates the potential for almost unlimited court action for prisoners willing to pursue every avenue for relief. Prisoners take advantage of the advice of *jailhouse lawyers,* prisoners who become versed in criminal procedure, including appellate and habeas procedure. Because prisoners have a great deal of time to read and draft legal papers, some prisoners spend virtually their entire prison term filing for post-conviction relief. As one commentator notes, "The indigent criminal defendant has practically nothing to lose by appealing; he puts up none of the money. There is no good reason why, in these circumstances, indigent persons should not choose to litigate indefinitely, and some have shown themselves prone to do just that" (Geoffrey Hazard in Carrington et al. 1975, 63). Death penalty cases have been a particular concern. Critics point out that for the prisoner sentenced to death, filing successive petitions of habeas corpus becomes a strategy to indefinitely delay the execution of the death sentence:

> A State defendant convicted of a capital offense and sentenced to death may take advantage of three successive procedures to challenge constitutional defects in his or her conviction or sentence. His or her claims may be raised on appeal, in State and Federal *habeas* proceedings. As a consequence, there are extensive delays between sentencing and execution of the sentence. (Hazard in Carrington et al. 1975, 63)

Because trial court decisions on habeas petitions are routinely appealed, it is possible, although unusual, for a defendant to seek review in nine or more separate courts.

The opportunities for excessive and unnecessary litigation in any particular case are clearly substantial. Still, relatively few prisoners appeal their convictions. Even fewer seek collateral relief (Flanagan and Maguire 1990, 527–28). And still fewer prisoners actively and repeatedly seek to have their convictions overturned.

Nonetheless, two circumstances have combined to put habeas corpus on the reform agenda. First, the caseload of the appellate courts has traditionally been so small that increases in the number of prisoners filing appeals have had a dramatic effect. Second, growing death row populations dramatically emphasize the ability of death row prisoners to delay execution through successive petitions for habeas corpus.

■ OVERBURDENED APPELLATE COURTS

Concern about the growing volume of appeals and habeas actions increased during the 1970s. From 1960 to 1973 criminal appeals in the federal courts increased more than 250 percent, and federal actions brought by state prisoners (including habeas actions) increased 176 percent (see Figure 18–3). The Supreme Court also felt caseload pressures. Several groups were established to study the problem. Two major commissions (the Freund Study Commission in 1971 and the Hruska Commission in 1972) focused on the problem of caseload increases in the U.S. Supreme Court (Coleman 1983, 8). Other groups, such as the ABA and the National Center for State Courts, focused on the problems of caseload size in the intermediate appellate and state supreme courts.

The most recent period for which statistics are available is the decade between 1973 and 1983. During this period the rate of increase in the number of appellate

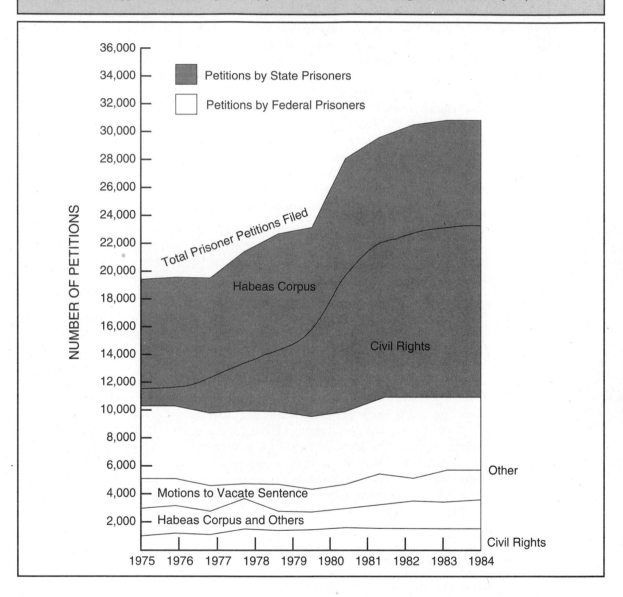

FIGURE 18-3   Petitions Filed by State and Federal Prisoners

Source: Reprinted from Howard Ball. © 1987. *Courts and Politics: The Federal Judicial System,* 2d ed. Englewood Cliffs, N.J.: Prentice-Hall, pp. 97, 221–223. Reprinted by permission of Prentice-Hall, Englewood Cliffs, New Jersey.

filings moderated slightly. Criminal and civil appeals grew at similar rates (107 percent and 114 percent, respectively), whereas criminal appeals had previously been growing much more rapidly than civil appeals. Nonetheless, criminal appeals continued to grow faster than the number of criminal cases in the justice system. Between 1973 and 1983 "criminal appeals grew more than twice as fast as the FBI Crime Index statistics and twice as fast as trial court criminal filings in the 29 jurisdictions with trial court statistics" (U.S. Bureau of Justice Statistics 1985, 4).

The causes of this explosion in the number of appeals and requests for post-conviction relief are not entirely clear. Some commentators speculate that the recognition of the right to counsel in criminal cases, especially in the first appeal of right, increased the number of defendants able to take advantage of the appellate process (Carrington et al. 1975). Several legal scholars also suggest that caseload increases were caused by an increase in the number of "frivolous appeals" brought by prisoners. As one commentator notes, "The fact that many a poor person appeals his conviction simply because he has nothing to lose by doing so means in turn that the appellate courts, to their great annoyance, are being called upon increasingly to hear and decide cases in which the legal issues raised are clearly without merit" (Robert Hermann in Carrington et al. 1975, 701).

New judgeships were created to accommodate the growing appellate docket, but the number of judgeships fell far behind the number of appellate cases. Although the total number of civil and criminal appeals filed between 1973 and 1983 increased by 112 percent (in the forty-three states for which data were available), the number of appellate judgeships increased only 36 percent. In 1973 an average of 85 appeals were filed per appellate judge; by 1983 the number had grown to 133 appeals per judge. The same trend can be seen in the federal courts of appeals. In 1982 a three-judge panel heard an average of 635 criminal and civil appeals. In 1993 the average was 902 cases per three-judge panel (Maguire and Pastore 1994, 550–551).

Because of mounting concern about overcrowding in the appellate courts, states and the federal courts began to change the appellate process in the 1960s. By the 1980s almost all appellate courts had made major changes, including policies designed to decrease the number of appeals, to increase the number of justices, or to decrease the amount of time devoted to each decision (Carrington et al. 1975, 3).

Efforts to Decrease the Number of Appeals

A number of Supreme Court rulings have sought to decrease the number of habeas corpus actions filed by prisoners in the federal courts and to limit the number of times a death sentence is reviewed. The general purpose of these rulings has been to promote finality and to decrease repetitive appeals by defendants who have had an opportunity for a full and fair review of their convictions. In decisions such as *Stone v. Powell* (1976) the Supreme Court has explicitly acted to limit the number of cases eligible for review by the federal courts. Congress has also shown an interest in this area by introducing bills that would revise federal habeas corpus procedure to limit the number of times a case could be reviewed and to impose time limits designed to prevent death row inmates from waiting until the eleventh hour to challenge their convictions (*Congressional Digest* 1992, 109). A study committee appointed by Chief Justice William H. Rehnquist and chaired by retired justice Lewis Powell has been particularly influential in this area.

Although federal habeas corpus in death penalty cases has received the most attention, many suggested reforms have targeted the growing number of direct appeals. Some have proposed limiting appeals to only certain kinds of cases, for example, to only those defendants sentenced to a term of incarceration (Hazard in Carrington et al. 1975, 60). Others have suggested that appeals of convictions for petty offenses should be discretionary rather than by right. Because there is no U.S. constitutional right to appeal, states are free to limit access to the appellate process in any way that does not violate the equal protection clause of the Fourteenth Amendment.

In addition to these changes, some courts have implemented prescreening procedures for direct appeals in an attempt to identify those cases that may not

U.S. JUDGES OK HABEAS REPORT,
WITH GREATER INMATE SAFEGUARDS

The national debate over streamlining habeas corpus procedures in capital cases continued last month as the Judicial Conference of the United States weighed in, endorsing a plan to restrict habeas corpus but calling for somewhat greater protections for death row inmates. The action was considered a setback for Chief Justice William H. Rehnquist, who has criticized the years of delay that typically occur between capital sentencing and execution.

The debate began last September, when a panel of the Judicial Conference, chaired by retired Supreme Court Justice Lewis F. Powell, Jr., proposed strict new limits on the extent to which death row inmates may challenge the Constitutionality of their convictions or sentences. Chief Justice Rehnquist, who serves as chairman of the Conference, reportedly angered some members of that body when he sent the Powell Committee report to Congress. The Conference members had hoped that Rehnquist would wait until the Conference reviewed the Powell recommendations.

The Judicial Conference, which consists of high-ranking federal judges from across the nation, considered the issue at its March 13 [1990] meeting and, over the objection of the Chief Justice, recommended the Powell Committee report be modified in two areas.

First, the Conference called for standards to ensure that capital defendants are represented by competent, adequately-paid attorneys. The Powell Committee would set new limits on habeas corpus challenges only in states that make lawyers available to death row inmates for the purpose of filing habeas challenges, but the Powell Committee did not lay down standards for the quality of lawyers provided. The Judicial Conference said: "Because many of the delays in habeas corpus procedures are related to the fact that the defendant was not represented by competent counsel at the trial level (as well as in the state post-conviction proceedings), specific mandatory standards similar to those set forth in the Anti-Drug Abuse Act of 1988 should be required with respect to the appointment and compensation of counsel for capital defendants at all stages of the state and federal capital punishment litigation." The 1988 drug law standards state that lawyers handling post-conviction work in capital cases must have been admitted to practice in the state appeals court for at least five years, and have at least three years' experience handling felony appeals in that court.

On the second issue, the Judicial Conference essentially endorsed the recent recommendations of an American Bar Association task force. The Powell Committee would bar an inmate from mounting more than one habeas corpus challenge in federal court unless new factual evidence had emerged undermining the court's confidence in the determination of guilt on the offense for which the death sentence was imposed.

The Judicial Conference would allow additional habeas petitions in a greater range of cases. The Conference said: "A federal court should entertain a second or successive petition for habeas corpus relief if: the request for relief is based on a claim not previously presented by the prisoner in the state and federal courts and the failure to raise the claim is the result of state action in violation of the Constitution or laws of the United States, the result of Supreme Court recognition of a new federal right that is retroactively applicable, or based on a factual predicate that could not have been discovered through the exercise of reasonable diligence; and the facts underlying the claim would be sufficient, if proven, to undermine the court's confidence in the jury's determination of guilt on the offense or offenses for which the death penalty was imposed, or in the appropriateness of the sentence of death."

SOURCE: Reprinted from Criminal Justice Newsletter. 1990. "U.S. Judges OK Habeas Report, With Greater Inmate Safeguards." *Criminal Justice Newsletter* 21 (April 2): 5–6. Reprinted courtesy of Pace Publications.

merit a full review or those that raise frivolous issues. Both the Freund Study Group and the Hruska Commission recommended the creation of a new court to relieve the Supreme Court of some caseload pressure (Coleman 1983, 8; Ball 1987, 67–69). The Freund Study Group recommended that a new National Court of Appeals prescreen cases filed with the Supreme Court, decide some cases on the merits, and refer others to the Supreme Court for decision. The Supreme Court would retain discretion concerning the granting of *certiorari* in cases referred from the National Court. The Hruska Commission recommended that the Supreme Court refer to a proposed National Court of Appeals those cases that the High Court deemed straightforward enough to justify eliminating the need for Supreme Court review.

There is little consensus among scholars regarding the effects of these kinds of changes. Disagreement about these remedies also reflects disagreement about the role of the appellate process and the proportion of appeals that are frivolous. Some argue that all defendants should have a right to appeal, because to deny an appeal is to undermine the legitimacy of the court process itself. Prescreening appellate cases would mean that some defendants are denied a review without a full opportunity to present their complaints about the process that led to their conviction. According to some commentators, this is likely to heighten the suspicions of convicted criminals about the fairness of the process by which they were imprisoned.

For this reason the American Bar Association concluded that "it is basically unsound to introduce a screening stage for the purpose of short-circuiting frivolous appeals" (ABA in Carrington et al. 1975, 75). Moreover, the ABA pointed out that the amount of work required by the appellant in preparing the appeal would not change. If appellate judges handle prescreening, their workload increases, with no significant time savings in eliminating frivolous appeals. If the trial court handles prescreening, its decision would have to be appealable, which again would not go far in reducing the burden on the appellate courts. In addition, the courts have found it difficult to specify what constitutes a frivolous appeal. "In the final analysis, a frivolous case is what the last judge who rules on the question says it is" (Sokol 1969, 195). Because frivolousness is not self-evident, these commentators find little merit in the suggestion that any prescreening device can fairly and efficiently reduce the appellate caseload.

Despite the difficulty of specifying what constitutes a frivolous appeal, some critics argue that defendants who clog the courts with frivolous appeals ought to be penalized. Noting that indigent defendants have nothing to lose by appealing, Hazard argues, "It might be worth considering whether a rule should not be adopted that a convicted criminal offender runs the risk of having his sentence revised upward if his appeal is found to be without significant merit" (Hazard in Carrington et al. 1975, 63). Such a system of penalties for unjustified appeals was actually used in Great Britain, where an unsuccessful applicant for appeal automatically lost six to nine weeks of good time credit. The American Bar Association's standards on criminal appeals recommended against such a system in the United States, noting that penalties might deter appeals by individuals with valid issues to raise on appeal (Carrington et al. 1975, 81).

Another suggestion along the same lines is to pay defendants not to appeal. The idea here is to give indigent defendants the same sort of monetary stake in the decision to appeal that nonindigent defendants face. Under this proposal an indigent defendant would be given an option: pursue an appeal at public expense or be paid a sum of money equal to the cost to the state of providing

WAS GIDEON'S APPEAL FRIVIOLOUS?

An example of the difficulties involved in determining whether an appeal is frivolous is found in the landmark case of *Gideon v. Wainwright* (1963) discussed in Chapter 3. Gideon, a poor defendant convicted of burglary, insisted that the Constitution guaranteed the right to counsel. At the time, the leading Supreme Court case on the issue of right to counsel for indigents was *Betts v. Brady* (1942). Under *Betts,* a defendant was entitled to appointed counsel only if the case presented unusual circumstances. For example, if the charges were especially complex or if the defendant was mentally disabled, the Court required that counsel be appointed. In a simple burglary prosecution against a reasonably intelligent adult, such as Gideon, *Betts* was clear: the trial court need not appoint counsel. In other words, the applicability of the right to

counsel for Gideon was a matter of settled law. In appealing his conviction to the Florida Supreme Court, the state court correctly applied existing U.S. Supreme Court precedents. Ultimately, however, the U.S. Supreme Court heard Gideon's argument and reversed its own previous holdings. The Court held that the Sixth Amendment, through the Fourteenth Amendment, requires the appointment of counsel for indigent defendants such as Gideon.

How differently might this case have turned out if Gideon's petition to the Supreme Court had been screened for frivolousness? Would such a screening process slow the evolution of law? What recourse would an appellant have after his or her claims were denied without review because they were frivolous?

counsel for an appeal on the condition that the defendant forego appealing the conviction.

At present, only prescreening devices appear to have any serious support, whereas penalties for frivolous appeals and rewards for not appealing have gained few proponents. Other proposals for dealing with appellate caseload pressures have focused on the problem of increasing the capacity of the appellate courts to handle the cases coming to them, either by increasing the number of appellate judges or decreasing the amount of time spent on cases.

Increasing the Number of Appellate Judges

The number of appellate judges increased throughout the 1970s and 1980s. From 1974 to 1984, the number of intermediate appellate court judges increased 73 percent. In large part this increase came about through the creation of three-tiered court systems, which required additional judges. From 1957 to the end of the 1980s twenty-four states created intermediate appellate courts. In addition, other states expanded the appellate bench by adding appellate positions (Chapper and Hanson 1989, xi).

The creation of intermediate appellate courts acknowledges the dual role of the appellate process in general. One role is to review cases for the correctness of procedures and results in individual cases. A second role is to ensure uniformity in cases and to address policy questions for the police and courts in light of constitutional and statutory law. Intermediate appellate courts, although fulfilling both roles, focus on the first role by providing a review for individual defendants. This allows the supreme court to focus on those cases that raise significant institutional questions of uniformity and policy. In other words, the creation of an intermediate appellate court shields the highest court from routine business (Carrington et al. 1975, 10).

Some commentators have expressed fear that expanding the number of appellate judges would "threaten the quality of the process by diminishing the status of the judges and by increasing the difficulties of harmonious and uniform administration of the law" (Carrington et al. 1975, 3). Although this may be true, the potential threat to the quality of the process posed by such strategies as decreasing access to the appellate courts and decreasing the amount of time spent on each case is probably more serious than any decline in quality resulting from a comparatively lower status of appellate judges.

Decreasing the Time Spent on Cases

panel,
en banc

Several suggestions focus on making appellate courts more efficient by making the most of their limited time and personnel. One measure designed to conserve appellate court time has become common in intermediate appellate courts: deciding cases in panels (Marvell 1989, 285). Rather than having all appellate judges hear every case, a smaller **panel** of judges, typically a group of three, sits to hear the case. The entire appellate court sits *en banc* only when extraordinary circumstances warrant. A court will sit en banc to resolve conflicting decisions from different panels, or when the full court wishes to reconsider a panel's decision in a particular case, or when the case presents legal issues of such significance that the court deems it prudent to speak to the issue with a single authoritative voice. In most instances, however, intermediate appellate courts make decisions in panels.

per curiam
decision,
memorandum
decision

Another response to increasing caseloads has been to increase the use of summary dispositions. In some cases the court merely makes an oral ruling from the bench at the conclusion of oral arguments. In other cases, particularly when oral arguments have not been made, the court issues brief written orders, sometimes called *per curiam* or **memorandum decisions,** without providing an extensive recounting of the facts or discussion of the rationale or justification for its decision (Meader and Bernstein 1994, 85). These practices are becoming more common, accounting for a large majority of all decisions in some appellate courts (Stern 1981, 483).

Such practices have been sharply criticized. Some scholars argue that providing written reasons for a decision is essential to maintaining the integrity and legitimacy of the appellate process:

> Litigants and the public are reassured when they can see that the determination emerged at the end of a reasoning process that is explicitly stated, rather than as an imperious ukase [decree] without a nod to law or a need to justify. Especially in a case in which there is no oral argument, the opinion is an essential demonstration that the court has in fact considered the case. (Carrington et al. 1976, 31–32)

Another suggestion for reducing the amount of time appellate courts spend on each case is to dispense with the publication of opinions (Marvell 1989, 282). Not publishing saves time, because the judges do not have to provide a description of the facts of the case. In addition, unpublished opinions can be written less formally and require less revision and polishing (Stern 1981, 486). Many states and the federal circuit courts have adopted policies for deciding which opinions ought to be published and which need not be published. Sixty percent of all federal appellate court decisions are unpublished (Meador and Bernstein 1994, 87). In general, if the opinion "contributes something to an understanding of the law," it should be published (Stern 1981, 486). Electronic legal research services, such as Westlaw and Lexis, are attempting to include both published and unpublished opinions in their databases. Traditionally, unpublished opinions may not be cited or relied on as precedent. The availability of unpublished opinions through commercial databases used by lawyers could change this tradition.

Another strategy for increasing the efficiency of appellate courts is to reduce the amount of time devoted to oral argument. Appellate judges question the usefulness of oral arguments for routine cases. As a result, they have found this an easy way to streamline the appellate process, particularly because the judges retain control over which cases are given time for oral arguments.

Finally, some courts have hired additional personnel to do some of the routine work. Some courts have hired more law clerks or have assigned some tasks to central legal staff. Staff attorneys provide summaries, do legal research, and even draft opinions for justices.

None of these reforms has been completely successful. The number of appeals and petitions for habeas corpus has continued to rise (Maguire and Pastore 1994, 550–552), but departures from traditional appellate procedure have frequently been criticized (Chapper and Hanson 1990, xii). Defenders of traditional appellate practice and proponents of a right to appeal base their arguments largely on the presumed symbolic value of appellate processes. These commentators oppose curtailing access to the appellate courts or reducing the formality of appellate court proceedings, because they fear these practices will undermine the legitimacy of the appellate process and therefore the judicial system as a whole. Proponents of more streamlined appellate procedures assume that many appeals are hopeless last-ditch efforts by factually guilty criminal defendants who have nothing to lose by taking advantage of every appellate opportunity.

CONSEQUENCES OF APPEALS

Judging the actual effect of appeals is not easy. A study of four intermediate appellate courts found that only 20 percent of appellate cases resulted in a reversal (Chapper and Hanson 1990, 17). This finding tends to support the assumption that many appeals are without merit. Studies of the federal appellate courts result in similar findings. In the twelve-month period ending June 30, 1989, only 9.3 percent of criminal appeals in the federal Courts of Appeals resulted in reversal (Arkin 1992, 515). Findings such as these lead some experts on the appellate process to conclude that appellate caseloads could be dramatically reduced if the 80 to 90 percent of convicted defendants who appeal but do not gain a reversal could be persuaded to forego appeals or are screened out with minimal appellate court effort.

Although only a small proportion of all appeals results in reversal, the consequences for the defendant who gains a reversal are substantial. One study (Roper and Melone 1981) examined the final dispositions of cases remanded from the U.S. Courts of Appeals and subjected to reprosecution from 1975 to 1979. It found that more than 40 percent of these cases were ultimately dismissed by the trial court, often at the motion of the prosecutor. In other words, the prosecutor declined to reprosecute the case upon remand by the appellate court. An additional 7 percent of the cases resulted in an acquittal following retrial. The authors concluded that procedural rights make a difference in the substantive outcome of the case. When defendants were denied procedural rights in the original trials, they were convicted. On remand, almost half the defendants escaped conviction.

SANDRA LOCKETT'S POSTSCRIPT TO CONVICTION:
Case History of an Appeal

Sandra Lockett was convicted of murder for her involvement in the killing of an Ohio pawnshop owner (see Chapter 17 for a description of this case). Lockett had participated in planning the robbery, but stayed in the getaway car during the robbery and had not intended for the store owner to be killed. Although her co-defendant, Al Parker, had pulled the trigger, he agreed to testify against Lockett at trial in exchange for a plea agreement in which the prosecutor agreed not to ask for the death penalty. Lockett was convicted and sentenced to death.

Lockett first appealed her conviction and death sentence to the Ohio Court of Appeals and, subsequently, the Ohio Supreme Court. Lockett claimed that her case had been prejudiced by a death-qualified jury. Four veniremen had been dismissed because they said their opposition to the death penalty was so strong that they could not take an oath to carry out the law in a death penalty case. Lockett also claimed on appeal that the jury did not have sufficient evidence to find that she had purposefully intended the death of the pawnshop owner, and she claimed that counsel had been unconstitutionally ineffective. Both the Court of Appeals and the Ohio Supreme Court rejected her claim that the jury was prejudiced because it was death-qualified. The Ohio Supreme Court also rejected her claims regarding the sufficiency of evidence and ineffective assistance of counsel (*Ohio v. Lockett* 1976).

Lockett then petitioned the United States Supreme Court to request that she be allowed to file in forma pauperis; the Court granted her request (*Lockett v. Ohio* 1977). Then Lockett petitioned the United States Supreme Court to grant her a writ of certiorari to review her case. The Court granted her petition. After its review of the issues, the Supreme Court affirmed her conviction by a death-qualified jury, but it set aside her death sentence. The Supreme Court held that Ohio's death penalty statute violated the Eighth and Fourteenth Amendments because it did not permit the judge to consider mitigating factors with respect to the defendant's character and record (*Lockett v. Ohio* 1978).

Finally, Lockett appealed her confinement through a federal habeas corpus petition, still arguing that she had been harmed by ineffective assistance of counsel and adding a claim that the judge erred in giving instructions to the jury. The U.S. District Court dismissed the petition, and Lockett appealed the decision. The U.S. Court of Appeals for the Sixth Circuit rejected her claim of ineffective assistance of counsel on the merits and ruled that she could not now complain about the jury instructions because she did not object at the time. Exercising her last option, Lockett petitioned the U.S. Supreme Court to review the decision on her petition for habeas corpus. This time the High Court denied her request (*Lockett v. Arn* 1986).

A study of four intermediate appellate courts suggests some reasons that prosecutors decline to prosecute after a successful appeal (Chapper and Hanson 1990). This study found that 32 percent of the prejudicial errors identified by appellate courts related to rulings on admission or exclusion of evidence or the sufficiency of evidence in support of the conviction. If the appellate court rules that key evidence should not have been used to convict or that evidence was insufficient to support the charges, prosecutors may conclude on remand that they do not have a strong enough case to proceed, and they move for dismissal. Moreover, in some cases the defendant may be nearing the end of a prison term, and the prosecutor may decide that the case does not warrant an additional investment of resources because of the defendant's pending release.

■ SUMMARY

Appellate courts sit at the pinnacle of the judicial process and receive only a fraction of the cases processed through the trial courts. Few defendants appeal, and even fewer are successful in having their convictions reversed. Nonetheless, the availability and fairness of appellate procedures serve an important symbolic function in ensuring that trial court procedures are reviewed and that errors are corrected. For those defendants who are wrongly convicted because of trial court errors, the appellate process is of inestimable value. The two principal avenues for review of the procedures leading to conviction are direct appeal from the trial court and a civil action, called habeas corpus, which may be brought after direct appeals have been exhausted.

The growing appellate caseloads of the last several decades have alarmed many observers and have resulted in a variety of innovations to streamline appellate court processes. Some scholars have criticized the system for allowing criminal defendants to appeal their convictions without end. Others contend that although some defendants might abuse the opportunities to seek review of trial court decisions, efforts to curtail access to the appellate courts will only reduce the overall legitimacy of the judicial process while having only the most negligible effect on appellate court workloads.

Decisions of the U.S. Supreme Court influence appellate court workloads by increasing (or decreasing) the grounds available for appeal, increasing (or decreasing) ambiguity about the correctness of trial court proceedings, and increasing (or decreasing) access to federal habeas corpus for state prisoners. The impact of appellate decisions on criminal justice practice is not always apparent at the time of decision. Moreover, considering the practical policy effects of a decision may not be an appropriate basis for deciding individual cases.

Appellate policies are not among the most glamorous of the criminal justice process. Consequently, debates about appellate policy typically are confined to a relatively small group of appellate judges, attorneys, and scholars. Given continued concern about caseloads and finality of convictions, this constrained debate is likely to continue.

■ FOR FURTHER DISCUSSION

1. One issue related to appellate procedure that has received much attention in recent years is the lack of finality in appellate proceedings. In what ways is this perhaps more a problem of appearances than a serious factor in appellate court overcrowding? What steps have been taken to better define an end point?

2. Little information is available on the contribution of jailhouse lawyers to the volume of habeas corpus petitions, but many judges consider the repetitive attempts of prisoners to gain release an abuse of the review process. Can you devise a mechanism whereby inappropriate uses of the habeas process could be eliminated without increasing the potential for miscarriages of justice? How might you analyze this issue in relation to the due process model and the crime control model?

3. In recent decades efforts have been made at all levels of government to increase public access to government proceedings. Open records laws, open

meetings laws, and decisions to televise legislative and judicial proceedings are examples of this trend. Some kinds of proceedings remain off limits, including jury deliberations and the discussions of appellate judges. Does the public have an interest in observing these proceedings? Does the public have an interest in maintaining the secrecy of these proceedings?

■ REFERENCES

American Bar Association Commission. 1977. *Standards Relating to Appellate Courts, Final Draft.* Chicago: American Bar Association.

Arkin, Marc M. 1992. "Rethinking the Constitutional Right to a Criminal Appeal." *UCLA Law Review* 39 (February): 503–80.

Baker, Thomas E. 1994. *Rationing Justice on Appeal: The Problems of the U.S. Courts of Appeals.* St. Paul, Minn.: West.

Ball, Howard. 1987. *Courts and Politics: The Federal Judicial System,* 2d ed. Englewood Cliffs, N.J.: Prentice-Hall.

Carrington, Paul, Winslow Christian, Wilfred Feinberg, Jerold Israel, Delmar Karlen, and Bernard Witkin. 1975. *Appellate Justice: 1975,* Vol. 1. [s.l.] Advisory Council for Appellate Justice.

Carrington, Paul, Daniel J. Meador, and Maurice Rosenberg. 1976. *Justice on Appeal.* St. Paul, Minn.: West.

Cecil, Joe S., and Donna Stienstra. 1987. *Deciding Cases Without Argument: An Examination of Four Courts of Appeals.* Washington, D.C.: Federal Judicial Center.

Chapper, Joy A., and Roger A. Hanson. 1990. "Understanding Reversible Error in Criminal Appeals." *State Court Journal* 14 (Winter): 16–18.

———— 1989. *Understanding Reversible Error in Criminal Appeals, Final Report.* Williamsburg, Va.: National Center for State Courts.

Coleman v. Thompson, 501 U.S. 722, 111 S.Ct. 2546 (1991).

Coleman, William T. 1983. "The Supreme Court of the United States: Managing Its Caseload to Achieve Its Constitutional Purposes." *Fordham Law Review* 52 (October): 1–36.

Congressional Digest. 1992. "Federal Habeas Corpus." *Congressional Digest* (April): 102–3, 109.

Douglas v. California, 372 U.S. 353, 83 S.Ct. 814 (1963).

Duker, William F. 1980. *A Constitutional History of Habeas Corpus.* Westport, Conn.: Greenwood.

Flanagan, Timothy, and Kathleen Maguire. 1990. *Sourcebook of Criminal Justice Statistics—1989.* Washington, D.C.: U.S. Department of Justice, Bureau of Justice Statistics.

Graham v. Collins, 113 S.Ct. 892 (1993).

Griffin v. Illinois, 351 U.S. 12, 76 S.Ct. 585 (1956).

Herrera v. Collins, 113 S.Ct. 853 (1993).

Judicial Conference of the United States. 1990. Proceedings. *Annual Report of the Director of the Administrative Office of the United States Courts.* Washington, D.C.: U.S. Government Printing Office.

McClesky v. Zant, 499 U.S. 467, 111 S.Ct. 1454 (1991).

McKane v. Durston, 153 U.S. 684, 14 S.Ct. 913 (1894).

Maguire, Kathleen, and Ann L. Pastore. 1994. *Sourcebook of Criminal Justice Statistics—1993.* Washington, D.C.: U.S. Government Printing Office.

Martineau, Robert J. 1987. "Appeals and Appellate Practice." In R. J. Janosik, ed. *Encyclopedia of the American Judicial System,* Vol 2. New York: Charles Scribner's Sons.

Marvell, Thomas B. 1989. "State Appellate Court Responses to Caseload Growth." *Judicature* 72 (March): 282–91.

———— 1978. *Appellate Courts and Lawyers. Information Gathering in an Adversary System.* Westport, Conn.: Greenwood.

Meador, Daniel J. 1991. *American Courts.* St. Paul, Minn.: West.

Meador, Daniel John, and Jordana Simone Bernstein. 1994. *Appellate Courts in the United States*. St. Paul, Minn.: West Publishing Co.

North Carolina v. Pearce, 395 U.S. 711, 89 S.Ct. 2072 (1969).

Pennsylvania v. Finlay, 481 U.S. 555, 107 S.Ct. 1990 (1987).

Peyton v. Rowe, 391 U.S. 54, 88 S.Ct. 1549 (1968).

Resnik, Judith. 1985. "Precluding Appeals." *Cornell Law Review* 70 (March): 603–24.

Roper, Robert T., and Albert P. Melone. 1981. "Does Due Process Make a Difference? A Study of Second Trials." *Judicature* 65 (September): 136–41.

Ross v. Moffitt, 417 U.S. 600, 94 S.Ct. 2437 (1974).

Sokol, Ronald P. 1969. *Federal Habeas Corpus,* 2d ed. Charlottesville, Va.: Michie.

Stern, Robert L. 1981. *Appellate Practice in the United States*. Washington, D.C.: Bureau of National Affairs.

Stone v. Powell, 428 U.S. 465, 96 S.Ct. 3037 (1976).

Traynor, Roger J. 1970. *The Riddle of Harmless Error*. Columbus: Ohio State University Press.

U.S. Bureau of Justice Statistics. 1985. *The Growth of Appeals*. Washington, D.C.: U.S. Department of Justice.

INDEX

Dershowitz, Alan, 176
Determinate sentencing, 401–2
Deterrence, 382–83
    general, 382
    specific, 382
Diminished capacity, 326, 327
Direct appeals, 417, 418–19
Directed verdict, 371
Direct evidence, 198, 200
Direct examination, 368, 369
Discovery, 282–83
Discretion of prosecutor, 163–64, 300–301
Disposition, 388
Disproportionate sentence, 399–400
Dispute resolution, 3
    adjudication, 7–8
    evaluating alternative, 229–30
    force in, 4
    mediation, 4
    medieval courts as forums for, 67–71
    negotiation, 3–4
    rule by fiat, 5–6
    rule of law in, 5, 6–7
Disputes
    adjudication of, 10–11
    negotiating, in criminal court, 14–15
    of fact, 10
    of law, 10–11
Dissenting opinion, 424
District attorney, 146
Diversion, 184–85
Diversion programs, 194
DNA evidence, 338
DNA identification techniques, 267–68
Documentary evidence, 199
Domestic abuse, 159–60
Dossier, 99
Double jeopardy, 54
Drug testing, pretrial, 240
Drummond, Edward, 328
Dual court system, 20
Due process
    versus crime control, 15–16
    Magna Carta and the concept of, 75–76
    right to, 50–52
Due process clause, 45–46
Due process model, 15
Duren rule, 357
Duress as affirmative defense, 342, 343
Durham rule, 329
Dying person, declaration of, 269

Early representation, 235
Egan, Michael, 152
Eighth Amendment
    and the death penalty, 408–9
    and right to bail, 255, 257, 258
    and sentencing, 399
Eilberg, Jonathan, 152
Eilberg, Joshua, 151–52
Election of state court judges, 125, 126
Electronic monitoring, 391–92
Elements, 11
En banc, 29, 435
    appeal, 425
Entrapment as affirmative defense, 343
Environmental Protection Agency (EPA), 7
Equal protection, and death penalty, 409, 411
Error
    harmless, 424–25
    reversible, 424–25
Ethical standards, and plea bargaining, 300–301, 303–6
Evidence
    admissibility of scientific, 267–68
    assessing, 201–3, 270
    circumstantial, 198, 200
    clear and convincing, 52
    direct, 198, 200
    DNA, 338
    documentary, 199
    exclusions of, to protect other rights, 269–70
    material, 266–67
    physical, 199, 345–46, 347
    demonstrative, 345–46, 347
    preponderance of, 52
    presentation of, in trial, 368–72
    pretrial assessment of, 264–66
    probable cause in, 270–71
    probative, 266, 267
    role of prosecutor in weighing, 197
    rules of, 368
    standard of, 52
        in China, 109–10
    testimonial, 199, 202
Evidence advocacy, 266
Examination, direct, 368, 369
Excited utterance, 268
Exclusionary rule, 55–56
Exclusive civil jurisdiction, 217
Excuse, 341

Harmless error, 39
Hearing
  preliminary, 278–81
  sentencing, 399
Hearsay, 268–69, 370
Henry II, 72, 73
Henry VIII, 76
Heresy, 95
Hierarchical jurisdiction, 21
High-rate offenders, 383
Hill, Anita, 129
Hobbes, Thomas, 4
Hollow promise, 300
Horizontal prosecution, 159
Hostile witness, 369
House arrest, 391–93
Hruska Commission, 429
Hudud, 101, 102, 104
Hung jury, 375–76, 377

Ignorance as affirmative defense, 342
Immunity from prosecution, 275
Impartial jurors, 357–58
Implicit agreement, 291
Incapacitation, 383
  selective, 383
Incarceration, 387–90
Incompetency
  consequences of, finding, 325
  defining, for standing trial, 323
  motion for examination, 324–25
  purpose of proceedings on, 325
Incorporation, 45–46
Indeterminate sentencing, 401
Indictment, 35, 273
Indigents
  crisis in representation of, 186
  defense services for, 178–82
  determination of, 235
  right to counsel for, 48
Individuals, rights of, 84, 86
In forma pauperis, 427
Information, 35, 278
Information jurisdictions, 278
Initial appearance, 34, 222–24, 233
  bail bonding, 242–44
  and bail decision making, 246–50
    race and gender bias in, 248–50
  and bail reform movement, 244–46, 254–59
  functions of, 234

being informed of the charges, 234
determining pretrial release, 235
indigency and early appointment of
  counsel, 235
probable cause determination, 234–35
options for pretrial release, 235–37
  conditional release, 239–40
  monetary conditions of release, 241–42
  nonmonetary conditions of release, 237–39
pretrial release outcomes, 250
  effect of pretrial release on case outcome,
    251–53
  failure to appear, 250–51
  rearrests for pretrial offending, 253–54
Inquisition, 95
Inquisitorial process, 96
  contemporary, 96
  history of, 94–96
Insanity, recent reforms of definition of, 329–30
Insanity defense, 326–29, 342
  in perspective, 331
  procedures in, 330–31
Insanity plea, consequences of successful, 331
Insanity rule, development of, 328
Integrity, maintaining for prosecutor, 163
Intensive supervision probation, 393
Interlocutory appeal, 420
Intermediate sanctions, 390
Interrogation
  in French trial process, 98–99
  overbearing, 340
Investigation
  for defense, 183–84
  as function of grand jury, 201, 274–75
  role of defense counsel in, 173–74
  resources of prosecutor in, 199–200
Irresistible impulse test, 328–29

Jailhouse lawyers, 429
Jails, 388
Jefferson, Thomas, 88
John, King, 75
Judge(s), 116–43
  becoming, 116–23
  characteristics of, 119–22
  influence on bail decision, 247–48
  learning ropes as, 130
  maintaining integrity, 139–42
  qualifications of, 117, 216
  reputations of, 132